READING FOR COLLEGE WRITERS

READING FOR COLLEGE WRITERS

Laurence Behrens University of California, Santa Barbara

Leonard J. Rosen Bentley College

 Little, Brown and Company

Boston ■ Toronto

Library of Congress Cataloging-in-Publication Data

Behrens, Laurence.
    Reading for college writers.

    1. College readers.   2. English language — Rhetoric.
I. Rosen, Leonard J.   II. Title.
PE1417.B3958   1987   808'.0427   96   86-27237
ISBN 0-316-75727-6

Library of Congress Catalog Card No. 86-27237

ISBN 0-316-75727-6

9   8   7   6   5   4   3   2   1

MV

Published simultaneously in Canada by Little, Brown & Company (Canada) Limited

Printed in the United States of America

CREDITS

Part One

p. 18: H. L. Mencken. "George Washington," in *The Vintage Mencken,* ed., Alistair Cooke. New York: Vintage. Copyright 1958. Reprinted by permission of Random House.

pp. 5, 27–30, 45: Patricia Curtis. "The Case Against Animal Experiments," in *Reader's Digest.* February 1980, pp. 181–186. Condensed from *The New York Times Magazine,* December 31, 1978. Reprinted with permission from the February 1980 Reader's Digest. Copyright © 1978 by The New York Times Company. Reprinted by permission.

pp. 23–24, 51–52: Blythe Hammer. "The Thick and Thin of It" taken from "The Successful Animal." Reprinted by permission from the January/February issue of *Science 86.* Copyright © 1986 by the American Association for the Advancement of Science.

pp. 38–39: Peter Steinhart. "The Edge Gets Thinner," *Audubon,* November 1983, p. 98 and 102. Reprinted by permission of the author.

p. 60: Stuart L. Koman. "Conducting Short-term Inpatient Multiple Family Groups," in *Handbook of Adolescents and Family Therapy,* eds., Marsha Pravder Mirkin and Stuart L. Koman. Gardner Press, Inc. Copyright 1985, pp. 173–174. Reprinted by permission of Gardner Press, Inc.

p. 76: Frederick Douglass. *My Bondage and My Freedom.* Dover Publications, Inc. Copyright 1969, pp. 16–17. Reprinted by permission of Dover Publications, Inc.

pp. 76–77: Alfred Kazin. From *A Walker in the City.* Copyright 1951, 1979 by Alfred Kazin. Reprinted by permission of Harcourt Brace Jovanovich, Inc.

p. 83: Studs Terkel. "Sharon Atkins," in *Working.* New York: Pantheon Books, copyright 1974. Reprinted by permission of Random House.

pp. 86–89: Julia Kagan, "Top Ten Motivators and Satisfiers," *Working Woman,* July 1983, pp. 16–18. Reprinted with permission from *Working Woman* magazine. Copyright © 1986 by HAL Pulications, Inc.

(Continued on page 555)

⊏═⊐ A Note to the Instructor

Reading for College Writers is a freshman-level text-reader ideally suited for students in open-admissions colleges (and elsewhere) who need an introduction to composition that is more patient than the approach taken in many texts. *Reading for College Writers* follows the successful format used in our *Writing and Reading Across the Curriculum*. Part One (Chapters 1 through 6) is devoted to the skills and techniques of reading and writing at the college level. Part Two (Chapters 7 through 13) presents a series of interdisciplinary readings clustered around specific topics that provide the student with occasions to practice the skills learned in Part One. The purpose of the book is to teach students how to read carefully and how to write papers based on sources.

Beyond its shared format with *Writing and Reading Across the Curriculum, Reading for College Writers* is very much its own book. Written to the specific needs of a well-defined student audience, it proceeds with a slower-paced, interactive pedagogy, is written in a less-formidable style, and contains reading selections more accessible than those found in *Writing and Reading Across the Curriculum*. In this book we have completely rethought and re-presented the skills (except for critique) discussed in Part One of *Writing and*

Reading Across the Curriculum. We begin *Reading for College Writers* with a definition and discussion of *active reading* and then review how one identifies the structure of a passage and distinguishes between fact, opinion, and fact-influenced-by-opinion.

The chapters in Part One include numerous and creative exercises presented in a pedagogically sound, developmental sequence and designed to improve students' skills and enable instructors to assess student mastery. The exercises are a fundamental component of the book, intended to involve students in our discussion of the writing process and complement the writing assignments in Part Two.

The writing of summaries is treated in Chapter 2. Then, in Chapter 3, we introduce the skill of inference-making, organizing our discussion and exercises around five questions that students will be able to apply to their readings in Part Two and elsewhere. We are careful to stress how multiple inferences can be drawn from a single source; this topic leads us to Chapter 4, where we discuss using multiple sources. Chapter 4 corresponds to the synthesis chapter in *Writing and Reading Across the Curriculum,* but it is far less abstract. Again, numerous exercises help the student understand concepts. The most extensive discussion of rhetorical forms and their uses is deferred until Part Two, where it is presented in the context of readings that students will use as they write. In Chapter 4 we also give considerable attention to developing the thesis and the relation between it and the paper that follows. The chapter concludes with the first draft of an actual student paper that draws on the articles in Chapter 3. Students who have read that chapter will thus be able to observe how source articles can be incorporated into an essay.

The example paper, presented in its first draft in Chapter 4, is exceedingly rough, but serves our purposes of instruction. In Chapter 5 we introduce the skill of revision and work much of our discussion around revisions of the paper. We treat revision at the levels of the essay, paragraph, and sentence. At the end of the chapter we present the completed final draft of the example paper, which is a considerable improvement over the first draft and which represents a realistic achievement for the student using this book. In Chapter 6 we turn to finishing touches: using quotations and writing introductions and conclusions. We provide guidelines for quoting (when and what one should quote) and offer advice on the mechanics of quoting, including notes on syntactic and grammatical requirements. We also discuss the principles of introducing and concluding a paper and provide specific techniques for doing both.

Part Two, the anthology section of the book, consists of seven chapters, each of which is focused on a particular topic and includes extensive apparatus. Five of the chapters introduce specific skills for incorporating source materials into papers. Students learn how to cite sources as examples, to compare and to contrast sources, to use sources when writing descriptions or arguments, and to use sources when inferring cause and effect.

Typically, the chapters in Part Two are organized as follows:

- *Introductory material:* A brief essay introduces the subject of the chapter. One or two passages on the subject are presented and analyzed for content and structure. A particular method for combining sources is presented (i.e., description, example, argument, comparison/contrast, cause/effect).
- *Body of chapter:* A preview assignment helps the student keep basic issues in mind when reading articles that will become the basis of a formal paper. Each of five or more articles presents a distinct point of view on the subject and is preceded by a headnote. Each article is followed by the four types of questions discussed at length in Part One (i.e., content, structure, fact/opinion, inference).
- *Conclusion of chapter:* A summary assignment, based on one of the articles in the chapter, helps the student organize a reading and structure a summary. Several paper assignments help students see different sets of source readings *in relation* to one another.

Throughout the text we urge students to remember that college-level papers based on sources are *not* cut-and-paste affairs in which a summary of one source is butted up against the summary of another *ad nauseam* until a conclusion is reached. Rather, we counsel that papers based on sources *use* those sources in support of the writer's unique thesis. We also are careful to remind students that seldom, if ever, is one of the individual techniques learned for relating one source to another (e.g., comparison and contrast) the *only* technique used in writing a paper. A single paper is more likely to exhibit several techniques, guided by the writer's unique thesis.

Although our first book, *Writing and Reading Across the Curriculum,* continues to serve its segment of the freshman writing population, we recognize — thanks to the responses of many instructors — that its level of discussion and its reading selections are inappropriate for many students. *Reading for College Writers* is our response to that sentiment. We approached our work with a different audience in mind; though our basic format remains the same as in our earlier book, our manner of presentation, our selection of readings, and the skills we chose to emphasize all have changed — we think to better serve the needs of students at the many open-admissions colleges (and kindred institutions) around the country.

A comprehensive Instructor's Manual for this text is available from the publisher. Please feel free to write — care of Little, Brown and Company — with your comments and suggestions.

Acknowledgments

We take pleasure in acknowledging the advice of the reviewers who helped us hammer the early manuscript into a readable, usable text. Thanks to

Gary Columbo and Malcom Kiniry, UCLA Writing Program; Robert J. Kloss, William Paterson College; Cecilia Macheski, LaGuardia Community College; Robert Schwegler, University of Rhode Island; Louise Smith, University of Massachusetts; Judith Stanford, Merrimack College; and Harvey Wiener, LaGuardia Community College. We would also like to thank Sheridan Blau, Angus Dunstan, Valerie Hobbs, Joan Mitchell, Lydia White, and Muriel Zimmerman, all of the University of California, Santa Barbara, Gary Waynesmith of Triangle Publications, Inc., and Annabel Nelson, of the Los Angeles Unified School District, for their suggestions for readings and their review of sections of the manuscript. Our copy editor, Barbara Flanagan, brought that profession's special quality of mind to bear on the work and helped us address the various inconsistencies and dubious phrasings. To the book editor, Andrea Cava, our thanks for shepherding the manuscript through production. To Nan Upin, our praise for helping expedite reviewers' notes and other material needed in a timely fashion. And to Joe Opiela, editor, our special thanks for expert guidance through all stages of writing and production.

A Note to the Student

When you applied to college, you made a decision to extend your experience in a special way. Of all the possibilities available to you on graduating from high school, you pursued higher learning. To learn in a college setting requires that you understand and add to what others have said about our world. Since the material you will study is stored mainly in written records, you will devote considerable time to books, essays, and reports. To succeed, you will need to read, and read well. You will also need to write well.

In academic life, what you write depends largely on what you read. A typical assignment requires you to locate a number of articles on a topic — say the ways in which aerosol sprays affect the ozone layer of the atmosphere. A professor expects you to understand what you've read, to reflect on it, to compare and contrast differing points of view, to develop your own responses to these points of view, and eventually to write an essay. Two main purposes are served when you engage in such tasks. The first is that you begin the long process of accumulating information. Whether you intend to devote a lifetime of study to a subject or to gain only a general appreciation, as a newcomer to the academic community you must begin with the same task: reading texts.

You will do this in each of your courses, and the information you acquire will become increasingly complex the longer you study. Yet memorizing facts and theories alone does not constitute understanding. To understand, you must *do* something with those facts and theories. Professors therefore assign papers for a second reason: to get you to respond to source materials and in the process develop habits of careful, critical thinking.

This text will introduce you to college-level reading and writing. You will learn to read carefully and actively for information; you will also learn to use that information as you develop essays guided by your unique point of view.

Contents

CHAPTER **8** **Passion in Print** 235

CHAPTER **9**

Who Needs College?   285

Introduction   285

CHAPTER **10** ## Anatomy of a TV Success: "Hill Street Blues" 333

CHAPTER **11** ## Children of Divorce 362

CHAPTER **12**   **Ethnic Identity/Cultural Assimilation**   426

P A R T

Introduction

In Part One of this book you will learn through examples and exercises how to write college-level essays based on written sources. A great deal of academic writing relies on the work of others, and as a writer you will need to understand source materials well enough to incorporate them into essays of your own design. Accordingly, in Part One you will learn techniques for reading accurately and creatively as you respond to individual sources. You will also learn how to infer relationships among sources; how to develop a working thesis in which you combine your ideas along with other ideas and information; how to convert a working thesis into a first draft; and how to revise that first draft to achieve a final, polished essay.

By actively responding to the exercises throughout Part One, you will become familiar with the *process* of writing—a process that involves numerous steps and is inherently messy. First you will gather information and plan your essay, and then you will actually write. Very few *good* writers are satisfied with their work after a first attempt; we hope to impress upon you the value of revising as a way to clarify ideas both to yourself and to your readers. You will learn to rewrite your essays two or more times, improving your effort with each revision. After you have acquired the skills discussed in Part One, you will have the opportunity to practice in Part Two. There you will be asked to write papers based on source materials—articles, essays, and reports on specific topics designed to stimulate and hold your interest.

CHAPTER 1

Active Reading

Introduction

To a certain extent, all reading is active. Even the most leisurely review of the Sunday paper or a popular magazine requires that you sit in a chair, take the printed material in hand, and focus attention on a page: your eyes begin to work as your brain deciphers graphic symbols. Soon a puzzled expression comes over your face as words form at your lips: "Weight-loss plan encourages dieters to eat cheesecake?" You have read and understood and responded—a sophisticated, uniquely human activity. College-level reading requires even more activity: you are asked not simply to follow the general drift of a passage but also to identify its main idea, to identify parts of the whole and understand how those parts relate to the whole, and, perhaps most important, to use what you have read as a basis for further thought. To read actively in college requires that you *watch* an author developing his or her presentation. You are attentive to tone, to the author's method of organizing evidence, and to the validity of the author's assertions. As an active reader you are wary, always on the lookout for information and ideas of value, always ready to question, always ready to form a critical, intelligent response.

A "critical" response to an essay or book is not necessarily negative; rather, it is well reasoned and thoughtful, either positive *or* negative. Assume for the moment that you have found an article on the proposed construction of a tunnel system spanning the English Channel. You think the article will be especially helpful for a paper assigned in your introductory engineering course, and you would like to use a portion to help develop your ideas. Why not refer to the article in your paper, using another author's expertise to help with your assignment? This is exactly how professionals of all persuasions write: by making references to and building on the work of others. This act of referring is known as *writing from sources,* and it forms the basis of all academic discussion—which is no surprise, for articles, essays, and books are important repositories of our culture's knowledge. And since knowledge is the central object of concern in a university, everyone (both teachers and students) must use sources regularly. They must also use them well—with accuracy and care—and this is the goal of critical, intelligent reading.

What constitutes an intelligent reading? In a word, *activity.* Let's take our example of the article on the proposed tunnel system. You would not use this source in a paper solely because you "liked it." Statements of likes and dislikes are valid initial responses, but as carefully considered points of view they are limited. A critical, active reading enables you to understand *why* you like or dislike something—to say (in the case of this example) that the level of technical detail, the use of schematic drawings, and the discussions of obstacles to construction all combine to make a convincing presentation.

This ability to explain your reactions depends to a large extent on experience. The more you know about a subject, the more sophisticated your observations and questions will be and the more intelligent your reading will be. As a marathon runner, an expert in the field, you would have many observations and questions to raise when purchasing a pair of running shoes. By contrast, someone who runs one-half mile every other month would not be so intimately involved with the sport and would not likely be as shrewd a critic as you. Likewise with academics. As a newcomer to college, you will not be an expert in your courses (as your professors are); thus you may feel ill equipped to make good, sharp observations about what you read. No matter. What you need is experience, and that's why you've come to college. Be patient, and you'll find that as you study and absorb new bodies of information your ability to read will improve.

With an eye toward improvement, then, let's begin our discussion of critical, active reading and its relation to writing.

Active Reading

The first stage in a critical, active reading is to have a response. Be interested enough in what you read to react. Challenge the author's ideas and let the author's ideas challenge you. (See Chapter 3 for a discussion on possible responses.) Once you've had a response, begin to develop it by knowing precisely *what* an author has said and *how* he or she has said it. Three fundamental skills are involved: reading a passage for the main idea; making distinctions among facts, opinions, and facts influenced by opinions; and outlining the structure of a passage. For ease of presentation, we present these skills separately; but realize that in practice a critical reading requires you to use the skills simultaneously.

Reading for the Main Idea

When you read, you should be able to identify an author's main idea. Consider this paragraph:

> No one knows exactly how many animals American researchers sacrifice each year, but estimates range from 64 million to 90 million. These animals, which include dogs, cats, monkeys, horses, ponies, calves, sheep, goats, pigs, birds, rats and mice, are used in experiments that often involve intense suffering.[1]

Now put your hand over the paragraph and recall what it is about. Can you express its subject in just a few words? If you said "animal experimentation" or "animals suffering in experiments," you have correctly identified the main idea of the paragraph. But if you want to use that idea for your own purposes (for instance, in a paper you are writing), then you need to express it in a sentence. If you write, "Millions of animals suffer in research experiments every year," then you will have accurately represented the views of the paragraph's author.

What we have just done may seem like an easy task, but it is not, especially when the passages to be read are lengthy and complex, as academic material tends to be. In fact, being able to restate briefly what someone else has written requires considerable skill and is one of the essential activities of academic life. So important is the skill of accurately restating another's main idea that not much else can be done in an academic setting before it is mastered. The reasons should be apparent: we can make advancements in knowledge only if we understand what is already known. That is, we rely on the work of others to provide the basis of our own intellectual activity. It follows that we can profit from another's writing only when we are able — beyond question — to read accurately and to read for the main idea. These are the skills on which academic success largely depends.

Try reading the following passage for its main idea. Experienced critical readers often read with a pencil in hand. If they own the book or journal being examined or if they are working with a photocopy, they underline important words and phrases. Critical, active readers also jot down their own notes of explanation in the margins. Try these techniques and see if they help you identify the main idea.

[1]Patricia Curtis, "The Case Against Animal Experiments," *Reader's Digest* (February 1980): 181; condensed from *New York Times Magazine* (December 31, 1978).

The Civil War caused more death and destruction than any previous war in modern history. No other war had been fought on such a grand scale or had employed with such deadly effect a technology designed for peacetime. This first modern war saw the employment for tactical purposes of the railroad, the telegraph, and the balloon. American ingenuity, stimulated by the war, created the railway gun, the electrically exploded torpedo, the Gatling gun, the repeating rifle, and more efficient cannons. The results could be seen in the casualties. Over 110,000 Union soldiers were killed in action out of the 360,000 lost from all causes. Total deaths in the Confederate armies came to 258,000, of whom 94,000 died in battle. Disease killed more men than bullets, since antiseptics were unknown. And hundreds of thousands of men were permanently disabled. It has been estimated that the war cost the North close to $4 billion in initial outlays and several billions more for pensions and other payments later on. For the nation as a whole, the price of the war ultimately came to $20 billion.[2]

If you have identified the subject of this paragraph as the death and destruction caused by the American Civil War, then you are correct. To express the main idea briefly in a sentence so that you could use it in your own work, you would write something like the following: "The American Civil War resulted in enormous death and destruction." We have stated this main idea in our words; but note that the same idea has already been expressed in the first sentence of the paragraph, where main ideas (otherwise known as topic sentences) are often found: "The Civil War caused more death and destruction than any previous war in modern history." If you wished to include all or part of the author's actual language in an essay you were writing, you would use quotation marks. And whether you have quoted the exact words of an author or have paraphrased (as we did), you are obligated to credit your source—to let your reader know that the ideas presented have been borrowed from another writer. We discuss the ways in which a writer gives such credit in later chapters. For the moment, as a guide to your own underlining and notemaking, consider the way in which we have marked up the paragraph on the Civil War. We have underlined essential information and circled and made marginal notes on supporting information.

> The Civil War caused more death and destruction
> than any previous war in modern history. No other war
> had been fought on such a grand scale or had em-
> ployed with such deadly effect a technology designed
> for peacetime. This first modern war saw the em-   *Modern tech.*
> ployment for tactical purposes of the railroad, the   *applied to war*
> telegraph, and the balloon. American ingenuity, stimu-
> lated by the war, created the railway gun, the electri-
> cally exploded torpedo, the Gatling gun, the repeating

[2]Richard Hofstadter, William Miller, and Daniel Aaron, *The United States: The History of a Republic* (Englewood Cliffs: Prentice-Hall, 1957), 381.

rifle, and more efficient cannons. The results could be seen in the casualties. Over 110,000 Union soldiers were killed in action out of the 360,000 lost from all causes. Total deaths in the Confederate armies came to 258,000, of whom 94,000 died in battle. Disease killed more men than bullets, since antiseptics were unknown. And hundreds of thousands of men were permanently disabled. It has been estimated that the war cost the North close to $4 billion in initial outlays and several billions more for pensions and other payments later on. For the nation as a whole, the price of the war ultimately came to $20 billion.[3]

Death by bullets and disease

Overall cost of war

Why did we underline, circle, and make notes in the way we did? (This is another way of asking, How did we know what counted as important information?) First, we began with the assumption that every sentence of every paragraph, just as every paragraph of an essay, has a purpose: a passage is about *something,* and that something we take to be the subject. In the paragraph above, the subject is the *Civil War,* and we underlined it.

Next we sought to determine what claim is being made about the Civil War. The answer is easily apparent: the Civil War *caused more death and destruction than any previous war in modern history.* Now we have isolated the most important information of the passage — its main idea. All other information supports this one underlined sentence.

Finally, we circled supporting information—individual words and phrases—and wrote very brief explanatory notes in the margins. We circled "first modern war" and wrote "Modern tech. applied to war." From our note we then drew lines to specific examples: the railway gun, the torpedo, and so on. We also circled the casualty figures and wrote another explanatory note: "Death by bullets and disease." And we circled the figure $20 billion, writing "Overall cost of war."

Our method of marking the passage — underlining the main idea and circling supporting ideas — is one of many methods, and it may differ from yours. The essential point is to mark every paragraph of an article in such a way that you can easily recall information. It takes more time to read carefully, with pencil in hand, than to read quickly. But careful reading saves time in the long run: when you write a paper or study for an exam, an earlier, thorough reading of pertinent articles allows you to review material quickly, as opposed to having to reread entire articles because you've forgotten their contents. The adage "You can pay now or pay later" applies here: read comprehensively early on and you'll save yourself time in the long run.

Now identify the main idea of one more paragraph before we move on to other elements of critical reading. Here's a test to determine whether you've

[3]Hofstadter, Miller, and Aaron, *History of a Republic,* 381.

correctly identified an author's main idea: you and your classmates, when asked to write down the main idea, should produce some version of the same sentence. Make notes according to the method we just described or some other method that you devise; express the content of the paragraph in a single sentence; and then in class compare that sentence to your classmates'.

> Why is it that the thought of going to jail is abhorrent to the average person? It is not that he fears physical discomfort. He can go roughing it on a camping trip and have a wonderful time even though both the food and the mattress may be worse than a good jail would provide. Nor is the sheer threat of confinement any great concern in itself. No, the average law-abiding man is abhorrent of jail because by going there he would lose too much. He has a good job or good career prospects that would be jeopardized by a jail record. He enjoys the affection and respect of parents, wife, children, friends, and associates. Just as important, he enjoys his own self-respect, and none of these important emotional satisfactions does he want to reduce by getting a record as a jailbird. In other words, it is mainly the stigmatic potential of jail that gives it a deterrent effect for Mr. Average Man. But this is quite enough. In fact, it means that the threat of jail is a powerful deterrent force to the well-adjusted and law-abiding man or woman. Unfortunately, as a voter and taxpayer he supports this crime control concept based on his own personal reaction to penal sanctions, and he fails to consider the man who has never had any of these personal advantages to lose.[4]

Distinguishing Between Fact and Opinion

Not everything you read is factual, and to be a critical reader you must learn to make certain basic distinctions. Consider the following:

> Approximately three hundred trees must be harvested to build an average-sized house.

> Timber companies exterminate entire forests so that middle-class Americans can realize their dream of home ownership.

> More Americans should live in apartment buildings.

If you were writing a paper on the resources required for building homes in America and came across these statements, you would be faced with a dilemma: Are the statements equally dependable? Are they true? How can you tell? In what ways could you use each statement in your paper? The answers to these questions depend on your ability to make fundamental distinctions. Specifically, you should be able to classify the material you read as fact (the first statement); as opinion (the third statement); and as fact influenced by opinion (the second statement). The experienced reader approaches and uses facts and opinions differently.

[4]Paul W. Kebe, *Prison Life and Human Worth* (Minneapolis: University of Minnesota Press, 1974), 7–8.

Statements of Fact

A fact is a statement about the world that is generally regarded to be true, a statement that can be verified by direct, independent research (if you are willing to go to the library and do a bit of checking). Facts do change, even though some people would prefer they did not. The earth, after all, was once thought to be flat; and there are now some scientists who believe that it is slightly pear-shaped! What then counts as a fact? For the most part, a fact is the collective judgment of people who pride themselves on objectively observing the world. Traditionally, this has meant scientists, physicians, and other scholars. But there is no substitute for your own common sense. When an author states that sixty million animals are experimented on every year, common sense tells you that that statement could be verified—checked for truthfulness—if you chose to do so. In other words, the statement could be regarded as a fact, as unbiased, objectively presented information.

EXERCISE

Following are five sentences. In the space provided, state whether or not each appears to be factual—to provide information that is either true or likely to be discovered as true if you had time to research the subject. If the sentence appears to be factual, describe how you would go about verifying it.

1. Steel is stronger than iron.

_____

_____

2. On June 28, 1914, the assassination of Archduke Francis Ferdinand at Sarajevo triggered the beginning of World War I.

_____

_____

3. The development of photography has changed the way people remember.

_____

_____

4. The speed limits posted on interstate highways are a nuisance.

_____

_____

5. George Washington soaked his false teeth in Madeira every night before going to bed.

_____

_____

Notice that we did not ask you to state which phrases *are* factual because neither you nor we possess sufficient knowledge to know in each case whether the statement is actually true. When some item is presented to us as a fact — that George Washington soaked his false teeth in wine every night or that the moon lies 200,000 miles from the earth — we cannot be sure that the information is factual until we do some checking. What we can be sure of, however, is that the statement falls into the category of things about which facts can be known. The category of potential facts includes objects that can be counted; objects that can be measured for distance, weight, volume, and speed; objects whose constituent elements can be identified; and objects whose history is a matter of record. The following statements are all potentially factual:

Henry Adams was born in 1838.

Pasta is made from eggs, flour, and water.

The Union consists of fifty states.

Marsupials carry their young in pouches.

You should know on a *first* reading of a passage which if any items of information are potentially factual. Certainly the statement about the moon's distance from the earth appears to be a fact. It is also incorrect; the moon lies 240,000 miles (not 200,000) from the earth. But this discrepancy is of little consequence on a first reading. Only when you are prepared to make use of a fact must you establish its accuracy.

Now consider two brief paragraphs. The first presents material that falls into the category of potential fact. The paragraph explains, among other things, why the sky is blue.

> As the sun's rays pass through the earth's atmosphere, some are scattered, and a play of colors results. Blue rays are scattered most, and therefore a clear sky is typically blue. Yellow rays are scattered less than blue; thus the sun itself, so long as it is well above the horizon, looks yellow. But just after sunrise and just before sunset the sun is reddish. At these times the sharply slanting sun's rays must travel a longer path through the atmosphere, and more of the blue and yellow rays are filtered out. The red rays, which are scattered least, come through in the largest numbers, giving the sun its reddish hue. If there are clouds and dust in the air, many of the red rays which filter down into the lower atmosphere are reflected, and large areas of the sky may be reddened.[5]

Every sentence in this paragraph on sunlight could be verified either by your own direct observations of the sun or by a few hours of research in a library. All of the information on sunlight is potentially factual. Now consider a second paragraph.

> We can understand...how the poet got his reputation as a kind of licensed liar. The word poet itself means liar in some languages, and the words we use in literary criticism — fable, fiction, myth — have all come to mean

[5]Herbert S. Zim and Robert H. Baker, *Stars* (New York: Golden Press, 1956), 26–27.

something we can't believe. Some parents in Victorian times wouldn't let their children read novels because they weren't "true." But not many reasonable people today would deny that the poet is entitled to change whatever he likes when he uses a theme from history or real life.[6]

Northrop Frye is not as specific with his information as is the author on sunlight. He does not, for instance, name the languages in the world in which "poet" means "liar"; nonetheless, this is a statement we could verify and is thus potentially factual, as is the statement about Victorian parents. But the very last sentence of the paragraph is most definitely not a fact:

> But not many reasonable people today would deny that the poet is entitled to change whatever he likes when he uses a theme from history or real life.

This sentence has not even the potential of becoming a fact, for it is a *belief,* based on the author's private experience, about the ways in which people would react. Perhaps it is a well-founded belief, but it is not potentially true in the way that "*poet* means liar in Swahili" is potentially true. In other words, Frye's last sentence is an *opinion.*

Statements of Opinion

An opinion is a belief, a statement that may be regarded as true by one person or a group of people but that cannot be proved as true by independent, direct observation of the world. Statements of opinion cannot be verified by measuring, examining constituent elements, reviewing historical records, and so on. The following are some varieties of opinions with which you are doubtless familiar: Statements of preference (or value)—"Chocolate is the best-flavored ice cream";—"Autumn is the most beautiful season." Statements of prediction (or speculation)—"The Cardinals will win the pennant this year." Advice—"You'll live longer if you lay off the red meat." Interpretation—"Hamlet's greatest flaw is his inability to make decisions." Though these statements differ, they share an important feature: each expresses a view held by some one person or, conceivably, a community of people. And none of these views can be directly verified by independent observation of the world in the way that the preceding paragraph about sunlight can be verified.

Philosophers disagree over what exactly distinguishes a fact from an opinion. Some feel that the two do not actually differ at all. (The argument goes this way: "Facts" are agreed-upon truths held by a community such as scientists. When the "opinions" of the group change because of some new observation about the world—that it is round, not flat, for instance—the "facts" are adjusted accordingly. Isn't "fact," then, just another word for shared "opinion"?) Others believe that facts are perceived by the senses, and opinions arise from the mind. But critics object and say that the senses cannot always be trusted and that certainty comes only from within the mind. All kinds of interesting

[6]Northrop Frye, *The Educated Imagination* (Bloomington: Indiana University Press, 1964), 63.

philosophical questions lie in this direction, but we cannot pursue them here. We can only keep a skeptical mind as we return to the proposition that when reading and preparing academic work it is important to *try* to distinguish between fact and opinion or between "objective" writing (based on fact) and "subjective" writing (based on opinion or feeling).

Before we provide another group of sentences for you to analyze, let's review two statements from the exercise on page 9 and discuss what makes them opinions:

> The development of photography has changed the way people remember.
>
> The speed limits posted on interstate highways are a nuisance.

Some people may regard speed limits as a nuisance; but just as many or more people would regard posted speed limits to be a valuable safety measure. So the statement, while a truthful expression of one person's views, is not factual, a true expression for all people. The statement about photography certainly looks as if it could be true, and the person who wrote this is probably convinced that it is. But how could we test the accuracy of such a claim? People alive during the first years of photography are now dead. To what written records could we look for evidence that people in the nineteenth century remembered differently from the way we do? Or if we could locate a modern community in some remote part of the world that had never seen photographs, how could we determine differences in ways of remembering? By comparing brain tissues? By simply asking questions? If we found a difference, could we conclude that the absence or presence of photographs was essential to the difference? Probably not, for other variables, such as differences in language, are likely to be involved.

Even though the statement that photography has changed the way people remember is not factual, it is certainly intriguing and of great value. Think of what we could learn from an essay built around such an idea. The opinions of the author would challenge us to consider the impact of photography on our lives, and this — like any effort that enables us to see the commonplace differently — would be a meaningful exploration. The point is that opinions are crucially important to the way we live, and they can be powerful. Passionately expressed opinions have gotten people elected and lynched and have led to revolutions, all of which are surely facts. Still, if you are to read well, you must make the important distinction between facts and opinions. Appreciating the distinction enables you to know how to respond to a statement. You accept potential facts as accurate and true for the moment, pending verification. You read, for instance, that warm water freezes into ice cubes more quickly than cold, so you change your behavior to take advantage of this "fact." When you discover that the "fact" is wrong, you return to filling the ice cube trays with cold water. You respond to opinions with opinions: you regard them as debatable and use them as challenges to help clarify your own thinking about a subject.

Fortunately, distinguishing fact from opinion is usually not very difficult to do. In most cases, writers of books or articles make it clear that they consider what they are describing to be good or bad, worthy or unworthy, important or trivial. And even if a writer seems unaware that what he or she considers facts might be considered opinions by others, we as readers are often able to make the distinction. We are able to do this simply because of our experience with the world — with other people, such as advertisers, who try to persuade us that their opinions are true.

| **EXERCISE** | |

Examine the following eight statements and determine whether they appear to be fact or opinion. If a statement is potentially factual, explain how you would verify the information. If a statement is an opinion, classify it as a preference (a statement of value), a prediction (or speculation), advice, or interpretation.

1. Mary Shelley conceived the idea for her novel *Frankenstein* when she was challenged to write a ghost story by the English poet Lord Byron.

_____

_____

2. In terms of climate, agreeableness of inhabitants, sweetness of air, and intellectual excitement, New York City is the most desirable place to live on the North American continent.

_____

_____

3. Marble and chalk are both varieties of limestone.

_____

_____

4. Despite its success as a futuristic thriller, George Lucas's *Star Wars* is actually a remake of medieval romances.

_____

_____

5. Today's students profit most from their college education when they train for specific jobs in the business world.

_____

_____

6. Unless patterns of consumption change drastically, our grandchildren will inherit a world devoid of wilderness areas and clean rivers.

_____

_____

7. The artificial language Esperanto was created by Ludwig Zamenhoff in 1887.

_____

_____

8. Summer temperatures in Antarctica rarely climb above 0° Fahrenheit.

_____

_____

Statements of fact and opinion are regularly mixed together in the presentations of authors, who may switch from one to the other and back to the first again. It is up to you to detect the mix. Often a pattern develops in which an author presents information that we could accept as factual and follows with an assessment (that is, an opinion) about that information.

EXERCISE	

In the following paragraph, place an asterisk (*) at the beginning of each sentence that appears to be factual. Place a check beside sentences that provide the author's opinion or assessment of those facts.

Perhaps a total of 100 billion humans have walked the planet since the appearance of the earliest hominids. Of these, about six per cent have been agriculturists, fewer than four per cent have lived in industrialized societies, and all the rest—approximately ninety per cent—have lived as hunters and gatherers. Only during the past 12,000 years in a few places, and for less than 5000 years in most of the world, have humans domesticated plants and animals, lived in settled villages, developed complex societies, and harnessed other sources of energy besides human muscle. The 12,000 years since the earliest agriculture represent only about five hundred human generations, surely too few to allow for overwhelming genetic changes. Therefore the origins of the intellect, physique, emotions, and social life that are universal to human beings must be traced to preagricultural times. Humans are the evolutionary product of the success of the hunting adaptation, even though almost all of _Homo sapiens_ alive today have abandoned that way of life. The traits acquired over millions of years of following this adaptation continue to provide the basis for human adjustment to the modern world. Still influencing us today is the fact that hunting and gathering is more than simply a particular means of subsistence. It is a complete way of life: biologically, psychologically, technologically, and socially.[7]

Statements of Fact Influenced by Opinion

Often you will encounter facts that are wrapped, so to speak, in an opinion. Consider: "Researchers sacrifice sixty million animals yearly." Here we

[7]Peter Farb, _Humankind_ (Boston: Houghton Mifflin, 1978), 89.

have a fact (sixty million animals are used in research experiments every year) presented to us with a belief about that fact (the animals are "sacrificed"). The word *sacrifice* implies that laboratory animals are killed needlessly. The word *used* would have been a neutral, opinion-free way of stating the fact: "Sixty million animals are *used* in experimental research every year."

Certainly there is nothing wrong — and much that is right — with you as a writer interpreting information that you present in a paper. If you believe that animals are sacrificed — as opposed to used — then say so! Express yourself! But as a critical reader, you should be on the alert for emotionally charged words that reveal an author's opinions, or *bias*. Consider the difference between the following two sentences.

Three hundred thousand anarchists marched on Washington.

Three hundred thousand freedom fighters marched on Washington.

EXERCISE	

In the preceding statements, we are given factual information, which we could verify. What is that information?

_____

_____

We also have the facts interpreted for us. How so?

_____

_____

The statements about animals being sacrificed and protesters marching in Washington reveal the way in which an opinion can lead a writer to an interpretation that colors, or biases, a fact. Sometimes a writer's opinion can bias a fact by unconsciously limiting the writer's focus. An example: If you attended a world-cup soccer match with an engineer, an anthropologist, and a fanatical sports fan, the chances are that each of you would report on that experience differently. When asked what happened at the game, the anthropologist might report on a spectacle of eighty thousand people watching grown men kick a ball up and down a playing field; the engineer might report on the design of the stadium; the sports fan might well ignore everything except the game itself and, when asked for details, provide an impassioned, play-by-play description. When reading an article, then, you should know or try to know the profession of the writer, for this in part will determine what the writer considers — and reports — as important information.

None of us can possibly observe every detail about the world around us. Assume that as you read this you're lying on the floor on a carpet. What would the world be like if you could not block out information? A million—more than a million—questions would bombard you every instant and disrupt your ability to concentrate. Say the carpet is made out of wool. Where did the wool come from? When was it sheared? What happened to the lamb? Where was it born? Who cared for it? On whose table did it end up as lambchops? Were the lambchops tasty? And so would go the questions, *ad infinitum,* if you could not selectively filter out information. Every item in your room could be put to similar questions, which, if asked, would be utterly immobilizing.

Thus, to guarantee sanity, we selectively block out information by employing filters, some of which are unconscious and others of which are wholly conscious—like a professional affiliation. In the case of the soccer match, the affiliation (as engineer, sports fan, or anthropologist) determines what the observers allow their minds to perceive. Unconscious filters that affect the ways in which we perceive the world include race, religion, and socioeconomic status—filters that have powerful effects on both writers and readers. In an active, critical reading, your job is to be alert to the author's conscious (and, when you gain experience, unconscious) filters, identifying them as best you can. If you start your critical reading by finding out the profession of the writer, you can anticipate what the writer might and might not say about a topic. Try this experiment. Read the following paragraphs, both written on the subject of quartz crystals, and identify the professions of the writers.

> Quartz, one of the most widespread of minerals, [is] a naturally occurring silica, SiO_2. It can be distinguished from all other minerals by its hardness (7), vitreous luster, and lack of cleavage. Quartz constitutes about forty percent of the average granite and granite gneiss, and these rocks compose about ninety percent of the earth's crust.[8]

> In early British folk belief quartz pebbles were called star-stones and were constantly sought for their curative properties. Nine star-stones collected from a running brook, boiled in a quart of water from the same brook, would impart their curing power to the water, which was given to the patient for nine successive mornings. In the Shetland Islands quartz pebbles were said to cure sterility; they were collected by women and thrown into a pool wherein they washed their feet. In Persian folk practice quartz crystals are sometimes put on babies to insure their getting enough mother's milk.[9]

The first writer is a geologist and the second a folklorist. Each brings to the topic of quartz crystals a particular point of view, or set of concerns, that limits the way the crystals are seen and described. The geologist is concerned with the mineral components of quartz, while the folklorist is interested in the beliefs that people have attached to quartz crystals. Who we are, which in large part is determined by our schooling, significantly affects the ways in which we see.

---

[8]*Collier's Encyclopedia* (New York: Macmillan, 1981), s.v. "quartz."
[9]*Funk & Wagnalls Standard Dictionary of Folklore, Mythology, and Legend* (New York: Harper & Row, 1972), s.v. "quartz."

Other factors also affect our vision by allowing opinions to influence the selection or presentation of facts. It is standard practice for writers to supply evidence to support a conclusion; sometimes, however, writers will supply only those facts that support and omit those that do not—hardly ethical, but it's done all the time. (This last statement is a mixture of fact and opinion, isn't it?) A building contractor trying to land a large job may include in his proposal testimonials from satisfied customers (some perhaps written more than fifteen years ago) while, naturally enough, omitting the complaints of dissatisfied customers. His proposal appears to support the "fact" that he is a reliable contractor. Thus an opinion—that he is the best contractor for the job—can lead to a careful but unrepresentative and not entirely truthful selection of facts.

To demonstrate this point, read the following three assessments of George Washington. Then review each assessment in light of the other two and list potential facts about Washington's character; the author's opinions about Washington; and the ways in which these opinions may have influenced the facts selected.

Article 1

The greatest asset America possessed was the leadership of General Washington. His greatness, as his contemporaries insisted and as posterity has adjudged, lay in the wonderful balance of a group of qualities. Taken singly not one was brilliant, but in combination they presented an almost matchless array of virtues. His soundness of judgment, never showy or merely clever, impressed every associate. When Patrick Henry was asked who was the greatest man in the Continental Congress, he replied: "If you speak of eloquence, Mr. Rutledge of South Carolina is by far the greatest orator; but if you speak of solid information and sound judgment, Colonel Washington is unquestionably the greatest man on that floor." He was wise not merely as to his immediate problems, but in foresight. The consummate illustration of that foresight was his masterly plan of campaign in 1781, which culminated in the capture of Cornwallis and ended the Revolution.[10]

Article 2

Washington was in personal command of the American forces in the New York region, which he rightly judged would be the scene of the principal British offensive. The American commander-in-chief was cold and reserved by nature, resentful of criticism, and sometimes jealous of other American generals. He was not a professional soldier and in his inexperience sometimes made mistakes that might well have had fatal results for the American cause. But his mistakes became less frequent as the war went on, and his courage, integrity, selfless devotion, and balanced judgment were of enormous value to the patriots. As a commander and a leader he had no equal on either side of the struggle.[11]

---

[10]Michael Kraus, *The United States to 1865* (Ann Arbor: University of Michigan Press, 1959), 224.
[11]Dexter Perkins and Glyndon G. Van Dusen, *United States of America: A History*, vol. 1 (New York: Macmillan, 1962), 154.

Article 3

If George Washington were alive today, what a shining mark he would be for the whole camorra of uplifters, forward-lookers and professional patriots! He was the Rockefeller of his time, the richest man in the United States, a promoter of stock companies, a land-grabber, an exploiter of mines and timber. He was a bitter opponent of foreign entanglements, and denounced their evils in harsh, specific terms. He had a liking for forthright and pugnacious men, and a contempt for lawyers, schoolmasters and all other such obscurantists. He was not pious. He drank whiskey whenever he felt chilly, and kept a jug of it handy. He knew far more profanity than Scripture, and used and enjoyed it more. He had no belief in the infallible wisdom of the common people, but regarded them as inflammatory dolts, and tried to save the Republic from them. He advocated no sure cure for all the sorrows of the world, and doubted that such a panacea existed. He took no interest in the private morals of his neighbors.

Inhabiting These States today, George would be ineligible for any office of honor or profit. The Senate would never dare confirm him; the President would not think of nominating him. He would be on trial in the newspapers for belonging to the Money Power. The Sherman Act would have him in its toils; he would be (under indictment by every grand jury south of the Potomac; the Methodists of his native State would be denouncing him (he had a still at Mount Vernon) as a debaucher of youth, a recruiting officer for insane asylums, a poisoner of the home. And what a chance there would be for that ambitious young district attorney who thought to shadow him on his peregrinations—and grab him under the Mann Act!*[12]

EXERCISE	

Based on your reading of these passages, list the statements about Washington that you regard as potentially factual.

Article 1: _____

_____

_____

Article 2: _____

_____

_____

---

*The Mann Act (1910) forbade the transport of women across state lines for indecent purposes.
[12]H. L. Mencken, *The Vintage Mencken,* ed. Alistair Cooke (New York: Vintage, 1958), 67–68.

Article 3: _____

_____

_____

State in a sentence the opinion each writer holds about Washington. Then support your statement by referring to lines from the passage.

Article 1: _____

_____

_____

Article 2: _____

_____

_____

Article 3: _____

_____

_____

Speculate on information that may not have been considered by each author as he wrote his
assessment of Washington.

Article 1: _____

_____

_____

Article 2: _____

_____

_____

Article 3: _____

_____

_____

EXERCISE

You have analyzed three passages and have seen how writers' opinions can affect the
ways in which they select facts for presentation. Now consider four individual sentences and
explain how each contains *biased* information — that is, potential facts presented in a way that
reveals the author's opinion about those facts.

1. The growing presence of birth control clinics in public high schools is a national disgrace.

Fact-based content: _____

_____

Opinion-based content: _____

_____

2. Psychoanalyst Erich Fromm was correct in asserting that many Americans devote excessive hours to work not because they love their jobs but because they dread the freedom of unscheduled time.

Fact-based content: _____

_____

Opinion-based content: _____

_____

3. Recent government patterns in funding university research establishes a clear and unwholesome relationship between science and the military.

Fact-based content: _____

_____

Opinion-based content: _____

_____

4. Grave robbers have threatened to raise the recently discovered remains of the *Titanic* by use of floats and pumps.

Fact-based content: _____

_____

Opinion-based content: _____

_____

Examining the Structure of an Essay

You have learned to identify the main idea of an essay (or a passage from a longer work, such as a book) and to make important distinctions among facts, opinions, and facts influenced by opinions. One further skill must now be developed as you train to become a critical reader: the ability to observe the ways in which writers organize their work. As a critical reader, you should be able to make observations about an essay's *structure*.

To explain the role of structure in an essay, let's begin with an analogy. Imagine that you are an architect whose job is to design affordable housing. Imagine also that for each new project you are working with guidelines specified by your employer. You have a loosely defined sense of the whole house: how large it can be, what quality of materials can be used, and so on. You also work with individual customers. You have limits, then, placed on you by your employer and preferences expressed to you by the customer. You sit down to design a house and—in an effort to offer the customer the most economical, spacious arrangement—you experiment with designs by placing rooms in various relationships to one another. In this way, you build a model house with parts (i.e., individual rooms) that snap together and apart with ease.* How many closets should be built on the first floor? Upstairs? In the basement? You snap the rooms together according to your hunches and see what works best. Within a few days, you arrive at a satisfactory arrangement that meets the requirements of both your employer and the customer. But there's a slight problem. In the best configuration, the dimension of two rooms will have to be reduced. You call the customer; she arrives for a review of the design, and says: "Terrific. But I want a place to do my woodworking." She leaves and you grumble, returning to your drawing board; but it is not long before you've restructured the parts again, this time to everyone's satisfaction.

How has an appreciation of *structure* helped the architect to design the house? What has this to do with the way writers work? First, having a sense of the whole project and how parts might fit together to make up that whole provided the architect with just enough of an outline, an overall sense of things, to make a beginning. Beginnings are crucial, for even though your final design of a project may look nothing like your original conception, the freedom to begin has allowed you to start the process whereby you change parts as the project develops. Few obstacles are as crippling to a writer as dwelling on a project in its entirety. Ten- or fifteen-page papers are not written at once. *Parts* of papers are, however, and if you have developed a sense of how the parts fit together—that is, a sense of structure—then slowly but surely you will work on one part at a time until a whole paper emerges from your efforts.

As a writer, you will usually begin with an assignment that places constraints on you. How do you respond? By considering your assignment in the way the architect considered his: first, start with a clear sense of what is expected—that is, review the assignment carefully—and then discover ways in which you can divide the assignment into parts. This takes creativity on your part. The sketchy outline that you produce as you break the subject into parts should be enough to get you started. (In Chapter 4, we discuss in detail how a writer develops the ability to divide an assignment into workable parts.) During the process of writing, you will discover that parts get developed, redeveloped, positioned, and repositioned (just as the rooms of the house did) until, by the second or third attempt to make the paper succeed (that is, by the second or third "draft"), your ideas have gained clarity and force. At this point you may want to give your work to reviewers who will make suggestions that force you to revise again, perhaps grumbling as you do so. But if you want your paper to work well, then you will welcome constructive criticism as a guide to

*The *i.e.* in the parentheses is an abbreviation of the Latin term *id est,* meaning "that is." Other abbreviations of Latin you'll likely encounter in academic writing: *e.g.,* for *exempli gratia,* meaning "for example"; *viz.,* for *videlicet,* meaning "namely"; *et al.,* for *et alii,* meaning "and others"; and *cf.,* for *confer,* meaning "compare."

help you along. Ultimately, you reach a final draft with which you, your instructor, and reviewers are pleased.

Why do you need to appreciate how writers use structure in order to appreciate the importance of structure in critical reading? We'll respond by stating what we take to be a general principle about academic work: Writing and reading are closely interdependent skills; to do one well often means to do the other well. In fact, we'll go so far as to say that a student is only as sophisticated a reader as he or she is a writer, and vice versa. It is crucial to know, for instance, both as a reader and as a writer, that ideas in well-written papers are always developed in component parts, or in stages. What makes a paper well structured and easy to follow (or to write) or poorly structured and difficult to follow (or to write) is whether these stages are recognizable and whether the relationship among them is clear. You must, in brief, know how structure is used well in order to ascertain its use when you read an article. When you as a reader can divide an article into its component parts, understanding how the author has positioned each to create a meaningful and well-developed whole, you have gone a long way toward understanding what you've read.

Study the following diagram and the accompanying explanations:

The structure of an essay

Introduction _____ *The introduction provides a transition from the world of the reader to the world of the essay.*

_____ Thesis _____ *of the reader to the world of the essay.*

The thesis is the most general statement of the essay. It organizes and is explained by the paragraphs that follow.

Paragraph 2 _____ ↓ _____

—Body of essay.

Paragraph 3 _____ ↓ _____

Notice how each paragraph refers back to and develops some part of the thesis.

Paragraph 4 _____ ↓ _____

The arrows between paragraphs indicate that each paragraph leads logically to the next. The order of presenting details in the essay is important.

Conclusion _____ ↓ _____

The conclusion provides a transition from the essay back to the reader's world.

Observe the placement of arrows in the diagram; they signify the logical relationship among elements of the passage. All academic essays should have a clearly stated thesis, a one-sentence, general statement that describes the content of the essay to follow. The thesis is usually found at the end of the first or second paragraph, after the general topic of the essay has been introduced.* Following the thesis is a series of paragraphs, each of which is written to supply supporting information that will make the thesis convincing to a reader. Only paragraphs that are related to the thesis belong in the essay. This is why you see arrows in the diagram leading from each paragraph back to the thesis. (Essays that are not academic and intended for an audience outside of the university often do not follow this tight structure and may succeed brilliantly. So if the structure just described seems to "lock you in," realize that it is a structure for academic occasions. We should say, however, that readers of all persuasions, inside academics and out, expect writing to be clear and carefully structured, whatever that structure happens to be.)

In addition, paragraphs supporting the thesis must lead logically from one to the next. The reader must know why, for instance, paragraph 3 has been placed after paragraph 2 and not before, which means that the writer must be very sure of where in the essay supporting information is placed. Hence, arrows in the diagram also lead from one paragraph to the next. Finally, after the thesis has been stated and supported, the writer ends the presentation with some concluding remarks.

To summarize the essential elements of a well-structured essay: (1) the essay should contain a thesis that allows the reader to anticipate the paragraphs that follow; (2) the essay should contain paragraphs whose information supports and clarifies the thesis; and (3) the paragraphs of the essay should be arranged in a way that makes sense to the reader. We will discuss later the terms introduced here; but for now it is enough that you appreciate the very broad requirements of a well-structured paper.

EXERCISE	

Let's put this discussion to use by examining the structure of an eight-paragraph article. Read Blythe Hamer's "The Thick and Thin of It" with pencil in hand, and mark the passage as discussed on page 25. On a separate piece of paper, write in a single sentence the main idea of each paragraph.

If every person in Macau were given equal portions of land, each would   1
live in a space a quarter the size of a tennis court. If you take into account the
room necessary for streets, stores, and offices, people living in Macau (like
people living in Manhattan) are more likely to end up with an apartment the

---

*On pages 119–126 we discuss the ways to write a thesis.

size of a Ping-Pong table. With more than 63,000 people per square mile, Macau, a tiny city-state off the coast of China, is the most densely populated place in the world.

Every Falkland Islander, by contrast, could roam over two and a half square miles without ever seeing another human. But he'd better watch where he steps; sheep outnumber people by more than 300 to one.

No single cause explains why some areas of the world are so much more thickly settled than others. But high population density can be an accident of political history, as it is in city-states such as Macau. And it is often the result of geography: the three most densely populated countries in the world—Macau, Hong Kong, and Singapore—are all islands. Many larger island countries, such as Malta, Taiwan, and Barbados, also rank among the most densely settled parts of the world.

Density can also be the result of the economy of an area. "The Falkland Islands are so thinly settled because they have no resources other than sheep," says Tom Merrick of the Population Reference Bureau in Washington, D.C. "The population doesn't grow because so many people emigrate."

The countries that are least densely populated often have obvious climate or geographical flaws, like Mongolia (three people per square mile). Australia has a population density of five per square mile, and Canada has only seven, demonstrating the effect of huge hinterlands. The United States is not very crowded, despite perceptions to the contrary, with 65 people per square mile. "A lot of our land is uninhabitable," says Ken Hill, a demographer at the National Academy of Sciences in Washington, D.C. "The Rockies, the desert, and the rangeland are not places people want to live, so they crowd together in pleasanter surroundings."

If high population density were a measure of pleasantness, then Bangladesh would be pleasant indeed. With 1,800 people per square mile, it is the most densely settled nonisland nation in the world. Nearly 100 million people live in an area the size of Arkansas. All of Bangladesh is arable, and that explains its density. "There are no deserts, mountains, or impenetrable forests," says Hill. "There's plenty of rainfall, so most fields yield two crops a year."

Socioeconomic factors also influence population density. In Bangladesh, mothers and fathers see additional children as contributing to the family labor force, not detracting from the family food supply. Children often work 10-hour days on their families' subsistence-level farms. Women usually have seven or eight children, partly to compensate for the high infant mortality rate. Falkland Islanders, in comparison, have only two children per family. "They have a European attitude toward children," says Hill. "They don't see the need for more, even though for years emigration has been causing the country's population to decline."

When is a place too empty or too crowded? That's a judgment everyone has to make for himself. In Manhattan people press together in subways and on street corners without batting an eye. But in America a hundred years ago, the sound of an axe in the next clearing signalled that it was time to move on.[13]

---

[13]Blythe Hamer, "The Thick and Thin of It," *Science* 86 (January/February 1986): 58.

Hamer's "The Thick and Thin of It" meets all the requirements of a well-structured essay. In examining the organization of Hamer's work, first identify on a separate piece of paper the main idea of each paragraph. Compare your listing of main ideas with ours below. If at any point one of your sentences differs from our corresponding sentence, reread the paragraph in question until you are certain of its main idea.

Paragraph 1: "Macau, a tiny city-state off the coast of China, is the most densely populated place in the world."

Paragraph 2: The Falkland Islands are thinly populated.

Paragraph 3: Population density has many causes. One is the "accident of political history"; another is geography.

Paragraph 4: Economy can affect population density.

Paragraph 5: "Climatic or geographical flaws" result in low population density.

Paragraph 6: Bangladesh's entirely arable land and favorable climate have resulted in a highly dense population.

Paragraph 7: "Socioeconomic factors also influence population density."

Paragraph 8: Each person's tolerance of population density is a matter of individual taste.

Now that we understand the content of Hamer's brief essay, let us turn our attention to the way in which she has organized this content. In the sentences above, underline the one sentence about which everything else in the essay is written; that is, identify the thesis. Recall that a thesis is the most general statement of an essay—a statement that leads a reader to anticipate all supporting information that follows. For instance, consider the general statement "A rainbow has seven colors." If this were a thesis organizing an entire essay, one would not be surprised to find that seven paragraphs—or sections of the paper—would follow, each discussing one of the seven colors. Now locate and underline the thesis in the list above.

Paragraph Outlines and Section Outlines

If you underlined the first sentence in number 3 as the most general sentence of those listed, then you have done well. Every other sentence in the list, every other sentence in the entire passage, in some way supports that thesis: "Population density has many causes." Now let's examine the overall organization of the essay, using the diagram offered earlier as a guide. You will notice that it is possible to create an outline of a passage both by paragraph and by section. We can define a section as a grouping of paragraphs all related to one broad statement, which itself supports the thesis. The section outline thus follows from (or is a generalized version of) the paragraph outline. Both the section and the paragraph outlines have their uses, and you should be familiar with each. The section outline allows you to examine groups of paragraphs and thus to gain a broad sense of the essay's development. The paragraph outline enables you to focus closely on details. Section outlines, in which you condense groups of paragraphs, work best with lengthy passages. In shorter passages, where one or two paragraphs may account for an entire section, the paragraph outline works well. Keep in mind that any useful critical reading allows you to appreciate broad patterns of development *and* specific

26 ACTIVE READING

details; you will therefore want to be aware of both methods when determining the structural outline of a passage.

Section Outline	Paragraph Outline	
Part I Introduction Extremes of density	Paragraph 1:	Description of the most densely populated place is given.
	Paragraph 2:	Description of the least densely populated places is given.
	Thesis:	Follows directly from two introductory examples: "No single cause explains why some areas of the world are so much more thickly settled than others."
	Paragraph 3:	Two causes—political history and geography—are suggested as explanations for varying densities.
	Paragraph 4:	A third reason is offered: "Density can be the result of the economy of an area."
Part II Various causes of population densities	Paragraph 5:	A fourth reason is offered: "Climatic or geographical flaws" can result in low population density.
	Paragraph 6:	A fifth reason is offered: Favorable geographic and climatic conditions, in contrast to flaws listed in paragraph 5, result in high population density.
	Paragraph 7:	A seventh reason is offered: "Socioeconomic factors also influence population density."
Part III Conclusion	Paragraph 8:	Conclusion.

A section outline of Hamer's essay reads as follows:

Part I: Introduction, paragraphs 1 and 2: Extremes of density.

Thesis: "No single cause explains" high and low population densities.

Part II: Body of the paper, paragraphs 3, 4, 5, 6, and 7: six possible causes that affect population density.

Part III: Conclusion.

Notice how every item of information in Hamer's essay refers to (and in some significant way supports) her thesis. Moreover, every paragraph leads logically from one to the next: one example is given (paragraph 1) and its opposite follows (paragraph 2); the opposition leads to the thesis (paragraph 3), and six possible causes for varying population densities follows (paragraphs 3–7). In sum, Hamer's brief essay is well organized. When you can appreciate this organization, you can better appreciate and understand the contents of the essay.

Demonstration: Reading for Structure

You have done a significant amount of work as a critical reader when you can identify the main idea of every paragraph in an essay; distinguish among facts, opinions, and facts influenced by opinion; and identify the structure that an author has used. Once you can develop your ability to perform each of these skills with accuracy, you will have taken the first important step to becoming an accomplished reader—*and writer*—of college-level work.

In the next chapter we will introduce the skill of summary, and you will be asked to formalize your reading for main ideas, facts and opinions, and structure by writing a paragraph or two. But for now, let's examine two more brief articles for their structures. We'll lead you through an analysis of the first passage, entitled "The Case Against Animal Experiments" by Patricia Curtis. We'll leave the analysis of the second passage up to you.

The professor was late leaving the medical school. His wife and young- 1
sters were asleep when he got home, and the professor suddenly felt lonely as he fit his key in the lock. But as he opened the door, Salome was there to welcome him. The little dog leaped ecstatically, wagging her tail and licking the professor's hand. Salome's exuberant joy at his return never failed to cheer him.

Early next morning, the professor drove back to the medical school and 2
entered the laboratory. He noticed that a dog on which one of his students had operated the previous afternoon still had an endotracheal tube in its throat and had not received pain medication. Another dog had bled through its bandages and lay silently in a pool of blood. Sloppy work, the professor thought—must speak to those students. The dogs made no sounds, because new arrivals were subjected to an operation that destroyed their vocal cords so that no barks or howls disturbed people in the surrounding buildings.

The professor looked over the animals to be used that day by his surgery 3
students. He came across a female dog that had just been received. Frightened, she wagged her tail ingratiatingly. The professor felt a stab. The small dog bore an amazing resemblance to Salome. Nevertheless, he made a note to remind himself to give orders for her to be prepared for experimental surgery.

No one knows exactly how many animals American researchers sacri- 4
fice each year, but estimates range from 64 million to 90 million. These animals, which include dogs, cats, monkeys, horses, ponies, calves, sheep, goats, pigs, birds, rats and mice, are used in experiments that often involve intense suffering.

The research establishment has generally insisted that live animals provide the only reliable tests for drugs, chemicals and cosmetics that will be used by people. Researchers also believe that animal experiments are necessary in the search for cures for human illnesses and defects. There is no question that many important medical discoveries, from polio vaccine to physiology of the stress response, have indeed been made through the use of animals. Thus universities, medical and scientific institutions, pharmaceutical companies, cosmetics manufacturers and the military have always taken for granted their right to use animals in almost any way they see fit.

But increasing numbers of scientists are beginning to ask themselves   6
whether all experiments which involve painful testing tools — such as stomach tubes, burn equipment, radiation devices and electric prods — are worth the suffering they entail. "Within the scientific community there is a growing concern for animals that has not yet had a forum," says Dr. F. Barbara Orlans, a physiologist at the National Institutes of Health and president of the newly formed Scientists' Center for Animal Welfare. "We will try to be a voice of reason between scientists and the humane organizations."

The cause of this rising concern among many scientists lies in the discov-   7
eries that science itself has made. We now know that many animals feel, think, reason, communicate and even, on occasion, behave altruistically toward each other. This information has narrowed the gap we perceive between ourselves and the rest of the animal kingdom, making it more difficult to rationalize inhumane experiments.

Paradoxically, the public tends to be "speciesist" in its reaction to animal   8
experimentation: For many people, a test is permissible when it inflicts pain on a "lower" animal like a hamster, but not on a dog. If U.S. Air Force researchers had used guinea pigs instead of beagles when they tried out a poison gas in 1973, they probably would not have provoked the public outcry that resulted in curtailment of their funding.

It is not known whether any single vertebrate species feels less pain than   9
another. Yet rats and mice, which compose about 75 percent of America's total lab-animal population, are exempted from a federal law designed to give some protection to laboratory animals. The Animal Welfare Act, passed in 1966 and amended in 1970 and 1976, covers only about four percent of all lab animals. The law sets some standards for housing and care, and indicates that pain-relieving drugs should be used. But the law places no restrictions on the kinds of experiments to which animals may be subjected and it includes a loophole — if a scientist claims that evidence of pain is a necessary part of an experiment, anesthetics or analgesics may be withheld.

Common today are psychological experiments in "learned helplessness."   10
Caged animals are given electric shocks until they learn certain maneuvers to obtain food. Then the researchers change the rules so that the animals have to learn more and more ways to avoid shocks. Ultimately, the animals simply lie down and passively receive shock after shock. Researchers have attempted to draw parallels between this "learned helplessness" and depression in humans.

In another experiment typical of a series under way since 1966 at the   11
Armed Forces Radiobiology Research Institute in Bethesda, Md., ten monkeys were starved for 18 hours and then "encouraged" with electric prods to run on treadmills. This went on for several weeks before the monkeys were sub-

jected to gamma-neutron radiation. Then they were retested on the treadmills for six hours, and subsequently for two hours each day until they died. The purpose was to get an idea of the effects of radiation on human endurance.

One argument in favor of animal tests is that under laboratory-controlled   12
circumstances they are likely to be objective and consistent. But the results of the same tests conducted on the same kinds of animals often differ from one laboratory to the next. Many investigators concede that the stresses caused by crowded cages, callous treatment, pain and fear can affect the metabolism of the animals and thus confuse test results.

Another rationale for many animal tests is that they predict human reac-   13
tions. Yet different species can respond differently to substances or situations. Thalidomide, for example, did not produce deformities in the fetuses of dogs, cats and hamsters.

According to veterinarian Thurman Grafton, executive director of the   14
National Society for Medical Research, people who talk about alternatives to animals are creating false hopes. "These new technologies can only be adjuncts to the use of animals," he claims. "While they furnish clues as to what direc- tion a type of research might take, you will ultimately need an animal with its interchanging biochemical functions to properly assay a drug."

Yet, in some instances, such as the production of certain vaccines, animals   15
have already been replaced by other test methods. To encourage the search for more alternatives, groups like the American Fund for Alternatives to Animal Research and, in England, the Lord Dowding Fund have given grants to scientists engaged in research aimed at finding experimental substitutes for animals.

In 1978 the American Fund made its first grant, to biology professor Earl   16
William Fleck at Whitman College in Walla Walla, Wash. The award will help finance his development of a test substituting one-celled organisms called tetrahymena for animals in screening substances for teratogens, agents that can cause birth defects. It is expected that the test will be cheaper, quicker, more accurate and more humane than killing thousands of pregnant animals. And Dowding Fund recipient John C. Petricciani, a research physician now with the Food and Drug Administration, has devised a method of assessing how tumors grow by inoculating tumor cells into skin from nine-day-old chicken embryos instead of into animals.

Alternative testing methods are frequently discovered by scientists who   17
are searching for simpler and more cost-efficient ways to achieve their goals. Berkeley biochemistry professor Bruce Ames, for example, invented a widely used technique that tests *Salmonella* bacteria to predict carcinogenic proper- ties of chemicals. Hans Stich, a Canadian cancer researcher, has devised a test for carcinogenicity that uses human cells, takes one week and costs only about $1000. The usual method, using rats and mice, takes three years and costs about $200,000. While these methods do not yet rule out the use of some ani- mals as the final test of a chemical's safety, they can spare the lives of countless more by serving as an initial screen.

In his book, *Alternatives to Animal Experiments,* British physiologist D. H.   18
Smyth says there is hope that the ever-increasing numbers of lab animals can be considerably reduced. But he also warns that it is unlikely that a complete phasing out of animal experimentation will happen soon. Still, he asks, "Does

this mean we can perpetrate any cruelty on animals to satisfy scientific curiosity in the hope that it will one day be useful? To me it certainly does not."

British psychologist Richard Ryder calls experimenters to task for trying   19
to have it both ways. They defend their work scientifically on the basis of the
similarities between humans and animals, but defend it morally on the basis of
the *differences.*

And there's the rub: the differences aren't as reassuringly clear-cut as they   20
once were. We now know that some animals have a more highly developed
intelligence than some humans—for example, infants and the severely retarded.
Ryder asks, "Suppose we were to be discovered by more intelligent creatures
from elsewhere in the universe. Would *they* be justified in experimenting
on *us?*"[14]

Your first response to this or any article will *not* be to analyze its structure.
You'll save that for the time when you have a reason to study the article closely.
What will that reason be? What could motivate you to analyze how an author
has pieced together material in such a way as to achieve certain effects? The
reason, very simply, is *interest*: your interest. As you're assigned material in
your classes, you will read articles and will respond to them—sometimes
emotionally, other times intellectually, often with a combination of the two. An
active, intelligent reading begins with honest, felt reactions to whatever you've
read. Once you know that you feel something and have a response, you're in a
position to explore both the article and your own reaction to it.

Take this article on animal experimentation. No one would spend the time
scrutinizing the structure of this piece if there weren't a good reason to do so.
What might that reason be? Perhaps you've had a strong reaction to Curtis's account. Perhaps you're outraged at the treatment animals receive in research
laboratories. Or you're skeptical. You're inclined to support animal experimentation and find yourself suspecting that Curtis has not been entirely fair in her
presentation. Both of these reactions provide you with a reason for examining
the structure of "The Case Against Animal Experiments." You want to understand your response.

So with this article, as with others, *have* a reaction. Respond to what you
read. And then allow your response to be a motivation for examining structure.

Examining the Structure of
"The Case Against Animal Experiments"

The length of this article (twenty paragraphs) leads us to adopt the section
approach as we write an outline of the structure. Examining sections, or parts,
allows us to gain a broad sense of the article and how Curtis has constructed it.

We will divide Curtis's discussion into seven parts. Why seven? Why not
three or twelve? The choice of seven depends on our particular reading of the
article. You might well have perceived sections differently, which is fine. For
now, accept seven as the number of sections; when you're experienced, you'll

[14]Curtis, "The Case Against Animal Experiments," 181–186.

be able to make your own determinations. The seven parts, as we understand them, are defined by the following paragraphs (we give the content of the first three parts here and let you describe the content of parts IV–VII in the exercises).

Part I (paragraphs 1–3): The story about Salome

Part II (paragraphs 4–6): A statement of the problem

Part III (paragraphs 7–9): Background information

Part IV (paragraphs 10–11)

Part V (paragraphs 12–13)

Part VI (paragraphs 14–18)

Part VII (paragraphs 19–20)

The main idea of the article (its thesis) we take to be the following: *Animal experimentation is inhumane and should be abandoned or made more humane as other means of research become available.* Every part of the article, every paragraph belonging to a part, directly supports this thesis. Let's examine the first two parts in detail.

Part I: The story about Salome

On reading the article we make the obvious observation that Curtis begins with a story. The first three paragraphs of "The Case Against Animal Experiments" clearly differ from the remainder of the article. How so, and what is the relationship of this story about Salome to the thesis and to the material that follows?

The introduction to this article is a story, whereas what follows is an argument. The story makes an appeal to our hearts; the argument (paragraphs 4–20) makes an appeal to our intellects. The purpose of the story is clearly to create sympathy for the author's case against animal experimentation. When the dog in the lab is compared to the faithful and affectionate Salome, we feel a pang of remorse, for both Salome and the lab animals are presented as humanlike in their emotions, and we are urged—though not directly—to pity them. The effect of the story is to prepare us to accept the argument that follows.

Part II: A statement of the problem

Paragraphs 4–6 mark a second beginning of the article; Curtis drops the guise of storyteller and speaks directly to her readers, attempting to change our minds (as opposed to our hearts) through the force of logic. These three paragraphs form a section in that each paragraph *defines* the issue under examination—that is, the thesis. By contrast, the next section, beginning with paragraph 7, provides a *history* of the issue, or background information.

Consider how paragraphs 4–6 can be grouped into an identifiable section: in paragraph 4, Curtis defines the current state of affairs in animal experimentation, which she takes to be a problem (suggested by her use of "experiments that often involve intense suffering"). Paragraph 5 provides the standard justification for using animals in laboratory experiments. The word "but" introducing paragraph 6 signals a turn away from the scientists' justifications and toward the position Curtis herself will take, a position that she establishes by quoting Dr. Orlans. Considered as a unit, paragraphs 4–6 amount to a statement of the problem that Curtis will address in the paragraphs to follow. Now let's examine those paragraphs:

EXERCISE

Part III: Background information

Explain how paragraphs 7, 8, and 9, considered together, form an identifiable section of the article that could be titled "background information."

_____

_____

_____

_____

How is paragraph 8, in its mention of "speciesism," related to paragraph 7?

_____

_____

_____

    Now state the content of the remaining parts of "The Case Against Animal Experiments," which we've defined by paragraph numbers. Then answer the questions that follow.

Part IV (paragraphs 10–11): _____
                                     (Provide a title for the part.)

What is the purpose of this part of the article? Explain how paragraphs 10–11 constitute an identifiable section. How are these paragraphs related to one another?

_____

_____

_____

How is this section related to the main point of the article, that animal experimentation is inhumane and should be abandoned or made more humane as other means of research become available?

_____

_____

_____

How is this part of the article related to parts III and V?

_____

_____

_____

Part V (paragraphs 12–13): _____
(Provide a title for the part.)

What is the purpose of this part of the article? Explain how paragraphs 12–13 constitute an identifiable section. How are these paragraphs related to one another?

_____

_____

How is this section related to the main point of the article, that animal experimentation is inhumane and should be abandoned or made more humane as other means of research become available?

_____

_____

_____

How is this part of the article related to parts IV and VI?

_____

_____

_____

Part VI (paragraphs 14–18): _____
(Provide a title for the part.)

What is the purpose of this part of the article? Explain how paragraphs 14–18 constitute an identifiable section. How are these paragraphs related to one another?

_____

_____

How is this section related to the main point of the article, that animal experimentation is inhumane and should be abandoned or made more humane as other means of research become available?

_____

_____

_____

How is this part of the article related to parts V and VII?

_____

_____

_____

Part VII (paragraphs 19–20): _____
                                              (Provide a title for the part.)

What is the purpose of this section of the article? Explain how paragraphs 19–20 constitute an identifiable section. How are these paragraphs related to one another?

_____

_____

How is this section related to the main point of the article, that animal experimentation is inhumane and should be abandoned or made more humane as other means of research become available?

_____

_____

_____

How is this part of the article related to part VI?

_____

_____

_____

You have now completed your structural analysis of "The Case Against Animal Experiments." Usually you'll write such an analysis in the margins of the article itself (provided you are working with your own copy or a photocopy). To gain a sense of how a structural analysis looks when written as notes in the margins of an article, transfer the seven content labels to their appropriate locations in Curtis's article. If, in a few weeks, you had occasion to refer to the piece — as you might if you decided to write a paper on animal experimentation — your structural notes plus the assorted underlinings made in an effort to define the main ideas would help considerably in refreshing your memory. And they would also help if you were asked to write a summary of the article (as you will be asked to do in Chapter 2).

EXERCISE

With pencil in hand, read the final assignment for this chapter: "Where the Jobs Are" by Carrie Tuhy, on pages 229–232 in Chapter 7. As you read, label the parts in Tuhy's article. Be confident enough in your groupings of paragraphs that you could defend each group as a distinct, identifiable part of the whole article. Remember that to recognize the parts of an article you must, with confidence, be able to recognize the author's thesis.

The techniques we have described in this chapter for making notes based on active reading take time; but we hope you can appreciate in the long run they are time savers and an aid to understanding. When you have made your notes well, when you understand an author's main idea, when you can read for structure and distinguish between facts and opinions, you should seldom if ever need to reread an entire article to recall its contents.

CHAPTER 2

Summarizing

Using the Summary

A summary is a brief restatement, in your own words, of the contents of a piece of writing (a group of paragraphs, a chapter, an article, a book). Used by itself in response to an exam question, a summary demonstrates how well you've understood the reading material. Consider a typical question: "What was the Supreme Court's decision in the case of *Brown vs. the Board of Education?*" In a physics class you might be asked: "Why does a navigator's use of a sextant to plot a ship's position at sea assume that the sun and stars revolve around the earth?" In some cases, exam or paper questions will call for both summary and evaluation: "Explain (film director) Eisenstein's approach to editing as discussed in his chapter in *Film Form*. Then evaluate his use of editing in his film *Battleship Potemkin.*" In each of these assignments, the instructor is calling for a brief restatement of material with which students in the class should be familiar. Students can demonstrate how well they have read by writing summaries.

Testing your mastery in this way is useful, but more useful still is the summary that you include in papers, for it is in papers that you *apply* what you

have learned. Assume that you're working on a report in which you will recommend for or against building a "bullet" train in your section of the country.
(A bullet train, after the French and Japanese models, travels at speeds of
200 mph on heavily used commuter routes.) You need a wide variety of information for such a report: cost studies, commuting schedules, projected use of
the system, reports on systems installed in other countries, and so on. To make
use of this information, you need to present in your paper the material collected during your research, writing summaries of articles and parts of articles
to suit your needs. By applying what you have learned, you do something far
more sophisticated than answering exam questions that call for a summary.
You use material you've mastered for your *own* purposes, according to your
own design. This is the way in which new knowledge gets created.

Often you will summarize information in a paper both to help establish
a point you are making (as you would do in the report on bullet trains) and
to comment on or to interpret that point (as in answering the question on
Eisenstein). By way of example, examine the few sentences below, taken from
a paper on the difficulties of combating terrorism. Take special note of the way
in which the writer offers an opinion only *after* he has provided an accurate
summary (in this case a summary of two newspaper accounts):

> In December 1985, terrorists attacked civilians in two European air-   1
> ports—one in Rome and one in Vienna. The gunmen struck their targets   2
> within minutes of each other, indicating a carefully planned operation that
> President Reagan attributed to the Libyan leader Muammar Kaddafi. Reagan   3
> followed the charge with economic sanctions against Libya. But economic   4
> sanctions are of dubious value in discouraging terrorism.

This pattern of summary followed by comment is used time and again in
academic writing, with good reason. Virtually all of our discussions in college
are based on established bodies of knowledge. If you are to speak intelligently
about that knowledge, if you are to add to it in any way, then you must demonstrate your ability to summarize accurately and objectively; for it is only when
you have understood what someone has said that you have earned the right
to respond.

Observe more closely the pattern established in the paragraph on terrorism: information is summarized (sentences 1, 2, and 3) and then commented
on (sentence 4). Notice how the author holds his opinions in reserve until the
summary is completed. As a reader, whether or not you agree with the assessment that economic sanctions are of dubious value in discouraging terrorism,
you depend on the summary's accuracy so that you can draw your own conclusions, which you then compare with the author's.

Consider the consequences of an inaccurate summary:

> In December 1985, freedom fighters attacked civilians in two European air-
> ports—one in Rome and one in Vienna....

This revised lead sentence fails the test of objectivity, for by using the term
"freedom fighters," the writer implies that the attacks were justified. Certainly

the writer is entitled to this opinion, but only *after* he offers an accurate, complete, opinion-free summary. Before commenting on any information — be it an event gleaned from newspaper accounts (as in our example); some other writer's opinion, summarized from an article; or a series of facts summarized from a report — you owe your readers objectivity so that they can form their own opinions independent of yours.

You will write summaries of varying lengths as you work on your papers. At times, a summary will be no longer than a sentence or two, and in such cases you will be summarizing only the part of an article that is useful in developing a particular point in your paper. Consider this example:

> R. Neil Sampson, executive vice-president of the National Association of Conservation Districts, estimates the current loss from sheet erosion — the movement of soil by water — is equivalent to a million acres of farmland a year. Wind erosion on the Great Plains costs another 250,000 acres. Over the next century, says Sampson, at this rate, we'll lose the equivalent of 62 million acres, an area the size of Oregon and roughly the amount of land we needed to produce our entire export of food in 1980. Norman Berg, former chief of the Soil Conservation Service, predicts that if present trends continue, world food supplies will be imperiled in less than a century.[1]

Imagine yourself as the author of this paragraph excerpted from an article on soil erosion. In your research you have discovered a twenty-page report written by R. Neil Sampson and a ten-page essay written by Norman Berg. Both the report and the essay are wide ranging and cover a variety of topics. As you write your paper, you plan — in this particular paragraph — to devote attention to *predictions*. It makes sense, therefore, to summarize and use only those parts of the reports by Sampson and Berg that involve predictions.

In another part of the paper on soil erosion, you might need a longer summary of a different source:

> American farming has always been troubled by overproduction, which keeps prices low. The answer has been for the individual farmer to try to produce more and to hope that other farmers will produce less. In 1972, the United States sold grain to the Soviet Union, and the following year Secretary of Agriculture Earl Butz determined that the world market would accommodate the surpluses which had kept prices low. He called upon farmers to "plant fencerow to fencerow." For several years, the price of grain went up as Americans sold overseas and the surpluses declined. It looked like a long-term trend, so the value of farmland rose. And farmers bought more land to take advantage of both higher grain prices and increasing land values. They bought at high interest rates.
>
> They were sanguine. They were eager. The acreage devoted to export crops increased from 50 million in 1950 to 100 million in 1975, to 133 million in 1978. Since 1978, there has been a 39 percent increase in the acreage planted to wheat. One-third of America's farmland is now planted in crops

---

[1] Peter Steinhart, "The Edge Gets Thinner," *Audubon* (November 1983): 98.

grown for export. Most of the export goes not to feed the world's hungry, but to affluent countries like Japan and Russia, which can afford to buy it.
That expansion, however, caused serious erosion problems.[2]

Again, imagine yourself the author of these paragraphs. You've come to the part of your paper in which you'll discuss the overproduction of crops and its effect on soil. To make your point, you need to summarize a large section—twelve pages—of a U.S. government agricultural review. You devote two full paragraphs of your article to this summary and then follow with an interpretation in which you observe a cause and effect relationship.* Again, note the pattern: first comes the accurate, objective summary; *then* comes the opinion.

So you will use summaries, both long and short, to assemble and perhaps (though not necessarily) to comment on information and ideas contained in various sources. A caution, however: Good writers are careful not to allow summaries to become a substitute for original thinking. Use a summary in the service of *your* ideas. A paper consisting of summaries stitched together with transitions may demonstrate that you've done some research and have thought about your sources in a minimal way. But it does not demonstrate an active, original mind at work; and this, in combination with a mastery of source material, is what professors value most in a student.

Writing the Summary

If you have read and completed the exercises in Chapter 1, then you have already acquired the skills needed to write a summary. Recall that an active reading requires you to identify the main idea of an article; to distinguish between facts and opinions; and to discern an article's structure. We presented these skills separately in Chapter 1. Here we join them because to summarize what another writer has written, you must first know the main idea of the passage in question, how the author has organized parts to present that main idea, and what proportion of the material presented is likely to be factual. In other words, before sitting down to prepare a summary, you must understand an article thoroughly; practicing the skills discussed in Chapter 1 enables you to do that.

We begin the discussion on writing summaries by examining a single paragraph that you have seen before:

> As the sun's rays pass through the earth's atmosphere, some are scattered, and a play of colors results. Blue rays are scattered most, and therefore a clear sky is typically blue. Yellow rays are scattered less than blue; thus the sun itself,

---

*A cause and effect relationship is one in which a writer establishes a sequence of events and attempts to prove that the circumstances surrounding one event have led to, or caused, the following event(s). In the example paragraphs the author argues that the excessive planting of crops for export has caused problems with soil erosion.

[2]Steinhart, "The Edge Gets Thinner," 102.

so long as it is well above the horizon, looks yellow. But just after sunrise and just before sunset the sun is reddish. At these times the sharply slanting sun's rays must travel a longer path through the atmosphere, and more of the blue and yellow rays are filtered out. The red rays, which are scattered least, come through in the largest numbers, giving the sun its reddish hue. If there are clouds and dust in the air, many of the red rays which filter down into the lower atmosphere are reflected, and large areas of the sky may be reddened.[3]

We will frame the discussion in terms you already know: main idea, fact/opinion, and structure. When writing a summary of a passage, first identify its main idea. You can usually do this by underlining a sentence. In the preceding paragraph you would underline the first sentence:

> As the sun's rays pass through the earth's atmosphere, some are scattered, and a play of colors results.

Next determine how the passage is structured. Reread the example paragraph, examining its organization, and you will discover a very definite pattern — from most to least: from rays that are most scattered to those that are least scattered. Finally, determine what part of the passage you could accept as factual, pending further investigation. Having previously read this paragraph on sunlight in Chapter 1, you know that all of its information is potentially factual; and this, as you will see, will affect the way that you write the summary.

As we use the categories *main idea, fact/opinion,* and *structure* to guide our critical reading, the information we derive will provide the basis for a summary. First we should examine the sentence we've underlined as the main idea of the paragraph. Would this serve as a summary?

> As the sun's rays pass through the earth's atmosphere, some are scattered, and a play of colors results.

Yes it would, for this is the *topic sentence* of the paragraph, the one that organizes the information that follows. Every sentence of the paragraph explains, or provides some detail about, the topic sentence. So the sentence would serve as a summary; yet we would prefer not to use it, for two reasons. We often feel restricted when quoting an author's language for the first sentence of a summary. By freeing ourselves from the language of the original passage, we are usually better able to condense material. Also, we more clearly understand a passage restated in our own words: something about the process of translation from the author's vocabulary to our own forces clarity. With these considerations in mind, we organized our notes on the paragraph as follows:

Main idea

Sunlight scatters as it passes through the atmosphere, resulting in a "play of colors."

---

[3]Herbert S. Zim and Robert H. Baker, *Stars* (New York: Golden Press, 1956), 26–27.

Supporting details

The sky appears blue at midday and red at sunrise and sunset.

Structure

The paragraph is arranged as a progression from rays that are scattered most to rays that are scattered least.

Fact/opinion

All of the information appears to be factual.

Using these notes, we write a one-sentence summary:

Sunlight scatters as it passes through the atmosphere, making the sky appear blue at midday and red at sunrise and sunset.

Requirements of the Summary

A summary must pass three tests to be successful. It must be brief, complete, and objective.

Brevity

Though the length of a summary depends on the length of the passage summarized, a good rule of thumb is that a summary should be no longer than one-quarter of the original passage. Often it will be shorter, as when you summarize an entire chapter of a book or a book itself. (You wouldn't very well write a 100-page summary of a 400-page treatise.) And as you have seen, the length of a summary also depends on how you intend to use it. At times, you will summarize a small portion of an article, and the result will be brief; at other times, you will summarize an entire article, and the result will be far longer.

Completeness

By definition, a summary is not as long or detailed as the original passage. This creates a dilemma: how do you delete information and at the same time achieve completeness? You will resolve the difficulty only when you develop the ability to sense important information in a passage. Easy rules for developing this sense don't exist. You must read articles carefully and critically and understand them; once you have done this, you will be able to separate the more important material from the less, using the more important as you write your summaries.

To test for a summary's *completeness*, you can pose a question: Having read your work, will readers in any way *mis*understand the essential content of the passage on which the summary is based? If they won't, then the summary is complete. It contains only the most important details and an example or two. To learn about other details, readers will have to go to the original passage.

Objectivity

Summarizing Facts

Finally, a summary must be objective, and you can establish this by making certain that you have not interpreted any of the material you've summarized. One way of demonstrating objectivity is by writing the summary as the original author would have written it, making yourself "transparent" in the process. As the writer of a summary, you are like a window through which readers see the passage that was written by someone else. If you are transparent, a reader sees directly through you, with no distortions, to the article being summarized. Adopting a transparent stance as a writer is appropriate when you've determined that most, if not all, of the information in the passage you're summarizing is potentially factual. When this is the case, you can write the summary as you would if you were the author of the original. (Therefore, the body of the summary needn't mention the author; credit your source in the heading, the introduction, or the footnote.) Our example summary on sunlight demonstrates this transparent stance:

> Sunlight scatters as it passes through the atmosphere, making the sky appear blue at midday and red at sunrise and sunset.

Notice that our presence as writers of this summary cannot be detected at all. We are transparent to the reader and have presented the main idea of the original passage without interpretations. It is as if the authors of the original passage had written the summary themselves.

EXERCISE

The following two paragraphs—from Carl Sagan's *Dragons of Eden* and from the entry "Rough Riders" in the *Encyclopedia Americana*—contain potentially factual information. Read each and then try your skill at writing summaries. Because an active, critical reading provides the basis for any summary, underline and make marginal notations as you read. Answer the questions that follow each selection in preparation for writing the summaries.

Bloodhounds have a widely celebrated ability to track by smell. They are presented with a "trace"—a scrap of clothing belonging to the target, the lost child or the escaped convict—and then, barking, bound joyously and accurately down the trail. Canines and many other hunting animals have such an ability in extremely well-developed form. The original trace contains an olfactory cue, a smell. A smell is merely the perception of a particular variety of molecule—in this case, an organic molecule. For the bloodhound to track, it must be able to sense the difference in smell—in characteristic body molecules—between the target and a bewildering and noisy background of other molecules, some from other humans who have gone the same way (including those organizing the tracking expedition) and some from other animals (including the dog itself). The number of molecules shed by a human being while walking is relatively small. Yet even on a fairly "cold" trail—say, several hours after the disappearance—bloodhounds can track successfully.[4]

Base your response to the following questions on your underlining and marginal notes.

1. If you underlined a sentence in the paragraph as the main idea (or topic sentence), this was probably sentence 1. Why, based on your understanding of the paragraph, would this sentence *not* serve as a particularly useful summary?

_____

_____

_____

_____

2. What information is essential to understanding the paragraph?

_____

_____

_____

3. What information would you *not* include in a summary? Why?

_____

_____

_____

4. Is there a clear organization of information in the paragraph? If so, what is it?

_____

_____

_____

Now combine information from your answers to questions 1, 2, and 3 into a one- or two-sentence summary of the paragraph by Carl Sagan. Because the paragraph is largely factual (or potentially so), adopt a transparent stance as you write the summary. Summarize the paragraph as though you were Sagan.

_____

_____

[4]Carl Sagan, *The Dragons of Eden: Speculations on the Evolution of Human Intelligence* (New York: Random House, 1977), 155.

_____

_____

_____

EXERCISE

Now read and make notes on a second passage, this one on the Rough Riders.

Rough Riders, [was] the popular name given to the First U.S. Volunteer Cavalry, which fought in the Spanish-American War. The Volunteer Service Act of April 1898 authorized "raising a regiment of cowboys as mounted riflemen" in anticipation of the war in Cuba. On May 17th the Rough Riders, consisting of Western ranchers, prominent businessmen, college athletes, and a number of adventurous bluebloods, were officially mustered in. Col. Leonard Wood took command, and Theodore Roosevelt, then the under secretary of the Navy, resigned his post to join the unit as a lieutenant colonel.

Forced to leave their horses behind, the unit arrived in Cuba on foot and participated in the battles of the Santiago campaign. After the battle at Las Guásimas, Wood was promoted to brigade commander, and Roosevelt assumed command. He led the Rough Riders in a successful charge up "Kettle Hill" (July 1st), and supported the fight on San Juan Hill from that location. After their departure from Cuba on August 8, they were disbanded at Montauk Point, N.Y.[5]

Base your response to the following questions on your underlining and marginal notes.

1. Will you make a reference in your summary to Col. Leonard Wood? Why or why not?

_____

_____

_____

2. Will you include in your summary a mention of the Volunteer Service Act of 1898? Why or why not?

_____

_____

3. On May 17, 1898, the cavalry unit was "mustered in." On August 8 of the same year it was disbanded. How will you *briefly* restate this information?

_____

_____

[5]*Encyclopedia Americana* (Danbury, Conn.: Grolier, 1983), s.v. "Rough Riders."

4. A successful summary will answer as many of the following questions as seem appropriate for a passage. Briefly answer these questions as they relate to the passage on the Rough Riders.

Who? _____

_____

What? _____

_____

Where? _____

_____

When? _____

_____

Based on your notes and response to these questions, write a two-sentence summary on the passage about the Rough Riders. As with the previous summary, because the information you are treating appears to be factual, adopt a transparent stance. Write the summary as though you were the author of the original passage.

Summarizing Opinions

At times, based on your active, critical reading, you will determine that a passage contains as many or more of an author's opinions as it does potential facts. Consider what is by now a familiar example: you read the statement "Sixty to ninety million animals are sacrificed every year in lab experiments" and observe that the word *sacrificed* is an opinion, not a fact. The act of making this distinction, which is so important to an intelligent, critical reading, is an act of interpretation. How will you reflect this interpretation in a summary, which by definition is supposed to be objective (or free of interpretations)? The difficulty is resolved by being honest and direct with your readers. If you have distinguished between an author's apparent facts and opinions, then say as much. Following is a paragraph by Patricia Curtis on animal experimentation. How would you summarize it?

> No one knows exactly how many animals American researchers sacrifice each year, but estimates range from 64 million to 90 million. These animals, which include dogs, cats, monkeys, horses, ponies, calves, sheep, goats, pigs, birds, rats and mice, are used in experiments that often involve intense suffering.[6]

An accurate summary of this paragraph will clearly identify Curtis's use of the word *sacrificed* as an opinion, but it will do so in a neutral way:

[6]Patricia Curtis, "The Case Against Animal Experiments," *Reader's Digest* (February 1980): 181; condensed from *New York Times Magazine* (December 31, 1978).

> Patricia Curtis believes that the sixty to ninety million animals used in lab experiments every year are being "sacrificed."

Note that the distinction we've made in reading the paragraph is reflected in our summary. We've split Curtis's opinion away from her fact by using the word *believes* with reference to *sacrifice* and by stating the information about animals as though it were true. Compare this summary to our next one, where we make no reference to Curtis:

> Sixty to ninety million animals are used every year in lab experiments.

Which summary would you use in a paper? This depends on the purpose of the paper. If you intend to comment on Curtis's views, then you would include her name in the summary; if you want only the apparently factual information — the number of animals used in experiments every year — then you would omit any mention of Curtis.

The goal of a summary is objectivity, and this is still possible when you make distinctions between fact and opinion for a reader. Compare the summaries above with the following:

> Patricia Curtis correctly believes that the sixty to ninety million animals used in lab experiments every year are being "sacrificed."

This summary is biased and therefore unacceptable. Why? The word *correctly* reveals a judgment on our part — that we agree with Curtis's opinion. Our responsibility in the summary is to present material neutrally, not to take sides. We have every right to agree or disagree with an author, but only after we have *neutrally* presented her views. Using the following present-tense verbs helps establish this neutrality:

Curtis *believes*	Curtis *argues*
Curtis *states*	Curtis *asserts*
Curtis *claims*	Curtis *agrees*
Curtis *disagrees*	Curtis *objects*
According to Curtis	Curtis *remarks*

When you use one of these expressions, you are inserting your voice into a summary so that readers, detecting your presence, can infer that you've made a distinction between fact and the author's opinions. Moreover, the distinction must be *neutral* and *accurate*. If you wrote, "Curtis believes that all animal experimentation is unjustified," you would be misrepresenting the author's position.

It should come as no surprise that the source materials you'll use in writing papers are often a mixture of opinion and fact. After all, other writers are like you: they use source materials as a basis on which to draw conclusions about the world and the way it works. When you read source materials critically, you will often need to distinguish between facts and opinions; therefore, when writing summaries you will need to be both transparent and present.

We'll take a typical example. Assume that you are writing a paper on the behavior problems of adolescents and you come across the following paragraph by Peter Farb. It is intriguing enough that you would like to summarize and use it.

> Perhaps a total of 100 billion humans have walked the planet since the appearance of the earliest hominids. Of these, about six per cent have been agriculturists, fewer than four per cent have lived in industrialized societies, and all the rest—approximately ninety per cent—have lived as hunters and gatherers. Only during the past 12,000 years in a few places, and for less than 5000 years in most of the world, have humans domesticated plants and animals, lived in settled villages, developed complex societies, and harnessed other sources of energy besides human muscle. The 12,000 years since the earliest agriculture represent only about five hundred human generations, surely too few to allow for overwhelming genetic changes. Therefore the origins of the intellect, physique, emotions, and social life that are universal to human beings must be traced to preagricultural times. Humans are the evolutionary product of the success of the hunting adaptation, even though almost all of *Homo sapiens* alive today have abandoned that way of life. The traits acquired over millions of years of following this adaptation continue to provide the basis for human adjustment to the modern world. Still influencing us today is the fact that hunting and gathering is more than simply a particular means of subsistence. It is a complete way of life: biologically, psychologically, technologically, and socially.[7]

(Line numbers in margin: 1, 2, 3, 4, 5, 6, 7, 8, 9)

You will recall reading this paragraph in Chapter 1 (page 14), where you were asked to read critically. If your first reading was successful, you have already made important distinctions between Farb's use of potentially factual statements and his use of interpretations based on those facts. Return to page 14 and skim your notes. How effective was your reading? Compare your critical analysis to ours. We list the following as potential facts:

Sentence 1: Approximately 100 billion humans have lived.

Sentence 2: Approximately 90 percent have been hunters and gatherers.

Sentence 3: Only for 5000 years have humans in most of the world lived as agriculturalists (and, later, as industrialists) in villages.

Sentence 4: Humans have been predominantly agriculturalists for 500 generations.

Sentence 6: "Humans are the evolutionary product of...the hunting adaptation"; almost all humans "alive today have abandoned that way of life."

Sentences 8–9: "Hunting and gathering is...a complete way of life: biologically, psychologically, technologically, and socially."

We feel confident that each of these statements is potentially true, though we might want to confirm that by conducting further research (which could well

---

[7]Peter Farb, *Humankind* (Boston: Houghton Mifflin, 1978), 89.

reveal to us that one of these supposed facts is an opinion). Farb also makes statements of opinion in the paragraph.

| EXERCISE | |

Consider the following sentences. In the space provided, explain why each appears to be an opinion.

Sentence 4: "Surely [five hundred human generations are] too few to allow for overwhelming genetic changes."

_____

_____

_____

Sentence 5: "Therefore the origins of intellect, physique, emotions, and social life that are universal to human beings must be traced to preagricultural times."

_____

_____

_____

Sentence 7: "The traits acquired over millions of years of following this [hunting] adaptation continue to provide the basis for human adjustment to the modern world."

_____

_____

_____

Sentence 8: Hunting and gathering as a way of life is "still influencing us today."

_____

_____

_____

In preparing to write our summary of Farb's paragraph, we have distinguished between his use of fact and opinion. Notice that in sentence 8 Farb combines the two. We can agree that the *fact* "that hunting and gathering is more than simply a particular means of subsistence" is potentially true. But Farb asserts in the same sentence that this fact is "still influencing us today." Here is an interpretation, and we need to say that it is in our summary.

Before we begin writing, let's outline the paragraph according to the categories we established in Chapter 1. Recall that these are the categories you use whenever you choose to read an article carefully, whether or not you intend to write a summary.

Main idea

"The traits acquired over millions of years of following [the hunting] adaptation continue to provide the basis for human adjustment to the modern world."

(Note that Farb locates the main idea toward the end of the paragraph. The main idea is an *opinion* based on the facts that he presents.)

Structure

Part I: Three and a half statements of fact.

Part II: Predominantly statements of opinion.

Fact/opinion

The distinctions have been made in the preceding discussions.

Our strategy for writing the summary will be to divide the paragraph into two parts (fact and opinion), following the paragraph's structure; we will then write a one-sentence summary of each part.

> For millions of years, the great majority (90 percent) of the 100 billion people who have lived on earth have been hunters and gatherers, though modern humans have largely abandoned this way of life for agriculture and technology. According to Peter Farb, our behavior today continues to be influenced by the biological and psychological traits that enabled 90 billion of our predecessors to succeed.

This summary is the result of five revisions. Notice that in the first sentence we report potential facts in Farb's own voice. In this sentence we are transparent as writers. The second sentence begins with the phrase "according to Peter Farb," and with this phrase we "enter" the summary to make an important distinction: the statement that our behavior continues to be influenced by primitive impulses is not a fact but an interpretation of facts, or a theory. The introductory phrase notes this interpretation and distinguishes it from the facts presented earlier. Thus in our summary we have been both transparent and present, depending on the information we summarized. Note also that we have presented Farb's views *neutrally,* without comment.

EXERCISE

Now practice your skills by summarizing a paragraph that contains both facts and opinions, from *The Restless Earth* by Nigel Calder. Distinguish between facts and opinions and then, as a preparation for writing the summary, arrange your notes according to three categories: main idea, fact/opinion, and structure:

> The peak of the Matterhorn, rising to nearly 15,000 feet at the frontier of Switzerland and Italy, is not the highest in the region, but it has always been a special challenge to mountaineers in the Alps, because of its sharp profile. This pointed pyramid of rock was carved, by the action of ice, out of a much larger sheet of rock that formerly covered the area. We can now suppose, with considerable confidence, that the top section of the Matterhorn is a piece of Africa that was pushed on top of Europe. By Africa we mean Italy, originally a part of Africa, which was torn, rotated and driven towards Switzerland.[8]

What is the main idea? _____

_____

_____

List potential facts: _____

_____

_____

List opinions: _____

_____

_____

How is the paragraph structured? _____

_____

_____

Now write a one- or two-sentence summary. Because the paragraph contains fact and opinion, you will need to be both transparent and present, as we were in summarizing the paragraph by Farb. Check the accuracy of the summary by comparing your version with others'.

_____

_____

_____

_____

_____

Two Methods for Organizing Summaries

The Paragraph Method

One effective way of preparing a summary is to summarize every paragraph of an article. If you place the resulting list of sentences on a sheet of

[8]Nigel Calder, *The Restless Earth: A Report on the New Geology* (New York: Viking, 1972), 33–34.

paper *beneath* what you understand to be the author's thesis, you will in effect have written the first draft of a summary. You will need to revise to achieve smoothness and eliminate repetition, but the content of the summary will have been established. The paragraph method of summarizing works best with short articles. Given an article longer than twenty paragraphs, you'll want to use a different method for summarizing; but more on that later. Reread "The Thick and Thin of It," which you saw before in Chapter 1.

If every person in Macau were given equal portions of land, each would live in a space a quarter the size of a tennis court. If you take into account the room necessary for streets, stores, and offices, people living in Macau (like people living in Manhattan) are more likely to end up with an apartment the size of a Ping-Pong table. With more than 63,000 people per square mile, Macau, a tiny city-state off the coast of China, is the most densely populated place in the world. 1

Every Falkland Islander, by contrast, could roam over two and a half square miles without ever seeing another human. But he'd better watch where he steps; sheep outnumber people by more than 300 to one. 2

No single cause explains why some areas of the world are so much more thickly settled than others. But high population density can be an accident of political history, as it is in city-states such as Macau. And it is often the result of geography: the three most densely populated countries in the world—Macau, Hong Kong, and Singapore—are all islands. Many larger island countries, such as Malta, Taiwan, and Barbados, also rank among the most densely settled parts of the world. 3

Density can also be the result of the economy of an area. "The Falkland Islands are so thinly settled because they have no resources other than sheep," says Tom Merrick of the Population Reference Bureau in Washington, D.C. "The population doesn't grow because so many people emigrate." 4

The countries that are least densely populated often have obvious climatic or geographical flaws, like Mongolia (three people per square mile). Australia has a population density of five per square mile, and Canada has only seven, demonstrating the effect of huge hinterlands. The United States is not very crowded, despite perceptions to the contrary, with 65 people per square mile. "A lot of our land is uninhabitable," says Ken Hill, a demographer at the National Academy of Sciences in Washington, D.C. "The Rockies, the desert, and the rangeland are not places people want to live, so they crowd together in pleasanter surroundings." 5

If high population density were a measure of pleasantness, then Bangladesh would be pleasant indeed. With 1,800 people per square mile, it is the most densely settled nonisland nation in the world. Nearly 100 million people live in an area the size of Arkansas. All of Bangladesh is arable, and that explains its density. "There are no deserts, mountains, or impenetrable forests," says Hill. "There's plenty of rainfall, so most fields yield two crops a year." 6

Socioeconomic factors also influence population density. In Bangladesh, mothers and fathers see additional children as contributing to the family labor force, not detracting from the family food supply. Children often work 10-hour days on their families' subsistence-level farms. Women usually have seven or eight children, partly to compensate for the high infant mortality rate. Falkland Islanders, in comparison, have only two children per family. "They have a 7

European attitude toward children," says Hill. "They don't see the need for more, even though for years emigration has been causing the country's population to decline."

When is a place too empty or too crowded? That's a judgment everyone has to make for himself. In Manhattan people press together in subways and on street corners without batting an eye. But in America a hundred years ago, the sound of an axe in the next clearing signalled that it was time to move on.[9]

8

On page 25 you will find that we already wrote one-sentence summaries of each paragraph. We reprint them here, leaving a space above for the thesis.

Thesis: _____

_____

_____

Paragraph 1: "Macau, a tiny city-state off the cost of China, is the most densely populated place in the world."

Paragraph 2: The Falkland Islands are thinly populated.

Paragraph 3: Population density has many causes. One is the "accident of political history"; another is geography.

Paragraph 4: Economy can affect population density.

Paragraph 5: "Climatic or geographical flaws" result in low population density.

Paragraph 6: Bangladesh's entirely arable land and favorable climate have resulted in a highly dense population.

Paragraph 7: "Socioeconomic factors also influence population density."

Paragraph 8: Each person's tolerance of population density is a matter of individual taste.

Based on our critical reading of the passage, we've determined that Blythe Hamer's thesis is "No single cause explains why some areas of the world are so much more thickly settled than others." When writing a summary, you should look for a thesis sentence in the original passage and determine whether or not it would be suitable as a thesis for the summary. Generally, we prefer to write our own thesis; we reserve quoting an author for two occasions: when the original language is particularly apt, as is the case when the author coins a phrase or uses a colorful expression (this would help make the summary interesting), and when the original language is particularly clear on a difficult point that we've had trouble summarizing (this would help make the summary clear). In this case, there are no elements in Hamer's thesis that we could not summarize well, so we'll use our own version:

Many factors contribute to population density.

[9]Blythe Hamer, "The Thick and Thin of It," *Science* 86 (January/February 1986): 58.

Wherever it occurs in an original passage, the thesis in a summary is placed first. When we place our thesis at the head of the preceding eight-sentence list and then run the sentences together into paragraph form, the resulting paragraph looks like this:

> Many factors contribute to population density. "Macau, a tiny city-state off the coast of China, is the most densely populated place in the world." The Falkland Islands are thinly populated. Population density has many causes. One is the "accident of political history"; another is geography. Economy can affect population density. "Climate and geographical flaws" result in low population density. Bangladesh's entirely arable land and favorable climate have resulted in a highly dense population. "Socioeconomic factors also influence population density. Each person's tolerance of population density is a matter of individual taste.

You should expect this first draft of the summary to be rough. As yet, there are no transitions, and we have not revised to eliminate repetition. Though we have distilled the important content of Hamer's article, we would not feel comfortable in calling this paragraph complete. More to the point, we would not want to call the paragraph a paragraph: it lacks smooth transitions from one sentence to the next; the words *population density* occur more times than we would like to count; and some sentences, notably sentences 2 and 3, appear to be out of order. The last situation is no surprise since these are one-sentence summaries of paragraphs intended to *introduce* a thesis that we have shifted to the beginning of the summary. As a result, we are left with two sentences of introduction in the summary that introduce nothing. This paragraph clearly needs work!

What we must do for this — for any — summary is create a new context that is independent of the original passage. We need to regard the paragraph we are writing as an entity unto itself that should have its own beginning, middle, and end. We want a paragraph that is *unified,* one in which all sentences clearly refer to the thesis. We want a paragraph that is *coherent,* one in which every sentence leads logically to the next. And we want a paragraph that will read smoothly, without repetitions. Follow us as we revise our very rough first draft of the summary. Notes in the margins explain our handwritten changes.

Part of original intro. Delete

Delete reference to Bangladesh as an example of climate's and geography's effect on density.

Many factors contribute to population density. ~~"Macau, a tiny city-state off the coast of China, is the most densely populated place in the world." The Falkland Islands are thinly populated. Population density has many causes.~~ *cause of population density* One is the "accident of political history"; another is geography. Economy can affect population density~~,~~ *as well as* "~~Climate or~~ *and* geographical flaws" result in low popu~~lation density. Bangladesh's entirely arable land and favorable climate have resulted in a highly dense population.~~ "Socioeconomic factors~~, also influence population density.~~" Each person's tolerance of population density is a matter of individual taste.

Geography mentioned in previous sent.

Mostly what we have done to this paragraph is to delete material. In the revised version we've cut all examples, making the summary's second draft considerably shorter than the first:

> Many factors contribute to population density. One cause of population density is the "accident of political history"; another is geography. Economy can affect population density as well as climate and socioeconomic factors. Each person's tolerance of population density is a matter of individual taste.

We can streamline the summary further by combining all of the factors mentioned by Hamer into one list. Notice that we will shift the order of elements, placing "economic" and "socioeconomic" factors together to avoid awkwardness. When writing a summary, do not hesitate to rearrange information according to your needs. The summary should function as a coherent and unified paragraph. These criteria often require that you alter the order in which information is presented in the original passage.

> Many factors contribute to population density. ~~One cause of population density is~~ the "accident[s] of political history"; ~~another is~~ geography. ~~Economy can affect population density as well as~~ (climate;) and socioeconomic~, and economic~ factors. *[handwritten: among them]* Each person's tolerance of population density is a matter of individual taste.
>
> ⇓
>
> Many factors determine population density, among them the "accident[s] of political history"; geography; climate; and socioeconomic and economic factors. Each person's tolerance of population density is a matter of individual taste.

Unfortunately, the result of all of our cutting and streamlining is that the summary has a skimpy feel. The more we read it, the more we want an example or two. So we'll resurrect the examples from the introductory paragraphs (we had cut them earlier) and place them just before the summary's final sentence—which, without a mention of specific examples, seems strangely unrelated to the list of factors. Read the next revision, its new sentence in italics:

> Many factors determine population density, among them the "accident[s] of political history"; geography; climate; and socioeconomic and economic factors. *Many people live on Macau, the world's most crowded place; fewer live on the Falkland Islands, among the world's least crowded places.* Each person's tolerance of population density is a matter of individual taste.

Notice how we reworked the information from Hamer's first two paragraphs back into the summary, after we had cut it initially. Recall that our one-sentence summaries of Hamer's introduction were as follows:

Paragraph 1: "Macau, a tiny city-state off the coast of China, is the most densely populated place in the world."

Paragraph 2: The Falkland Islands are thinly populated.

We modified these sentences so that we would have a single, short, parallel construction that did two jobs: to fill out the summary by providing some detail and to create a transition between the list of factors and the summary's final sentence. We did this by providing the briefest possible examples that would lead into (and create a context for) the summary's conclusion about population density and individual preference. The result proved only partially effective, for the first and (new) second sentences of the summary seemed unrelated, as did sentences 2 and 3. Better transitions were needed, so we tried again. Here is our solution, with the additional phrases set in italics:

> Many factors determine population density, among them the "accident[s] of political history"; geography; climate; and socioeconomic and economic factors. *These factors can combine to create a high density,* as on Macau, the world's most crowded place; *and a low density,* as on the Falkland Islands, among the world's least crowded places. *Wherever one lives,* tolerance of population density is a matter of individual taste.

At last, we have arrived at a summary that works. Note how the two new transitions function: In "these factors can combine," the repetition of the word *factor* ties the content of sentence 1 into the content of sentence 2. The final transition, "wherever one lives," depends for its sense on the previous sentence (and thus creates a strong logical connection between the last sentence and the rest of the paragraph). In this final draft we've arrived at an acceptable summary of Hamer's article. You'll notice that the summary contains virtually no details, just major points (the exception being the reworked summary of the introduction). If readers need particular examples of any factors contributing to high or low population density, they can refer to the original article. Finally, note that since the information in Hamer's article is potentially factual, we adopted a transparent stance as we wrote; we have offered no distinctions between fact and opinion.

The Section Method

If the article you are summarizing is short—say, twenty paragraphs or less—then using the paragraph method of summary works well. But for longer articles, this approach can be tedious. A second approach is the section method. To use this method, you divide an article into its component parts, or sections. Instead of writing a summary of every paragraph, you write a one- or two-sentence summary of every *section*. The length you determine for a section depends on the length of the source material. When you are summarizing a book, each section would consist of a chapter, or even a group of chapters if the book is exceptionally long. When you are summarizing a long article, a section may consist of two or three pages.

EXERCISE	

In Chapter 1 you spent time working on a structural outline of Patricia Curtis's "The Case Against Animal Experiments." It is time now to put that close reading to work by writing a summary. Refer to pages 31–34, where you provided four content labels for the article after we had provided three. Use these content labels in the following outline. If you read the article well and spent time underlining and making notations in the margins, then the following exercise should not take long. If you have not completed the exercise on pages 31–34, do so before attempting the summary here.

After each of the article's seven part headings, write a one- or two-sentence summary. Remember that if you have made any distinctions between Curtis's use of facts and opinions, then you must reflect these distinctions in the summary itself. (When making distinctions, remember to use present-tense verbs, as discussed on page 46.)

We begin these notes for the summary by writing a thesis, which (based on our reading in Chapter 1) we've cast as follows:

> *Thesis*: Patricia Curtis believes that animal experimentation is inhumane and should be abandoned or made more humane as other means of research become available.

Part I (paragraphs 1–3): The story about Salome

_____

_____

_____

_____

Part II (paragraphs 4–6): A statement of the problem

_____

_____

_____

_____

Part III (paragraphs 7–9): Background information

_____

_____

_____

_____

Part IV (paragraphs 10–11): _____

_____

_____

_____

_____

Part V (paragraphs 12–13): _____

_____

_____

_____

_____

Part VI (paragraphs 14–18): _____

_____

_____

_____

_____

Part VII (paragraphs 19–20): _____

_____

_____

_____

_____

Use the thesis we've provided to organize a summary of the article. As with the paragraph method for writing summaries, position the thesis as the first sentence; place the subsequent section summaries below it, in paragraph form. The result of this effort will most certainly be repetitive and choppy and in need of revision. Revise the paragraph several times until you achieve a brief, accurate, and readable summary. Compare your final effort with those of your classmates. You and others working with Curtis's article should be able to agree on what counts as essential information. You should also be able to agree on the portions of the article that are potentially factual and those that are predominantly opinion. Be sure to reflect these distinctions in the summary itself.

EXERCISE

For your next assignment, use either the section method or the paragraph method and write a summary of "Growth Industries of the Future," which appears on pages 215–217 in Chapter 7. Be sure to identify Nicholson's main idea and to use that idea as the thesis—the first sentence of the summary. Identify the structure of the article and write summaries of each section (or each paragraph). Distinguish between facts and opinions, and call attention to these distinctions.

For quick reference, here is a step-by-step approach for writing summaries. Realize that every article presents unique challenges; to write an effective summary, you must show flexibility, determination, and insight.

- *Read* the article or other piece of writing carefully. Determine its structure.
- *Reread.* This time divide the article into sections. The author's use of paragraphing will often be a useful guide. *Label,* on the article itself, each section. *Underline* key ideas and terms and make marginal notations.
- *Write one-sentence summaries* of each section on a separate sheet of paper. If the article is brief, write one-sentence summaries of each paragraph.

- *Write a thesis, a one-sentence summary of the entire article.* The thesis should express the central idea of the article, as you have determined it from the preceding steps. You may find it useful to keep in mind the information contained in the lead sentence or paragraph of most newspaper stories—the *what, who, why, where, when,* and *how* of the matter. *Note:* In some cases a suitable thesis may already be in the original article. If so, you may want to quote it directly in your summary.

- *Write the first draft of your summary* by combining the thesis with your one-sentence summaries. Eliminate repetition. Eliminate less important information. Disregard minor details or generalize them. Use as few words as possible to convey the main ideas.

- *Check your summary against the original article* and make whatever adjustments are necessary for accuracy and completeness.

- *Revise your summary,* inserting transitional words and phrases where necessary to ensure coherence. Check for style. *Avoid a series of short, choppy sentences.* Combine sentences for a smooth, logical flow of ideas. Check for grammatical correctness, punctuation, and spelling.

Summary and Paraphrase

A summary is a *brief* restatement, in your own words, of the content of a piece of writing. A paraphrase is also a restatement, but it is often as long as the original work. Compare a summary and a paraphrase of the following paragraph.

> The honeybee colony, which usually has a population of 30,000 to 40,000 workers, differs from that of the bumblebee and many other social bees or wasps in that it survives the winter. This means that the bees must stay warm despite the cold. Like other bees, the isolated honeybee cannot fly if the temperature falls below 10°C (50°F) and cannot walk if the temperature is below 7°C (45°F). Within the wintering hive, bees maintain their temperature by clustering together in a dense ball; the lower the temperature, the denser the cluster. The clustered bees produce heat by constant muscular movements of their wings, legs, and abdomens. In very cold weather, the bees on the outside of the cluster keep moving toward the center, while those in the core of the cluster move to the colder outside periphery. The entire cluster moves slowly about on the combs, eating the stored honey from the combs as it moves.[10]

A summary of this paragraph would read as follows:

> Honeybees, unlike many other varieties of bee, are able to live through the winter by "clustering together in a dense ball" for body warmth.

[10]"Winter Organization," in Helena Curtis, *Biology,* second edition, (New York: Worth, 1976), 822–823.

A paraphrase of the same passage would be considerably more detailed:

> Honeybees, unlike many other varieties of bee (such as bumblebees and wasps), are able to live through the winter. The 30,000 to 40,000 bees within a honeybee hive could not, individually, move about in cold winter temperatures. But when "clustering together in a dense ball," the bees generate heat by constantly moving their body parts. The cluster also moves slowly about the hive, eating honey stored in the combs. This nutrition, in addition to the heat generated by the cluster, enables the honeybee to survive the cold winter months.

As you can see, the paraphrase is more detailed than the summary. You must determine, based on the needs of a particular paper, which of these techniques to use. Use the summary when a brief recounting will do. Use the paraphrase when detailed information is needed—when, for instance, your paper requires that you closely follow the logic of a presentation as it is developed in a source. Remember also to use quotation marks whenever you use someone else's language. (See our discussion on using quotations on pages 171–183.)

EXERCISE	

Two passages follow. Summarize and paraphrase each. The first passage is taken from Jacob Bronowski's *The Ascent of Man.*

> It took at least two million years for man to change from the little dark creature with the stone in his hand, *Australopithecus* in Central Africa, to the modern form, *Homo sapiens*. That is the pace of biological evolution—even though the biological evolution of man has been faster than that of any other animal. But it has taken much less than twenty thousand years for *Homo sapiens* to become the creatures that you and I aspire to be: artists and scientists, city builders and planners for the future, readers and travellers, eager explorers of natural fact and human emotion, immensely richer in experience and bolder in imagination than any of our ancestors. That is the pace of cultural evolution; once it takes off, it goes as the ratio of those two numbers goes, at least a hundred times faster than biological evolution.[11]

Write a one-sentence summary of the passage.

_____

_____

Write a paraphrase of the passage.

_____

_____

[11]Jacob Bronowski, *The Ascent of Man,* text edition (Boston: Little, Brown, 1973), 59.

_____
_____
_____
_____

The second passage concerns "multiple family groups" (MFGs) and is excerpted from a book by Stuart Koman on adolescent and family therapy. A multiple family group, led by a trained psychologist or psychiatrist, is a therapeutic technique in which four to seven families are brought together in one place to actively work on and resolve family difficulties.

There is a metaphor that's useful for conceptualizing a multiple family group: the symphony orchestra. Taking each member of the group as an instrument, and each family or subgroup (children, adults, males, females, etc.) as a section, the orchestra develops its potential by learning to blend and contrast all of its sounds. Through the building of themes that are played and replayed in seemingly unending variations, each instrument establishes its own unique place and the orchestra expands its repertoire. With this in mind, the jobs of the leader/conductor become clear. These are: (1) to help choose the pieces that will challenge the orchestra to evolve beyond its present ability; (2) to control and structure the orchestra so that all of the instruments can be heard; (3) to provide guidance, nuance, feeling, and interpretation so that the resulting product has meaning beyond the notes played; and (4) to model tolerance and respect for each sound and family of sound.

The MFG is far more like the orchestra in rehearsal than the orchestra in performance. Imperfection, the constant reworking of themes, and striving for improvement are the main fare. Drama, elegance, excitement, and resolution are extremely powerful, but less often seen. The leader/conductor has some control over the group, but the metaphorical crutch fails to describe adequately the mutual development and participation of the group and the leader in writing the "symphony" as the group evolves. Unlike the real orchestra, the MFG has no finished piece to play. Rather, the group works on each other's problems, aided by the leader's expertise in promoting a context for resolution.[12]

Write a two-sentence summary of the passage. (You can assume that you've already defined the term "multiple family group." You need not define it in the summary or paraphrase.)

_____
_____
_____

Write a paraphrase of the passage.

_____
_____

[12]Stuart L. Koman, "Conducting Short-term Inpatient Multiple Family Therapy," in _Handbook of Adolescents and Family Therapy,_ eds. Marsha Pravder Mirkin and Stuart L. Koman (New York: Gardner, 1985), 173–174.

Review your work. Have you stated clearly whose material you're summarizing or paraphrasing so as to avoid plagiarism? If you've borrowed any language from other sources, have you used quotation marks? In both paraphrase and summary, are you satisfied that most of the language is your own?

CHAPTER 3

◻︎▭ **Making Inferences**

███ **Introduction**

Suppose that one afternoon you walk to the local high school to watch a basketball game. The tipoff is at 4:00 P.M., you arrive at the school at 3:50, and there are *no* other people to be found! For a few moments you stare in disbelief. And then your mind starts to work furiously.

What happens next is a process known as *inference*. You are presented with certain facts and attempt to draw conclusions based on those facts. Fact number 1 is that the game was supposed to begin at 4 o'clock. Fact number 2 is that there are no people standing about. Your first conclusion—or *inference*—is that the game is obviously not going to start at 4 o'clock because if it were, there would surely be other people around by this time. Your second inference is that you must have gotten your first "fact" wrong. If this is the case, there are, you infer, two possibilities. Either you have the time wrong (perhaps the game was played yesterday at 4:00, or perhaps it won't be played until later in the day or even until next week); or you have the place wrong (perhaps this is not, as you had thought, a home game). At this point you can't be certain of which inference is correct until you have more facts on which to base a decision. And so you call a friend to get those facts.

Whether you realize it or not, you make inferences all the time — successfully. You have an *implicit* understanding of the process. Our goal here is to make this understanding *explicit,* for you will need to make inferences carefully, and quite consciously, in order to read and write well. An *inference* is a conclusion that you must draw for yourself using information presented to you. This conclusion could not be drawn were you not able to make careful observations about what you encounter and then to make educated guesses based on those observations. Note that inferences differ from summaries and opinions. A *summary* is brief restatement, in your own words, of the contents of a piece of writing. When summarizing, you do not draw conclusions; you simply say what has already been said, but in fewer words and in your own words. An *opinion* is an idea, an interpretation, a judgment that someone (either you or another) states directly. But when you draw a conclusion from evidence and that conclusion has not been previously stated, then you are making an *inference.*

You might recall an example of inference at work in the Mike Nichols film *The Graduate.* Benjamin, fresh from four years of college, has just driven home from his graduation party the attractive, middle-aged Mrs. Robinson, a friend of his parents.

> *Benjamin:* For God's sake, Mrs. Robinson! Here we are — you got me into your house, you give me a drink, you put on music, now you start opening up your personal life to me and tell me your husband won't be home for hours. . . . Mrs. Robinson, you're trying to seduce me! Aren't you?

Benjamin has correctly inferred the significance of Mrs. Robinson's actions; but the older woman, still playing with the young man she hopes to ensnare, assures him that he has drawn the wrong conclusion — and Benjamin humbly apologizes!

We are constantly drawing inferences based on what we see and hear and on how others behave. The world is filled with facts that, by themselves, are lifeless: they have no value or significance unless you can integrate them into your own thinking and experience through the process of inference making. This integration requires effort. No one awakes one morning able to make sophisticated inferences about academic material without first having devoted many hours of work to such tasks. The ability to make an inference is a skill, and above all you need a willingness to be *interested* in what you read and hear. When you are interested, you question; when you question, you create for yourself an urge to seek answers, and this urge leads directly to the process of inference making. Without a commitment of interest on your part, the process cannot begin.

Assume that you are reading an article on genetic engineering. You sense that the author does not support experimentation with DNA. You wonder: Why do I get this impression? This question suggests that you are interested enough in the article to have had a response—the crucial first step. Now you begin the process of making an inference: you've posed a question that needs answering. The next step is to return to the article and reexamine the evidence presented. On rereading, you notice that the author never directly states that genetic engineering is dangerous and should be discontinued. However, you've observed that the author presents only evidence *against* gene splicing and its consequences. You now understand your hunch. On the basis of evidence, you have inferred the author's views. Imagine that your roommate has read this same article and has nothing to say other than a perfunctory "Oh, wasn't that interesting." This response is not followed by a detailed, thoughtful reaction. If your roommate had not been interested enough in the subject to pose questions, then he would be in no position to infer anything useful about the article. (A *useful* observation is one that clarifies or intelligently comments on important issues in an article.) Perhaps you find that this process of making initial observations, posing questions, and then searching out evidence resembles the investigative work of Sherlock Holmes or Agatha Christie's Miss Marple. What distinguishes these fictional sleuths from their more prosaic counterparts is an ability to draw accurate conclusions based on the scantiest evidence—what has appeared, in fact, not to be evidence at all to other observers. (Think of your roommate's and your response to the article on genetic engineering.) What will distinguish you as a college student is your ability not only to master a collection of facts but also to draw interesting inferences from them. Realize that you must *do something* with the information you acquire; for this to happen, you must be interested, willing to question, ready to reexamine evidence, and able to make inferences. In sum, you must be observant, creative, and willing to take an intellectual risk.

Active Questioning

As you gain experience, you will improve your ability to pose good questions about what you read. Here we discuss five questions you might consider. Each assumes that you're examining a single source. When you write a paper, you will need to question and draw inferences from several sources, the subject of Chapter 4. For the moment, we'll consider individual sources.

Questioning What Has Happened

In the example that began this chapter, we placed you at the gymnasium doors of a local high school. You arrived for a basketball game and did not see what you expected. Questions occurred to you: What's happened here? Where is everyone? You considered possibilities, *inferred* certain conclusions, and then attempted to gain more facts that would most likely confirm one of your inferences.

Knowing what has happened is not always easy, and when it is not you must review events carefully and assemble all available and pertinent facts. Observe them and speculate about possibilities: make inferences about what has happened. Then pose questions that will suggest ways to gather more facts until you have assembled enough information to confirm one of your inferences and know what has happened — or, alternatively, not to know. (There are many cases in which no one besides those immediately involved in an action knows what has happened. Think of all the crimes that go unsolved every year.)

Just as we can end an exploration with understanding, we can end with uncertainty; but assume for the moment that, based on your powers of observation, you can review a set of clues and piece together events as they occurred. Now you will have a chance to try your skills.

EXERCISE	

Read the following two vignettes, or sketches, and state as clearly as possible the facts as you understand them. Next make inferences: speculate about what might have happened. Finally, list the additional information you think would be needed to confirm one (or more) of your inferences.

You are walking down a street in your hometown and see a limousine parked before a church.

You are walking down a street in your hometown and see a limousine parked before your house.

Facts: How do the facts differ in these two cases?

_____

_____

_____

Inferences: What can you infer has happened in each case?

_____

_____

_____

What further information would you need to confirm one (or more) of your inferences?

_____

_____

_____

_____

Explain why your inferences change depending on the facts presented.

_____

_____

Your college roommate is a psychology major interested in how and whether animals can learn. Already she has adopted and trained a dog that can catch Frisbees and a cat that can press a lever, dispensing milk into a bowl. Your roommate buys a canary. One day on returning from classes, you see an empty bird cage, its door open, sitting in an empty lot adjacent to your apartment building.

Facts: _____

_____

_____

_____

Inferences: What has happened? (There are several possibilities.)

_____

_____

_____

What further information would you need to confirm one (or more) of your inferences?

_____

_____

_____

_____

Questioning the Cause of an Event

Often you will observe the outcome of an event and know what has happened, but you won't know why. *Why* is a question that can prompt inference making and a reexamination of evidence. To know why something has happened is to know its cause. You can kick a ball and see that it travels in an arc from your foot, five yards through the air, until it strikes the ground and rolls along for another five yards. Here is a simple instance of cause and effect, of an obvious action and reaction. Human relations, however, are not usually so clear-cut. Your younger brother walks into the kitchen, sobbing. His pants leg is ripped and he says in a broken voice: "I fell." That's obvious enough. Now you want to know *why*, so you ask — but he's not talking. If he had simply tripped and fallen, he would likely have said so. Why did he fall? You look out the window, up the street, and observe several schoolchildren leaping from a ledge, trying to land feet first on a concrete sidewalk a yard and a half below. You infer that your brother had been playing with his daredevil friends. But is that the only possible explanation for the fall? Why did he join his friends to begin with? You recall that a week earlier you overheard a conversation in which a schoolmate of your brother's called him a baby because he wouldn't play football. So you infer a new, and more complex, cause for the crying: he jumped from the ledge because he did not want his friends taunting him. And *why* is he so sensitive about being taunted? What's the reason for *that?*

Attempting to understand the causes of an event can become complicated, and one is never certain when to stop considering possibilities. Giving advice on this point is not easy since every event (along with its causes) differs from every other event. We can say that you should be sensitive to complexity. Don't be tempted by the simple answer, the impulse to explain a complex event by pointing to a single cause. Many people find that the more they read, the more complex the world seems to become — not because the world has changed but because their understanding of it has. When you are sensitive to complexity, you will find that cause and effect can be a very tricky business.

How thorough should you be in exploring causation? This depends. At times an event will have a simple, direct cause; at other times it will not (as, for instance, when you try to understand the motivations for someone's actions). The safest course is to assume that causes are complex unless you can prove them otherwise.

EXERCISE

Try your hand at inferring cause and effect. Read the following sketch and respond to the questions.

Before returning home one evening, you purchase an out-of-town newspaper, on an inside page of which you read a headline: "Vice-President [of U.S.] Appears in [Your Town] on Platform with Indicted Labor Leader." On arriving home, you reach for the local newspaper. Printed in bold letters across its front page is the headline: "Vice-President Graces Local Dedication Ceremony."

Facts: _____

_____

_____

_____

_____

Inferences: *Why* has this event been reported so differently in the two newspapers?

_____

_____

_____

_____

_____

Inferences: What can you infer about the objectivity of news accounts?

_____

_____

_____

_____

What further information would you need to confirm one (or more) of your inferences?

_____

_____

_____

_____

You are driving along a deserted, rainswept road late one night. You pass a car, its hood raised and its emergency lights blinking. You do not stop.

Facts: _____

_____

_____

Inferences: Why did you not stop? What inferences did you make about what you had seen?

_____

_____

_____

_____

Inferences: What other inferences could you have made about the disabled car? How would these other inferences have led to a different action on your part?

_____

_____

_____

_____

_____

What further information would you need to confirm one (or more) of your inferences?

_____

_____

_____

_____

Questioning Qualities of Character or States of Mind

When you read, you invariably react to the person who is writing or to the persons or events being described. This reaction can be so strong that you begin inferring character traits or various states of mind such as optimism, pessimism, rationality, irrationality, cynicism, sincerity, insincerity, and so on. To infer a state of mind, to infer from what you read or hear what somebody else is thinking but not stating directly, requires great care. No one can see directly into the mind of another, and any claims about what someone else is thinking must be based on clearly observable evidence. The inferences you make about someone's state of mind will never be confirmed in the way that inferences about some event (a basketball game not taking place) can be confirmed. In the case of an event you can make a phone call, gain new information, and learn whether or not your inference was correct. In the case of a person's character or unstated ideas you can seek out additional information, but such information, like your own inferences, will consist of informed opinion, not fact. Nonetheless, your speculations can be of great value. Consider the following example, the first line from F. Scott Fitzgerald's *The Great Gatsby:*

> In my younger and more vulnerable years my father gave me some advice that I've been turning over in my mind ever since.

In rereading this line, we determined that it reveals something important about the speaker. What? The speaker or narrator (Nick Carraway, as we are soon to learn) is no longer young and has become less vulnerable. Why? And what has vulnerability to do with age? Our (tentative) answer: We often associate innocence and vulnerability with youth. One characteristic of innocent children is that they hold no part of themselves in reserve. They are entirely involved with relationships and have not learned to erect emotional defenses. The result can be painful, for when relationships fail the innocent are hurt badly, never having considered the need to be distrustful. Innocence makes one vulnerable; bitter experience teaches one to become guarded. When Nick implies that he is less vulnerable than he used to be, we *infer* that he has been hurt.* Once we make this inference, we are eager to read on to determine its accuracy.

*A note on vocabulary: When you read an article, you may find that an author *implies* a conclusion—that is, hints at it but does not state it directly. You as the reader, picking up on the implication, would *infer* the conclusion.

Nick states that for some time he has been considering his father's advice. We infer from this that he's a reflective sort. We can count on him to think about things carefully. We can also speculate on a bond between Nick and his father, though at the moment we have no clue as to what that bond may be.

So from a single sentence we have inferred that the narrator is reflective, has been hurt (though we don't know how), and has retreated psychologically so that he is "less vulnerable." Are these inferences true? Are they factual? No. They are interpretations based on the evidence of a single sentence. We believe that the inferences are well founded since we can relate them to specific words. We had not, after all, inferred that the narrator was wildly insane. (We could have done so, but the inference would have lacked credibility since there are no words in the sentence that would support such a conclusion.) Though our inferences are not facts, they serve as valuable guides to our reading: the more we infer, the more questions we pose, the greater our interest in what follows, and the richer our reading experience.

Notice that we've confined our observations to the person who is narrating the story—Nick Carraway. We have no basis on which to speculate about Fitzgerald himself, for Nick is not the author, but the author's creation. Only when we have read *The Great Gatsby* and most of Fitzgerald's other stories, only when we have read biographies and letters, only when we have assembled a great amount of information would we risk making inferences about the author himself. Even if we did all this, we'd have to realize that the evidence for such inferences is indirect. Compare our inferences concerning Nick with the ones we made about the basketball game, where the evidence we needed to make our inferences could not have been more direct and explicit. Inferring psychological states, as opposed to inferring what has happened in the observable world, is a complicated business. Of course, people do this all the time; but, as we said, you must be sensitive to the complexities of psychological analysis. A reasonable guideline is to make no inferences that you cannot support.

EXERCISE

The following story by Thomas Bailey Aldrich is, perhaps, the world's shortest. Read it and see what inferences you can make about the main character.

A woman is sitting alone in her old, shuttered house. She knows that she is alone in the whole world; every other thing is dead.

The doorbell rings.

Facts: _____

_____

_____

_____

_____

Inferences: What can you infer about the psychological state of the woman? Cite supporting evidence for each inference.* (In posing this question we make an assumption that the events described are not true. We'd be the first to say that this assumption may be wrong.)

_____

_____

_____

_____

List as many questions about the story as occur to you. (A discussion with one of our classes produced a list of thirty-one questions.)

_____

_____

_____

_____

What further information would you need in order to respond to these questions?

_____

_____

_____

_____

Questioning a Writer's Implied Opinions

Writers do not always express their opinions directly. At times (so as not to be heavy-handed) this omission is by choice. Imagine that a cousin writes you a letter, inviting himself for a two-month stay in your apartment. You certainly could write and state directly that he is not welcome. You could have several reasons for feeling this way: one could be that you become competitive whenever he's around, a quality you don't much admire in yourself and would like to avoid; another reason might be that your apartment is small and that you

---

*By _cite_ we mean that you should point to specific sentences or phrasings within a passage that support the point you're making.

have three roommates who don't want to be more crowded than they already are. You'd be justified in giving both reasons to your cousin, but you choose the second. After all, you'd rather not be insulting. So you take pen in hand and write the following letter:

Dear Sam,

Thanks for the note last week. I realize you need to get away from home for a while, but I'm not going to be able to put you up. My three roommates and I live in a small apartment on campus, and we don't have enough space as it is. The hotels around here are expensive, and you'd have to rent a furnished apartment for at least six months. So I'd recommend not coming to Boston right now. Besides, I'm pretty busy with school. See you at home over the semester break.

Sincerely,

Sam receives the letter, reads it, and then calls to say that he's angry and hurt. Where did you go wrong? You were careful not to come out and tell your cousin that he wasn't welcome. But if you reread the letter, you'll see there are no signs of encouragement. In fact, every sentence besides the first, perfunctory one says "no." You implied that you did not care for your cousin's company, and he correctly inferred it. Should you be surprised, then, that he has read between the lines and called to say, stiffly, "You didn't write that letter to spare my feelings. You wrote it because it was easier than being honest."

The point here is that writers often imply opinions that they do not state directly. In academic writing, when writers consciously or (as you may determine) unconsciously withhold their opinions, you are in a position to infer what those writers believe, based on what they have written. For example, recall the essay from Chapter 1 on animal experimentation. Nowhere in her twenty paragraphs does Patricia Curtis state directly that experimentation on lab animals is wrong and should be discontinued. Though she has chosen a title—"The Case Against Animal Experiments"—to provide a clue as to what follows, we cannot know conclusively what she thinks from the title alone. (An article with the same title might present the case against experimentation and then attack the reasoning as flawed.) As critical readers we must infer Curtis's opinions based on the evidence she presents. Recall the story about Salome, calculated to win our sympathy; recall also that evidence was presented unevenly so as to favor the position against experimentation. Based on these observations we felt justified in making our inference.

Whether Curtis purposefully withheld her opinion we do not know; we do know, however, that writers are sometimes so passionately involved in their topics that they are unable to see, let alone present in clear and unambiguous terms, their own opinions. Consider the arguments of someone who in a heated discussion with his neighbor lists all of the reasons why she should be selective about showing her home to potential buyers. He's making the argument that Ms. Jones shouldn't sell her house to a person of this race or that religion. "Don't you see that the property values in the neighborhood will go down? That those people drive motorcycles and fight all night long? That they'll hold weird rituals that will corrupt my Jody?" The person making these claims may well believe his stereotypes to be factual. What he does not understand, however, is that his "facts" are actually opinions; it is up to you as a shrewd listener (or reader, if the exchange were printed) to infer this man's views, which he does not (and could not) state for himself: namely, that people are not born as equals and that skin color, national origin, and religious conviction are the criteria that distinguish decent folk from less decent. You may find these beliefs to be repugnant, as we do; but before you say or write as much, you must be able to name them. And to do that you must first make inferences.

EXERCISE

Read the following paragraph by Eva Salber, a home-care physician who attends to the elderly and rural poor in North Carolina. You should be able to infer certain opinions she holds but does not state directly.

I do not want to romanticize the lives of these rural people. Their lives are hard and have almost always been ones of unremitting toil with little economic return. Many of us might well consider their lives monotonous and narrow. But we must remember that their values, and their way of life, are different from the lives of those of us who study them and plan their care. Much could be done at small expense to make their lives easier: higher Social Security payments, insulation of homes, and installation of indoor plumbing, would increase their physical comfort and help maintain independent living. Provision of physical comfort in an institutional setting does not fit the pattern of their lives. The expectations of the elderly themselves, their values, their wants, their desires, must prevail. They are oriented to their own people and home place rather than to things. Their horizons may be narrow, limited in the main to kith and kin, neighbors, friends, and church, but their emotional attachments, their human relationships, their social supports in the community are strong and make their lives fulfilling.[1]

What facts has Salber presented? _____

_____

_____

_____

Inferences: (1) What does Salber believe about her patients, though she does not say so directly? (2) What does she believe about the role of home-care physicians?

_____

_____

[1]Eva J. Salber, *Don't Send Me No Flowers When I'm Dead* (Durham, N.C.: Duke University Press, 1983), xxiii.

_____

_____

_____

_____

What evidence can you cite for the inferences you have made?

_____

_____

_____

_____

Questioning Your Response to a Piece of Writing

When you are interested in what you read, you can expect to have emotional as well as intellectual responses to articles, essays, and books. Trust these responses. If you are confused, then say so and ask why. Whatever the response, listen to yourself, identify the way you feel, trust the integrity of your feelings, and then return to the passage in search of an explanation. Find particular sentences that affect you most deeply and ask: What is it about these lines that gets me feeling angry? Elated? Confused? Wistful?

These questions will likely lead you to the process of inference making — this time not about your reading material so much as about yourself. Memories from childhood might be stirred and come rushing back to you, as might thoughts about a book you once read or some remark you overheard in a theater. Whatever your response, try to understand it by posing questions: Why do I recall these particular memories when I read this line? What was it about that remark I overhead that reminds me of this passage? And so on. *Use* your responses to these questions as a way of helping you to approach the original source material.

Read the following paragraph:

Nothing has been more productive of injury to young literary students than those stories — or legends — about great writers having written great books in a very short time. They suggest what must be in a million cases impossible, as a common possibility. You hear of Johnson having written *Rasselas* in a few weeks,* or of Beckford† having done a similar thing, of various other

---

*Samuel Johnson (1709–1784), English poet, critic, journalist, conversationalist, writer of essays, and author of *Dictionary of the English Language. Rasselas, Prince of Abyssinia,* a famous prose work that Johnson allegedly wrote in a week's time, tells the story of a man who leaves home in search of a happy life only to discover that in his searching he has neglected to live.

†William Beckford (1760?–1844), an enormously wealthy Englishman who built Fonthill Abbey and wrote the Gothic novel *Vathek.*

notables never correcting their manuscript—and the youth who has much self-confidence imagines that he can do the same thing and produce literature. I do not believe those stories. I do not say exactly that they are not true; I only say that I do not believe them, and that the books, as we have them now, certainly represent much more than the work of a few weeks or even months. It is much more valuable to remember that Gray[‡] passed fourteen years in correcting and improving a single poem, and that no great poem or book, as we now have the text, represents the first form of the text. (Take, for example, the poets that we have been reading. It is commonly said that Rossetti's "Blessed Damosel" was written in his nineteenth year.[§] This is true, but we have the text of the poem as it was written in his nineteenth year, and it is unlike the poem as we now have it; for it was changed and corrected and recorrected scores of times to bring it to its present state of perfection.) Almost everything composed by Tennyson was changed, and changed, and changed again, to such an extent that in almost every edition the text differed.[‖] Above all things, do not imagine that any good work can be done without immense pains.[2]

[‡]Thomas Gray (1716–1771), English poet, author of the lyric *Elegy Written in a Country Churchyard.*

[§]Dante Gabriel Rossetti (1828–1882), member of a prominent Anglo-Italian family. Rossetti was a poet and painter. "The Blessed Damosel" is one of his better-known poems.

[‖]Alfred, Lord Tennyson (1809–1892), famous English poet, appointed poet laureate in 1850 by Queen Victoria. His major works include *In Memoriam, Maud,* and *The Idylls of the King.*

This paragraph by Lafcadio Hearn, a Greek-born, English-educated, American newspaperman and (ultimately) naturalized citizen of Japan, was clipped by one of us, who placed it in a journal along with a note. The note is an attempt to understand a very definite, personal reaction to Hearn's remarks. As such, the note is an example of what we're suggesting you do when you read:

> Though I don't know Hearn just yet, I intend to find out who he is; the man speaks with an assurance about writing that is a tremendous comfort. I've often sat at my desk intimidated by the number of drafts it will take to make something readable. Lafcadio Hearn offers hope and assurance when he says: "Above all things, do not imagine that any good work can be done without immense pains"—although I do quibble with his use of the word "pains." Effort is required at writing—yes. But not necessarily pain. In any event, the myth of the genius who can play chess while composing a brilliant novel or essay does no one any good. To see the myth attacked, and attacked intelligently, with confidence, is encouraging. Use this paragraph somehow—with students in class; maybe in a book. Use it.

The response, as you see, is a personal one. Hearn's paragraph stirred emotions. Taking time to respond personally yields pleasure, and for this reason alone we recommend it. But there are practical uses as well for personal

[2]Lafcadio Hearn, *Talks to Writers,* ed. J. Erskine (Salem, N.H.: Ayer, 1967). Reprint of 1920 edition.

responses. Here, for example, we used Hearn's paragraph along with a journal entry to demonstrate how one can use the process of inference making to explore one's own reactions. When the time came for writing this section of the text, we recalled the paragraph and put it to use. Similarly, you can expect to use personal responses to the material you've read. Whether this use is immediate and anticipated or unanticipated, follow through with your initial reactions. Trust them, develop them, make inferences about them in an attempt to better understand yourself.

EXERCISE

Two brief paragraphs follow. The first is from Frederick Douglass's *My Bondage and My Freedom,* and the second is by Alfred Kazin, *A Walker in the City.* Choose one that you respond to, in whatever way: all that's needed is a firmly felt reaction. Then write for five minutes without stopping. Develop your response without worrying about spelling or punctuation. Pose questions to yourself repeatedly and answer them as best you can.

Col. Lloyd was not in the way of knowing much of the real opinions and feelings of his slaves respecting him. The distance between him and them was far too great to admit of such knowledge. His slaves were so numerous, that he did not know them when he saw them. Nor, indeed, did all his slaves know him. In this respect, he was inconveniently rich. It is reported of him, that, while riding along the road one day, he met a colored man, and addressed him in the usual way of speaking to colored people on the public highways of the south: "Well, boy, who do you belong to?" "To Col. Lloyd," replied the slave. "Well, does the colonel treat you well?" "No, sir," was the ready reply. "What! does he work you too hard?" "Yes, sir." "Well, don't he give enough to eat?" "Yes, sir, he gives me enough, such as it is." The colonel, after ascertaining where the slave belonged, rode on; the slave also went on about his business, not dreaming that he had been conversing with his master. He thought, said and heard nothing more of the matter, until two or three weeks afterwards. The poor man was then informed by his overseer, that, for having found fault with his master, he was now to be sold to a Georgia trader. He was immediately chained and handcuffed; and thus, without a moment's warning he was snatched away, and forever sundered from his family and friends, by a hand more unrelenting than that of death. *This* is the penalty of telling the simple truth, in answer to a series of plain questions.[3]

It was never learning I associated with that school: only the necessity to succeed, to get ahead of the others in the daily struggle to "make a good impression" on our teachers, who grimly, wearily, and often with ill-concealed distaste watched against our relapsing into the natural savagery they expected of Brownsville boys. The white, cool, thinly ruled record book sat over us from their desks all day long, and had remorselessly entered into it each day — in blue ink if we had passed, in red ink if we had not — our attendance, our conduct, our "effort," our merits and

---

[3]Frederick Douglass, *My Bondage and My Freedom* (New York: Dover, 1969), 16–17.

demerits; and to the last possible decimal point in calculation, our standing in an unending series of "tests" — surprise tests, daily tests, weekly tests, formal midterm tests, final tests. They never stopped trying to dig out of us whatever small morsel of fact we had managed to get down the night before. We had to prove that we were really alert, ready for anything, always in the race. That white thinly ruled record book figured in my mind as the judgment seat; the very thinness and remote blue lightness of its lines instantly showed its cold authority over me; so much space had been left on each page, columns and columns in which to note down everything about us, implacably and forever. As it lay there on a teacher's desk, I stared at it all day long with such fear and anxious propriety that I had no trouble believing that God, too, did nothing but keep such record books, and that on the final day He would face me with an account in Hebrew letters whose phonetic dots and dashes looked strangely like decimal points counting up my every sinful thought on earth.[4]

Review

An inference is a conclusion about a passage that you must draw for yourself. In the articles you read, writers will make their presentations, offering facts and opinions; frequently they will interpret information for you and argue for a certain conclusion. When conclusions are not developed or when they are developed but you disagree, then you are entitled to infer your own conclusions. You may, on considering the information presented, piece together a pattern, guess at an opinion, or speculate on a motivation. These initial hunches, or inferences, will often lead to questions. And questions will lead to a closer examination of the passage, the result being carefully observed details that will help you to confirm or refute your conclusions. The more you read, the more natural this process of inference making becomes. If the process feels unnatural at first and you find yourself unable to make initial hunches, then begin with this brief list of questions. Read an article, pose the questions (when they are appropriate), and develop inferences in response.

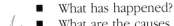

- What has happened?
- What are the causes of this event?
- What qualities of character or states of mind can be inferred about the writer or the persons described?
- What opinions does the writer hold but not state directly?
- What is your response to the piece of writing?

In responding to these questions, make sure that your inferences are valid. *Valid* does not mean *true*. A valid inference is merely defensible, which means that it can be supported by reference to particular lines in a text. If you conclude, for instance, that author Maxie Smith is against liberal parole policies but does not state as much in his essay, then you must be able to cite particular lines in the essay that support your conclusion. When such support is present,

[4]Alfred Kazin, *A Walker in the City* (New York: Harcourt, 1951), 17–18.

your inferences are said to be *valid,* and readers must respect them even though they may disagree.

Same Facts, Different Inferences

Disagreement is an engine that drives the academic world. Disagreement stimulates debate; it inspires participants and observers; it leads to expanded research; it provides a motivation to learn. At times, people will disagree on which facts should be accepted as correct and authoritative. In a court case, for instance, one lawyer might argue that her client did not violate the terms of a contract; another might argue the opposite. What are the facts? The disagreement has been brought into a courtroom so that facts can be established and a resolution reached. Disagreements can also arise when people accept the same set of facts as correct but differ over interpretation. It is this second case that interests us here. As you have probably inferred (we have not yet directly stated the point), inference making depends just as much on the reader as on the article being analyzed. Each reader brings a unique set of values and a unique history to a passage, and it is no surprise that different readers react differently to a single set of facts and opinions. How you respond to a passage reveals just as much about who you are as it does about the passage itself.

Consider: You and a friend emerge from a building on campus at 11 o'clock one evening to find a crowd of students sitting on the library steps. There is no speaker, apparently. The students seem to be enjoying themselves as they watch a full moon. A number are wearing jackets with Greek symbols on them. Somewhere you hear a radio playing. What's going on? As an officer in a fraternity, you conclude that a party is in progress and that the people who are gathered belong to a rival organization. But your friend, a physics major, says: "They must be waiting for an eclipse or a meteor shower."

As it turns out, both of you are right. You've stumbled onto a party, the reason for which (as if there needed to be one) is a partial eclipse of the moon. Because you brought different perspectives to the same facts, you and your friend emerged with different conclusions; actually, you based your inferences on somewhat different facts. Your friend observed people watching the full moon but did not register the significance of the Greek letters on their jackets. You observed the letters but failed to notice the moon. Both inferences are valid, though neither is entirely correct.

The perspective you bring to a set of facts obliges you to see in a certain way. We can never get outside of or drop our personal perspective in order to see something as it "really" is. That attitude itself is a perspective. The best we can do is to understand the virtues and limits of how we see and to appreciate that different people will regard the same facts differently. Let's consider an example. Read the following paragraph.

Dear Ms. Flynn:

I am a 28-year-old woman working as a registered nurse in a large metropolitan hospital. I've worked for seven years and am happy with my profession. Yet I have difficulty communicating with the hospital management. Although other nurses on the staff and patients agree that my work is competent, my managers express dissatisfaction at biannual reviews. On a day-to-day basis, however, they are silent, offering no encouragement or constructive criticism. As a result, I go to work feeling unsure of myself and come home feeling crabby. I'm losing confidence and am in need of some advice.

Struggling RN

As we read this paragraph, a question occurs to us: What is the source of this person's difficulties? The question leads us to reexamine the evidence. When we reread the letter, we can establish potentially factual information about the working environment in the nurse's hospital:

Management
  — conducts biannual reviews
  — provides no daily feedback
RN
  — competent worker with seven years' experience
  — happy with her profession
  — unhappy with the management in this particular job

For each of these apparent facts we would want corroborating evidence. There's no reason to think that the information in the nurse's letter is inaccurate. But then again, since we have to be sure of our facts before making inferences based upon them, we would certainly want to verify that the writer is a competent nurse. Other nurses on the hospital staff, along with physicians, would be in a good position to evaluate Struggling RN's competence. And patients with whom she's worked could help us verify her interpersonal skills.

Assuming the nurse's information is reliable, we can make certain inferences. But let us establish, first, the perspective from which we're writing, since this will largely determine the inferences we make. We'll assume that we are sociologists whose job it is to observe the functioning of groups. Two questions organize the way we see: (1) How do groups function within the larger society? (2) How do individuals interact to create a group? Given this perspective, we can make the following inferences:

> This writer describes a working environment that is flawed. In a well-managed workplace, employees are for the most part content and productive. That the nurse has lost confidence in her skills and is unhappy suggests that the hospital management is in need of reorganization. It's possible that her frustrations are due more to her problems than to her employers'; so before agreeing with her assessments we would want to hear the views of other staff members.

Our inclination, however, is to believe that the nurse's lack of confidence is a problem caused by ill-trained managers. Our advice would be that the woman look for new employment in a workplace that is structured differently — one that is not so rigidly hierarchical in the sense that employees feel they always have someone over them, evaluating their performance. In a smaller hospital or in a hospice center, the organization's structure would be completely different and better suited to the nurse's personality.

For this inference to be valid, we must demonstrate how we arrived at it by citing certain information in the two paragraphs. First we begin with our belief that the observations made by the nurse are accurate descriptions of her working environment. We want to verify her observations by checking with other employees; but for the moment we'll assume that her report is accurate. Here is our rationale for the inference we've made. Again, remember that we are writing as sociologists, interested in group behavior.

> Individuals work in groups, and when individuals are frustrated the source of their frustrations often lies within the organization or, more properly, the disorganization of the larger group. Groups must function well in order for individual members to do so. In this case, the group structure appears to be flawed: this employee feels that her managers offer no constructive criticisms. When this happens, even the most resilient individuals begin to doubt their worth—both professionally and personally—which is what we see happening with the nurse. For organizations to work well, communication must be clear and open; responsibilities must be understood; good work must be rewarded; and employees must feel free to vent dissatisfactions with the hope of having them addressed (without the fear of getting themselves fired). Because communication is clear in the well-managed, well-organized company, an employee will know whether or not she is performing adequately.

We've made our inference—that the writer's working environment is flawed—and we've demonstrated its validity by referring to and discussing material in her letter. The paragraph on which we've based our inference appeared in an advice column. Read the columnist's—Juliette Flynn's—response to the nurse. It could not be more different from ours, and yet the inferences that Ms. Flynn makes and the ones that we have made are based on identical information. See if you can guess the perspective from which the columnist is writing.

> Dear Struggling:
> I advise that you go to your supervisors and express your concerns over the lack of feedback. If they are unresponsive, you might want to consider looking for another job, either in your hospital itself or in another hospital. Having new managers with no preconceived (negative) notions about your abilities will provide the breathing room necessary to start over and regain your confidence. Assuming, as you say, that you're good at your job, a change of scenery should do the trick. However, if you *do* have problems communicating or if your technical skills *are* in need of improvement, then your new managers will express dissatisfaction, too—in which case you'll need to take a hard look within and realize that you may need to change in both performance and attitude.
> Unless you own a business, you'll always be working for someone and will thus be in the position of proving yourself. This can be stressful, I agree. But like it or not, having managers who evaluate your performance is a fact of working life. You must satisfy the expectations of your superiors, knowing that

as a rule they will not indulge you. *Their* superiors do not pay them to indulge you, but rather to ensure that you do the best work possible. I agree that an employee should be able to expect encouragement and advice. For whatever reason, you're not getting these now, so you should look elsewhere. But be prepared to look within as well. If the problems you describe recur, it is time for some limited, goal-specific counseling that will help you to accept the advice and criticism of others better. The object is to communicate effectively with the people you work for. After all, you may one day be a manager, and the lessons you learn now will surely come in handy.

Juliette Flynn

You will see how different are the conclusions that we and the columnist draw. As you reread the two responses to the nurse's letter, you should be able to make your own inferences: first about the columnist and next about us. For instance, you should be able to infer that we organize our analysis around conditions in the working environment, while Flynn organizes her discussion around the *individual's* functioning (or in this case, not functioning) in the working environment. We examine the larger group; Flynn examines the individual in that group. We infer that the group dynamic is flawed; Juliette Flynn infers that the individual is flawed. Thus we have two very different inferences drawn from identical information. Assuming that you've observed these different inferences in articles that you've read, your next job is to determine what *you* believe about the facts. Who seems to be right—Juliette Flynn or us? Perhaps neither of us is right. Why? You answer these questions by making your own inferences, realizing that what you infer has a great deal to do with your perspective as a critical reader.

When you read a primary (or uninterpreted) source, like the letter from Struggling RN, then you will make inferences based directly on that piece of writing. When you read a secondary source—an interpretation of a passage, as our inferences and Flynn's inferences would be—then you will make two sets of inferences: the first about the original source, if it is provided, and the second about the interpretations of that source.* That is, you would make inferences about *our* inferences.

EXERCISE	

Make inferences now as you answer these two questions:
Based on your reading of our response to the nurse, what do we feel about the potential for employees to be satisfied with their managers? What evidence can you find in what we've written to support your answer?

---

*See page 113 for more on the distinction between primary and secondary sources.

_____

_____

What does Juliette Flynn feel about the potential for employees to be satisfied with their managers? What evidence can you find in what she's written to support your answer?

_____

_____

_____

Your efforts to understand your own perspective as a reader are easier
when you have other responses to compare yours against. When comparison is
not practical, try asking yourself how someone else—a *worthy* opponent—
would see identical evidence. If you give the exercise your best effort, you will
learn to appreciate how differing (but still valid) inferences can be made about
a single source.

Combining Your Skills in a Single, Coherent Analysis

Having learned to distinguish facts from opinions in Chapter 1, to write
summaries in Chapter 2, and now to make inferences, you are in a position to
bring sophisticated skills to bear on the articles you read. When the occasion
requires, you should develop a single, comprehensive analysis of a source
based on three categories: *facts,* the author's *opinions,* and your *inferences.*

1. Read for facts.
   Be able to write a summary of the article.
   Identify the thesis, the main idea of the article.
   Understand supporting material.
   Understand the structure.
2. Read for the author's opinions.
   Clearly distinguish between potential facts and the author's opinions.
   Identify facts that have been influenced by opinions.
3. Respond to the article with questions and make inferences about what
   you read.
   Be aware of conflicting inferences that can be made about the same
   source.

EXERCISE	

We turn now to a sample article, "Sharon Atkins—Receptionist" from Studs Terkel's
Working, and ask you to develop a critical reading. As you read, distinguish facts from opinions, and then make what inferences you can. We'll help by prompting you with questions.

(A receptionist at a large business establishment in the Midwest. She is 24. Her husband is a student. "I was out of college, an English lit. major. I looked around for copywriting jobs. The people they wanted had majored in journalism. Okay, the first myth that blew up in my face is that a college education will get you a job.")

"I changed my opinion of receptionists because now I'm one. It wasn't   1
the dumb broad at the front desk who took telephone messages. She had to be something else because I thought I was something else. I was fine until there was a press party. We were having a fairly intelligent conversation. Then they asked me what I did. When I told them, they turned around to find other people with name tags. I wasn't worth bothering with. I wasn't being rejected because of what I had said or the way I talked, but simply because of my function. After that, I tried to make up other names for what I did — communications control, servomechanism. (Laughs)

You come in at nine, you open the door, you look at the piece of machin-   2
ery, you plug in the headpiece. That's how my day begins. You tremble when you hear the first ring. After that, it's sort of downhill — unless there's somebody on the phone who is either kind or nasty. The rest of the people are just non, they don't exist. They're just voices. You answer calls, you connect them to others, and that's it.

I don't have much contact with people. You can't see them. You don't   3
know if they're laughing, if they're being satirical or being kind. So your conversations become very abrupt. I notice that in talking to people. My conversations would be very short and clipped, in short sentences, the way I talk to people all day on the telephone.

I never answer the phone at home. It carries over. The way I talk to peo-   4
ple on the phone has changed. Even when my mother calls. I don't talk to her very long. I want to see people to talk to them. But now, when I see them, I talk to them like I was talking on the telephone. It isn't a conscious process. I don't know what's happened. When I'm talking to someone at work, the telephone rings, and the conversation is interrupted. So I never bother finishing sentences or finishing thoughts. I always have this feeling of interruption.

You can think about this thing and all of a sudden the telephone rings   5
and you've got to jump right back. There isn't a ten-minute break in the whole day that's quiet. I once worked at a punch press, when I was in high school. A part-time job. You sat there and watched it for four, five hours. You could make up stories about people and finish them. But you can't do that when you've got only a few minutes. You can't pick it up after the telephone call. You can't think, you can't even finish a letter. So you do quickie things, like read a chapter in a short story. It has to be short-term stuff.

I notice people have asked me to slow down when I'm talking. What I do   6
all day is to say what I have to say as quickly as possible and switch the call to whoever it's going to. If I'm talking to a friend, I have to make it quick before I get interrupted. . . .

I do some drawings — Mondrian, sort of. Peaceful colors of red and blue.   7
Very ordered life. I'd like to think of rainbows and mountains. I never draw humans. Things of nature, never people. I always dream I'm alone and things are quiet. I call it the land of no-phone. . . ."[5]

---

[5]"Sharon Atkins," in *Working*, by Studs Terkel (New York: Pantheon, 1974).

Let's consider the inferences we can make based on Sharon Atkin's account of her life as a receptionist. First we must review the facts that she presents. Reread paragraph 1. What are the facts? (1) Atkins had to change her image of receptionists ("dumb broad at the front desk") because she became a receptionist herself. (2) When people at press parties discovered what she did for a living, they turned away to talk to "other people with name tags." (3) After that, she tried to think of more elevated-sounding names for herself.

Given these three facts, what can you infer about the following?

The social status of receptionists:

_____

_____

_____

The relationship between the word "receptionist" and one's own self-image:

_____

_____

_____

People who look down on receptionists (including, at one point, Sharon Atkins herself):

_____

_____

_____

The remaining paragraphs of the interview deal mainly with the ways in which Atkins's relationships to other people have changed as a result of her job. Reread paragraphs 2–7 and state the facts as Atkins presents them:

Facts: _____

_____

_____

_____

What opinions about these facts does Atkins state explicitly?

_____

_____

_____

Now consider what Atkins does not state explicitly. Reread paragraphs 2–7 and make inferences based on the following questions. Cite evidence (actual lines in the passage) in support of each inference.

How does Atkins feel about her job?

_____

_____

_____

_____

_____

What kind of working atmosphere would she prefer?

_____

_____

_____

_____

Why does she draw pictures of nature, not people?

_____

_____

_____

_____

What would she like to do instead of being a receptionist?

_____

_____

_____

_____

Although Sharon Atkins does not come right out and say that she hates her job, it is clear that she does. Listen to the mechanical way in which she describes how her day begins: "You come in at nine, you open the door, you look at the piece of machinery, you plug in the headpiece." She must, you infer, feel like a piece of machinery herself. Then: "You tremble when you hear the first ring." The next statement is even more revealing: "After that, it's sort of downhill—unless there's somebody on the phone who is either kind or nasty. The rest of the people are just non, they don't exist. They're just voices." One would expect pleasant voices to be an exception to the downhill course of the day, but why should the _nasty_ voices help things out? Possibly, we conclude, even nasty people are preferable to "non" people. At least nasty people seem human—not like disembodied, mechanical sounds.

We can make other inferences about Atkins's feelings: her increasing hatred of the telephone and telephone conversations; her changed relationships to people even when she sees them face to face; her yearning to get away from people altogether, to the land of "no-phone," where things are peaceful, ordered, and quiet.

We present now two more articles on the subject of working. In Chapter 4 we'll use these articles as the basis for a paper; but before we do so, we ask that you develop an analysis of each. By *analysis* we mean that you should use the skills you've developed to illuminate your reading material: distinguish fact from opinion; observe the writer's use of thesis and structure; and make inferences. Realize that the papers you write in college will only be as good as your analyses of individual sources. Resolve now to concentrate on your work. Read the following two articles and produce a careful analysis of each.

EXERCISE

In "The Top Ten Motivators and Satisfiers," Julia Kagan reports on a survey conducted by the Public Agenda Foundation. Surveyors questioned both blue-collar and white-collar workers, male and female, to determine the effect of certain rewards on a worker's happiness and productivity. Read the article and analyze it in three ways: (1) Underline every inference that Kagan makes based on the survey results. (2) Examine Kagan's use of sources—to whom does she refer in the article? Where? Why? (3) Make your own inferences based on the survey.

...Would giving workers what they want make them work harder? A growing body of research indicates that this would not necessarily be the result. For many years, researchers have made distinctions between rewards that make workers more satisfied (satisfiers) and rewards that motivate them to work harder (motivators). Yet this message has been slow to reach management.

In a major 1975 study of job satisfaction and productivity, Daniel Yankelovich, president of the Public Agenda Foundation, and Raymond A. Katzell, Ph.D., professor of psychology at New York University, found that many policymakers assume that these two goals are causally linked, that increasing job satisfaction automatically increases productivity. This turns out to be an expensive mistake. Efforts based on this assumption, they found, "are more likely than not to leave productivity unchanged, or at best to improve it marginally, and may even cause it to decline." The jobholders in the Public Agenda survey confirm the motivators/satisfiers distinction.

...

Intrinsic rewards

The most obvious difference between the lists of motivators and satisfiers is that motivators concern the job itself almost exclusively. Working conditions and fringe benefits—both considered important to workers—do not appear to promote productivity, although these factors are prominent satisfiers.

Ambition, in the form of a desire for money and advancement, tops the lists of motivators. In some groups, though, good pay is surprisingly low on the list—for male managers and professionals, it ranked number 11 and doesn't even appear here. What is most interesting about the lists is the importance of the content of the job itself. Managers also would do well to notice that the nature of work, the degree

THE TOP TEN MOTIVATORS

Managers and Professionals		Blue-Collar Workers	
Men	**Women**	**Men**	**Women**
A good chance for advancement (48%)	A good chance for advancement (47%)	Good pay (50%)	Good pay (44%)
A great deal of responsibility (45)	A job that enables me to develop my abilities (44)	A good chance for advancement (47)	A good chance for advancement (42)
Recognition for good work (44)	Recognition for good work (43)	Pay tied to performance (47)	Pay tied to performance (41)
A job where I can think for myself (44)	A great deal of responsibility (40)	Recognition for good work (42)	A challenging job (37)
A job that enables me to develop my abilities (41)	A job where I can think for myself (38)	Interesting work (38)	A job where I can think for myself (35)
A challenging job (42)	Good pay (37)	See end results of my efforts (38)	Interesting work (35)
A job that allows me to be creative (41)	Pay tied to performance (37)	A job that enables me to develop my abilities (36)	A job that enables me to develop my abilities (34)
A job with pay tied to performance (40)	A challenging job (35)	A challenging job (34)	See end results of my efforts (34)
A say in important decisions (39)	A say in important decisions (32)	A job that allows me to be creative (34)	A job that allows me to be creative (33)
A place that does quality work (39)	A place that does quality work (32)	A job where I can think for myself (33)	Recognition for good work (32)

to which it allows an employee to grow and develop her abilities, is also important to blue-collar...workers.

There is a difference, though, in what one could call the power need of managers and professionals and that of lower-level workers: Managers are more hungry for a great deal of responsibility and a say in important decisions. There is little difference, however, between what motivates male and female managers.

. . .

More backing for the importance of intrinsic rewards in job motivation comes from *In Search of Excellence,* the thoughtful book on America's best-run companies by Thomas J. Peters and Robert H. Waterman, Jr. (Harper & Row, 1982). Concerning recognition for good work, Peters and Waterman note that the best companies design reward systems that make most employees feel like winners. (For example, IBM's sales quotas are set so that 70 to 80 percent of the sales force can meet them.) The authors also stress the importance of immediate and positive reinforcement.

The peaceable kingdom

The lists of satisfiers provide a dramatic contrast to the motivators. What everyone wants most of all, it seems, is peace and quiet—a job without too much rush and stress. Judging by their reaction, male managers and professionals feel particularly hard-pressed. Another stereotype that bites the dust is that women are more concerned with human relations. Both sexes value working with people they like and getting along with their supervisors.

Why don't fringe benefits, lack of stress and good working conditions produce motivation to hard work? In the 1950s, industrial psychologist Frederick Herzberg found that factors extrinsic to a job (he called them hygiene factors because they

THE TOP TEN SATISFIERS

Managers and Professionals		Blue-Collar Workers	
Men	**Women**	**Men**	**Women**
Job without too much rush and stress (71%)	Job without too much rush and stress (57%)	Job without too much rush and stress (57%)	Job without too much rush and stress (55%)
Good working conditions (67)	People really care about me as a person (57)	Good working conditions (57)	Being informed about what goes on (55)
Convenient location (65)	Working with people I like (56)	Convenient location (53)	Getting along well with supervisor (51)
Being able to control work pace (61)	Convenient location (55)	Working with people I like (52)	Working with people I like (48)
Flexible working hours (61)	Getting along well with supervisor (54)	Getting along well with supervisor (52)	Flexible working hours (48)
Working with people I like (56)	Good fringe benefits (52)	Being informed about what goes on (50)	Being able to control work pace (45)
Good fringe benefits (53)	Job security, little chance of being laid off (52)	People who listen to your ideas (50)	People treat me with respect (45)
Never asked to do anything improper or immoral (53)	Good working conditions (51)	Informal work environment (49)	Convenient location (44)
Place I'm so proud of I want everyone to know I work there (53)	Never asked to do anything improper or immoral (50)	Being able to control work pace (47)	Good working conditions (44)
Employer with good reputation (52)	Flexible working hours (48)	Fair treatment (46)	People who listen to your ideas (44)

included working conditions as well as supervision, company policies, interpersonal relations, benefits and job security) had the power to make people feel dissatisfied and perform poorly if they fell below a certain level but did not increase job performance if they rose to an optimum level. In their 1975 study, Yankelovich and Katzell pointed out that many people are satisfied with their jobs precisely because their work is undemanding and requires minimal effort.

The reader should not leave this article with the impression that it would be wise—to say nothing of moral—to mount a full-scale attack on fringe benefits and other satisfiers in the company compensation plan in order to replace them with motivator-based benefits. As Herzberg found, when "hygiene" factors become unacceptably low, they make employees so unhappy that negative effects on productivity result. What is important is that companies pay attention to designing jobs to create maximum levels of intrinsic interest and to provide financial and nonfinancial rewards for those who put in maximum effort.[6]

You have underlined the inferences Kagan has made, based on her analysis of the survey results. In abbreviated form, list those inferences here:

1. _____

_____

2. _____

_____

3. _____

_____

4. _____

_____

5. _____

_____

6. _____

_____

7. _____

_____

8. _____

_____

Kagan refers to three sources in her article other than the survey she's reporting on. Identify these sources. Where do they appear? What is their function in the article?

1. _____

_____

[6]Julia Kagan, "The Top Ten Motivators and Satisfiers," *Working Woman* (July 1983): 16–18.

2. _____

_____

3. _____

_____

Now study the survey results yourself. What inferences can *you* make? After you have stated your inferences, provide a rationale for them; explain how you arrived at these particular conclusions.

1. _____

_____

_____

2. _____

_____

_____

3. _____

_____

_____

4. _____

_____

_____

EXERCISE

The following is the introduction to the best-selling *The 100 Best Companies to Work for in America* by Robert Levering, Milton Moskowitz, and Michael Katz. Distinguish between facts and opinions; note any facts presented with a bias (that is, wrapped in an opinion); determine the thesis; and observe the structure. Read with pencil in hand so that you can mark up the passage as you see fit. Finally, use your notes to write a summary.

> Finding a good place to work is not easy. It's not easy for a job hunter, and it wasn't easy for us.   1
>
> Over the years everyone hears about great places to work—that such-and-such a company has a country club for employees, that a certain firm has such a terrific profit-sharing plan that a $5-an-hour warehouseman retired with a half-million dollars, or that some corporations treat their people so well that executive recruiters find it impossible to lure them away. But how do you go about finding America's superlative employers?   2

We had some ideas to begin with. One of us has covered the business scene for more than 25 years. All three of us had worked together to produce *Everybody's Business: An Almanac,* a book published by Harper & Row in 1980, which profiled 317 large companies. 3

Our previous research made us painfully aware that we were entering unexplored territory. It's odd—but telling—that American companies are rarely examined from the standpoint of their employees. The literature of business is rich with stories about companies and analyses of their operations. The *Wall Street Journal* chronicles these activities so well that it has become the largest-selling daily newspaper in the nation. During the course of a year, *Business Week, Forbes,* and *Fortune* publish 103 issues that are crammed with lists, tables, and charts tracking the progress of companies in a multitude of categories. And there are hundreds of trade magazines that rank, grade, and otherwise evaluate companies in their industrial settings: biggest hotels, biggest candy makers, biggest airlines, and on and on. 4

Yet none of these sources regularly spotlights the human condition inside business. They don't, as a rule, tell how employees are treated. They don't discuss which companies have the best benefit programs. They hardly ever do company-by-company comparisons of workplace environments. 5

We knew we had to cast a wider net to confirm our hunches and inspire new ones. If a company is a good place to work, its employees make no secret of it. Talking about where you work is one of the most common pastimes in America (and who isn't at least curious about whether the grass is greener somewhere else?). The better employers usually acquire a good reputation within their communities and within their industries. We realized that, at first, reputation would have to be our guide, so we resorted to the grapevine. 6

We asked all kinds of people to recommend great places to work: friends, relatives, executive recruiters, management consultants, market researchers, publishers, public relations counselors, business school teachers, newspaper reporters, magazine editors, radio and TV news staffers, advertising agency employees. We literally solicited prospects from everyone we met, including doctors and dentists we visited. A notice that we were looking for superior workplaces appeared in three widely circulated business publications. We rarely conducted interviews inside a company without asking the people we were talking with for additional recommendations. 7

After we had compiled a list of 350 candidates, we wrote to all of them for information about themselves and their employee policies. We received a wide range of responses. Some sent elaborate descriptions of their employee philosophy; at the other extreme was a terse letter informing us that the company was already besieged with job applications and that the last thing they needed was more attention of this kind; still others, suspecting a vanity press venture, told us they chose "not to participate." 8

Sifting through this material and listening to what people told us, we narrowed our candidate roster to 135 companies. But we quickly realized that the material was thin and rather lifeless, and that the only way to get in-depth information and lend substance to hearsay was to look for ourselves at every company on our list. We took a deep breath and telephoned our travel agents. 9

We crisscrossed the country for the better part of a year, visiting 114 companies in 27 different states—from a textile mill in South Carolina to a plywood coop in Oregon, from banks on Wall Street to oil companies in 10

Texas. In between plastic trays of airline food, we settled down to lengthy conversations with employees, from the factory floor to the executive suite. We typically interviewed at least half a dozen people at each company, and sometimes we talked with several dozen. We made a point of asking the companies to set up interviews with people who had previously worked elsewhere. We found group interviews to be particularly useful, because comments by one person would spark reaction from another.

It was heartening to discover how well earned are the reputations of the companies on our list; people really like to work at these places. Employee satisfaction is a factor you can't measure by reading company pamphlets. It's one thing to listen to presidents or chairmen talk about the great companies they head; they do it all the time. It's something else to talk, as we did, to the head of the mailroom at Time Inc., or an usher at the Los Angeles Dodgers stadium, and to see the pride they felt about working for their companies. 11

People are proud to work for companies that treat them well. They become linked to these companies in more than just an employer/employee relationship. It's the presence of this feeling more than any other, perhaps, that sets these 100 companies apart from the great mass of companies in America. 12

Our methods were journalistic rather than scientific. We did not try to impose a preconceived set of standards. The firms vary too much for systematic comparison. Working in a bank in Southern California is very different from working in a steel mill in Indiana. And IBM, with over 200,000 U.S. employees, is a world apart from Celestial Seasonings, with about 200 workers. 13

Despite the diversity, almost every one of the "100 Best" has something distinctive to offer its employees. At some the benefits are very tangible, from the huge fortunes attainable at Trammell Crow to the 25-cent gourmet lunch prepared by a French chef at Merle Norman Cosmetics or the million-dollar employee center with swimming pools, Jacuzzis, and handball courts at ROLM. Other places, like Gore and Kollmorgen, offer unusual management styles. Each company is unique, but there were certain themes we heard over and over again, and the urge to draw a kind of composite picture of the ideal company is irresistible. Beyond good pay and strong benefits, such a company would: 14

1. Make people feel that they are part of a team or, in some cases, a family.

2. Encourage open communication, informing its people of new developments and encouraging them to offer suggestions and complaints.

3. Promote from within; let its own people bid for jobs before hiring outsiders.

4. Stress quality, enabling people to feel pride in the products or services they are providing.

5. Allow its employees to share in the profits, through profit-sharing or stock ownership or both.

6. Reduce the distinctions of rank between the top management and those in entry-level jobs; put everyone on a first-name basis; bar executive dining rooms and exclusive perks for high-level people.

7. Devote attention and resources to creating as pleasant a workplace environment as possible; hire good architects.

8. Encourage its employees to be active in community service by giving money to organizations in which employees participate.

9. Help employees save by matching the funds they save.

10. Try not to lay off people without first making an effort to place them in other jobs either within the company or elsewhere.

11. Care enough about the health of its employees to provide physical fitness centers and regular exercise and medical programs.

12. Expand the skills of its people through training programs and reimbursement of tuition for outside courses.

We found, in general, that small companies are better than big companies — as places to work. So you will find here some companies you may never have heard of, like Odetics or Moog. The big companies on our roster have maintained many small-company traits: they break down their operations into small units, they push responsibility down into the ranks, they don't mangle people. We were pleased also to find three divisions of large companies that qualified (though their parent companies didn't): Bell Labs (American Telephone & Telegraph), Physio-Control (Eli Lilly), and Westin Hotels (United Airlines). 15

Midway through our process the Thomas Peters/Robert Waterman book, *In Search of Excellence,* was published. We examined their list of "excellent" companies with interest to see how it compared with our "100 Best." Finding some overlap but also significant divergences, we observed that management for profits, growth, and contented stockholders does not always yield a good place to work. We rejected many companies to which they gave accolades — Boeing, National Semiconductor, Frito-Lay, and McDonald's . . . , to name a few. 16

By the time we completed our research we had gained a better understanding of the difference between the traditional employer/employee relationship, which is often adversarial, and the kinds of practices we encountered on our journey. We feel that the "100 Best" may be part of the first wave in a major change that will affect for the better the way all of us think of our jobs and conduct our businesses. A phrase that expresses this change is "beyond technique." Whether a technique is drawn from a management handbook or an organization psychologist, the whole framework tends to be manipulative: "we" are looking for a way to get "them" to work harder or do something we want them to do. (One of the most alienated groups of employees we met was a Japanese-style quality circle at a Honeywell bomb factory in Minneapolis.) Among the "100 Best" we found many firms which have transcended that manipulative framework and achieved a sense that "we are all in it together." This unwritten pact among employees often begins with one or more key individuals who genuinely care about the quality of the experience of everyone in the company. 17

It can be argued that both conventional managerial techniques and the innovative practices described in this book enhance productivity and create a healthy economy. But the "100 Best" offer an added benefit of such high value that it's difficult to place on the same scale: a working life for thousands of people really worth living and worth looking forward to every waking day.[7] 18

[7]Robert Levering, Milton Moskowitz, and Michael Katz, *The 100 Best Companies to Work for in America* (Reading, Mass.: Addison-Wesley, 1984), vii–x.

The following is a list of the 100 best companies to work for in America, arranged by industry, as compiled by Levering, Moskowitz, and Katz. An asterisk is placed next to the companies that made the authors' list of ten best.

Consumer Goods
Anheuser Busch
Celestial Seasonings
Eastman Kodak
General Electric
General Mills
H. J. Heinz
Johnson Wax
Johnson & Johnson
Mary Kay Cosmetics
Maytag
McCormick
Merle Norman
  Cosmetics
Philip Morris
Polaroid
Procter & Gamble
Ralston Purina

Drugs & Health Care
Baxter Travenol
Hospital Corporation of
  America
Johnson & Johnson
Marion Laboratories
Merck
Physio-Control

High Technology
Advanced Micro
  Devices
Analog Devices
Apple Computer
Bell Laboratories*
Control Data
Digital Equipment
Electro Scientific
General Electric
Hewlett-Packard*
Intel
IBM*
Kollmorgen
3M
Moog
Odetics
ROLM
Tandem Computer

Tandy
Tektronix

Oil & Chemicals
Atlantic Richfield
Borg-Warner
Du Pont
Eastman Kodak
Exxon
H. B. Fuller
Gore
3M
Polaroid
Raychem
Shell Oil
Tenneco

Steel & Auto
Borg-Warner
Cummins Engine
Dana
Deere
Donnelly Mirrors
Inland Steel
Nissan
Nucor
Tenneco
Worthington

Conglomerate
General Electric
General Mills
3M
Tenneco

Office Equipment
Apple Computer
Control Data
Digital Equipment
Eastman Kodak
Exxon
Hewlet Packard
IBM
Liebert
3M
Pitney Bowes*
ROLM
Tandem Computer
Tandy

Clothing
General Mills
Gore
Levi Strauss
Olga
Springs Mills

Shelter
Armstrong
Trammell Crow*
CRS Sirrine
Linnton Plywood
Herman Miller
Weyerhaeuser

Utility
Southern California
  Edison

Media & Entertainment
Leo Burnett
Walt Disney
Doyle Dane Bernbach
Hallmark Cards*
Knight-Ridder
Los Angeles Dodgers
Quad/Graphics
Random House
Reader's Digest
Time Inc.*

Retailing
Dayton Hudson
General Mills
Lowe's
Mary Kay Cosmetics
Merle Norman
  Cosmetics
Nordstrom
J. C. Penney
Publix Super Markets
Tandy
Wal-Mart Stores

Banking & Finance
Borg-Warner
Citicorp
Control Data

A. G. Edwards	Northwestern Mutual	Preston Trucking
General Electric	Life*	Ryder
Goldman Sachs*	J. C. Penney	Viking Freight
J. P. Morgan	Ryder	**Restaurants & Hotels**
Rainier National Bank	Tenneco	General Mills
Security Pacific Bank	**Transportation**	Ralston Purina
Insurance	Delta Air Lines*	Saga
Erie Insurance	People Express	Westin Hotels

What is the thesis of this article?

_____

_____

_____

_____

Divide the article into sections, giving each a title. Write a one- or two-sentence summary for each section, making sure these summaries reflect the distinctions you have made between fact and opinion. (See pages 8–20 to refresh your memory on presenting the distinction.) When you've completed your outline, combine section summaries with the thesis and write a one- or two-paragraph summary.

To conclude your critical analysis of the introduction to *100 Best Companies,* develop inferences in response to the following questions. Support each inference by citing lines from the text.

What is the relationship between job satisfaction and working environment?

_____

_____

_____

_____

What is a manager's proper function?

_____

_____

_____

What are the virtues of working?

_____

_____

_____

_____

The authors say that their "methods were journalistic rather than scientific" (paragraph 13). What is your reaction to this?

_____

_____

_____

_____

What other inferences have you made?

_____

_____

_____

_____

You now are able to read single sources—articles, essays, reports—and respond to them thoroughly and systematically. You can read for the main idea; you can identify an article's structure; you can write a summary; you can distinguish between facts and opinions; and you can make inferences based on what you've read. One task remains: to *synthesize,* or combine, a number of sources on a single topic into a coherent paper. In Chapter 4 you will use the notes on the articles you have read here to help you combine sources and write a paper of your own design.

CHAPTER 4

▭ Using Multiple Sources

▮ Introduction

Writers of all persuasions rely on source materials, looking to them for background information, important facts, and ideas and theories on which to build responses. Not to rely on the work of others to help you on your way is to deny that other people have useful knowledge. But of course other people do have useful knowledge. Whatever your field of interest, other writers have most likely researched or commented on it, recording their investigations in articles, essays, and reports that you—both as a student and as a professional—will devote considerable time to reading.

This chapter is designed to show you how to draw on multiple sources when writing a paper. You will have the opportunity to make use of material you've already read and to synthesize, or combine, that material—along with your own ideas—into a coherent and (one would hope) exciting paper. But before we begin that effort, we'll examine a completed product: an article by David Chandler, reporter on scientific matters for the *Boston Globe*. Written in early 1986 after the explosion of the space shuttle *Challenger* and the death of its seven astronauts, Chandler's "Unmanned Rockets vs. the Shuttle" represents an effort much like the ones you will make in your composition course and elsewhere: to write the article, Chandler combined information from a variety of sources to complement his own ideas. Notice how he narrowly defines his topic and then *uses* his sources to establish background information and to develop each position of the controversy he plans to explore. To get the most out of this demonstration, read with pencil in hand and place an asterisk (*) in the margin wherever Chandler relies on the statements of others to help with his own presentation. Remember: your focus here is to understand how a writer has used the work of others as an aid to his own work.

The rocket thundered skyward from its launch pad, arcing gracefully out over the Atlantic ocean on its column of smoke — and then, suddenly, a devastating explosion reduced it to a shower of debris. Launches were halted indefinitely pending a full investigation of the causes and a determination of how to prevent any further such accidents. 1

It was a setback and a financial loss, but in this case it was not a tragedy: The Ariane 3 rocket that was blown up in flight last September was an unmanned rocket. Two satellites were destroyed, but no lives were lost. 2

"If it's an unmanned rocket, it's only a waste of money," says Thomas Gold, a Cornell University physicist who has long opposed what he views as excessive emphasis on the manned space program. Gold believes that it is senseless, and perhaps even immoral, to risk human lives to launch satellites that could just as easily be sent aloft on unmanned rockets like Ariane. 3

Most of the satellites launched by the shuttle so far, and most of those scheduled for future launches, could be launched by available unmanned rockets with little or no modifications. 4

But, despite some advantages of unmanned flight and exploration, there remain powerful arguments and strong political support for continuing the shuttle program. 5

It's clear, for starters, that certain major payloads could be launched in no other way. For example, the Hubble Space Telescope, a billion-dollar instrument that may revolutionize astronomy, was built specifically to take advantage of the shuttle's huge capacity and of its capability to provide repair and refurbishment services. 6

Built to use the full dimensions of the shuttle's payload bay, it is far too large to be launched by any other space vehicle. And as astronomer and former NASA official Robert Jastrow points out, no one would ever have contemplated launching such an expensive and intricate instrument into orbit without having the ability to make repairs; the idea of a billion-dollar telescope floating uselessly in space because of a failure of some tiny electronic part is simply unthinkable. 7

Much other planned research requires the use of the shuttle as well. For example, the kind of research that can be done aboard the European-built Spacelab module in the shuttle's cargo bay — including studies of the effects of weightlessness on human physiology, the growing of crystals for electronic components and the manufacture of medicines — cannot be done anywhere else. 8

The pros and cons have left the scientists themselves sharply divided on   9
the issue of the relative emphasis placed on manned and unmanned programs. But virtually no one argues that it should be entirely one way or the
other; the questions center on what the balance should be. Many scientists are
now calling, more forcefully than ever, for an increase in the unmanned part
of the space program.

A few scientists—notably James Van Allen, discoverer of the Earth's radia-   10
tion belts—have decried the expense of the manned space program and
called for an almost exclusive concentration on unmanned scientific exploration instead, saying this would be far more cost-effective.

Peaked during Apollo era

Other space scientists dispute that idea. Joseph Allen, physicist and for-   11
mer shuttle astronaut, says, "It seems to be argued that one takes away from
the other. But before there was a manned space program, the funding on
space science was zero. Now, it's about $500 million a year."

Allen points out that expenditures on unmanned scientific research have   12
followed the trend of spending on the manned program, reaching a peak during the Apollo era.

"I was in the manned program for many years," Allen says. "But basically   13
my background is the science program, since I'm a physicist." Overall, he
feels, the relative spending on manned and unmanned programs has been "a
pretty good balance."

Another scientist working for the space agency put it more forcefully: 14
"The unmanned [science] program gets plenty of money. They just spend it all
like a bunch of drunken sailors."

But in the wake of the tragic Challenger explosion, astronomer Gold says: 15
"My feeling is that it's almost inevitable that unmanned boosters will make a
strong return."

NASA has been fighting tooth and nail against that notion, however. Just   16
last year, the agency lost a major battle with the US Air Force that had raged
for years. The Air Force wanted to continue using some unmanned rockets
rather than relying entirely on the manned space shuttle, and finally won a
concession that it would be allowed to order 10 unmanned Titan rockets for
use over a five year period, starting in 1988.

NASA wants mixed fleet

But even NASA has recently begun to modify its hard-line stance that the   17
shuttle should handle everything.

Ivan Beke, NASA director of advanced programs, says: "We want both. We   18
want a mixed fleet of manned and unmanned." Beke is directing a study, due
to be presented to the President in May, of possible new launch vehicles for
NASA's long-range future.

But for the short run, because of NASA's phasing-out of unmanned boost-   19
ers, payloads that had been scheduled for launch by the shuttle this year have
few alternatives. Some companies and governments are willing to sign up customers for unmanned satellite launch services, but most are either still in the
organizational stages or else booked solid for the near future.

Ariane, the world's first launch vehicle owned by a corporation rather   20
than a government, is now back in business after an investigation into last

September's accident resulted in some changes to valves in the rocket's third stage. A successful launch last Friday night from a site in French Guiana, launching two scientific satellites, was to be the first of seven scheduled for this year.

But Arianespace, the company that handles bookings for the European-built rocket, has no definite openings in its launch schedule before May 1987, although there is a possible opening on a test launch of the first Ariane 4 rocket in August or September of this year. At a maximum, assuming that several scheduled payloads will not be ready on time, Arianespace estimates that there might be openings for nine satellites in the next three years, out of 22 planned launches. Each Ariane 3 rocket can carry two satellites.* 21

3 firms may enter business

Jacqueline Schenkel of Arianespace said last week that there have been inquiries from potential satellite launch customers since the Challenger accident, but such inquiries were just part of normal business planning. No shuttle customers have signed up for an Ariane launch since the accident, she said. 22

At least three American companies are planning to enter the commercial launch business, by picking up contracts that NASA had allowed to lapse with the companies that have been manufacturing some of the extensively tested and used unmanned rockets already phased out by the agency. These would probably be launched at facilities leased from NASA, although some companies are studying the feasibility of building launch pads. 23

General Dynamics is trying to market a commercial version of NASA's Atlas-Centaur, Transpace Carriers would like to market the Delta rocket, and Space Services Inc. has designed, but not built, a rocket called the Conestoga II that resembles a scaled-down version of NASA's Titan III, using available rocket motors. 24

Other companies are also seriously considering entering the market, some using completely new designs. But it takes at least 30 months to build even a rocket of known design, such as a Titan III, so even if these companies were to swing into full operation right away, it would do nothing to alleviate the immediate crunch in launch availability. 25

Long list of commitments

Ten commercial satellite launches were scheduled for the shuttle over the next year, and 11 others scheduled for launch by Ariane rockets during the same period. The shuttle has other, higher-priority launch commitments as well. There were three Defense Department missions scheduled over the next 12 months, as well as two military satellites that were to be included with civilian payloads on other missions, and those military missions will have top priority when shuttle flights resume. 26

Other missions that have time-critical launch requirements, such as the Galileo and Ulysses space probes, will have second priority. Paying commercial customers come next, and all NASA scientific payloads that do not have specific time constraints will go to the end of the line. 27

Science, in short, may be the area hardest hit by the interruption in the shuttle program, particularly if the delay is a long one. The longer the hiatus, 28

*In May 1986, after this article was written, an Ariane rocket exploded, prompting Arianspace to postpone all launches until early 1987 [Authors].

the more Defense missions and time-critical missions will be piling up, waiting for launch dates. With many experts now predicting a one- to two-year delay before the shuttle flies again, the impact on space research could reverberate through the end of the decade.

Nature magazine, the prestigious British science journal, editorialized recently that "one of the lasting casualties of [the Challenger] accident will be…the notion that the entire ambition of the United States in space can be sustained by one chief launching instrument. It would be safer and probably also cheaper to keep the shuttle for the jobs that only the shuttle can carry out, using some other rocket to put everyday satellites into orbits."[1] 29

Imagining the Paper as a Conversation

When you write a paper, you in effect are creating a conversation in which both you and others, usually experts in a field, "talk" about a particular topic. Experienced writers establish background information for their papers by referring to one set of sources; they document a controversy, perhaps, by referring to another set of sources; they may review interpretations of controversial events by referring to still another set. By using information and ideas from a variety of sources, writers act as organizers of conversations about their topics, conversations in which they themselves participate. This is precisely what David Chandler has done in his "Unmanned Rockets vs. the Shuttle."

Notice first that in paragraphs 1 and 2, Chandler introduces his topic, relying on his own information. Perhaps he had read news accounts of the explosion of Ariane 3; perhaps he was present at the launching of the unmanned rocket. Whichever, here is background information that Chandler himself provides. He has begun a conversation about rockets exploding and "cargo" being lost. In paragraph 3, he turns for the first time to an outside source (that is, someone other than himself): Cornell University physicist Thomas Gold. Chandler could very well have summarized Gold's remarks by writing, "Some scientists have argued that the danger of manned flights is not warranted for payloads that could be launched on unmanned rockets." But Chandler chooses instead to name Gold and have him participate directly in the conversation of the paper. First Gold is quoted (notice how Chandler establishes his source's credentials to speak as an authority):

> "If it's an unmanned rocket, it's only a waste of money," says Thomas Gold, a Cornell University physicist who has long opposed what he views as excessive emphasis on the manned space program.

Next we're given a summary of Gold's very distinct and forceful views:

> Gold believes that it is senseless, and perhaps even immoral, to risk human lives to launch satellites that could just as easily be sent aloft on unmanned rockets like Ariane.

[1]David Chandler, "Unmanned Rockets vs. the Shuttle," *Boston Globe* (February 24, 1986): 41, 43.

How has Chandler gotten this information? Perhaps he talked with Gold directly; perhaps he read someone' else's interview. Or he may have read an article by or about Gold. Wherever he got his information, he has *used* the statements made by an authority to continue the discussion of his paper. And certainly a discussion—whether it's held in your dorm room, in a newspaper article, or in a term paper—profits from intelligent contributions.

Now examine what happens after Chandler refers to his first source. In paragraph 4, he builds on Gold's remarks by contributing new but related information:

> Most of the satellites launched by the shuttle so far, and most of those scheduled for future launches, could be launched by available unmanned rockets with little or no modifications.

This contribution to the discussion represents an extension to Thomas Gold's remarks. Gold believes "it is senseless, and perhaps even immoral" to risk human lives when they do not need to be risked. Chandler's sentence assumes the validity of this view and then, by presenting precisely the right information at the right moment, raises an important and unsettling prospect: have the officials in charge of the shuttle program behaved recklessly?

The answer, if we accept the views of Thomas Gold, would seem to be yes. Yet Chandler knows, based on his research, that there are those who disagree with this conclusion. Significantly, paragraph 5 begins with the word *but,* which signals to the reader that the opinion just presented will be challenged. Just as in a conversation in which one person speaks, establishing a particular point of view, and is followed by someone who disagrees, so too in Chandler's written conversation, one statement is followed by counterstatement. The word *but* informs the reader that the conversation continues:

> But, despite some advantages of unmanned flight and exploration, there remain powerful arguments and strong political support for continuing the shuttle program.

Reread paragraphs 6, 7, and 8—the paragraphs forming the response to Gold. Observe how Chandler again refers to an outside source. Paragraph 6 begins with a discussion of the Hubble Space Telescope. What is the source of this information? Most likely Chandler has done some research. He has explored information from various sources and has taken notes; he uses this information at the precise point in his article where it is most helpful, in forming the first response to Thomas Gold's position (that unnecessary manned flight is senseless). Chandler builds on the response by calling on a second expert witness, physicist Robert Jastrow. And so the conversation develops, with the author carefully presenting information and placing sources in relation to one another so as to allow for intriguing disagreement.

We asked Chandler to tell us something about the way he gathered and arranged his source materials. This is how he replied:

> Many of the sources for this story were people that I had already spoken to when I was working on other stories. Others were people I had seen talk-

ing about this subject in television interviews or people who were quoted in other newspaper or magazine stories.

What I was looking for, in choosing people to talk to, were these factors:

- People who were connected with NASA (now or in the past) or who were connected with other rocket companies or agencies (such as Arianespace) or who worked on scientific research that has to do with space.
- People who had strong opinions on this subject. In some cases, I knew this from having talked to them before or having seen other interviews with them. In other cases, it just seemed like a good bet (Joe Allen is a former astronaut, so I figured that he would think manned space flight was a good idea).
- People on both sides of the issue. Fairness is crucial in a newspaper story, so it was important to find people who could make the best, strongest arguments for each side. In that sense, a newspaper story is a bit like a court case, with each side presenting its best points.

Reading every article I could get my hands on about this subject helped to identify several people who met these criteria. Also, often one person would refer me to other people who could provide useful information.

For example, I tried to get information about a report by the National Commission on Space, which was supposed to contain detailed plans for the future of the U.S. space program. When I finally reached one member of the commission, she refused to talk about the report because it was not finished yet. But she gave me the name and number of Ivan Beke, a NASA official in charge of another, similar report. He was helpful and ended up in the story.

I also talked to several people, such as representatives of companies that plan to get into the launch business, who provided me with information that helped me to understand the situation but that I didn't quote in the story.

Since people on both sides of the question had strong opinions, I structured the story as sort of a debate, letting each side make its points and then answering each other's points.

Because it was a newspaper story, I could not have expressed my own opinions in the piece even if I had wanted to—that's strictly against the rules. If it had been a magazine article or a newspaper column, then I could have let my own feelings show rather than always using other people's words.

But even though I let both sides have their say, my own opinions may have shown through. You may notice that the beginning of the story (the "lead") and the quote at the end of the story (the "kicker") both make the same point: that there are advantages to including unmanned rockets in the space program.

EXERCISE

To impress on you the vigilance with which a professional writer keeps the conversation of his work alive, reread "Unmanned Rockets vs. the Shuttle." Beginning with paragraph 6, explain *briefly* how each subsequent paragraph represents an effort to continue the conversation begun in paragraph 1. We'll make notes for paragraphs 7–11; you make notes for the others.

Paragraphs 7–9: Chandler summarizes, stating the pros and cons of the arguments just presented; the issue is balance — of unmanned versus manned flight.
Paragraph 10: James Van Allen argues for one sort of balance: more unmanned flights.
Paragraph 11: Joseph Allen argues the opposite.

Paragraph 12: _____

Paragraph 13: _____

Paragraph 14: _____

Paragraph 15: _____

Paragraph 16: _____

Paragraph 17: _____

Paragraph 18: _____

Paragraph 19: _____

Paragraph 20: _____

Paragraph 21: _____

Paragraph 22: _____

Paragraph 23: _____

Paragraph 24: _____

Paragraph 25: _____

Paragraph 26: _____

Paragraph 27: _____

Paragraph 28: _____

Paragraph 29: _____

You have read and analyzed an article in which a writer has placed himself in the prestigious company of an astronaut and renowned physicists and astronomers. Even though David Chandler is a newspaper reporter, not an astrophysicist, he was able, by conducting research and by making reference to numerous, authoritative sources, to create a lively and informative conversation. Chandler could have participated a great deal more in the exchange: he might have argued, for instance, for or against fewer manned space flights. But he doesn't, since his job (defined by his editor) is to report on the controversy, not to take sides.

Like Chandler, you will be asked to write papers; and to do so successfully, you will have to do what he has done: define and limit a topic; gather information from various authoritative sources; and then actually write a paper by selectively *using* that information, according to a specific purpose. If your paper succeeds, it too will be a conversation. As a contributor, you may be more or less present. Like Chandler, you might choose to remain invisible, serving as the person who arranges sources in interesting ways. You might also choose to participate actively in the conversation by presenting your views along with those of your sources.

Consider the following essay, "A Nation Is United and Touches Mystery," by James Wall, as an example. Wall, like David Chandler, chooses space flight as a general topic. Like Chandler, Wall relies on sources; but unlike Chandler, he uses sources as a point for personal departure and comment.

"It was sad when that great ship went down." The folk song with that line 1 was written after the sinking of the U.S.S. *Rueben James,* an American ship enroute to England just before the United States entered World War II. All aboard were killed. The sudden destruction and the loss of life galvanized the nation.

When the space shuttle *Challenger* blew up 74 seconds after lift-off, a na- 2 tion that had become casual, even bored, about space travel experienced grief and entered what sociologist Robert Bellah called a "moment of profound national unity." The deaths of seven crew members — including the first "citizen passenger," schoolteacher Christa McAuliffe — became a personal loss to an entire population.

Media images soon displayed faces of schoolchildren, puzzled and pained 3 over an awareness of a mortality that most had avoided noticing. A teacher was dead. Death had become real.

Bellah, who was lecturing in Chicago the day after the tragedy, noted that 4 the feeling of national unity that emerged out of the shock of the disaster is a rare occurrence in national life. Our individualism is so rampant that we seldom feel a sense of oneness with the larger community. This observation is the theme of *Habits of the Heart,* the well-known book that Bellah wrote with four other scholars. It is difficult to acknowledge that we live in communities of "memory and hope" when our memories are unrelated to our common life, and our hopes are focused not on the whole, but on personal gain.

It may be hard to recall now, but most Americans who watched the 5 launching of the space shuttle most likely perceived its crew members primarily as persons traveling upward on career paths. But when they died, a larger truth seems to have struck the nation, albeit briefly: these were certainly career-oriented professionals, but they had also risked their lives in service to the larger community.

Responding to a question about the difference between the terms 6 "career" and "calling," Bellah observed that the term "career" did not enter the English language until the 19th century. Before that, people had considered themselves "called" to a vocation, a term derived from the biblical understanding of being "called by God." A career, in contrast, has become a journey upward to personal achievement.

Seven careers ended at Cape Canaveral. But we now realize that these 7 seven astronauts were involved in a "calling," pursuing tasks to serve others.

In this sudden shift in perception, our nation experienced a special moment in its life, a moment that included sadness but that also gave us a sense of one-ness. As a people we were bound together in the same kind of grief we knew on the day that President John F. Kennedy died while on a political mission to unify the Texas Democratic Party. The ambiguity of personal glory involved in that political journey—and in launching *Challenger* in search of national glory and scientific advancement—was transcended in a fleeting moment of sorrow. When such moments occur, we connect with a divine mystery. For we are driven beyond tragedy into the wonder of a relationship with God who alone grasps the full meaning of our every puzzling moment.

In the months ahead, there will be debate over whether it is worth the   8
risk to send humans into space. In a monumental display of bad timing, one Chicago television commentator tried to raise that question a few hours after the explosion. Angry listeners forced him to apologize. Without realizing it, the commentator had intruded into a time of personal mystery for a people who rarely are touched in this manner.

Ambiguity is erased—though fleetingly—when death strikes. In our re-   9
cent "moment of profound national unity" we experienced gratitude to those who presented themselves to us as gifts, persons who became "heroes," and who, in death, suddenly became much larger than life.

· · ·

Seven *Challenger* crew members died much too early. Why? We do not   10
know. But we do recall their earlier glory, like that of Housman's young athlete:

The time you won your town the race
we chaired you through the market-place;
man and boy stood cheering by
and home we brought you shoulder-high.

To-day, the road all runners come,
Shoulder-high we bring you home,
And set you at your threshold down,
Townsman of a stiller town.

Drawn together in this time of sadness, our nation is now a "stiller town."   11
In the seven deaths we received a gift: an opportunity to feel united as a people. When that "great ship went down," we rose, for one brief moment, above our individualism and found a connectedness....[2]

James Wall's treatment of the shuttle explosion differs greatly from Chandler's. Wall has used sources to enhance and to provide further opportunities for developing his own reflections on the death of the seven *Challenger* astronauts. Whereas Chandler's editor required that he not take sides in his discussion, Wall (given that he *is* the editor of the weekly magazine in which this editorial appeared) very definitely takes sides and states a position—that is the

[2]James M. Wall, "A Nation Is United and Touches Mystery," *The Christian Century* (February 5–12, 1986): 107–108.

purpose of his essay. Yet even in a reflective piece such as this, you'll notice that Wall refers to source materials.

EXERCISE	

Examine Wall's use of sources in each paragraph. First list the source referred to and then describe the use to which Wall puts the source:

Paragraph 1: _____

_____

_____

_____

Paragraph 2: _____

_____

_____

_____

Paragraphs 3–5: _____

_____

_____

_____

_____

Paragraphs 6–7: _____

_____

_____

_____

Paragraphs 8–9: _____

_____

_____

_____

Paragraphs 10–11: _____

_____

_____

_____

_____

If you were to summarize your observations, you'd find Wall using source materials as occasions to expand on his thinking about the shuttle explosion. He uses a source and then applies its point to the *Challenger* and its crew. For instance, Wall cites sociologist Bellah's distinction between "career" and "calling." As soon as the distinction is made, Wall uses it to discuss how the astronauts had a calling to serve others as well as a career to serve themselves. Wall repeats this pattern throughout the essay. So you see that writers can respond to source materials neutrally, as Chandler does, and personally, as Wall does.

You've arrived at the point in your studies at which you've read material and have developed responses to it. Now is the time to consider how you will use sources to enhance your discussion of a topic. Will you use sources to set the terms of a debate, like Chandler does? Will you use them to elicit your own reflections on the topic, like Wall does? Will you use them for some other reason? Now, as you make the transition from being a perceptive reader to a perceptive writer, you have some decisions to make; and that's what we'll be discussing in the next section.

Writing Your Papers in Five Stages

1. *Read and understand what others have written about your topic.* To write a paper based on source materials, you must begin by reading about a topic. You've already done this first step in Chapters 1, 2, and 3, in which you learned to read critically and actively. For every source you read, you should be able to observe the following:

The author's main idea(s)

The author's supporting ideas

Differences among facts, opinions, and facts influenced by opinions

The structure of the piece of writing

In addition, you should be able to write a summary of the articles you read and make useful inferences. If you are unsure of your skills in any of these areas, you should return to the discussions in the first three chapters. To write an effective paper based on source materials, you must be able to understand the individual sources you plan to combine.

2. *Make inferences among your sources.* As you observed in his article on manned versus unmanned space flight, David Chandler was able to make connections among his sources when writing his paper. These connections are crucial. As you read one source, often you are reminded of another. How are the sources related? That's your job to figure out. If the relationship is significant, then you will want to say that in your paper. Note how in paragraph 10 of his article Chandler refers to James Van Allen and then, in paragraph 11, to Joseph Allen:

A few scientists—notably James Van Allen, discoverer of the Earth's radia- 10
tion belts—have decried the expense of the manned space program and
called for an almost exclusive concentration on unmanned scientific exploration instead, saying this would be far more cost-effective.

. . .

Other space scientists dispute that idea. Joseph Allen, physicist and for- 11
mer shuttle astronaut, says, "It seems to be argued that one takes away from
the other. But before there was a manned space program, the funding on
space science was zero. Now, it's about $500 million a year."

Imagine Chandler at work gathering sources for his article. He discovers two
articles—one by Van Allen and another by Allen—and sees that they are related: specifically, that the two authors hold opposite views. Chandler then
arranges his paper to take advantage of this disagreement. In so doing, he provides an important contrast for his readers. There are numerous ways in which
sources can be related. We will introduce you to several as you read further in
the text.

3. *Write a thesis.* A thesis is a sentence that establishes the topic you wish
to discuss in your paper and the claim you wish to make about the topic. Assume that two people, Jones and Simpson, are writing papers on an identical
topic: draft registration. The *claims*—what Jones and Simpson have to say
about their topic—may radically differ. Jones may claim that draft registration
in peacetime is justified, while Simpson may claim the opposite. People can
(and do) discuss the same topic and make widely different claims about it.
That's why you must do more than simply choose a topic when you write a
paper: you must also make an assertion about the topic. You must declare
your views.

By limiting a topic and by establishing a claim you wish to make, your thesis will govern the paper that follows. If your paper is to be successful, every
sentence that you write must in some way support or develop your thesis. If
sentences or paragraphs drift from the stated focus of your paper, then you
must change the thesis to accommodate the new material or must delete the
new material.

4. *Anticipate the structure of the paper, based on your thesis.* Recall that in
Chapter 1 we discussed what *structure* in an article refers to and how you, as a
critical reader, need to be aware of structure in order to read well. As a reader,
you are able (or are becoming able) to observe how writers fashion the parts
or sections of a paper to create a whole. The writing of an accurate summary
often depends on your ability to understand an article's overall structure.

As a writer, your job is to *create* a structure for your paper that allows you
to develop the whole thesis by systematically developing it in parts. Reading
for structure requires skills of observation; writing (that is, creating) a structure
requires skills of invention. Once you have settled on a thesis, you will need to
develop at least a tentative structure in order to begin writing your paper.
Which sources will you use where? You must have a sense of the whole—what

you wish to accomplish—in order to begin working on the parts. Look to your thesis for guidance.

5. *Write the first draft of your paper.* Once you have written a working thesis that identifies the purpose of the entire paper and once you have developed a structure for the paper that will allow you to achieve your purpose, your time has come to begin writing. When we say write a "first draft," we mean that you should make a first attempt, an initial and rough effort, at completing the outline of the paper that you've sketched for yourself. A *draft* is a version of your work. Obviously, a first effort will not be as polished as a third, and so you should not expect perfection early on. What you can expect of a first draft is to have gotten something down on paper that is more or less related to your thesis. In subsequent drafts, you will refine what you've written (You may change your thesis; you may delete or add information.) The principal challenge of the first draft is to get from nothing—a blank page—to something. Once you have material to work with, even if to discard and replace, you at least have made a start. And a start, a place to begin, is crucial.

Now we'll take the five stages in turn and discuss each in detail. As the basis of both our discussion and the paper that you will write, we rely on the reading selections from Chapter 3. Our broad subject area will be *job satisfaction.* We will examine the reading selections in detail, make inferences among them, develop a thesis and outline, and write a paper based on sources. In sum, what we will do between this point and the end of the chapter is what you will do when writing a paper.

When making use of source materials, you have an obligation to your readers to cite sources and not to plagiarize. The matters are related: when other writers contribute ideas to your paper, you give credit to their contributions by acknowledging them. You *cite* your sources by stating the name of the contributor and the place from which you have borrowed the material. To borrow information and ideas from an author—by quoting, paraphrasing, or summarizing—without giving credit to the author (thereby creating the impression that someone else's work is your own) is *plagiarism,* the most serious of academic offenses.

So when working with source materials, as we will do here and as you are about to do, remember to provide *citations* whenever you rely on another source to help your discussion along. Any good college-level English handbook offers detailed instructions on how to cite sources.

Read and Understand What Others Have Written About Your Topic

As we've said, to write an effective paper based on source materials you must first have a response, which will help you to understand the single sources you wish to combine. By *understand* we mean that you should be able to identify the following:

The author's main idea

The author's supporting ideas

Differences among facts, opinions, and facts influenced by opinions

The structure of the passage

You must also be able to write a summary based on this information, and you should be able to make inferences.

We'll take the five sources you've read on job satisfaction and make notes about each on the basis of the criteria just stated. Though you have already read these selections, we suggest that you reread them as we make notes and as you prepare to combine sources along with your own ideas into a paper. The first source, you will recall, is a description by Sharon Atkins from Studs Terkel's book, *Working,* about her job as a receptionist. Turn to page 83 and reread her account.

Source 1

Our notes on Sharon Atkins are as follows.

Content The main idea of this piece is clear: Sharon Atkins has a job that she feels demeans her and that she detests for clearly stated reasons. In her interview with Studs Terkel, Atkins presents the following facts: (1) She changed her image of receptionists when she became one, a change prompted by such slights as people turning away from her at a company party not because of who she was and what she was saying but because of her job description. (2) Her day is filled with the mechanical routine of working a switchboard. (3) Her phone conversations on the job become abrupt. Since Atkins cannot know the feelings of people calling (whether they're laughing, kind, satirical), she prefers to end conversations quickly. (4) Her habit of quick, abrupt conversation developed at work carries over to her phone conversations in private life, so much so that her friends ask her to "slow down" when speaking with her. Atkins prefers to speak with people in person and dreams of a land of "no-phone," where she is surrounded by peaceful scenes of nature.

We find two opinions expressed in this passage. The first (from paragraph 2) is that kind and nasty people are preferable to "non" people (callers whose personalities she cannot assess) since they at least offer the prospect of life on the other end of the phone line. Atkins also believes that working a punch press is preferable to working a switchboard since at a punch press she could concentrate and finish her thoughts. At her present job she cannot do either.

By reviewing the facts and opinions presented in this source, we have in effect written a summary. In making notes on a source you needn't write formal summaries unless you plan to use them in part of your paper, which you will often do. Usually you will summarize not an entire source in the paper you're writing but only the sections of the source pertinent to your main idea.

Structure Though this passage by Atkins is transcribed from an interview (so we wouldn't expect as neatly planned a presentation as we would in a paper), we can observe a method to her response. Atkins develops her response in four parts, with paragraph 1 constituting the first part. Here Atkins discusses the image she had of receptionists before she took the job. The image changes once she begins her work: she is not "the dumb broad at the front desk" but a sensitive, intelligent individual who requires a minimum of respect, just like everyone else. Part II, consisting of paragraphs 2 and 3, concerns life on the job. Part III consists of paragraphs 4, 5, and 6 and concerns the effects of her being a receptionist, both at home and at work. In the final part, paragraph 7, Atkins reflects on pastimes such as painting that allow her some measure of escape from the tedium of work.

EXERCISE	

Write a summary of this passage, using the information we've provided. Try writing one or at most two sentences for each of the four parts we've identified.

_____

_____

_____

_____

_____

_____

_____

_____

Inferences We can make the following inferences about Sharon Atkins and her job, based on this passage: (1) Both in the eyes of the public and in the eyes of Sharon Atkins, the status of receptionists is exceptionally low—a status not warranted. (2) Those who condescend to receptionists (as did the people at the party who turned away from Atkins) hold a job in high or low esteem according to its title, not according to the person holding it. The attitude is arrogant and misinformed. (3) Sharon Atkins detests her job as a receptionist. (4) She would prefer a calm and peaceful working atmosphere, where she could think in complete thoughts and speak in complete sentences. She would also prefer a job that she and others held in high esteem. (5) Atkins draws pictures of nature, not people, to escape the demeaning relationship with the public that her work forces on her every day.

Source 2

The second source article we're considering for our paper is the brief letter written by Struggling RN to columnist Juliette Flynn. We are considering the letter and response as two separate sources: The nurse's letter is a primary source, like the transcription of the interview with Sharon Atkins. A primary source provides significant, uninterpreted information from which original conclusions can be drawn. A short story would be a primary source, as would letters written by Thomas Jefferson on his plans for constructing Monticello. A secondary source consists of commentary on and interpretations of primary sources. A critic's review of Faulkner's short fiction would be a secondary source, as would a historian's account of the building of Monticello. Following this logic, Juliette Flynn's response to Struggling RN is a secondary source. Reread the nurse's letter on pages 78–79.

Content Struggling RN presents both facts and opinions in her letter. The apparent facts (apparent because we would want to check them for accuracy) are as follows: The writer is a nurse with seven years of experience. She has difficulty communicating with her managers. The hospital management is not responsive. The nurse is dissatisfied with a working environment that makes her feel uncertain about her abilities.*

Inferences In Chapter 3, we made several inferences about Struggling RN and her predicament. Recall that we were careful to identify a particular point of view (as sociologists) when making the inferences, our reasoning being that who a person is determines to a large extent what sorts of inferences he or she will make. Based on our reading of the nurse's letter, we said the following:

> This writer describes a working environment that is flawed. In a well-managed workplace, employees are for the most part content and productive. That the nurse has lost confidence in her skills and is unhappy suggests that the hospital management is in need of reorganization. It's possible that her frustrations are due more to her problems than to her employers'; so before agreeing with her assessments we would want to hear the views of other staff members. Our inclination, however, is to believe that the nurse's lack of confidence is a problem caused by ill-trained managers. Our advice would be that the woman look for new employment in a workplace that is structured differ-

---

*When we designate a sentence such as this — "The nurse is dissatisfied..." — as a fact, we are saying only that a person has made a statement about her own experience. The *act* of making that statement is a fact. She made it. Whether the statement is true is another matter. It's possible that she is deceiving herself; to claim this, we'd have to make an interpretation, or refer to the views of some informed source (her psychiatrist?). In any event, Struggling RN's saying "I'm dissatisfied" differs from her saying "The grass is green in springtime." In the first case, she's describing an internal state, a feeling; in the second case, she's describing something in the physical world that we can verify. We consider both statements to be factual. The one we have to assume is true; the other we can verify.

ently—one that is not so rigidly hierarchical in the sense that employees feel they always have someone over them, evaluating their performance. In a smaller hospital or in a hospice center, the organization's structure would be completely different and better suited to the nurse's personality.

Source 3

Columnist Juliette Flynn responds to Struggling RN differently than we do. Reread pages 80–81 and you will see that the inferences she makes about the writer's complaints have a great deal to do with her focus on the individual's responsibility in an organization. For instance, Flynn states that "[H]aving managers who evaluate your performance is a fact of working life. You must satisfy the expectations of your superiors...." Here, she is concentrating on the individual employee's position with respect to a system of management that she—Flynn—does not question. In differing with Flynn, we imply that there *are* alternative systems of management in which constant evaluations by superiors is not a "fact of working life." So you see that so-called facts may actually be opinions. We are able to make this observation because our perspective as readers of the nurse's letter differed from Flynn's. In making our inferences, we focused on the organization's role in making employees content and productive.

Source 4

Our fourth source is the article "The Top Ten Motivators and Satisfiers" by Julia Kagan. Reread the article on pages 86–89.

Content In "The Top Ten Motivators and Satisfiers," Julia Kagan reports that the Public Agenda Foundation interviewed white-collar and blue-collar workers and then collected its findings into table form. These findings are factual. We could verify, if we wanted, that 48 percent of the professional men interviewed considered "a good chance for advancement" to be a top motivator in a job. We could similarly check any other percentage stated in the tables. Kagan presents basically two facts: the information in the two tables and the information that Yankelovich and Katzell conducted a study of job satisfaction and productivity in 1975, concluding that the two are not necessarily related. (*Note:* That Yankelovich and Katzell conducted a study and reached a certain conclusion is a fact. The conclusion itself, however, is an opinion.)

Whenever Kagan interprets percentages from the table, she is presenting her opinions. Her most important opinion is that the factors motivating workers to be productive in their jobs do not necessarily result in their being satisfied. The opposite is also true: satisfied workers are not necessarily more productive than dissatisfied workers. Based on her reading of the survey, Kagan discusses specific "motivators" and "satisfiers": working conditions and fringe benefits do not appear to promote productivity; they do appear, however, to promote job satisfaction. Ambition promotes productivity, while peace and quiet on a job promote worker satisfaction.

Toward the end of her discussion, Kagan refers to the work of Frederick Herzberg, who concluded from his own research that when "hygiene factors" in the workplace fall below a certain standard, worker satisfaction can adversely affect productivity. Yet optimal "hygiene" in the workplace does not appear to increase job performance.

Inferences Surveys are conducted both to gain information about a specific set of people and to generalize from that information to a larger population. We see Kagan taking the results of the Public Agenda Foundation survey and making interpretations—which seem valid to the extent that she limits her opinions to the group of people surveyed. It appears, however, that she wants to generalize from the survey results and make claims about workers who weren't interviewed by the Public Agenda Foundation.

Source 5

Our next source is from *The 100 Best Companies to Work for in America* by Levering, Moskowitz, and Katz. Reread the article on pages 90–93.

Content In Chapter 3 you wrote a summary of *100 Best Companies.* In that summary you should have noted the following facts: A large amount of information exists on the financial aspects of business, though relatively little on the conditions for workers. The authors therefore set out to observe these conditions and found that America's "100 Best" companies share twelve "themes."

Levering and his cowriters present opinions whenever they make claims about companies that they did not observe directly. This is to say that they, like Kagan, tend to generalize. Specific claims made about the one hundred companies studied can be regarded as potentially factual. Generalized claims, like the following, cannot: "People are proud to work for companies that treat them well." We're hesitant to generalize beyond the one hundred companies studied, even though we tend to agree with the authors' conclusion. Some employees could be indifferent toward companies that treat them well (perhaps they expect good treatment and take it for granted).

Three other opinions are offered: (1) "Techniques" for improving employee productivity alienate employees from management; these techniques are manipulative and are based on an "us" versus "them" mentality. (2) The good company offers good pay and strong benefits. (3) Incentives that increase a worker's pride and loyalty improve the quality of working life. Though we tend to agree with these statements, they are opinions.

Structure The main idea of *100 Best Companies* is expressed in paragraph 1: "Finding a good place to work is not easy. It's not easy for a job hunter, and it wasn't easy for us." Notice how these two sentences, the authors' thesis, organize the rest of the two-part essay. Paragraphs 2–11 are a factual recounting of *how* the authors went about finding their "100 Best" companies. Paragraphs 12–18 provide definitions of the "good" company. Not surprisingly, the second part of the essay consists largely of opinions. Though you might read this entire essay in conducting background research for a paper on job satisfaction, it is likely that if you were to write a summary of the piece, you would do so based only on the second part; for it is here that the authors present the thrust of their research.

Inferences Based on our reading of this article, we can make three inferences: (1) A manager's proper function is to encourage an employee's sense of belonging to the organization. (2) Since working accounts for a majority of a person's day, having a rewarding, satisfying job is essential to successful, happy adjustment in life. (3) It is the company's responsibility to create the working conditions that promote worker satisfaction.

Make Inferences Among Your Sources

After closely examining several sources that bear on your topic, your next step in writing a paper is to make inferences *among* these sources. In theory, source materials can be related in an infinite variety of ways; but in practice, there are a few patterns or relationships that are used time and time again in the "conversation" of a paper. After selecting a topic for discussion, you will call on various authors to contribute ideas and information. One author will speak and you, or another, will respond. Your reader, the one who is "listening in" on this conversation, must be able to follow. Your responsibility is to establish clear relationships among the ideas and information discussed by the various authors. The relationships we will discuss here are *example, comparison and contrast,* and *description.* We'll discuss other relationships later in the text.

Example

Imagine that you have read three articles on a very broad topic: *jobs.* How are the sources related? One might provide an *example* of a statement made in another. Inferring the relationship of *example* between sources requires that you understand the difference between a general statement and a specific one. Consider the following:

1. Many jobs are endangered.
2. Certain jobs on auto assembly lines are endangered.
3. Sophisticated, computer-driven robots have replaced welders, painters, and bolt tighteners on auto assembly lines.

The most general statement is number 1, and the most specific is number 3. Why? A general statement concerns a broad subject area — in the case of sentence 1, "jobs." A specific statement concerns a narrowly defined topic — in the case of sentence 3, auto assembly line welders, painters, and bolt tighteners. The term "jobs" is general and could apply to any number of endeavors: construction, nursing, teaching, and so on. Notice that sentence 2 is more specific than 1 since a particular class of jobs is named: autoworkers. But sentence 3 is more specific still since it names particular types of autoworkers and explains how their jobs are endangered. The information in sentence 3, therefore, can be considered an example of the claims made in sentences 1 and 2. This same relationship of general to specific can exist among source materials. (See Chapter 8 for a more detailed discussion of examples.)

Comparison and Contrast

Often you will find that different authors agree or disagree on a point, and when you observe them doing either, you have cause to infer comparisons (similarities) and contrasts (differences). Though we will discuss this relationship in some detail later, we can say here that a writer is obliged to compare and contrast elements of the same class: a comparison between a maple tree and working at a subway station would not yield much that is useful, except to a poet. But a comparison between a maple and a palm would allow you to examine important elements of both. One of the chief virtues of a comparison/ contrast is that, in the search for similarities and differences, you focus on details in each source that might have escaped your attention had you examined only a single source. Without the comparison of a palm tree, would you have noticed that the wood of the maple is particularly dense? That the tree does not grow well in sandy soil? That it cannot tolerate even mildly brackish water? That it sheds its leaves yearly? Effective comparisons and contrasts contribute to the conversation of a paper by establishing multiple points of view (in the case of contrasts) and a consensus of opinion (in the case of comparisons). (See Chapter 12 for a more detailed discussion of comparison and contrast.)

Description

You may read source materials and realize that, when considered together, they provide a description of a place, of an event, or of a condition of one sort or another. Imagine finding several articles on trekking in Nepal. Five or six newspaper articles, considered together, might provide an accurate account of the *Titanic*'s sinking or an account of factory life during the Industrial Revolution. You'll find that the most effective descriptions—when you are both writing them and discovering them in your sources—use vivid language to create specific images for the reader. (See Chapter 7 for a more detailed discussion of description.)

Typically, when writing a paper you will refer to several sources and you will relate them to one another in a variety of ways. One section of a paper might be devoted to a description; another to a comparison and contrast; a third to examples. At times you might summarize portions of your sources and then, perhaps, comment on your summaries. In any one paper you will most likely infer a variety of relationships among your sources, depending on your purpose.

What relationships can be inferred among the five sources on job satisfaction? To help you see sources in relation to one another, we suggest that you write a brief, schematic summary that lists the essential features of each source on a single page. We do so here:

Atkins: Alienated worker, feels diminished by her job.

Struggling RN: Confused worker; does not communicate well with management; does not know whether she or the management is responsible for her loss of confidence.

Flynn: Responds to Struggling RN; assumes that it is the worker's responsibility to adjust to the requirements of management.

Kagan: Presents and interprets Public Agenda Foundation survey; distinguishes between job satisfiers and motivators, claiming that the two are not necessarily related.

Levering, Moskowitz, and Katz: The authors identify the job satisfiers that distinguish America's "100 Best" companies; satisfaction in one's job leads to pride, loyalty, sense of belonging; best companies minimize distinctions among employees.

Here are the inferences we can make *among* these five sources.

1. The pieces by Atkins and Struggling RN, when considered together, can provide a *description* of unsatisfactory working conditions.
2. Columnist Juliette Flynn believes that individuals must resign themselves to a hierarchical workplace in which managers have more power than lower-level employees. Flynn believes it is primarily the employee's responsibility to adjust to the dictates of management. On the other hand, Levering and his cowriters suggest that management can establish a nonthreatening work environment in which work can be personally satisfying. Therefore, we can *contrast* the views of Flynn and Levering and his cowriters.
3. We can infer that Flynn and Levering and his cowriters would cite Atkins and Struggling RN as *examples* — albeit examples demonstrating different points. Flynn cites the nurse and, one guesses, would cite Atkins as people who have failed to adjust appropriately to the conditions of the workplace. Levering and his cowriters would cite the same examples in support of their view that an attentive management will keep employees satisfied while an inattentive one will likely frustrate them. Atkins and the

nurse would be cited as examples of frustrated employees. Their places of work would provide examples of mismanaged organizations.

4. Kagan makes a distinction between the factors in a job that satisfy employees and the factors that motivate them, observing that the two are not necessarily related. In paragraph 18 of their introduction, Levering and his cowriters say essentially the same thing: that workers can be productive without being satisfied (though satisfaction adds a crucial component to the quality of working life). We can therefore *compare* the views of Kagan and Levering and his cowriters on this point.

In considering our five sources, we've observed the three relationships just mentioned: we relate our sources to each other by inferring examples, comparisons and contrasts, and descriptions. Whether we will use all these relationships in our paper depends entirely on our purpose. And we will not understand our purpose until we write a working thesis.

Write a Working Thesis

As we've said, a thesis is a sentence that establishes the topic that you (or any author) wish to discuss in a paper and the claim to be made about that topic. When you can identify an author's thesis, then you can anticipate broad sections of the articles that you read. Assume that, on reading a magazine, you've come across an essay and identified the following thesis: "During the decade leading up to 1929, stock speculation, the land boom in Florida, and bank failures helped lead America into the Great Depression." On the basis of this sentence, what sections of the essay would you expect the author to develop?

We've seen the value of identifying a thesis as a reader. Now we change perspectives and focus on the ways in which a writer creates and works from a thesis. To begin the actual writing of a paper, you must have a purpose in mind, and the thesis establishes this purpose. Imagine your writing the statement about the Depression. Had you done so, you would have understood your purpose, and you would have known that any paper based on such a statement would need to be developed in three parts. We'll speak at length about how writers must look to their thesis for guidance on structuring a paper. For now, understand that the thesis is a crucial tool for organizing your work. In the following pages, we discuss in detail how you go about choosing a thesis.

Pose Questions About Your Sources

One excellent way to discover a thesis is to pose questions about a topic, questions such as *what, why, how,* and *who.* If, in answering these questions, you can refer in specific ways to your sources, then you have established the basis for writing a paper. The more sources that you can refer to in an answer, the more lively will be the conversation that you create. We can pose several questions about our sources on job satisfaction:

1. What is the importance of working?
2. Does work need to be satisfying?
3. Who is responsible for making work satisfying?
4. What are the qualities one should look for in a job?

EXERCISE	

Let's propose some initial answers. Wherever you find a blank space, you provide the answer.

1. What is the importance of working?
   a. Work is important because it keeps economies running.
   b. Work is important because it provides people with something to do every day.

   c. _____

   _____

2. Does work need to be satisfying?
   a. It makes no difference to the health of the economy if workers are satisfied as long as they are productive.
   b. A job must be satisfying in order for workers to maintain their self-respect.

   c. _____

   _____

3. Who is responsible for making work satisfying?
   a. No one. Work is not and never was intended for satisfaction. A person works to make a living.

   b. _____

   _____

   c. _____

   _____

4. What are the qualities one should look for in a job?
   a. When job hunting, one should apply to companies that experiment with innovative programs for personnel.
   b. When job hunting, one should consider _____

   _____

Each of these answers is a potential thesis and could be used to organize a paper. Notice that each answer would allow a writer to refer to several of the five sources on job satisfaction. Consider:

It makes no difference to the health of the economy if workers are satisfied as long as they are productive.

In a paper organized by this sentence, we could refer to Levering, Kagan, and Atkins. Levering and his cowriters (*100 Best Companies*) state that "conventional managerial techniques...enhance productivity and create a healthy economy," even though they would prefer to see companies employ the techniques that provide for their workers "a working life...really worth living and worth looking forward to every waking day." Kagan ("Top Ten Motivators and Satisfiers") states that productivity is not affected by a lack of a worker's satisfaction. We could cite Atkins, the receptionist, as an example and say that regardless of her being unhappy in her job, she performs adequately—which, from the management's point of view, might be all that's expected. A mundane working life might be all that Atkins can reasonably expect.

We could also use our sources to support a very different thesis:

A job must be satisfying in order for workers to maintain their self-respect.

In a paper organized by this sentence, we could—in addition to developing our own thoughts on the subject—refer to the articles by Atkins and Struggling RN, citing them as examples of the lost self-respect that follows from working in an unrewarding job. We could refer to Levering and his cowriters, who state that employees are proud to work at jobs they find satisfying. We could also refer to Kagan's article and the information in the Foundation survey.

You see, then, that source materials can be used to support statements that are quite different, even diametrically opposed. In writing a paper, you will use sources according to the needs of your thesis. (A basic commitment to honesty requires fairness, however: you must consider the views of those who disagree with you. We'll discuss this requirement at a later point.)

EXERCISE	

Take the following statements, each a potential thesis, and list the sources you would use to develop them. Also provide brief phrases summarizing the key information from these sources that support the thesis.

Work is important because it keeps economies running.

_____

_____

_____

_____

Work is important because it provides people with something to do every day.

_____

_____

_____

_____

Take one of *your* answers to the questions on page 120 and list the sources you would use to develop it.

_____

_____

_____

_____

You can never be sure, before actually writing a paper, of what your thesis will be. That's why we say that the answers to our questions about job satisfaction are *potentially* theses. Once you've identified a purpose for your paper and have gotten down to writing, you may discover new ideas and find, on reflection, that these do not develop your thesis. To keep the focus of your paper clear and distinct, you will often need to revise the original thesis to make room for newly discovered material. Or you may need to delete material.

Whenever you begin the writing process, the sentence you choose to organize your paper is called a *working thesis*. Once you have written a draft and have made adjustments so that every element of the working thesis is developed and no section of the paper drifts from the purpose set out in the working thesis, then you (and your reader) are entitled to refer to your organizing statement as *the* thesis.

What happens when no questions occur to you about your topic? You've read your sources and have drawn a blank. You need to begin writing, but you haven't a thesis. What do you do? When you find yourself in such a predicament, try a different technique for discovering your working thesis.

Begin with a Broad Subject Area and Narrow It

Suppose you have been assigned a ten-page paper in History 204, a class on democratic forms of government. Not only do you not have a thesis, you don't have a subject! Where will you begin? You need to select a broad area of interest and make yourself knowledgeable about its general features. What if no broad area of interest occurs to you? Don't despair—there's usually a way to make use of discussions you've read in a text or heard in a lecture. The trick is to find a topic that can become personally important, for whatever reason. (For a paper in your biology class, you might write on the digestive system because a relative has stomach troubles. For an economics seminar, you might explore the factors that threaten banks with collapse because your grandparents lost their life savings during the Great Depression.) Whatever the academic discipline, try to discover a topic that you'll enjoy exploring; that way, you'll be writing for yourself as much as for your professor. Some specific strategies to try if no topics occur to you: review material covered during the semester, class by class if need be; review the semester's readings, actually skimming each assignment. Latch onto any subject that has held your interest, even if for a moment, and use that as your point of departure.

So you've reviewed each of your classes and you recall that a lecture on the democracies in the city-states of ancient Greece aroused your curiosity. You are interested in the subject of *democracy.* * At this point, the goal of your research is to limit this subject to a manageable topic. Though your initial focus will often be more specific than our example, "democracy," we'll take the most general case (the subject in greatest need of limiting) as our starting point.

A subject can be limited in at least two ways. First, a general article like an encyclopedia entry may do the work for you by presenting the subject in the form of an outline, with each item in the outline representing a separate topic (which, for your purposes, may need further limiting). Second, you can limit a subject by asking several questions about it:

Who?

What aspects?

Where?

When?

How?

Which ones?

These questions will occur to you as you conduct your research and see the ways in which various authors have focused their discussions. Having read several sources and having decided that you'd like to use them, you might limit the subject "democracy" by asking, "What aspect?"

Subject: democracy

Limited subject: modifications to democracy

Certainly, "modifications to democracy" offers a more specific focus for your paper than "democracy," but the focus is still not specific enough. A paper that thoroughly explored this limited subject would have to begin with the first democracy in Greece and then discuss the ways in which democracy has been

---

*Is your curiosity aroused by city-states? Some people quite naturally like to know about our traditions, where we came from, what we can learn from the past. You may say, "City-states— who cares?" This is understandable, but remember that as a college student you wander at first in unfamiliar territory, where city-states and what they can teach us about the human enterprise are important. If you need more practical motives for showing interest in academic subjects, recall that you are preparing to enter a professional world whose most valued members are always asking questions, willing to show interest in something new, and willing to take risks to make gains. If you are not such a person, presumably you are in college to teach yourself to be one. A good way to start is to question everything and everyone and, through questioning, develop interests that will extend your experience.

modified over the past 2000 years to accommodate the needs of particular peoples. You might write on Greek democracy, parliamentary democracy, French democracy, and so on. Your limited subject might be appropriate for a book-length inquiry, but not for a ten-page paper. It therefore needs further limiting. Such limitations might be suggested to you by other sources. You can also narrow a limited subject by continuing to ask questions of it, in this case, "Where?"

Subject: democracy

Limited subject: modifications to democracy

Initial topic: modifications to American democracy

Now we have progressed to an initial topic by identifying features of our limited subject that bring it into realistic focus. But think again. Could "modifications to American democracy" be thoughtfully discussed in the assigned length? Probably not, since the scope is still too broad. To develop this initial topic, we would need to list and explain modifications to American democracy over the past 200 years. The focus can be made even more specific by asking another question, "When?"

Subject: democracy

Limited subject: modifications to democracy

Initial topic: modifications to American democracy

Topic: modifications to American democracy during the next twenty years

At last we have a satisfactory topic. It answers as many of the questions about the subject of democracy as seems appropriate for a paper of roughly ten pages. (Specifically, it answers "What aspect?" "Where?" and "When?") The topic we've chosen, "modifications to American democracy during the next twenty years," strikes what appears to be an acceptable balance between the specific and the general. We say "appears" because we can't be sure until we complete the thesis statement and sketch the outline of our paper. However, the topic shows promise: limited as it is, it allows room for a detailed, complex discussion that will illuminate for the reader what these modifications to democracy may be during the next twenty years.

Clearly, the process of narrowing the topic to a subject has depended directly on our experiences as researchers. Had we found but one proposed modification to democracy mentioned in the literature, had we found no discussion of proposals for modifying *American* democracy, or had we found that most commentators agree that American democracy is in fine shape for the immediate future, we could not have limited the topic as we did.

Make an Assertion

Once you have identified the topic, develop it into a thesis by making an assertion about it. If you have spent enough time gathering information, you should be fairly knowledgeable about your topic. You should have gained enough information—enough experience—to have a valid opinion (and to defend it). But if you are having trouble making an assertion, try writing your topic at the top of a page and then listing everything you now know and feel about it. Often from such a list you will discover an assertion that you can then use to fashion a working thesis. A good way to gauge the reasonableness of your claim is to see what other authors have asserted about the same topic. In fact, keep good notes on the views of others; the notes will prove a useful counterpoint to your own views as you write, and you may want to use them in your paper.

Let's make three assertions about our topic, in order of increasing complexity. The assertion in each sentence is italicized:

1. *Several critics have suggested* that we modify American democracy during the next twenty years.
2. *We should seriously consider* modifying American democracy during the next twenty years.
3. *The most sensible plan* for modifying American democracy during the next twenty years *has been proposed by Deborah Sloane*.

Keep in mind that these are *working theses.* Since we haven't written a paper based on any of them, they remain hypotheses to be tested. After completing a first draft, we would compare the contents of the paper to the thesis and make adjustments as necessary for unity. The working thesis is an excellent tool for planning broad sections of the paper, but don't let it prevent you from pursuing related discussions as they occur to you.

You will have observed that identical source materials (in this case, articles by critics who suggest changes in American democracy) can be used to develop a number of theses.

EXERCISE	

In the space provided, list the elements that you would expect to find in three papers organized by the sentences above.

Several critics have suggested that we modify American democracy during the next twenty years.

What sections of the paper can you anticipate, based on this working thesis?

_____

_____

_____

_____

We should seriously consider modifying American democracy during the next
twenty years.

What sections of the paper can you anticipate, based on this working thesis?

_____

_____

_____

_____

The most sensible plan for modifying American democracy during the next twenty
years has been proposed by Deborah Sloane.

What sections of the paper can you anticipate, based on this working thesis?

_____

_____

_____

_____

Why does working thesis number 2 promise a more complex paper than thesis number 1?
And why would working thesis number 3 be the most complex of them all?

To review: a thesis (a one- or two-sentence summary of your paper) helps
you to organize and your reader to anticipate a discussion. A thesis is distinguished by its carefully chosen subject and predicate, which should be just
broad enough and complex enough to be developed within the length limitations of the assignment. You can develop a thesis by posing—and then answering—questions about your sources; and by beginning with a broad subject
area and narrowing it. Both novices and experts in a field typically begin the
initial draft of a paper with a working thesis—a statement that provides writers
with structure enough to get started but with latitude enough to discover what
they want to say as they write. Once you have completed a first draft, you
should test the "fit" of your thesis with the paper that follows. Every element of
the thesis should be developed. Discussions that drift from your thesis should
be deleted or the thesis changed to accommodate the new discussions.

Anticipate the Structure of the Paper
Based on Your Working Thesis

Once you have read your source materials and have understood how they
are related, and once you have developed a working thesis that allows you to
use your sources as well as your own ideas, you are ready to create a rough
outline that will give your paper a structure. In Chapter 1 (pages 3–35), we

discussed the importance of understanding, both as reader and as writer, the relation of the whole paper to its parts. That discussion is essentially the same one we need to make here, so we ask that you reread it. Before proceeding any further, review pages 20–35. We will assume that you are familiar with this material when we ask you to complete the various exercises that follow.

One important difference between your life as a reader and your life as a writer is this: readers get to observe completed essays and articles; writers must create them from scratch, through trial and error. Typically, to work through a paper from first draft to last, you must experiment with a number of elements—the thesis, your paper's structure, your sources, and your own ideas—until, gradually (never all at once), a finished paper emerges. As a reader your job is to be analytical, to work with what others have created; as a writer your job is to do the creating. Any artist will tell you that creation is a messy process. You must be willing to experiment, to take chances—and then, when you see an element of your work that has the promise of being success- ful, you must revise and revise again until you have completed your effort. Be willing to experiment, and you will succeed.

Begin with the following sentence as a working thesis:

> Many causes helped lead America into the Great Depression.

As a potential working thesis, this statement is somewhat helpful—it lets you and your readers know, for instance, that your paper is not about rogue ele- phants. But just how helpful is this sentence? While we know that the subject of the paper will be the causes of the Great Depression, the working thesis gives us *no* clue as to which causes; and so a reader might expect a discussion of *all* the causes of the Depression. Certainly, you aren't prepared to deliver on this promise; after all, you're writing a ten-page paper, not a book. The working thesis provides no clear idea of the parts of the paper, so we need to revise it. Following our technique on pages 122–124 for clarifying thesis statements, we therefore pose two questions: *When* and *Which ones?* Our result:

> During the decade leading up to 1929, stock speculation, the land boom in Florida, and bank failures helped lead America into the Great Depression.

A working thesis such as this allows us to anticipate three sections of the paper: one on stock speculation, one on the land boom, and one on bank fail- ures. The thesis also focuses our discussion on a specific period of time so that we are not obligated to discuss the very early causes of the Depression. Once you have a working thesis that seems manageable in scope, your next chal- lenge is to experiment with the structure of your paper.*

You will recall from Chapter 1 a diagram that resembles the following.

---

*By *manageable* we mean a thesis that sets for you an amount of work appropriate for your assignment. The modified thesis just developed would set a manageable amount of work for a ten-page paper. The original thesis, "Many causes helped lead America into the Great Depression," would be a manageable thesis—for a book.

Thesis: During the decade leading up to 1929, stock speculation, the land boom in Florida, and bank failures helped lead America into the Great Depression.

Part I: _____ ↓ _____

_____

_____

_____

Part II: _____ ↓ _____

_____

_____

_____

Part III: _____ ↓ _____

_____

_____

_____

Conclusion: _____ ↓ _____

_____

_____

_____

You see here the shell of a section outline. Notice that just as with the paragraph outline on page 22, each section, or part, refers back to and develops some part of the thesis. And each section leads logically to the next. A section is a group of paragraphs that develops one specific part of the thesis. Here is our section outline for our paper on the Depression:

Thesis: During the decade leading up to 1929, stock speculation, the land boom in Florida, and bank failures helped lead America into the Great Depression.

↓

Part I: The land boom contributed to the economic collapse.

↓

Part II: Stock speculation contributed to the economic collapse.

↓

Part III: Bank failures contributed to the economic collapse.

↓

Conclusion: These three factors worked together, contributing to the collapse of the American economy.

As a writer you need to understand why you place the sections of a paper in a particular order. In our case, we knew from our source material that stock speculation and land speculation both strained the resources of the country's banking system. The discussion in parts I and II lead to the discussion in part III. This general principle, of one part of the paper leading logically to the next, applies to all academic writing.

Once you have arranged the broad sections of your paper according to your purpose, you can concentrate on developing the content of each section—which you do by writing a series of paragraphs. Notice the relationship of each paragraph to what we call the subthesis:

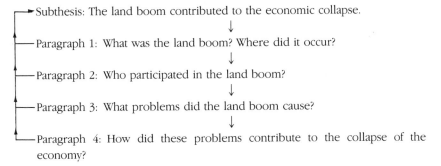

Subthesis: The land boom contributed to the economic collapse.

Paragraph 1: What was the land boom? Where did it occur?

Paragraph 2: Who participated in the land boom?

Paragraph 3: What problems did the land boom cause?

Paragraph 4: How did these problems contribute to the collapse of the economy?

A subthesis organizes one section of a paper and is developed much like a thesis: every paragraph of a section should develop the subthesis in the same way that the sections of the paper should develop the main thesis. Moreover, every paragraph of a section should lead logically to the next, just as every section of a paper should lead logically from one to the next. Whether you are writing a five-paragraph report or a fifty-paragraph article, these same structural requirements apply.

Creating an outline based on your working thesis allows you to begin writing a paper. If you discover several new ideas in the act of writing, you should pursue them, even if you drift from your working thesis. In later drafts you'll have the opportunity to revise your work. In the first draft, your job is to write, and an outline will provide enough structure to get started. Work on one part of the outline at a time, and you will eventually write the whole paper.

Consider the sections of a paper you could develop based on this thesis:

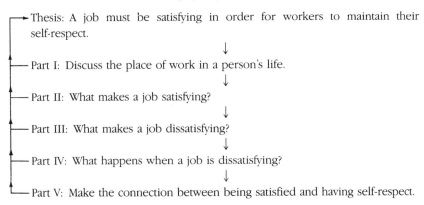

Thesis: A job must be satisfying in order for workers to maintain their self-respect.

Part I: Discuss the place of work in a person's life.

Part II: What makes a job satisfying?

Part III: What makes a job dissatisfying?

Part IV: What happens when a job is dissatisfying?

Part V: Make the connection between being satisfied and having self-respect.

Each of these sections is implied by our working thesis. If we want to discuss job satisfaction, we should examine what a job is and how one achieves a measure of satisfaction by working at it. What importance does work play in a person's life? Part I of the outline attempts an answer. Part II addresses the definition of job *satisfaction*. The headings for parts III and IV are also implied by the thesis. The choice of verb "must be" in the thesis ("A job *must be* satisfying...") suggests that there are consequences for being both satisfied and dissatisfied at work. But we have yet to define dissatisfaction. We do that in part III and then treat the consequences of dissatisfaction in part IV. Finally, in part V, we discuss how being satisfied at work leads to self-respect, the point we wish to demonstrate in our paper.

As an alternative, we considered placing part V after part III, after the discussion of what makes a job satisfying. This placement would make for a nicely balanced paper:

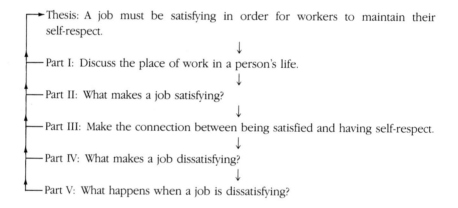

Thesis: A job must be satisfying in order for workers to maintain their self-respect.
↓
Part I: Discuss the place of work in a person's life.
↓
Part II: What makes a job satisfying?
↓
Part III: Make the connection between being satisfied and having self-respect.
↓
Part IV: What makes a job dissatisfying?
↓
Part V: What happens when a job is dissatisfying?

We finally decided on the first arrangement because delaying the discussion about the relationship between self-respect and job satisfaction made for a strong conclusion. Certainly, we could have organized (and justified the writing of) the paper by following either section outline. In fact, you'll usually have choices to make when organizing your papers, with two or three choices being equally valid. Our advice is to choose the organization that you think will be most interesting to write — and to read. Whatever your choice, remember that the sections of a paper are derived from, and are implicit in, the working thesis. Look to your working thesis for guidance when creating an outline for your paper.

Now that we've developed section headings based on a thesis, we need to create a content for each section. We'll do so with a combination of our own ideas and those of the authors in our five sources on job satisfaction.

Thesis: A job must be satisfying in order for workers to maintain their self-respect.

Part I: Discuss the place of work in a person's life.

Typically, American adults work 50 weeks a year, 8 hours a day for 5 days a week. Most people sleep 8 hours a day, which leaves another 8:

8 hours working
8 hours sleeping
8 hours doing other things (being with family, etc.)

One-half of a person's waking life is spend away from family and close friends, working.

Part II: What makes a job satisfying?

Refer to Levering, Moskowitz, and Katz, *100 Best Companies*

Refer to results from survey conducted by Public Agenda Foundation

Part III: What makes a job dissatisfying?

Refer to Levering and cowriters: discuss management "technique" and the "us" versus "them" mentality.

Refer to Atkins: discuss her being snubbed at the company party (the assumption by others that her job is not important); discuss the mechanical routine of her job.

Refer to Struggling RN: failure to communicate well with management (regardless of fault) leads to nurse's loss of confidence on the job and general crabbiness at home.

Refer to Kagan: use the survey results to show that neither Atkins nor the nurse benefits from what those in the survey thought to be strong job satisfiers.

Part IV: What happens when work is dissatisfying?

Refer to Atkins: discuss her feelings of alienation and the ways in which her job as a receptionist affects her private life.

Refer to Struggling RN: discuss her confusion and self-doubt.

Part V: Make the connection between being satisfied at work and having self-respect. In the conclusion, tie together the points made in the preceding sections. Then discuss why self-respect is important.

Notice how our outline allows us to use source materials — the work of Levering and cowriters, Kagan, Atkins, and Struggling RN — in support of our own thesis. You can now see how important it is to understand your sources thoroughly so that you can call on them as needed to develop the different sections of your papers. If your efforts succeed, then you — like David Chandler, writing on the space program — will have created conversations among your sources, conversations with experts in which you will have participated.

Here is a second working thesis you could use as the basis of a paper:

Management and individual employees share equally in the responsibility for creating a productive, satisfying workplace.

By now you should be able to examine a working thesis and determine the sections that would be needed to develop a paper. On the basis of this thesis, we can anticipate the author's discussing the following topics, each of which we can see developed around a different question:

What is management's responsibility for creating a productive, satisfying workplace?

What is the individual's responsibility?

What is job satisfaction?

What does it mean to be productive at work?

How is productivity related to job satisfaction?

Two methods of arranging this paper occur to us:

Arrangement 1

Thesis: Management and individual employees share equally in the responsibility for creating a productive, satisfying workplace.

Part I: What does it mean to be productive at work? What is job satisfaction?

Part II: What is management's responsibility for creating a productive, satisfying workplace?

Part III: What is the individual employee's responsibility?

Part IV: How is productivity related to job satisfaction?

Arrangement 2

Thesis: Management and individual employees share equally in the responsibility for creating a productive, satisfying workplace.

Part I: Being Productive at Work

What does it mean to be productive at a job?

What is management's responsibility for making workers productive?

What is the individual employee's responsibility for being productive at the job?

Part II: Job Satisfaction

What is job satisfaction?

What is management's responsibility for making workers satisfied with their jobs?

What is the individual employee's responsibility for being satisfied with a job?

Part III: Discuss the relationship between productivity at work and job satisfaction.

In the first outline, you'll note that we group together our planned discussion of job satisfaction and productivity (Part I). This initial grouping has consequences for the rest of the paper, for in part II we plan to discuss management's role in fostering a productive *and* satisfying workplace and in part III we plan to discuss the individual's role. By contrast, in the second outline, we separate the discussions of productivity and job satisfaction. Again, our decision has consequences for the rest of the paper: in the second outline, management is discussed in two places—parts I and II—whereas it was discussed in only one section before. Likewise, we discuss the employee's responsibilities (for being productive and satisfied) in two places as opposed to one.

Which arrangement works better? It's difficult to say before writing the paper. If we had to choose, we'd be inclined to try the second arrangement. Since in the conclusion we want to explore the relationship between productivity and job satisfaction, perhaps it would be better to define those ideas as distinctly as possible beforehand—which suggests that we discuss job satisfaction and productivity in separate sections of the paper.

So we would work with the second outline, though we would have a concern: the sources we're using have more to do with job satisfaction than with productivity. Aside from a brief mention in Levering and cowriters (paragraph 18) and Kagan's assertions that a worker's satisfaction with a job is not necessarily related to his ability to produce, we seem to have few source materials on the subject of productivity. Our concern is that, given our outline (in which productivity plays so large a part, forming one-half of the outline), the first section of our paper may be underdeveloped.

The only way to know whether an outline would work is to write a first draft. Soon enough we would discover whether our concerns were justified. If they were, we could change our thesis so that not so much attention needed to be given to a worker's productivity. The larger point to bear in mind is this: when you choose among section outlines, every choice will have its advantages and disadvantages. Choose the outline that you think will make for the strongest paper, and then write. You can always rewrite; you can always change an outline or a working thesis. What's required at this initial stage is your willingness to experiment.

EXERCISE

Now review the other working theses on page 120. (Consider your own as part of the list.) Choose one working thesis and write a section outline based on it. Then develop a content for your outline, as we have, using at least three of the five sources on job satisfaction.*

Thesis: _____

_____

*If you use your own working thesis, then make sure you have sufficiently limited your subject and the claim you wish to make about that subject. Remember: your working thesis guides the development of the entire paper. A thesis that is too broad will commit you to writing too long a paper (or, conceivably, a short paper in which you treat complex ideas superficially). A thesis that is too limited will not allow you material enough to develop a paper. Before writing a section outline based on your own working thesis, ask your instructor to review the thesis.

Part I: _____

Part II: _____

Part III: _____

Part IV: _____

Part V*: _____

In a sentence or two, explain how each part develops some aspect of your working thesis.

Part I: _____

_____

Part II: _____

_____

Part III: _____

_____

Part IV: _____

_____

Part V: _____

_____

Next explain how each section leads logically to the next. Justify the order you've selected.

_____

_____

_____

_____

_____

Now write a detailed section outline in which you list (and explain briefly) the sources you will use to develop each section of the paper. Prepare this outline on a separate sheet of paper. You will use it as your guide for writing a first draft.

Write the First Draft of Your Paper

With a working thesis, section outline, and rough idea of the material to be used in developing each section of your paper, you are ready to begin writing—one paragraph of one section at a time. You may, if you choose and your instructor agrees, write a paper on the basis of the section outlines that we've developed—one for the thesis "A job must be satisfying in order for workers

---

*We choose a five-part outline merely as a point of departure. The thesis you're working with may require more or fewer parts.

to maintain their self-respect" or for the thesis "Management and individual employees share equally in the responsibility for creating a productive, satisfying workplace." We would, however, encourage you to work with a thesis that *you've* selected and developed into a section outline.

We've asked a student in one of our freshman composition courses to write a paper. Saundra Goulet began the process of writing a paper by reading the five sources on job satisfaction, just as you did. She selected a working thesis on the basis of which she developed a section outline, which she then used as a guide to writing her paper. We present Saundra's first draft, below, reprinted with *no* editorial changes so that the draft will be much like your own (and ours)—complete with awkward phrasings, underdeveloped paragraphs, misspellings, and the like. There is no need in a first draft to attend to these matters since your primary task is to get something down on paper, something that you can refine later. In Chapter 5, we'll use Saundra's draft as the basis of our discussion on revision.

When it comes time to begin looking for a job a person should find a job that will satisfy his needs as an employee as well as a human being. The job market holds many jobs for many different kinds of people. There are jobs for teenagers, that may not be the right job for someone who has a college degree and is looking for a place to start. The quality of the job and its benefits help employees to be satisfied with themselves and their work. A satisfying job supplies workers with self-respect and maintains their productivity producing a healthy economy.

For a person to be successful in his work, he must first decide what exactly it is that he wants to do. He should ask himself questions such as, "Do I need a college education to perform to must best work?", "Does this job supply the amount of salary I am looking for?", "Is there room for improvement?" "Is this a challenging job?" The list of questions could go on and on. One should list his own questions in the order inwhich he sees their importance.

Once the type of job has been established, the job hunting begins. The employee first finds the type of job that is interesting to him and then he tries his experience and determination at his job. Often times people find themselves liking their job for various reasons. The first few months at a job could make or break one's chances at working for the particular company. In the beginning of the job the employee is more interested in meeting new people and becoming familiar with the company. It is usually later in the job when one discovers he is unhappy with his work. The reasons for his unsatisfaction maybe from the company's benefits, the little extras that come with your weekly paycheck, or the lack of movement up the job ladder. By this I mean lack of advancement to top management jobs.

One of the worst reasons for being unsatisfied could be losing your 4 self-respect, as described in the article by Studs Terkel entitled "Sharon Atkins." Sharon is a receptionist who finds herself unsatisfied with her work, not because of the salary or the lack of advancement, but because of her title. When people ask her about her job she is embarassed to say she is a receptionist because of their reaction. The fact that she feels embarassed should not give her a viable reason to quit her job. She, as well as anyone else in this type of predicament, should be proud of her work because it has importance to her and the company she works for. The job in which you wish to work must give you the self respect you need and deserve. This can be achieved by being proud of one's work and when people ridicule one's work he should back up himself with the better qualities of the job.

Finding a satisfying job entales alot of aspects for one to look at. Several of these have been discussed, but still there are more. The preceding 5 aspects have been strictly related to the person finding the job. Now we shall look at the company and what one should expect from it. When people begin looking for work or even begin trying to plan their career, they should expect to be able to communicate well with their workmates and their managers. Poor communication can lead to dissatisfaction. For instance, take the case of the "Struggling RN." She is a nurse who cannot communicate well with her managers and she feels insecure and unhappy as a result. All she gets is negative feedback, when what she needs is encouragement and suggestions on how to improve.

If an individual enters the job with an open mind, he should be able   6
to recognize exactly what a company has to offer and if he is right for the
particular job. In one of the articles entitled "Beyond Technique," an article taken from the book *The 100 Best Companies to Work for in America,*
the authors of the book were looking for ways to describe and find the
best companies in America as well as why people work for these companies. The authors found that by merely speaking with the presidents of
the companies and managers, they were not going to find the absolute
real reasons. The employees were the ones to provide the answers. Most
of these answers dealt with the way the companies treat their employees,
they discovered it was not always the company nefits that made their job
satisfying. A satisfying job ntales many important qualities. Some of
theses qualities maybe that the employees wish to feel like they are a
"part of a team" or that the company cares enough about the employees
that they provide fitness centers for them or that they care enough that
they wish to expand the skills of the employees through training programs. These and many other qualities of a company attract and keep
people working at the company.

A final aspect in job satisfaction is somewhat different from those   7
previously stated. It was thought earlier that if a company was to
increase job satisfaction then the productivity of the company would
increase. This however, was proven to be very wrong. When finding facts
to support this assumption researchers found that if anything increasing job satisfaction "are more likely than not to leave productivity
unchanged, or at best improve it marginally, and may even cause it to
decline" (Kagan). Therefore it can be stated that job satisfaction does not
necessarily increase or decrease productivity, but the two can be indirectly related. The satisfied employee may maintain his productivity but
he may also slack off because he feels he can get away with it.

Job satisfaction is caused by many factors which may not effect the   8
productivity of the workers but it does have an effect on the economy. If

workers are satisfied with themselves and the work they do the economy will tend to be much healhtier. People will find themselves more involved in their work making life in general more pleasant as well as promoting the health of the economy.

A satisfying job supplies workers with self-respect and maintains 9 their productivity producing a healthy economy. When it come time for people to enter the job market they should remember to make a list of questions to assist them in finding a job suitable for their needs. They should also remember that a satisfying job entales more than company fringe benefits. People should find self-respect within their work which will help the health of the economy as well as make their life more pleasant as well.

CHAPTER 5

Revising

Revision is sometimes regarded as an afterthought to the writing process, a luxury one indulges in only when time is available. In the discussion that follows, we will argue (and demonstrate through Saundra Goulet's work) that revision is central to the writing process, that to write effectively means to revise.

Introduction

Whether or not Saundra's final paper closely resembles the draft you've just read does not matter, for she has made an attempt at developing a working thesis and outline. She may have deviated from her outline, but that's as it should be, since in first drafts writers should feel free to discover what they want to say as they are writing. First drafts are necessarily sloppy: some parts of the working thesis will be developed well, and other parts will be developed partially or not at all. On rereading, you may discover paragraphs that have nothing to do with the original thesis; yet the paragraphs may be interesting enough to warrant changing the design of the paper. As a writer you'll need to make your peace with the sloppiness of first drafts, coming to expect not a finished effort but a rough, initial attempt that will, after many revisions, yield a well developed, clearly written final product.

Presumably, you have written a paper just as Saundra Goulet has. Follow us as we work with Saundra to revise — literally, to resee — what she has done. On the basis of her analysis and our own, she will begin the process of rewriting, taking what she has produced and adding to it, deleting, and clarifying so as to more fully achieve her purpose.

We recommend that you evaluate and then rewrite a paper enough times to answer the following:

Essay-level concerns

Is the entire essay, considered in all its parts, coherent, unified, and well developed?

Paragraph-level concerns

Is each paragraph, considered as an individual unit, coherent, unified, and well developed?

Sentence-level concerns

Is each sentence expressed with clarity and force? Is each sentence of the paper grammatical?

When reviewing a first draft, experienced writers will consider these questions simultaneously. We've asked Saundra, and we advise you, to take these questions in the order presented and to apply them separately. The advantage in doing so is that you are more likely to understand the separate but equally important requirements of a successful paper. As you gain experience, you will be able to make multiple revisions — working simultaneously at the levels of the essay, the paragraph, and the sentence. But for now we urge that you work with each level separately. As we discuss the levels of revision, we'll present our reactions to Saundra's paper. She, in turn, will revise her work based on our recommendations.

Essay-level Revisions

Turn briefly to page 128 and review the diagram explaining the relationship between a thesis and the component parts of a paper. You'll recall from the discussion about reading for structure that a finished essay allows a reader to anticipate, on the basis of the thesis, which sections of a paper will follow and be developed. The successful essay creates these expectations and then lives up to them. Every component of the paper implied in the thesis will be defined; moreover, sections of the paper will be arranged in a way that allows for ready understanding.

Unity

When every group of paragraphs in a paper develops some aspect of the thesis and when there are *no* paragraphs present that drift from the thesis, developing some unrelated point, then a paper is said to be *unified* or to have *unity.* A writer's most important and often most difficult task in revising a first draft is to ensure unity. A paper cannot succeed unless it is unified—unless all of its parts clearly relate to the thesis, the one sentence that summarizes the purpose of the whole. Use the following questions to help evaluate your first drafts for unity, and then revise them as needed:

What is the working thesis of your paper?

What sections of the paper should a reader expect to encounter based on the working thesis? List these sections.

Are all of these sections present? If not, you have two options if your paper is to be unified:

Add the omitted material to the paper so that in the second draft all elements of the thesis will be developed.

Do not add any material; instead, delete parts of the thesis so that you are no longer obligated to discuss the sections overlooked in the first draft.

Are there any sections of the paper unrelated to the working thesis? If there are, you have two options if your paper is to be unified:

Delete the new sections if you decide that they do not add substantially to the ideas you wish to pursue.

Keep the new sections but revise the thesis so that a reader could expect to encounter this discussion in the paper.

When working on the second draft of a paper, you should be able to identify a *thesis,* as opposed to what (in your first draft) was a working thesis. The distinction is important. In the first draft the working thesis gave you direction enough to begin writing. Almost certainly the first draft will not be unified. There will be material (a sentence, a paragraph, or even a group of paragraphs) that does not develop any part of the working thesis; and there will be parts of the working thesis that you haven't developed. Your responsibility in the second draft is to add and delete material until you've established a tight fit between your thesis and the sections of the paper that follow. By the completion of the second draft, all paragraphs should relate directly to the thesis, and all elements of the thesis should be discussed.

Coherence

In a second draft you should also work to establish the coherence of your paper. Turn again to page 128 and notice the arrows in the diagram leading from one paragraph to the next. These arrows suggest that, if your work is to make sense, every section of your paper must follow logically from the preceding section. Again, imagine your paper as a conversation being overheard by readers. Your responsibility is to ensure that an audience can follow the exchange and flow of ideas. To discuss in one section of your paper the economic challenges of urban renewal and in the next, without apparent connection, alleged corruption among building contractors is to risk disorienting your audience. As the organizer of the conversation, you must provide clear transitions between paragraphs and between groups of paragraphs, or sections.* The most forceful transition is the one that clearly joins the content of two paragraphs (or sections). The transition will act like a bridge by summarizing preceding material and announcing material to follow. In this manner, the transition enables a reader to pass without difficulty from one part of a discussion to the next. You will have written a coherent paper when an audience can read your paper without having to stop and consider how one paragraph or group of paragraphs is related to another.

| **EXERCISE** | |

Examine the three sentences below. Consider each as a transition excerpted from papers you haven't yet read. On the basis of these transitions, identify the discussion that has just taken place and the discussion that is about to take place.

Mr. Thompson's behavior at the Paris Exposition of 1899 was not the only reason he was considered dangerous.

From the Indians' point of view, the American frontiersmen moving westward in the mid-nineteenth century were aggressive and often brutal. Yet the frontiersmen felt they were justified in their actions, principally for two reasons.

Lawrence Shales and Hannah Wolfe have offered their theories on why movies affect us so deeply. I propose a different explanation.

*See pages 128–129 for a discussion about how individual paragraphs constitute sections of a paper and how sections constitute the whole.

You can see that a transition provides a passageway in a paper: back to the content of a preceding paragraph and forward to the content of coming paragraphs. Every transition serves this double purpose. A transition can be a sentence or a group of sentences, as above, or a single word or phrase. Recall how David Chandler, writing on the space program, used a variety of techniques for making transitions:

> "I was in the manned program for many years," Allen says. "But basically my background is the science program, since I'm a physicist." Overall, he feels, the relative spending on manned and unmanned programs has been "a pretty good balance."
>
> Another scientist working for the space agency put it more forcefully: "The unmanned [science] program gets plenty of money. They just spend it all like a bunch of drunken sailors."
>
> But in the wake of the tragic Challenger explosion, astronomer Gold says: "My feeling is that it's almost inevitable that unmanned boosters will make a strong return."[1]

The words "another scientist" at the beginning of the second paragraph announces an immediate connection between the preceding paragraph and the paragraph to follow. And in the third paragraph, the single conjunction "but" similarly establishes a connection — this time, a contrast. Consider these brief expressions when writing transitions:

yet	in addition
however	moreover
by contrast	consequently
on the other hand	and
but	another

To ensure coherence in your paper, place transitional words, phrases, or sentences between paragraphs within sections and between sections themselves. Regard any difficulty in making transitions as a clear sign that you should revise your paper; for when the content of adjoining paragraphs is not related, making an effective transition between them will be impossible. To meet the requirements of coherence, you will often need to shift the location of paragraphs within a paper. When your revision is successful, every paragraph will lead logically to the next, and you will have made clear and effective transitions.

[1]David Chandler, "Unmanned Rockets vs. the Shuttle," *The Boston Globe* (February 24, 1986): 41, 43.

Development

Read the following paragraph:

> We went to New York City and did a lot of interesting things. We had a great time. Then we took the train north to New England, where we spent another two weeks. After that, we returned home.

The problem with this paragraph is its undeveloped content. What does the writer mean by "a lot of interesting things"? What constitutes a "great time"? What did the writer do in the two weeks in New England? The paragraph promises a content that it doesn't deliver. The writing is superficial.

Individual paragraphs like this one can be undeveloped, and so can broad sections of a paper. Recall that a thesis establishes for a reader certain expectations about what will follow in a paper. When a paper is unified, all the sections promised by the thesis will be present. But for the discussion to be useful, it must be more than merely present; it must be developed — and developed adequately. "Adequate," of course, is a relative word. A discussion that's detailed enough (i.e., adequate) for one person might not satisfy another. Your best guide in this matter is to anticipate what your reader needs to know in order to understand your topic. Consider, for instance, that you began a paper with the following as a working thesis:

> Successful urban planning largely depends on the health of a city's tax base, the involvement of neighborhood action groups, and the leadership of city officials.

After reviewing the first draft, you see that you've devoted three pages to defining and discussing the importance of a city's tax base and another four pages to discussing neighborhood action groups. You also discover that you've devoted only two brief paragraphs to the role of city officials in achieving successful urban renewal. It should occur to you that your discussion is imbalanced, that you've developed two parts of your thesis in detail and have left a third part virtually undeveloped. Recall that your working thesis creates certain expectations for the reader. If the promised third section on the role of city officials is not substantially expanded, then you will not have met your obligation to the reader. What can you do? You have two options: either revise the thesis to omit references to material you do not intend to develop (that is, delete all references to city officials in this thesis) or revise the paper and develop the missing content.

To define what constitutes "adequate" development of a topic is impossible in the abstract; judgments of adequacy depend on the purpose of a paper and on the needs of an audience. Still, the following questions may help clarify the extent to which you've developed various sections of a paper.

> What is the importance of this section to the paper's overall effectiveness? Does the section constitute a principal part of your thesis? If so, you need to devote a considerable amount of attention to it.

What are the expectations of your audience? What level of detail are you expected to provide?

Once you've identified the sections of a paper that you will need to discuss, do you find yourself unable to develop these sections? If so, try the following strategies:

Define your terms. If an experience was enjoyable, discuss exactly what you mean by "enjoyable."

Discuss the *component parts* of your topic. If you are writing about combustion engines, list the components of the engine and then discuss these components separately.

Discuss the *process* by which something works or the steps involved in producing something. Examine each step separately.

Provide *examples* of all general statements. Refer to source materials and use quotations. (See the discussion on quotations in Chapter 6.) Comment on quotations and examples. Discuss why they are important.

Develop *comparisons* and *contrasts*. (See pages 433–435 for a detailed discussion of comparison and contrast.)

At some point in the writing of every paper you'll need to determine whether you've adequately developed each of the component sections. Rely on your judgment (which will improve the more you read and write). Ask yourself: Would intelligent people reading the different sections of this paper learn what they need to know to follow my discussion? If your considered answer is yes, then you can let well enough alone and begin attending to the other aspects of revision. You will have a chance to concentrate on developing papers in different ways as you work through Part Two of this book.

Reactions to Saundra's Paper

What follows is the note we wrote to Saundra in response to her first draft. We base our reactions and suggestions on the three essay-level concerns just discussed: unity, coherence, and development.

Saundra:

You've made a beginning—good job. You've identified the following as your working thesis:

A satisfying job supplies workers with self-respect and maintains their productivity, producing a healthy economy.

Based on this thesis, I would expect to encounter four sections in this paper:

1. A definition of a satisfying job
2. A discussion of the relationship between a satisfying job and self-respect
3. A discussion of the ways in which a satisfying job maintains a worker's productivity
4. A discussion of the ways in which a worker's productivity ensures a healthy economy

It appears that you do something other than develop these four points. In fact, you've attempted to write two papers here: the first on how one should go about looking for a job and the second roughly on the sentence you've identified as your working thesis. (Reexamine the very first sentence of the paper. That, too, seems to be a working thesis.) As might be expected, confusion results. Notice how paragraph 2 is devoted to job hunting, as is paragraph 3, while paragraph 4 turns to job dissatisfaction (the word is *dissatisfied*, not *unsatisfied*). But paragraph 5 then turns back to *finding* a satisfying job — or so states your opening sentence.

I'll leave it to you to determine the ways in which your subject shifts about in the remaining paragraphs. Suffice it to say that, at present, you haven't written on one topic; your paper therefore lacks unity and coherence. My advice is to choose one thesis and to develop it systematically. If you stay with your original thesis, be sure to develop each of its four component parts. If you choose the thesis on locating a good job, then you'll need to identify the components of *that* thesis and then organize accordingly. And if you choose the original thesis, write it out in two sentences for the moment. Begin the second draft with these sentences. You can work on an introduction later.

On the basis of these notes, Saundra revised her work. The paper she produced in her second draft was superior to the first. But still there were paragraphs that seemed out of order, and there were parts of the thesis that were left undeveloped—most notably on the relationship between job satisfaction and productivity and between productivity and a healthy economy. So after two drafts, difficulties remained with essay-level unity and coherence. We advised Saundra to develop all aspects of her thesis or to delete the references in it to productivity and the economy. She responded in this way:

> I've decided to delete part of my thesis in order to develop a better organized and more coherent paper. I found it easier to base the paper on two topics (job satisfaction and self-respect) and develop those completely than to have four topics that I did not develop well.

We present Saundra's second revision—the third draft of her paper. You will notice immediately how she has limited her thesis. Also observe that, at the level of the essay, the draft is for the most part coherent and unified.

A satisfying job supplies workers with self-respect. —— *The new thesis is well focused and can be developed adequately in a 5-page paper. The old thesis (page 145) committed Saundra to a much longer paper.*

In order to fully understand what a satisfying job is, it must first be defined. The definitions of a satisfying job vary from each person's own personal view and opinion. A satisfying job is a job that a worker wants to arise for every morning. The job is something the worker is proud of and it gives the worker rewards. These rewards range from the fringe benefits that a company has to the worker feeling proud of his work. A company car, free membership to a fitness club are some examples of these benefits. A job can provide a worker with a sense of responsibility. That responsibility may only be answering phones but to the employee and the company it is important. The satisfying job also usually includes an enjoyably large paycheck. This paycheck is a reflection of how hard the employee works and how proud he is of his work. To complete his understanding of a satisfying job, the employee should develop his own idea as well as understand the importance of a satisfying job. The importance of a satisfying job adds meaning and enjoyment

1st section of ¶ has a definite purpose and is unified.

This second ¶ works to define job satisfaction, whereas the attempt was never made in the first draft.

Attempted transition only partially successful.

to a person's life. A worker who is satisfied with his work finds pleasure in more than just his job. His entire life cannot be based on a job, but a job can indirectly affect other factors in one's life. A satisfying job provides the worker with a better attitude toward himself. This attitude makes the job more satisfying as well as any other encounter he may come across.

Second section of ¶ develops slightly different idea. But considered alone, it is also unified.

For the employee to acquire a satisfying job, a company must have the qualities of a satisfying job. These qualities provide the employee with an easier time of deciding whether the job will be satisfying to him. Each company has many different fringe benefits and certain qualities that "attract" and keep people working for them. These qualities differ from company to company with some similar qualities. By comparing the particular qualities of each company the employee should be able to find the job he is looking for. In one of the articles entitled "Beyond Technique," the authors of the book were looking for ways to describe and find the best companies in America as well as why people work for them. By merely speaking with managers and company presidents, they were not able to find the absolute real reasons. So they went to employees who provided them with the answers. Most of these answers dealt with the way the companies treat their employees. They discovered it was not always the company benefits that made the job satisfying. A satisfying job entails many more important qualities. Some of these qualities may be that the employees wish to feel like they are "part of a team" or that the company cares enough about the employees that they provide fitness centers for them or that they care enough that they wish to expand the skills of the employees through training programs. These

This ¶ succeeds, in part, because it avoids the "how-to-find-a-good-job" approach of the first draft.

Again ¶ has a clearly defined topic, and contents of the ¶ stick to that topic.

This ¶ furthers the definition of job satisfaction by discussing industry's role.

and many other qualities "attract" and keep people working at the company.

The definition of the preceding 2 P's is extended here with an attempt to define an unsatisfying job.

Up until now we have looked at what a satisfying job is, but to understand fully what a satisfying job entails the definition of an unsatisfying job should be discussed. An unsatisfying job supplies the worker with discontent and makes the worker feel miserable. The worker finds himself dreading work every waking day. His unhappiness may be caused by a number of reasons. The reasons range from the employee's weekly paycheck to lack of advancement up the management ladder. Having a stressful working environment is another reason for people to be dissatisfied. One example would be the case of a registered nurse who writes to an advice columnist and says that because she cannot communicate well with the managers at her hospital, she has become insecure about her work and generally unhappy.

Good example, but develop.

In order for the employee to remain content with his job he must find pride as well as self-respect in his work. The job in which he works must give him the self-respect he needs and deserves. This can be achieved by being proud of one's work and when people ridicule one's work he should respond with the important qualities of his work. A job that is important to the employee supplies him with a sense of self-respect. Self-respect can be related to a satisfying job in that it gives the employee a sense of belonging, it makes him feel good about himself and his job. If the employee feels good about himself and his work he will find other things in his life much more enjoyable and worthwhile.

Some version of this ¶ might work well as a conclusion. (It seems out of place here.)

Distinction between this example and first one would be good to make.

This, however, is not always the case. In fact, there are people who find themselves dissatisfied with their work which may even cause the worker to lose his self-respect. In the article entitled "Sharon Atkins," written by Studs Terkel, *A second example of a dissatisfied worker. Overall unity of paper remains strong. All pts of thesis are being developed. But could this example be placed next to the one about the nurse?*

a case of the loss of self-respect is described. Terkel uses his article to show the reader that a satisfying job as well as a dissatisfying job can provide a person with a lack of self-respect. Sharon Atkins finds herself very unhappy with her job. It seems that her job is taking over her entire life. She finds that the qualities that go with a receptionist are taking over in her social life. She finds herself being short and sometimes rude with people whom she cares about and loves. She wants her life out of work to be very different from her work life. By painting pictures of nature she achieves this dream. The dissatisfaction that the job creates also

All aspects of the thesis are discussed in this draft, whereas in the first draft 2/3 of the thesis went undeveloped. With 1 exception, it's lead logically from one to the next here -- there is essay-level coherence, whereas in first draft there was little. This draft is unified: the first was not. Work still needs to be done at the level of the ¶ and the sentence. Revision on these levels will now yield results, given that the essay as a whole succeeds.

causes her to lose her self-respect. Her problem begins when she has to tell people what type of job she has. She found herself embarrassed to say she was a receptionist because of people's reaction. This reaction provided her with an insecurity and she found it difficult to go to work and enjoy her work as she did before. This could lead up to her quitting her job. But the fact that she is embarrassed should not give her viable reason to quit her job. She, as well as anyone else in this type predicament, should be proud of her work because it has importance to her and the company she works for.

Often, as in this particular case, it will take two or three attempts to produce a draft that is coherent and unified at the level of the essay. With diligent effort, Saundra was able to achieve her first objective of the revision process — to create a tight fit between her thesis (which she needed to revise) and the subsequent paragraphs of her paper. You will have observed in this last draft that every element of the thesis is discussed and that paragraphs, for the most part, flow logically from one to the next. Once these fundamental requirements of essay-level unity and coherence are met, writers should turn their attention to the second level of revision: examining the effectiveness of individual paragraphs.

Paragraph-level Revisions

A paper can succeed only when its component parts—its paragraphs—succeed. We use the terms *unity, coherence,* and *development* in discussing individual paragraphs as well as entire essays because the principles involved in the writing of both the essay and its component parts are identical. As you've seen, the successful essay is unified: blocks of paragraphs, or sections, develop a single, organizing sentence—the thesis. In the same way, paragraphs must be unified: every sentence in a paragraph must in some way develop adequately the paragraph's organizing, topic sentence. And just as the logical relationships between paragraphs must be clear in order to establish the coherence of a paper, so too the logical relationships between sentences *within* a paragraph must be clear.

Paragraph Unity

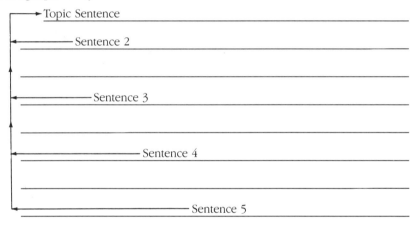

The arrows in this diagram suggest that the relationship between a topic sentence and the sentences constituting a paragraph is parallel to the relationship between a thesis and the sections constituting an entire essay. A topic sentence is the most general statement in a paragraph. Like a thesis, a topic sentence governs the selection and placement of the material that follows.* When a sentence in a paragraph fails to develop some aspect of the paragraph's stated topic, that sentence should be deleted or the topic should be altered. The same principle that guides the revision of essays with respect to unity guides the revision of paragraphs. What you should look for in a unified paragraph is a tight fit between the topic sentence and the sentences that follow. Unless you achieve such a fit, your paragraph will lack unity and your writing will not communicate.

*If you are uncertain about how to write a topic sentence and place it in a paragraph, consult a good handbook, where you'll find a detailed discussion of the matter.

To demonstrate these points, we'll examine two examples—one written by economist John Kenneth Galbraith and the other by Saundra Goulet. Of course, such a comparison is unfair: Galbraith is an accomplished, practicing professional; Saundra Goulet is a freshman beginning her professional studies. Nevertheless, we want to demonstrate that both professional and beginning writers need to work their papers through several stages of revision. Galbraith the writer is committed to the revision process. He once told an interviewer that it takes him *five* drafts to complete a manuscript. Such is the relationship between writing we respect and the effort that goes into that writing. Ideas gain clarity and force when they are revised. This is as true for our best writers, our Galbraiths, as it is for our freshman writers, such as Saundra—and you. Let's turn to three paragraphs from Galbraith's *Affluent Society:*

One can think of modern poverty as falling into two broad categories.	1
First there is what may be called *case* poverty. This one encounters in every	2
community, rural or urban, however prosperous that community or the times.	3
Case poverty is the poor farm family with the junk-filled yard and the dirty	4
children playing in the bare dirt. Or it is the grey-black hovel beside the rail-	5
road tracks. Or it is the basement dwelling in the alley.	6

Case poverty is commonly and properly related to some characteristic of	1
the individuals so afflicted. Nearly everyone else has mastered his environ-	2
ment; this proves that it is not intractable. But some quality peculiar to the in-	
dividual or family involved—mental deficiency, bad health, inability to adapt	3
to the discipline of modern economic life, excessive procreation, alcohol, in-	
sufficient education, or perhaps a combination of several of these handicaps—	
have kept these individuals from participating in the general well-being.	

Second, there is what may be called *insular* poverty—that which mani-	1
fests itself as an "island" of poverty. In the island everyone or nearly everyone	2
is poor. Here, evidently, it is not so easy to explain matters by individual in-	3
adequacy. We may mark individuals down as intrinsically deficient; it is not	4
proper or even wise so to characterize an entire community. For some reason	5
the people of the island have been frustrated by their environment.[2]	

Within a paragraph, a writer establishes unity by constant reference to a single topic. These references should be made without awkward repetitions of words or phrases, and for this purpose pronouns work well. Especially useful are the demonstrative pronouns: *this, that, these,* and *those.* In Galbraith's first paragraph, for instance, observe how he uses pronouns to keep our attention focused on the topic *case poverty.* Sentence 3 begins with the pronoun *this,* which renames *case poverty,* mentioned for the first time in sentence 2. To repeat the term in sentence 3 would have been unacceptably awkward:

> First there is what may be called case poverty. Case poverty one encounters in every community, rural or urban.

Galbraith chooses the pronoun *this* to create a link between sentences. Sentence 4 begins by repeating *case poverty,* the repetition being far enough re-

[2]John Kenneth Galbraith, *The Affluent Society* (Boston: Houghton Mifflin, 1958).

moved from the first mention of the term to avoid awkwardness. With the repetition we have another direct link established between a sentence in the paragraph and the paragraph's topic. And in sentences 5 and 6, the connection is continued by the repeated use of *it* — a pronoun that again refers to *case poverty*. Thus, on rereading paragraph 1, you realize that Galbraith has worked to achieve unity by making *every* sentence relate clearly to a single topic.

EXERCISE	

Now examine paragraphs 2 and 3. In the spaces provided, identify the topic of each paragraph and explain how Galbraith has achieved paragraph unity.

What is the topic of paragraph 2? _____

_____

Examine each sentence of the paragraph. What noun in the topic sentence is repeated in subsequent sentences? _____

_____

_____

What is the topic of paragraph 3? _____

_____

Examine each sentence of the paragraph. What noun in the topic sentence is repeated in subsequent sentences? _____

_____

_____

Now let's turn to Saundra Goulet's second paragraph, presently in its third draft. Examine Saundra's work for unity. Identify her paragraph's topic sentence, and use that sentence as a basis on which to determine whether the paragraph is unified.*

*Saundra has not yet revised the word choice in particular sentences, so some of the phrasings in this first paragraph are stilted; you'll also find errors in grammar and mechanics. But at this point in the revision process, correcting grammar and mechanics is not as important as establishing the paragraph's unity. We advise students to attend to grammar, mechanics, spelling, and word choice in the latest stages of revision.

Some writers, however, are not able to restrain themselves and must, when they spot an awkward phrase or a grammatical error, rewrite — then and there. Whether you revise individual sentences for clarity and force *while* you are revising a paragraph for coherence and unity or *after* makes little difference as long as you can complete each level of revision successfully. Ultimately, you must do what's comfortable for you.

In order to fully understand what a satisfying job is, it   1
must first be defined. The definitions of a satisfying job vary   2
from each person's own personal view and opinion. A satis-   3
fying job is a job that a worker wants to arise for every
morning. The job is something the worker is proud of and   4
it gives the worker rewards. These rewards range from the   5
fringe benefits that a company has to the worker feeling
proud of his work. A company car, free membership to a   6
fitness club are some examples of these benefits. A job can   7
provide a worker with a sense of responsibility. That responsibility may only be answering phones but to the employee
and the company it is important. The satisfying job also   8
usually includes an enjoyably large paycheck. This paycheck   9
is a reflection of how hard the employee works and how
proud he is of his work. To complete his understanding of a   10
satisfying job, the employee should develop his own idea as
well as understand the importance of a satisfying job. The   11
importance of a satisfying job adds meaning and enjoyment
to a person's life. A worker who is satisfied with his work   12
finds pleasure in more than just his job. His entire life   13
cannot be based on a job, but a job can indirectly affect other
factors in one's life. A satisfying job provides the worker   14
with a better attitude toward himself. This attitude makes   15
the job more satisfying as well as any other encounter he
may come across.

In her topic sentence (the first sentence of the paragraph), Saundra announces her intention to define a satisfying job. Sentence 2 builds directly
from sentence 1 by stating that definitions vary from person to person. But
nowhere other than in this sentence does Saundra discuss different definitions.
On rereading the paragraph you find that she presents a *single* definition;
therefore, sentence 2 should either be deleted from the paragraph or somehow modified so that the reader no longer expects multiple definitions. Sentence 3 actually begins to define terms, a process that continues for six

sentences—until the sentence we've circled, sentence 10, where Saundra apparently wants to make a transition.

Whether it is used between paragraphs or between sentences within a paragraph, a transition begins with a summary that is either stated directly or implied. The summary's function is to prepare the reader for new material by reviewing the sentences (or paragraphs) just presented. The second part of the transition establishes a relationship between the material summarized and the material about to be presented. In the case of the transition we've circled, the initial summary could be clearer: "To complete his understanding of a satisfying job, the employee should develop his own idea as well as understand the importance of a satisfying job." The term "understanding" has been left far behind—in the first sentence of the paragraph—and yet Saundra uses the term prominently in the first part of her transition. This is confusing. Nevertheless, Saundra is correct to attempt a transition here since she's trying to shift discussion away from defining a satisfying job to the importance of having a satisfying job. In effect, she is telling herself with this sentence that she wants to develop a new topic. And she does exactly that in the sentences following the circled transition. In her final draft, Saundra moved this discussion into a separate paragraph.

Saundra's paragraph, as written, is not unified: its first part develops one topic and its second part another. After we made the same types of comments on Saundra's paper as we've made here, she revised accordingly. The following is the final version of her second paragraph. Notice how in the revision every sentence works to define job satisfaction. Notice also that Saundra uses pronouns and repetition to keep our attention (and hers) focused on what constitutes a satisfying job. To achieve unity in her final draft, she has used the same techniques employed by John Kenneth Galbraith.

> The definitions of a satisfying job may vary from person to person, but certain basic characteristics are common to all satisfying jobs: for instance, a satisfying job is one for which a worker wants to get up every morning. He enjoys the atmosphere that his fellow employees and his job-related responsibilities create. This atmosphere, the friendliness of fellow workers, and the overall feeling of "family" at the company give the worker reasons to go to work. The job also gives the worker certain fringe benefits, such as a company car and free membership in a fitness club. Last but not least, the satisfying job usually includes an enjoyably large paycheck. This paycheck is a reflection of how hard the employee works and how proud he is of his work.

We've used Saundra's topic sentence as a basis on which to examine every subsequent sentence and to determine whether or not it (1) develops the topic sentence and should be retained; (2) does not develop the topic sentence and should be deleted from the paper; or (3) does not develop the topic sentence and should be removed from the paragraph but developed elsewhere. Be certain that each of the paragraphs in your paper is unified by conducting such an analysis. When you are revising a paragraph, attempt to repeat words or to use pronouns to remind your reader (and yourself) that you are discussing a single topic.

Paragraph Coherence

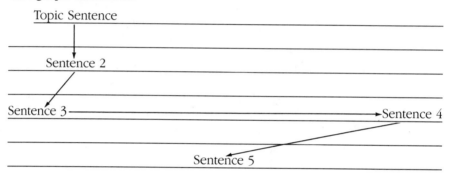

For a paragraph to be coherent, individual sentences must lead logically from one to the next, as the arrows in this diagram suggest. You'll recall that in our discussion of essay-level coherence we reviewed the use of transitions and the ways in which they establish clear relationships between paragraphs. We emphasized the importance of paragraphs being closely related in content before transitions are attempted. Unless the relationship between the content in two paragraphs is clear, transitions will be awkward.

Transitions also can and should be used *within* paragraphs to clarify relationships between sentences. When the content of two sentences is closely related, a transition between them is easily made; when the content is unrelated, the transition will be strained and the paragraph incoherent. In contrast to phrase- or sentence-length transitions between paragraphs, transitions within paragraphs are usually brief, often one-word conjunctions such as *and, but,* and *or.* These one-word conjunctions operate in the same way as full sentence-length transitions: they require a reader to understand the content of the previous sentence and then to anticipate the content of the sentence that follows. Use the following brief expressions to establish clear, distinct relationships between sentences within a paragraph:

The words *and, in addition, another, moreover,* and *also* establish a relationship of *addition* from one sentence to the next.

The words *but, however,* and *yet* establish a relationship of *contrast* from one sentence to the next.

The expressions *for instance* and *for example* establish a relationship of *example* from one sentence to the next.

The words *accordingly*, *consequently*, *therefore*, and *thus* establish a relationship of *cause and effect* between one sentence and the next.

Read once again the following paragraphs by John Kenneth Galbraith. Underline every use of a transitional word or phrase. As you do so, note how Galbraith links the content of his sentences.

> One can think of modern poverty as falling into two broad categories. 1
> First there is what may be called *case* poverty. This one encounters in every 2
> community, rural or urban, however prosperous that community or the 3
> times. Case poverty is the poor farm family with the junk-filled yard and the 4
> dirty children playing in the bare dirt. Or it is the grey-black hovel beside 5
> the railroad tracks. Or it is the basement dwelling in the alley. 6
>
> Case poverty is commonly and properly related to some characteristic 1
> of the individuals so afflicted. Nearly everyone else has mastered his environ- 2
> ment; this proves that it is not intractable. But some quality peculiar to the 3
> individual or family involved — mental deficiency, bad health, inability to adapt
> to the discipline of modern economic life, excessive procreation, alcohol, in-
> sufficient education, or perhaps a combination of several of these handicaps —
> have kept these individuals from participating in the general well-being.
>
> Second, there is what may be called *insular* poverty — that which mani- 1
> fests itself as an "island" of poverty. In the island everyone or nearly everyone 2
> is poor. Here, evidently, it is not so easy to explain matters by individual in- 3
> adequacy. We may mark individuals down as intrinsically deficient; it is not 4
> proper or even wise so to characterize an entire community. For some reason 5
> the people of the island have been frustrated by their environment.

Every sentence in these paragraphs is related to the sentence that precedes it. How does Galbraith achieve this coherence? Let's examine paragraph 1 and map out the way in which the content of each sentence leads to the next. As we've noted, sentence 2 establishes the paragraph's topic: *case poverty*. Sentence 3 tells us where one encounters the topic — in both rural and urban settings. Sentence 4 defines the topic more specifically by providing a rural example; sentences 5 and 6 provide specific urban examples. Note especially the transitional word *or* in sentences 5 and 6, used to establish alternative examples of case poverty.

EXERCISE	

Map out the coherence of paragraphs 2 and 3. Underline each of Galbraith's transitional expressions and explain how one sentence leads logically to the next.

Analysis of Paragraph 2: _____

_____

Analysis of Paragraph 3: _____

We present again the second paragraph of Saundra's paper in its third draft, revised for unity but not yet for coherence. Recall that in order to be coherent, a paragraph must consist of sentences that are clearly related to one another. Has Saundra's second paragraph met this requirement?

In order to fully understand what a satisfying job is, it 1 must first be defined. The definitions of a satisfying job vary 2 from each person's own personal view and opinion. A satis- 3 fying job is a job that a worker wants to arise for every morning. The job is something the worker is proud of and 4 it gives the worker rewards. These rewards range from the 5 fringe benefits that a company has to the worker feeling proud of his work. A company car, free membership to a 6 fitness club are some examples of these benefits. A job can 7 provide a worker with a sense of responsibility. That respon- sibility may only be answering phones but to the employee and the company it is important. The satisfying job also 8 usually includes an enjoyably large paycheck. This paycheck 9 is a reflection of how hard the employee works and how proud he is of his work. To complete his understanding of a 10 satisfying job, the employee should develop his own idea as well as understand the importance of a satisfying job. The 11 importance of a satisfying job adds meaning and enjoyment to a person's life. A worker who is satisfied with his work 12 finds pleasure in more than just his job. His entire life 13 cannot be based on a job, but a job can indirectly affect other factors in one's life. A satisfying job provides the worker   14

with a better attitude toward himself. This attitude makes   15

the job more satisfying as well as any other encounter he

may come across.

This paragraph contains a problem with coherence. Sentences 5 and 6, for the most part, treat fringe benefits; sentence 7 treats the topic of pride (as it is developed through responsibility); and sentence 8 treats a separate topic: paychecks, a primary (as opposed to fringe) benefit. Sentences 5 through 8 do not lead logically from one to the next and, therefore, need to be revised for coherence. Saundra has two options: she could begin with sentence 4 and present the rest of the paragraph as follows:

A satisfying job will provide a worker with benefits and a sense of pride.
    —Discuss the benefits.
    —*Then* discuss the sense of pride.

Or she could phrase sentence 4 differently and arrange the remainder of the paragraph in this way:

A satisfying job will provide a worker with benefits.
    —Discuss the benefits.
A satisfying job will provide a worker with a sense of pride.
    —Discuss pride.

Either method of arranging sentences would lead to a coherent paragraph in which each sentence would be directly related to a preceding or following sentence. In fact (as you saw when you read her final, revised second paragraph on page 155), Saundra chose this second option with a slight modification: she moved her discussion of pride into a separate paragraph.

Note that in her revised paragraph Saundra has used several transitions to establish clear relationships between sentences: *but, for instance, also, last but not least.* When you successfully revise a paragraph for coherence, you will use these and other brief transitions. (Again, refer to the listing of transitions on page 156.)

Paragraph Development

Reread the following sentences excerpted from the third draft of Saundra's second paragraph, along with our marginal notations.

A satisfying job is a job that a worker wants to arise for

why? Develop.

every morning. The job is something the worker is proud of

Discuss pride and rewards separately.

and it gives the worker rewards. These rewards range from

the fringe benefits that a company has to the worker feeling

proud of his work. A company car, free membership to a

Coherence: while you're discussing material benefits, discuss paychecks

fitness club are some examples of these benefits. A job can provide a worker with a sense of responsibility. That responsibility may only be answering phones but to the employee and the company it is important. The satisfying job also usually includes an enjoyably large paycheck.

Develop. Add to discussion of pride and responsibility. Define both.

As you've seen and as we've noted in the margins, this section of the second paragraph is not coherent. Saundra switches from one topic (benefits) to another (responsibility) and then back to the first. At two separate points in this draft we wrote notes in the margin, advising Saundra to develop the content of her sentences. She did so, and we'd like you to compare the original sentences against Saundra's more thoroughly developed revisions. Consider the following sentence, for instance:

A satisfying job is a job that a worker wants to arise for in the morning. *Why? Develop.*

Now read the revision:

…a satisfying job is one for which a worker wants to get up every morning. He enjoys the atmosphere that his fellow employees and his job-related responsibilities create. This atmosphere, the friendliness of fellow workers, and the overall feeling of "family" at the company give the worker reasons to go to work.

EXERCISE	

Explain briefly how the revision differs from the original.

_____

_____

_____

_____

_____

_____

Consider another two sentences:

A job can provide a worker with a sense of responsibility. That responsibility may only be answering phones but to the employee and the company it is important.

Develop. Add to discussion of pride and responsibility. Define both.

And the revision:

A job can also provide a worker with a sense of pride and responsibility. When an employee is hired, the company lays out all of the responsibilities the job entails, and by accepting the job the employee takes on these responsibilities. The responsibility may only be answering phones or typing letters, but to the employee and the company these jobs are important. By having responsibilities the employee finds pride in his work — the pride of being a member of a team, a team that works hard and together. He develops pride by being a contributing member in the company's success. The more responsibility and pride an employee has, the more satisfying his job will be.

EXERCISE

Discuss the differences between the two drafts.

_____

_____

_____

_____

_____

_____

_____

_____

In response to our suggestions, Saundra developed her ideas more fully. You have probably defined *development* for yourself by this point, and your definition, based as it is on examples, will be more precise than any abstract definitions we could offer. We could say that in a well-developed paragraph the writer takes each idea and discusses it thoroughly. But of course this definition depends on the definition of *thoroughly* — the same problem we had with *adequate* earlier. It is better to define the term *development* by reference to specific examples. When some point in a paragraph is not well developed, as you've seen, a reader is left with questions: Why? What does the writer mean? What's the point of the example? And so on.

Anytime a reader stops to puzzle in this way over the meaning of a passage, the writer has defeated himself or herself by interrupting the process of communication. It is entirely legitimate to expect readers to think seriously and deeply about a passage that is *fully* communicated: this is the very purpose of writing. But for a reader to stop in confusion because a writer has *in*completely communicated his or her content — this is a problem. More particularly, it is a problem in development.

How well developed should a sentence or paragraph be? In the abstract, this is difficult to answer. What counts as "well developed" will differ depending on a writer's audience and its expectations. If in the course of a paper you must refer to a book — say, *Huckleberry Finn* — and know that your audience is familiar with the novel, then you would be justified in mentioning only the title. Nothing further about the story and its significance in American literature is needed. But if your audience doesn't know the book, you are obligated to discuss it in enough detail that any references you make to it can be understood. The point to remember is that *all* writing must be clearly understandable regardless of audience. When terms important to the meaning of a discussion are not clearly defined or when a discussion raises the need for an explanation that is not supplied, confusion results.

The writer has a dual responsibility, therefore, when developing a paper. The first is to achieve, regardless of audience, a basic level of understanding in which essential information is provided. Terms are defined; examples given; explanations offered. The content offered to the reader has no obvious gaps. The writer's second responsibility in developing a paper is to provide a level of detail appropriate to a particular audience. Common sense, if not the specific requirements of an assignment, will dictate the level of detail needed. Know your audience; know the expectations they will have for your writing.

When testing your paragraphs for development, question the content of every sentence. Let your questions guide you in clarifying and developing your ideas. We suggest that you begin the process by posing four questions:

1. *Have I assumed any connections between events that might not be clear to my readers?* Consider the following example. What apparent relationship has the writer made? Why would a reader need clarification?

   A satisfying job is one for which a worker wants to get up every morning.

2. *Have I defined terms clearly?* Underline the terms that need defining in the following sentence.

A job is satisfying when it provides a worker with a sense of pride and responsibility.

3. *Have I used examples to illustrate the points I want to make?* Provide two possible examples for the following statement. How would you develop each?

A working environment can indirectly affect other parts of a person's life.

4. *Have I explained the significance of examples and quotations?* Left undiscussed, the following quotation would be inadequate. Why?

There is no clear relationship between the satisfaction of workers and their productivity. Researchers speculate that "many people are satisfied with their jobs precisely because their work is undemanding and requires minimal effort."

These example sentences are taken from context, so it is impossible to tell whether in fact the writer has adequately developed them. But assuming that the sentences were not developed, they should have been; for in each the writer assumes that information or certain relationships are clear to the reader, when they may well not be. Actually, these connections may not be clear to the writer either. When writers fail to show evidence of posing and responding to questions about their own work, they frequently do not understand their ideas. It is deceptively easy to skim superficially along the surface of a discussion when what is needed is a conscious attempt to pause and probe deeply, to explore significance, to wrestle with complexity. After a time, when you realize that a writer does not pause anywhere to discuss in detail at least some aspects of a paper, you begin to wonder: is the writer capable of developing, of thinking carefully and in detail about his ideas?

For your own benefit and that of your readers, pose questions about what you write, just as you pose them about what you read. And then respond to those questions. Your paper needn't read like an interview; but it should show evidence that you have challenged your own thinking and have attempted to develop ideas. Saundra had not made this attempt as late as her third draft. Some of her paragraphs were developed well and others poorly. By her fourth draft, however, she had given each of her paragraphs careful attention. Guided by our notes and her own questions, Saundra developed her ideas, achieving a completeness in her entire paper that she had achieved in her revised second paragraph.

Sentence-level Revisions

Many writers cannot wait until a fourth or fifth draft to rewrite their sentences for clarity, force, and correctness of grammar. Some writers must, by force of habit, revise on all levels (essay, paragraph, and sentence) simultaneously. If you can do this and achieve the desired results, fine. We advise at least three separate revisions because many writers new to college find it easier to focus on one aspect of revision at a time. At whatever point you revise the wording of particular sentences, realize that certain aspects of revision are absolute and others are relative, varying from person to person.

The absolute requirements of revision are grammar, mechanics, and spelling. English grammar is a contract of sorts among speakers of the language. The contract is arbitrary, and its rules are rules not of nature but of convention. *On March 21 of every year, spring comes to the Northern Hemisphere:* this is a fact of nature, and there's nothing people can do to alter it. *When joining two sentences, use a conjunction or a semicolon:* this is an arbitrary rule made by people and is certainly not a fact in the way that spring always begins on a certain day of the year is a fact. Rules of nature we must abide by; but rules of grammar, spelling, and mechanics we can choose to accept or ignore.

We advise you to adhere to the rules, not because they are "correct" or "true" in any absolute sense—they aren't—but because people will expect you to adhere. Rightly or wrongly, the "King's English" (the language spoken and written in the manner urged on you by your teachers from the first grade through the twelfth) has become a ticket of admission into the world of commerce, government, and the professions. If you wish to gain entrance, you must speak and write according to certain rules. This, the political argument for following the rules of grammar, offends many people, who claim that the King's English is used by the powerful to oppress those who happen to speak and write a nonstandard form of the language. Valid as this objection may be, the fact remains that a writer has two choices: to write according to the standard rules and to be accepted as a member of the academic and professional communities or to disregard (or never fully learn) the rules and be regarded, unfairly, as someone who will never gain entry into those communities. If you do not learn the rules, you do so at risk, for many people—not just English teachers but also employers and prospective clients—will hold you accountable for spelling correctly and writing grammatically. Our advice is to not put yourself at a disadvantage by ignoring or failing to learn the conventions of standard English.

We will not review here any specifics of grammar, mechanics, and spelling. For that you have a handbook and a dictionary, which you should use regularly to ensure that there are no "errors" in your sentences. You can also refer to your handbook to learn how writers make sentences stylistically appealing. Sentence style, like fingerprints, varies from one person to the next. Even so, certain fundamental elements underlie all stylistically successful sentences. For instance, accomplished writers generally avoid awkward repetitions. "A satisfying job is a job that..." contains a double and awkward use of the word *job*. The sentence could be reworded: "A satisfying job is one in which...."

Accomplished writers also vary their sentence patterns, use parallel structures, choose words to be concise, and so on. You can learn all this from a handbook, and we urge that you do so.

After you've revised a paper for essay-level concerns and again for paragraph-level concerns, you will have enough invested in your work to want to make it read smoothly. By the third draft you should have clearly defined the purpose of your paper and developed your ideas. Both the paper as a whole and individual paragraphs will be unified and coherent by this point. Now strive to present your work in the most compelling manner possible, examining each sentence of your paper and determining whether, or to what extent, it needs to be revised for grammar, spelling, mechanics, and style.

By way of example, we present a final, sentence-level revision of a paragraph from Saundra's fourth draft. Notice Saundra's willingness to make her word choice both precise and concise — to say exactly what she needs to say in as few words as possible. Her revisions also show a willingness to vary sentence patterns. Thus, not only is the paragraph unified and coherent (the product of four previous drafts), it is also stylistically pleasing and easy to read. Saundra has striven for and achieved a direct, clear expression.

Every ~~To complete his understanding of a satisfying job, the~~ employee should understand ~~its~~ *the* importance ~~to his working~~ *that a satisfying job has to both his* career ~~as well as~~ *and* his personal life. A satisfying job adds meaning and enjoyment to a person's life. A worker who is satisfied ~~with his work~~ finds pleasure in more than just his job. *For instance,* ~~His entire life cannot be based on a job, but a job can~~ *He will be* ~~indirectly affect other factors such as the employee being~~ healthier, more energetic, and outgoing. ~~A satisfying~~ *when a* job makes ~~the worker~~ *him* feel good about himself, ~~therefore making~~ ~~his personal life more exciting and fulfilling.~~ The *satisfying* job will provide less stress and strain *than a dissatisfying one,* so that when the employee leaves work for the day he leaves his work behind him. A satisfied employee ~~leaves~~ *goes to* his office for work and his home for play. ~~A~~ *Thus, a* satisfying job provides the worker with a better attitude toward himself. ~~This attitude makes the~~ *We can call this attitude self-respect.* ~~job more satisfying as well as any other encounter he may~~ ~~come across.~~

We worked in conference with Saundra on this and every other paragraph of her paper, carefully reviewing word choice and helping her revise for clarity and style. The result is an exemplary draft, her fifth and final effort.

Work and Self-Respect

A satisfying job means more to a worker than just a large weekly paycheck. A worker has certain expectations about a job—that it will be enjoyable and worthwhile. When these expectations are met and a job is satisfying, a worker will feel happy and self-respecting.

The definitions of a satisfying job may vary from person to person, but certain basic characteristics are common to all satisfying jobs: for instance, a satisfying job is one for which a worker wants to get up every morning. He enjoys the atmosphere that his fellow employees and his job-related responsibilities create. This atmosphere, the friendliness of fellow workers, and the overall feeling of "family" at the company give the worker reasons to go to work. The job also gives the worker certain fringe benefits, such as a company car and free membership in a fitness club. Last but not least, the satisfying job usually includes an enjoyably large paycheck. This paycheck is a reflection of how hard the employee works and how proud he is of his work.

A job can also provide a worker with a sense of pride and responsibility. When an employee is hired, the company lays out all of the responsibilities the job entails, and by accepting the job the employee takes on these responsibilities. The responsibility may only be answering phones or typing letters, but to the employee and the company these jobs are important. By having responsibilities the employee finds pride in his work—the pride of being a member of a team, a team that works hard and together. He develops pride by being a contributing member in the company's success. The more responsibility and pride an employee has, the more satisfying his job will be.

Every employee should understand the importance that a satisfying job has to both his career and his personal life. A satisfying job adds meaning and enjoyment to a person's life. A worker who is satisfied finds pleasure in more than just his job. He will be healthier, more energetic, and outgoing when a job makes him feel good about himself. The satisfying job will provide less stress and strain than a dissatisfying one, so that when the employee leaves work for the day he leaves his work behind him. A satisfied employee goes to his office for work and his home for play. Thus, a satisfying job provides the worker with a better attitude toward himself. We can call this attitude self-respect.

Companies can do a great deal to contribute to a worker's satisfaction by offering fringe benefits that attract and keep people working for them. These benefits and "perks" differ from company to company, and by comparing the particular qualities of each company the employee should be able to find the job he is looking for. The authors of *The 100 Best Companies in America* (Levering, Moskowitz, and Katz) found the best companies in America as well as an explanation for why people work for them. The researchers discovered that it was not always the company benefits that made the job satisfying. A satisfying job entails many more important qualities, such as an employee's wish to feel like he is a "part of a team" or that the company cares enough about the employee to provide fitness centers or training programs. These and many other qualities attract and keep people working at the company.

A worker would be fortunate to be employed by one of the "100 Best" companies. Unfortunately, many workers are not and are dissatisfied with jobs that make them miserable. Some workers find themselves dreading work every waking day. Their unhappiness may be caused by a number of reasons, one of which might be the weekly paycheck. An employee may find himself doing more work than he is being paid for. His feelings of being insufficiently paid could cause dissatisfaction. Another reason for dissatisfaction could be the lack of advancement up the management ladder. After working for a number of years an employee usually expects a promotion. A promotion gives the employee new and challenging duties that keep him satisfied. If the employee finds little or no advancement, he becomes dissatisfied with himself and his work. One final reason for dissatisfaction may be a stressful working environment. Stress often stems from an employee's inability to communicate with a company's management. In her advice column, journalist Juliette Flynn answers a letter from a nurse who signs herself "Struggling RN." This woman is 28 years old and writes a letter to Flynn because she is unhappy with managers who give her negative feedback at twice-yearly reviews but no constructive criticism on a daily basis. As a result, the nurse—who believes she is a competent professional—feels insecure on the job and crabby at home. Her loss of self-respect in the workplace has affected her ability to be happy elsewhere.

Receptionist Sharon Atkins is unhappy with work for a different reason; but the effects of this unhappiness are identical to the nurse's: a loss of self-respect and difficulty being happy both on and off the job. Atkins is a receptionist interviewed by Studs Terkel in *Working*. Every morning Atkins goes into the office, sits at her desk, puts on her headset, and begins plugging in wires and connecting one person's voice to another. She is a switchboard operator. She finds that the disagreeable qualities that go with being a receptionist are taking over her social life. She is short and blunt on the phone, pretending to be happy and pleasant when she is not. Sometimes she is rude with people whom she cares about and loves. She wants her life outside of work to be very different from her work life, and it is only by painting pictures of nature that she achieves this dream.

Sharon Atkins has lost her self-respect. Her problem begins when she has to tell people what type of job she has. She finds herself embarrassed to say she is a receptionist because people react (at company parties) by ignoring her. This reaction makes her insecure, and she finds it difficult to go to work and enjoy herself as she did before, when she worked at a punch press. This lack of self-respect could lead to her quitting her job. If she is that dissatisfied she probably should quit. By remaining a receptionist, she will disrupt her social life as well as her working career. If an employee finds his work as dissatisfying as Atkins finds hers, he should begin looking for a new job.

In order for the employee to remain content with his job, he must find pride as well as self-respect in his work. A satisfying job will give an employee a sense of belonging. It will make him feel good about himself. And if the employee feels that way about himself and his work, he will find other things in his life much more enjoyable and worthwhile.

After writing her first draft, Saundra revised her paper four times:

	Time to complete
1st draft	4 hours
2nd draft	4 hours
3rd draft	3 hours
4th draft	2 hours
5th draft	1 hour

10 hours spent on revision

14 hours

Note that Saundra spent decreasing amounts of time on successive drafts of her paper, a pattern we've seen in our own work and that of other students and colleagues. Also familiar is the ratio of time spent revising to time spent on the first draft: roughly 2½ hours of revision to every hour of initial drafting.

Saundra's final draft is superior in every respect to her first draft—which comes as no surprise since she worked long and hard on revising her paper. You can expect to make similar progress when you make a similar commitment. And by this point, you are certainly capable of such a commitment. You've learned to respond to single sources by making inferences and by writing summaries in which you distinguish between facts and opinions. You've learned to infer relationships among sources and to use these inferences to create a working thesis—and, subsequently, a first draft. And if you have followed the progress of Saundra's revision, you have learned to revise your work for essay-, paragraph-, and sentence-level concerns, fully recognizing that it will take you roughly twice as long to achieve a final draft as to write the initial one.

In working through these first five chapters, you've seen what is required to write a paper based on sources and guided by your unique ideas (for example, Saundra referred to three sources, all of which she put to use in developing her own thesis). Now it is your turn to write—to put into practice what you've learned. The chapters in Part Two of this book provide the occasions you'll need to begin writing papers. Each presents a group of readings clustered around a narrowly defined topic. You'll be asked to develop a personal response to these readings, and, based on this response, you'll formulate a paper in much the same way Saundra formulated hers: by using sources in support of your own ideas.

Part Two begins with Chapter Seven. In Chapter Six, we discuss techniques for introducing and concluding your papers and for using quotations.

CHAPTER 6

Using Quotations and Writing Introductions and Conclusions

Using Quotations

A quotation records the exact language used by someone in speech or in writing. In contrast, a summary is a brief restatement in your own words of what someone else has said or written. And a paraphrase is also a restatement, though one that is often as long as the original source. Any paper in which you rely on sources will depend heavily on quotation, summary, and paraphrase. How will you choose among the three?

Realize that the papers you write should be your own—for the most part your own language and certainly your own thesis, your own inferences, and your own conclusions. It follows that references to your source materials should be written as summaries and paraphrases, both of which are built on restatement, not quotation. You will use summaries when you need a *brief* restatement, and paraphrases, which provide more explicit detail than summaries, when you need to closely follow the development of a source. When you quote too much, you risk losing ownership of your work: more easily than you might think, your voice can be drowned out by the voices of those you've quoted. So use quotations sparingly, as you would a pungent spice.

Nevertheless, quoting just the right source at the right time can significantly improve your papers. The trick is to know when and how to use quotations.

Choosing Quotations

- Use quotations when another writer's language is particularly memorable and will add interest and liveliness to your paper.
- Use quotations when another writer's language is so clearly and economically stated that to make the same point in your own words would, by comparison, be ineffective.
- Use quotations when you want the solid reputation of a source to lend authority and credibility to your own writing.

Quoting Memorable Language

Assume you're writing a paper on Napoleon Bonaparte's relationship with the celebrated Josephine. Through research you learn that two days after their marriage, Napoleon, given command of an army, left his bride for what was to be a brilliant military campaign in Italy. How did the young general respond to leaving his wife so soon after their wedding? You come across the following, written from the field of battle by Napoleon on April 3, 1796:

> I have received all your letters, but none has had such an impact on me as the last. Do you have any idea, darling, what you are doing, writing to me in those terms? Do you not think my situation cruel enough without intensifying my longing for you, overwhelming my soul? What a style! What emotions you evoke! Written in fire, they burn my poor heart![1]

A summary of this passage might read as follows:

> On April 3, 1796, Napoleon wrote to Josephine, expressing how sorely he missed her and how passionately he responded to her letters.

You might write the following as a paraphrase of the passage:

> On April 3, 1796, Napoleon wrote to Josephine that he had received her letters and that one among all others had had a special impact, overwhelming his soul with fiery emotions and longing.

How feeble this summary and paraphrase are when compared to the original! Use the vivid language that your sources give you. In this case, quote Napoleon in your paper to make your subject come alive with memorable detail:

> On April 3, 1796, a passionate, lovesick Napoleon responded to a letter from Josephine: "Do you have any idea, darling, what you are doing, writing to me in those terms?" She had written longingly to her husband, who, on a military campaign, acutely felt her absence. "What emotions you evoke!" he said of her letters. "Written in fire, they burn my poor heart!"

[1]Francis Mossiker, trans., *Napoleon and Josephine* (New York: Simon and Schuster, 1964).

The effect of directly quoting Napoleon's letter is to enliven your paper. A *direct* quotation is one in which you record precisely the language of another, as we did with the sentences from Napoleon's letter. In an *indirect* quotation you report what someone has said, though you are not obligated to repeat the words exactly as spoken (or written):

> Napoleon asked Josephine whether she realized what she was doing by writing to him so passionately.

Notice the difference between a direct and indirect quotation of the same sentence:

> *Direct Quotation:* Franklin D. Roosevelt said: "The only thing we have to fear is fear itself."
>
> *Indirect Quotation:* Franklin D. Roosevelt was the one who said that we have nothing to fear but fear itself.

The language in a direct quotation, which is indicated by a pair of quotation marks (" "), must be exactly faithful to the language of the original passage. When using an indirect quotation, you have the liberty of changing words (though not changing meaning). For both direct and indirect quotations, you must credit your sources, naming them either in (or close to) the sentence that includes the quotation or in a footnote.

Quoting Clear and Concise Language

You should quote a source when its language is particularly clear and economical — when your language, by contrast, would be wordy. Reread a passage from Patricia Curtis that we used in Chapter 2:

> The honeybee colony, which usually has a population of 30,000 to 40,000 workers, differs from that of the bumblebee and many other social bees or wasps in that it survives the winter. This means that the bees must stay warm despite the cold. Like other bees, the isolated honeybee cannot fly if the temperature falls below 10°C (50°F) and cannot walk if the temperature is below 7°C (45°F). Within the wintering hive, bees maintain their temperature by clustering together in a dense ball; the lower the temperature, the denser the cluster. The clustered bees produce heat by constant muscular movements of their wings, legs, and abdomens. In very cold weather, the bees on the outside of the cluster keep moving toward the center, while those in the core of the cluster move to the colder outside periphery. The entire cluster moves slowly about on the combs, eating the stored honey from the combs as it moves.[2]

A summary of this paragraph might read as follows:

> Honeybees, unlike many other varieties of bee, are able to live through the winter by "clustering together in a dense ball" for body warmth.

[2]"Winter Organization," in Patricia Curtis, *Biology,* second edition (New York: Worth, 1976), 822–823.

A paraphrase of the same passage would be considerably more detailed:

> Honeybees, unlike many other varieties of bee (such as bumblebees and wasps), are able to live through the winter. The 30,000 to 40,000 bees within a honeybee hive could not, individually, move about in cold winter temperatures. But when "clustering together in a dense ball," the bees generate heat by constantly moving their body parts. The cluster also moves slowly about the hive, eating honey stored in the combs. This nutrition, in addition to the heat generated by the cluster, enables the honeybee to survive the cold winter months.

In both the summary and the paraphrase we've quoted Curtis's "clustering together in a dense ball," a phrase that lies at the heart of her description on wintering honeybees. For us to describe this clustering in any language other than Curtis's would be pointless since her description is admirably brief and precise.

Quoting Authoritative Language

You will also want to use quotations that lend authority to your work. When quoting an expert or some prominent political, artistic, or historical figure, you elevate your own work by placing it in esteemed company. Quote respected figures to establish background information in a paper, and your readers will tend to perceive that information as reliable. Quote the opinions of respected figures to endorse some statement that you've made, and your statement becomes more credible to your readers. For example: in an essay that we might write on the importance of reading well, we could make use of a passage from Thoreau's *Walden:*

> Reading well is hard work and requires great skill and training. "[It]...is a noble exercise," writes Henry David Thoreau in *Walden,* "one that will task the reader more than any exercise which the customs of the day esteem. It requires a training such as the athletes underwent....Books must be read as deliberately and reservedly as they were written."

By quoting a famous philosopher and essayist on the subject of reading, we add legitimacy to our discussion. Not only do *we* regard reading to be a skill that is both difficult and important; so too does Henry David Thoreau, one of our most influential American thinkers. The quotation has elevated the level of our work.

You can also quote to advantage well-respected figures who've written or spoken about the subject of your paper. Recall David Chandler's discussion of space flight and his reference to a physicist and an astronaut:

> A few scientists — notably James Van Allen, discoverer of the Earth's radiation belts — have decried the expense of the manned space program and called for an almost exclusive concentration on unmanned scientific exploration instead, saying this would be far more cost-effective.

. . .

Other space scientists dispute that idea. Joseph Allen, physicist and former shuttle astronaut, says, "It seems to be argued that one takes away from the other. But before there was a manned space program, the funding on space science was zero. Now it's about $500 million a year."

Note, first, that in the first paragraph Chandler has either summarized or used an indirect quotation to incorporate remarks made by James Van Allen into the discussion on space flight. In the second paragraph Chandler directly quotes his next source, Joseph Allen. Both quotations, indirect and direct, lend authority and legitimacy to the article, for both James Van Allen and Joseph Allen are experts on the subject of space flight. Note also that Chandler has provided brief but effective biographies of his sources, identifying both men so that their qualifications to speak on the subject are known to all:

James Van Allen, *discoverer of the Earth's radiation belts* ...

Joseph Allen, *physicist and former shuttle astronaut* ...

The phrases in italics are called *appositives*. Their function is to rename the nouns they follow by providing explicit, identifying detail. Any information about a person that can be fit in the blank in the following sentence pattern can be made into an appositive phrase:

Name is _____ .

The information that would be placed in the blank after the linking verb *is* becomes the appositive:

James Van Allen is *the discoverer of the Earth's radiation belts.*

James Van Allen has decried the expense of the manned space program.
⇓
James Van Allen, *discoverer of the Earth's radiation belts,* has decried the expense of the manned space program.

EXERCISE

Write sentences with appositives using the following sentence pairs. (A note on punctuation: appositive phrases that follow proper nouns are placed within a *pair* of commas.)

William Henry Harrison was the ninth President of the United States.

William Henry Harrison died after one month in office.

_____

_____

Victor Cline reports that "behavioral scientists have finally established a causal relationship between some children's exposure to TV violence and increased aggressive behavior."

Victor Cline is a professor of psychology at the University of Utah.

Incorporating Quotations into Your Sentences

Quoting Only the Part of a Sentence or Paragraph That You Need

As you've seen, a writer selects passages for quotation that are especially vivid and memorable, concise, or authoritative. Now we will put these principles into practice. Suppose that while conducting research on the topic of college sports you've come across the following, written by Robert Hutchins. (Hutchins is a former president of the University of Chicago.)

> If athleticism is bad for students, players, alumni and the public, it is even worse for the colleges and universities themselves. They want to be educational institutions, but they can't. The story of the famous halfback whose only regret, when he bade his coach farewell, was that he hadn't learned to read and write is probably exaggerated. But we must admit that pressure from trustees, graduates, "friends," presidents and even professors has tended to relax academic standards. These gentry often overlook the fact that a college should not be interested in a fullback who is a half-wit. Recruiting, subsidizing and the double educational standard cannot exist without the knowledge and the tacit approval, at least, of the colleges and universities themselves. Certain institutions encourage susceptible professors to be nice to athletes now admitted by paying them for serving as "faculty representatives" on the college athletic board.[3]

Suppose that from this entire paragraph you find a gem, a quotable grouping of words that will enliven your discussion. You may want to quote part of the following sentence:

> These gentry often overlook the fact that a college should not be interested in a fullback who is a half-wit.

Incorporating the Quotation into the Flow of Your Own Sentence

Once you've selected the passage you want to quote, work the material into your paper in as natural and fluid a manner as possible. Here's how we would quote Hutchins:

> Robert Hutchins, a former president of the University of Chicago, asserts that "a college should not be interested in a fullback who is a half-wit."

Note that we've used an appositive to identify Hutchins. And we've used only the part of the paragraph — a single clause — that we thought memorable enough to quote directly.

---

[3]Robert Hutchins, "Gate Receipts and Glory," *The Saturday Evening Post* (December 3, 1983).

EXERCISE	

Read the following two passages, the first by John Gardner and the second by Stendhal. Incorporate the underlined material into a sentence. We provide the name of the author for each passage as well as some biographical information that you can use in an appositive phrase. Here's the sentence pattern you should follow:

		present-tense	(optional)	
		tense	(optional)	
Author,	appositive phrase,	verb*	that	quotation.

		Present-tense
Author	Appositive Phrase	Verb
Robert Hutchins,	a former president of the University of Chicago,	asserts that

Quotation
"a college should not be interested in a fullback who is a half-wit."

Passage 1

Good grades in English may or may not go with verbal sensitivity, that is, with the writer's gift for, and interest in, understanding how language works. <u>Good grades in English may have more to do with the relative competence, sensitivity, and sophistication of the teacher than with the student writer's ability.</u> It is not quite true to say that every good writer has a keen feeling for sentence rhythms—the music of language—or for the connotations and diction levels (domains) of words. Some great writers are great in spite of occasional lapses—clunky sentences, feeble metaphors, even foolish word choices. Theodore Dreiser can write: "He found her extremely intellectually interesting"—language so cacophonous and dull most good writers would run from it; yet few readers would deny that Dreiser's *Sister Carrie* and *An American Tragedy* are works of art. The writer with a tin ear, if he's good enough at other things, may in the end write deeper, finer novels than the most eloquent verbal musician.[4]

John Gardner was a novelist, critic, and teacher of creative writing.

_____

_____

_____

Passage 2

<u>There is no such thing as ingratitude in love;</u> the pleasure of the moment always seems worth, and more than worth, the utmost sacrifice. The only thing that can

---

*When incorporating a quotation into a sentence, you'll frequently need to introduce the passage with a verb, and often that verb will be expressed in the historical present tense. This example sentence is typical. Hutchins wrote what we quoted in 1938; but still we introduce the quotation with the present-tense "Hutchins asserts" because what he wrote is present to us in his essay as we read it, every time we read it. You'll need to use the historical present tense for a while before you become comfortable with it. In these exercises, use verbs such as *believes*, *says*, *states*, *claims*, *remarks*, and *asserts*. (You'll find a longer list of suitable verbs on page 46.)

[4]John Gardner, *On Becoming a Novelist* (New York: Harper and Row, 1983), 3.

be regarded as wrong is a lack of frankness; one *must* be honest and open about one's heart.[5]

Stendhal was a nineteenth-century French novelist and essayist.

_____

_____

_____

Using Ellipsis Marks

Using quotations is somewhat complicated when you want to quote the beginning and end of a passage but not its middle — as was the case when we quoted Henry David Thoreau. Here's part of the paragraph in *Walden* from which we quoted a few sentences:

> To read well, that is, to read true books in a true spirit, is a noble exercise, and one that will task the reader more than any exercise which the customs of the day esteem. It requires a training such as the athletes underwent, the steady intention almost of the whole life to this object. Books must be read as deliberately and reservedly as they were written.[6]

And here was how we used this material.

> Reading well is hard work and requires great skill and training. "[It] . . . is a noble exercise," writes Henry David Thoreau in *Walden*, "one that will task the reader more than any exercise which the customs of the day esteem. It requires a training such as the athletes underwent. . . . Books must be read as deliberately and reservedly as they were written."

Whenever you quote a sentence but delete words from it, as we have done, indicate this deletion to the reader by placing an ellipsis mark, three spaced periods, in the sentence at the point of deletion. Use ellipsis marks at the beginning of a quotation if you begin the quotation in the middle of a sentence.*

> Reading well " . . . is a noble exercise," writes Henry David Thoreau in *Walden,* "one that will task the reader more than any exercise which the customs of the day esteem."

If you are deleting the end of a quoted sentence, place the ellipsis mark after the last word you are quoting and add one extra period to indicate the end of the sentence:

> "It requires a training such as the athletes underwent. . . . Books must be read as deliberately and reservedly as they were written."

*The rationale for using an ellipsis mark is as follows: A direct quotation must be reproduced *exactly* as it was written or spoken. When writers delete or change any part of the quoted material, readers must be alerted so they don't think that the changes were part of the original. Ellipsis marks and brackets (discussed below) serve this purpose.

[5]Stendahl, *On Love,* trans. Gilbert and Suzanne Sale (New York: Penguin, 1982), 130.

[6]Henry David Thoreau, "Reading," in *Walden* (New York: Signet Classic, 1960), 72.

And if you are deleting the middle of a sentence, use an ellipsis mark in place of the deleted words:

"To read well...is a noble exercise, and one that will task the reader more than any exercise which the customs of the day esteem."

| **EXERCISE** | |

The first passage below is from an article titled "Scenario for Scandal" by Mark Naison, and the second is from *How to Read a Book* by Mortimer Adler and Charles Van Doren. Quote only the italicized words and incorporate the quotations into sentences of your design. Use ellipsis marks, as appropriate, to indicate where you have deleted some words from the quoted passage.

Passage 1

At the Ivy League colleges, which assumed the mission of training a social elite, *popular sports programs managed to survive without the recruitment of semi-literate athletes or illegal cash payments for their services.*[7]

Use the following information to identify Naison with an appositive phrase; also use a present-tense verb to introduce the quotation.

Mark Naison is a sports historian and an associate professor of Afro-American studies at Fordham University. Naison is referring here to collegiate sports in the 1890s.

_____

_____

_____

_____

Passage 2

There is some feeling nowadays that reading is not as necessary as it once was. *Radio and especially television have taken over many of the functions once served by print,* just as photography has taken over functions once served by painting and other graphic arts. *Admittedly, television serves some of these functions extremely well; the visual communication of news events, for example, has enormous impact. The ability of radio to give us information while we are engaged in doing other things* — for instance, driving a car — *is remarkable, and a great saving of time.* But it may be seriously questioned whether the advent of modern communications media has much enhanced our understanding of the world in which we live.[8]

Assume that you would indent this quotation since it is rather long. (Generally, you should set off in its own indented paragraph any quotation that is longer than five lines.)

[7]Mark Naison, "Scenario for Scandal," *Commonweal,* vol. CIX, no. 16 (September 24, 1982).
[8]Mortimer J. Adler and Charles Van Doren, *How to Read a Book* (New York: Simon and Schuster, 1972), 3–4.

Introduce the quotation with a sentence that includes an appositive phrase, and use a colon instead of a period at the end of this introductory sentence. The appositive phrase should consist of the title of Adler and Van Doren's book.

_____

_____

_____

_____

_____

_____

_____

_____

Using Brackets

Use square brackets whenever you need to add or substitute words in a quoted sentence. The brackets indicate to the reader a word or phrase that does not appear in the original passage but that you have inserted to avoid confusion. We used brackets in one of the sentences quoted from *Walden* to add the pronoun *it*. In deleting the first part of Thoreau's sentence on reading well (we wanted to quote only the second part), we deleted the sentence's subject. To begin our quotation as follows would have confused the reader:

> Reading well is hard work and requires great skill and training. "... is a noble exercise," writes Henry David Thoreau in *Walden,* "one that will task the reader more than any exercise which the customs of the day esteem."

So to fill in a subject and make the sentence comprehensible, we included the pronoun *it* in brackets:

> Reading well is hard work and requires great skill and training. "[It] ... is a noble experience," writes Henry David Thoreau in *Walden.*

You'll sometimes want to quote a passage containing an ambiguous pronoun. When the pronoun's antecedent (the word "it" refers to) would be unclear to readers, delete the pronoun from the sentence and substitute an identifying word or phrase in brackets. When you make such a substitution, no ellipsis marks are needed. Assume that you wish to quote the italicized sentence in the following passage:

> Golden Press's *Walt Disney's Cinderella* set the new pattern for America's Cinderella. This book's text is coy and condescending. (Sample: "And her best friends of all were — guess who — the mice!") The illustrations are poor cartoons. And Cinderella herself is a disaster. *She cowers as her sisters rip her homemade ball gown to shreds.* (Not even homemade by Cinderella, but by the mice and birds.) She answers her stepmother with whines and pleadings.

She is a sorry excuse for a heroine, pitiable and useless. She cannot perform even a simple action to save herself, though she is warned by her friends, the mice. She does not hear them because she is "off in a world of dreams." Cinderella begs, she whimpers, and at last has to be rescued by—guess who—the mice![9]

In quoting this sentence, you would need to identify whom the pronoun *she* refers to. You can do this inside the quotation by using brackets:

Jane Yolen believes that Walt Disney's "[Cinderella] is a sorry excuse for a heroine, pitiable and useless."

If the pronoun begins the sentence to be quoted, as it does in this example, you can identify the pronoun outside of the quotation and simply begin quoting your source one word later:

Jane Yolen believes that Walt Disney's Cinderella "is a sorry excuse for a heroine, pitiable and useless."

If the pronoun you want to identify occurs in the middle of the sentence to be quoted, then you'll need to use brackets. Newspaper reporters do this frequently when quoting sources, who in interviews might say something like the following:

After the fire they did not return to the station house for three hours.

If the reporter wants to use this sentence in an article, he or she needs to identify the pronoun:

An official from City Hall, speaking on the condition that he not be identified, said, "After the fire [the officers] did not return to the station house for three hours."

You will also need to add bracketed information to a quoted sentence when a reference essential to the sentence's meaning is implied but not stated directly. Read the following paragraphs from Robert Jastrow's "Toward an Intelligence Beyond Man's":

These are amiable qualities for the computer; it imitates life like an electronic monkey. As computers get more complex, the imitation gets better. Finally, the line between the original and the copy becomes blurred. In another 15 years or so—two more generations of computer evolution, in the jargon of the technologists—we will see the computer as an emergent form of life.

The proposition seems ridiculous because, for one thing, computers lack the drives and emotions of living creatures. But when drives are useful, they can be programmed into the computer's brain, just as nature programmed them into our ancestors' brains as a part of the equipment for survival. For example, computers, like people, work better and learn faster when they are motivated. Arthur Samuel made this discovery when he taught two IBM com-

---

[9]Jane Yolen, "America's 'Cinderella,'" APS Publications, Inc., in *Children's Literature in Education,* vol. 8 (1977): 21–29.

puters how to play checkers. They polished their game by playing each other, but they learned slowly. Finally, Dr. Samuel programmed in the will to win by forcing the computers to try harder—and to think out more moves in advance—when they were losing. Then the computers learned very quickly. One of them beat Samuel and went on to defeat a champion player who had not lost a game to a human opponent in eight years.[10]

If you wanted to quote only the italicized sentence, you would need to provide readers with a bracketed explanation; otherwise the words "the proposition" would be unclear. Here is how you would manage the quotation:

> According to Robert Jastrow, a physicist and former official at NASA's Goddard Institute, "The proposition [that computers will emerge as a form of life] seems ridiculous because, for one thing, computers lack the drives and emotions of living creatures."

EXERCISE

Write sentences in which you quote the italicized words in the following passages. Use brackets to enclose information as needed to clarify the quotations.

Passage 1

The following is excerpted from "Adventures in the Skin Trade," a *Time* article by Anastasia Toufexis on illegal traffic in wild animals.

> Wildlife traffickers often launder items: if a country bans the export of a species, smugglers spirit animals into a nearby nation that permits their export. An official of an accommodating government can be bribed to list his country as the origin of items. Says Paul Gertler, a biologist with the federal wildlife permit office: "Inspectors at ports of entry are put in the position where they have to take the word of another government."
>
> As an example, conservationists cite Bolivia, which has an estimated 500 hyacinth macaws. In 1980–81 Bolivia exported 800 of the birds, each worth up to $5,000; wildlife experts believe that most were caught in Brazil. Sudan, which has fewer than 100 white rhinos, exports scores of horns annually. Prized as an aphrodisiac in the Orient, horns fetch $250 per lb.
>
> The seemingly legitimate documents shielding these shipments make the illegal trade difficult to detect. But the World Wildlife Fund has recently helped the U.S. Government computerize international export-import records and has begun matching them with census counts of endangered species. *Stopping the illegal trade in the future may depend not only on catching poachers in the act but on following the document trail they leave behind.* Says the fund's Linda McMahan: "It's not just a cloak-and-dagger operation any more. It's becoming a complex paper chase."[11]

Introduce the sentence you're quoting with the author's name and affiliation.

---

[10]Robert Jastrow, "Toward an Intelligence Beyond Man's," *Time* (February 20, 1978).
[11]Anastasia Toufexis, "Adventures in the Skin Trade," *Time* (May 28, 1984): 82.

_____

_____

_____

_____

Passage 2

The following is excerpted from an article in *Science 84* titled "Year of the Tornado" by Steve Olson.

> Large tornadoes pack the strongest winds on the face of the Earth, as fast as 300 miles per hour. Winds of such magnitude can reduce a house to splinters in seconds. These winds are also responsible for some of the side-show oddities left behind. Old hands tell stories of tornadoes shearing the wool from the backs of sheep, sucking the soda from open bottles, driving wooden planks through steel girders, pelting people so hard with grit that they are tattooed for life, and driving pieces of straw into tree trunks.
>
> For researchers, a twister's winds have another, particularly unwelcome effect: They make tornadoes very difficult to study. Tornadoes destroy any standard meteorological instruments over which they pass. So researchers have to rely on indirect measurements and eyewitness accounts to check their theories. One atmospheric scientist has called tornado research the "last frontier" in meteorology. In fact so little is known that in the 1970's a quartet of scientists seriously suggested that tornadoes get their start from the eddies created when cars pass each other on the highway.
>
> A more conventional explanation holds that the swirl in a tornado comes from the strong, shifting winds within a thunderstorm. *When these winds blow from the right directions, they can create horizontal columns of spinning air, like great invisible tubes rolling over the countryside. A combination of updrafts and downdrafts may then lift these tubes into the air and tilt them on end. Once vertical, the tubes may build toward the ground and intensify to form tornadoes.* [12]

Introduce the sentence you're quoting with the author's name and affiliation. Since this is a lengthy quotation, you'll need to indent it. What bracketed information will you add to the quoted sentence?

_____

_____

_____

_____

_____

_____

_____

_____

[12]Steve Olson, "Year of the Tornado," in *Science 84,* vol. 5, no. 9 (November 1984): 177–178.

Introductions and Conclusions

Introductions

The purpose of an introduction is to prepare the reader to enter the world of your essay. The introduction makes the connection between the more familiar world inhabited by the reader and the less familiar world of the writer's particular subject; it places a discussion in a context that the reader can understand.

Many writers put off writing their introductions until they've completed a draft of their paper. There's a lot to be said for this approach. Since you presumably spent more time thinking about the topic itself than about how to introduce it, you are in a better position to begin directly with your presentation (once you've settled on a working thesis). And often it's not until you've actually seen your essay on paper and read it over once or twice that a "natural" way of introducing it becomes apparent. Even if there is no natural way to begin, you are generally in better psychological shape to write the introduction after the major task of writing is behind you and you know exactly what you're leading up to. Perhaps, however, you can't operate this way. After all, you have to start writing *somewhere,* and if you have evaded the problem by skipping the introduction, that blank page may loom just as large wherever you choose to begin. If this is the case, then go ahead and write an introduction, realizing that you will need to revise it later on. But in the meantime you will have gotten started.

There are many ways to introduce a reader to the topic of your paper. We consider three: leading from the general to the specific, posing questions, and writing a historical review.

From the General to the Specific

In this common technique for introducing a paper, you begin with a general statement and, with successive sentences, make increasingly specific statements until you arrive at a thesis. Saundra Goulet used this technique. Though her introduction is brief, it provides the reader with the necessary transition into the paper:

> A satisfying job means more to a worker than just a large weekly paycheck. A worker has certain expectations about a job — that it will be enjoyable and worthwhile. When these expectations are met and a job is satisfying, a worker will feel happy and self-respecting.

Saundra's first statement is her most general one; the second statement builds upon the first in specific ways; and the third follows with a still more specific claim, the thesis of her paper. You can observe the same pattern in this next introduction to a paper on the 1968 massacre at My Lai, Vietnam:

> Though we prefer to think of man as basically good and reluctant to do evil, such is not the case. Many of the crimes inflicted on humankind can be

dismissed as being committed by the degenerates of society at the prompting of the abnormal mind. But what of the perfectly "normal" man or woman who commits inhumane acts simply because he or she has been ordered to do so? It cannot be denied that such acts have occurred, either in everyday life or in war-time situations. Unfortunately, even normal, well-adjusted people can become cruel, inhumane, and destructive if placed in the hands of unscrupulous authority. Such was the case in the village of My Lai, Vietnam, on March 16, 1968, when a platoon of American soldiers commanded by Lt. William Calley massacred more than 100 civilians, including women and children.

Using Questions

Frequently, you can provoke the reader's attention by posing a question or a series of questions:

> In a world of advancing technology, new techniques in prenatal testing are being developed, and amniocentesis, a test for birth defects, is one of them. Are the risks involved with amniocentesis worth the benefits?

Note again the use of a first sentence that orients the reader to the general subject of the paper. A direct question follows, the answer to which will be the author's thesis. The same technique is used in the following introduction. Here the writer offers an answer (that is, a thesis) in the introduction along with her question:

> Are gender roles learned or inherited? Scientific research has established the existence of biological differences between the sexes, but the effect of biology's influence on gender roles cannot be distinguished from society's influence. According to Michael Lewis of the Institute for the Study of Exceptional Children, "As early as you can show me a sex difference, I can show you the culture at work." Social processes, as well as biological differences, are responsible for the separate roles of men and women.

Historical Review/Review of a Controversy

You will sometimes need to prepare readers for your discussion by presenting a historical review. Such a review is especially useful when you plan to make an argument. Presumably, you've chosen to argue a position about which people will disagree; and an effective way of introducing the topic is to review the history of that disagreement, as in the following opening paragraph to a student essay:

> For many years, laboratories and hospitals have used animals in medical experiments. Certain animals such as the dog and monkey have been used more frequently than others because they are easily obtainable and because of their physiological similarities to humans. It is because of these similarities that many medical discoveries have been possible. But these same similarities have given rise to a controversy: those against animal experimentation argue that if dogs and humans are used in experiments because they resemble humans physiologically, then subjecting these animals to lab experiments is as

cruel as subjecting humans to the same experiments. I disagree with this view and believe that researchers who use animals in the lab should continue their work in order to continue making medical discoveries that will benefit both humans and animals.

The following introduction also is also built on a review of a controversy:

> The *American Heritage Dictionary*'s definition of civil disobedience is rather simple: "the refusal to obey civil laws that are regarded as unjust, usually by employing methods of passive resistance." However, despite such famous (and beloved) examples of civil disobedience as the movements of Mahatma Gandhi in India and the Reverend Martin Luther King, Jr. in the United States, the question of whether or not civil disobedience should be considered an asset to society is hardly clear cut. For instance, Hannah Arendt, in her article "Civil Disobedience," holds that "to think of disobedient minorities as rebels and truants is against the letter and spirit of a constitution whose framers were especially sensitive to the dangers of unbridled majority rule." On the other hand, a noted lawyer, Lewis Van Dusen, Jr., in his article "Civil Disobedience: Destroyer of Democracy," states that "civil disobedience, whatever the ethical rationalization, is still an assault on our democratic society, an affront to our legal order and an attack on our constitutional government." These opposite views are clearly incompatible. I believe, though, that Van Dusen's is the more convincing. On balance, civil disobedience is dangerous to society.

Each of these introductions clearly prepares a reader for the discussion to follow. You can choose a brief or a lengthy introduction as long as you establish the general topic of your paper and then state, or at least suggest that you will state, a thesis.

Conclusions

One way to view the conclusion of your paper is as an introduction worked in reverse, a bridge from the world of your essay back to the world of your reader. A conclusion is the part of your paper in which you restate and (if necessary) expand on your thesis. Essential to any conclusion is the summary, which is not merely a repetition of the thesis but a restatement that takes advantage of the material you've presented. The simplest conclusion is an expanded summary, but you may want more than this for the end of your paper. Depending on your needs, you might offer a summary and then build onto it a discussion of the paper's significance or its implications for future study, for choices that individuals might make, for policy, and so on. You might also want to urge the reader to change an attitude or to modify behavior. Certainly, you are under no obligation to discuss the broader significance of your work (and a summary alone will satisfy the formal requirement that your paper have an ending); but the conclusions of better papers often reveal authors who are "thinking large" and want to connect the particular concerns of their papers with the broader concerns of society.

Consider the summary-conclusion used by Saundra Goulet in her paper on job satisfaction and self-respect:

> In order for the employee to remain content with his job, he must find pride as well as self-respect in his work. A satisfying job will give an employee a sense of belonging. It will make him feel good about himself. And if the employee feels that way about himself and his work, he will find other things in his life much more enjoyable and worthwhile.

The following two conclusions from other essays differ from Saundra's in that they imply a summary. All that is necessary in a conclusion is that you remind your readers of the ground you covered in the paper. Once this is done—either directly with a summary or indirectly with a reference back to the paper (a reference that asks the reader to provide the summary)—you have met the first obligation of a conclusion. The following conclusions also differ from Saundra's in that they attempt to place the discussion in a larger context. These conclusions go beyond a simple summary and attempt to make a comment about society in general.

> Even though the evidence suggesting that animals, like humans, have consciousness seems persuasive, the evidence is not conclusive; and until it is, scientists should continue to experiment on animals in the laboratory. Too many benefits have come to both humans and animals not to continue experimentation. If we stop now, we would never know the goals we could have achieved, the diseases we could have conquered. Successful experiments on animals have made for a healthier, longer, and more bearable human life. If we discontinue medical experiments on animals today, there may be little hope for a disease-free life tomorrow. Scientific experimentation has its costs. Benefits must be weighed against risks, and whenever benefits promise to be great, risks must be taken.

As you see, the author begins with an implied summary: "Even though the evidence suggesting that animals, like humans, have consciousness seems persuasive...." This sentence forces the reader to reconstruct and review evidence already presented; that is, the sentence acts as an implied summary. From this point, the conclusion develops as a commentary both on animal experimentation and on the risks of science in general. The author wants to move beyond the limited topic of the paper to a more general topic. This is an example of a writer's "thinking large," a trait also shared by the following conclusion. (The following example concludes a paper begun with the question "Are the risks involved with amniocentesis worth the benefits?" The writer did not provide her answer—her thesis—until the conclusion, an excellent technique when one wants to lay out all the evidence before stating a decision.)

> I feel that amniocentesis is a very helpful test. Although there are indeed risks involved with the procedure, there are risks in every type of medical test. Women these days are establishing careers for themselves before even considering settling down to marry and start a family. If a career woman were to become pregnant and have a child afflicted with some genetic disease, a child

whose care would require more attention than normal, the woman may be resentful. Because she has already put a great deal of time into her career, she may not be willing to give it up to care for her infant. Although right-to-lifers have labeled amniocentesis a "search and destroy" mission for those who want perfect babies, I feel that the test is a big help. Some parents may not be financially stable enough to raise a child with a major handicap that may require great amounts of money to care for. Some parents may not be capable of loving a severely retarded child while others may. Choosing to take the test and gaining advance knowledge of a fetus with some form of disease or handicap will give the parents a few extra months to prepare themselves, other family members, and friends for the birth of a child who will have special and complex needs. Such a child will be cared for by parents who really want him; these parents will be responsible parents. Any pregnancy is a gamble, and even perfect-looking babies can have serious medical or behavioral problems. Despite all its advances, medical science still cannot tell us that our babies will, for certain, be all right. But we can at least be informed.

As in the first example, the author implies her summary. By writing "Although there are indeed risks involved with the procedure..." she reminds the reader of important points she raised earlier in the paper. The conclusion continues with a balanced, thoughtful discussion on the topic and concludes with a broadening of the discussion: "Despite all its advances, medical science still cannot tell us that our babies will, for certain, be all right. But we can at least be informed."

View your introductions and conclusions as you would transitions within a paper. All serve the same purpose: to act as bridges that ease the reader's way through your work. By providing transitions at the beginning, middle, and end of your papers; by helping readers along with unified, coherent paragraphs; and by being as complete as possible in the development of your ideas you cannot help but succeed in achieving your purpose: to communicate.

The sure sign of success will be when your papers generate a reaction. No one will be distracted by incomplete presentations or ungrammatical sentences. People will agree or disagree with your *ideas;* and when this happens, you will have joined the academic community, where students and teachers discuss what's on their minds as they attempt to learn more about themselves and their world.

P A R T
T W O

Introduction

Part Two gives you the opportunity to practice the skills you have learned in Part One. Each chapter consists of a group of articles dealing with a particular topic. These topics include career prospects in the 1990s, romance novels, the dispute over the value of a college education, "Hill Street Blues," the effects of divorce on children, the conflicts experienced by members of ethnic minorities in the United States, and the assassination of Abraham Lincoln.

Beginning with Chapter 8, questions following each article are organized under the following headings:

- **Content** (what does the article say?)
- **Structure** (how is the article organized, and why is it organized as it is?)
- **Fact/Opinion** (distinguish between statements of fact and statements of opinion in the article)
- **Inferences** (draw inferences from the article)

At the conclusion of each chapter, you will be asked to write essays based on your responses to some of these questions. In composing these essays you will draw upon the ideas and information in two or more source articles. The introductory material in each chapter will provide hints on how to develop and organize your essays, for example, how to write an essay that *compares and contrasts,* one that advances an *argument,* or one that draws *cause and effect* relationships.

Chapter 7, "Career Prospects in the 1990s," serves as a transition between Part One and Part Two. In this chapter, you will read a limited number of short passages and be guided step by step in preparing a *descriptive* essay on the topic. In later chapters there will be considerably less direct instruction, and you will take increasing responsibility for the preparation of your essays.

CHAPTER 7

Career Prospects in the 1990s

Introduction

After you finish college or graduate school, what will you do? What kind of jobs will be available to people with your background and education? Which career fields are booming with unlimited opportunities? Which ones are declining? How much money can you expect to make? In what parts of the country are the opportunities brightest?

Many educators deplore the fact that college students are so preoccupied with such mundane matters as jobs and "making a buck." But for students facing the non-summer job market for the first time, these are natural—in fact, critical—concerns.

As a student you may decide to apply your academic skills to discovering answers to some of these questions. Perhaps you are taking a course for which it is appropriate to investigate the career prospects of the immediate future—the 1990s. As part of your work in the course, you decide to research relevant information and to write a paper on what you discover.

In this chapter we provide several articles focusing on career prospects in the 1990s. After reviewing the skills that you learned and practiced in Part One, we demonstrate how to select key information from these articles in preparation for developing a thesis, preparing an outline, and then writing a paper in which you report your findings.

First Source

To begin, read "Bright Job Prospects for 1980s and 1990s."

Alex Poinsett

BRIGHT JOB PROSPECTS FOR 1980s AND 1990s

1   Where will you be working in 1990? In sales? Construction? Health care? If you haven't mulled over these questions, perhaps now is as good a time as any since you in a sense will be competing with 119 million other workers by 1990. Also, new technologies will both *create* and *eliminate* hundreds of thousands of jobs. You can already see this, for example, in the computer field which has generated an entire new group of occupations—programmers, systems analysts, peripheral equipment operators—while simultaneously decreasing the need for inventory clerks, bookkeepers, and other clerical workers.

2   Clearly, then, the time and trouble you take in planning your career will pay off eventually, especially since jobs are becoming more specialized and employers increasingly are seeking workers with marketable skills. In fact, the U.S. Labor Dept. estimates that the majority of jobs in the future will require some sort of trade or technical training.

3   Your first step in choosing a career is to be generally aware of the *more than 30,000 career specialties* that exist today. Talk to your counselor, visit a library, or consult your state's labor department about the career possibilities best suited to you. You will find helpful hints in the *Occupational Outlook Handbook* published by the U.S.

Bureau of Labor Statistics. At the very least, its projections will help you avoid preparing today for jobs that probably will not even exist in 1990. Guide your preliminary inquiries with the following considerations:

- *Your interests.* Do you enjoy helping people, working with your hands, playing with figures, creating, designing, being outdoors? Pinpoint your likes and translate them into career possibilities: mechanics, dress design, allied health, electronic technology, advertising, computer programming. Probably the most important factor in career satisfaction is liking what you do.   4

- *Salary.* What is the beginning salary in your chosen career? What can you expect to make after two or three years of experience? What about after 15 years? Check with employers. Get realistic estimates of what the return on your investment will be.   5

- *Advancement.* Is the career you've chosen open-ended? Where will it lead you? Will it allow you to eventually start your own business (if that's your goal)?   6

- *Job demand.* Is there a *need* for your career specialty? Will you be in demand or *are there more people than jobs?* Check long-range projections of demand. Choose a career with a good   7 future. *Make sure your job won't become obsolete in a few years.*

8 ■ *Job mobility.* Where are the jobs? In your locale? Or are jobs clustered in specific areas which would give you the opportunity to travel? For example, commercial divers usually have to relocate (sometimes overseas) while computer programmers work mostly in large and medium-size cities. Medical workers, on the other hand, are usually found everywhere.

9 ■ *Working conditions.* Find out exactly what a person in your chosen career does — know exactly what your duties and work environment will be. A career may *sound* glamorous or exciting, but before you make up your mind, get all the facts. Don't be unpleasantly surprised on the job.

10 ■ *Educational requirements.* Almost all good jobs today require *specialized training* beyond high school. But *quality* not quantity counts. *It's not how many years of education you have, it's what type.* Generally, specialized training is more "marketable" than a general education. *Find out what type of education you need in order to qualify in your career.* It may take a few months, or one or two years or more of training.

. . .

11 As you know, college education traditionally has been a gateway to better pay, higher status, and more challenging work. Consequently, the proportion of workers in the labor force who have completed at least four years of college has risen from eight to 17 percent between 1952 and 1978. Yet, recent experience suggests that *a college degree no longer guarantees success.* The number of college graduates employed in professional and technical occupations declined between 1968 and 1978 because these occupations did not expand as rapidly as did the supply of graduates. Consequently, one out of four college graduates took jobs traditionally filled by persons with less schooling,

and the number of graduates in clerical, lower-level sales, and blue-collar occupations grew.

12 In the future, more college graduates are likely to be available than will be needed to fill jobs requiring college degrees. But not all such occupations will be overcrowded. Despite widespread publicity about the poor job market for college graduates, they still hold a relatively high advantage over other workers. They are more likely to be employed and to hold the highest-paying professional managerial jobs. If you're interested in occupations that require college degrees, you should not be discouraged from pursuing careers that you believe match your interests and abilities.

13 While becoming knowledgeable about these broad occupational trends, keep in mind that *two-thirds of the nation's workers currently are employed in industries that provide services such as health care, data processing, trade, education, repair and maintenance, office careers, government, transportation, banking and insurance.* On the other hand, industries that produce goods through farming, construction, mining, and manufacturing employ *less than one-third* of the nation's work force. In the future, you can expect the service-producing industries to account for *seven out of every 10 workers,* while the goods-producing industries will increase their work force *by only 13 percent.* These are among general trends that will suggest your best and worst employment fields during the remainder of this decade. Consider the following broad projections:

14 *Clerical workers.* This, the largest occupational group, includes bank tellers, bookkeepers, cashiers, secretaries, and typists. Expect employment in these occupations to grow from 16.9 to 21.7 million workers or 28 percent between 1978 and 1990. You will see new developments in computers, office machines, and dictating equipment greatly affecting employment in many occupations within this group. For instance, *more than 250,000 positions will be created in the com-*

puter field by the end of this decade and the growth of many businesses will depend on their ability to expand computer operations. Meanwhile, dictation machines have sharply reduced the need for stenographers and will continue to adversely affect your employment prospects in that occupation. However, technological innovations will not affect clerical work if your job involves a high degree of personal contact. You can expect substantial opportunities, for example, if you wish to become a secretary or receptionist.

15   *Professional and technical workers.* Expect this group, which includes many highly trained workers, such as scientists and engineers, medical practitioners, teachers, entertainers, pilots and accountants, to add 2.7 million workers by 1990. Do not expect all professional jobs to be equally promising, however. For example, despite a growing demand for lawyers, competition for jobs will intensify because of a burgeoning supply of law graduates. Teachers will continue to face competition, as will artists and entertainers, airline pilots and oceanographers.

16   *Managers and administrators.* This group includes bank officers and managers, buyers, credit managers, self-employed business operators, etc. *Expect this group to grow from 10.1 to 12.2 million or 21 percent between 1978 and 1990.* However, the number of self-employed business managers will continue to decline as large corporations and chain operations increasingly dominate many areas of business. Some small businesses, such as quick-service groceries and fast-food restaurants, will still provide you opportunities for self-employment. And the demand for salaried managers will continue to grow as firms increasingly depend on trained management specialists, particularly in highly technical areas of operation.

17   *Sales workers.* Figure this group to generate about 1.6 million jobs by 1990, largely because of expansion in the retail trade industry which employs nearly one-half of these workers. Despite the use of labor-saving merchandising techniques, such as computerized checkout counters, more stores and longer operating hours will cause employment to increase.

18   *Blue-collar occupations. Look for craft workers, operatives and laborers to account for only one-quarter of the nation's employment growth by 1990.* Also, anticipate growth among highly skilled craft workers to add 2.5 million jobs to the economy. And expect employment in nearly all construction trades to grow, along with particularly rapid increases for heavy equipment operators, electricians, ironworkers and cement masons. Among mechanics and repairers, employment will increase most among workers who repair computers, office machines and industrial machinery. By contrast, figure the long-run employment decline in the railroad industry to result in drops in employment for some craft occupations concentrated in that industry. Also, look for very little growth in the printing crafts, because of advances in printing technology.

19   *Service workers.* Figure this group, which includes cooks and chefs, cosmetologists, police officers, practical nurses, and child care workers, to be the fastest growing occupational field, generating 4.1 million new jobs by 1990. The reasons for this rapid growth include rising demands for medical care and protective services and trends toward more frequent use of personal services, such as beauty salons.

20   Perhaps by now you have a better idea of where you will be working in 1990. Your decision, of course, will be heavily influenced by changes—either for better or worse—that are occurring in the working world. But ultimately, your decision should be influenced the most by you.

Content

This article is a good introduction to the subject of career prospects in the 1980s and 1990s. It provides a broad overview of the career issues most likely to be of concern to those students soon to enter the job market.

Notice that facts rather than opinions are central to this article. The writer, Alex Poinsett, does occasionally offer his opinion; for example, in paragraph 4 he says, "Probably the most important factor in career satisfaction is liking what you do." While this statement could not be classified as a fact, as an opinion it is so noncontroversial that it could almost be considered pure information. (Compare this opinion, for example, with the opinions behind the article on animal experimentation.)

Still, all the information in this article serves to reinforce the writer's *thesis:* that in the face of an ever-changing job market students should spend a good deal of time planning their career options before they actually start hunting for jobs. This thesis appears most explicitly at the beginning of the second paragraph:

> Clearly, then, the time and trouble you take in planning your career will pay off eventually, especially since jobs are becoming more specialized and employers increasingly are seeking workers with marketable skills.

The main purpose of a thesis like this one is less to argue a particular viewpoint (who could plausibly argue the opposite—that time spent planning will *not* pay off?) than to organize the discussion that follows.

Structure

The purpose of this article is to *describe* those areas that should be of most concern to future job-seekers as they consider their career options. To accomplish this purpose, Poinsett divides his article into three parts.

In the first part (paragraphs 1–10) Poinsett introduces the subject and notes that the reader's first inquiries about career planning should concern such basic matters as the reader's own interests, the salaries and advancements offered by various careers, the demand for certain jobs, where these jobs are located, working conditions, and educational requirements.

In the second part (paragraphs 11 and 12) Poinsett focuses more specifically on educational requirements, discussing the importance for many jobs of a college education.

In the third part (paragraphs 13–19), after noting that two-thirds of the nation's workers are employed in service industries and only one-third in production industries, Poinsett discusses six broad career areas: clerical workers, professional and technical workers, managers and administrators, sales workers, blue-collar workers, and service workers. He indicates the particular occupations that fall into each area and the social, economic, and technological changes that will cause growth or decline in each area.

The article concludes with a one-paragraph summary (paragraph 20) in which Poinsett wraps up his discussion.

The article can be represented in outline form as follows:

I. Planning for a career
   A. Introduction: Planning is crucial (¶1–2)

        B. Get information (¶3)
            1. Interests (¶4)
            2. Salary (¶5)
            3. Advancement (¶6)
            4. Job demand (¶7)
            5. Job mobility (¶8)
            6. Working conditions (¶9)
            7. Educational requirements (¶10–11)
    II. The role of a college education
        A. College degree no longer guarantees success (¶11)
        b. College degree still an advantage (¶12)
    III. Career trends
        A. From a goods-based economy to a service-based economy (¶13)
        B. Six broad career areas (¶14–19)
            1. Clerical workers (¶14)
            2. Professional and technical workers (¶15)
            3. Managers and administrators (¶16)
            4. Sales workers (¶17)
            5. Blue-collar occupations (¶18)
            6. Service workers (¶19)
    IV. Conclusion (¶20)

Taking Notes

    Let's see how this article might look after you have finished taking notes on it.

Alex Poinsett

BRIGHT JOB PROSPECTS FOR 1980s AND 1990s

(Add star.)

Where will you be working in 1990? In sales? Construction? Health care? If you haven't mulled over these questions, perhaps now is as good a time as any since you in a sense will be competing with 119 million other workers by 1990. Also, new technologies will both *create* and *eliminate* hundreds of thousands of jobs. You can already see this, for example, in the computer field which has generated an entire new group of occupations — programmers, systems analysts, peripheral equipment operators — while simultaneously decreasing the need for inventory clerks, bookkeepers, and other clerical workers.

(Underline where shown.)

Clearly, then, the time and trouble you ✻ take in planning your career will pay off eventually, especially since jobs are becoming more specialized and employers increasingly are seeking workers with marketable skills. *Thesis* In fact, the U.S. Labor Dept. estimates that the majority of jobs in the future will require some sort of trade or technical training.

Your first step in choosing a career is to be generally aware of the *more than 30,000 career specialties* that exist today. Talk to your counselor, visit a library, or consult your state's labor department about the career possibilities best suited to you. You

(Handwrite summary words or phrases in the margin.)

Where to get information
will find helpful hints in the *Occupational Outlook Handbook* published by the U.S. Bureau of Labor Statistics. At the very least, its projections will help you avoid preparing today for jobs that probably will not even exist in 1990. Guide your preliminary inquiries with the following considerations:

Important considerations in choosing a career

✓ ■ *Your interests.* Do you enjoy helping people, working with your hands, playing with figures, creating, designing, being outdoors? Pinpoint your likes and translate them into career possibilities: mechanics, dress design, allied health, electronic technology, advertising, computer programming. Probably the most important factor in career satisfaction is liking what you do.

✓ ■ *Salary.* What is the beginning salary in your chosen career? What can you expect to make after two or three years of experience? What about after 15 years? Check with employers. Get realistic estimates of what the return on your investment will be.

✓ ■ *Advancement.* Is the career you've chosen open-ended? Where will it lead you? Will it allow you to eventually start your own business (if that's your goal)?

✓ ■ *Job demand.* Is there a *need* for your career specialty? Will you be in demand or *are there more people than jobs?* Check long-range projections of demand. Choose a career with a good future. *Make sure your job won't become obsolete in a few years.*

✓ ■ *Job mobility.* Where are the jobs? In your locale? Or are jobs clustered in specific areas which would give you the opportunity to travel? For example, commercial divers usually have to relocate (sometimes overseas) while computer programmers work mostly in large and medium-size cities. Medical workers, on the other hand, are usually found everywhere.

✓ ■ *Working conditions.* Find out exactly what a person in your chosen career does — know exactly what your duties and work environment will be. A career may *sound* glamorous or exciting, but before you make up your mind, get all the facts. Don't be unpleasantly surprised on the job.

✓ ■ *Educational requirements.* Almost all good jobs today require *specialized training* beyond high school. But *quality* not quantity counts. *It's not how many years of education you have, it's what type.* Generally, specialized training is more "marketable" than a general education. *Find out what type of education you need in order to qualify in your career.* It may take a few months, or one or two years or more of training.

Importance of college degrees
As you know, college education traditionally has been a gateway to better pay, higher status, and more challenging work. Consequently, the proportion of workers in the labor force who have completed at least four years of college has risen from eight to 17 percent between 1952 and 1978. Yet, recent experience suggests that *a college degree no longer guarantees success.* The number of college graduates employed in professional and technical occupations declined between 1968 and 1978 because these occupations did not expand as rapidly as did the supply of graduates. Consequently, one out of four college graduates took jobs traditionally filled by persons with less schooling, and the number of graduates in clerical, lower-level sales, and blue-collar occupations grew.

In the future, more college graduates are likely to be available than will be needed to fill jobs requiring college degrees. But not all such occupations will be overcrowded. Despite widespread publicity about the poor job market for college graduates, they still hold a relatively high advantage over other workers. They are more likely to be employed and to hold the highest-paying professional managerial jobs. If you're interested in occupations that require college degrees, you should not be discouraged from pursuing careers that you believe match your interests and abilities.

Add checks to subheadings to make them stand out from other underlined material.

Two-thirds of workers in service industries
Less than one-third of workers produce goods

While becoming knowledgeable about these broad occupational trends, keep in mind that *two-thirds of the nation's workers currently are employed in industries that provide services such as health care, data processing, trade, education, repair and maintenance, office careers, government, transportation, banking and insurance.* On the other hand, industries that produce goods through farming, construction, mining, and manufacturing employ *less than one-third* of the nation's work force. In the future, you can expect the service-producing industries to account for *seven out of every 10 workers,* while the goods-producing industries will increase their work force *by only 13 percent.* These are among general trends that will suggest your best and worst employment fields during the remainder of this decade. Consider the following broad projections:

Service workers will increase more than goods-producing workers

Clerical workers. This, the largest occupational group, includes bank tellers, bookkeepers, cashiers, secretaries, and typists. Expect employment in these occupations to grow from 16.9 to 21.7 million workers or 28 percent between 1978 and 1990. You will see new developments in computers, office machines, and dictating equipment greatly affecting employment in many occupations within this group. For instance, *more than 250,000 positions will be created in the computer field by the end of this decade* and the growth of many businesses will depend on their ability to expand computer operations. Meanwhile, dictation machines have sharply reduced the need for stenographers and will continue to adversely affect your employment prospects in that occupation. However, technological innovations will not affect clerical work if your job involves a high degree of personal contact. You can expect substantial opportunities, for example, if you wish to become a secretary or receptionist.

Computer jobs

✓ *Professional and technical workers.* Expect this group, which includes many highly trained workers, such as scientists and engineers, medical practitioners, teachers, entertainers, pilots and accountants, to add 2.7 million workers by 1990. Do not expect all professional jobs to be equally promising, however. For example, despite a growing demand for lawyers, competition for jobs will intensify because of a burgeoning supply of law graduates. Teachers will continue to face competition, as will artists and entertainers, airline pilots and oceanographers.

✓ *Managers and administrators.* This group includes bank officers and managers, buyers, credit managers, self-employed business operators, etc. *Expect this group to grow from 10.1 to 12.2 million or 21 percent between 1978 and 1990.* However, the number of self-employed business managers will continue to decline as large corporations and chain operations increasingly dominate many areas of business. Some small businesses, such as quick-service groceries and fast-food restaurants, will still provide you opportunities for self-employment. And the demand for salaried managers will continue to grow as firms increasingly depend on trained management specialists, particularly in highly technical areas of operation.

✓ *Sales workers.* Figure this group to generate about 1.6 million jobs by 1990, largely because of expansion in the retail trade industry which employs nearly one-half of these workers. Despite the use of labor-saving merchandising techniques, such as computerized checkout counters, more stores and longer operating hours will cause employment to increase.

✓ *Blue-collar occupations. Look for craft workers, operatives and laborers to account for only one-quarter of the nation's employment growth by 1990.* Also, anticipate growth among highly skilled craft workers to add 2.5 million jobs to the economy. And expect employment in nearly all construction trades to grow, along with particularly rapid increases for heavy equipment operators, electricians, ironworkers and cement masons. Among mechanics and repairers, employment will increase most among workers who repair computers, office machines and industrial machinery. By contrast, figure the long-run employment decline in the railroad industry to result in drops in employment for some craft occupations concentrated in that industry. Also, look for very little growth in the printing crafts, because of advances in printing technology.

✓ _Service workers._ Figure this group, which includes cooks and chefs, cosmetologists, police officers, practical nurses, and child care workers, to be the fastest growing occupational field, generating 4.1 million new jobs by 1990. The reasons for this rapid

growth include rising demands for medical care and protective services and trends toward more frequent use of personal services, such as beauty salons. _Conclusion_

Perhaps by now you have a better idea of where you will be working in 1990. Your decision, of course, will be heavily influenced by changes — either for better or worse — that are occurring in the working world. But ultimately, your decision should be influenced the most by you.

Summary

Here is a summary of Poinsett's article, based on our reading and our notes:

Background information

Thesis →

If you are planning to begin your career in the 1990s, you will be competing with millions of other workers in a job market that will be very different from the one that exists today. "Clearly, then, the time and trouble you take in planning your career will pay off eventually, especially since jobs are becoming more specialized and employers increasingly are seeking workers with marketable skills."

One paragraph summarizing first part of article

Get as much information as you can about the ← _Topic sentence_ career specialties in which you are interested. Concern yourself especially with the following questions: (1) What are your interests? What do you most like to do? (2) What are the salary prospects in your chosen career? (3) What are the opportunities for advancement? (4) Is there a significant demand for workers in your chosen career field? (5) Where will you have to go to find job opportunities? (6) What are the working conditions of people in the field? (7) What are the educational requirements to qualify for your chosen career?

Each subheading in article covered in summary

One paragraph summarizing second part of article

Although more jobs than ever require college degrees, people with college degrees are not always able to find jobs in professional and technical fields. Still, those with college degrees have an advantage in the job market over those without degrees.

Main ideas about college education & jobs covered in summary

One paragraph summarizing third part of article

In the future, seven out of ten workers will be employed in service occupations and three out of ten ← _Topic sentence_ in goods-producing occupations. The largest occupational group will be clerical workers. Included in this group are hundreds of thousands of new positions in the computer field. <u>Professional and technical workers</u> will increase their numbers by nearly 3 million workers, but there will be stiff competition for jobs in many occupations in this field. There will be more than 10 million more <u>managers and administrators</u>, though there will be a decline in self-employed managers. The number of <u>sales workers</u> will increase by about 1.6 million. <u>Blue-collar workers</u> who will be most in demand are highly skilled craft workers, construction workers, and those who can repair computers and industrial machinery. The fastest-growing group will be <u>service workers</u>, whose numbers will increase by over 4 million by 1990.

Each subheading in article covered in summary

Some key statistics and other details mentioned

Additional Sources

The information in this article is important, but it represents only a small quantity of the material you will need if you are to present a thorough and well-balanced paper on career prospects. Accordingly, you will want to read and consider additional sources on this topic. Presented below are two such additional sources.

Second Source

The second source for the topic is an article titled "Careers with a Future." Read it carefully, taking notes, and then answer the questions that follow.

Marvin Cetron ■ Thomas O'Toole

CAREERS WITH A FUTURE
WHERE THE JOBS WILL BE IN THE 1990s

1   There will always be lawyers, but there won't be as many lawyers in the year 2000 as there are today because the demand won't be as great. There won't be as many doctors 20 years hence either, in part because there won't be the demand for doctors in 2000 that there is today. In fact, to turn a phrase on an old nursery rhyme, there won't be as many rich men, poor men, beggarmen, and thieves as there are today because the world's job markets will change dramatically in the next 20 years.

2   Well, maybe there will be just as many thieves in 2000 as there are today. But there won't be as many textile workers, automotive workers, or steel workers. The robotizing of the assembly line will see to that. There won't be as many clerical workers either— or as many sales people and stock clerks. The computer will see to that. Only one thing is sure about tomorrow's job markets: There will be major shifts in employment patterns—though it doesn't mean there will be major changes in the numbers of people employed anywhere inside the job market.

3   Take yourself ahead to the 1990s and imagine the help-wanted ads appearing in your local newspaper. This is what we antici-

pate for the classified pages of the *Washington Post* in the nineties:

4

HELP WANTED

GERIATRIC SOCIAL WORKER — Inner-city private nursing home, immediate opening for capable, reliable person. Must be L.P.N. or have equivalent education. Salary $15,000 thru $22,000 depending on experience. References required. Equal Opportunity Employer.

LASER PROCESS TECHNICIAN — Near Prince William County heliport and the metro rapid transit system. Northern Virginia high-technology firm needs dependable, experienced laser technician. Should have two years related laser cutting machine experience or will train. Flex time and day care available. Job sharing and shared dividends. Salary $15,000 to $25,000 negotiable. E.O.E.

GENETIC ENGINEERING — Positions available for both process technicians and engineering technicians. Relocation. New plant in Wyoming. Must have two years technical education and training. Additional education paid by company. Moving expenses paid by firm. Company will buy your present home. Right to work. $20,000 to $29,000. E.O.E.

BATTERY TECHNICIANS — Near Route 66 and Manassas. Large oil firm needs five technicians with previous experience in fuel cells or high-energy batteries. High-school diploma or equivalent. Shift work. O.T. available, dressing rooms and private locker, discount on all corporate products. Education and managerial training available. $12,000 to $18,000. E.O.E.

5   These four ads will typify the shifts that are coming in the nation's job market, changes that are bound to affect the work force of the future.

300 Million Unemployed

6   The key question facing us in the 20 years ahead is, Can the six billion people who will be alive in the year 2000 find work when so many of today's four billion are unemployed? Put it another way: Where will the new jobs come from in the next 20 years if we start to lose the old jobs to robots and computers? There's little question many of the old jobs will disappear, and not just because of robots and computers. Take textiles, an industry that has had wanderlust since the spinning wheel that started it all in the north of England. Pity the poor Hong Kong shirtmaker. The business he stole from the United States and Western Europe is already migrating to Mexico and Thailand, where the labor is cheaper than it is in Hong Kong. It won't be long before the Thais and the Mexicans lose their shirts to Egypt and Bangladesh. The same kind of thing is happening in steelmaking and shipbuilding. The business migrated out of the U.S. and Western Europe to Japan, where labor was cheaper. Now, it's moving to Korea and Taiwan, where labor comes cheaper than it does in Japan.

Concerns and worries about unemployment are hardly new to our society. After all, nineteenth-century steel barons thought their businesses would die when all the railroads were built. The railroad barons thought their businesses would die when cars and trucks and airplanes came along. One of their contemporaries talked about the "growing armies of the unemployed." Who was that? His name was Karl Marx. Well, the 1930s justified many of his fears, but the fifties and sixties should have buried them. Now, it's time to rejustify the fears of Karl Marx. At a rough guess, there are now 300 million unemployed people in the world. Almost 10 million of this army of the unemployed are in the United States, with another nine million in the industrialized countries of Western Europe.

7

One of 30 Works the Land

There's little question that employment patterns are shifting and will continue to shift throughout the world. Take agriculture. When Ronald Reagan was born, almost one-third of America worked down on the farm.

8

Now, barely one out of 30 works the land in the U.S. The same trend is true in Europe and Japan, where one out of 20 works on a farm. The mechanization of the American farm led the American worker to heavy industry in World War II, then to the service industry after the postwar period. Nowadays, one-third of America's blue-collar workers are in services, meaning they don't manufacture anything. They simply service the machines and people who do the manufacturing in the blue-collar industry and the machines and people who grind out the paperwork in the white-collar industry. This shifting trend will continue as robots — the so-called "steel-collar" workers — take more of the jobs in manufacturing and computers take more of the jobs in the office.

9   We think one of the major jobs of the future will be the robot technician, whose numbers could run to more than two million by 2000. We say that because the robotizing of America (and all other industrial countries) will be the only way to raise industrial productivity. General Motors has already said it will spend $1 billion installing 14,000 robots on its assembly lines by 1990. Chrysler and Ford plan to follow suit. In fact, Chrysler put robots into its welding operation at its Jefferson plant outside Detroit and increased productivity 20% with 200 fewer workers. But robots aren't perfect. They have to be cared for. They have to be programmed before they go to work, maintained so they don't break down, and fixed when they do break down. If they break down, they have to be replaced by other robots ready to go to work. Who's going to see that the backup robots are ready? The robot technicians, that's who.

Robot Technicians

10   The next generation of robots will be able to see, touch, hear, smell, and even speak. They'll need extra loving care, which means lots of service jobs for the robot technicians. We predict there will be as many as 1.5 million robot technicians on the job in the U.S. alone by 1990, making a starting salary of $15,000 a year and a midrange salary of $24,000 a year. Unless you are the kind of pessimist who thinks robots will build robots to repair robots, you can count on a robot technician's job to be a ticket into the twenty-first century. Of course, if there are robot technicians, there will have to be robot engineers. We think you can count on a robot engineer's degree to be a first-class ticket into the twenty-first century, to a job that pays $28,000 a year to start. The robot engineers of the next century will design a third generation of robots.

Computer Programmers

          The robots of the future will only be as   11 smart and dexterous as the computer software that programs them, which spotlights another major job of the future. Nobody will be in demand in the next 20 years like computer programmers. Harvard University now insists that all of its undergraduates be able to write a simple, two-step computer program before graduating. That is a sign of the times to come. Another sign of the times to come is the microprocessing chip, which has inspired new electronic products like pocket computers and talking toys. The chip has also transformed old products into new ones, like washing machines programmed to use cooler water for gentler washing and telephone switchboards that will take and store messages. Some estimates suggest that in the U.S. alone, the demand for computer programmers already outstrips the supply by anywhere from 50,000 to 100,000. We think those estimates are conservative. We think that by 2000 there will be almost one million new jobs generated for computer programmers in the U.S., with starting salaries of $13,000 and midrange salaries of $25,000 a year.

Laser Technicians

          It is often difficult to predict what new   12 jobs will be created by new technologies.

Often, we identify new technologies with job elimination instead of job creation. But when the invention of the transistor was announced in 1948, few technologists predicted the mushroom cloud that would follow it. Few people realized that this tiny electronic gate was the foundation of what soon will be the world's biggest business. Why should they have? After all, the transistor was conceived to be a replacement for the vacuum tube and no more. Even a few years after it was invented, one transistor still cost $15 and its use was restricted to things like hearing aids. The developments had not come along that cut its cost to a fraction of a cent and increased its use to thousands of new products. So it is with the laser, which came along 15 years after the transistor and which promises so many new uses that we predict it will be the transistor of the next 20 years. The laser will replace machine and foundry tools in every tool- and die-making shop in the world. The tool- and die-makers of the future will be laser technicians, whose numbers will mount so rapidly in the next 10 years that they will reach 2.5 million by 1990 and whose salaries will match those of the robot technicians.

Energy Technicians

13   Two industries that will spawn numerous new jobs are energy and hazardous wastes.... We predict that by 1990 there will be as many as 1.5 million new jobs for energy engineers and technicians. We think demand for energy technicians, making midcareer salaries of $26,000 a year, will exceed the supply for years to come in nuclear power plants, in coal, shale oil, and tar sands extraction plants, even in solar engineering plants....

Waste Technicians

14   We're not as certain about the hazardous wastes industry, but we'll go out on what we think is a short limb and predict 1.5 million new jobs for hazardous waste technicians,

whose most experienced practitioners will earn $28,000 a year by the year 2000. While it's true that robots will be used to clean up the worst of our industrial wastes, there won't be enough robots in the world to clean it all up. Environmentalists estimate that decades, and billions of dollars, will be needed to clean up the nation's industrial mess. When the requirements for collection, transportation, disposal, and monitoring of radiological, biological, and chemical wastes are included, the number of workers needed will exceed 1.5 million. The cleanup of Three Mile Island alone will take an estimated 10,000 workers 10 more years to complete. It doesn't seem futuristic to us to predict that they'll be joined by an army of more than one million to clean up the rest of America.

The Gene Machine

No new industry will make more of an   15 impact on America and the industrial world in the next 20 years than the gene-splicing business, whose ranks of high-technology firms staffed by Ph.D. biologists and chemists will explode far beyond the turn of the century. Who can predict what the world of genetic engineering will bring? Already, gene splicing has been hailed as one of man's most awesome accomplishments, like splitting the atom was half a century ago. The "Gene Machine" is with us, whether we like it or not. Behind us are the laboratory synthesis of insulin, interferon, human growth hormone, new antibiotics to treat bacterial infections, and new anticoagulants to break up blood clots in the arteries. Ahead of us are things like genetically altered corn and wheat that will suck nitrogen right out of the air and eliminate the need for ammonia fertilizers. Genetic engineering will produce fuels from wastes, plastics from sugar, and sweeteners from cheese. It will even leach metals from ores and clean up oil spills. Says Britain's *Economist* magazine: "It is one of the biggest industrial opportunities of the next 20 years." Our prediction? It's a modest one. We predict there will be at least 150,000 new jobs by 1990 for genetic engineering technicians alone, whose salaries will top $30,000 a year.

Paramedics

16   There will be major new job breakthroughs in the delivery of health care in the next 20 years. If the demand for doctors goes down as we expect it will, the demand for paramedics to do the jobs once done by nurses and doctors will explode. One reason is the tools that medicine will have to diagnose what's wrong with people. These tools will eliminate the jobs of doctors at the same time they create jobs for paramedics. The increase in population and in the numbers of elderly people can only accelerate the demand for paramedics, whose numbers we think will increase by 1.3 million by 1990 and whose salaries will reach $29,000 a year by midcareer. Another explosive medical field will be that of the geriatric social technician, who will be essential to the mental and social care of the nation's aging. We forecast a need for one million workers, starting out at $16,000 a year, by 1990. Finally, we think that a distinctive job of the future will be a job we'll call bionic technician. These people won't be bionic themselves; they'll range from mechanics who make the bionic arms, legs, hands, and feet of the future to those who are involved in letting the blind see and the deaf hear with new bionic instruments. We think there will be at least 200,000 new jobs for bionic technicians in the next 10 years. They'll be paid well— $32,000 a year after a few years' experience.

17   It's coming, all of it. Robots are coming that will eliminate jobs and create jobs in the factories, and computers are coming that will do the same things in the office. The U.S. Department of Labor now identifies 28,000 job titles in the American economy, many of them either obsolete or on their way to obsolescence (e.g., tea taster, linotype operator). By the time the Labor Department gets around to revising its list (it changes it every 10 years), most of the jobs on the list will have changed. That is one of the prices we pay to keep up with technological change....

18   Artists who can create something original will be more richly rewarded than they are today. So will entertainers and professional athletes, who will be made America's richest people by cable television in the years ahead. Imagine the way cable television will bid to broadcast professional baseball's playoff and World Series games. The cable will offer baseball at $1 per seat for each first-round playoff game, $2.50 for each second-round game, and $5.00 for each World Series game. Assuming 35 million cable television sets and seven World Series games, that comes to a potential gross for the World Series alone of more than $1 billion. Now, imagine what the players will ask for as their rightful share of those receipts. If you want to grow up to be rich, be a baseball player.

. . .

Solar Technicians in the Sun Belt

19   Some well-known trades and some brand new trades will flourish in the coming years. Among the old trades whose futures are bright are opportunities for what we might call operating engineers: people who can run cranes and bulldozers; automobile mechanics; heating, cooling, and refrigeration mechanics; and appliance servicemen. The most promising new trades are in the energy fields. Solar technicians in the Sun Belt, for instance. Energy conservation technicians in the Northeast. Reagan's deregulation of oil and natural gas will surely be followed by stepped-up drilling for both, so it's not hard to predict that there will be a rising demand for oil-field technicians of every stripe. These jobs involve long hours and hard work but the compensations are enormous. Oil-field workers often earn as much as $60,000 a year. Drilling for oil and gas at sea will trigger a new demand for an unusual job, that of professional diver. The

risks of jobs like divers have come way down in the past 10 years. There is little risk at all to the divers staffing professional diving companies, most of which are located in Houston and New Orleans. Remember, jobs are concentrated in locations. You can't expect to graduate from a technical school in your hometown and right away find work as an aircraft mechanic if your hometown is in Maine and you don't live near an airport. For example, jobs in the electronics industry are mostly in California, Arizona, Massachusetts, Texas, and New York. If you want to work in electronics, move to those states and you'll have a better chance.

20   We'll forecast three new jobs for the future that the Bureau of Labor Statistics leaves out. One of these jobs we'll call housing rehabilitation technician, a catchall word for somebody who's expert at making a new house out of an old house or making a new house out of brand new materials. World population will double in the next 35 years, and that will intensify demand for housing so strongly that we think as many as 1.75 million new housing technicians will be needed by 1990. Our second new job is holographic specialist, a cousin of the robot technician, who will work in the robotized factory of the future specializing in servicing the optical computers that compare the inputs they're getting from the factory floors to the three-dimensional holographic data stored in other computers. We forecast a demand for 200,000 holographic specialists by 1990. Finally, there is the battery technician, the person who will service the next generation of fuel cells and batteries that will be used to power the cars and homes of the future. We think the demand for battery technicians will be 250,000 by 1990. In short, we do not believe there will be a shortage of jobs in the next 20 years. Only a shortage of creative, imaginative people to fill them.

21   All the future jobs we've mentioned so far are jobs we are predicting for the next 20 years. Are there other occupations that might take off out to the end of the century?

Let's speculate for just a moment. Restaurant chefs could be in enormous demand, due to the increase in leisure time and the dual careers of husbands and wives. The rapid increase in the quality and quantity of frozen foods will cause a demand for more chefs and nutritionists by food packaging companies. There may be more city managers because there will be more satellite cities in need of them. The boom in leisure time will create vast numbers of new jobs for hotel managers and for public relations and advertising specialists, whose job it will be to promote new uses for leisure time. Rental assistants will proliferate because people will want help in finding vacation spots and summer rentals as well as homes. The same will hold true with dieticians, who will be consulted frequently as people become more conscious of their appearances. Geriatric food consultants will also be in demand, as well as licensed practical nurses for the elderly. The number of pharmacists will double in the next 20 years. After all, if the people of the future are going to live longer, they will need their corner druggists more than ever.

22   Does this article sound futuristic? Maybe, but 10 years ago, did we have any idea what a solar engineer did for a living? The impact of new discoveries and new technology is here now and much more is on the horizon. Accelerated change in these and other technologies will open up whole new arrays of occupations and careers. Indeed, Clyde Helms, president of Occupational Forecasting (Arlington, Virginia), has a whole firm that does nothing but forecast and train individuals for new occupations. These forecast occupations aren't limited to our children. If you have found yourself thinking of a career change, interesting possibilities are already here! Extensive updating of our current training and educational programs will be required to meet the demands of these new occupations, and educators of the future had better start making plans now for what's coming next.

| EXERCISE |

Before writing a summary of this article, answer the following questions. You will use the answers as the basis of your summary.

1. What is the thesis of the article? At what point does the thesis first appear?

2. What subject are the authors discussing in paragraph 6 when they tell us about the Hong Kong, Thai, and Egyptian shirtmakers?

3. At the turn of the twentieth century, about a third of all American workers earned their living through agriculture. To what areas has work shifted since that time—during and after World War II?

4. Make up a chart indicating the main occupations discussed by Cetron and O'Toole. Include columns that show (1) how many workers the authors expect will be employed in each occupation by the end of the century and (2) what kind of starting and mid-career salaries these occupations will command. (The article does not provide enough information for you to fill in all areas of the chart.)

5. Why do the authors see such a bright future for laser technicians?

6. Which three separate occupations are covered in paragraph 16, in which the authors discuss the paramedic field?

7. Why will professional athletes make even more money than they do now?

8. Why will relocation be necessary for many who enter the job market?

9. What three occupations are discussed in paragraph 20?

10. Which service occupations, discussed in paragraph 21, will see great expansion by the end of the century?

11. In their conclusion, the authors see a need for what kind of new programs?

Structure

Following is an outline of Cetron and O'Toole's article.

I. The changing job market
  A. Introduction: Shifts in employment patterns (¶1–2)
  B. Typical jobs of the future (¶3–5)
  C. Unemployment (¶4–7)
  D. Shift from agricultural to industrial to service economy (¶8)
II. New careers
  A. Robot technicians (¶9–10)
  B. Computer programmers (¶11)
  C. Laser technicians (¶12)
  D. Energy and hazardous waste technicians (¶13–14)
  E. The gene machine (¶15)
  F. Paramedics (¶16)
  G. Summary: The changing job market (¶17)
  H. New opportunities for artists, entertainers, athletes (¶18)
  I. Flourishing well-known trades (¶19)

J. Flourishing new trades (¶20)
K. Opportunities in other traditional areas (¶21)
III. Conclusion: Possibilities and requirements (¶22)

| **EXERCISE** | |

Write a summary of Cetron and O'Toole's article, using your answers to the questions in the first exercise. Also use the summary of "Bright Job Prospects in 1980s and 1990s" as a model.

Third Source

Here is the third source on career prospects in the 1990s, "How to Forecast Your Own Working Future." Read it carefully, taking notes, and then answer the questions that follow.

James O'Toole

HOW TO FORECAST YOUR OWN WORKING FUTURE

1   Let's suppose you are a typical, 21-year old college senior, womb-weary after 32 semesters of formal schooling and institutional mollycoddling. You are about to cut the umbilical cord to family and school and make your own way in the terrifying jungle of mortgages, car payments, taxes, utility bills, and, alas, work. Work, the necessity of adult life that provides the wherewithal for tape decks, Perrier, designer jeans, and the little luxuries as well.

2   Here's what a labor economist might say about your prospects: Look forward to a job as a bank teller or secretary at a much lower salary than that earned by the pimply-faced kid who dropped out of your high school class and became a plumber. Because of unfortunate demographic realities, don't count on much upward mobility, or to retiring with a nice nest egg. You'll slave away in a lousy job until the day they plant you.

But you don't like that scenario. You feel 3 it is your God-given right to find an economist who'll tell you what you want to hear. But economists are all so depressing these days. So you turn to your local, franchised futurist who, for a modest consulting fee, offers the following forecast: You'll have many exciting jobs in the course of your life, punctuated intermittently with educational stop-outs during which you'll be retooled for entirely different careers. You'll work flexitime, flexiweek, flexiyear, flexicareer — most of the time at home, interacting with the computer terminal linking you to offices flung far around the globe. Since robots will do all the grunt work, there'll be abundant leisure and affluence for everybody. When the time comes, you won't want to retire because your latest part-time job is the most fulfilling and self-actualizing yet.

Bad Track Records

4   Who should you believe, the labor economists or the futurists? Probably not the former because no one — not horserace touts, Federal Energy Department planners, Chrysler executives, or the Hunt brothers — has a worse forecasting record than labor economists. Labor economists are the folks who were still predicting teacher shortages in the late 1960s, even while demographic trends clearly foreshadowed the impending "baby bust" and empty classrooms.

5   In general, the economists' forecasts of labor supply and demand, career opportunities, emerging professions, and future working conditions have a fantastical air. So should we trust the futurists? Although most futurists have been spared the mind-addling effects of a traditional economic education, most members of this breed, too, have pathetic track records when it comes to workplace forecasts. Recall Alvin Toffler's prediction (in *Future Shock*) of workplace "ad-hocracy" — "a new freeform world of kinetic organizations" — following the demise of traditional, regimented, bureaucratized organizations. Thus far, he's been one of the few to find gainful employment in that abstract environment.

6   Why are the experts so often wrong in their forecasts about work? Having tracked the forecasts of both economists and futurists with decreasing amusement over the last dozen years, it seems to me that almost all of their prognostications contain one of two mistakes.

7   Error Number One: Most labor economists assume that the future is going to be a simple extrapolation of current trends. For example, the U.S. Bureau of Labor Statistics (BLS) forecasts in the 1970s were predicated on the following assumptions: high levels of employment; adequate energy availability; softening of the inflationary spiral; continuation of the pace and nature of technological change; peace; and no significant change in defense spending. In short, they saw a continuation of the general economic and political trends of the last two decades. But

experience teaches us little else than that the future is always full of surprises. It is no wonder, then, that when we review the past forecasts of labor economists in light of what actually occurred, their forecasts are found not only to be wrong, but embarrassingly and consistently so.

8   Error Number Two: Most futurists are wont to base their forecasts on a singular view of what will transpire, not an array of alternatives, because that would never sell. Here we have Alvin Toffler's "third wave," in which new values and new technology produce work choices galore; Marilyn Ferguson's "Aquarian Conspiracy," in which radical chic becomes *de rigueur* and everyone experiences simultaneous, multiple self-actualization at work; Willis Harman's "voluntary simplicity," in which we all find job satisfaction in small but beautiful settings; Herman Kahn's brave new industrial world, in which American manufacturers ape the Japanese and produce affluence untold; and Robert Heilbroner's "human prospect" of dog-eat-dog fighting over the shrinking spoils of an economy gone rotten in the teeth.

9   Who's correct? Your guess is as good as theirs. After all, each of these alternatives — and several more I could just as easily have cited — is *possible*. What is *probable* is that no single vision represents a future that is certain enough for you to bank on while doing your own career planning. In fact, there is no single future. There are only many alternative futures, each with unique consequences for the workplace.

10   The future that comes will depend on the myriad actions taken by private citizens (acting as consumers, voters, and participants in the labor market), business managers, public officials, foreign competitors, Middle East oil potentates, and about half a zillion other players in the game of contemporary world history. This makes the forecasting of working conditions, unemployment rates, career opportunities, and other aspects of the future of work rather difficult, to say the least.

11   On the one hand, we don't want to be like those labor economists who predict a

future that will flow inevitably out of the past and present—because ayatollahs, entrepreneurs, and mad scientists are sure to make fools of us if we do. On the other hand, we don't want to be like those over-exuberant futurists who predict one future out of many possibilities—the one that they *want* to happen. That approach naively compresses the contingencies and complexities of life into a simplistic vision that makes great theater, but lousy raw material for national, corporate, or personal career planning.

An Exercise Program

12   Frustrated? Don't be, for there are at least two exercises on the future of work that you can undertake responsibly and usefully. For starters, you could identify a broad range of possible futures, cluster them for purposes of analysis around some logical principle, and then ask yourself what conditions could lead to these various alternatives. My colleague Kenneth Brousseau and I did just that to create four scenarios of the small industrial workplace, circa 1995.

13   Workplace A is a meritocracy in which rewards go to those hard-working employees who are most successful in climbing the corporate hierarchy. President Reagan would approve of this model. Workplace B represents the psychological school of behaviorism as espoused by the Harvard emeritus psychologist, B. F. Skinner. Here employee behavior is closely regulated and monitored: workers who are efficient and productive are quickly and elaborately rewarded. Workplace C is entitlementarian, characterized by numerous rights (or entitlements) that limit managerial prerogatives and protect employees against virtually every form of insecurity and risk. This view is compatible with Senator Edward Kennedy's political philosophy. Workplace D reflects the humanism of the late E. F. Schumacher. This organization is designed to enhance personal growth and development through employee participation in decision-making.

14   Which scenario is most likely? Let me give you a clue. There are three elements that will determine the future: continuity, change, and choice.

Continuity

The future is always influenced by the   15 past and present. Thus, the seeds of the future of work are sprouting in today's workplaces. Indeed, if one looks closely, one can find aspects of all four 1995 workplaces in operation today in one American company or another. This might be an important hint about the future: If pluralism is the mode of work in America, can we think of any plausible reason to assume that this diversity would be lost in the future, abandoned in favor of a monolithic workplace paradigm? In fact, were we to trace the trend, we would find that American workplaces are even more varied in the conditions of work they offer than they were 20 years ago.

Nonetheless, just because a trend has   16 been going in one direction for a long time is no guarantee that it will continue indefinitely in the same direction. (That is, after all, the error made regularly in economic forecasts.) To understand deviations from continuity we must understand the process of change.

Change

The future is always influenced by unexpected events—those developments that break the continuity of history. In the workplace, the Depression broke the long trend of laissez-faire and led to the introduction of government programs designed to increase employee security. In the late 1960s, the youth, environmental, and anti-war movements paved the way for the minor inroads made recently by humanism in some American corporations.

What could happen in the 1980s to drastically alter current trends? Would a severe energy crisis foster the need for efficiency-minded behaviorism in order to save our standard of living? Would a decade of stagflation lead to a return to 1930s-type unionism and entitlementarianism?

Economic, technological, and political   19 change will no doubt lead to readjustments in the world of work, but how far can we expect these changes to go? To understand the effects of change on historical patterns we must understand the process of choice.

Choice

20   The future is always influenced by the choices that people make when confronted with a new development. Managers often respond to a recession by substituting machines for workers in the hope of increasing efficiency. Politicians respond to recessions by creating public service jobs or using macroeconomic policy to stimulate the economy. Individual workers might respond to changing environmental conditions by choosing one job over another, choosing to invest or to spend, or choosing to return to school for further training. Importantly, such choices cannot be predicted solely on the basis of a "rational" response to technological, economic, and other environmental events. What people *want* — their values — is an important determinant of their future actions.

Toward a Pluralistic Future

21   Based on historical behavior, futurists seem wrong to assume that most workers can, will, or would want to throw out the old and ring in the new. People resist change, and sometimes with good reason. For example, many futurists and economists predict that American workers will substitute the convenience of a computer terminal in their homes for the long, increasingly expensive commute to work. Rationally, that is what they should do (if we limit rationality to the logic of economics). But workers have other values besides economics and convenience. For most adults, almost all friendships are formed at work. We're only able to drag ourselves out of bed and into the plant or office each morning because we look forward to shooting the breeze with our workmates.

22   In the final analysis, workers will decide whether the continuity of commuting to central workplaces or the change of decentral-

ized working in homes will prevail in the future. It seems reasonable to conclude that some will choose the convenience of working at home, some will choose the pleasures of socializing with co-workers, and some will mix the two. What any one individual will choose will depend on his or her age, family responsibilities, experiences, personal values, and the nature of the job to be done.

23   Choice — what people want — is thus a central determinant of the future of work. For what it is worth, our research shows that trade unionists want entitlementarianism, corporate executives want meritocracy, and intellectuals and students want humanism (behaviorism is the popular favorite only in the Harvard Psychology Department). Again, this points toward a pluralistic future of work and away from the monolithic forecasts of the popularizing futurists.

24   Still frustrated by the blurred image in the crystal ball? There is only one way to clear it up: Make your own forecasts. Write your own scenarios, taking continuity, change, and choice into account, and see which one (or ones) seems most likely. If you are ambitious, you might even try a second exercise. Begin by identifying the elements of continuity and change that you believe will influence the work world of the future; then analyze how you think these factors will interact with the choices of key players, and you'll have a forecast you can trust more than anything any expert could dream up.

...

Your Personal Work Future

25   As you analyze your forecast of the future of work, be careful not to assume that this will *determine* your own career changes. Clearly, the general environment will *influence* the options available to you but, even in bad times, individuals have a greater opportunity to create their own futures than career counselors, labor economists, and other experts would have you believe.

26   In addition to the general opportunities available, there are two other key factors in your own work future: What you want to do, and what you are good at (including what you are qualified by education or training to do in careers where this is a prerequisite). That is, even if you want a job as seemingly difficult to obtain as that of a blacksmith, you *can* get it if you are willing to go where there are horses. It helps if you are good at it, but even this may not be an absolute constraint if you are willing to work at it or to apprentice yourself to a qualified blacksmith (or bookbinder, plumber, radio announcer, etc.)

27   The BLS might tell you that the odds against getting a job in journalism are a million to one. But if you are willing to devote yourself single-mindedly to getting such a job, and if you have some objective evidence that you have a smidgen of writing talent, the odds simply don't apply to you because official odds don't take the factors of desire and ability into account.

28   Remember: for any given job, most people don't want it, most don't have the talent for it, and even fewer are willing to make an effort to obtain it. Thus, if you have ambition and talent the odds are almost always in your favor for any career. With the exception of most professional organizations, few employers will turn down an applicant who persistently and convincingly says, "This is the job I want; I'm willing to work for it, even if I have to start at the bottom and work up."

29   The secret of forecasting your personal work future, then, consists not so much in analyzing the opportunities in the general environment, but in deciding what you want to be when you grow up. And that can be a lot harder than learning to adjust the vertical hold on a crystal ball.

Content and Structure

An outline of this article will provide a clear idea of how it has been put together.

I. Introduction: What are your prospects? (¶1)
   A. What the gloomy economists predict (¶2)
   B. What the optimistic futurists predict (¶3)
   C. Bad track record of economists (¶4)
   D. Bad track record of futurists (¶5)
II. Why the experts are wrong (¶6)
   A. Error number 1 (economists) (¶7)
   B. Error number 2 (futurists) (¶8–9)
   C. Why accurate forecasting is difficult (¶10)
   D. Summary: Don't predict the way economists and futurists do (¶11)
III. Four possible scenarios for the future (¶12)
   A. Workplaces A, B, C, and D (¶13)
   B. Factors on which these workplaces depend (¶14)
      1. Continuity (¶15–16)
      2. Change (¶17–19)
      3. Choice (¶20–23)
   C. Your own scenario (¶24)
IV. Your personal work future
   A. Continuity, change, and choice influence but do not determine your own personal work future (¶25)

B. What counts: what you want to do; what you are good at (¶26–28)

C. Conclusion: You are in control of your own future (¶29)

```
┌──────────────┬──────────────────────────────────────────────────┐
│  EXERCISE    │                                                  │
└──────────────┴──────────────────────────────────────────────────┘
```

Write a summary of the article based on the preceding outline and on your own notes.

Writing the Paper

Now that you've read three sources on the subject career prospects for the 1990s, you can begin developing a thesis.

Using Description in Papers

In this chapter and in Chapter 8 we focus on *description*. A description is a re-creation, in words, of some object, person, place, emotion, sensation, or state of affairs—such as the prospective job market. This re-creation is accomplished when the writer divides a subject into its component parts and then offers a detailed account of those parts, presenting them to the reader in some clear and orderly fashion. As a reporter, your job might be to describe an event—when, where, and how it took place. As a scientist, you would observe the conditions of an experiment and record them for review by others. As a student writer and future job-seeker, you would consider the various aspects of the career situation as it will exist in the foreseeable future and provide an account of these aspects for your own and others' benefit.

Your job in writing a description paper is not to argue a particular viewpoint but rather to present the facts in a reasonably objective manner. Of course, description papers, like other academic papers, should be based on a thesis. But the purpose of a thesis of a descriptive paper (e.g., "Ireland is a beautiful place to visit") is less to advance a particular opinion or point of view than to provide focus and direction to the various facts contained within that paper.

Limiting the Subject

Let's review the process of generating a thesis from a subject. In Chapter 4 we suggested that you ask yourself a series of questions to limit the subject to a topic and then make an assertion about the topic to generate a thesis. These were the main questions:

Who?

What aspects?

Where?

When?

How?

In selecting the subject matter of this chapter, we have already done some of the limiting. We began with the subject of careers. But this was too broad. One way of limiting the subject to make it more interesting to people who are about to begin careers during the next ten years was to ask *When?* One answer was career prospects in the 1990s.

To further limit this subject to a topic, we can ask the question *What aspects* of career prospects in the 1990s? Any number of topics are possible, but let's take one as an example: planning your work future.

This topic may still be too broad for a relatively short paper, particularly when it is based on such a limited number of sources. So let's ask another question: *Where?* And for the sake of example, we'll select one of the many possible responses: planning for your work future in a changing world.

Thesis

To generate a thesis we must make an assertion about the topic. The kind of assertion you can make—and back up with evidence—depends on what you already know about the subject (which depends to some extent on how much you have read about it) and what you think about the subject. If you are having trouble making an assertion, try writing down your topic at the top of a page and then listing everything you know and feel about it. Often from such a list you will discover an assertion that you can then use to fashion a working thesis.

Let's make three assertions about our topic—assertions that our reading leads us to believe we can back up:

1. When planning your work future, it is important to keep in mind that the world of work is rapidly changing.
2. When planning your work future, keep in mind that although high-tech careers are booming, it is still possible to succeed in more traditional fields.
3. When planning your future, consider that you may devote your working life to a career that does not even exist yet.

Notice that none of these theses is highly argumentative. It is difficult to imagine anyone disagreeing with any of them. As we've suggested, the purpose of such theses—of any thesis for a descriptive paper—is less to persuade the reader to your own point of view than to give focus and unity to your discussion.

The Working Outline

Having selected one of the theses, your next step is to develop a working outline. We sketch outlines for papers using the first two theses. We've indicated next to each topic and subtopic the paragraph(s) from each source where evidence may be found. (Abbreviations: P, Poinsett, "Bright Job Prospects for 1980s and 1990s"; C/O, Cetron and O'Toole, "Careers with a Future"; O, O'Toole, "How to Forecast Your Own Working Future.")

> Thesis 1: When planning your work future, it is important to keep in mind that the world of work is rapidly changing.

I. Shifts in work patterns
   A. The shift from a goods-oriented to a service-oriented economy (P, ¶9; C/O, ¶8)
   B. A variety of possible workplaces (0, ¶13)
II. More workers needed for traditional jobs
   A. Jobs in broad areas: clerical, professional, management, sales, blue collar, service (P, ¶13–19)
   B. Jobs in specific areas: paramedics, geriatric social workers, oil field workers, chefs, city managers, pharmacists (O, ¶16, 19, 21)
III. Workers needed for new jobs
   A. Computer programmers (P, ¶14)
   B. Other jobs: robot technicians, laser technicians, etc. (C/O, ¶9–22)
IV. The career planning process
   A. Decide what you want to do (P, ¶4–10; O, ¶26–29)
   B. Plan to educate and train yourself for your chosen career (P, ¶11–12; O, ¶29)

> Thesis 2: When planning your work future, keep in mind that although high-tech careers are booming, it is still possible to succeed in more traditional fields.

I. The changing world of work
   A. The shift from a goods-oriented to a service-oriented economy (P, ¶9; C/O, ¶8)
   B. A variety of possible workplaces (0, ¶13)
II. High-tech opportunities
   A. Opportunities in broad areas (P, ¶14–15)
   B. Opportunities in specific fields (C/O, ¶9–15, 19–21)
III. Opportunities in traditional fields
   A. Unreliability of futurists' predictions (O, ¶5–8)
   B. Continued importance of traditional careers (P, ¶13–19; C/O, ¶21)
   C. Continuity (O, ¶15)
   D. Control of your own destiny (O, ¶25–29)

A paper based on thesis 3 ("When planning your future, consider that you may devote your working life to a career that does not even exist yet") would use much of the same material in sections I and II of the preceding outline; but of course it would not focus on the traditional fields covered in section III.

EXERCISE

At this point you are ready to write a paper on the topic career prospects for the 1990s. You have two options: (1) Write a paper that uses any of the theses discussed above. (2) Develop your own thesis by making a different assertion about the limited subject. Based on this new thesis, prepare an outline, have it approved by your instructor, and then write a paper.

Additional Readings

You may wish to develop a paper that is based on a wider selection of sources than the three you have read. If so, here is some additional material on this subject. Questions following the selections will help focus your attention on important points.

Tom Nicholson

GROWTH INDUSTRIES OF THE FUTURE

1   Ten years ago the automobile was still the main source of jobs in the American economy. Detroit's automakers and their satellites—the steel, glass, rubber and aluminum industries, railroads and car dealers on Main Street—employed one in every five American workers. But with that industry now in its worst slump since the Great Depression, there are nearly 1 million unemployed workers in what is known as the "auto cluster"— and even if the industry comes roaring back, automation will make most of their old jobs obsolete.

2   So where will they and others entering the labor force find work in the years ahead? There is no real answer; the computer might replace the auto as the symbolic soul of the economy, but the future is far more complex and unpredictable than that. Government manpower economists predict a massive increase in the number of computer programmers, for instance, but some independent experts warn that to plan for that would be foolish and wrong. The reason? "New generations of computers will be directly accessible to their users," says Marvin Cetron, president of Forecasting International, Ltd. "You won't need programmers in between."

Cetron also believes the government has greatly underestimated the impact—on job destruction as well as job creation—of robotics, biotechnology and lasers.

3   There is also disagreement over the future of more traditional jobs. Elementary-school teaching, for example, may make a comeback by the mid-1980s if in fact a new baby boom is under way. The National Education Association predicts that a significant number of new teaching jobs will open up starting with the 1983–84 school year. On the other hand, labor economists such as Audrey Freedman of the Conference Board warn that the old baby-boom group "just isn't having the large number of kids you might expect"—and that fewer teachers will be needed. The Reagan administration expects to see a substantial rise in employment in the defense industry, but there, too, the growth may not be as impressive as predicted. For the time being, aerospace plants in California are retooling; even when they start to hire, however, the jobs won't be forever. Rockwell's B-1B production, for example, is expected to peak in two and a half years with a total of 20,500 workers. Many of them could be back job hunting

by 1989. Increased employment in military aerospace programs may also be offset as major defense contractors like Lockheed and McDonnell Douglas lay off workers in their commercial-airliner businesses due to the current glut of wide bodies.

4   There is also a great deal of argument among experts about what the technology explosion will bring in the way of new occupations. "There are jobs out there that no one has ever heard of," says W. Clyde Helms Jr., president of Occupational Forecasting, Inc., and a pioneer in the field. "The whole complex of notions about our occupational infrastructure is obsolete. Everyone knows what a 'sunrise' industry is. But what are the new sunrise occupations? We're only beginning to identify them. And until we do we can't train for them, or even advertise for them."

5   While they find it difficult to get too specific, most government and private-indus-try experts do agree that the biggest future job growth will come in two general areas: information, and what is commonly termed "conservation." Information will include computers, robotics, biotechnology and transmission technologies such as laser and fiber optics. Conservation will include both the human and ecological kinds, from health care to already established conservation efforts such as solar energy, more efficient use of raw materials and waste disposal. The Labor Department's list of the fastest-growing job titles (see table) is illustrative of those trends. Of the top 12 occupations, five are in information or information-related fields: computer-service technicians, systems analysts, business-machine repairmen and computer programmers and operators. With Americans living longer and increasingly concerned with good health, experts anticipate tremendous growth in such fields as occupational and physical therapy and speech

THE SHIFTING JOB MARKET

Jobs in the smokestack industries will continue to decline, but there will be new opportunities in service and high-tech sectors.

SOME JOBS ARE GOING...		OTHERS ARE GROWING...		BUT THE FUTURE IS HERE.	
Occupation	Percent decline in employment	Occupation	Percent growth in employment	Occupation	Estimated employment by 1990
Shoemaking-machine operators	−19.2	Data-processing-machine mechanics	+157.1	Industrial-robot production	800,000
Farm laborers	19.0	Paralegal personnel	143.0	Geriatric social work	700,000
Railroad-car repairers	17.9	Computer-systems analysts	112.4	Energy technicians	650,000
Farm managers	17.7	Computer operators	91.7	Industrial-laser processing	600,000
Graduate assistants	16.7	Office-machine services	86.7	Housing rehabilitation	500,000
Housekeepers, private household	14.9	Tax preparers	77.9	Handling new synthetic materials	400,000
Child-care workers, private household	14.8	Computer programmers	77.2	On-line emergency medical	400,000
Maids and servants, private household	14.7	Aero-astronautic engineers	74.8	Hazardous-waste management	300,000
Farm supervisors	14.3	Employment interviewers	72.0	Genetic engineering	250,000
Farmers, owners and tenants	13.7	Fast-food restaurant workers	69.4	Bionic medical electronics	200,000
Timber-cutting and logging workers	13.6	Child-care attendants	66.5	Laser, holographic and optical-fiber maintenance	200,000
Secondary-school teachers	13.1	Veterinarians	66.1		

Sources: Bureau of Labor Statistics, Forecasting International, Ltd., Occupational Forecasting, Inc.

pathology, as well as medical and dental programs administered by nurses and technicians rather than doctors.

6   There also will be rapid growth in occupations that barely exist today. Genetic-engineering technicians and bionic-medicine specialists are expected to account for 450,000 jobs by 1990, while the number of laser-process and robot-production technicians may reach more than 1 million. But college students preparing for more "conventional" careers still have reason to hope. Several professions will continue to be a source for jobs in the 1980s: petroleum engineering, medicine, law, banking. Honorable professions all—but suddenly sounding a bit old-fashioned when compared with many of the new skills that will be needed to manage and service an extraordinary new technological age.

EXERCISE

Content

Recall the main ideas in this article by answering the following questions. Respond to some of the questions in your own words. Respond to others by finding quotations from the article that provide the answers.

1. Why might the field of computer programming not enjoy the boom that so many people have been predicting for it?

2. What factors help account for the uncertain employment prospects in aerospace programs?

3. Which two career areas will enjoy the biggest job growth? Cite examples of occupations in each area.

Structure

1. What is the purpose of paragraph 1?

2. Explain how paragraphs 3 and 4, considered together, form an identifiable section of the article. Give this identifiable section a title.

Fact/Opinion

Classify each of the following statements as either a fact, an opinion, or a fact wrapped in an opinion. If the statement is a combination of fact and opinion, identify which part is fact and which opinion.

1. "Ten years ago the automobile was still the main source of jobs in the American economy."

2. "There will also be rapid growth in occupations that barely exist today."

3. "Honorable professions all—but suddenly sounding a bit old-fashioned when compared with many of the new skills that will be needed to manage and service an extraordinary new technological age."

Inferences

In your responses to the following questions, incorporate some of the quotations you located in response to the Content questions. You may decide to use either all or only part of each quotation.

1. What kind of jobs will be plentiful in the near future that will most appeal to those who want to work in the helping professions?

2. What kind of job prospects would you face if you decided to go into the same line of work as one or both of your parents?

TEN BEST CAREERS FOR BLACK MEN

Ebony has chosen ten "best" careers for Black men who want to take on some of the many challenges of the '80s. The choices were made based on novelty, present and projected demand as seen by the Bureau of Labor Statistics, projected expansion of the discipline and practicality.

Physician Assistants

1   The title is deceiving, since many of these professionals are authorized to administer medical care and prescribe treatment. Physician assistants came into being in the '60s, when medically trained corpsmen in Vietnam were asked to contribute during a physician shortage. Most physician assistants worked in health care before completing a two-year curriculum of biological sciences. About 40 percent practice in medical centers in counties with populations under 50,000. Labor experts hesitate to predict demand, but the increase of physician assistants from 100 in 1970 to 9,500 in 1980 suggests a real need.

Laser Process Technicians

2   There will be great demand here. More and more, technically trained persons are needed to operate the laser equipment that is fast replacing machine and foundry tools. Interested workers should have a solid technical foundation and a willingness to be re-trained. Salaries start at about $15,000; the average salary is $25,000.

Systems Analysts

3   Opportunities will be great for these workers, who must find more efficient ways of processing data for businesses. While there is no standard avenue of entry, employers favor those who are familiar with programming languages. A degree or training in computer science, accounting, information systems, information science or data processing is recommended. Almost half of the systems analysts have transferred from other occupations, and many of them were promoted from computer programmer. Beginning systems analysts earned about $330 a week in 1980, while experienced ones earned from $390 to $460 a week.

Hotel Managers and Assistants

4   As hotels and motels spring up and chain and franchise operations spread, more management personnel are needed to ensure that the many phases of the business work efficiently. General managers of these operations need middle management workers who can oversee certain phases of the business, such as accounting, security, food service, housekeeping and maintenance. Over 80 colleges and universities offer four-year degree programs in hotel and res-

taurant administration. General managers earned between $20,000 and $80,000 a year in 1981. It is not uncommon for a department head or other middle management worker to earn $50,000 a year.

Engineers

5   The supply of professionals needed to steer us through a sophisticated technical world still lags dreadfully behind the demand. Any well-prepared engineer, regardless of discipline, should find opportunities virtually knocking at his or her door. Demand is equally great in the major engineering disciplines—petroleum, chemical, civil, aeronautical, electrical, metallurgical, mechanical, industrial and mining. Petroleum engineers are the highest paid on average, with starting salaries of $24,000 in 1980. A strong background in mathematics and science before college makes the curricula less rigorous.

Accountants

6   The typical major for today's college student is accounting—justifiably. Expanding businesses and government agencies need people who can handle the financial records and help make business decisions. Accountants can specialize in auditing, taxation, budgeting, costs or investments. Their earnings ranged from $18,400 to $31,900 in 1980. Experienced specialists, such as certified public accountants, earn much more.

Technical Writers

7   While specialists produce and operate technical devices, someone has to turn their professional jargon into clear, readable language for the lay person who must know how to use the devices. Technical writers have this responsibility, in addition to preparing reports on research, writing instructional materials and preparing proposals. They are often employed by firms in the electronics, energy, aircraft, chemical,

and computer manufacturing industries. Good writing skills should be combined with some knowledge of a scientific or technical field. About ten colleges and universities offer a technical writing curriculum. Starting salaries in 1980 averaged about $15,000 annually; some experienced writers earned as much as $31,000 annually.

Occupational Therapists

People who are mentally, physically or   8 emotionally disabled need occupational therapists to facilitate their activities. These therapists usually work with specific types of disability groups, and may supervise student therapists and volunteers. Opportunities for occupational therapists are expected to be quite favorable, due chiefly to continued support for various rehabilitation programs. A bachelor's degree is required, and 15 states require a license.

Bank Officers/Managers

Many careers are available for persons   9 who specialize in banking services. Loan officers, trust officers, operations officers, data processing managers, customer service representatives and correspondents are all important cogs in the banking business. More of them will be needed as the industry calls for improved quality control in the computer age. Business will also be stimulated by international trade and investment. A business administration major, or a concentration in accounting, economics or commercial law is appropriate; a master of business administration degree is ideal. Salaries for officer trainees are quite competitive. Salaries of M.B.A. holders rival those of engineers.

Robot Production Technicians

Many people will be replaced by robots   10 as the microprocessor industry becomes the third largest industry in the United States by 2000. Robots will not, however, be able to keep their own operations in line. New workers with the skills of computer programmers and electronics technicians will be needed to ensure that the robots' exacting applications remain just that. These workers can start at $15,000 a year, and the average is about $24,000.

Anita Gates

FAST-TRACK JOBS

1   The trouble with many of today's most promising careers (the ones that are expected to increase by the thousands between now and 1995 or so) is that you probably wouldn't wish them on your worst enemy.

2   The news that there will be 1.2 million jobs for auto mechanics, 2.3 million positions for cashiers and a 94-percent increase in the number of jobs for legal assistants does not thrill the average American college graduate. Nowadays, most young women want more than a mundane job that just helps to pay the rent and the grocery bills. They want a career in a field where there's plenty of money and glamour—and a chance to go straight to the top.

3   Luckily, growth and glamour do exist side by side in a few careers. It's even possible to combine big money and a work style that's slightly less demanding than the presidency.

4   Where and how do you get in on these impossible dream jobs? The really smart career planner today doesn't let herself get stuck in a field that's going nowhere by choosing a particular occupation first. Instead, she takes a look at the overall fastest-growing industries, and then finds her niche within one. Here are a few possibilities to consider.

Health Care

5   Taking care of the sick and the old is a big business today. And, as our population continues to gray (even some baby boomers will be in their fifties by 1999!), it's going to get even bigger. Going into health care doesn't have to mean becoming a doctor or nurse, though. Hospitals and clinics are businesses, and they need every kind of specialist—from secretaries to programmers.

Bionics Engineer

6   *"The Six Million Dollar Man"* may have been fiction when it was first broadcast on TV in 1973, but bionics is a real and growing field. Ask the man who designed the first artificial heart or the teams working to create "biochip" organs. The job title they hold is biomedical engineer, and it usually calls for a master's degree in biomedical engineering—not medical school. Average income: $37,000.

Hospital Administrator

7   Somebody has to run the hospital, allotting budgets to pay for test tubes and keeping peace between the nurses and doctors. If you get a master's degree in public or health-services administration, and learn to manage people and money expertly, you could end up earning $85,000 or more as the head of a big-city hospital.

Medical Writer

8   When researchers finally discover a cure for cancer, somebody will have to write up the news. It could be you, a wordsmith who knows medical terminology and the health-care business. Medical brochures and technical articles for scientific journals might be part of your work. Possible employers: hospitals, drug companies, research labs. It's not the same as writing a bestseller, but you'll get a good income ($30,000 average) and great benefits.

Optometrist

9　　Eye doctors simply don't have the same kind of demands on them that other physicians have: No one calls for an emergency eye test at 3 A.M. And patients with serious eye problems are sent to the ophthalmologist. So get your O.D. (four years after college), earn $50,000 a year (much more is possible in private practice) and get used to the prestige, Doctor.

Drug Marketer

10　　There are now at least 100,000 prescription drugs for sale in the United States. But you don't have to be a pharmacist to profit from the boom. An M.B.A. in marketing and some chemistry in your past can get you a product manager's job at one of the big pharmaceutical companies. Your responsibilities may range from coordinating ads and market research to overseeing drug pricing and distribution. Average income: $38,000.

The Computer Industry

11　　Remember the TV ads that urged you to sign up for Bill and Harry's Technical Institute to "join the fast-growing computer industry"? Lots of people rushed in to fill the jobs for programmers and systems analysts, which increased by more than 100 percent. Unfortunately, that added up to about a 500-percent increase in people qualified to do those jobs.

12　　Yes, the computer industry is still expanding faster than you can pull out your floppy disk. But the real winners here will take their computer knowledge into non-programming careers.

Computer Lawyer

13　　In 1983, there were 3,500 computer-related cases in U.S. courts—but only a few universities offered studies in computer law. An attorney who knows her software, though, and who keeps up with laws concerning computer contracts, theft and rights is worth her weight in gold. U.S. lawyers average $52,000, but those in a needy specialty like this could make $100,000 or more.

Service Technician

14　　It's the blue-collar job where you wear a white collar—all dressed for success. The people who service and repair computers earn almost as much ($22,360 median) as the programmers ($23,140). Becoming a technician only takes a year or two of training at a vocational school or junior college. And some earn as much as $34,000 or more.

Computer Salesperson

15　　Take computer-science courses to know your product, keep up with changing technology, and then offer your sales ability to the best computer manufacturer you know. With base pay and commission, the average computer-sales representative with only two or three years experience earns $35,000 per year. Top salespeople across the country take in $100,000 to $300,000 or more. Probable bonus: a company car.

Information Systems Manager (MIS)

16　　The woman who has computer knowledge *and* top-notch people-management skills can rise to the industry's most prestigious jobs. Get a business, computer science or information-systems degree. Start as a systems analyst ($20,000–$25,000 average; $50,000–$60,000 for the top 10 percent). Then move up the corporate ladder, taking on responsibility for the design, development and implementation of projects. Top MIS people average $25,000–30,000 in the education sector to $45,000 at public utility companies.

Software Developer

17　　Inventing the next superstar program is a lot like writing a novel. You come up with an idea for new software and submit it to a video "publisher." If they like it, they'll market it for you. First step: learn programming. Then concentrate on a specialty, be it word processing, spreadsheets or games. Your income is mostly from royalties (2) to 25 percent of the wholesale price of each program sold).

Travel

18   The travel industry has never been healthier. People are taking business trips more frequently; more retired Americans with nest eggs and baby boomers who consider "seeing the world" a normal middle-income budget item are hitting the roads. Expect stiff competition, however, for the opportunities ahead.

Hotel Manager

19   You could live rent-free in a luxurious suite and order room service every morning. On top of that, you'd earn good money ($32,000 average; $80,000 at the largest hotels). Be sure, though, to marry a househusband or stay single; next year, you may be transferred to Paris or Athens or Anaheim. And of course, you're on call at all hours. A bachelor's degree in hotel and restaurant administration is the best credential to get you started. Any summer or part-time hotel work, even as a waitress, is a plus.

Travel Agent

20   You won't get rich helping people plan their vacations and business trips—unless you make a killing with your own agency. Salaried agents average only $14,000 a year. But they can travel free on "familiarization" trips. Take a course on travel and tourism, bone up on your geography and get to know a computer keyboard. This is one of the country's fastest-growing occupations.

Tourist-Board Manager

21   Work for France, Ireland, Denmark— you name it. Somebody in the U.S. has to promote these countries so Americans will want to travel to them. You may arrange for travel agents or journalists to visit the coun-

try you work for, make speeches, create vacation packages and act as liaison to hoteliers and tour operators. Foreign language skills help. Average income: $30,000–$35,000. Drawback: These jobs are available only in major cities.

Air-Traffic Controller

22   If you're quick, articulate and can handle the stress, this is one of the best government jobs around. A $34,000 average income, long vacations and a great retirement plan are the pluses. After passing an aptitude test, you'll undergo 12–16 weeks of training at the Federal Aviation Administration Academy. Then you'll be assigned to an airport or traffic-control center. A college degree or an aviation background will help you beat the competition.

Airline Pilot

23   Earn $75,000 a year (national average for major airlines) for flying 18 hours a week— and see the world without spending a cent. Even better, the airlines need women: Right now, it's estimated that a woman's chances of getting hired as a pilot are twice as good as a man's. To fly for a major airline, you need a commercial pilot's license. A college degree is recommended.

Communications

24   Newscaster jobs will be very tight: At least half of the semifinalists in last year's Miss America pageant seem to have already announced their intentions to corner that market. But there are other fascinating media careers, with almost as much glamour—and less competition.

TV Producer

25   The local talk-show host may have a household name and face, but it's the producer who really puts the show together. One of your jobs would be to plan segments. You'd also keep an eye on budgets and ratings. Career advice: Get a degree in broadcasting. Take a job at any station that will hire

you, which is likely to mean relocating (don't bypass cable TV or even radio). And be willing to start at rock bottom—it'll pay off later, but more with status than salary. The average income on local shows is $17,000. Only network producers earn $100,000 or more.

Meetings Planner

26   Plan conventions, conferences, seminars and trade shows, by working on a corporation's or association's staff, or as a consultant. The job requires long hours, sometimes considerable travel and great organizational skills to choose the site and take care of everything from the audiovisual setup to menus and name-tag distribution. Locations range from big-city hotels to Caribbean resorts. A business degree helps here. Average income: $31,000.

Publicist

27   Your job (at a corporation or public-relations firm) would be to get your client on TV and radio and in print. You might book authors on talk shows, write press releases for a new cosmetic or help a TV crew film the latest diagnostic techniques at a hospital. Writing skills are important, but a persuasive sales personality is the real key to success. Average pay: $38,500.

Advertising Account Executive

28   At the ad agency, copywriters come up with the words and the artists create the layouts and sets. But they take their direction from the account executive. It's her job to sell the campaign to the client. For the winning edge, you need to be an expert on the client's product, whether it's a computer or cereal. A degree in marketing is also a plus. The average account executive makes $28,000 a year.

Media Escort

29   Where would celebrity authors be if they had to promote their books in 12 cities without help? Many are met by an official escort who's hired and paid for by the publisher. As an escort, you'd drive the visitor to interviews at newspapers and TV stations, introduce her or him to contacts there and handle any problems that arise. People who are organized and who know how to take charge make the best escorts. It's a new field and usually a freelance one, paying $50–$150 or so a day.

Sales

Sexism has a hard time surviving here. 30 In sales, when you produce for the company, they know it—and you get ahead. But there are many kinds of sales ability and specialties to choose from.

Auctioneer

The secret is out: Auctioneers make 31 good money. Whether you're taking bids on livestock, antiques or modern art, knowing your specialty is half the game. Breaking in can be tough, though, so go to an auctioneering school and then take any entry-level job at a company—an art auction house, for instance—that hires auctioneers. Expect $40,000–$50,000 a year if you're good, $100,000 or more if you're great.

Commercial Real-Estate Broker

Let bored housewives sell that charming 32 ten-room colonial. You'll do better handling office space, industrial properties and hotels. First, get your agent's license. After some sales experience and additional study, you can become a broker—and arrange everything from title searches to loans. Average pay: $34,000. Top brokers have six-figure earnings.

Institutional Stockbroker

If you perk up at the sight of dollar signs 33 and know you can really sell, head for Wall Street—or your city's equivalent. New brokers go into a securities firm's formal training program. The smart ones then specialize in selling to institutions rather than to individual investors. The average stockbroker earns $80,000 a year. The few who handle institutional accounts average $200,000!

Manufacturer's Representative

34   Some companies can't afford or don't need a full-time sales staff, but they'll hire you to sell their product line to stores in your city, state or region. Set up your office at home, and represent one company or several. Reps average $50,000 a year; those who start their own firms average $94,000.

Agent

35   Some people who couldn't sell an ad for the high-school yearbook can really shine at selling people instead. Hollywood agents negotiate contracts for the stars, while literary agents are the middlemen between authors and publishers. Beginners often start at an agency for a set salary that ranges from $15,000 to $20,000. When they branch out on their own, they can make 10 to 25 percent of whatever their clients earn through their efforts.

Money

36   These days, Americans are more finance-conscious than ever. This is good news for accountants, but there are other ways to cash in on the trend.

Financial Planner

37   Remember when only the very rich had people to manage their money? Now Mr. and Ms. Middle-Income have started seeing a financial planner — an expert who can advise them on savings, investments, budgets and how to meet their particular financial goals (retirement, education, etc.). Get experience in banking, insurance or the securities industry and take the tests to become a Certified Financial Planner. Then find a job with an established planner or build your own clientele. Average income $30,000–$50,000.

Securities Analyst

38   You don't have to be a fast-talking sales type in order to make it big on Wall Street. The analyst's daily routine is more like that of an author. She reads (trade journals, financial reports), interviews people and writes reports — evaluating a company's stock as a good or bad buy for the firm's clients. An M.B.A. is usually necessary. The average yearly pay is $40,000–$45,000, plus bonuses, and there are jobs in every city large enough to have a major brokerage firm.

Lending Officer

39   Going into any big bank's training program can be a good career move. But when they ask you what you want to specialize in, forget the international division. Tell them lending. That's the straightest route to the top. Having an M.B.A. is best, but any business degree makes you a good job candidate. The average salary is $24,500, but it's much higher in large banks.

Securities Trader

40   Dedicate yourself to work days in the business world's fast lane, and you might be able to retire rich at 35. Traders often work right on the stock-exchange floor, filling buy and sell orders from their brokerage firms. If you can predict which stocks will be hot, you'll make money fast. Any financial or business degree will get you started. Expect $35,000–$45,000 a year, plus bonuses. Superstar traders literally make millions.

Investment Banker

41   When a company needs to raise money, it issues stocks. The investment banker's job is advising them how to do this, as well as helping them sell the stocks. With bonuses, this job can pay an average of $100,000 a year. Most people either make it big in investment banking or change careers altogether. An M.B.A. is very important.

City Life

42   You can be a doctor or a lawyer in even the smallest town. Some jobs, though, are more commonly found in urban settings. As long as there are restaurants, health clubs

and theaters, there will be special careers for city people.

City Manager

43   You don't have to run for office to help run city hall. Today, cities of all sizes (from Dallas to Blacksburg, Virginia) hire people to manage the municipality as if it were a business. The first city manager ever (in Staunton, Virginia) won his job by getting a bridge repaired for 80 percent less than the contractor's estimate. Your duties would range from overseeing traffic control to setting up concerts in the park. Get a master's in public administration for this $40,000-a-year career.

Fitness Director

44   All the people running health clubs aren't former dancers or movie stars. A degree in exercise physiology, physical education or the health sciences will get you started. Manage a private club or design fitness programs for corporations (salary range: $19,000–$45,000). Entry-level jobs include exercise instructor and fitness technician.

Urban Anthropologist

45   If Margaret Mead were starting out today, she might skip Samoa and study cultural patterns in New York or Los Angeles instead. Corporations hire anthropologists to look into questions like "Why do workers from one ethnic community react differently than those from another?" A Ph.D. is almost a must in this growing social-science specialty. Average earnings: $34,800.

Chef

46   Cooks at fast-food spots don't take home big paychecks, but chefs in fine big-city restaurants do. If you think you have the talent, take a formal course at a culinary school and work your way up through the restaurant kitchen hierarchy. Successful chefs can earn $40,000 or more. The very best can name their own price—and write their own cookbooks.

Theatrical Engineer

47   In Shakespeare's day, theaters didn't have sophisticated audio systems and lasers. Today's theaters do—but they have very few engineers trained to understand them. Get an electrical, mechanical or civil-engineering degree—plus training in theater management. (Only Purdue University offers an M.F.A. in theatrical engineering.) The average salary is $37,500.

48   Even if you decide to home in on one of these fields, don't expect the job search to be a snap. America has a "glut" of working-age people. But the right credentials, a clear career goal that employers will understand, good interviewing skills and a little persistence will pay off in these fields with the best growth prospects.

49   Oh, yes—we haven't yet mentioned the *least* promising careers for the '80s and '90s: These are the fields expected to have zero or negative job growth (not only won't any new jobs be created, some will be eliminated). If you had your heart set on being a college professor, a butcher, a merchant marine or on having any career in the post office, take our advice—have a change of heart.

John W. Wright

CAREER PROSPECTS IN THE 1980s

To determine which professions stand to fare best—and worst—in the 1980s, *Money* magazine studied data from the Bureau of Labor Statistics and from colleges, professional associations, and recruiting firms. Occupations then were ranked by weighting the four factors detailed in the table below. Computer systems analysts placed first partly because of their excellent prospects of getting jobs and promotions. Doctors earn much more but rank second because of an expected surfeit of them in major cities. A more acute oversupply pushes lawyers farther down the list. By contrast, opportunities abound for military officers, but low pay reduces their ranking. In the table, the typical starting salary is for those with bachelor's degrees; for doctors, dentists, and lawyers, it's for the first year of practice. The mid-career salary is for ten years' experience.

CAREER PROSPECTS IN THE 1980s

Occupation	Estimated growth in jobs to 1990	Prospects for job seekers	Starting salary	Mid-career salary	Comments
The Sunniest					
Computer systems analyst	37%	Excellent	$16,500	$34,000	Add management skills and you can write your own program for advancement.
Doctor	38%	Good	45,000	82,000	Best of both worlds; the demand is in small towns, the money is in big cities.
Health service administrator	57%	Good	18,000	37,500	Health care is booming, but a master's degree in business or health management is a must.
Geologist	36%	Good	17,600	31,000	Domestic oil exploration will easily soak up the supply of degree holders.
Engineer	27%	Good	19,200	35,000	Energy specialists strike a gusher, but budget cuts cap need for civil engineers.
Dentist	29%	Good	27,000	53,000	New bridges to prosperity; corporate dental plans and in-store offices.
The Variables					
Dietitian	43%	Good	14,000	25,000	Nutrition-consciousness feeds ample growth, but salaries are far from fat.
Economist	39%	Good	14,500	45,000	Bad times are good for the dismal science, but beginners start low.
Banker	55%	Good	12,500	27,000	Plenty of security, but when it comes to pay, the money stays in the vault.
Accountant	29%	Good	14,000	31,000	In a money-maddened era, starting out is easy, but management spots are elusive.

Occupation	Estimated growth in jobs to 1990	Prospects for job seekers	Starting salary	Mid-career salary	Comments
Personnel administrator	17%	Good	12,500	29,500	Job growth may be even faster than expected but competition may be stiff.
Physicist	9%	Good	16,000	30,400	Bad news—jobs are few. Good news—number of qualified grads is fewer.
The Cloudiest Teacher	2%	Poor	11,000	17,000	Budget cuts and declining enrollments teach a bitter lesson to newcomers.
Military officer	1%	Good	10,000	22,000	Housing and living allowances (not included) won't shore up sorry pay scales.
Newspaper reporter	20%	Poor	12,500	25,000	Writers blocked; Woodward, Bernstein, and company inspired too many.
Public relations manager	24%	Poor	12,000	32,000	When the economic news turns sour, the publicity people are the first to go.
Lawyer	25%	Poor	18,000	50,000	Verdict: oversupply; sentence: less courtly compensation for years to come.
Architect	43%	Poor	12,000	28,700	Some room at the top, but ground level jobs are scarce and pay is poor.

EXERCISES

Content

Recall the main ideas in the three preceding articles by answering the following questions. Respond to some of the questions in your own words. Respond to others by finding quotations from the article that provide the answers.

1. According to many experts, future job growth will be greatest in two general areas—information and conservation (see "Growth Industries of the Future," paragraph 5). Which of the careers discussed in the three preceding articles would fall into the area of information? The area of conservation?

2. For careers about which salary information is provided in the articles, what are the five highest-paying occupations? What are the five lowest-paying?

3. To what extent does this assessment of "sunniest," "variable," and "cloudiest" career prospects in "Career Prospects in the 1980s" correspond with the assessments of career areas in other articles in this chapter? Note especially the brief comments about each occupation.

Structure

1. Explain how paragraphs 1–4 of "Fast-Track Jobs," considered together, form an identifiable section of the article. Give this identifiable section a title.

2. How are the occupations in "Fast-Track Jobs" organized?

Fact/Opinion

Classify each of the following statements as either a fact, an opinion, or a fact wrapped in an opinion. If the statement is a combination of fact and opinion, identify which part is fact and which opinion.

1. "About 40 percent [of physician assistants] practice in medical centers in counties with populations under 50,000" ("Ten Best Careers for Black Men").

2. "The supply of professionals needed to steer us through a sophisticated technical world still lags dreadfully behind the demand" ("Ten Best Careers for Black Men").

3. "The trouble with many of today's most promising careers (the ones that are expected to increase by the thousands between now and 1995 or so) is that you probably wouldn't wish them on your worst enemy" ("Fast-Track Jobs").

4. "Banker: Plenty of security, but when it comes to pay, the money stays in the vault" ("Career Prospects in the 1980s").

5. "You don't have to run for office to help run city hall" ("Fast-Track Jobs").

6. "Lawyer: Verdict: oversupply; sentence: less courtly compensation for years to come" ("Career Prospects in the 1980s").

Inferences

In your responses to the following questions, incorporate some of the quotations you located in response to the Content questions. You may decide to use either all or only part of each quotation.

1. According to the introduction to "Ten Best Careers for Black Men," the choices of occupations discussed were "based on novelty, present and projected demand as seen by the Bureau of Labor Statistics, projected expansion of the discipline and practicality." Based on the information in the article itself and on information in other articles in this chapter, what seems to be the main reason for each choice in this article? For example, do you think hotel managers and assistants were chosen because they are in great demand now or because they will be or for their "novelty" value?

2. What seem to be the main differences between the types of careers described in "Ten Best Careers for Black Men" and those described in "Fast-Track Jobs"? What are the main similarities?

3. To what extent does the information in "Career Prospects in the 1980s" coincide with that in "Ten Best Careers for Black Men" and "Fast-Track Jobs"?

4. Select the occupation from these three articles in which you are most interested and try to estimate how the variable factors of continuity, change, and choice may affect your own prospects for this career.

Carrie Tuhy

WHERE THE JOBS ARE

1   True, Arizona's Sandra Day O'Connor and California's Ronald Reagan had to head where the sun also rises to realize their lofty ambitions. But unless they yearn for a seat on the top bench or for an oval office, more and more Americans will find in this decade that they can satisfy their career goals—and often live where they like—in the West. Most cheering news of all: their chances for success are far better there now than at any time in its turbulent, boom-bust history. For they will find a region whose fortunes are increasingly buoyed by the major role it is playing in meeting the nation's energy, defense and technological needs.

2   The Commerce Department forecasts 3.8 million new jobs in the West by the decade's end, a rise of 18%. Two out of three of the people who will fill them may have to be recruited from elsewhere. Simply being in the right place at the right time isn't enough; you need the right education or training too. Says Philip Burgess, executive director of the Western Governors' Policy Office: "All too often the wrong people come out here. The man in Detroit is laid off the assembly line, sells his house, gets in his camper, drives west—and then finds out that he can't get a job."

3   Those who are likely to be most successful in the West combine needed professional or technical skills and the flexibility to follow the demand—be it in the region's cities or its developing rural areas. Engineers, scientists and craftsmen will find opportunity seemingly limitless. Jobs in service businesses as diverse as banking and bakeries will grow even faster than those in manufacturing or energy development. As the entire Pacific basin from Seattle to Singapore bene-

fits from an unprecedented burst of commerce over the next decade, employment in international trade will also expand mightily at West Coast ports and beyond.

4   Much of the overall job growth will be spurred by two powerful developments. First, as the search for more domestic energy supplies intensifies, resource-rich regions will boom. The Rocky Mountain states sit on the nation's most opulent supplies of undeveloped coal, oil, natural gas, uranium and other prized minerals. Previously developed fields in California, Colorado and elsewhere will become more productive with improved technology for recovery and a heightened incentive: oil selling for $34 a barrel, compared with $10 only two years ago. Offshore drilling will help the coastal states. While all this activity will create thousands of jobs in directly extracting these resources, still more openings will develop in financial, legal, administrative and other support services.

5   The second development: what Patricia Hill Hubbard, a director of the American Electronics Association in Palo Alto, calls "the golden decade of electronics." Technology will fashion new careers in telecommunications, health care, the military and other fields. The need for people who can provide computer programming has become—and will remain—insatiable. The West stands to profit proportionately more than any other region from development of the machines and their software.

6   Openings in energy-related fields will come in gushes rather than trickles. By mid-decade, the number of jobs tied to energy development in Colorado, Wyoming, Montana, Utah, Idaho, Nevada, Arizona and New Mexico could jump by 200,000, an increase

of 50%. Demand in that group of states for engineers will jump 50%, for managers 66% and for draftsmen 80%. Craftsmen with skills from carpentry to pipe fitting will be needed the most. Employment opportunities will be richest on the Eastern Slope of the Rockies. Denver will remain the energy center and Billings, Salt Lake City, Albuquerque and Phoenix-Tucson will be increasingly important satellites. In the less populated areas, Casper, Wyo. will offer jobs related to oil, gas and mineral — particularly uranium — development, and Grand Junction, Colo. will be the capital of oil shale.

7　　The oil and gas drilling rush shows little sign of slowing. During this year's first nine months, 7,725 wells were drilled in the western states, up nearly 38% from the same period last year. In Colorado alone, the number of wells drilled increased 50%. The decade's hottest talent search will continue to be for petroleum engineers, geologists and geophysicists. Result: a bidding war for new graduates and company raiding for veterans.

8　　In the past six months, salaries for the sought-after have increased 10% to 20%, the years of required experience have been trimmed and relocation benefits have been fattened with company cars, front money and generous stock plans. Says Gordon Scheig, a vice president at Fleming Associates, a headhunting firm in Denver: "There's not a geologist in town who needs to take any offer. He can wait for a better one next week."

Perks aplenty

9　　The shortage of seasoned professionals is the severest of all. Typical example: searching for an exploration manager with five to eight years' experience, an oil company offered a $60,000 base salary, plus a company car, $3,000 for incidental needs above the annual expense account and one-half of 1% interest in any projects he worked on. No takers. To deflect raiders, companies make defensive counteroffers. Getty Oil allows employees in engineering, geology and geophysics to borrow up to 80% of their annual salary at 11% after they've been with the company for three years. For each additional year they stay, Getty forgives 25% of the loan.

10　　Among the graduates of the class of '81, petroleum engineers received the highest average starting salaries, more than $26,600. Placement directors at the University of Idaho report that 65% of the employment requests were for engineers in general, who made up only 13% of the class. At the Colorado School of Mines, earth-science grads are getting offers with salaries in the mid-to-high 20s; in the past year, those bids have increased 19% for geologists and 13.5% for geophysicists.

11　　Demand is developing new academic disciplines and expanding some old ones. While the critical technical skills are most valued, major energy companies are courting new graduates in finance, accounting, law and computer science. The Universities of Oklahoma, Colorado and Texas now offer degrees in petroleum land management. The graduates are called landmen, and they scout potential exploration sites, research property titles and negotiate rights with farmers, ranchers and companies that control leases. Diane Lukowicz, 34, a former fine arts major at the University of Wisconsin, left the Midwest and looked for work as an interior decorator in Denver. Discouraged by limited opportunities and low pay, she spent three years earning a degree in land management at the University of Colorado. One month after graduating, she started work at Amoco's Denver office. Less than two years later, this landman earns $37,000.

12　　While the West's energy boom is an accident of geography, its high-tech surge is strictly a matter of design. Individual states actively recruit electronics firms by offering low — and sometimes no — taxes, relatively cheap land, and a willing work force. Electronics is the kind of clean, light, white-collar industry all states seek, even environmentally hypersensitive Oregon. Ten years ago, former Governor Tom McCall encouraged people to visit the state but not to stay. Today, facing a 10% unemployment rate and a devastated lumber industry, Governor Victor Atiyeh says candidly: "Oregon is open for business—and the kind of business we want most is high tech."

13   In California, one out of every four workers is employed in electronics. Companies in Silicon Valley south of San Francisco are so cramped for expensive space that they are expanding to Colorado, Arizona, Washington and Oregon. Mini-Silicon Valleys are taking shape: in the 160-mile stretch from Fort Collins to Colorado Springs, in the arc of suburban communities north of Seattle, in Boise, Albuquerque and the Tucson-Phoenix corridor.

14   High-tech companies, whose prime raw materials are brains, can afford to locate anywhere; they often choose to cluster in small communities because those highly prized brains prefer to live there. Beaverton (pop. 32,000), just west of Portland, has landed 34 electronics manufacturers in the past five years. Employees are easy to attract too. Says Roger Rees, 31, an electronics engineer in Floating Point Systems in Beaverton: "I had many offers from firms in Southern California, but I couldn't stand the smog, congestion and crime. So I started looking for a place that was more livable."

15   The competition for such professionals will surely intensify. The American Electronics Association forecasts that by 1985 electronics jobs in the West will more than double. Demand for electrical, mechanical and industrial engineers will continue to be strong throughout the decade; the most acute shortages will be among software engineers, computer analysts and programmers.

16   The opportunities and pay for job candidates with bachelor's degrees in engineering, computer and other sciences are so enticing that few students stay to get advanced degrees, and fewer still choose to take the 25% lower salaries offered to teach the subject. Last June's computer-science graduates received salary offers of $20,712 on average while electrical engineers got $22,584. Nearly 75% had accepted jobs before graduation. New engineering and science grads often can decide where they want to live as well as where they want to work. "We urge students to tell us if they prefer Boise or Fort Collins, manufacturing or marketing," says Jack Grout, an executive of Hewlett-Packard which recruits 1,500 new graduates annually.

17   Increased defense and aerospace spending by a determined Reagan Administration is good news for the West, where government contracts have long propped big segments of the economy. As in energy and electronics defense and aerospace employers will be locked in combat for people with technical skills. Three western states alone—Washington, Oregon and California—account for more than 16% of defense spending. And nearly a quarter of the Pentagon budget for prime contracts is going to companies in the western states. Rockwell International, Lockheed and Boeing are key manufacturers for the B-1 bomber and AWACS aircraft and the space shuttle. Many of the military armaments and aerospace testing sites are also in the region's vast expanses.

18   Denver Aerospace, a Martin Marietta division, has stepped up hiring in part to fill $750 million of missile contracts. The Denver plant is responsible for the assembly and testing of the MX missiles, which are scheduled to be launched beginning in 1983. In the past two years, the company has hired 5,500 people to handle the MX, the space shuttle and other government orders totaling $1.7 billion. To attract such volume, personnel director Robert E. Burnett is using electronic want ads, 30-second radio and television commercials advertising for engineers in Los Angeles, Seattle and Detroit to relocate to Denver. He also has raised employee rewards for successful referrals from $250 to $2,000. Last year, if they had helped to recruit candidates, employees were also eligible for an annual drawing for a two-week trip to Hawaii for two. This year the destination has been changed to Tahiti and biweekly raffles have been added for shorter trips to Las Vegas and Acapulco.

How services soar

19   Just as energy development and electronics manufacturing draw new people, that swelling population underwrites many more

new opportunities. As a rule, every basic job brought into an area creates three or four additional openings—usually in services. Arnold Kraus, 35, vice president of investments for Bache Halsey Stuart Shields Inc. in Tucson, can attest to that. After all, those hordes of new people showing up in Tucson make a rich market for a stockbroker. The New Jersey native, who will earn $150,000 in commissions this year, sees no reason to feel that he's missing the action on Wall Street. Says Kraus: "Someone with my kind of job used to have to live in New York or some other money center to really do well. But with WATS lines and airplanes, I can live and prosper in the place I love."

20   Health care is another high-growth service. Even in Idaho, Oregon and Washington, where the economy is less robust than in many other western states, jobs in the health-care field increased at least 30% from 1975 to 1980. Severe shortages of doctors and dentists persist in the more remote parts of the West where the energy boom has brought a rapid influx of people. Wyoming, which has no medical schools, has contracted with Omaha's Creighton University and the University of Utah to pay for all but $1,000 a year of the training of doctors who agree to practice in the state for three years. Throughout the West, demand during this decade will remain intense for laboratory technicians, nurses, hygienists and nutritionists.

21   While much of the opportunity for both primary industries and service businesses will be in smaller communities, larger cities will grow in importance as hubs of finance, transportation and trade. "The future of international trade automatically leads you to the West," says Roy Herburger Jr., a University of Southern California business professor. Jobs in banking, maritime law and freight forwarding will expand in ports from Long Beach to Seattle. Import and export volume at western ports will nearly double

by 1990. To prepare for such growth, Los Angeles is spending more than $150 million to deepen its harbor and add new terminals, a railroad yard and coal-handling depot. Seattle, the largest container port after New York City, is planning to capitalize on its geographic advantage: one day closer than California ports to the Far East.

22   Environmentalists argue that growth is endangering the land, taxing a limited water supply and polluting the air, but even such adversity brings job opportunities in resource management, both in government and private companies. A critical shortage of timberland will occur by the late '80s; as a result, forest planners are needed to develop ways of fattening the harvest and rejuvenating lands stripped of their timber. The West will also require agricultural engineers and hydrologists to develop improved methods of irrigation as energy and other development continues to squeeze land and the water supply available for crops. Aquaculture—farming the sea—and desalinization—removing the salt from the ocean water—will provide a new crop of specialized occupations for scientists by the decade's end.

23   There will be plenty of surprises. While those aquaculturists resume the push west—right into the Pacific—others will be turning east to find their New West. Says James Vashro, 32, a production manager for Hewlett-Packard, who relocated four years ago from the company's plant near San Jose, Calif. to its facility in Boise: "I've advanced faster than I ever thought possible. The future looks bright for me in Boise." Perhaps the most positive point about working in the West is that you no longer run the risk of getting lost there. After all, it is the place that launched a movie star on the path to the presidency and a woman to the highest court in the land.

EXERCISE	

Content

Recall the main ideas in this article by answering the following questions. Respond to some of the questions in your own words. Respond to others by finding quotations from the article that provide the answers.

1. Why isn't the booming West the right area for everybody?

2. Which "two powerful developments" are responsible for most of the West's job growth?

3. What types of support industries will enjoy growth along with the primary industries they are supporting?

4. Expansion in the West may create environmental problems. What kinds of job opportunities will develop from the effort to deal with such problems?

Structure

1. Explain how paragraphs 4 and 5, considered together, form an identifiable section of the article. Give this identifiable section a title.

2. How is paragraph 7 related to paragraph 6?

3. How is paragraph 4 related to the thesis of the article?

Fact/Opinion

Classify each of the following statements as either a fact, an opinion, or a fact wrapped in an opinion. If the statement is a combination of fact and opinion, identify which part is fact and which opinion.

1. "The Commerce Department forecasts 3.8 million new jobs in the West by the decade's end, a rise of 18%."

2. "Openings in energy-related fields will come in gushes rather than trickles."

3. "Throughout the West, demand during this decade will remain intense for laboratory technicians, nurses, hygienists and nutritionists."

Inferences

In your responses to the following questions, incorporate some of the quotations you located in response to the Content questions. You may decide to use either all or only part of each quotation.

1. In paragraph 15 Tuhy shows how a socially desirable development—higher employment—can arise from an environmentally undesirable one. What other areas occur to you in which an undesirable development has generated a desirable one?

2. On what factors does the continued development of the West seem to depend? What factors might bring an end (or at least a slowdown) to such development and thus to employment prospects?

3. Although the West has enjoyed remarkable development and prosperity during the past decade or so, other areas should not be overlooked. For example, many people assumed not too long ago that the industrialized cities of the Northeast were irreversibly decaying. Yet Massachusetts (and Boston especially) has enjoyed a resurgence recently, largely due to the computer industry; and New York City, long ailing among eastern cities, is more prosperous than it has been in years. To what extent do you think that other areas of the country are just as occupationally desirable as the West? Why?

CHAPTER 8

⊏▭⊐ **Passion in Print**

▮▮▮ Introduction

You've seen them in special racks at the supermarket and at your local library. The Harlequins. The Silhouettes. The Candlelight Ecstasies. They're featured in TV ads, sensuous, soft-focus ads showing deserted, windswept beaches, soulful stares, swiftly closing window shutters. They feature rugged but sensitive men; passionate yet independent women. They have titles like *Dare to Love; Rich, Radiant Love; Flames of Passion; Lovely, Loving Lips; Forbidden Rhapsody; Passport to Nirvana; Life of Oblivion;* and *Surrender to Love.* Perhaps (just out of curiosity, of course) you've picked one up yourself and leafed through a few pages. And perhaps you've even read one—or two—all the way through.

If so, you're not alone. Although the audience for romance fiction seems to have peaked in 1983, when it was estimated at 20 million readers, American women still are spending about $100 million a year on what one critic calls "love-conquers-all schmaltz." Witness the case of one avid reader:

> She spends $2,500 a year on pulp. After packing husband [Donnie] and son off to work, she likes to read one in the morning.

"Then I'll fix lunch and if there's nothing really pressing, I'll read another one. Then I cook supper and if Donnie's out in the woodshop working, I'll read another one." She never takes them to bed. "Once you get started, you want to finish them, and I know I can't stay up all night reading."

Over the years she has managed to read, collect and catalogue some 7,000 romances. Donnie turned one room into wall-to-wall shelves. They're filled. Basement and attic groan under the weight of boxes of paperbacks.[1]

Although this particular woman is—not surprisingly—unemployed, about 40 percent of romance readers, according to one survey, have full-time jobs, about the same percentage have family incomes above $30,000, and about half of them are college-educated.

Romance novels, then, are a cultural phenomenon. Some questions arise. What are they like? Why are they so popular? What do they offer their readers? Who writes them? Serious authors who can't get their more serious work published? Or people who are writing nothing but romance fiction? What do they think of their work? (Are they embarrassed or unapologetically proud?) What advice have they for others who might want to break into romance writing?

This chapter supposes that you have decided to investigate one or more of these questions for a paper—perhaps a paper for an American civilization, psychology, or mass media course. We will also focus on a particular technique of essay development, the technique of *example*.

As an introduction to the subject, here is a short piece that originally appeared in *The New Yorker*.

THE BEST-SELLING AUTHOR OF ALL TIME

1   When last we spoke with Barbara Cartland, it was at her home outside London, the year was 1976, her years were seventy-five, and her vital statistics looked like this: two hundred and seventeen books—a hundred and seventy of them novels—with a total of seventy million copies in print. We are happy to report that Miss Cartland, whom we encountered last month in the lobby of Penn Station, where she was greeting people coming to the second annual Romantic Book-Lovers' Conference, has since our last talk set aside her idling ways and got down to some serious work. In the intervening seven years, in which she has attained the age of eighty-one, she has had something or other to do with the Princess Di side of the Royal Wed-

ding *and* she has written a hundred and forty-five more books—an average of more than twenty a year—to bring her total to three hundred and sixty-two. Now, with something more than three hundred and fifty million copies bought and paid for, she may well be the best-selling author of all time. "I was in Honolulu recently, and I wrote 'Island of Love,' and on the way back we stopped in San Francisco, so I wrote 'Love Goes West.' No, it's 'Love Comes West,' I think," she told us. A book takes the disciplined Miss Cartland a week to complete, and she writes for only a shade over two hours each day.

And Miss Cartland, though she is the 2 reigning speed queen, is not alone in her lit-

[1]Art Harris, "The Love Bloat," *Washington Post*, 1 July 1985.

erary approach, we found as we wandered through the corridors of the Hotel Roosevelt, where the conference was held, and talked to some of its participants — who were almost uniformly female and were nearly all either published writers of romance fiction or unpublished writers of romance fiction. For instance, the second-best-selling romance author, Janet Dailey, who has produced seventy-eight novels, announced, "By trial and error, I've found the best ways to write — at least for me — and now I finish a book in about nine days." One reason romance writers write so quickly is that the market for their products never dries up. Rebecca Brandewyne, who was promoting her latest work, "Love, Cherish Me," at the conference, said she sometimes reads from seven to ten Harlequin romances (which stretch a hundred and eighty-odd pages) in a single evening. And apparently there are others like her. We picked up the following facts about Harlequin Books, the leading publisher in the romance industry:

3   Fact: Last year, Harlequin sold over two hundred million books — about six books per second.

4   Fact: If all the Harlequin books sold *in a single day* last year were stacked one on top of another, the pile would be sixteen times as high as the World Trade Center (or, alternatively, eight times as high as the two towers of the World Trade Center stacked one on top of the other).

5   Fact: If all the pages of all the Harlequin books sold over the past ten years were laid side by side in the proper places and in the proper configurations, they would completely cover Colorado and Pennsylvania.

6   Fact: If all the *words* in Harlequin books sold last year were placed end to end, they could stretch ninety-three times to the moon (a fact that is especially noteworthy when you consider that many Harlequin authors avoid long words).

7   Fact: If the Harlequin books sold last year were placed end to end, they could run along both sides of the Nile, both sides of the Amazon, and one side of the Rio Grande.

8   (During that last paragraph, we got up from our desk, bought a diet Coke, joked with several friends about their writing speed, and, in general, *wasted time*. All the while, the clock was ticking.)

9   One reason some writers can do romances with such dispatch is that thoughtful publishers provide recipes for them to follow. For example, we talked with Denise Marcil, who, with her partner Meredith Bernstein, "came up with the whole concept" for a new series of Avon paperback romances, which will appear once a month under the over-all title Finding Mr. Right. Ms. Marcil said, "In most romances, what happens is the woman falls in love with a man, there's a little conflict, and things work out. What's different in our books is that there are two heroes, not one. And the woman has to choose between them." Ms. Marcil assured us that none of the jilted heroes do anything rash, and that the breakups are always "handled in an adult way." As an example of the new genre, Ms. Marcil cited "Dancing Season," by Carla Neggers, the second title in the series, which features a young woman who runs a bakeshop in her native Saratoga Springs and must decide between a hometown boy and a dancer in a New York City ballet company. She takes the local, leaving the dancer to leap morosely, one of her reasons being that she doesn't want to give up her ambitious plans for culinary expansion.

10   It would be less than honest of us to report that the seas of romance fiction are altogether glassy. On the contrary, they're stormy and roiling — even tempest-tossed — when it comes to the issue of decorous behavior for female characters. Such a fog of photographers had enveloped Miss Cartland at Penn Station that we couldn't hear everything she said, but we distinctly made out the words "disgusting" and "animals." And her voice was resolute when she declared that romance fiction was "in rather a torrid period, where everyone feels they must be modern and put in some dirty bits." Miss Cartland, none of whose heroines find themselves in bed until the necessary vows have

been traded in the presence of a cleric, said it was a "medical fact" that promiscuity could damage young women. "Anyway," she added as she walked off, clutching a bouquet of red roses, "the most exciting thing in the world is still to hear someone say, 'I love you.'"

Content

This brief article provides some fascinating glimpses into the world of romance fiction, but it does not attempt to explore the entire world. Rather, it focuses on one particular writer, Barbara Cartland, and her astonishing literary productivity. The article opens and closes with a description of Cartland, who has been called "the Queen of Romance." Cartland is chosen as the main subject perhaps because she is the best *example* of a successful romance writer. The statistics about the number of Harlequin romances sold every year (the other important subject of the article) provide graphic indications of the vastness of Barbara Cartland's readership. Thus, the two main focal points of the article — Barbara Cartland and the unusual statistics on romance publishing — correspond with one another: Cartland has a vast literary "output," but there is also a huge readership eager for "input."

How can you use such material in your own papers? Let's take a closer look at the use of examples in writing.

Using Examples in Papers

A common technique for developing paragraphs is to provide examples of a general statement. This statement frequently is the topic sentence. Examples are a crucial form of evidence that writers use to support their claims. If, for instance, you wrote, "The councilwoman from my district is the most active member of the city government," no one would have reason to agree unless you provided examples, specific instances that would document your claim. But what if you had a hundred examples and were making the claim in a letter to the editor of your local paper? Would you use all of your examples? Not likely. You would want to choose examples judiciously, using only the most vivid. A few well-chosen examples are sufficient to support the points you wish to make.

Suppose you want to provide examples of successful romance writers in a paper you are writing. The information in this article would be useful to you. You would need to summarize the part of the article dealing with Barbara Cartland and use that summary as one of your examples. You would have to get more examples from other articles. (Other romance writers, such as Janet Dailey, are discussed in the article, but not in enough detail for you to derive a good example.) The part of your paper that deals with Cartland might read as follows:

> One of the best-known writers of romance novels is Barbara Cartland. By the time she was seventy-five years old she had written 217 books. During the

next seven years she wrote 145 more, for a grand total of 362. Writing for only two hours a day, Cartland can produce a book every week. During a recent trip to Honolulu, she wrote two, one while going and the other while coming back. Cartland objects to the recent trend toward "torrid" romances and to the "dirty bits" that today's romance writers feel compelled to include in their work. Her heroines never engage in sex until they are married. For Barbara Cartland, "the most exciting thing in the world is still to hear someone say, 'I love you.'"

Notice that we have summarized only those parts of the article that deal with Barbara Cartland. (We might be able to use some of the other information in other parts of our essay.) From the first paragraph of the article we got the information that we used in the first four sentences of our summary. From the final paragraph of the article, we got the information that we used in the last three sentences of our summary.

We used direct quotation (that is, material taken word for word from the source) three times in our paragraph. We quoted briefly Barbara Cartland's comments about the "torrid" nature of some modern romances and the "dirty bits" she finds in them. And we quoted at greater length her feeling that "the most exciting thing in the world is still to hear someone say, 'I love you.'" In these instances, it would have been difficult, if not impossible, to find other words as effective as Cartland's own. But we thought the other material, dealing mainly with numbers, could be effectively summarized in our own words.

Let's say you wanted to use information from this article as an example of the popularity of romance novels. For this purpose you could summarize some of the unusual statistical information. You might produce a paragraph like this:

> Romance novels sell in staggering quantities. Harlequin, the industry's leader, sold over two hundred million books in one year. If these books were placed end to end, they could line "both sides of the Nile, both sides of the Amazon, and one side of the Rio Grande." The books Harlequin sells in a single day would make a pile sixteen times as high as the World Trade Center.

In this paragraph the first, or topic, sentence announces the generalization: romance novels sell in staggering quantities. Using the two hundred million sales a year as a basis, we then cited some of the other information to exemplify these "staggering quantities." First we pulled out the only example from the article that also relied on *yearly* sale — the example of the books lining the rivers. Then we pulled out one more interesting example, the one about the World Trade Center. Having provided our two examples, we concluded that we had made our point (it isn't necessary to use *all* of the relevant information from the source) and ended the paragraph.

Assignment Preview

At this point we will give you a paper assignment that you can think about as you go through the articles in this chapter. As you read, select material you can use that will help you to write the assignment. If necessary, review Chapter 4 for advice on dealing with information in multiple sources. (This assignment will be reprinted as the first paper assignment at the end of the chapter.)

EXERCISE

After you have finished reading the selections in this chapter, write a paper in which you provide examples of some of the following:

- Successful romance writers
- Typical romance plots
- The popularity of romance novels
- Feelings of romance writers about their work
- The way romance novels satisfy their readers' needs
- Rules for writing romance novels
- Problems with romance novels

Questions following each selection will direct you to some of the more important information and ideas.

Please keep in mind that when we suggest you use examples in a paper, the body of your paper need not consist entirely of examples. Part of your paper may indeed use one or more examples, but another part may use description. Still another part may use explanation through such techniques as comparison and contrast or cause and effect analysis, and another part may use argument. (We will cover these techniques in later chapters.) How you present your material is up to you. The key question to ask yourself is: At this point in my paper, what is the most effective way of presenting my ideas?

Bethany Campbell

ONLY A WOMAN

One of the crucial parts of any romance novel deals with the early relationship between the hero and the heroine. Quite often the initial chemistry between them seems distinctly unpromising, though there are numerous hints of mutual attraction. Such is the case in Bethany Campbell's Harlequin romance, *Only a Woman.* In the first two chapters we meet the heroine, Scotty Morgan, a young but knowledgeable TV sports reporter, and the hero, Jed Quinn, a former basketball star who is now a coach. Quinn appears to hate reporters, particularly women reporters. Scotty's first attempts to interview him are unceremoniously rebuffed, and later, at a press conference, Quinn pointedly ignores her questions while responding freely to the male reporters.

Humiliated but determined, Scotty goes to Quinn's farmhouse. She encounters him chopping wood, stripped to the waist. ("She...hadn't seen a man who looked quite like this—who exuded such raw masculinity. **Quinn...looked like a blue-jeaned warrior god, wielding his battle-ax in the fading light. He looked very, very male, and for Scotty that was a disturbing revelation.")** **This encounter is no more successful than the earlier ones: Quinn insults her, sneers at her qualifications, and orders her off his property. Just before she drives away, however, he leans over to her and says, "I'd ask you in...if you wanted to come in as a woman—not as a reporter." ("For a dizzying moment, his face was so close to hers that she thought he was going to kiss her, and her heart seemed to spring out of her to join her breath in the starry cold.") As this excerpt begins, Scotty is discussing her experiences with the new director, Wally Walltham.**

Bethany Campbell, an English major, teacher, and textbook consultant, calls her writing world her "hidey hole," that "marvelous place where true love always wins out." In addition to *Only a Woman,* **she has written** *After the Stars Fall,* **also for Harlequin.**

1 "So did you beard Quinn in his den last night?" Wally Walltham asked Scotty the next afternoon. He was sitting at his desk with a hand mirror and tweezers, plucking some nose hairs he thought the camera might spot.

2 Scotty winced, watching him. "We talked. He understands my position much more clearly," she answered, which wasn't exactly a lie but not completely true, either.

3 "The position he'd like you to take is flat on your back, from what I hear," Wally hazarded. "Ouch! This smarts!"

4 "Wally, do you have to do that here?" Scotty asked, grimacing. "And what did you mean by that crack?"

5 "I have an image to keep up as a handsome hunk," Wally replied, examining his nose in the hand mirror. "This face is beloved by countless thousands. And what I mean is Quinn's got a reputation for cutting a swath through the ladies like General Sherman through Georgia. That may be one reason

you put him off. He's not used to seeing women standing up."

6 Scotty rubbed a finger under her nose in an unconscious registration of Wally's nasal ministrations. "That's comforting," she said, an edge of sarcasm in her voice. "Did you know all this before you assigned me to him?"

7 Her voice was flip, but her spirits were somber. It would be flattering to think that Quinn's words the night before had some grain of sincerity; that he found her attractive; that he could be interested in her as a woman, if not as a reporter; that he even felt some begrudging degree of concern about her. No, she thought. He probably said those things to all women with microphones in their hands.

8 "Oh, I knew he wasn't going to be easy to deal with," Wally allowed, raising his eyebrows. "But I figured you could handle him. If you can't, you're obviously not cut out for the job. But listen to a warning from old Uncle Wally: the guy's a real Don Juan. If he can't bully you out of his life, his next step will be a seduction attempt. Besides, he's got a score to settle."

9 Scotty was determined to remember Wally's warning, no matter what. But she frowned in puzzlement at his last statement. "What score? What's he got to settle?"

10 Wally shrugged elaborately, putting away his tweezers and hand mirror and taking out a nail file and emery board. He began to work on his nails.

11 "A score against women in sports. You've heard of Helena Schaffer of Boston?"

12 Scotty nodded. A bell seemed to ring inside her head, and suddenly things were beginning to make more sense. Helena Schaffer was a beautiful, russet-haired velvet-eyed woman—one of the first women to break to TV sportscasting. And she worked in Boston, where Quinn had played for almost nine years.

13 "What about Helena Schaffer?" Scotty asked as casually as she could manage. She'd read an article in *TV Guide* on the woman. Helena Schaffer was tough. She'd made

more than one startling exposé, and through those exposés she'd made her fortune. She was one of the few women who had a top position in television sportscasting, and it didn't hurt that she was described as "drop-dead beautiful."

14   "Quinn and Schaffer were an item," Wally informed her, scowling at a hangnail that had been presumptuous enough to intrude upon his life. "We're talking a serious item, Morgan—altar-bound. I was in the East then. It was a big local gossip story. You know—gorgeous, TV celeb from fine old Connecticut family to marry Oklahoma cowboy-type basketball star. My, she's a beautiful thing."

15   Scotty swallowed painfully. To call Helena Schaffer a beautiful thing was an understatement. She was the kind of woman who made the rest of the female race want to give up the fight and enter the nearest convent. Of course, she thought, that's just the type Quinn would go for—the woman with everything.

16   "What happened between them?" she asked, as if her concern were merely academic. She ought to be engraving every word of this conversation permanently on her brain cells. She found Quinn attractive—too attractive for her own good, especially as his tastes ran to women like Helena Schaffer.

17   "Oh, I don't know," Wally said carelessly, buffing his nails. "Career conflicts. That sort of thing. He's not the kind who can share a spotlight. Wanted her to give up broadcasting. Stay home and raise little Quinns. Well, she's not that kind of lady. She's strong. She told him she had a life of her own. She told him to take a walk. A wise decision. Quinn's not the type to settle down."

18   Scotty felt an unfamiliar sensation creeping into her bones. It was a mixture of jealousy and bitterness. "So she dumped him, and now I'm paying for it," she said. It wasn't fair, she brooded. Why should she, or any other woman for that matter, have to be punished because Helena Schaffer was smart enough to drop Quinn? He must have the ego of a spoiled child.

19   "Listen, Morgan," Wally said, examining his nails, "I knew Quinn would be tough, but not this tough. I didn't expect him to be this hard-headed. After all, you're certainly not the same type as Helena Schaffer."

20   Scotty nipped her inner lip at his left-handed compliment. She certainly wasn't the same type as Helena Schaffer. She wasn't beautiful, glamorous, celebrated, or even established. By implication, she wasn't tough, strong or smart, either. She was just plain old Scotty Morgan. Wally was probably surprised Jed Quinn had even noticed she was a woman.

21   "Besides," Wally went on blithely, "you're really in a kind of sympathetic position. Quinn's over-bearing, he's cocky, and he's riding for a fall. He's sure not going out of his way to court the press, and he should. Because those negative feelings will filter down to the fans—and they'll hate him too. Boy—he's going to have one hell of a season. That team of his can't win anything but the booby prize this year."

22   Scotty looked at him in frustration. "Are you saying it doesn't matter whether or not he talks to me? Because there's really no story anyway?"

23   "No-o-o," Wally said, musingly. "I'm just saying that if you get rough and tough on him, nobody's going to blame you—the guy's practically begging for it. That is, if you *can* get rough and tough. And if you can't—well, I guess nothing much is lost. Maybe it isn't much of a story—and I can always assign you to the junior high school circuit or something."

24   Scotty's full lips thinned in determination. She was tired of Wally's warnings, and she was sick to death of Jed Quinn looming between her and her future like some impassable mountain. "I can get as tough as I have to," she murmured. "I'm going to that game tonight. After his team gets their socks beaten off, I may be the only reporter who wants to talk to him."

25   "Suit yourself," Wally replied, sounding bored. "But there's not going to be much to report. The fans always hate to hear that the home team took a blood bath in their own blood."

26   "The poor Timberwolves," Scotty muttered. "They might be a terrible team, but at

least they deserve a decent coach." She unfolded the Fayetteville paper and scanned the story on the Wolves again.

27 The reporter, obviously unimpressed by Quinn's press conference, waxed sardonic:

This season's Wolves don't promise much. They're not only short, they're green with inexperience. Perhaps Quinn should petition to change the team's name. A team of little green men like this could more suitably be called the Martians. Yet Quinn claims to have great faith in them. This proves the old saying, "Hope springs eternal..."

28 She nodded to herself in satisfaction. The Mighty Quinn was about to be humbled, all right. She could think of nobody in greater need of humbling.

29 He thought he'd scare her, did he? He thought he'd charm her, did he? He thought he'd stop her, did he? She'd show him, and she'd show Wally Walltham, too. She hadn't even begun to fight.

30 It was a subdued band of Timberwolf fans that filled Benton Arena that night. Their famous Wolf howls lacked conviction. The cheerleaders, in their black and gold uniforms, performed disheartened cartwheels, as if they knew the cause was already lost.

31 Scotty stood on the sidelines, her green press ticket tied to the button of her blazer, a tape recorder slung over her shoulder with a strap. Hassledorf was rechecking his camera as the teams warmed up, each shooting baskets at their end of the court.

32 "The Wolves look like a pack of dwarfs," Hassledorf grumbled, eyeing the taller Taryton team, whose seven-foot center looked as if he could beat the Wolves all by himself. "This is going to be a slaughter."

33 The Mighty Quinn, looking confined in his three-piece dark suit, sat broodingly beside the assistant coaches on the bench. His flame-blue eyes rested on Scotty once, briefly, and he allowed himself a crooked half smile out of the corner of his mouth.

34 Scotty's heart seemed to skid away and hang momentarily over an abyss. With effort, it regained itself and began beating almost normally again. She had to remind herself Quinn was everything a sensible woman didn't need. He was a chauvinist, a womanizer, a manipulator, and, if he was not quite so rugged-looking, he'd even qualify as a pretty boy with those black-lashed electric-blue eyes. Her interest in him was strictly business.

35 "Might as well go sit under the basket Taryton's aiming for," Hasseldorf predicted gloomily. "There's not going to be any action at the other end and I won't get any highlights there. Too bad. I could use the exercise.

36 "Let's F-I-G-H-T—fight!" urged the desperate cheerleaders from the sidelines.

37 "Fight," responded a few laconic Wolf fans, sounding highly doubtful.

38 But the Wolves fought. By half time, Benton Arena seemed to tremble on its foundations as the fans howled with demented abandon—the place had gone stark raving mad. Hassledorf got more exercise than a whole legion of men would want, racing up and down court following the ceaseless action.

39 The score was tied. Out of nowhere, Channel 37's Duff Freely had appeared at the edge of the court, fastening his press tag to the button of his sports coat.

40 "What in the name of all that's holy is happening here?" he demanded. The cameraman from Channel 37, like Hassledorf, was winded. Channel 3, which initially hadn't bothered to send a cameraman at all, had suddenly produced one, who was setting up to tape game highlights.

41 Scotty blinked at Duff in exhausted surprise. She had been so caught up in the unexpected excitement that her blood seemed to be circulating at twice its normal speed. She had the peculiar high known only to true basketball fanatics, witnessing the kind of game that seemed to have dropped to earth from some frenetic basketball heaven.

42 "I think a miracle is happening," she said dazedly. "The short guys are running the pants off the tall guys."

43 "Lord," Duff said almost bitterly. "I wasn't even listening to the stupid game on radio. How'd things get so close? Taryton beat the

Wolves out for the division title last year. Taryton's got the height. They've got the experience. This shouldn't be happening."

44   "Exactly," Scotty said dryly, her head still feeling sublimely dizzy.

45   "What did Quinn do?" Duff asked. "Sell his soul to the Devil?"

46   Quinn, she thought, dropping back to reality with a small dull thud. "He's done the impossible," she admitted with grudging admiration. "And he's done it the hard way. Tough offense, tough defense. I never saw so many fast breaks."

47   "He can't keep it up," Duff said contemptuously. "You can't keep kids playing that hard."

48   "It's been done," Scotty informed him, but she, too, wondered if Quinn could pull it off. She'd heard of teams with short players performing like this, but she'd never actually seen it.

49   "No, it can't be done," Duff disagreed, as if that were that.

50   "John Wooden did it at UCLA," Scotty countered, naming college basketball's most phenomenal coach. "He took a team like this to a national championship."

51   She shook her head, still amazed at what she'd seen in the first half. If Quinn could pull this kind of playing out of his team, and if he could keep it up, the Timberwolves were going to be a team to conjure with. And if it was, she might be sitting on the brink of a sports fan's most beloved fantasy: a bona fide, straight-out-of-dreamland Cinderella team.

52   "They can't keep it up," Duff insisted. "It's a fluke." He looked at her shining face, her dazzled eyes. "Isn't it?"

53   "I don't know," she said softly, staring at the Wolves' empty bench. Suddenly she pictured Quinn's ice-blue eyes, his one-sided smile, and they seemed somewhat more dangerous than before. Maybe, just maybe, he was as good as he thought he was. And if he was that good, he was nothing short of a genius.

54   The second half took off like a rocket heading for the outer rim of the galaxy. Hassledorf, trying to chase the fastbreaking Wolves up and down the court, was wheezing when he passed Scotty and Duff. "Heart attack!" he puffed wildly. "Giving me — a heart attack!"

55   "Why doesn't he stop shooting?" Duff grumbled. "Everybody else has. At least till the end of the game. The old coot ought to relax."

56   "He doesn't quit because he's Hassledorf," Scotty said fondly. "You'd have to tie him down to stop him at this point. He was born to do this."

57   And so was she, Scotty thought, watching the Wolves force Taryton into another error. If there was anything in the world more exciting than this she had yet to discover it.

58   The Wolves were running their taller opponents off their feet. And Hobie Grant, a freshman from Chicago, was the fastest and most daring Wolf of all.

59   Lithe, black, handsome and six-foot five, Grant was also the one player Quinn didn't seem to have control of. He took some wild shots that bounced off the rim, but he jumped as if his legs were atomic powered. Taryton's weary seven-foot center seemed to be visibly shrinking.

60   Quinn, on the sidelines, was almost as active as the players, striding up and down the sidelines with his stiff-kneed walk, barking orders, his eyes shooting cold fire.

61   He'd done the usual striptease of a coach under pressure — doffing first his coat, then vest, then tie. He'd loosened his collar and rolled his shirt sleeves up over his powerful forearms. The back of his white shirt showed a wide stripe of perspiration down the spine, and his curly hair was falling over his forehead.

62   His face displayed an impressive array of emotions: amazement, disgust, anger, determination, encouragement, worry, elation and, once in a while, a pure cockiness. Like many coaches, he was not above dramatics, and his outrage at certain calls by the referee would have done a Shakespearean actor proud. He would straighten up like a man about to smite down a heathen temple, or bend into the crouch of an angry disbelieving man

about to revert to the law of the jungle. The crowd loved it.

63   When the final buzzer signaled the end of the game, the Timberwolves had won by two points, and the ecstatic yowls of the fans reverberating through the arena seemed to bounce off the surrounding mountains. They were cries of the purest joy, announcing that the Timberwolves were not only alive, but very well indeed. This winter would not be a time of darkness and mourning, but of celebration. Life was worth living, after all.

64   Quinn had done it, Scotty thought with amazement, trying to come down from her euphoria. He had actually done it. He was probably coaching those players the way a slave master would, but he had done it. She couldn't have been more surprised if he had subdued a rogue elephant with a team of ants.

65   She watched him stride off court. His face was as controlled and blank as a man merely boarding a commuter train—not the face of a coach whose team just pulled off an astounding victory.

66   Good grief, she thought. He didn't even look happy. He looked preoccupied, like a general already figuring the costs of this battle and planning the next.

67   Duff and Channel 3's Mahony, as well as a few radio and newspaper reporters, were making a beeline to follow him. Scotty clenched her mike, seized a flushed, gasping Hassledorf by the arm and followed the crowd out of the gym and down the hall toward the locker room.

68   Quinn paused in front of the locker-room door, looked around the corridor almost absently as if he had more important things on his mind. He saw Scotty in the press corps at his heels, set his jaw, lifted his brows in an expression of exasperation and stepped into the locker room.

69   Duff, Mahony and the rest streamed right in behind him. Hassledorf stopped short, shaking his head in disgust. Scotty could tell by the look on his face that he would have uttered a curse had he any breath left.

70   Scotty stood staring at the door, still riding high on the surge of adrenalin from the game. She thought about Wally's warning that she'd better get tough—and Quinn's claim that she wasn't tough enough. That sent enough energy surging through her to make her feel momentarily invulnerable.

71   "Come on," she urged Hassledorf, nodding at the locker room. "It's only a door. It's not going to stop us now. You've got us better footage on this game than any other station, and we might as well get the whole story."

72   Hassledorf shook his head again, looking frustrated and wild-eyed. "Locker—room," he panted, jerking his thumb toward the door.

73   "News team!" she countered, pointing first at him, then at herself. "He's not stopping us this time, Hassledorf. He's got me too charged up. I'm going in—with you or without you."

74   "Without—me," Hassledorf panted. His face went rigid with wariness.

75   "Okay," she said, looking grim. "I go alone."

76   She opened the door, and feeling like Alice entering Wonderland, marched into the men's locker room.

77   Hassledorf heaved a gigantic sigh and followed her.

78   A holler came from somewhere in the section of the showers, and Hobie Grant, dressed only in blue jockey shorts, looked down at Scotty as if a black widow spider had just scuttled into his presence.

79   "Can we keep up the pace?" Quinn was saying into a microphone that was held in front of his mouth. "Yes. These guys are training as if they had to play three halves, not two. They work about as hard as men can—"

80   His voice broke off and he stared in disbelief at Scotty and Hassledorf.

81   "What the—" Quinn started to say.

82   Duff Freely turned and laughed in her face. Whatever Quinn had to say was drowned out by the hollers and hoots of his players.

83 "Hey, guys, one of the reporters is wearing a skirt!"

84 "Quick, grab your towels!"

85 "Hey, baby! Interview me any time—in the shower."

86 "Tryin' to be one of the guys? You're certainly the cutest one—"

87 "Get her out, coach. This is men's territory."

88 Quinn waved his hand, instantly silencing them.

89 "Better reach for your towels, boys," he drawled to the naked and half-naked players. "We've just been invaded. Nothing is sacred any longer."

90 Scotty tried to ignore the fact that she was in a room filled with men in various states of undress, but silence, she noticed, was beginning to weigh a bit too heavily on the sweaty air.

91 Jed Quinn ran a large hand through his dark locks. The muscles of his jaw tightened ominously and his mouth became a threatening line.

92 "Well," he said, his gaze lancing through her. "Well, well, well. Came to see some more belly buttons, did you? What's the matter? Didn't you like mine?"

93 The remark embarrassed her, but she was determined that she was no longer to play games with him, nor let him set the tone.

94 "Do you plan to stick to a man-to-man defense all season?" she asked. "Will you play that way against Augustana, for instance?" She held the microphone out toward Quinn, noting with amazed satisfaction that her hand wasn't trembling.

95 He placed his fists on his lean hips, cocked his head slightly and stared at her from beneath his thick brows. "Miss Morgan. This is a men's locker room. And you're a woman. My players aren't stupid. They noticed that little fact almost immediately."

96 She held her ground. "Have you thought of going to a 2-2-1 zone press?" she asked, undaunted.

97 He made an impatient motion with his wide shoulders as if he were shrugging away a pesky mosquito. He looked around him, addressing the men in the room his mouth still tense with anger.

98 "Yes, boys," he said with a little sigh. "It's a woman. How do we know? Why, there are certain signs..." His eyes moved up and down her body, pausing to rest on her breasts and hips. "One of those signs is that it doesn't listen. No, boys, it just never wants to listen."

99 Scotty reminded herself not to be intimidated. "I asked you about zone defense," she started as calmly as she could, but she was beginning to feel her control slipping away.

100 "Now, boys," he went on, his hands still on his hips. "I'm as liberated as the next man, but I'll tell you something. A woman isn't a good thing at all to have in a men's locker room. Please note that I'm not saying women aren't good for anything. Indeed they're good for many things. Watch closely, and I'll demonstrate."

101 He took two long steps, and then he was hulking over her.

102 *Uh-oh,* thought Scotty, her eyes widening. She heard the whirl of Hassledorf's camera and a snicker from Duff Freely.

103 "Women are good for holding," Quinn said, with a smug smile of satisfaction.

104 Suddenly his arms were around her, and she felt herself being hoisted up like a child into his strong arms, her feet leaving the floor. She kicked ineffectually, trying to keep her microphone free. Her shoulder was pressed against the hardness of his broad chest. She could smell the faint scent of bay rum, mingled with fresh sweat and tobacco smoke.

105 Desperately she held the microphone toward his grimly set lips. "Zone defense?" she asked. Her voice was a frightened squeak.

106 "Women are good for holding," he repeated. "Holding very tightly."

107 His arms squeezed her more closely against him, and she gave an involuntary gasp. Being caught in his arms was like being pinned in a steel vise.

108 "And women are good for kissing,"

Quinn drawled, the dimple twitching in his bronzed cheek. "Especially for kissing good-bye. Goodbye, Miss Morgan."

109   His lips bore down on hers, roughly at first, inflexible and dominating. She tried to gasp again, but could not.

110   He kept on kissing her, just as tenaciously as before, his mouth growing gentler for a moment, then strengthening for an even more irresistible assault.

111   Dizzied by his warm male scent, she could feel the strength of his lean hands imprisoning her body and could taste the hot moistness of his practiced mouth. For a spinning moment her eyes had widened, and she had an unfocused look at the dark sweep of his lashes. Then in automatic self-defense she squeezed her own eyes shut, her head bending back, trying to escape the pressure of that too-expert mouth.

112   "Hey, coach! All right!"

113   "Good work, coach!"

114   "Whoo!"

115   "Get her, cowboy!"

116   The hoots of the players began to blur in her ears. She felt helplessly dazed — a woman trapped in a nightmare that had turned erotic. He was kissing her in a way she had never been kissed before, and it was doing something horrible to her muscle control. Her knees seemed to have gone numb, her whole body nervelessly pliant, and still he kissed her in that unyielding embrace, as if to prove that the superiority of his force must never again be questioned.

117   Suddenly his mouth relented, releasing hers. Her microphone she realized, was jammed rather painfully against her shoulder. His face drew away from hers and, still holding her, he stared down into her dazed eyes with satisfaction.

118   "As I said," he murmured, his voice husky with feigned tenderness, "Goodbye, Miss Morgan. Anytime you want more of the same, just walk in that door. I'll be happy to comply."

119   She felt herself being carried back toward the door, heard the force with which

he kicked it open. In a surge of humiliated rage, she realized he was actually throwing her out.

120   He set her down outside the door none too gently. "You've got a nice mouth," he said, the intimacy of his voice insulting. "But don't come back. Bye."

121   She straightened her blazer and glared up at him furiously. "Mr. Quinn," she said, her voice shaking with emotion. "I think you just violated about eighteen of my civil rights!"

122   "Come back in," he smiled, "and I'll violate something a lot more interesting than your civil rights. Parting is such sweet sorrow. *Adieu,* nevertheless. Beat it."

123   He closed the door, and she kicked it as hard as she could.

124   The door opened again, and Hassledorf was propelled out, pushed firmly by Quinn's long arms. "And keep your cameraman away. From now on you and Channel 50 are *persona non grata* around here. Keep out. You're henceforth banned. Expelled. Cast out. Finished. Kaput. Good-bye."

125   He gave her a mocking little wave, then closed the door again. Again Scotty kicked it, so hard it brought tears to her eyes.

126   The pain ebbed, but the tears stayed. "Oh, Hassledorf," she moaned, "What have I done? Can he really get away with this?"

127   Hassledorf looked strangely calm, even pleased.

128   "You did great, kid," he said, nodding in satisfaction.

129   "Great? Oh, sure," she wailed. She turned and gave the cold smooth wall of the corridor an impotent smack with her fist. "If I'd done any better, I'd have to commit suicide. Oh, I hate that man! I hate him!"

130   "Hey!" Hassledorf said, with the same strange smile. "Not to worry, kid." He patted his camera affectionately, as if it were a faithful dog. "I got it all. You just might become the heroine of one of the greatest sex discrimination cases ever."

131   "What?" she said, blinking at him from under her tousled bangs. If Quinn had just

stunned her nearly insensible, Hassledorf was finishing off the job quite neatly. She wasn't sure she had heard him correctly. "What?" she repeated, feeling slightly sick to her stomach.

132   "He just got too cute for his own good," Hassledorf said, smirking with evil satisfaction. "We've got him now." He patted his camera again. "Stick with me, kid. I'll make you famous."

133   He turned, whistling, and set off down the hall toward the exit door for the parking lot.

134   Scotty felt almost faint with confusion. She wanted Quinn to cooperate. She didn't want to turn this stupid controversy into a discrimination case. She wanted to do her job, not be Joan of Arc. She wanted to report news, not make it.

135   "Hassledorf," she called after him, "I don't want to be famous!"

136   Hassledorf kept on walking and whistling. Dazed, Scotty rubbed her tender swollen lips, looked around her like a small trapped animal, then ran after Hassledorf, her heels tapping out a rapid patter on the tile floor.

137   She had the sickening sensation that once again a chain of events was being set into motion that would carry her to some destination that she could not name, or even imagine.

EXERCISES

Content

Recall the main events in this chapter by answering the following questions. Respond to some of the questions in your own words. Respond to others by finding quotations that provide the answers.

1. What is the significance of Helena Schaffer?

2. Select examples of Scotty's conflicting feelings toward Quinn.

3. What are the prospects for the Timberwolves (and for Jed Quinn) this season?

4. How does the game surprise everyone? How does Quinn react after the game?

5. How does Scotty react during and after Quinn's kiss?

6. Why is Hassledorf happy about the locker room incident? What is Scotty's reaction to Hassledorf's attitude?

Inferences

In your responses to the following questions, incorporate some of the quotations you located in response to the Content questions. You may decide to use either all or only part of each quotation.

1. Did you find this chapter interesting? Why or why not? Did you find yourself in suspense as the chapter progressed? Would you like to read the rest of the novel?

2. Do you find this scene romantic? Sexy? Explain.

3. How are Scotty and Quinn characterized?

4. To what extent do you find that this scene relies on stereotypes of male and female behavior and attitudes?

5. What conclusions can you draw about Quinn based on his experiences with Helena?

6. Evaluate this scene as fiction. How does it compare with other fiction you have read? How does it compare with other romance fiction you have read? Consider such matters as the devices Campbell uses to characterize her hero and heroine, the dialogue, and the descriptions of their feelings.

7. Write your version of the chapter that follows Chapter 3 in *Only a Woman*. As an alternative, write an outline of the rest of the novel.

Alice Turner

JANET DAILEY: QUEEN OF HEARTS

Alice Turner is a freelance writer. This article, which first appeared in *Redbook*, will provide an example of a romance novelist discussing her work. The article begins with an excerpt from Janet Dailey's
1 ***Ride the Thunder.***

> His breath was warm against her lips an instant before his mouth covered them in a long, drugging kiss. Slipping free of the gown's shoulder straps, her hands explored the flexible steel bands rippling along his upper arms...Leaving a trail of golden fire, his mouth followed the slanting curve of her jaw to the hollow below her ear, down the smooth column of her neck all the way to the base of her throat. Her head was tipped back to allow him greater access to whatever area pleased him while Jordana trembled with quaking desire.

2 Could any woman resist? Millions of Janet Dailey's readers wouldn't dream of it. Ardently they devour the romance novels that Janet Dailey writes with such record-breaking speed — 79 since 1975, including *Ride the Thunder, Night Way* and the extremely popular "Calder" series. With almost 100 million of her books in print and her work translated into 17 languages and sold in 90 different countries, this compelling creature, who could easily double for one of her heroines, is among the half-dozen best-selling authors in the entire world.

3 Janet Dailey lives deep in the heart of the Ozarks, on the shores of Lake Taneycomo, with her husband Bill. A farmer's daughter from Early, Iowa, she is the youngest of four girls. Her sisters still live in Iowa, where the oldest is a truck driver, the second works in a dress shop and the third, a farmer's wife, is the accountant in a feed mill. Janet was a "tomboy bookworm," haunting the library, digging into Nancy Drew, the Hardy Boys, Mark Twain, and later surreptitiously reading *Forever Amber* and the works of Frank Yerby. Like one of her heroines, she left high school to become a secretary, went to work for a fascinating older man and, reader, she married him. At the age of nineteen.

4 Janet claims that Bill Dailey is her model for the romance hero. Sixteen years older than she, he was the independent and successful owner of an Omaha construction company when they met. They worked together there for more than ten years after their marriage, and he was only 44 when he decided to "retire," sell the company and set out on the road with Janet in a 33.5-foot Silver Streak house trailer.

5 To pass the time, Janet took along a stack of Harlequin romances given her by one of her sisters. "Shoot," she said as she finished one after another. "I could do better than that."

6 She said it a lot, and finally Bill was fed up. "If you think you're so darned smart," he said, "why don't you just get off your duff and do one?"

7 Janet accepted the challenge, and several months later sent her first manuscript to Harlequin Books, in Toronto, where it was accepted. She wrote a second. After the third, Bill came up with a scheme.

8   "I went to Jan and laid out a plan for doing these stories," he recalls. "She would do the writing, and I would manage her career and take care of all the research and the business. We would be a team. And that's the way we've done it."

9   Curled in a big corduroy armchair, her little Yorkshire terrier, Mandy, asleep in her lap, Janet speaks quietly, with great self-assurance. Her thick hair, woven in two braids and bound with bright-yellow ribbon, falls to her shoulders. In a dining alcove around the corner of the room, Bill has business visitors, and the hum of their conversation forms a backdrop that never breaks Janet's concentration. Dressed in white slacks and sweater, this slim, graceful woman knows her own beauty, her sensual strength, her power over men. And women.

10   *Q. Can you define romance?*
A. Romance is a mood, a state of mind. That's why we say, "I'm in the mood," or sometimes, "Wait until I'm in the mood." When I write, I try to create that state of mind, that feeling. It's a nice feeling, and it's one of the reasons romance novels are so popular.

11   *Q. What sort of behavior or attitude is romantic in a man?*
A. On the whole, I think it's thoughtfulness. That may not sound very sexy, but it is. In courtship, a man can't do enough for a woman. He tells her she looks nice, gives her flowers, kisses her hand, is attentive to everything she does and says. Disillusionment with marriage sets in at the point when he stops acting that way, and the woman feels a tremendous loss. She has lost that wonderful part of courtship when she felt important because he treated her as if she were the most important person in the world.

12   *Q. Do you have any advice on how you can keep that feeling going?*
A. You have to work at it. You can get a man to be romantic by doing something for him. You can bring him his coffee and orange juice in bed, and the minute he feels like the pampered king of the kingdom, he wants to

do something benevolent. It's just the way courtship worked with you, but turned around. In a real relationship you have a two-way situation.

13   *Q. The men in your novels are rich, glamorous, successful. Why aren't they more like the guy next door?*
A. Most people would say, "Oh, that's because women want security, and they fantasize about having a lot of money and pretty clothes — high living." But that's not why at all. What a woman wants is real access to her man — she doesn't want to compete with his boss for his attention or for his time. She wants him to be the boss and to give his time to her. So in a romance, if a man isn't rich, he's always in some way independent. He can be a dashing scoundrel or a hunting guide or an oil wildcatter. But he's always in control of his fate.

14   *Q. But don't the men in your books run to a certain type?*
A. In a romance novel, you must remember, the man is the sex object. The heroine spends a lot of time thinking about him, so he's observed in a lot of detail, described much more carefully than the woman is. He tends to run to type, but it's a very attractive type. Women want a man who is gentle, who has a sense of humor; a man who seems arrogant but is strong enough to be vulnerable, strong enough to change — like Rhett Butler.

15   *Q. Your books are pretty sexy. Aren't you underplaying the sexual part?*
A. Sexual desire is a very strong element in romances — and in romance too! And we writers certainly don't back away from it. But there is always a point where the man stops saying, "I want you — I desire you," and says, "Hey, I like you." The heroine becomes a person for him. He begins to appreciate her humor, her way of talking, the things that make her a person. And it's that — not just the sexual element — that makes the romance work.

16   *Q. How do you handle sex in your books?*
A. I know the reader wants to be titillated, but subtly. That's why the dialogue is so im-

portant. It's filled with innuendo, double meanings, the kinds of retorts you often wish you could think of. To keep the sexual tension going, the love scenes must be sensual, not graphic. You use a word like "stroke" or "caress" without being too specific. You say "his roaming hand" without saying where it's roaming. The reader's imagination will supply that! To go too far in print is not romantic at all.

17 *Q. Were the early romances you wrote for Harlequin and Silhouette that sexy?*
A. [*laughing*] When I was doing the Harlequins and Silhouettes, the rules kept changing. First, kissing was all that was allowed. Then gradually petting was okay, as long as it stayed above the waist and you didn't use the word "nipple." "Rosebuds," "peaks" and "crests"—oh, we were kept busy thinking of alternatives!

18 *Q. Do you think there's some truth in the criticism that romance novels are sheer fantasy—a means of escape for readers?*
A. It's true that they're called escape novels, but they won't work unless there's an element of reality too. I show a genuine conflict between the hero and heroine. Real or imagined, the conflict exists and they can't wish it away. The characters cope with it, find a way to resolve it, and that resolution involves change—it brings them closer together. We can all recognize that kind of pattern from our own relationships, even if the setting is idealistic and escape-oriented.

19 *Q. But you agree that women are, to a certain extent, looking for escape?*
A. Romance novels, don't forget, allow women to see other women moving into jobs and careers, competing with men, having identity crises. But they retain their femininity. They find love—and that's what readers want, so the books are reassuring. I think teen-agers read my books to find out what life is going to be like. In a way, romances deal with the realities of love and romance, not what goes on during adolescent dating. In romance novels, love includes communication, emotional respect, comprehension—not just sex.

20 *Q. How would you describe the women in your stories?*
A. I don't put great beauties in my books. I like down-to-earth, straightforward, plain-spoken women. Of course, I've had some fun with other types—manipulative flirts and such—but my favorite heroines are more like Jessie in *Calder Born, Calder Bred.*

21 *Q. Would you say there's romance after marriage?*
A. As you grow older, your notions about romance stay pretty much the same but your ideas about love change. Romance still means walking through the woods on a clear autumn day or sharing a glass of wine in front of the fireplace. You always think of it in those strong courtship terms. But love is stronger than that. Love comes from shared situations, shared feelings. The link of friendship holds you together. As time goes on you learn to value this even more, because you discover the rarity of it.

22 *Q. Then love, not romance, is the important thing?*
A. Remember I said there's a point in a book where romance begins to turn into love? That's what we hope will happen in our own lives. The erotic element is fun, but the relationship is really more what it's about. Courtship is exciting, and it's wonderful to be able to experience that in the context of love.

23 *Q. I'm beginning to get the idea that love is romantic. Would you agree?*
A. Well, I'll tell you a story. I remember that once when Bill and I were on the road, we ended up walking on the coast of Cape Cod on a dreary, blustery, cold, miserable day. We had to go down a long stretch of beach to get to the car. It was so cold that we could hardly walk, and at one point we had to huddle behind some rocks to get away from the wind. We cuddled up to each other to get warm and we watched the waves, which looked pretty threatening. We felt especially close at that moment, and it has become a memory we both cherish. It wasn't erotic, but it sure was romantic!

EXERCISES

Content

Recall the main ideas in this article by answering the following questions. Respond to some of the questions in your own words. Respond to others by finding quotations from the article that provide the answers.

1. To Dailey, what constitutes romance and romantic behavior?

2. Why does Dailey make all of her heroes "rich, glamorous, successful"?

3. How does Dailey treat sex in her novels?

4. How does Dailey respond to the charge that her novels are escapist, allowing readers to flee the real world and find comfort in a fantasy world?

5. What, for Dailey, is the relationship between love and romance?

Structure

1. Explain how paragraphs 1 and 2, considered together, form an identifiable section of the article.

2. Explain how paragraphs 3 through 7, considered together, form an identifiable section of the article. Give this section a title.

3. How is paragraph 9 related to the rest of the article?

Fact/Opinion

Classify each of the following statements as either a fact, an opinion, or a fact wrapped in an opinion. If the statement is a combination of fact and opinion, identify which part is fact and which opinion.

1. "With almost 100 million of her books in print and her work translated into 17 languages and sold in 90 different countries, this compelling creature, who could easily double for one of her heroines, is among the half-dozen best-selling authors in the entire world."

2. "Her thick hair, woven in two braids and bound with bright-yellow ribbon, falls to her shoulders."

3. "To keep the sexual tension going, the love scenes must be sensual, not graphic."

Inferences

In your responses to the following questions, incorporate some of the quotations you located in response to the Content questions. You may decide to use either all or only part of each quotation.

1. Why does Turner quote the passage from Dailey's novel *Ride the Thunder?*

2. In what way does Dailey's experience parallel that of a typical romance heroine?

3. To what extent does Turner describe Dailey as if she were a romance heroine?

4. From the evidence in this article, what seems to be the main appeal of romance novels for their readers?

5. Based on Dailey's comments, what kind of episodes would you expect to find in her novels?

6. What kind of elements would not work in romance novels? What kind of characters would not make good heroes or heroines? To what extent do the kinds of things that would not work in such novels indicate a problem with this kind of writing?

7. How does Dailey appear to feel about her work? About her life?

Will Stanton

WOMAN IN THE MIRROR

Will Stanton's books include *The Golden Evenings of Summer* and *The Old, Familiar Booby Traps of Home*. He has written for the *Saturday Evening Post* and *Reader's Digest*, where the following article first appeared. Here Stanton provides a humorous example of how overindulgence in romances can ruin wives and mothers.

1 My wife, Maggie, always made fun of paperback romances — right up to the time she got the flu and her friend Lucille brought her a stack of them. By the time she was well, she had read *Bride of Raventhorne, Bride of Falconhurst, Bride of Monkshaven, Bride of Ottercombe* and all the others. Then she returned them — and came back with an even higher stack.

2 I wasn't really concerned until I noticed one evening that there weren't any holes in the newspaper. No coupons had been cut out. No recipes. Nothing. I realized that she wasn't even *looking* at the paper anymore.

3 I went out to the kitchen. Maggie was reading *Forbidden Rhapsody* while some cookies baked. "Maggie," I said, "I can't help wondering...."

4 "Why I read such dumb books?" She smiled. "There's something about the world of Scottish castles, private jets and French châteaux. And the little things too. The spray of hibiscus on the breakfast tray, the flamenco guitarist at the café, the drive through orange and olive groves...."

5 "So you wish you were the heroine in the story."

6 Maggie got up, stepped over the curled-up corner of the linoleum and unhooked the coat hanger that secures the oven door. "How can you say that," she asked, "when I have so much?"

7 Lucille's husband, Roscoe, claimed to have read some of the books, so I asked him what it was that had the women so worked up.

8 "Hard to say," he said. "All the heroes are tall, dark, and have eyes that seem to conceal something. They are named Lance, Rance, Quinn or Damien. And the girl is a cute little thing who gets a job as companion for Lance's or Quinn's or Damien's 16-year-old ward.

9 "Sometimes the heroine loses her memory. Hurrying to catch the last train, she steps off the curb, hears the screech of brakes and wakes up in this château. When she looks in the mirror, a stranger's face looks back. Then this tall fellow with piercing blue eyes comes in, tells her she has had a long illness, and must rest and not ask questions. This goes on for 180 pages."

10 I checked out some of Maggie's books. Roscoe had, indeed, captured their essence.

11 "I've been reading some of your books," I said to Maggie one night. "Why keep struggling through the same plot? Like, in *Castle Limbo,* the young librarian steps off the curb, there is a screech of brakes, and darkness descends. She wakes up in this seaside villa

with no idea of where she is, and when she looks in the mirror, a strange woman looks back."

12   "And the same thing happens in *Isle of Oblivion*," Maggie agreed, "and in *Passport to Nirvana*." Her eyes softened. "It's what I look forward to most."

13   "You look forward to some poor girl getting clobbered by a cab?"

14   "I don't suppose a man could understand," she said. She thought for a minute. "You remember last Thursday? That was the day the TV burned out, and the house smelled of barbecued plastic. I'd tried that home perm the night before and wound up looking like Orphan Annie's grandma. Then the school nurse called—Sammy was sick, and I had to pick him up. Naturally, the car battery was dead. So there I was, standing at the curb in the rain with my jumper cables, trying to get somebody to stop." She took a deep breath. "There was a screech of brakes. I closed my eyes and thought, *If it's ever going to happen, let it be now.*"

15   I noticed the boys standing bewildered in the doorway. "Even if you lost your memory," our older son, Roy, said, "everybody else would know where you were."

16   "I don't have all the bugs worked out," she said. "But maybe the hairdo would throw them off long enough for the hospital records to get switched. Anyhow, I wake up in a strange tower. A man named Konrad is standing by the window. A Mediterranean breeze ruffles the curtains...."

17   The boys were looking at each other. "Who's going to fix our cinnamon toast?" demanded Sammy, "And drive us to the movies? And pick us up?"

18   Maggie tousled his hair. "As soon as I started to remember, I'd have Konrad send for you in his private jet."

19   "What about me?" I asked. "What'll Konrad do for me?"

20   "You?" Maggie said. "I, uh, haven't worked that out yet."

21   The following day I complained to Roscoe. "All those heroes—tall, trim, taciturn, curly hair, piercing eyes, landed, titled—how can I compete?"

He thought for a minute. "Taciturn?" he suggested.   22

Big help.   23

"It's no good," I told Maggie a few days later. "There's no way I can compete with Konrad and Lance and Quinn."   24

"Nobody wants you to," she said. "Those books don't have anything to do with you. They're just a way of keeping the dream alive."   25

"The dream?"   26

"Yes," she said. "When you're a girl, you dream about Prince Charming. One day you look in the mirror, and its not the face of a princess that looks back; it's the face of a woman who has ironed an acre of shirts, defrosted a glacier's worth of refrigerators and built a Great Wall of peanut-butter sandwiches. You know then that even if the prince should come riding up, he wouldn't get off his white horse."   27

"Serve him right," I said. "He'd never know what he was missing."   28

"So naturally...." She stopped and looked at me. "What does *that* mean?"   29

"Just that a cardboard hero wouldn't know what to do with a three-dimensional woman."   30

Maggie glanced down, smoothing her dress. "You'd say I was three-dimensional?"   31

"At the very least." I got up and walked over to the window. "And another thing. Any time you step off the curb, you be sure to look both ways. Okay?"   32

"Okay," she said.   33

She came over and stood beside me. "Nice breeze tonight." She sighed. "I love to look at the olive trees in the moonlight."   34

"Those are oranges," I said. "The olives are around back, next to the pimentos."   35

"Whatever." She took my arm, resting her head on my shoulder. "Must be getting late."   36

She began to stack her paperbacks on the table. As I started down the hall, I could hear her voice: "*Au revoir*, Rolph, Lance, Damien, Quinn."   37

I stopped and waited for her, touched by those good-bys. Good-bys? A vague feeling of uneasiness began to stir, and I reached back   38 for my eighth-grade French. *Au revoir?* Until the next time?

39   "Maggie," I whispered, "what do you mean by *au revoir?*"

"No questions, my prince," she said, 40 smiling mysteriously. "I've had a long illness and need my rest."

EXERCISES

Content

Recall the main ideas in this article by answering the following questions. Respond to some of the questions in your own words. Respond to others by finding quotations from the article that provide the answers.

1. How does Maggie get hooked on romance novels?

2. What is the narrator's response to Maggie's new obsession?

3. How does Maggie herself account for the appeal of novels like *Castle Limbo?*

4. To what extent can the narrator not compete with Konrad, Lance, and Quinn? To what extent can he do better than his paper rivals?

5. Why does Maggie finally decide to say *au revoir* to Rolph, Lance, and the rest?

Fact/Opinion

Classify each of the following statements as either a fact, an opinion, or a fact wrapped in an opinion. If the statement is a combination of fact and opinion, identify which part is fact and which opinion.

1. "My wife, Maggie, always made fun of paperback romances—right up to the time she got the flu and her friend Lucille brought her a stack of them."

2. "There's something about the world of Scottish castles, private jets and French châteaux."

3. "I noticed the boys standing bewildered in the doorway."

Inferences

In your responses to the following questions, incorporate some of the quotations you located in response to the Content questions. You may decide to use either all or only part of each quotation.

1. To what extent do you find that this article contains stereotyping of husbands and wives— to what extent, that is, does Stanton suggest that the attitudes of the wife he portrays in his article are typical of the attitudes of all wives and that the attitudes he portrays in himself are typical of the attitudes of all husbands?

2. What kind of marriage, what kind of family life, do the narrator and Maggie seem to have had?

3. To what extent do this marriage and family life account for Maggie's addiction to romance novels?

4. Does it seem, from the last two or three paragraphs, that Maggie is ready to give up romances once and for all? Why or why not?

5. How do Janet Dailey's comments on love and romance help account for Maggie's state of mind?

Lee Fleming

TRUE CONFESSIONS OF A ROMANCE NOVELIST

Lee Fleming, author of *Someone Special*, is a freelance writer residing in Washington, D.C. Like Turner's interview with Janet Dailey, this article provides examples of a romance novelist's feelings about her work—feelings that are different from those of Dailey.

1   I'm in it for the money. For years, through college literature classes, I railed against writers who sent bad books into the world. I remained pure but poor, destined to write fiction that might not sell but might get a review.

2   But there is the rent, and eating. I was tired of getting by on a free-lancer's income, tired, too, of hearing "Free-lance writer? Are you unemployed?" I was justified, I told myself. I decided to write a romance novel. After all, it would give me the freedom to write a *real* novel.

3   The embarrassment lingers, but not always. I still list my romance novels under "other" on my résumé. But recently, at a Washington social event where everyone asks everyone what they do, my response elicited: "You write romance novels? How marvelous! You're going to be rich."

4   Yes, delighted, I'm sure.

5   I had never read one, but a friend voiced my thought: "All you have to do is set it in some place like Zanzibar, call the hero Lassiter, and have him sneer most of the time. You can't miss." The first attempt took 39 hours, is something of a parody and got me a swift rejection. The second try, however, took 84 hours—36 to write, 48 to revise—and brought a $5,000 advance. If peo-

ple actually buy the book, there will be more. Depending on retail price (most sell for about $2.50) and numbers sold (suppose I sell 50,000) I could get $7,500—minus the advance. Maybe that's not such a big deal. But I indulge in fantasy: over a period of several years I could sell 200,000. I might net $20,000—or $30,000.

6   Publishers are hazy about first printings: a low figure is 50,000; the average is 250,000. Many publishers reprint again and again, selling through clubs as well as stores.

7   A writer with several books out can do very nicely. Take my 29-year-old friend who left waitressing two years ago to write romances: with five due for release, she estimates an initial income of $90,000.

8   Publishers are also in it for money. Mills & Boon, which puts out Harlequin romances, is the second largest paperback publisher in the world. Silhouette estimates it will account for three-fourths of Simon & Schuster's revenue in the coming year. Combined sales of Silhouette and Harlequin books for 1981 are estimated at 90 million copies. Even Random House has joined in with a Love and Life (my publisher) venture under Ballantine's imprint.

9   I focus on these figures. They're my justification. They offset the embarrassment. I do encounter barbed comments from academic acquaintances who say I have "let down" literature to make a buck. And one man at an embassy party turned his champagne glass upside down and left muttering under his breath when told of my new adventure. Another waved a knife under my nose, telling me I should die for writing drek.

10   My favorite people are the ones who say, "Romances? I've been meaning to write one myself. A cinch." They don't.

11   So I turn to lawyers and say, "Defendants? Heck, I could get them off. No sweat, only takes a minute."

12   Despite what others think, there is no formula. And while I may scorn much of the writing in the hundreds of romances released each year, when it's a matter of my books, beware. I won't disown them: within their boundaries I've honed my craft. Even in the parody, I set description-writing as the task. The result was a texture I would cheerfully transfer to a more "serious" work.

13   Claire Harrison, who writes for Silhouette and Harlequin, has plots that sound like mainstream fiction, plots that depend on psychological motives and barricades to fulfillment rather than on coincidence or circumstance. Kathleen Seidel, whose two books will launch Harlequin's American line, uses the lesson of her PhD from Johns Hopkins University in 19th-century novels to bring devices like symbolism and color imagery into play. English stylists, American storytellers: these are the "schools" developing. Most committed practitioners are very serious, holding strong opinions about individual authors and the romance genre in general.

14   My first encounters with Washington romance writers, where I discovered this unapologetic attitude, astonished me. They were secure and I was not. I was ambivalent about writing and had yet to read a romance, even after selling the book to Ballantine. I felt like a freak.

15   What I knew about various lines of romance novels came from the tip sheets that tell where to locate the action (either the United States or an exotic island—seldom both); what the hero can be (if he's a doctor, the heroine cannot be a nurse); what time frame should be used (it must be present day; if not, it's a historical romance); and what mystery is allowed (in a contemporary romance it must be why the hero and heroine can't get together, but a romance where mystery is central is a "gothic," regardless of time period, ruined castle or supernatural occurrences).

16   Tip sheets also give the length— between 50,000 and 75,000 words, depending on the line—and guidelines for characters' ages and appearance. Unlike mainstream fiction, where it is conceivable a hero could be ugly, no one buys a romance with that in mind. The heroine is pretty-to-beautiful, although, if beautiful, she a) doesn't know it or b) would never "use" her looks. That's left for the "other woman."

17   The sheets also outline acceptable sex. Until 1978, passion was allowed but not described; all that has changed. Jeanie Wilson, Harlequin's area representative, is succinct: "Harlequin Romances take you to the bedroom door; the Presents series open the door; the Superromances actually show them doing it." The newer lines are the result of the market stress on "real-life" situations, of which sex seems to be the major part.

18   I tried to compromise between sacred and profane by involving my heroine graphically with nonheros while she regained her sexual confidence in a pool, on a yacht and overlooking the Hollywood Hills. Trysts with hero Bill were left discreetly to the imagination.

19   "Wrong," said my editor. "Bill's the one. Get rid of the others and give us more with him."

20   Unlike erotica and pornography, where genitalia are named and nicknamed, the romance is bound by a vocabulary of "good taste." A penis is suggested but never named, although "breast" is acceptable. My favorite euphemism, having finally read some romances, is "insistent manhood," although colleagues have others on their Top 10 list of allusive phrases: powerful thighs, hardening muscles, animal attraction reaching out, muscled weight of his body, sheer looming force, rigid muscular tension straining, vibrant muscular body, tensile bulge of his thighs, velvet-skinned muscles of his back.

21   There are always happy endings, at the heart of which is the idea of commitment. "Yes, the woman needs the man, but by the book's end, he'd had to commit to her and her needs," Harrison points out, talking of the feminist backlash to romances.

22   With the idea of striking a blow for feminism in romance fiction, I had drawn my first heroine so strongly she was strident. Now, I've settled for giving her a career and self-esteem. The audiences do not want tracts; they want romance—believable romance. Because for every neurotic figure in a book, there are more vivid examples in life.

23   "I need these," a powerhouse trial lawyer told me. "Do you know what men are like out there?"

24   A close friend read my manuscript and called: "I'm miserable. Bill is wonderful and he's a figment of your imagination. Why is it only the creeps are real?"

25   There are perils to creating the perfect man and relationship. People assume my life's in the book, and that they're in it. An old boyfriend first told me he didn't mind if I put him in.

26   "Don't worry," I said. "No one you know will read it"—a lie. I freely plagiarized his life, from apartment and job to hair and eye color, although I did not steal his character. However, after reading the book, he gradually asked me to change things, from the pets and bungalow location to the foods the hero ate.

27   "It's not you," I pointed out.

28   "Everyone will think it's me," he countered.

29   Since the hero has numerous character quirks—despite being a generally terrific guy, the kind romances call for—I complied, removing the bothersome externals. He wanted out, but others have begged me to transcribe names, careers and even whole lives in the next book.

30   I have that option, but I have no control over title or cover. My working title (I thought) resonated with psychological implications, but *Giant Step* became *Someone Special* because the phrase popped up throughout. When my editor announced this, I groaned but agreed, reasoning that I owed her. She took me, based on a proposal and three chapters culled from the parody—almost unheard of in this business. And good relations with editors are essential. Loyalty is at a premium: I've heard horror stories about authors exorcised for having wandering eyes and pens.

31   I had wanted to use "Genevieve Haymond," my grandmother's name, as my nom de plume. The cover editor thought it a blatant pseudonym. "What about 'Ginny Haymond'?" my editor asked. "Virginia" is my middle name, mercifully remembered only by my mother and aunt in Boston. From out of the air, I snatched at two names from book bindings, and came up with "Carolyn Martin." For a week. I thought the novel would come out under CM, envisioned as sultry and darkhaired, rather than GH, who was clearly a fragile, blond southern flower. But recently I found out that the advance sheet uses "Ginny Haymond." I have no image of her at all.

32   Claire Harrison is "Laura Eden" and "Claire St. John," the first because Silhouette required that name, the second because it is the name she wants. "Laura" is a sexy blond; Harlequin's "Claire," on the other hand, is a sophisticated Gibson-style brunet.

33   Kathleen Seidel scrapped her pseudonym, deciding that using one meant she was ashamed; she is not.

34   I demanded anonymity. I was saving my name for the cover of that "serious" book. Arguably, by writing this I have defeated my purpose. But where I once felt that no one outside my circle should ever know the name behind the name, increasingly I tell people to look for the book when it comes out in June. As confidence increases that the writing is good, I may lose all vestiges of embarrassment.

35   I have a friend of critical bent who for years has looked pained when I've mentioned my fictive ambitions. The other day,

he read some chapters. Although he said nothing then, he told a party the next night, "She writes well. The plot's simple but the writing isn't."

36   I was touched that he saw what I wanted seen. But sweet though praise is, I'm still putting that pseudonym between me and the genre. I still have my doubts about the romance novel. Yet there is one part of the business about which I am sure: printed love is money nowadays.

EXERCISES

Content

Recall the main ideas in this article by answering the following questions. Respond to some of the questions in your own words. Respond to others by finding quotations from the article that provide the answers.

1. What sort of guidelines are offered by the publishers' tip sheets?

2. In what ways has the feminist movement influenced Fleming's depiction of her female characters?

3. What role does Fleming's editor play in the creation of her novels?

4. Why does Fleming continue to have mixed feelings about using her real name in connection with her occupation?

Structure

1. Explain how paragraphs 6–9, considered together, form an identifiable section of the article. Give this identifiable section a title.

2. How is paragraph 13 related to paragraph 12?

3. How is paragraph 36 related to the thesis of the article?

Fact/Opinion

Classify each of the following statements as either a fact, an opinion, or a fact wrapped in an opinion. If the statement is a combination of fact and opinion, identify which part is fact and which opinion.

1. "I'm in it [writing romance novels] for the money."

2. "Many publishers reprint again and again, selling through clubs as well as stores."

3. "Kathleen Seidel, whose two books will launch Harlequin's American line, uses the lesson of her Ph.D. from Johns Hopkins University in 19th-century novels to bring devices like symbolism and color imagery into play."

4. "I have a friend of critical bent who for years has looked pained when I've mentioned my fictive ambitions."

Inferences

In your responses to the following questions, incorporate some of the quotations you located in response to the Content questions. You may decide to use either all or only part of each quotation.

1. Why does Fleming feel embarrassed about writing romance novels? Why does she feel less embarrassed now than she used to?

2. Why do you think Fleming spends so much time on the financial realities of romance novel publishing?

3. From the evidence in the two articles, compare and contrast the ways that Janet Dailey and Lee Fleming appear to feel about their work.

4. Reread paragraphs 10 and 11. Fleming has herself saying to lawyers, "Defendants? Heck, I could get them off. No sweat, only takes a minute." How does this quotation help to crystallize one aspect of her attitude toward her work?

5. For what purpose do you think Fleming discusses (in paragraph 13) her fellow romance novelists Claire Harrison and Kathleen Seidel? How does this discussion tie in with her oft-stated embarrassment at being the author of romance novels?

6. Do you notice any difference in attitude between Janet Dailey's discussion of sex in romance novels (paragraphs 16 and 17 in Turner's article) and Fleming's discussion of the same subject (paragraph 20 in her article)?

7. What differences do you discern between the attitude of Maggie's husband in "Woman in the Mirror" and Fleming's friend Bill concerning the relationship between themselves and romance heroes?

Barbara Delinsky

WRITING THE CATEGORY ROMANCE

Barbara Delinsky has written more than twenty category romances under the pen names Bonnie Drake and Billi Douglas. Included in her recent titles are *Gemstone* and *Time to Love*. This article also appears as a chapter in *Writing and Selling the Romance Novel*. It will provide examples of many of the aspects of romance novels that are mentioned in the Assignment Preview at the end of the introduction to this chapter.

1   Category romance has come of age. Even when a weak economy put many other areas of publishing on hold, the genre thrived. What started as a field dominated by the Harlequin Romance expanded to include monthly entries by Dell, Simon and Schuster, Jove, Bantam, and New American Library, among others.

Why do readers flock to buy category romances by the millions? For one thing, they find romance novels shorter, easier to read, and therefore more pleasurable than some of the heavier fare on the bookstore shelves. Each new romance title is a self-contained entertainment unit, a predictably good read. For another, the category romance is priced lower than most mainstream novels, and finally, and most important, it offers a story of love and happiness, a story in which problems are met and resolved, a story in which two people discover, in their union, something far greater than the simple sum of their parts.

Sound trite? Or corny? Then, read no further! For the most fundamental prerequisite to writing romance is *loving* romance. It is the one element that unites romance writers with their readers, and it is inescapable.

4   My own entry into the field of romance novel writing was quite by accident. As opposed to many of my colleagues, I had not been a fan first. A romantic, yes; a regular reader of romance, no. Indeed, I was quite ignorant of the field until I spotted a newspaper article on the category romance and its authors. Call it fate ... or destiny ... or a certain spark kindled in that instant—but something appealed to me at the thought of giving it a try.

5   Enthusiastically, if systematically, I pored over forty or fifty Harlequin Romances, outlined them with paper and pencil, tried to discern the much-touted "formula," then set out to write my own novel. After an intense three-and-a-half weeks of near-constant work, I sent off that first manuscript. Six weeks later, it was picked up from the slush pile and bought by Dell, who brought it out as *The Passionate Touch,* under the pseudonym Bonnie Drake. Less than three years after finishing that first romance novel, I mailed number twenty-one off to my editor in New York.

6   How does one go about writing category romance? First, one reads. One reads *widely.* One reads widely *in the field.* It is not enough to pick up one or two romances that were published even as recently as a year or two ago. The field is changing so rapidly that one must buy last month's books, *this* month's books to get an accurate glimpse of what is being bought now for publication next year. For category romance *is* different from the mainstream novel in that it stays within certain guidelines—ever-widening guidelines, but guidelines nonetheless. Which leads to the second step in writing romance—setting your eye on a market.

7   Identify the publishing houses that publish category romance and send for tip sheets. First and foremost, such tip sheets indicate the length of manuscript a particular house wants, a figure that varies from 50,000 to 100,000 words, depending on the line.

Some imprints, such as Simon and Schuster's Silhouette, have multiple lines, each with its own length requirements and guidelines. Today, most category romances are in either a 188-page or a 256-page format, though this, too, may change.

8   Tip sheets suggest the preferred ages of hero and heroine (most commonly between 25 and 40); types of setting (some American, others European or "exotic"); and occupations (often professional, always interesting), plus the kinds of conflicts preferred for a given line—physical or emotional, internal or external. Tip sheets also indicate the acceptable level of sensuality, varying from sweet (as in a typical Silhouette Romance) to provocative (as in a Dell Ecstasy, a Silhouette Desire, an NAL Rapture, or a Bantam Loveswept). Finally, tip sheets list those taboos—such as violence, infidelity, and overwhelming tragedy—which, if included in your work, would guarantee a speedy rejection.

9   Much as these guidelines might be scoffed at, we who regularly write category romance respect them, just as we respect the hundreds of thousands of readers who inspire them. These readers are primarily women, as often married as single, with as many college and post-graduate degrees as high school diplomas, ranging widely in age but being above average in intelligence and increasingly sophisticated in taste. They find our books enjoyable, in part because they have no fear of finding endless profanity or immorality, or page upon page of depression to add to what they read in the newspaper every morning. For that matter, I know of no author of category romance who would write any other way. Like our readers, we are positive people, looking at the brighter side of life, dedicated to problem-solving and, yes, happy endings.

10   Before the matter of tip sheets and guidelines is set aside, let me say a final word about the "formula" often mentioned by those new to or unfamiliar with the genre. "Formula" has a nasty sound ... and rightfully so, since it implies that a writer

composes a story mechanically. None of us does that! There are no clones in category romance. One doesn't simply sit down and write the same thing over and over again following some elementary set of rules. Each book is written, created, and produced by an author whose emotional investment in the project is monumental. Indeed, with so many books on the market, my colleagues and I spend much of our time laboring to make each plot line, each sentence, paragraph or chapter, unique.

11   To those cynics who so often ask about the "formula," therefore, my answer is very simple: If there is a "formula" to speak of, it consists ever so broadly of a man, a woman, a love story, and a happy ending. Voilà!

12   After thoroughly familiarizing yourself with the genre, you will probably want to pick up a specific line at which to aim. Based on each publisher's tip sheets, find a line whose specifications most closely resemble your personal preferences. For example, if you want to write a longer novel, something in the range of 70,000 or 75,000 words, set your sights on a Silhouette Special Edition or a Harlequin American Romance. If your proclivity is toward action and adventure, as opposed to inner psychological conflict, think about writing a Silhouette Intimate Moments. If you feel most comfortable with a sensually explicit style, aim for an Ecstasy or one of the other more sensual lines.

13   With a definite goal in mind, and having read the very latest books published by your target company, you are ready to begin.

14   Pick a theme that interests you. Since your contemporary romance will be told primarily from the woman's point of view, its theme will most often emanate from her. You may want to write about the conflict between career and family, the problems of love the second time around, the struggle for sexual equality. Whereas in the past, the most common theme was a woman's virginity and her preservation of it, themes have changed drastically, as have the times. Nowadays, with most heroines in their mid-twenties or older,

few are virgins, and if they are, they must have extremely good reasons for being so . . . which may indeed be the major theme of the story. Further, the governess-heroine of old has yielded to the female executive, lawyer, photographer, geologist, or architect, hence a corresponding widening of theme possibilities.

15   Themes today may relate to a woman's attitude toward men based on a past hurt, her attitude toward marriage based on a family trauma, her attitude toward the world based on her own lofty ambitions. You may choose issues of trust, love versus lust, freedom and its many meanings; in short, any of the issues facing a woman of today. Most important, be sure *you* feel comfortable with the major theme, since it is one in which you'll be as emotionally involved as your heroine.

16   Next, create your characters, giving them names, physical characteristics, occupations and backgrounds, in a sense composing a case study working from present to past. Your characters must be complete, interesting and modern. Research their occupations as though you were entering the field yourself, though you may include only a small fraction of that information in your actual manuscript. Before you ever lift a pencil, you should know your characters intimately. If they are composites of people you've known from time to time, fine. The better you understand them, the easier it will be to write about them. Remember, if *you* aren't drawn to them, your reader won't be!

17   Above and beyond the conflicts encountered, often created, by the hero and heroine, these two characters must be likable. Indeed, the reader should want to identify with the heroine *and* fall in love with the hero—which does not mean to say that these characters must be perfect. Small faults, when acknowledged by either hero or heroine, often make them all the more endearing.

18   Conversely, don't hesitate to idealize your characters in some ways. Remember, romance is, in its way, a fantasy. It's all right to make your characters larger than life, as long

as they remain, by some stretch of the imagination, believable.

19   Now, find a situation to introduce your characters to one another. This will be the start of your novel, and is critical to the establishment of both characters and theme. Since category romances are, by definition and guideline, shorter than mainstream novels, there is no time to dally with past relationships that can be handled in summarized flashbacks as the story progresses. Rather, the hero and heroine must meet early on, preferably in Chapter 1, certainly no later than the start of Chapter 2, in circumstances that are enticing — or they will arouse the interest of neither editor nor reader. With the number of new romance novels appearing on the bookstore racks and shelves each month, readers are growing understandably picky. They will give the author ten, perhaps twenty pages (all skimmed as they stand at the shelves) in which to capture their fancy. If the reader is bored, she will put the book down — and you've lost a sale. Worse, if the editor is bored, your book will never make it to the shelf!

20   Having chosen an introductory situation that excites you, now sit down and plot out the rest of the story. I prefer to do this with pencil and paper, listing first the general course of events to take place, then gradually filling in detail with each go-round.

21   At the start of the story, hero and heroine either meet for the very first time, are reunited after a long separation, or are forced, by some twist of fate, to see each other as they've never done before. At story's end, they quite surely declare their love and head toward a future of rainbows and sunshine together. Between these two points… the storm rages! Use your imagination; be innovative. Stretch the guidelines as much as possible without breaching them. Look to your everyday life for realism, to your fantasy life for exhilaration. Be conservatively daring… and have fun.

22   Given the limited number of pages allotted, the story must be tight. I find that I work most comfortably with one major theme and its conflict, and one or two lesser sources of tension, all intertwined to keep the whole flowing quickly and bring about the ultimate confrontation and resolution.

23   Whereas mainstream fiction can handle many more sub-themes and sub-plots, the category novel is self-limiting. Indeed, the true challenge of writing category fiction — be it romance, mystery, western or science-fiction — is in presenting the most meaningful story possible, given the limitations of a mere 200 or 250 pages. And it *is* a challenge. Ask any established writer of another genre who has ever attempted to write in category!

24   Time can't be wasted with unnecessary detail. Hence, I haven't even *mentioned* the locale of the story. Whereas originally there was a touch of the travelogue in category romance, today the emphasis is on the *relationship,* the love story itself. Indeed, the fact of location has become so inconsequential that I have, on more than one occasion and with remarkable ease, changed it *after* I've begun a book. Obviously, if one plans to write about a hero and heroine meeting and working together as part of an anthropological study on a tiny South Pacific island, things are different. And, in either case, what little or lot you portray of a particular locale should be accurate. With a worldwide readership, there will always be one fan or foe who *knows* whether what you've described is correct.

25   Just as the setting must be introduced lighthandedly, the use of secondary characters must likewise be soft-pedaled. There is simply not enough room to give them depth. Therefore, I usually conceive of these characters last, using them solely to further the storyline, to move the hero and heroine toward one another.

26   There are times when my plot outline undergoes more editing as I write than the manuscript itself does. It never fails to thrill me when my characters and story take off by themselves, and I find newer, more exciting things occurring than I had ever planned. In light of this, I reserve the right to toss that

original plot outline in the trash if I see fit. Spontaneity, within bounds, can't be beaten!

27   Plot outline, character descriptions, theme synopses in hand, you are finally ready to begin writing. Choose your words with care, leaning freely toward the sensual, being ever aware that a romance must be abundantly romantic, that you must seduce your reader.

28   The reader should quickly identify with the heroine and begin to experience life through her eyes. Make it a vibrant life! Let the heroine *do,* rather than constantly ponder, brood, or recall. If she is relaxed and happy, let her warm to the hero, open up in conversation, return his gentle banter. If she is frustrated, let her snap at him waspishly. If she is angry, let her make his scrambled eggs too dry. If she is nervous, let her knot her fingers in a telephone cord or fidget with the folds of a sheet. Such attention to detail makes her all the more real, all the more human.

29   I cannot stress strongly enough the importance of dialogue in today's category romance. It may be intelligent, thought-provoking, poignant, blunt, or humorous. It should be used freely and often, as the most effective vehicle for allowing two people to get to know each other and, indeed, fall in love.

30   Alas, you are now on your own. For, in actual word-by-word working of a manuscript, your specific writing style will be as different from mine as night from day. Contrary to popular notion, the field of the category romance welcomes this, just as it welcomes originality and freshness of plot ideas and characters. Herein is the challenge: to work within the guidelines of the category to produce a work that is new and exciting.

31   Marvelous things have happened in the past few years. Our heroes and heroines have matured and grown more real, more modern. Their situations have broadened to include a whole gamut of circumstances, many in direct turnaround to those of tradition. One thing remains the same, though. Love.

32   First and foremost, a category romance is a novel about love: finding it, recognizing it, perhaps momentarily losing a grip on it, before finally capturing it forever. To write category romance, one must *feel* romance. One must blend fact with fantasy, emotion with imagination, to produce a story that leaps out to embrace the reader in a fiercely gentle grip. It's not easy, this writing of romance. It takes hour upon hour of intense concentration, week after week of steady work. But for the pride of the finished product, and the pleasure it brings to reader after reader, it is truly a labor of love!

EXERCISES

Content

Recall the main ideas in this article by answering the following questions. Respond to some of the questions in your own words. Respond to others by finding quotations from the article that provide the answers.

1. For what three reasons, according to Delinsky, are category romances thriving?
2. For Delinsky, what is "the most fundamental prerequisite to writing romance"?
3. Why is it important for aspiring romance authors to read widely in the field?
4. Why are the guidelines important for both writers and readers of romance novels?

5. How does Delinsky respond to criticisms that romances are formula novels?

6. How have themes in romance novels shifted in recent years?

7. What advice does Delinsky have to offer on characterization?

8. Why is the locale of the story—where the action takes place—relatively unimportant?

9. During the past few years what has changed and what has remained the same in romance novel writing?

10. How does Delinsky use examples to illustrate her general points in the final section of her article (paragraphs 24–32)?

Structure

1. Divide the article into its major parts (groups of paragraphs). Indicate with a phrase what each part is about.

2. Explain how paragraphs 14–26, considered together, form an identifiable section of the article. Give this section a title.

3. How is paragraph 25 related to paragraph 24?

4. What is the purpose of paragraph 31?

Fact/Opinion

Classify each of the following statements as either a fact, an opinion, or a fact wrapped in an opinion. If the statement is a combination of fact and opinion, identify which part is fact and which opinion.

1. "What started as a field dominated by the Harlequin Romance expanded to include monthly entries by Dell, Simon and Schuster, Jove, Bantam, and New American Library, among others."

2. "Finally, tip sheets list those taboos—such as violence, infidelity, and overwhelming tragedy—which, if included in your work, would guarantee a speedy rejection."

3. "Time can't be wasted with unnecessary detail."

Inferences

In your responses to the following questions, incorporate some of the quotations you located in response to the Content questions. You may decide to use either all or only part of each quotation.

1. To what extent (if any) do you think there is a contradiction between Delinsky's protestations that romance writers do not use formulas and her advice on developing plots in paragraphs 19–23?

2. Delinsky seems to have a different attitude toward writing romance novels from Lee Fleming. At what points in her article do her attitudes become most clear?

3. What attitudes toward the romance novel do Delinsky, Fleming, and Dailey seem to share?

4. From the evidence of Delinsky's article as well as the articles by Lee Fleming and about Janet Dailey, to what extent must a romantic spirit on the one hand and a hard business sense on the other work together in a successful romance writer? Cite quotations from each article that show how these different impulses are both at work.

5. Based on the excerpt from *Only a Woman,* do you think that Bethany Campbell has followed the kind of advice offered by Delinsky? Explain.

ROMANCE TIP SHEETS

Most romance publishers have prepared tip sheets to guide aspiring writers. Presented here are tip sheets from three major romance lines: Harlequin, Silhouette, and Caprice.

Harlequin

A FINE ROMANCE... is hard to find!

1   EDITOR seeks manuscripts for publication in women's Category Romance market. Applications should be between 50–55,000 words long and concerned with the development of true love (with view to marriage) between lady, 17–28, and gentleman, 30–45 (must be rich and/or powerful). Exotic location preferred, happy ending essential. Applications in writing to Editorial Department, Romance Fiction, Mills & Boon Ltd., 15–16 Brook's Mews, London, W1A 1DR.

2   If only it were as easy as that! Every Mills & Boon reader and every aspiring Mills & Boon writer has a very clear picture of what makes our books so successful; some people have even tried to reduce it to a formula which, in its essentials, would look very like the fake ad above. But in order to keep up the high reputation which rests at the core of Mills & Boon's success we have to be a lot tougher than that.

3   We believe that the so-called formula is only the beginning, and that originality, imagination and individuality are the most important qualities in a romance writer. Any competent novelist can follow a detailed recipe for success, but we want writers who have the sort of star quality that makes their books instantly recognisable as *theirs*. The Mills & Boon editorial office, which originates most Harlequin Romances and Harlequin Presents, receives nearly 4,000 manuscripts for consideration every year from aspiring authors. If a dozen new authors are selected for publication in that time, we reckon we are having a bumper year!

4   In a very short space of time, the world of romantic fiction has grown into a big business, and it's not easy to stay businesslike *and* romantic. However, we still believe that quality is more important than quantity—that romance readers deserve the best we can find. A book that simply 'makes the right noises' will *not* make a Mills & Boon.

5   What do we look for when we read a manuscript for the first time? Many would-be authors have tried to find exactly the right note, but have had to admit defeat in the end. Surprisingly, we don't worry too much about flawless presentation; a book that has been written with genuine feeling can be forgiven a few typing mistakes. What is more important is a genuine love of storytelling, combined with a freshness and originality of approach. Sincerity, and belief in the characters as real people, communicate themselves to the reader; if a writer is less concerned about conveying her heroine's innermost thoughts so that the reader understands and sympathises, than making sure the hero first kisses her on page 18 as laid down by the tip-sheet, that preoccupation will show up on the page. Similarly, although imitation is the sincerest form of flattery, we don't want new authors whose work echoes the style of our readers' current favorites. Each of our authors must possess an individual touch, her own particular way of telling a story, and this quality is vital. The great artist is not simply someone who can paint a human figure with the right number of arms and legs, and the

great musician does more than hit the correct notes in the correct order! In the same way, it is what a romance writer creates with her material that makes her special (and successful); a good book is not simply a question of constructing a plot with a hero, a heroine, two quarrels and a happy ending, and spinning it out for 200 pages.

6   The story doesn't necessarily have to be complicated—in fact, a simple tale introducing only a few characters besides the hero and heroine is often very successful. Make sure, however, that the characters are convincing in both their actions and their words. If the hero is meant to be a man of authority, used to being obeyed, he should be shown as such and the other characters should react to him accordingly. With such clues of behaviour, too, it is not always necessary to state bald facts; you can afford to keep the reader guessing by stimulating his/her imagination. For instance, if you include a scene in which the heroine quarrels violently with someone, there is then no need to state that she has an unpredictable temper! If such behaviour is unusual, the reason for it (nervous strain, a headache, a feeling of apprehension) immediately gives the reader a deeper understanding of the heroine's character, and one that has been arrived at by guesswork; the reader who guesses about a character in a book is an interested reader. In general, the dialogue should be completely unstilted. A would-be writer should be aware all the time of everyday patterns of speech, and should try to make the characters as true to life as possible.

7   Equally important is the background against which the principal characters are set. It is vital that this should be as accurate as research allows, although there is no substitute for an author's personal knowledge of a particular background. All Mills & Boon authors spend a good deal of time checking the material used in their books, because they realise how quickly the recognition of a fault or inaccuracy can spoil the reader's enjoyment of a scene. This care should be extended to small details, as well as the more obvious points such as foreign locations and customs; if, for instance, a would-be writer has no idea about office life, it is a mistake to make the heroine a secretary! A working knowledge of the practical details is essential at such points. All this may sound like obvious common sense, but it is surprising how often the obvious is ignored!

8   When attempting a Mills & Boon novel, concentrate on writing a good book rather than a saleable proposition. A good book sells itself and is good indefinitely, while a 'saleable proposition' tends to be based on what is saleable *at the time of writing*— even if a publisher snaps it up, the world will have moved on by at least nine months by the time it finally appears. Think of what you, as a reader, would like to read, rather than what you think an editor will buy—the one will lead to the other if all goes well.

9   A Mills & Boon has a standard length of about 190 printed pages—between 50,000 and 55,000 words. From a purely practical angle, any manuscript which differs so greatly that its author cannot reduce or expand its size to fit this requirement is unsuitable. The most important consideration in accepting or rejecting a manuscript is, however, whether the story lives up to the high standard that Mills & Boon readers have set for us. We know from their letters what they like and dislike about our books, and their opinions matter to us. Maybe we can't please every one of our readers all the time, but it isn't for want of trying!

Silhouette Books*

10   This tip sheet is a guide. It is not a substitute for extensive reading of Silhouette Romances. To find out what a Silhouette Romance is, read as many as possible.

*Silhouette Books no longer sends detailed tip sheets to its writers. The tip sheet included here is out of date and does not reflect the type of romance novels Silhouette Books currently publishes.

11   Though Silhouette Romances are always written in the third person, the point of view is almost exclusively the *heroine's*. She is almost always a virgin, young (19–29), but not beautiful in the high fashion sense. She is basically an ingenue, and wears modest make-up and clothes. The book should open with an unexpected change, challenge, or adventure in her life which she accepts eagerly, although sometimes with trepidation. Her reaction to the amorous advances of the hero mirror the conflict between her desire for him and her strong belief in romantic love. *The hero* is 8 to 12 years older than the heroine. He is self-assured, masterful and tempered, passionate and tender. He is rich and successful in the vocation of his choice, or independently wealthy with some interest to which he devotes his time. Not necessarily handsome, but above all virile, he is never married to anyone but our heroine, though he may be widowed, and even divorced, providing it is made clear that the divorce was not his fault. *The plot* of Contemporary Romance is built around the conflict between the heroine and hero; by the end of the novel this conflict is resolved and the lovers are together. The novel explores their developing relationship. We prefer their initial meeting, or the events leading up to their meeting, to be in the first chapter. Background material should be kept to a minimum of memories and flashbacks. After the lovers meet, the narrative should be sequential and straightforward. A Silhouette Romance is not a Gothic or a Novel of Suspense or Adventure. Murder, gunplay, abductions, beatings, spies, and the occult are not suitable elements for Silhouette Contemporary Romance. *Love scenes* should be frequent and escalate in intensity. The lovers should not consummate their love without marriage. Descriptions of their lovemaking should be sensuous, not graphic. Rape and Violence do not belong in a Silhouette Contemporary Romance. *The setting* is always contemporary, preferably exotic or lush. Sense, taste, touch, are all important. Dialogue should be natural. The writing, while contemporary, should

not be slangy, obscene, or profane. Local idioms, dialect, foreign words and phrases should be used with extreme discretion.

Caprice Romances

12   Caprice Romances are contemporary young adult first-love novels that will express the restlessness of youth and the wonder of falling in love.

13   *Plot:* The first meaningful romantic interlude in a young woman's life. Although she may have dated before, she believes that this romance is the real thing. The development of emotional and physical feelings toward a young man, the confusion these feelings bring on and the happiness which results when confusion gives way to caring...this is the world of CAPRICE.

14   The young people are basically good. One or the other may be selfish or vain on occasion, any number of pitfalls are allowed as long as they are acknowledged and rectified by the end of the book, and as long as both members of the relationship remain likeable to some extent.

15   A strong subplot is encouraged. The plots will reflect current day attitudes and themes that are of interest to teen readers. There can be family or school traumas, problems or joys, as long as the focus remains on the love aspect.

16   Although these books are traditional romances in that they are comparatively innocent, our young people are not unaware of sex. They experience the stirring of sexual desire but these descriptions must be sensitively handled and our characters will not follow through on their desires.

17   *Characters:* The girl is fifteen or sixteen. Her experience with dating up to this point is the author's choice but it is within this relationship that the girl's emotions blossom.

18   The boy is sixteen or seventeen and has had varied experience with girls. Again his prior experience is up to the author.

19   We strongly recommend that other characters be developed...a best friend, possibly

an understanding adult (not a parent), an ex-girlfriend or boyfriend, etc.

20 *Point of view:* From the girl's point of view, either first or third person.

Length: 50,000 to 60,000 words. Dia- 21 logue is an important element in each of these stories.

EXERCISES

Content

Recall the main ideas in these passages by answering the following questions. Respond to some of the questions in your own words. Respond to others by finding quotations from the article that provide the answers.

1. What is the main idea projected in the first four paragraphs of the Harlequin tip sheet?

2. What qualities in a manuscript are most important, according to Harlequin? What qualities are less important?

3. Why does Harlequin discourage imitation and slavish adherence to its own tip sheets?

4. Why is research important, according to Harlequin?

5. To what degree do the specifications for Harlequin, Silhouette and Caprice romances compare (reflect similarities)? To what degree do they contrast?

Inferences

In your responses to the following questions, incorporate some of the quotations you located in response to the Content questions. You may decide to use either all or only part of each quotation.

1. To what extent do the guidelines in the various tip sheets reveal traditional expectations about women and men? To what extent do they reveal post–women's liberation concerns?

2. How are these guidelines reflected in some of the things that Dailey and Fleming say about their characters and their plots?

3. In "Writing the Category Romance," Barbara Delinsky writes, "'Formula' has a nasty sound...it implies that a writer composes a story mechanically. None of us does that! There are no clones in category romance. One doesn't simply sit down and write the same thing over and over again following some elementary set of rules." But as one critic, Kathleen L. Campion, observed, "If you can follow a cake recipe, you can write a romance novel, or so it appears." To what extent does the information in the tip sheets support or contradict Delinsky's denial of the romance "formula"?

4. In what way are the requirements for Caprice Romances different from those for Silhouette romances? (Focus on the hero, the heroine, and the plotting.)

5. What qualities of an ideal romance (from the point of view of one or more of the tip sheets) would prevent it from qualifying as "literature"?

6. Compare and contrast the various comments about the importance of formula in romance writing in (1) Fleming's "True Confessions" (especially paragraphs 12 and 13); (2) Delinsky's "Writing the Category Romance" (especially paragraphs 10 and 11).

7. To what extent do you think Bethany Campbell, in the excerpt from *Only a Woman,* relies on the kinds of formula devices indicated in the tip sheets?

8. To what degree do the specifications in the tip sheets reflect sexist, outdated, or otherwise undesirable attitudes?

9. Some critics feel that romances not only promote and perpetuate outdated attitudes but also may be a device to keep housewives in their proper place. (Recall the housewife mentioned in our introduction who reads three romances a day and so has neither the time nor the inclination to do anything more productive. Recall also Will Stanton's wife, who reads romances to take her mind off the frustrations of her household chores.) Write an essay either agreeing or disagreeing with this charge.

John Gross

A ROMANTIC REFERENCE BOOK

1   It's the tone that makes the music and it's the tag that makes the romance. Tags, if you are unfamiliar with the term, are short descriptive phrases used to raise the temperature of romantic fiction. Where an amateur novelist might be content to have her hero merely smile, for instance, a tag-wielding professional will substitute something stronger and stranger—"His mouth quirked with humor," or "There was a pale blue lightning of amusement between his lashes." And it can make all the difference—the difference, as Jean Salter Kent rightly says, "between a cold, factual report and an eager, pulsating, sensuous story."

2   Miss Kent first heard about tags from a helpful literary agent who was trying to explain to her why her novels kept being turned down by publishers. She already belonged to a writers' group that met every week "to critique each other's manuscripts," and taking the agent's advice to heart she and another member of the group, Candace Shelton, decided to put aside the stories they were working on and concentrate on thinking up tags instead. With a dedication Bouvard and Pécuchet might have envied they gradually stockpiled and sorted out over

3,000 suitable items, and they have now published the results of their labors in the shape of *The Romance Writers' Phrase Book* (Perigee Books, $6.95), a work they see not exactly as a reference book—they don't encourage aspiring writers to borrow phrases from them wholesale—but as an example and an inspiration. In Miss Kent's own case, collecting tags certainly seems to have done the trick; she has now had seven of her novels published.

3   Many of the individual entries in the *Phrase Book* are irresistible, and few are of the kind that would gain much from extended critical analysis. "She paused, broadcasting a regal certainty"; "She saw his eyes, large glittering ovals of repudiation"—what more is there to say? "She could be as playful as a girl or as composed as an intelligent woman"—the most you feel inclined to add is an accompanying drawing by James Thurber.

4   As you read on, however, a few general reflections inevitably start coming to mind. Whether they intended to or not, the authors have in fact provided quite a good structuralist (or is it poststructuralist?) guide to some of the recurrent patterns and underlying ten-

sions of the genre. You begin to notice key words like "fluid" or "exude," for example ("He rose in one fluid motion"); you become aware of the extent to which cynicism is seen as the chief enemy, of how many thin lips and mocking looks there are. But perhaps the most striking characteristic of the phrases in the book, taken as a whole, is the way in which they oscillate between the utterly vague and the unnaturally specific. On the one hand, "There was a spark of some indefinable emotion in his eyes"; on the other, "She was entranced by the chocolate of his eyes," "His wild sapphire eyes mellowed subtly," "The expression of his currant-black eyes seemed to plead for friendship." And allied to this there are frequent switches of tempo, from the languorous to the hectic ("She quickly chastised herself") and back again.

Despite such contrasts, a formula is a 5 formula, and the final effect is one of monotony. The men in particular tend to be almost repulsively handsome and rugged, "tall and straight like a towering spruce," endowed with "long, sturdy Viking legs." What a relief it is to come across the odd, presumably villainous exception ("His bulbous nose dominated his meaty features").

Still, far be it from me to critique. If you 6 want help composing the kind of books in which they specialize, the authors deliver the goods, and they left me pondering on how difficult it is to describe moments of high romantic passion convincingly, at any literary level. There are probably phrases in D. H. Lawrence or Charlotte Brontë they could have slipped into their book without anyone noticing—not that I would ever suspect them of attempting anything so subversive.

EXERCISES

Content

Recall the main ideas in this article by answering the following questions.

1. What are "tags"? Why are they important in romance novels?

2. In what way do Kent and Shelton advise aspiring authors of romance novels to make use of *The Romance Writers' Phrase Book?*

Structure

1. What is the purpose of paragraph 2?

2. How is paragraph 2 related to paragraphs 3 and 4?

Fact/Opinion

Classify each of the following statements as either a fact, an opinion, or a fact wrapped in an opinion. If the statement is a combination of fact and opinion, identify which part is fact and which opinion.

1. "Tags, if you are familiar with the term, are short descriptive phrases used to raise the temperature of romantic fiction."

2. "Despite such contrasts, a formula is a formula, and the final effect is one of monotony."

Inferences

In your responses to the following questions, incorporate some of the quotations you located in response to the Content questions. You may decide to use either all or only part of each quotation.

1. John Gross remarks that "few [of the phrases recommended for romance novels] are of the kind that would gain much from extended critical analysis." What do you think he means by this? What can you gather from this comment about his attitude toward *The Romance Writers' Phrase Book?*

2. Gross also says that after studying these phrases, you will conclude that "cynicism is seen as the chief enemy." What does he mean by this? Why is cynicism the chief enemy?

3. What correspondences can you discover between the desirable qualities of the romantic hero as implied from the *Phrase Book* and the desirable qualities of the hero as implied from the publishers' tip sheets and in Barbara Delinsky's "Writing the Category Romance"?

4. Does Gross's attitude toward *The Romance Writers' Phrase Book* change at all in the final paragraph of his article? If so, how? Why, for example, does he mention D. H. Lawrence and Charlotte Brontë?

5. Do you find evidence of tags in Bethany Campbell's chapter from *Only a Woman?* Explain.

6. Do you see any connection between the kinds of things discussed in "A Romantic Reference Book" that account for Maggie's decision (in "Woman in the Mirror") to say good-bye to Rolph, Lance, Damien, and Quinn?

7. What connections, if any, do you see between Lee Fleming's ambiguous feelings toward her profession and the subject matter of "A Romantic Reference Book"?

Margaret Atwood

JUST LIKE A WOMAN

Born in Ottawa, Canada, author Margaret Atwood has taught at the University of British Columbia, York University, and the University of Toronto. She has won numerous awards for her fiction, her poetry, and her critical essays. Among her volumes of poetry are *Double Persephone*, *Poems for Voices*, *You Are Happy*, and *Two-Headed Poems*. Her novels include *The Edible Woman*, *Lady Oracle*, *Bodily Harm*, *Murder in the Dark*, and, most recently, *The Handmaid's Tale*. Atwood's article, and the one that follows by Margo Jefferson, offer examples of the problems with romance fiction.

1   Men's novels are about men. Women's novels are about men too but from a differ-ent point of view. You can have a men's novel with no women in it except possibly the landlady or the horse, but you can't have a women's novel with no men in it. Sometimes men put women in men's novels but leave out some of the parts: the heads, for instance, or the hands. Women's novels leave out parts of men as well. Sometimes it's the stretch between the belly button and the knees, sometimes it's the sense of humor. It's hard to have a sense of humor in a cloak, in a high wind, on a moor.

Women do not usually write novels of the type favored by men but men are known to write novels of the type favored by women. Some people find this odd.

2   I like to read novels in which the heroine has a costume rustling discreetly over

her breasts, or discreet breasts rustling under her costume; in any case, there must be a costume, some breasts, some rustling, and, over all, discretion. Discretion over all, like a fog, a miasma through which the outlines of things appear only vaguely. A glimpse of pink through the gloom, the sound of breathing, satin slithering to the floor, revealing what? Never mind, I say. Never never mind.

3   Men favor heroes who are tough and hard: tough with men, hard with women. Sometimes the hero goes soft on a woman, but this is always a mistake. Women do not favor heroines who are tough and hard. Instead they have to be tough and soft. This leads to linguistic difficulties. Last time we looked, monosyllables were male, still dominant but sinking fast, wrapped in the octopoid arms of labial polysyllables, whispering to them with arachnoid grace: *darling, darling.*

4   Men's novels are about how to get power. Killing and so on, or winning and so on. So are women's novels, though the method is different. In men's novels, getting the woman or women goes along with getting the power. It's a perk, not a means. In women's novels you get the power by getting the man. The man is the power. But sex won't do; he has to love you. What do you think all that kneeling's about, down among the crinolines, on the Persian carpet? At least say it. When all else is lacking, verbalization can be enough. *Love.* There, you can stand up now, it didn't kill you. Did it?

5   I no longer want to read about anything sad. Anything violent, anything disturbing, anything like that. No funerals at the end, though there can be some in the middle. If there must be deaths, let there be resurrections, or at least a heaven so we know where we are. Depression and squalor are for those under twenty-five; they can take it, they even like it, they still have enough time left. But real life is bad for you; hold it in your hand long enough and you'll get pimples and become feeble-minded. You'll go blind.

6   I want happiness, guaranteed, joy all around, covers with nurses on them or

brides, intelligent girls but not too intelligent, with regular teeth and pluck and both breasts the same size and no excess facial hair, someone you can depend on to know where the bandages are and to turn the hero, that potential rake and killer, into a well-groomed country gentleman with clean fingernails and the right vocabulary. *Always,* he has to say. *Forever.* I no longer want to read books that don't end with the word *forever.* I want to be stroked between the eyes, one way only.

7   Some people think a woman's novel is anything without politics in it. Some think it's anything about relationships. Some think it's anything with a lot of operations in it, medical ones I mean. Some think it's anything that doesn't give you a broad, panoramic view of our exciting times. Me, well, I just want something you can leave on the coffee table and not be too worried if the kids get into it. You think that's not a real consideration? You're wrong.

8   *She had the startled eyes of a wild bird.* This is the kind of sentence I go mad for. I would like to be able to write such sentences, without embarrassment. I would like to be able to read them without embarrassment. If only I could do these two simple things, I feel, I would be able to pass my allotted time on this earth like a pearl wrapped in velvet.

9   *She had the startled eyes of a wild bird.* Ah, but which one? A screech owl, perhaps, or a cuckoo? It does make a difference. We do not need more literalists of the imagination. They cannot read *a body like a gazelle's* without thinking of intestinal parasites, zoos, and smells.

10   *She had a feral gaze like that of an untamed animal,* I read. Reluctantly I put down the book, thumb still inserted at the exciting moment. He's about to crush her in his arms, pressing his hot, devouring, hard, demanding mouth to her as her breasts squish out the top of her dress, but I can't concentrate. Metaphor leads me by the nose, into the maze, and suddenly all Eden lies before me. Porcupines, weasels, warthogs, and skunks,

their feral gazes malicious or bland or stolid
or piggy and sly. Agony, to see the romantic
frisson quivering just out of reach, a dark-
winged butterfly stuck to an overripe peach,

and not to be able to swallow, or wallow.
Which one? I murmur to the unresponding
air. *Which one?*

EXERCISES

Content

Recall the main ideas in this article by answering the following questions. Respond to
some of the questions in your own words. Respond to others by finding quotations from the
article that provide the answers.

1. Summarize the chief negative qualities Atwood finds in women's novels.

2. How is the hero of a man's novel different from the hero of a woman's novel?

3. Why does Atwood have trouble with the sentence "She had the startled eyes of a
wild bird"?

Inferences

In your responses to the following questions, incorporate some of the quotations you
located in response to the Content questions. You may decide to use either all or only part of
each quotation.

1. Atwood makes considerable use of *irony* in this brief essay; that is, she often means the opposite of what she says. When, for example, she says (in paragraph 5), "I no longer want to
read about anything sad," she clearly means that she finds the attitude of people who only
want to read about happy things appalling. What other examples of irony do you find? Why do
you think she uses irony instead of saying straightforwardly what she likes and dislikes?

2. What criticism of romance novels is Atwood making when she says, "real life is bad for you;
hold it in your hand long enough and you'll get pimples and become feeble-minded. You'll
go blind"?

3. What criticism is Atwood making of characterization in romance novels in paragraph 6?

4. What is Atwood saying about the language of romance novels in the final three paragraphs?

Margo Jefferson

SWEET DREAMS FOR TEEN QUEENS

**Margo Jefferson, formerly of *Newsweek*,
teaches journalism at New York University.**

1   It seems appropriate to begin a piece on
books for teen-age girls with the words of
the adults who produce them.

"After years of being deluged with young 2
*adult books dealing with the unhappy reali-
ties of life, such as divorce, pregnancy outside of marriage, alcoholism, mental illness,
and lately child abuse, teenagers seem to*

want to read about something closer to their daily lives." (Wildfire Romances)

3   *"Caprice Romances are contemporary young adult first-love novels that will express the restlessness of youth and the wonder of falling in love."*

4   *"Each Sweet Dreams romance features a heroine who is about sixteen years old—an ordinary, middle-class suburban girl, with a family to match. The romantic interest, a boy of the same age or a little older, should appear early in the story—the sooner the better."*

5   *"The tension in these novels lies in the heroine's struggles with common adolescent problems, her romantic fantasies as opposed to the realities, and in her desire to define herself.... The ending of a First Love, though, is always upbeat."*

6   *"Wishing Star ... plots should deal with some of the more serious problems of young girls today, like divorce, school difficulties, loneliness, death, parental things, etc. No books will deal with sexual matters, like abortion, unmarried pregnancy, affairs. There should, however, be a romance in every book."*

7   *"Our young people are not unaware of sex. They 'make-out' and may have the first stirrings of sexual desire but description must be sensitively handled and they will not follow through on their desires."* (Caprice)

8   *"Lastly, there should be no profanity, no religious references, and no explicit sex. We endorse hugging and kissing, of course. Where would romance be without them?"* (Sweet Dreams)

9   You can find these books in the young adult sections of bookstores, sometimes displayed in white plastic racks, sometimes in boxed sets, prettily done up in pink with touches of blue, mauve and dove gray. You can also find them in shopping malls and advertised in the brochures of teen book clubs owned by Xerox and by Scholastic Books, which brought out the first of these series,

the Wildfire Romances, in 1979. Teen romances bring their publishers millions in sales, and the publishers are willing to lavish millions on advertising in return. Although the romances were originally marketed through schools and libraries, Bantam, Simon and Schuster, Scholastic, and Grosset and Dunlap have now captured a large trade audience as well. They have an eye to the future and say they want their girl readers to experience a literary upward mobility that will allow them to move (eventually) from *Small Town Summer* and *I'm Christy* to *Wuthering Heights* and *Jane Eyre.*

10   These books, which cost less than $2 for some 200 pages of text where words that exceed two syllables are kept to a tasteful minimum, reproduce rapidly, at the rate of two new titles per series each month. Bookstores usually shelve them very near their adult romance counterparts, but you can distinguish between them immediately. The covers of adult romances feature illustrations of exotic fantasy; the teen ones offer photographs of adolescent models gazing into a boyfriend's, a mentor's or the camera's eye with tender, lively or sweetly mournful expressions. Grown-up girls are expected to kick off their shoes and abandon reality with a defiant toss of the head. Teen-age girls are supposed to wander in a state of suspension where fantasy and reality cannot be torn asunder. You fix your hair, put on a record, turn a few pages of *In My Sister's Shadow,* watch television, go through your Sweet Dreams slumber party kit, call your best friend, try to decide whether to wear the pink, the yellow or the white sweater tomorrow and gaze at the face on the cover of *Terri's Dream.*

11   If, dear adult reader, you're confused as to which decade you're in, you'd be no less so if you'd actually read a few of these books. I did, and I found that they're grown-up nostalgia repackaged for the young, very like those remakes of 1950s and 1960s songs done by people in their 30s and 40s pretending to be ten or twenty years younger. It's the silliest sort of ventriloquism: sentimentality about one's own past, piped through the mouths of another generation. The titles

alone betray their authors' generation. Remember Ray Milland in *The Lost Weekend* when you read about teen-age alcoholism in *The Lost Summer;* see Pat Boone and Shirley Jones stroll through the woods when you read about teen-agers on a farm in *An April Love Story.* Fuse the Gershwin brothers with the Jefferson Airplane when you read *Please Love Me...Somebody* or *Someone To Love.* One writer is named Veronica Ladd (all these writers are women, or at least all have women's names—the girls' and ladies' book world has always supported a few men who use female pen names). V. L. dedicates her novel to "L.L.: Romantic Hero, Leading Man in My Private Movie."

12   Listen to the voices of these modern teen-agers as they are rendered by the writers of young adult fiction in a language taken from old soap operas and magazines: " 'Lisa, beautiful Lisa,' Rick murmured as he turned her toward him. 'You will always be surrounded by flowers and love.' " "Dan seemed to be mine, all mine," one heroine declares. Another meets the boy of her dreams when he seeks shelter from a storm in her "simple country kitchen."

> "I'll get you a towel." Another crash of thunder interrupted her words.... "The lightning's close," she shuddered, frozen in place.
>
> "As long as we're inside we're safe," Jeff reassured her soothingly.
>
> *(Terri's Dream)*

One pair of aspiring teen rock stars dream of being the new Sonny and Cher, but their school dances feature The Bump, The Hustle, and The Funky Chicken, all nearly ten years out of date.

13   Yes, but if these books are so false, why do teen-age girls buy them? And why was I unable to put any one of them down once I'd begun reading, despite being enraged or sickened? Well, they're written according to a formula, and the formula is as neat and efficient as that of sitcoms or pop songs or the advertising ditties we commit to memory in spite of ourselves. But the formula also re-

flects our earliest learning experiences—the belief that good behavior brings rewards, bad behavior punishments; the notion that a threatening world can be made benign and orderly through external means (magic and fate) or internal means (conformity and submission).

Fairy and folk tales depend on these   14 primitive notions, as do any number of literary classics that appear on the approved reading lists of high-schoolers. Think of Dickens, the Brontës, Jane Austen, and Shakespeare's comedies: fortunes are whisked away and rebestowed, lost parents and relations are found suddenly and lost again if necessary, siblings are joined in matched-set marriages. But of course there's so much more; the classics permit a range of responses and readings. The young adult romances allow only one of two responses— you can either reject them or comply with them, and they offer no compensations of setting, character or style.

Still, they do have one virtue that may be   15 worth all their faults. They ease fears by offering just enough of the real to make the unreal seem irresistible and attainable. The reader of teen romances feels like Dorothy in *The Wizard of Oz,* lulled to sleep in the poppy field, or like one of those fictional children who trudge through snowy woods longing to lie down and sleep forever. Somehow the torpor of these romances, the lassitude of their writing and plotting, accommodates the beguiling somnambulance of adolescence—form trots obediently after function. It's all here: the yearning to be as conventional as possible, which coexists with the desire to be singled out as particularly worthy of love, admiration and success. Not that the books aren't filled with moral lessons; it's just that the lessons are small and dainty, like the feet and hands pretty girls were once supposed to have. Don't be slothful, snobbish or deceitful. Be a nice person and be well groomed. If your girlfriends and boyfriends are from a higher social class than you are, that proves people are just people. If they're from a respectably lower one, that proves the same thing. (The lack of *mise en scène* helps shield the mythologies of class difference from the realities.) Once a heroine has learned to be herself—to make good grades and get along with her parents and cultivate her athletic or artistic gifts diligently but without undue extravagance—she'll be given a boyfriend and a future full of vague promise. Happily ever after is the time it takes to finish one romance and begin another.

16 "Rumpelstiltskin" and "The Three Spinsters" are fairy tales that feature girls of humble birth who are hustled off to palaces to win princes with their spinning skills. Teen romance writers are spinning into straw whatever gold exists in our childish longings, but the raw materials of fairy tale and teen romance are the same. Dutiful daughters get good boys. The nasty little men and the ugly old women have been banished. The heroines are always talking about "learning to be me," but what a richly rewarded little me that is. I know that teen-age agonies, however shallow—not buying the right dress, not getting a place on the cheerleading squad—are genuine sorrows, but I wonder if they're not also propitiations of a sort: if we're not hoping, while we suffer, that this may be all life demands in the way of trials and tribulations. I noticed that even those teen romance heroines who are aspiring Olympic athletes or gifted fledgling artists never ask themselves what every teen-age girl would, has and does: Am I really talented? What will I do if I meet someone who has more talent? ("You must say what you really want most," Laurie tells Jo March in *Little Women*. "Genius," Jo answers, "don't you wish you could give it to me, Laurie?")

17 What happens when self-discovery has to be its own reward, when talent isn't enough and parents thwart one's wishes while boyfriends sulk and pull away? When Louisa May Alcott wasn't dashing off pseudonymous thrillers or—her words—"providing moral pap for the young," she wrote *Work,* a spirited and earnest look at the opportunities for employment, love and self-respect available to nineteenth-century middle-class women in America. What happens when teen-age girls discover what *Work*'s heroine, Christie Devon, did: that "it's *so* hard to be patient and contented when nothing happens as you want it to, and you don't get your share of happiness, no matter how much you try to deserve it." Our young adult romance writers remain silent on these points. Their publishers assure us that inexperienced young adult readers prefer it that way and are better off if such questions aren't asked.

18 Critics of teen romances, notably the Council on Interracial Books for Children, have excoriated them for sexism, racism and class smugness. All true, but it's fascinating to watch how the books try to accommodate modern views on such issues without endangering the status quo. Boys are offered as rewards here because they bring out the best in girls who are struggling to find themselves. Some of the boys are shy and sensitive, others are jock heroes eager to bring their shy, sensitive sides to light. The boy encourages the heroine to pursue her talent; he nurtures her efforts to be honest and independent. I'll be the feminist for you, he seems to be murmuring in soft but manly tones—I'll be man and woman for both of us. Parents are usually supportive and sketchily drawn, providing sitcom-style reproaches and rapprochements. Only divorced or separated parents, most often mothers, are given any dimension. That the writers only feel free to criticize those parents who have broken the marriage bond doesn't alter the fact that they are the most interesting parents in the books. Most broken marriages are mended by the book's end, of course, which is quite an accomplishment. A girl who reads more than three of these books will not only feel worthless if she doesn't have a boyfriend; she will feel worthless if her parents can't be reconciled in the real-life equivalent of 200 pages.

19 Given this landscape, it's hopeless to expect minority groups to be portrayed intelligently. Jews aren't mentioned directly, though an occasional Jewish-sounding name

drifts across the page. (For instance, I found Jason Steiner, rejected as a possible date for Frannie Bronson in *The Popularity Plan* because he was "too loud.") Hispanics appear in walk-on parts and are treated with that squeamish courtesy that marks the appearance of a new Token in Our Town: Dr. Gomez, the "dark-skinned" physician, Mrs. Lopez, the art teacher "with just a trace of a Spanish accent." Blacks, who have had token status longer than Hispanics, play larger roles in several books—as school friends, as neighbors who behave like tough but loving housekeepers, or as maids who behave like loving but tough mothers and teachers. I came upon one Native American (the best friend of a wealthy white businessman's son) and no Asians.

20   Both a blind and a paralyzed girl appear in books from Wishing Star, the self-declared line of contemporary "non-sexual problem" books. So does a lot of wishful thinking. Blind Lee finds a shy, sensitive beau and passes for sighted at his school dance; paralyzed Andie finds a protectress in the mother of the drunk driver responsible for her condition. In not one of the books is there a whisper about homosexuality. Writers who feel obliged to countenance the occasional member of a minority group draw the line at homosexuals. And even if writers and publishers could decide what line to take, homosexuality would still raise the issues of sex—its force, its repercussions, its effect on identity—far too clearly.

21   The guidelines are distinct: the only lust allowed is the lust for romance and stability. Otherwise, titillation must suffice. And so heroines feel warm sensations and unbearable thrills at "his touch"; they are transfixed by his gaze and prey to "stabs" of excitement when he passes them in the hall. Dreams, which are "like being with him all night," are good for a few illicit snickers, and so are sports, especially horseback riding. ("Maura lifted into a hunt seat, squeezed her legs into Blackfire's sides, and the rhythm began—up, over, land, squeeze.") Only a few books mention "going all the way," and I found myself wondering, given the rising number of girls reading these novels and the rising number of girls getting pregnant, whether there was any overlap of the two constituencies. It is not impossible; it is, in fact, likely. What these books are really marketing is wishful thinking—the state of mind many teen-age girls are in when they experience intercourse, pregnancy, abortion or childbirth.

22   What do the writers of these books actually think about their products? I'm not sure, but they display a certain anxiety of influence, rapping the adult romances their readers will graduate to in a few years firmly on the knuckles. "He didn't have a rock jaw or Roman nose or pearly teeth, or any of the stock attributes of the heroes of the romantic novels she read by the dozens," says the heroine of *I've Got a Crush on You.* She's speaking of her high school English teacher, who will praise her poetic gift, admit that he could fall in love with her, but leave her free to pursue college, fame and a local boyfriend instead. Adult romances soften the brain and teach you a lot of outdated slang, a friend tells the heroine of *Dreams Can Come True,* who later exclaims, "Why couldn't things be the way they were in books? She had met the most important man in her life and he hadn't even looked at her....Wryly, she thought of her silly little dreams she'd written in her secret notebook."

23   I'd like to leave you with brief summaries of my two favorite teen romances. *Honey* (Wishing Star) is about a young girl who lives with her mother in a Boston suburb. Father left them years ago; now all mother, who is from a fine old New England family, does is whine and read adult romances. Honey, who is a promising art student, cooks and cleans for both of them. Into this drudgery comes the family next door— the elegant Redfields of Mississippi with their maid, Vanilla. Vanilla, as her name playfully indicates, is black, and not really a maid. The Redfields discovered her singing in a Las Vegas club to earn money for college tuition and were so impressed that they brought

her into their home so she could earn her Boston University tuition by working for them. Suddenly, Honey's father returns, eager to make a new life for his family in Maine. The Redfields go off to Europe and Honey stays behind for a while, feeling deserted by everyone. But Vanilla, who has just graduated *summa cum laude,* sits her down and explains a few things about love and mothering. Honey's self-absorbed mother is only one slice of a "Mother Pie," Vanilla says; other slices are teachers, mentors and friends, even men. And, of course, "mean old chocolate Vanilla." So Honey goes happily off to Maine, leaving behind a boyfriend who will visit her regularly and taking with her the knowledge that it is still possible to make a loving mammy out of a college-educated maid.

24   *P. S. I Love You* (Sweet Dreams) tells of young Mariah and her dream of being a famous novelist like Rosemary Rogers or Kathleen Woodiwiss. She meets Paul Strobe in Palm Springs where she, her mother and her sister have gone to house-sit for the summer. Paul is from a wealthy but enlightened and artistic family; he befriends a Native American and his father writes novels and owns a bookstore. Paul wants to be an architect, and it is he who encourages Mariah to look beyond romantic novels to realistic ones. But shortly after they fall in love, Paul is stricken with cancer, and when Mariah returns to California he enters the hospital. She is loving and loyal throughout his decline, and when he dies her mother reminds her that "no true love story has a happy ending."

But this one does. Mariah has grown through her pain; she is young and pretty, her parents are getting back together and she has a new typewriter. We know that when she is a little older her love story with Paul will be the subject of her first novel. She will take it to Paul's father, who, remembering her kindness to his son, will get it published and sell it in his bookstore.

And that's where we began—in book- 25 stores, where First Love, Caprice, Sweet Dreams, Wildfire and Wishing Star will be joined this month by Windswept, a "contemporary gothic" series. If I were a 16-year-old, would I buy these books? Well, perhaps if I had limited financial and emotional resources, knew about rising unemployment among teen-agers and cutbacks in college loans and scholarships, had at least heard of liquor and drugs, felt uncertain about sex, had some awareness of divorce and the correlation between poverty (genteel or crude) and single women (with or sans children), and didn't want to think too much about any of this—yes, I would buy these books.

And if I were an adult writer, editor or 26 publisher who knew all of this and had experienced some of it, and perhaps wanted to recreate my memory or fantasy of a care-free adolescence—a memory that would not only soothe and please me but would see to it that, for their own good, teen-age girls were no more prepared for the world than I had been and made no fewer mistakes than I had—well, I'd write, edit, advertise, and sell these books.

| **EXERCISES** | |

Content

Recall the main ideas in this article by answering the following questions. Respond to some of the questions in your own words. Respond to others by finding quotations from the article that provide the answers.

1. What are some of the differences between teen romances and adult romances?

2. Jefferson believes that teen romances are "grown-up nostalgia repackaged for the young." Why?

3. According to Jefferson, why do teen-age girls continue to buy romances?

4. Since both teen romances and literary classics by Dickens, the Brontës, Jane Austen, and Shakespeare rely on such "primitive notions" as good being rewarded and evil punished, what is the difference, according to Jefferson, between the young romances and the classics?

5. These romances, according to Jefferson, "do have one virtue that may be worth all their faults." What is this virtue?

6. What kind of hard questions are *not* asked in teen romances, according to Jefferson? Why is this a problem?

7. What other criticisms have been directed at teen romances?

8. How do the summaries of *Honey* and *P. S. I Love You* exemplify the kind of positive and negative qualities of teen romances that Jefferson has discussed in the earlier part of her article?

Structure

1. Divide the article into its major parts (groups of paragraphs). Indicate with a phrase what each part is about.

2. How is paragraph 14 related to paragraph 13?

3. Explain how paragraphs 18–20, considered together, form an identifiable section of the article. Give this section a title.

4. What is the purpose of paragraphs 25–26?

Fact/Opinion

Classify each of the following statements as either a fact, an opinion, or a fact wrapped in an opinion. If the statement is a combination of fact and opinion, identify which part is fact and which opinion.

1. "These books, which cost less than $2 for some 200 pages of text where words that exceed two syllables are kept to a tasteful minimum, reproduce rapidly, at the rate of two new titles per series each month."

2. "If, dear adult reader, you're confused as to which decade you're in, you'd be no less so if you'd actually read a few of these books. I did, and I found that they're grown-up nostalgia repackaged for the young, very like those remakes of 1950s and 1960s songs done by people in their 30s and 40s pretending to be ten or twenty years younger."

3. "[Teen romances] ease fears by offering just enough of the real to make the unreal seem irresistible and attainable."

4. "Critics of teen romances, notably the Council on Interracial Books for Children, have excoriated them for sexism, racism and class smugness."

5. "Given this landscape, it's hopeless to expect minority groups to be portrayed intelligently."

Inferences

In your responses to the following questions, incorporate some of the quotations you located in response to the Content questions. You may decide to use either all or only part of each quotation.

1. In the early part of her article, Jefferson discusses some of the differences between teen and adult romances. From reading the other articles in this chapter, does it seem to you that there is a significant difference?

2. How does Jefferson feel about teen romances? Point out passages in which her attitude is clear, either from what she says or from the way she says it.

3. Some readers have found a good deal of irony in this article. (Writers use irony when they say the opposite of what they mean — for example, saying, "This is a truly profound movie" but meaning, "This is a truly stupid movie.") Examine the last three paragraphs and see if you can determine how Jefferson is being ironic. Does she use irony in other parts of the article?

4. Do you think that Maggie, as she is portrayed at the end of "Woman in the Mirror," would agree with Jefferson about the deficiencies of romances? To what extent?

5. To what extent do Delinsky's and Gross's comments about the romance "formula" and about romance "tags" support the comments made by Jefferson in "Sweet Dreams"?

6. Of the writers you have read in this chapter, which seems the most accepting of romances? The least accepting? Which have ambiguous responses?

7. To what extent do you think that romances are harmless — even appealing? At what point does the appeal of romances become a problem — even harmful?

8. Do you agree with such critics of teen romances as the Council on Interracial Books for Children? Why or why not?

9. Some readers have found this article snobbish in its attitude toward teen romances. These readers have suggested that Jefferson is looking down her nose at these novels and the people who read them. Do you agree with this charge? In what passages, if any, do you find examples of snobbery?

10. To what extent do Delinsky, Fleming, Dailey, and Jefferson agree on the appeal of romance novels for their readers? Examine the parts of each article in which the appeal of romance novels is discussed.

11. Have you ever read teen romances? If so, write an essay on your thoughts and feelings about this genre. What attracted you (or still attracts you) to these novels? To what extent do you agree with Jefferson? To what extent do you share her negative attitudes? Do you agree with her assessments about what motivates teenagers to read these novels? Have your feelings about teen romances changed since you first started reading them? If so, how?

SUMMARY ASSIGNMENT

Write a summary of Barbara Delinsky's "Writing the Category Romance." (You may need to review the procedures discussed in Chapter 2.)

Begin by writing one-sentence section summaries. Then write a thesis for the article as a whole. Next combine your thesis and the section summaries into a coherent summary of the entire article.

We will help get you started by suggesting one way that the article can be divided into sections and by writing two one-sentence section summaries.

Section 1 (paragraphs 1–3)
   In recent years category romances have become a major publishing success, as millions of readers eagerly buy these low-priced, easy-to-read, and emotionally satisfying works of fiction.

Section 2 (paragraphs 4–5)
   Barbara Delinsky got into the romance novel field "quite by accident," but three years later had written twenty-one romance novels.

Section 3 (paragraphs 6–7)

Section 4 (paragraphs 8–11)

Section 5 (paragraph 12)

Transition (paragraph 13)

Section 6 (paragraphs 14–15)

Section 7 (paragraphs 16–18)

Section 8 (paragraphs 19–20)

Section 9 (paragraphs 21–26)

Section 10 (paragraphs 27–30)

Section 11 (paragraphs 31–32)

Is there an easy way to identify the sections of an article? There is no ready-made formula; you must read the article carefully and think carefully about how the parts are related to one another. Still, you can be alert for *signs* of transition.

Look for transitional words and phrases at the beginning of paragraphs. Here are some of the common transitions that may introduce new sections:

First	In contrast
Second	Still
Third	On the other hand
Next	Although
Finally	At the same time
Furthermore	All in all
In addition	In summary
Also	In conclusion
Similarly	As a result
Now	

Notice, for example, that paragraph 16, which we have suggested begins a new section, opens with "Next," and paragraph 19, which also begins a section, opens with "Now."

Sometimes new sections open with questions, as, for example, paragraph 6: "How does one go about writing category romance?" However, such devices only indicate the *possibility* of a new section. You must ultimately use your own judgment. Paragraph 17, for example, begins with "Above and beyond" and paragraph 18 begins with "Conversely"; but neither of these paragraphs, in our judgment, begins a new section; they simply indicate relationships *within* the section. Paragraph 3 begins with two questions, but based on the way that this paragraph relates to the previous ones, paragraph 3 seems to us the end of the first section rather than the beginning of the second one.

PAPER ASSIGNMENT

We reprint here the assignment on romance novels that we gave before the main body of readings.

Write a paper in which you provide examples of some of the following:

- Successful romance writers
- Typical romance plots
- The popularity of romance novels
- Feelings of romance writers about their work
- The way romance novels satisfy their readers' needs
- Rules for writing romance novels
- Problems with romance novels

Now work through the following stages in writing your synthesis:

1. Develop a possible list of thesis statements.

2. Narrow these thesis statements as necessary.

3. Select the one thesis that most appeals to you.

4. From the quotations you have selected, your answers to the questions, and your notes, select appropriate evidence to support your thesis.

5. Work up a preliminary outline. Indicate which evidence you will use.

6. Write a draft of your paper based on your outline.

ADDITIONAL WRITING ASSIGNMENTS

1. Go to the supermarket and select a romance for research. Report on what you find. What sort of power does the book you've chosen exert? Do you see the operation of a formula?

2. Try your hand at writing the opening chapter of a romance.

3. Have you ever read a love story that has had a powerful effect on you? If you can find the story, reread it and decide whether its effect is due to the way it fits a formula or to something else.

4. Explain how some of the articles in this chapter throw light on the chapter from Bethany Campbell's *Only a Woman*. For example, does what happens in this chapter appear to be in line with Janet Dailey's ideas about romance? How well does the chapter show Barbara Delinsky's principles at work? To what extent does the chapter make use of the formula in the tip sheets or of Gross's "tags" from the romance reference book? To what extent does the scene conform with the requirements specified in the tip sheets? What do you think Margo Jefferson would say about this chapter?

CHAPTER 9

Who Needs College?

Introduction

Who needs college? Obviously, you think that you do, or you wouldn't be reading this. But what do you expect to get from college? An education? An opportunity to further develop your mind and your outlook? A ticket to graduate school or a job? Time to decide what you want to do with your life?

During the last couple of generations it was taken for granted that college served a useful purpose, usually one or more of the purposes just suggested. It was also taken for granted that most academically inclined high school seniors would continue their education in college the following year. The past decade or so, however, has witnessed growing doubts about the value of a college education. In particular, critics have charged that colleges are educating many young people for jobs that may not be there when they graduate and that what students learn during their college years has little or no relevance to what they will be doing in the working world. In response to such critics, colleges have been compelled either to reaffirm their traditional values or to modify their curricula (often in a more vocationally oriented direction) to convince skeptical students and their parents that their offerings are indeed "relevant."

In this chapter we will provide readings that help throw light on this controversy, readings that you can use to develop a paper on the value of a college education. Some of the readings reaffirm the traditional values of a college education. Others take the position that many students are not well served by the traditional four-year college curriculum. Still others do not take a strong position one way or the other but rather present the subject for your consideration.

Since this subject lends itself very well to *argument,* we will also be focusing in this chapter on the technique of argument in academic essays.

As an introduction to the subject, read the following piece, "Does College Really Matter Anymore?" This article was first published in 1979.

DOES COLLEGE REALLY MATTER ANYMORE?

1   The college degree has lost some of its aura. The magic carpet to higher-paying, successful careers is dumping many passengers short of that destination.

2   From the heyday of the 60s, when a sheepskin was almost sure to open the way to a professional job or managerial position, we've come to this prediction from the Bureau of Labor Statistics: There's a one-in-four chance that students earning degrees between now and 1985 will wind up in blue-collar or clerical jobs or other occupations that traditionally haven't been filled by college-educated workers.

3   The change (some call it a collapse) in the college job market is neither new — it has been confronting grads for several years — nor difficult to explain. It's primarily the result of the bulge in the number of Americans who carry college credentials. During the 1960s an average of half a million students received bachelor's degrees each year; now the figure is close to one million and expected to hover around that mark for a few more years before beginning to decline. The supply of college grads is simply outstripping the number of jobs requiring them. Harvard economist Richard Freeman, who examines the shifting economic status of college graduates in his book *The Overeducated American,* concludes that "knowledge is power only if most people do not have it."

4   Today's plentiful supply of graduates means increasing competition for jobs, disappointment for many in terms of pay or type of work and, for some, no job at all. Tales of college graduates toiling in jobs once considered beneath them or carrying their expensive degrees along to the unemployment line have made a lot of people wonder whether it's still worth it to go to college.

Cost-Benefit Analysis

5   College is expensive and growing more so every year. The basic average cost per student at public universities is now estimated at $3,258. (That's 22% more than those in the class of '79 paid for their freshman year.)* Estimates of the nation's investment in higher education have run as high as 85 billion dollars annually, a figure that includes earnings students passed up by sitting in a classroom rather than working at a job.

6   Would going to college be worth the cost for you? To answer from a purely financial standpoint, you must gauge how much more money you could hope to earn with a college degree than without one and compare that with the cost of four or more years

*According to the College Entrance Examination Board, as indicated in the 1985 edition of its pamphlet "Meeting College Costs," the average cost of one year at a four-year public institution is now $5,314.

of college. This is a tricky business because, among other things, it depends on the type of degree and work you get and requires making and projecting assumptions for a 40- to 50-year working life.

7 Many attempts have been made to put a dollar value on a college diploma. Several years ago Census Bureau Figures provided this precise calculation for men: Getting a degree would add $231,695 to their lifetime earnings. One researcher found that each additional year of schooling after high school added an average of more than $800 to annual salaries. However, a recent BLS assessment of the payoff cited such variables as inflation and offered this conclusion: "How much more money does a college graduate make? Maybe a little, maybe a lot."

8 One thing is certain: While the cost of college keeps going up, the earnings advantage bestowed by a degree is slipping. Median income of college alumni has been running more than 30% higher than that of high school grads; ten years back the premium was about 50%. The narrowing gap reflects both better pay for high school grads and the growing number of degree holders in jobs that don't demand a college education.

Don't Jump to Conclusions

9 Although a degree has lost some of its financial clout, the economic advantages for those who go to college are still significant. The following table compares the median annual incomes of college graduates with those of workers who didn't go beyond high school. These are 1977 figures, the most current available.

Education	Income	
	Men	Women
High School	$15,434	$ 8,894
Four or more years of college	20,625	12,656

10 A college degree may not guarantee you a good job — it never could — but the lack of one can bar you from even being considered for certain positions. The BLS believes that by 1985, 18.1% of all jobs will be reserved for college graduates. And although the surging supply of graduates may deflate the economic value of their credentials, it can make things tougher for those without a degree. Other things being equal, many employers will choose a college grad over an applicant who didn't go beyond high school.

11 Higher education does carry protection against unemployment. In early 1976, for example, the jobless rate among young college graduates ages 20 through 24 was 6.1%; for high school grads of the same ages it was 14.1%. At that time the national unemployment rate was 7.5%, more than triple the 2.4% rate among all college graduates.* Certainly, college graduates are spilling over into job areas that used to be the province of nongraduates. But they're often getting those jobs at the expense of less-educated workers, outbidding them rather than being left unemployed.

12 Another advantage, although difficult to measure in dollars, is that a college education may enhance your ability to adapt to changes in the job market and other economic conditions. In his book *Investment in Learning,* Howard Bowen, professor of economics and education at Claremont Graduate School, writes that "education has the effect of keeping lifetime options open. If a person stops his education short of college, he may cut off access to further education, to many jobs and to other lifetime opportunities and satisfactions."

There's More to It Than Money

13 Judging the value of higher education only on its financial return would be a big mistake. Bowen, who argues that the monetary return is sufficient to cover the cost of

*According to the *1984 Statistical Abstract of the United States,* the national unemployment rate in 1982 was 9.7%. The unemployment rate for high school graduates was 10.3% and the rate for college graduates was 4.2%.

college, says other benefits — including "personal development and life enrichment" — are more significant.

14 We asked Freeman, whose *The Overeducated American* was taken by some as a broadside attack on the value of college, his advice for students wondering whether they should continue their education. "I think most people should still go to college, but not for the economic payoff," he responded. "You have to weigh the fact that a college degree doesn't guarantee a good job or high pay the way it used to against the obvious fact that it's going to widen your horizons to an extent few other experiences do."

15 How do you measure those other benefits? Grand concepts like the "whole person" or "educated man" are intangible and can't be tallied up like salaries. But that doesn't diminish their value.

16 College will introduce you to different people and new ideas and ways of thinking, and it can lead to what Loren Pope, director of the College Placement Bureau, calls "intellectual flexibility." The theme of self-discovery is woven through much of the commentary on the goals of higher education.

17 A great deal of research has been done to pinpoint the nonmonetary effects of higher education. Here's a collection of some of the findings:

- College graduates are, in general, more satisfied with their jobs than are less-educated workers. (This varies according to the job, however. A recent survey found that among secretaries the most dissatisfied were women with college degrees.)
- College grads are more likely to vote and to participate in political and civic organizations.
- They own and read more books than high school graduates and watch less television. College alumni also attend more motion pictures and are more likely to take advantage of adult education programs.
- When freshmen are asked why they decided to go to college, the number

one response is "to get a better job." By the time they graduate, though, they put more emphasis on getting a general education and less on vocation.

- College graduates are less likely to consider life routine or dull than are nongraduates.
- They save a higher percentage of their income than others do.
- The more education one has, the more tolerant and understanding of others he or she is likely to be. Bowen reports that most alumni say "getting along with people is one of the most significant results of their college education."
- Women who have been to college are more likely to be in the labor force, and college graduates in general are more likely to approve of women working.
- Husbands who have been to college are more likely to help around the house, and college-educated parents devote more time and money to their children. The effects of college on family life, Bowen concludes, may be among its most significant outcomes.
- College graduates are probably better able to cope with the growing complexities that confront Americans these days.
- Alumni are likely to work longer hours. One study found that each extra year of school added about one hour to the average workweek.
- College graduates enjoy better health and, on the average, live longer than nongraduates.

18 There's no assurance that going to college would affect you in any of these ways. In fact, it's impossible to conclude that college alone is responsible for the differences that have been cited.

Making Your Decision

19 So how do you decide whether you should go to college? As with any important and expensive decision, it's not easy. Aca-

demic ability and motivation are critical; so is the ability to meet the mounting bills you'll face if you pursue a degree. Relatives and friends may influence you, too.

20   If you have a certain career in mind—as a physician or a physicist, for example—you know college is essential. Being uncertain of what you want to do, however, doesn't mean you shouldn't go on in school. Somewhere between one-third and two-thirds of all students change their major fields of study or career plans during their college years, a fact that supports the view of college as an opportunity to broaden your outlook and make decisions about your future.

21   Don't be scared off by the knowledge that the financial promise of a degree, though still great, is diminishing. The demand for graduates depends mightily on their field. Currently, for example, the market for new engineering grads is booming while that for graduates with liberal arts degrees is in a slump.

22   Freeman sees an advantage in the declining "get ahead" appeal of college. He says people who aren't academically oriented and don't want to go to college aren't under so much pressure to do so for fear of "turning down the future." The growing emphasis on adult education means those who don't go directly from high school to college have opportunities to return to the classroom later, either to delve into a subject to satisfy intellectual curiosity or to specialize with an eye to entering a new profession. Remember, too, that college doesn't hold a monopoly on exposure to new ideas.

23   There are appealing jobs available that don't require a college education. For some occupations, such as skilled trades and some technical fields, special training can give you better credentials than a bachelor's degree in liberal arts. There are high-paying jobs that don't require college and positions that demand degree holders but don't offer hefty salaries. Last year, for instance, the average starting salary for a college graduate in the humanities was just over $10,000; a journeyman plumber could easily earn twice that amount or more.

24   There's no reason, of course, that a plumber or an electrician or a computer technician shouldn't have a college education or that a college grad should spurn these fields. In *Investment in Learning* Bowen challenges the "widespread but obsolete assumption that blue-collar work is in some sense inappropriate for educated men and women. This assumption is a carry-over from an aristocratic conception of both work and higher education."

25   As you weigh the question of whether you should go to college, consider all your options but don't overplay the financial factors at the expense of other results of higher education. Remember that the much-talked-about concepts of being "overeducated" or "underemployed" relate only to the 40 or so hours each week that a person devotes to earning a living. Many argue that even if college had no impact on that part of your life, it would still be a good investment.

26   Consider these remarks by an Oxford professor, as reported by a student who was to become Britain's prime minister, Harold Macmillan: "Except for [those who will become teachers], nothing that you will learn in the course of your studies will be of the slightest possible use to you in after life—save only this—that if you work hard and intelligently, you should be able to detect when a man is talking rot, and that, in my view, is the main, if not the sole purpose of education."

Content

This article explores both sides of the controversy over the value of a college education. Unlike some of the other readings in this chapter, it does not begin with a strongly defined point of view and argue that point of view all the way through. Rather, it begins with a proposition ("The college degree has lost some of its aura") and considers arguments that attempt to answer the question posed in the title — does college really matter anymore? As the article progresses, however, it becomes clear that the author believes that college *does* matter, and he presents his material to support this belief.

Notice how the article is put together. There are four main sections. In the first section (paragraphs 1–4), the author introduces the subject under discussion. His approach in the introduction is to explain why "the college degree has lost some of its aura" and to lead up to the question posed in the title. In the second section (paragraphs 5–12), the author focuses on the monetary value of a college degree. He provides a number of statistics that could be used to support either side of the argument about the value of a college education. The author, however, seems to emphasize the financial benefits of a college education.

In the third section (paragraphs 13–18), the author focuses on the non-monetary values of a college education. For the most part, the information provided in this section would be used in arguments supporting the value of a college degree. As the author points out in paragraph 18 (and as author Caroline Bird points out in an article appearing later in this chapter), there is no guarantee that college *will* result in the benefits listed or that it alone is the cause of these benefits. Still, it is unlikely that the author would have devoted so much space to these benefits unless he believed that they were genuine results of a college education. In the fourth section (paragraphs 19–26), the author focuses on some considerations that may determine a person's decision to go (or to not go) to college. On the surface the author may appear to be presenting a balanced argument, but notice how he weights the argument in favor of a college education; for example, notice what he says in the final two paragraphs (25 and 26).

Using Argument in Papers

When you *argue* in an academic paper, you begin with a point of view — a point of view that you announce in your thesis — and you then provide reasons for the truth or validity of that point of view. Along the way you may also provide reasons why the opposing point of view is untrue or invalid. You may show that both your point of view and the opposing point of view have merit but that your point of view has more merit. But whatever strategy you adopt, the main thing about an academic *argument* is that it is based on your own point of view.

You may wonder how a paper that uses argument is any different from a paper that uses description or one that uses example since all three types require that you begin with a thesis. The answer is that argument deals with a different type of thesis. Let's review what we said when we introduced the description paper:

Your job in writing a description paper is not to argue a particular viewpoint but rather to present the facts in a reasonably objective manner. Of course, description papers, like other academic papers, should be based on a thesis. But the purpose of a thesis of a descriptive paper (e.g., "Ireland is a beautiful place to visit") is less to advance a particular opinion or point of view than to provide focus and direction to the various facts contained within that paper.

In other words, in a description paper (as well as in an example paper), the thesis serves mainly to unify the information you present. Such a thesis ("Ireland is a beautiful place to visit," for example) is not controversial, is not opinionated, does not represent a particular point of view. It's simply a basis for discussion. (We suppose there might be one or two people who would argue that Ireland is *not* a beautiful place to visit; but we'll just arbitrarily say that that isn't a serious argument!)

What are some examples of theses that could serve as the bases of argument papers? Here are a few:

Capital punishment should be outlawed.

We need a constitutional amendment against abortion.

The United States should lift all restrictions on immigration.

All public school students in the United States should be required to read and write English.

All U.S. corporations should be required to pay a minimum percentage of their income in taxes.

The latest Clint Eastwood film is terrible.

Boxing should be banned.

For many students, college is a waste of time and money.

For many students, college is a worthwhile investment.

Notice that all of these theses are *debatable*. They are propositions about which reasonable people could disagree. They are propositions about which people could (given the right information and arguments) be persuaded to change their minds. This is generally not true of the kinds of theses that serve to unify description and example papers. For example, the thesis "While some romance writers are completely happy and confident in their chosen profession, others are less sure of themselves" serves to unify an essay. It is, for the most part, not debatable. It is one over which reasonable people would not disagree.

Notice also that *how* debatable a thesis is depends on how it is worded. For example, take the thesis about the terrible Clint Eastwood film. If the writer of an argument with that thesis were to provide several convincing examples of terrible qualities in the film under discussion, he or she would have a good chance of persuading an objective reader. But what if the thesis, instead of reading "The latest Clint Eastwood film is terrible" read "The latest Clint

Eastwood film is his worst"? This is a more debatable thesis and a much more difficult one to prove since the writer would not only have to cite terrible qualities in the present film but would also have to show that these qualities made the film worse than all other Eastwood films — all of which would have to be considered.

Let's consider the last two thesis statements on the list:

For many students, college is a waste of time and money.

For many students, college is a worthwhile investment.

One of the important words in both thesis statements is "many." Consider how difficult it would be to prove either thesis if "most" were substituted for "many" or, worse, if there were *no* qualifying phrase "For many students." The resulting statements would be seen by many readers as too extreme, and it would be difficult to persuade them of the truth of the theses without more evidence than is provided in the source "Does College Matter Anymore?." But with the qualifying phrase "For many students," the article can provide evidence to support one thesis or another.

Consider, for example, the first thesis, "For many students, college is a waste of time and money." Here is part of an argument paper based on this thesis that provides evidence from "Does College Really Matter Anymore?"

> For years people have justified the great expense of a college education (now averaging over $5,000 a year at a public four-year college) by pointing to the more prestigious jobs and the higher salaries that college graduates command. But since more people than ever before are college graduates, the advantages of a college degree are far less than they used to be. According to one article, the "supply of college grads is simply outstripping the number of jobs requiring them." As a result, many college graduates wind up settling for blue-collar or clerical jobs that require no college diploma. And there is less of a difference between salaries of college graduates and non–college graduates than there used to be. In particular, liberal arts majors are likely to find themselves earning less money after graduation than non–college graduates who are skilled in trades such as plumbing.

Part of our evidence was derived from the introductory section of the article (the quotation comes from paragraph 3); other evidence came from the second part, dealing with the financial considerations of a college education (e.g., paragraph 8), and from the final part (e.g., paragraph 23), about deciding whether or not to go to college.

The article could also supply evidence for the opposite thesis, "For many students, college is a worthwhile investment." Here is a paragraph from an argument paper based on such a thesis and using evidence from "Does College Really Matter Anymore?"

> Even though a college education is not as good a financial investment as it used to be, college graduates still tend to earn more money than non–college graduates. They are less likely to be unemployed than non–college graduates. And of course they are eligible for a whole range of professional

jobs—for instance, in law, medicine, or social work—that are open only to college graduates. But for many, the financial advantages offered by a college education are less important than other intangible advantages. College tends to broaden both your mind and your outlook on life. According to one article, "College will introduce you to different people and new ideas and ways of thinking, and it can lead to...'intellectual flexibility.'" There are other intangible aspects of a college education: researchers have found that, for whatever reason, college graduates are more satisfied with their jobs, and more active in civic affairs, show a greater tolerance and understanding of other people, are better able to cope with life's complexities, are healthier, and live longer. And one great advantage of being more highly educated was offered by the former British prime minister Harold Macmillan: "'...nothing that you will learn in the course of your studies will be of the slightest possible use to you in after life—save only this—that if you work hard and intelligently, you should be able to detect when a man is talking rot, and that, in my view, is the main, if not the sole purpose of education.'"

Our evidence for this paragraph was derived largely from the second section of the article (especially paragraphs 9–11), from the third section (especially paragraphs 16–18), and from the final section (paragraph 26, which includes our closing quotation).

It's possible, of course, that our thesis might take a middle-of-the-road position. For example, we might take the position that "Although college today is a less secure financial investment than it used to be, for most people college is a worthwhile investment." This thesis, of course, is the one that underlies the source article itself, and so you could cite evidence from both sides of the question, just as the article does.

Assignment Preview

As in the previous chapter, at this point we give you a paper assignment that you can think about as you read the remaining selections in this chapter. As you read, select material you can use that will help you write the assignment. If necessary, review Chapters 4 and 7 for advice on dealing with evidence in multiple sources. (This assignment will be reprinted as the first paper assignment at the end of the chapter.)

EXERCISE

Write a paper in which you argue a thesis of your choice. Either you may select a thesis in advance or, preferably, you may wish to formulate a thesis as you read through the articles. Having formulated a thesis, read or reread the selections with an eye to finding evidence that will support your thesis. Questions following each selection will direct you to some of the more important information and ideas.

Once again, please note that a paper that uses argument need not consist *entirely* of argumentative passages. An argument paper may (and indeed should) include description and example. The descriptions and examples, however, will be subordinate to the major argument of the paper.

Techniques of Argument

How does one organize a paper that effectively argues a case? Experienced writers seem to have an instinctual sense of how to present their ideas. Less experienced writers wonder what to say first, and when they've decided on that, wonder what to say next. There is no single method of argument. But the techniques of even the most experienced writers often boil down to a few tried and tested arrangements.

Two (or More) Reasons

In his book *A Short Course in Writing,* Kenneth Bruffee presents some of the most effective of these arrangements. The first one is simply called *Two Reasons,* but it could just as well be called *Three Reasons* or whatever number of reasons the writer has. Here is this method in outline form:

A. Introduction and thesis
B. Two reasons the thesis is true
  1. First reason
  2. Second reason (the more important one)

You can advance as many reasons for the truth of the thesis as you think necessary; but save the most important reason(s) for the end, since the end of the paper — its climax — is what will remain most clearly in the reader's mind.

Recall our analysis of the article "Does College Really Matter Anymore?" at the beginning of this chapter. Here is how that article is organized in terms of Professor Bruffee's *Two Reasons*:

A. Introduction (the writer does not make his thesis — that college *does* matter — explicit at this point)
B. Two reasons his *implicit* thesis is true
  1. First reason: there still are financial benefits
  2. Second (more important) reason: nonfinancial benefits, such as job satisfaction, greater tolerance of others
C. Conclusion (other factors that may determine your decision to go to college)

Nestorian Order

Another way of organizing arguments, according to Professor Bruffee, is called *Nestorian Order.* Here is how such an essay would be organized:

A. Introduction and thesis
B. Several reasons the thesis is true
   1. Second best reason
   2. Other reasons
   3. Best reason

This method of organization is useful when there are many reasons for the truth of the thesis. To avoid a sense of clutter, the two most important reasons are placed like bookends around the body of the paper, with the second most important reason first and the most important reason last. Professor Bruffee suggests that (1) and (2) in the outline above be combined in one paragraph and that (3) be discussed in the following paragraph. But if you have a great deal of material to present from multiple sources, you can use several paragraphs to cover each part of your essay. Recall from "Does College Really Matter Anymore?" that the first reason (financial benefits of college) was discussed in paragraphs 5–12 and the second reason (nonfinancial benefits) in paragraphs 13–18.

Strawman

The next way of presenting an argument is called *Strawman*. When you use the Strawman technique, you present an argument *against* your thesis, but immediately afterwards you show that this argument is weak or flawed. The advantage of this technique is that you demonstrate that you are aware of the other side of the argument and that you are prepared to answer it.

Here is how the Strawman argument is organized:

A. Introduction and thesis
B. Main opposing argument
C. Refutation of opposing argument
D. Main positive argument

The writer of "Does College Matter Anymore?" does in fact use elements of the Strawman argument:

A. Introduction
B. Opposing argument: some people suggest that there is no longer any financial benefit to a college education
C. Statistics show that this opposing argument is untrue
D. There are not only financial benefits, but also nonfinancial benefits to a college education

Concession

Finally, one can use *Concession* in an argument. Like Strawman, you present the opposing viewpoint, but you do not proceed to demolish the opposition. Instead, you concede that the opposition does have a valid point, but that even so, the positive argument is the stronger one. Here is an outline for a Concession argument.

A. Introduction and thesis
B. Important opposing arguments
C. Concession that this argument has some validity
D. Positive argument(s) developed

The writer of "Does College Really Matter Anymore?" also uses elements of the Concession argument:

A. Introduction
B. There are fewer financial benefits to a college education than there used to be
C. This is true; but college educated people, on the average, still earn more than non–college graduates
D. There are not only financial benefits, but also nonfinancial benefits to a college education

Sometimes, when you are developing a Strawman or Concession argument, you may yourself become convinced of the validity of the opposing point of view and change your own views. Don't be afraid of this happening. Writing is a tool for learning as well as for communication. To change your mind because of new evidence is a sign of flexibility and maturity, and your writing can only be the better for it.

These are some of the techniques you can use when developing your own argument papers. Your arguments may not be quite as elaborate as those in "Does College Matter Anymore?" (As we have seen, this essay demonstrates a variety of types of argument; you may use only one type in each paper.) As you become more experienced, however, you will become more comfortable handling a variety of techniques.

SHOULD YOU GO TO COLLEGE?

This article first appeared in *Senior Scholastic*. Anne Nelson is a graduate of Yale University.

1 Three out of every four college students in the U.S. are going to college for the wrong reasons.

2 That's [what] one statistic writer Anne Nelson came up with after doing research that led to her creation of the quiz on the following page.

3 Ms. Nelson reports that only about 25 percent of the nine million U.S. college students are interested in their classroom education. The rest may just be wasting a chunk of their life. Some are in college to please their parents, some because they think a diploma is a passport to success, and some because they simply don't know what else to do.

4 Making matters worse is the fact that a good many collegians are studying for

careers in overcrowded fields. And it's estimated that close to half are getting themselves or their families into debt in order to get that degree.

5 The 10 questions on this page are not meant to stop you from going to college if that's your dream. And they aren't meant to send you running off to college, if you haven't been planning to go.

6 All the quiz can do is this: Start you thinking, maybe in a new way, about college and career plans. If that happens, you might want to do research or talk with parents, teachers, or counselors. They may help you work out your own answers to questions such as these:

■ Should I go to college immediately after high school or should I wait — and work — awhile?

■ Is the career I'm planning on exactly right for me? Or should I look around for a "better fitting" one?

■ If I don't go to college, what other kind of training should I seek — and where?

Quiz

1. Do you like to learn things because
   a. they're interesting?
   b. they will be of immediate and direct use to you?
   c. they might come in handy some day?
2. Do you prefer to work
   a. on paper?
   b. with your hands?
   c. with people?
3. Which is your most important goal in life:
   a. status?
   b. a relaxed lifestyle?
   c. money?
4. Whom would your college education please the most:
   a. yourself?
   b. your parents?
   c. your high school guidance counselor?

5. Do you
   a. like high school?
   b. hate it?
   c. find some subjects interesting but most of it irrelevant?
6. If you couldn't go to college for some reason, would you prefer to spend four years
   a. getting by, spending time reading and traveling?
   b. finding a good steady job and starting to settle down?
   c. getting a head start on an interesting profession and trying to work your way up?
7. Do people from vastly different backgrounds than your own
   a. exhilarate you?
   b. make you defensive?
   c. bore you?
8. Do you think of books as
   a. friendly objects?
   b. enemies that you're sometimes forced to deal with?
   c. necessary tools to find out what you need to know?
9. Would you rather spend your time
   a. defining the problem?
   b. performing the tasks that need to be done?
   c. solving the problem?
10. If you went to college, would you go
    a. with some idea of what you wanted to do in life, but open to suggestion?
    b. with no preference for what you wanted to study, expecting to decide later?
    c. knowing exactly what you wanted to study and what you would do with it?

Answer Key

If you answered more questions with "a" than anything else, beg, borrow or steal your way into college; there's every indication that it will be both an enjoyable and worthwhile experience for you.

If you answered mostly "b," you might best look around at your other opportunities. There's no reason you should have to suffer through four years of education that you might not want and/or need.

If you answered with four or more "c's," you're an interesting case. You probably

wouldn't have a bad time in college, but at the same time you seem to have enough drive to do well without it. And, you may be so impatient to get started in life that college would be a bore. Think long and hard before you make a decision.

EXERCISES

Content

Recall the main ideas in this article by answering the following questions. Respond to one or two of the questions in your own words. Respond to one or two by finding quotations from the article that provide the answers.

1. On what evidence does Anne Nelson conclude that "Three out of every four college students in the U.S. are going to college for the wrong reasons"?

2. What are some of the "wrong reasons" for going to college?

3. What is the purpose of the quiz that accompanies this article?

Fact/Opinion

Classify each of the following statements as either a fact, an opinion, or a fact wrapped in an opinion. If the statement is a combination of fact and opinion, identify which part is fact and which opinion.

1. "Three out of every four college students in the U.S. are going to college for the wrong reasons."

2. "Some are in college to please their parents, some because they think a diploma is a passport to success, and some because they simply don't know what else to do."

Inferences

In your responses to the following questions, incorporate some of the quotations you located in response to the Content questions. You may decide to use either all or only part of each quotation.

1. After taking the quiz yourself, reread the answer key, noting the interpretations that Nelson gives to "a" answers, "b" answers, and "c" answers. Do the interpretations provided in the answer key seem justified in your own case? As a general rule? Why or why not? (Keep in mind that you don't have to answer *every* question—just most of them—with one particular letter in order to be tagged one way or another.)

2. Just before the quiz, three questions are asked. Do you believe the results of this quiz could help provide answers to these questions? Why or why not?

3. Do you think all graduating seniors (and others contemplating college) should be required to take a quiz such as this?

4. What do you think would be the reaction in college admissions offices to a quiz such as this? Explain.

PRINCIPLES OF THE LIBERAL ARTS COLLEGE

This statement, appearing in the *Mount Holyoke College Bulletin*, was drawn up by the Mount Holyoke Faculty Study Committee on the Principles of the College. It offers an eloquent argument for the values of the liberal arts college.

1   All human experience is education in some sense; and a liberal arts education does not exclude the sorts of learning that derive directly from the process of living itself. It differs from other varieties of education, however, because it places at its center the content of humane learning and the spirit of systematic, disinterested inquiry.

2   Its ultimate subject is humanity: the worlds, the works, the acts of human beings. It is therefore, first, an education in what we are and have been, and in the worlds we inhabit and have created: the worlds of thought and art, the social and physical worlds. It is, further, an education in the means of exploring those worlds and of creating new ones. Beyond this, it is an education that is evaluative, not merely factual and descriptive: it emphasizes the necessity of critical judgment, of respect for the finest in human achievement, together with the belief that a sense of the finest carries with it a capacity and even an imperative to live and act according to its demands.

3   The liberal arts college is therefore based on and defends certain central convictions and assumptions. It maintains that the search for knowledge, and with knowledge, compassionate understanding, is a central and not a peripheral human activity. It assumes a continuity in human endeavor, and therefore the necessity of learning in the present about and from the past. It maintains that in a diverse and increasingly divided world there is urgent need for a common language of educated awareness and rational discourse. It maintains that the perspective gained from knowledge of the nature, scope, and quality of our various worlds is not to be mistaken for disengagement from the world as it is or might become. It defends the right of all to seek knowledge for its own sake, without immediate regard to its utility, and affirms also that the world would suffer without the leaven of those who engage in this pursuit. Finally, it believes that the tools of thought and attitudes of mind acquired in a liberal arts college can be translated into the acts by which, without violence, things that do violence to the world are changed.

4   The college is ideally a society of students and faculty collectively and consciously committed to these convictions: to discovering, exploring, and upholding them. It is a *collegium,* a fellowship, with a proud but not prideful sense of its common purpose and of the values that govern its daily life. It brings together those who are serious but not solemn about learning, and humble but not hopeless before the complexity of knowledge: those who want to know what is to be known. It is a fellowship whose members are gentle of spirit and tolerant of human failing, but maintain unrelenting hostility toward any destruction of human dignity.

5   Such a college tries to encourage in all its members and in all their modes of en-

deavor not only a respect but a zest for truth and excellence. It encourages the capacity to admire and pursue excellence with intensity but without arrogance, and with some compassion for all who encounter the obstinacy of truth. It fosters an ability to accept and even welcome the necessity of strenuous and sustained effort in any area of endeavor. It specifically provides the tools of mental inquiry and tries to reveal their variety, their inner logic, and their relatedness. It tries also to encourage some daring in the use of these tools: the impulse to ask questions beyond found or accepted answers, the will and the disciplined ability to move from the foundation of the known toward that which is still to be known and done. It seeks to develop individuals committed to humane values, capable of rejecting oversimplification of ideology or method, and liberated from narrow definitions of themselves, of others, and of human problems in general.

6   These are utopian ideals, and rightly so, but the world of a college that seeks to live by them is nevertheless a real and a rigorous world. It is not a place of preparation for living; but a world where a life of a particular sort is intensely lived: a life of the mind above all, and of individual and joint endeavor.

7   This world has, however, its special characteristics. It is a world that recognizes human differences, but refuses to allow and seeks to eliminate all discriminations based on wealth, race, and sex. It imposes no limitations upon freedom of thought and speech beyond the obligations to respect the evidence of facts, and to honor the freedom and listen to the reasoned thought of others. It

provides the time, the freedom, and indeed the obligation to engage in reflection, in undistracted intellectual inquiry, in systematic and unhurried exploration of the world of knowledge, and of the self in relation to that world.

To this world the liberal arts college invites those who genuinely seek what it has to offer. It is not, however, a college designed or equipped to perform all possible roles in education, and will not redefine its nature to meet the expectations of those who may, legitimately, seek an education in something other than the liberal arts. It is hoped that after leaving college students can use what they have learned, but more importantly it is hoped they can be what they have learned. They are expected to continue to learn, whether in formal academic situations, in any of the professions, or independently, but Mount Holyoke's is not the task of preparing students professionally for what comes after any more than it is that of perpetuating that which came before. Mount Holyoke is, specifically, a "liberal arts college," concerned in a special way with the three ideas those three words bring together: freedom, learning, community of purpose. As a society of those who have come together for the sake of learning, the faculty and students profess and study those special arts of mind and spirit that they believe can free people — at least from ignorance, and perhaps from other poverties. The liberal arts are the arts of thought, perception, and judgment, the arts that foster humanity and civility of the spirit, and it is these arts that Mount Holyoke places at the center of its life.

8

EXERCISES

Content

Recall the main ideas in this passage by answering the following questions. Respond to some of the questions in your own words. Respond to others by finding quotations from the article that provide the answers.

1. How does a liberal arts education differ from other varieties of education? What is its subject?

2. Restate, in your own words, some of the "central convictions and assumptions" of the liberal arts college.

3. Cite and explain some of the oppositions described in paragraph 4.

4. Restate, in your own words, some of the "special characteristics" of the liberal arts college.

5. How does Mount Holyoke acknowledge and respond to expectations that college prepare students for the working world?

Structure

1. What is the purpose of paragraph 3?

2. What is the purpose of paragraph 6?

3. How is paragraph 7 related to paragraph 6?

Fact/Opinion

Classify each of the following statements as either a fact, an opinion, or a fact wrapped in an opinion. If the statement is a combination of fact and opinion, identify which part is fact and which opinion.

1. "All human experience is education in some sense, and a liberal arts education does not exclude the sorts of learning that derive directly from the process of living itself."

2. "The liberal arts college is therefore based on and defends certain central assumptions and convictions."

3. "[The liberal arts college] seeks to develop individuals committed to humane values, capable of rejecting oversimplifications of ideology or method, and liberated from narrow definitions of themselves, of others, and of human problems in general."

Inferences

In your responses to the following questions, incorporate some of the quotations you located in response to the Content questions. You may decide to use either all or only part of each quotation.

1. In paragraph 6, the authors acknowledge that the ideals they have been discussing are "utopian" — meaning "excellent, but existing only in fancy or theory." Why are such ideals utopian? And if they are utopian, then what is the value of discussing them, much less of proposing them as the underlying principles of an institution that exists in the real world?

2. How does this piece of writing contribute to the debate about the value of a college education?

3. Explain what you think is meant by the final sentence of paragraph 3: "Finally, it [the liberal arts college] believes that the tools of thought and attitudes of mind acquired in a liberal arts college can be translated into the acts by which, without violence, things that do violence to the world are changed." How do you think such things can be accomplished?

4. Paragraph 5 includes the statement that the college "encourages the capacity to admire and pursue excellence with intensity but without arrogance, and with some compassion for all who encounter the obstinacy of truth." What do you think is meant by that last phrase, "the obstinacy of truth"?

5. How can the world of the college be at the same time "a real and rigorous world" but "not a place of preparation for living" (paragraph 6)?

6. A hope is expressed (paragraph 8) that "after leaving college students can use what they have learned, but more importantly...[that] they can be what they have learned." Explain your understanding of the difference.

Caroline Bird

COLLEGE IS A WASTE OF TIME AND MONEY

Caroline Bird, who has attended Vassar College, the University of Toledo (B.A.), and the University of Wisconsin (M.A.), is the author of _Born Female, The Crowding Syndrome_ (on population growth), _Everything a Woman Needs to Know to Get Paid What She's Worth,_ and _The Case Against College._ Between books and lecture tours, Bird teaches courses on the status of women and writes for magazines as varied as _Ms._ and _Management Review._ The following article combines material from "College Is a Waste of Time and Money," which appeared in _Psychology Today,_ and "Where College Fails Us," from _Signature._ Although Bird wrote these articles in 1975 and some of the issues she discusses are no longer current, Bird's basic objections to the traditional college curriculum are still shared by many today.

1   A great majority of our nine-million college students are not in school because they want to be or because they want to learn. They are there because it has become the thing to do or because college is a pleasant place to be; because it's the only way they can get parents or taxpayers to support them without working at a job they don't like; because Mother wanted them to go, or some other reason entirely irrelevant to the course of studies for which college is supposedly organized.

2   As I crisscross the United States lecturing on college campuses, I am dismayed to find that professors and administrators, when pressed for a candid opinion, estimate that

no more than 25 percent of their students are turned on by classwork. For the rest, college is at best a social center or aging vat, and at worst a young folks' home or even a prison that keeps them out of the mainstream of economic life for a few more years.

The premise—which I no longer accept—that college is the best place for all high-school graduates grew out of a noble American ideal. Just as the United States was the first nation to aspire to teach every small child to read and write, so, during the 1950s, we became the first and only great nation to aspire to higher education for all. During the '60s we damned the expense and built great state university systems as fast as we could. And adults—parents, employers, high-school counselors—began to push, shove and cajole youngsters to "get an education." 3

It became a mammoth industry, with taxpayers footing more than half the bill. By 1970, colleges and universities were spending more than 30-billion dollars annually. But still only half our high-school graduates were going on. According to estimates made by the economist, Fritz Machlup, if we had been educating every young person until age 22 in that year of 1970, the bill for higher education would have reached 47.5-billion dollars, 12.5 billion more than the total corporate profits for the year. 4

The Baby Boom Is Over

Figures such as these have begun to make higher education for all look finan- 5 cially prohibitive, particularly now when colleges are squeezed by the pressures of inflation and a drop-off in the growth of their traditional market.

6 Predictable demography has caught up with the university empire builders. Now that the record crop of postwar babies has graduated from college, the rate of growth of the student population has begun to decline. To keep their mammoth plants financially solvent, many institutions have begun to use hard-sell, Madison-Avenue techniques to attract students. They sell college like soap, promoting features they think students want: innovative programs, an environment conducive to meaningful personal relationships, and a curriculum so free that it doesn't sound like college at all.

7 Pleasing the customers is something new for college administrators. Colleges have always known that most students don't like to study, and that at least part of the time they are ambivalent about college, but before the student riots of the 1960s educators never thought it either right or necessary to pay any attention to student feelings. But when students rebelling against the Vietnam war and the draft discovered they could disrupt a campus completely, administrators had to act on some student complaints. Few understood that the protests had tapped the basic discontent with college itself, a discontent that did not go away when the riots subsided.

8 Today students protest individually rather than in concert. They turn inward and withdraw from active participation. They drop out to travel to India or to feed themselves on subsistence farms. Some refuse to go to college at all. Most, of course, have neither the funds nor the self-confidence for constructive articulation of their discontent. They simply hang around college unhappily and reluctantly.

9 All across the country, I have been overwhelmed by the prevailing sadness on American campuses. Too many young people speak little, and then only in drowned voices. Sometimes the mood surfaces as diffidence, wariness, or coolness, but whatever its form, it looks like a defense mechanism,

and that rings a bell. This is the way it used to be with women, and just as society had systematically damaged women by insisting that their proper place was in the home, so we may be systematically damaging 18-year-olds by insisting that their proper place is in college.

Sad and Unneeded

10 Campus watchers everywhere know what I mean when I say students are sad, but they don't agree on the reason for it. During the Vietnam war some ascribed the sadness to the draft; now others blame affluence, or say it has something to do with permissive upbringing.

11 Not satisfied with any of these explanations, I looked for some answers with the journalistic tools of my trade — scholarly studies, economic analyses, the historical record, the opinions of the especially knowledgeable, conversations with parents, professors, college administrators, and employers, all of whom spoke as alumni too. Mostly I learned from my interviews with hundreds of young people on and off campuses all over the country.

12 My unnerving conclusion is that students are sad because they are not needed. Somewhere between the nursery and the employment office, they become unwanted adults. No one has anything in particular against them. But no one knows what to do with them either. We already have too many people in the world of the 1970s, and there is no room for so many newly minted 18-year-olds. So we temporarily get them out of the way by sending them to college where in fact only a few belong.

13 To make it more palatable, we fool ourselves into believing that we are sending them there for their own best interests, and that it's good for them, like spinach. Some, of course, learn to like it, but most wind up preferring green peas.

14 Educators admit as much. Nevitt Sanford, distinguished student of higher education, says students feel they are "capitulating to a kind of voluntary servitude." Some of them

talk about their time in college as if it were a sentence to be served. I listened to a 1970 Mount Holyoke graduate: "For two years I was really interested in science, but in my junior and senior years I just kept saying, 'I've done two years; I'm going to finish.' When I got out I made up my mind that I wasn't going to school anymore because so many of my courses had been bullshit."

15 But bad as it is, college is often preferable to a far worse fate. It is better than the drudgery of an uninspiring nine-to-five job, and better than doing nothing when no jobs are available. For some young people, it is a graceful way to get away from home and become independent without losing the financial support of their parents. And sometimes it is the only alternative to an intolerable home situation.

16 It is difficult to assess how many students are in college reluctantly. The conservative Carnegie Commission estimates from five to 30 percent. Sol Linowitz, who was once chairman of a special committee on campus tension of the American Council on Education, found that "a significant number were not happy with their college experience because they felt they were there only in order to get the 'ticket to the big show' rather than to spend the years as productively as they otherwise could."

17 Older alumni will identify with Richard Baloga, a policeman's son, who stayed in school even though he "hated it" because he thought it would do him some good. But fewer students each year feel this way. Daniel Yankelovich has surveyed undergraduate attitudes for a number of years, and reported in 1971 that 74 percent thought education was "very important." But just two years earlier, 80 percent thought so.

An Inside View of What's Good

18 The doubters don't mind speaking up. Leon Lefkowitz, chairman of the department of social studies at Central High School in Valley Stream, New York, interviewed 300 college students at random, and reports that 200 of them didn't think that the education they were getting was worth the effort. "In two years I'll pick up a diploma," said one student, "and I can honestly say it was a waste of my father's bread."

19 Nowadays, says one sociologist, you don't have to have a reason for going to college; it's an institution. His definition of an institution is an arrangement everyone accepts without question; the burden of proof is not on why you go, but why anyone thinks there might be a reason for not going. The implication is that an 18-year-old is too young and confused to know what he wants to do, and that he should listen to those who know best and go to college.

20 I don't agree. I believe that college has to be judged not on what other people think is good for students, but on how good it feels to the students themselves.

21 I believe that people have an inside view of what's good for them. If a child doesn't want to go to school some morning, better let him stay at home, at least until you find out why. Maybe he knows something you don't. It's the same with college. If high-school graduates don't want to go, or if they don't want to go right away, they may perceive more clearly than their elders that college is not for them. It is no longer obvious that adolescents are best off studying a core curriculum that was constructed when all educated men could agree on what made them educated, or that professors, advisors, or parents can be of any particular help to young people in choosing a major or a career. High-school graduates see college graduates driving cabs, and decide it's not worth going. College students find no intellectual stimulation in their studies and drop out.

22 If students believe that college isn't necessarily good for them, you can't expect them to stay on for the general good of mankind. They don't go to school to beat the Russians to Jupiter, improve the national defense, increase the GNP, or create a market for the arts—to mention some of the benefits taxpayers are supposed to get for supporting higher education.

23 Nor should we expect to bring about social equality by putting all young people

through four years of academic rigor. At best, it's a roundabout and expensive way to narrow the gap between the highest and lowest in our society anyway. At worst, it is unconsciously elitist. Equalizing opportunity through universal higher education subjects the whole population to the intellectual mode natural only to a few. It violates the fundamental egalitarian principle of respect for the differences between people.

The Dumbest Investment

24   Of course, most parents aren't thinking of the "higher" good at all. They send their children to college because they are convinced young people benefit financially from those four years of higher education. But if money is the only goal, college is the dumbest investment you can make. I say this because a young banker in Poughkeepsie, New York, Stephen G. Necel, used a computer to compare college as an investment with other investments available in 1974 and college did not come out on top.

25   For the sake of argument, the two of us invented a young man whose rich uncle gave him, in cold cash, the cost of a four-year education at any college he chôse, but the young man didn't have to spend the money on college. After bales of computer paper, we had our mythical student write to his uncle: "Since you said I could spend the money foolishly if I wished, I am going to blow it all on Princeton."

26   The much respected financial columnist Sylvia Porter echoed the common assumption when she said last year, "A college education is among the very best investments you can make in your entire life." But the truth is not quite so rosy, even if we assume that the Census Bureau is correct when it says that as of 1972, a man who completed four years of college would expect to earn $199,000 more between the ages of 22 and 64 than a man who had only a high-school diploma.*

*According to the 1984 *Statistical Abstract of the United States,* a person who completed four years of college in 1979 could expect to earn $309,000.

27   If a 1972 Princeton-bound high-school graduate had put the $34,181 that his four years of college would have cost him into a savings bank at 7.5 percent interest compounded daily, he would have had at age 64 a total of $1,129,200, or $528,200 more than the earnings of a male college graduate, and more than five times as much as the $199,000 extra the more educated man could expect to earn between 22 and 64.

28   The big advantage of getting your college money in cash now is that you can invest it in something that has a higher return than a diploma. For instance, a Princeton-bound high-school graduate of 1972 who liked fooling around with cars could have banked his $34,181, and gone to work at the local garage at close to $1,000 more per year than the average high-school graduate. Meanwhile, as he was learning to be an expert auto mechanic, his money would be ticking away in the bank. When he became 28, he would have earned $7,199 less on his job from age 22 to 28 than his college-educated friend, but he would have had $73,113 in his passbook—enough to buy out his boss, go into the used-car business, or acquire his own new-car dealership. If successful in business, he could expect to make more than the average college graduate. And if he had the brains to get into Princeton, he would be just as likely to make money without the four years spent on campus. Unfortunately, few college-bound high-school graduates get the opportunity to bank such a large sum of money, and then wait for it to make them rich. And few parents are sophisticated enough to understand that in financial returns alone, their children would be better off with the money than with the education.

29   Rates of return and dollar signs on education are fascinating brain teasers, but obviously there is a certain unreality to the game. Quite aside from the noneconomic benefits of college, and these should loom larger once the dollars are cleared away, there are grave difficulties in assigning a dollar value to college at all.

Status, Not Money

30   In fact there is no real evidence that the higher income of college graduates is due to college. College may simply attract people who are slated to earn more money anyway; those with higher IQs, better family backgrounds, a more enterprising temperament. No one who has wrestled with the problem is prepared to attribute all of the higher income to the impact of college itself.

31   Christopher Jencks, author of *Inequality,* a book that assesses the effect of family and schooling in America, believes that education in general accounts for less than half of the difference in income in the American population. "The biggest single source of income differences," writes Jencks, "seems to be the fact that men from high-status families have higher incomes than men from low-status families even when they enter the same occupations, have the same amount of education, and have the same test scores."

32   Jacob Mincer of the National Bureau of Economic Research and Columbia University states flatly that of "20 to 30 percent of students at any level, the additional schooling has been a waste, at least in terms of earnings." College fails to work its income-raising magic for almost a third of those who go. More than half of those people in 1972 who earned $15,000 or more reached that comfortable bracket without the benefit of a college diploma. Jencks says that financial success in the U.S. depends a good deal on luck, and the most sophisticated regression analyses have yet to demonstrate otherwise.

33   But most of today's students don't go to college to earn more money anyway. In 1968, when jobs were easy to get, Daniel Yankelovich made his first nationwide survey of students. Sixty-five percent of them said they "would welcome less emphasis on money." By 1973, when jobs were scarce, that figure jumped to 80 percent.

34   The young are not alone. Americans today are all looking less to the pay of a job than to the work itself. They want "interesting" work that permits them "to make a contribution," "express themselves" and "use their special abilities," and they think college will help them find it.

35   Jerry Darring of Indianapolis knows what it is to make a dollar. He worked with his father in the family plumbing business, on the line at Chevrolet, and in the Chrysler foundry. He quit these jobs to enter Wright State University in Dayton, Ohio, because "in a job like that a person only has time to work, and after that he's so tired that he can't do anything else but come home and go to sleep."

36   Jerry came to college to find work "helping people." And he is perfectly willing to spend the dollars he earns at dull, well-paid work to prepare for lower-paid work that offers the reward of service to others.

Psychic Income

37   Jerry's case is not unusual. No one works for money alone. In order to deal with the nonmonetary rewards of work, economists have coined the concept of "psychic income," which according to one economic dictionary means "income that is reckoned in terms of pleasure, satisfaction, or general feelings of euphoria."

38   Psychic income is primarily what college students mean when they talk about getting a good job. During the most affluent years of the late 1960s and early 1970s college students told their placement officers that they wanted to be researchers, college professors, artists, city planners, social workers, poets, book publishers, archeologists, ballet dancers, or authors.

39   The psychic income of these and other occupations popular with students is so high that these jobs can be filled without offering high salaries. According to one study, 93 percent of urban university professors would choose the same vocation again if they had the chance, compared with only 16 percent of unskilled auto workers. Even though the monetary gap between college professor and auto worker is now surprisingly small, the difference in psychic income is enormous.

40   But colleges fail to warn students that jobs of these kinds are hard to come by, even for qualified applicants, and they rarely accept the responsibility of helping students choose a career that will lead to a job. When a young person says he is interested in helping people, his counselor tells him to become a psychologist. But jobs in psychology are scarce. The Department of Labor, for instance, estimates there will be 4,300 new jobs for psychologists in 1975 while colleges are expected to turn out 58,430 B.A.s in psychology that year.

41   Of 30 psych majors who reported back to Vassar what they were doing a year after graduation in 1972, only five had jobs in which they could possibly use their courses in psychology, and two of these were working for Vassar.

42   Sociology has become a favorite major on socially conscious campuses, but graduates find that social reform is hardly a paying occupation. Male sociologists reported as gainfully employed a year after graduation from the University of Wisconsin included a legal assistant, sports editor, truck unloader, Peace Corps worker, publications director and a stockboy—but no sociologists per se. The highest paid worked for the post office.

43   Publishing, writing and journalism are presumably the vocational goal of a large proportion of the 104,000 majors in Communications and Letters expected to graduate in 1975. The outlook for them is grim. All of the daily newspapers in the country combined are expected to hire a total of 2,600 reporters this year. Radio and television stations may hire a total of 500 announcers, most of them in local radio stations. Nonpublishing organizations will need 1,100 technical writers, and public relations activities another 4,400. Even if the new graduates could get all these jobs (and, of course, they can't), more than 90,000 of them will have to find something less glamorous to do.

44   Other fields most popular with college graduates are also pathetically small. Only 1,900 foresters a year will be needed during this decade, although schools of forestry are expected to continue graduating twice that many. Some will get sub-professional jobs as forestry aides. Schools of architecture are expected to turn out twice as many as will be needed, and while all sorts of people want to design things, the Department of Labor forecasts that there will be jobs for only 400 new industrial designers a year. As for anthropologists, only 400 will be needed every year in the 1970s to take care of all the college courses, public health research, community surveys, museums, and all the archaeological digs on every continent. (For these jobs, of course, graduate work in anthropology will be required.)

45   Many popular occupations may seem to be growing fast without necessarily offering employment to very many. "Recreation work" is always cited as an expanding field, but it will need relatively few workers who require more special training than life guards. "Urban planning" has exploded in the media, so the U.S. Department of Labor doubled its estimate of the number of jobs to be filled every year in the 1970s—to a big, fat 800. A mere 200 oceanographers a year will be able to do all the exploring of "inner space"—and all that exciting underwater diving you see demonstrated on television—for the entire decade of the 1970s.

46   Whatever college graduates *want* to do, most of them are going to wind up doing what *there is* to do. During the next few years, according to the Labor Department, the biggest demand will be for stenographers and secretaries, followed by retail trade salesworkers, hospital attendants, bookkeepers, building custodians, registered nurses, foremen, kindergarten and elementary school teachers, receptionists, cooks, cosmetologists, private household workers, manufacturing inspectors and industrial machinery repairmen. These are the jobs which will eventually absorb the surplus archaeologists, urban planners, oceanographers, sociologists, editors and college professors.

47   John Shingleton, director of placement at Michigan State University, accuses the academic community of outright hypocrisy.

"Educators have never said, 'Go to college and get a good job,' but this has been implied, and now students expect it.... If we care what happens to students after college, then let's get involved with what should be one of the basic purposes of education: career preparation."

48   In the 1970s, some of the more practical professors began to see that jobs for graduates meant jobs for professors too. Meanwhile, students themselves reacted to the shrinking job market, and a "new vocationalism" exploded on campus. The press welcomed the change as a return to the ethic of achievement and service. Students were still idealistic, the reporters wrote, but they now saw that they could best make the world better by healing the sick as physicians or righting individual wrongs as lawyers.

No Use on the Job

49   But there are no guarantees in these professions either. If all those who check "doctor" as their career goal succeed in getting their MDs, we'll immediately have 10 times the target ratio of doctors for the population of the United States. Law schools are already graduating twice as many new lawyers every year as the Department of Labor thinks we will need, and the oversupply grows annually.

50   And it's not at all apparent that what is actually learned in a "professional" education is necessary for success. Teachers, engineers and others I talked to said they find that on the job they rarely use what they learned in school. In order to see how well college prepared engineers and scientists for actual paid work in their fields, The Carnegie Commission queried all the employees with degrees in these fields in two large firms. Only one in five said the work they were doing bore a "very close relationship" to their college studies, while almost a third saw "very little relationship at all." An overwhelming majority could think of many people who were doing their same work, but had majored in different fields.

Majors in nontechnical fields report even   51 less relationship between their studies and their jobs. Charles Lawrence, a communications major in college and now the producer of "Kennedy & Co.," the Chicago morning television show, says, "You have to learn all that stuff and you never use it again. I learned my job doing it." Others employed as architects, nurses, teachers and other members of the so-called learned professions report the same thing.

Most college administrators admit that   52 they don't prepare their graduates for the job market. "I just wish I had the guts to tell parents that when you get out of this place you aren't prepared to do anything," the academic head of a famous liberal-arts college told us. Fortunately, for him, most people believe that you don't have to defend a liberal-arts education on those grounds. A liberal-arts education is supposed to provide you with a value system, a standard, a set of ideas, not a job. "Like Christianity, the liberal arts are seldom practiced and would probably be hated by the majority of the populace if they were," said one defender.

The analogy is apt. The fact is, of course,   53 that the liberal arts are a religion in every sense of that term. When people talk about them, their language becomes elevated, metaphorical, extravagant, theoretical and reverent. And faith in personal salvation by the liberal arts is professed in a creed intoned on ceremonial occasions such as commencements.

Ticket of Admission

If the liberal arts are a religious faith, the   54 professors are its priests. But disseminating ideas in a four-year college curriculum is slow and most expensive. If you want to learn about Milton, Camus, or even Margaret Mead you can find them in paperback books, the public library, and even on television.

And when most people talk about the   55 value of a college education, they are not talking about great books. When at Harvard commencement, the president welcomes the new graduates into "the fellowship of educated men and women," what he could be saying is, "here is a piece of paper that is a passport to jobs, power and instant prestige." As Glenn Bassett, a personnel specialist at G.E. says, "In some part of G.E., a college degree appears completely irrelevant to selection to, say, a manager's job. In most, however, it is a ticket of admission."

56 But now that we have doubled the number of young people attending college, a diploma cannot guarantee even that. The most charitable conclusion we can reach is that college probably has very little, if any, effect on people and things at all. Today, the false premises are easy to see:

57 First, college doesn't make people intelligent, ambitious, happy, or liberal. It's the other way around. Intelligent, ambitious, happy, liberal people are attracted to higher education in the first place.

58 Second, college can't claim much credit for the learning experiences that really change students while they are there. Jobs, friends, history, and most of all the sheer passage of time, have as big an impact as anything even indirectly related to the campus.

59 Third, colleges have changed so radically that a freshman entering in the fall of 1974 can't be sure to gain even the limited value research studies assigned to colleges in the '60s. The sheer size of undergraduate campuses of the 1970s makes college even less stimulating now than it was 10 years ago. Today even motivated students are disappointed with their college courses and professors.

60 Finally, a college diploma no longer opens as many vocational doors. Employers are beginning to realize that when they pay extra for someone with a diploma, they are paying only for an empty credential. The fact is that most of the work for which employers now expect college training is now or has been capably done in the past by people without higher educations.

61 College, then, may be a good place for those few young people who are really drawn to academic work, who would rather read than eat, but it has become too expensive, in money, time, and intellectual effort to serve as a holding pen for large numbers of our young. We ought to make it possible for those reluctant, unhappy students to find alternative ways of growing up, and more realistic preparation for the years ahead.

EXERCISES

Content

Recall the main ideas in this article by answering the following questions. Respond to some of the questions in your own words. Respond to others by finding quotations from the article that provide the answers.

1. For what reasons does Bird believe the majority of students are in college?

2. Why is it now taken for granted in the United States that college is the next step for high school graduates?

3. Why did college growth grind to a halt during the 1970s?

4. How did the student unrest of the 1960s change the way administrators responded to students? How is current student unrest different from student unrest in the 1960s?

5. On what evidence does Bird make her assertions about students' "sadness" in college?

6. What objections does Bird have to universal college education as a means of bringing about social equality?

7. Bird believes that if anticipated financial rewards are the reason people pursue a higher education, "college is the dumbest investment you can make." Why?

8. How does Bird account for the increased average earnings of college graduates over non–college graduates?

9. What is "psychic income"? Why is it an important concept in any discussion of the value of a college education? What kind of occupations offer psychic income? What is the relationship between psychic income and financial income? Why will college graduates have trouble finding enough jobs that offer psychic income?

10. What evidence does Bird cite to demonstrate that even a professional education in college is usually not relevant to job success?

11. Summarize Bird's attitude toward the liberal arts curriculum.

Structure

1. Explain how paragraphs 3–6, considered together, form an identifiable section of the article. Give this section a title.

2. How are paragraphs 5 and 6 related to paragraphs 3 and 4?

3. How are paragraphs 20–23 related to paragraph 19?

4. How are paragraphs 24–29 related to the thesis of the article?

5. What is the purpose of paragraphs 57–60?

Fact/Opinion

Classify each of the following statements as either a fact, an opinion, or a fact wrapped in an opinion. If the statement is a combination of fact and opinion, identify which part is fact and which opinion.

1. "Just as the United States was the first nation to aspire to teach every small child to read and write, so, during the 1950s, we became the first and only great nation to aspire to higher education for all."

2. "Pleasing the customers is something new for college administrators."

3. "All across the country, I have been overwhelmed by the prevailing sadness on American campuses."

4. "My unnerving conclusion is that students are sad because they are not needed."

5. "If a 1972 Princeton-bound high-school graduate had put the $34,181 that his four years of college would have cost him into a savings bank at 7.5 percent interest compounded daily, he would have had at age 64 a total of $1,129,000."

Inferences

In your responses to the following questions, incorporate some of the quotations you located in response to the Content questions. You may decide to use either all or only part of each quotation.

1. What do you think Bird's reaction would be to the "Principles" of Mount Holyoke College (previous selection)? Explain.

2. How do Bird's arguments tie in with Anne Nelson's survey in the article "Should You Go to College?"

3. In light of your own experience and observations, how valid is Bird's belief about the real reasons most students are in college (paragraphs 1 and 2)?

4. In paragraphs 9–17 Bird discusses "the prevailing sadness on American campuses." Have you noticed such a sadness? Do you feel it yourself? Are the reasons for this sadness as you perceive it (if you do) the same as Bird's reasons?

5. In paragraph 9, Bird makes a comparison between the way society "damaged" women when it insisted that their place was in the home and the way society now damages 18-year-olds "by insisting that their proper place is in college." Is this a fair comparison? Why or why not?

6. In paragraph 13, Bird makes another comparison, in which college is compared to spinach (both are supposed to be "good for you"), although most students prefer "green peas." What do you think the green peas might be?

7. In what ways might it be possible to account for the discrepancy between the "Principles" of Mount Holyoke College and the comment by the Mount Holyoke student in paragraph 14 of Bird's article?

8. In paragraph 19, Bird quotes a sociologist who believes that so many people go to college unquestioningly because college is an institution, defined as "an arrangement everyone accepts without question." What other institutions of this kind have you encountered?

9. Bird asserts that "college has to be judged not on what other people think is good for students, but on how good it feels to the students themselves." Do you believe this is a valid criterion for judging the value of a college education? Why or why not?

10. Do "people have an inside view of what's good for them" (paragraph 21)? What evidence can you find that supports or refutes this thesis?

11. To what extent do you find validity in Bird's comparisons between the eventual financial return from a lump sum (equal to the cost of a college education) invested in a bank and the eventual financial return from the increased earnings of a college graduate?

12. On whom or what does Bird place the blame for the lack of fulfillment many students experience during college? On whom or what does she place the blame for the failure of many college graduates to find the jobs they have been preparing for?

13. In paragraph 52 Bird quotes one "defender" of the liberal arts concept as follows: "Like Christianity, the liberal arts are seldom practiced and would probably be hated by the majority of the populace if they were." Why do you think the speaker believes this? Do you agree? How do you think the authors of the Mount Holyoke "Principles" would respond to this assertion?

14. Bird notes that "when people talk about [the liberal arts], their language becomes elevated, metaphorical, extravagant, theoretical and reverent." To what extent do you think this statement accounts for the Mount Holyoke "Principles"?

15. After noting the "slow and expensive" professorial methods of disseminating ideas in college, Bird says that if "you want to learn about Milton, Camus, or even Margaret Mead you can find them in paperback books, the public library, and even on television." Comment on this statement.

16. What do you think Bird has in mind when she says in the final sentence, "We ought to make it possible for those reluctant, unhappy students to find alternative ways of growing up, and more realistic preparation for the years ahead"? What might be some "alternative ways" and "more realistic preparation"?

LETTERS IN RESPONSE TO BIRD'S "COLLEGE IS A WASTE OF TIME AND MONEY"

Caroline Bird's article "College Is a Waste of Time and Money," which first appeared in *Psychology Today*, generated many letters to the editor. Presented here is a sampling of those letters.

1   Even ice cream could become tasteless, if you were commanded to eat it. — *Gerta Farber, Newport Beach, Calif.*

2   To interview students in college regarding their thoughts on the value of higher education is ridiculous. Bird's own thesis is that at this age they don't know their asses from terrestrial apertures, and it is a rare college student who is sufficiently mature to know what life is about. — *Geoffrey D. C. Orton, Rensselaer, N.Y.*

3   Some students may be bored with 90 percent of their classes and be "interested" in only the remaining 10 percent. Does that mean that they are wasting their time and money? I don't think so. A valuable learning experience can be wrapped up in that 10 percent.
       I do agree with Bird that students are unable to recognize the relevance of most of the course work to their jobs. However, I have found that the longer people are out of school, the more they recognize the importance and relevance of many of their college courses. — *Jerry Horgesheimer, D.B.A., Ogden, Utah*

4   In some European countries the compulsory attendance age extends to ninth or 10th grade. Much of the emphasis is placed on reading, writing and arithmetic. Many college graduates in the U.S. lack the mastery of these vital skills. The lowering of the compulsory-attendance age in the United States would leave the opportunity of higher education only to those students who are attracted to education's liberality. — *Sam Maravich Jr., Steelton, Penn.*

5   I concur with Bird on the superfluous student situation in our college educational system. Anyone who can't maintain a 3.5 average should be drafted. — *Steven E. Barrett, West Point, N.Y.*

6   Bird doesn't recognize that a large proportion of the staggering sums asked collectively by colleges and universities are in the forms of loans, scholarships and grants that would not be available if one chose to invest in the world of business instead. — *John Michelsen, Gustavus Adolphus College, Mound, Minn.*

7   High schools should equip students with an awareness of society and the availability of jobs; provide them with marketable skills, and require courses that will help students examine and develop their own value systems, learn to make decisions and to achieve "personhood." Giving high-school students this knowledge would enable them to make better decisions as to what they chose to do after high school. Students who opted for work would have difficulty as the labor market, also, is certainly unprepared to accommodate a good percentage of high-school graduates. So college becomes a good stopgap.
       Parents who want their children to have it "as good as they do," if not better, feel that college will guarantee their children upward mobility (generally equated in dollar signs). This is unrealistic because of current and predicted labor demands, as well as the changing role of education that is becoming a life-long process instead of one ending at age 23. In addition, jobs will exist that cannot be prepared for now, as they do not exist. Flexibility is the key word, as well as societal reappraisal of the value of work and the prestige of vocational training. — *Judith Sacks, Counselor, Baldwin Senior High School, Baldwin, N.Y.*

8   How can a woman who has written a number of successful articles and books even hint that a college education is a waste of time and money? Was Bird's success based solely on a high-school education? — *Cathy Warren, Anaheim, Calif.*

9   I know a number of people with B.A.s who are for all intents and purposes ignorant of 90 percent of what they supposedly went to college to learn. I attribute this to immaturity at the time of instruction, poor secondary education, and the lowering of academic standards at many institutions. I started university study at 28. As an older student, I am self-motivated and have a clear goal I wish to attain. I feel strongly that students not academically inclined (as I was not, at age 18) should not be pushed into or pandered to at a university. — *Susan Gilbertsen, Eugene, Ore.*

10   We at the Boatshop raise our oar in salute to Caroline Bird.
We educators dropped our hammers and saws too soon! Observing that our college-degree success has led to Wall Street failure, we have turned to tools to discover excitement and satisfaction. Using their hands to discipline their minds, our apprentices create marketable products of both. — *Stefan P. Galazzi, Director, The Experience on Cape Cod, South Orleans, Mass.*

11   Perhaps the value of a college education is in learning to spot loose reasoning. The real financial question should've been "How much would the Princeton-bound man have to invest in an annuity paying $4,700 a year from age 22 to 64?" Bet it's more than $34,181. — *Russell Herman, Mississauga, Ontario*

12   I worked my way through a private college because I wanted to. As one of my professors once said, "The more we know, the more increase of mystery; the more we know, the more unknown we meet." He compared it to a light bulb of 60 watts that illuminates to a certain perimeter of light, and a 100-watt bulb that illuminates only to increase the perimeter of darkness. College, for me, was all this and more. — *Christine Masi, Maspeth, N.Y.*

13   In one sense I can say that college was indeed a waste of time and money. I am not working in my chosen field of study and the chances are that I won't be in the future. In another sense, college was an invaluable experience that I will never forget. I am not today the person I was when I entered college. My views on many subjects have made a 180° turn about. Some of these changes would have occurred anyway as a result of a process of maturing, but other changes needed the stimulus the university and its population provided. — *Linda Slepicka, Chicago*

14   College will continue to be a waste of time and money for the taxpayer and the student until colleges start getting what should be their product: trained students that can successfully and skillfully apply what they have learned and do. Of course the first prerequisite to this is that what is taught *can* be used. — *Glen J. Doe, Hamilton, Ontario*

15   Caroline Bird states that, if $34,181 be invested at 7.5 percent, compounded daily for a period of 42 years, the amount would be $1,129,200 at the end of that period. This statement is untrue. The amount would be $797, 392, but only if no income taxes were paid on the interest earned each year. — *Albert L. McCormmach, Walla Walla, Wash.*

16   Does Bird make a case against College (*College*, like Plato's *Republic*) or a case against the American postsecondary-education system that bores students for four (or more) years and then has the audacity not to reward those students for their stoical endurance (and dad's dough) with the lump of sugar, carrot or cigar? Worse, take her use of the word "good" like a college Freshman would — "I believe that college has to be judged not on what other people think is good for students but on how good it feels to students themselves [outrage mine]." But,

Caroline, at least in language one "good" does not another make. What about a case for wasting more time and money on education?—*John M. de Jong, Long Beach, Calif.*

17   College is not the most productive experience for every 18-year-old, or even for a majority of them. The danger, though, is not, as Bird suggests, imposing an "intellectual mode" on those not suited for it, but rather a dilution of the caliber of academic life.—*David Troup Risser, Graduate Student, Temple University, Philadelphia*

18   There are still students around who learn for the sake of learning. Witness those who "forsake" their training and move away from the busy city. I believe that the more education people acquire, the greater possibility they have of being eager-to-learn, open-minded and well-rounded persons. I especially applaud those who have good jobs and then seek to earn college degrees.—*Daniel D. Stuhlman, Cincinnati*

19   One overwhelming fact that Bird cannot explain is that once students grow into adulthood, they come back to the university, not for a degree ("that glorious piece of wallpaper," as Mark Twain called it), but to immerse themselves in ideas, literature, and the arts. Although undergraduate programs are finding themselves bankrupt—in more ways than one—programs for adults, schools of continuing education, are alive and flourishing all over the country. For the first time in American history, part-time, adult students outnumber fulltime undergraduates. This does not indicate that our universities are obsolete.

I certainly do not wish to "blame" undergraduates for not living up to our expectations. They, too, are victims of a society that systematically destroys intellectual curiosity and interpersonal sensitivity, a society that has replaced reading and discussion with the TV. But neither must we blame the universities for the widespread apathy found among undergraduates. And I suspect Bird knows this very well.—*Victor B. Marrow, Associate*

Director, Division of Liberal Studies, Assistant Professor of Social Philosophy, School of Continuing Education, New York University

Liberal arts should be taught in high   20
schools, community-based "continuing-education" programs, and small colleges. Vocational curricula should be available, in separate or coordinated programs, to complement the liberal arts. Large universities could then stick to academics and research. People could then know what to expect from whatever institution they attend, and clearer purpose would improve performances by both students and schools.—*Eric T. MacKnight, College Dropout, Washington, D.C.*

I'm not advocating four-year educational   21
degrees for everyone, but let's not annihilate one means for people, especially those just out of high school, to establish values and goals for themselves.—*Wayne McDonald, Dallas*

Individuals not familiar with the realities   22
of the career marketplace might take Bird's sophistry as truth and get ground up in 20th-century bureaucratic civilization. Her accusation that colleges sell education like soap is certainly true of her kind of exaggerations.—*Terry R. Armstrong, Coordinator, Portfolio Degree Program, Park College-Crown Center, Kansas City, Mo.*

I lasted one year on a State university   23
campus and three years later took up in an experimental University Without Walls program, primarily because I was faced with a salary cut without a degree. The responsibility of the UWW program was placed squarely on my shoulders. I learned not only the necessary academics and some practical skills that I was able to test out on the job, but I also learned to direct and take responsibility for my own learning, my own career, my own life.

I think most young people ought to give themselves a few years between high school and college (if they so desire—let's not go the other way and say that all 18-year-olds should delay college). They might see what the world is really like when one has to support oneself, and they might get the opportunity to discover what offers "psychic income" to them. — *Karen Trisko, Chicago*

24   To make higher education more relevant to more people would certainly make my job (recruiter for Education Opportunity Program applicants) a lot easier and more worthwhile. If the impact of your ideas has this effect, then I hope more people get wind of your message. If the waste in higher education is reduced by "better" selection procedures and more effective education methods, then I say let's push your ideas forward. If, on the other hand, what occurs is reduced funding that results in less incentives to create more relevant curricula, or, if "more" selectivity rather than "better" selectivity results in the continued "meat-market" tac-

tics of selection based only on GPAs and test scores (which have proved to discriminate against minorities and women), then I feel your statements may amount to a shortcut to the dark ages. — *Ramon Cruz, Assistant Director, Educational Opportunity Program, California State University, Long Beach*

After high-school graduation and two 25 years of junior college, I came to the very same conclusion as Bird. From there I tackled the working world via door-to-door sales, waitressing and, finally, assembly work. After only six months at the latter job, I was transferred to the engineering department and was trained as a draftsperson, my current position (note: I had only one semester of drafting in the 10th grade). I definitely feel anyone can get where they want to go with the right attitude, with a lot of persistence, and *without* a college diploma! — *Mrs. Cathy Emmett, Costa Mesa, Calif.*

EXERCISE

Inference Assignment

The writers of these 25 letters fall into three categories: those who agree with Bird (such as the writer of letter 1), those who disagree with her (letter 2), and those who, whether agreeing or disagreeing, wish mainly to make some additional comment on the subject (letter 4).

Reread the letters, classifying each into one of these three categories. Then look over the letters of agreement and the letters of disagreement for areas of similarity. (A number of those who agree with Bird, for instance, believe that most 18-year-olds are not intellectually or emotionally prepared to benefit from college; a number of those who disagree with her object to the way she makes her financial benefit projections.)

Next, prepare an outline for a three- or four-paragraph essay. (A four-paragraph essay would include a separate introductory paragraph.) In one paragraph summarize the agreements with Bird. In another, summarize the disagreements. (You can reverse this order if you like.) In the final paragraph, discuss some of the most interesting or important additional comments. Be sure to include a *thesis* that embraces all of the material you discuss.

Barbara Damrosch

REVIEW OF BIRD'S *THE CASE AGAINST COLLEGE*

Barbara Damrosch has taught English at four colleges. She is an editor of *The Little Magazine* and a freelance writer whose work has been published in *Esquire* and the *Village Voice*. Like many book reviewers, Damrosch uses her book review not only to discuss the book itself, but also to make an argument concerning the issues dealt with by the book.

1   Caroline Bird, according to the blurb on the jacket of her book, "has an uncanny knack for spotting trends in our society far ahead of the crowd." The "crowd" may indeed still subscribe to the "national myth that every 18-to-22-year-old American should go to college," but it requires no ESP to see flaws in that myth. Paul Goodman, ten years ago, maintained that college as he knew it was no more than a stage in a system of "compulsory miseducation," and riots on campuses since then have shown, among other things, that something is wrong with the college experience.

2   What *is* wrong with it? The argument that will sell Ms. Bird's book (though not her only argument) is that college isn't worth the money any more. Given recent job shortages, especially in the very fields that students newly greened by the counter-culture want to enter, such as forestry, oceanography and urban planning, college doesn't guarantee you a good living. Since college-aged people are not needed economically, they are stuck in these "youth ghettos" where they feel infantilized and unproductive. They are being driven to anomie, suicide, and the need to choose their own alternative solutions. "Sweeping changes will be needed" to provide them with sensible ones, says Bird, and she proposes several herself, including on-the-job vocational training and a system under which a liberal education might be offered to anyone who wants it, at whatever point in life.

3   Bird has written a well-researched survey of the facts that raises some good questions about college. But as an attempt at sorting out the problem it only confuses the reader, subjecting the institution of higher education to a variety of attacks without any thoroughgoing social analysis. The confusion stems from the relationship between two opposing views of what college is supposed to do. Both these views are popular ones.

4   The first, the rosy view, is that college is a banquet of the gods, where beauty is truth and truth beauty, and where a young person is made wiser, more humane and more tolerant. Bird ascribes this view to the "liberal arts religion" for which she can find no adequate definition beyond this one: college should teach "the habit of logical analysis and the conventions of rhetoric that make it possible to resolve differences of view on human affairs by debate and discussion." She must have asked the wrong people, for a good deal has been said and written on this subject. College may be the place for discussion, but this discussion is translatable into action (which a "resolution" might or might not be), and action is worthless if all the lessons of history must be relearned with each new generation. Even when it fails to instill values, a broad education gives people a belief in the possibility of choice. Bird pays this kind of education a series of backhanded compliments. Liberal arts graduates, she concedes, are more intelligent, more liberal than other people, but they were that way to start with and went to college for that reason. College encourages a high expectation of "psychic income" from a vocation, an expectation that is doomed to be unsatisfied, since few such pleasant jobs exist and only the job of college professor will fulfill it completely.

5   The second view of college, the practical one, is that it is a great Thanksgiving dinner from which people emerge successful, well-fed and middle-class. But here again, says

Bird, the prospects are gloomy. If the frost is on the rose, then the bloom is also off the pumpkin. If college provides entry into the elite, then college-for-everyone won't work. If college gives you the tools of management—certain kinds of discourse, the ability to manipulate abstract symbols—it must be for the few, since society can only use so many managers. The liberal arts religion is simply the mystery of class, the life of total fringe benefit, "instant operational prestige with strangers, the words and accents that make traffic cops believe your side of the story." Even professional training is a fraud, she claims, designed to corner the market for the pros. Skills such as general surgery could be picked up just as successfully by hanging around a hospital and watching the doctors at work.

6   I think that the split between the two goals is not a natural one, but one fostered by a distressed society: if college succeeds in its utopian aim it makes students unfit for the practical world. It produces "the Graduate" who comes home to L.A. and says "no" to plastics. The fact that both utopian and practical goals have existed simultaneously is one of the ironies of our culture. As political currents shift back and forth, college is the medium through which the middle class alternately replenishes and destroys itself. During the war in Vietnam the utopian element was of great social value to us. Do we no longer need it now that the war is over? Such trendiness is dangerous. If we pay attention to it, we lose our sense of history—even recent history.

7   I think that college does have something to offer the unintellectual or poorly prepared students, even if they must return to a proletarian job after graduation. If college raises expectations of psychic income, perhaps graduates will apply those standards to their working conditions, their leisure hours, the life of their communities and the way their society is governed. Between the people on the bottom (entering students) and the people on top (trustees, regents) there is often an argument that college is a track that leads to money. But in the classroom, theoretically, anything can happen. And sometimes remarkable things do.

EXERCISES

Content

Recall the main ideas in this article by answering the following questions. Respond to some of the questions in your own words. Respond to others by finding quotations from the article that provide the answers.

1. Damrosch claims that Bird's book confuses the reader. From what factor does this confusion stem?

2. Summarize Damrosch's account of the "rosy" or "utopian" view of college.

3. Summarize her account of the "practical" view of college.

4. Why does Damrosch think that college has something to offer even nonacademically inclined students who must work at intellectually undemanding jobs?

Structure

1. How is paragraph 4 related to paragraph 5?

2. How is paragraph 7 related to the thesis of the review?

Fact/Opinion

Classify each of the following statements as either a fact, an opinion, or a fact wrapped in an opinion. If the statement is a combination of fact and opinion, identify which part is fact and which opinion.

1. "Caroline Bird, according to the blurb on the jacket of her book, 'has an uncanny knack for spotting trends in our society far ahead of the crowd.'"

2. "Bird has written a well-researched survey of the facts that raises some good questions about college."

3. "Both these views [of what college is supposed to do] are popular ones."

Inferences

In your responses to the following questions, incorporate some of the quotations you located in response to the Content questions. You may decide to use either all or only part of each quotation.

1. Is Damrosch basically in agreement or disagreement with Bird over the value of a college education? Explain.

2. To what extent do you think the other readings in this chapter ("Does College Matter Anymore?" "Should You Go to College?," the Mount Holyoke "Principles," "College Is a Waste of Time and Money," and the responses to Bird) acknowledge the two opposing views of the purpose of college, as specified by Damrosch—the utopian view and the practical view?

3. How can the utopian and practical views exist simultaneously in our culture (paragraph 6)? Can one person hold both views at the same time?

4. Damrosch writes, "As political currents shift back and forth, college is the medium through which the middle class alternately replenishes and destroys itself." (She proceeds to give an example of the importance to society of the "utopian element" during the Vietnam era.) What do you think she means by this? In what way does the middle class "replenish" itself by means of college? In what way does it "destroy" itself?

Harvey A. Rubenstein

AN EDUCATION SYSTEM THAT FAILED

Harvey A. Rubenstein is president of V.I.P. Executive Search, a Los Angeles firm. This article, written in 1978, expresses an argument often made by businesspeople and others who believe that the liberal arts college is an impractical luxury in the modern world.

1   In the U.S., most college graduates today are incorrectly and inadequately educated as far as the business community is concerned. At best, many new graduates will find work in selling, which they did not plan on, or in manual labor, which they certainly did not have to devote four or more years of their lives preparing for.

The Changing Job Market

What many persons fail to realize is that 2 times have changed. Parents continue to be willing to sacrifice to pay or help pay the already lofty and rapidly rising costs of higher education for their children because of a long-held belief that a college sheepskin, as in the past, will continue to be a magic carpet to affluence and the good life for their sons or daughters. Cooperating with these aspirations, colleges for 14 years have lowered entrance standards to expand higher education opportunities for the poor and minorities.

3 Now, the job outlook for vast numbers of graduates after four or more years of college has soured. It is not because there are not and will not be jobs — although there are contracting career opportunities in the new persistent saturation of the highly educated labor market. Rather, the real problem is that large numbers of college students take the wrong courses and so can not qualify for many, if not most, present and expected job openings in an era of increasing specialization.

4 In short, a college diploma no longer is a *passe-partout* to good jobs. The right courses now are a must. Without them, college graduates will find, it will be another instance of the future that does not work. Already, disgruntled recent graduates are starting to call their college alma maters "unemployment factories" because they failed to train students for available jobs.

5 Far too many young people are going straight out of school into the labor force and becoming unemployed. As they eventually become middle-aged workers, one must wonder what the impact will be on their personalities, as well as on their employability, from never having had a suitable first job. Even today, eight of 10 middle-aged working people are misplaced in their careers and literally find it easier to change wives or husbands than jobs.

6 A symptom of the growing problem was disclosed in a recent survey of 185 major U.S. companies, which indicated that they planned to hire 3,845 engineering graduates and only 876 liberal arts graduates. That means they planned to hire over four-and-a-third times as many engineering graduates as liberal arts graduates. Yet, the colleges and universities are estimated to have bestowed nearly three times as many bachelor degrees to students of the humanities as to engineering students in 1976–77.

7 Universities try to get around such imbalance by having their placement services train graduates — after graduation — in ways to interview with a slick technique. They hope technique will hide from employment executives the fact that graduates are not qualified for available jobs. This approach is backward, archaic, and cloistered. The schools ought to start dealing with this problem with entering freshmen instead of with graduating seniors.

8 Since colleges and universities owe responsibility to their graduates, a new program must be adopted nationwide to help satisfy such responsibility. Such a program would force colleges to study the job market — present and future — and to teach this information in a required career-planning course to all entering freshmen before they are permitted to select a major.

9 In addition, the program would require each student upon selecting a major to sign a statement — printed in big, bold type — that he or she has been told what are the expected job opportunities in that field four years hence. The student would be told, for example, that 10,000 graduates are expected to be competing for only 1,000 job openings in the field of the major being selected. Then, students would have a more realistic idea about their chances for employment in the field they may be considering as a major.

10 However, the responsibility for making a success of this program does not rest solely with the schools. Business must start participating more actively with educators and students to rebuild the bridge over the widening gap between work and school.... The days simply are gone when companies could afford not to get involved.

11 Granted, many liberal arts students are not interested or talented in engineering. They ought to be encouraged to look hard at those non-engineering fields which hold the best expectations for future employment. While those 185 companies in the previously

mentioned survey were looking for 3,800 engineering graduates, they also were seeking 3,800 accounting graduates and 2,600 business administration majors (both marketing and non-marketing); chemistry, math, economics majors; and so on. Many available courses of study are related to business, where most graduates will spend the majority of their working days.

Education's Responsibilities

12   Most college graduates today are being victimized by the universities. It is time to get the universities back in line with their responsibilities to their students and the community. The universities ask business to recruit their graduates and for monetary donations. Yet, many educators remain insensitive to the needs of business—needs which really parallel the needs of the students as well, and the responsibilities of education to both.

13   Such educators are not even in tune with their own profession—education. There, you find a particularly bad discrepancy between the people available and the jobs available. Statistics indicate that one-third of the estimated 195,500 college seniors with education majors in 1977–78 will not find teaching jobs. That means one out of every three trained teachers will not find work in their chosen field—and this situation likely will worsen. Between 1974 and 1985, it is estimated, the number of college and university teachers will decrease by two per cent and secondary school teachers by eight per cent.

14   Education majors who are most likely to find teaching jobs are majoring in education of the handicapped, education of the mentally retarded, and adult education and those who speak a second language, particularly Spanish or whatever happens to be the dual language of their region.

15   Now somebody knew that a few years ago. Someone knew many future education graduates would not find jobs in teaching. Why weren't the students told? Employment

executives knew it, and so did the universities. Yet, the situation is not being remedied at all. The schools simply are not preparing their graduates for the careers and jobs which will be available.

16   Young people today just are not being told the cold, hard facts of life. Employment executives see the lamentable results every business day—all the education, anthropology, and art majors, and so on. Do you know how many annual job openings are estimated in such fields between 1974 and 1985?

17   Government statistics tell the sad story. There are expected openings for 600 political scientists, 900 actors and actresses, 850 dancers, 600 radio and TV announcers, 750 sociologists, 650 geographers, 250 anthropologists, and 100 oceanographers. Such limited opportunities make for keen competition.

18   Compare those with the estimated annual openings for 52,500 in engineering occupations, 6,400 chemists, 1,300 geologists, 1,700 physicists, 1,250 statisticians, 3,600 surveyors, 3,000 architects, 5,200 psychologists, 45,500 accountants, 11,700 purchasing agents, 17,300 drafters, 16,000 bank officers, and 4,500 credit managers. Or consider the estimated annual openings in the health field for 2,400 physical therapists, 3,200 dieticians, 6,500 pharmacists, and 71,000 registered nurses.

19   Even these statistics do not tell the whole story, though—we must include also the expected competition for projected job openings. Introducing this additional factor can change what appears to be a good opportunity into a highly competitive one and vice versa. Among the occupations where average annual openings are projected to exceed specializing graduates are accountants, computer systems analysts, other business and management areas, social service occupations, dentists, and medical practitioners.

20   On the other side of the coin, however, government projections indicate there will be more than 10 times the number of students receiving bachelor degrees in psychology as psychologist openings. There similarly

will be three times the number of graduating seniors in mathematics and statistics as openings in that field, nearly three times as many bachelor degrees awarded in the fine and applied arts as openings in that area, nearly twice as many in the physical sciences, and more than four times in the biological sciences.

21   Lest you think such odds are dismal, consider those in the social sciences — about one in 20 — then ask what is the occupational specialty of the estimated 66,270 seniors majoring in letters who are expected to be graduated in 1977–78.

22   Why are so many graduates so shocked when they apply for their first job in the rough, competitive, profit-oriented business world? The reason is clearly that they trusted and had faith in an education system which failed them — a system which failed not only the individual, but the entire community as well.

EXERCISE

Content

Recall the main ideas in this article by answering the following questions. Respond to some of the questions in your own words. Respond to others by finding quotations from the article that provide the answers.

1. In what way have times changed the value of a traditional college education, according to Rubenstein?

2. A college diploma is no longer sufficient for a job. What is essential, according to Rubenstein?

3. How do universities attempt to get around the fact that many of their graduating seniors are not adequately prepared for the job market, according to Rubenstein? Why is this approach ineffective? What do they need to do instead?

4. What specific programs does Rubenstein recommend that colleges institute to better prepare their graduates for the realities of the job market?

5. What responsibilities does business have in such preparation?

6. What does Rubenstein advise for the majority of students who have no talent or interest in engineering?

7. Why does Rubenstein feel that it is particularly outrageous for colleges to be so insensitive to the needs of business?

8. Rubenstein claims that many educators are not out of touch just with the business world but are even out of touch with their own profession. Why?

9. Why does Rubenstein so heavily emphasize statistics in paragraphs 17–21?

Structure

1. How are paragraphs 15 and 16 related to the thesis of the article?

2. How is paragraph 19 related to paragraphs 18 and 17?

Fact/Opinion

Classify each of the following statements as either a fact, an opinion, or a fact wrapped in an opinion. If the statement is a combination of fact and opinion, identify which part is fact and which opinion.

1. "Far too many young people are going straight out of school into the labor force and becoming unemployed."

2. "This approach [training liberal arts graduates to interview for engineering jobs] is backward, archaic, and cloistered."

3. "Statistics indicate that one-third of the estimated 195,500 college seniors with education majors in 1977–78 will not find teaching jobs."

Inferences

In your responses to the following questions, incorporate some of the quotations you located in response to the Content questions. You may decide to use either all or only part of each quotation.

1. Rubenstein concludes by claiming that the education system has failed not only the students and not only the individual, "but the entire community as well." Do you believe this is a fair statement? Why or why not?

2. To what extent would Rubenstein agree with Caroline Bird ("College Is a Waste of Time and Money")? How are their emphases and their perspectives different?

3. Outline the differences between Rubenstein's concerns and those expressed by the authors of the Mount Holyoke "Principles." Try writing a letter of response, either by Rubenstein concerning the "Principles" or by the authors of the "Principles" concerning Rubenstein's article.

Thomas J. Cottle

OVERCOMING AN INVISIBLE HANDICAP

Thomas J. Cottle, a sociologist and clinical psychologist, has lectured on psychology at the Harvard Medical School. His "Life Studies," which frequently appeared in *Psychology Today,* were psychological portraits of real people he interviewed. Among his many books are *Time's Children; Black Children, White Dreams;* and *Barred from School.* In this piece, Cottle's subject, Lucille Elmore, argues against the kind of viewpoint expressed by Rubenstein in the previous article.

1   On her 30th birthday, Lucille Elmore informed her husband that she was going through a crisis. "I was 30 years old, active, in good health—and I was illiterate," she recalls. "I didn't know books, I didn't know history, I didn't know science. I had the barest understanding of the arts. Like a physical condition, my knowledge limped, my intelligence limped."

She was not only the mother of two 2 young children but also was working full time as an administrative assistant in a business-consulting firm. Nevertheless, at age 30, with her husband's agreement, Lucille Elmore enrolled in college. "I thought getting in would be difficult," she says. "It was easy. I thought I couldn't discipline myself, but that came. Half the people in the library the first day thought I was the librarian, but that didn't deter me."

3   For Lucille, the awareness of her invisible limp came only gradually. As a young woman, she had finished high school, but she had chosen not to go on with her education. Her parents, who had never completed high school themselves, urged her to go to college but she refused. At the time, she was perhaps a bit timid and lacked a certain confidence in her own intellectual or academic abilities. Besides, a steady job was far more important at that point to Lucille than schooling: she felt she could read on her own to make up for any lack of education.

4   At 20, working full time, she married Ted Elmore, a salesman for a foodstore chain, a man on his way to becoming more than modestly successful. There was no need for her to work, but she did so until her first child was born; she was then 22. A second child was born two years later, and three years after that, she went back to work. With her youngest in a day-care program, she felt no reservations about working, but her lack of education began to nag at her as she approached the age of 30. She thus gave up her job, entered a continuing-education program at a nearby university, and began what she likens to a love affair.

5   "I'm carrying on an open affair with books, but like a genuinely good lover, I'm being guided. Reading lists, suggested reading, recommended readings — I want them all. I must know what happened in the 12th, 13th, 18th centuries. I want to know how the world's major religions evolved. Papal history, I know nothing of papal history and succession, or the politics involved. I read the Bible, but I never studied it. It's like music: I listened,, but it wasn't an informed listening. Now all of this is changing.

6   "I must tell you, I despise students when they talk about 'the real world,' as if college were a dream world. They simply don't understand what the accumulation of knowledge and information means. Maybe you have to be 30 at least, and going through a personal crisis, to fully appreciate what historical connections are.

7   "A line of Shakespeare challenges me more than half the jobs I'll be equipped for when I'm finished. I'm having an affair with him, too, only it's called Elizabethan Literature 606. I think many people prefer the real world of everyday work because it's less frightening than the larger-than-life world of college.

8   "There's a much more important difference between the rest of the students and me. We don't agree at all on what it means to be a success. They think in terms of money, material things. I suppose that's normal. They don't understand that with a nice home, and decent job prospects, and two beautiful children, I know I am a failure. I'm a failure because I am ignorant. I'm a failure until I have knowledge, until I can work with it, be excited by and play with ideas.

9   "I don't go to school for the rewards down the line. I want to reach the point at which I don't measure knowledge by anything but itself. An idea has value or it doesn't. This is how I now determine success and failure."

10   "'How can I use it?' That's what students ask. 'What good will this do me?' They don't think about what the question says about them, even without an answer attached to it. Questions like that only build up competition. But competition is the bottom line for so many students, I guess, getting ahead, getting a bit of a step up on the other guy. I know, it's my husband's life.

11   "I'll tell you what I think I like most about my work: the library. I can think of no place so exclusive and still so open and public. Millions of books there for the taking. A chair to sit in, a row of books, and you don't need a penny. For me, the library is a religious center, a shrine.

12   "Students talk about the real world out there. What about the free world in here? Here, no one arrests you for what you're thinking. In the library, you can't talk, so you have to think. I never knew what it meant to think about something, to really think it through. I certainly never understood what you had to know to even begin to think. I always thought it was normal to limp."

```
┌──────────────┬────────────────────────────────────────────────┐
│  EXERCISES   │                                                │
└──────────────┴────────────────────────────────────────────────┘
```

Content

Recall the main ideas in this article by answering the following questions. Respond to some of the questions in your own words. Respond to others by finding quotations from the article that provide the answers.

1. What was the nature of Lucille Elmore's "crisis"?

2. "Limping" is a metaphor used throughout this article (paragraphs 1, 3, and 12). What does Elmore mean when she uses the idea of limping in this way?

3. Why didn't Elmore go to college immediately after high school?

4. Why did she decide to go at age 30?

5. Why does Elmore say that she despises students who talk about "the real world"?

6. What is the difference Elmore perceives between the way she and her younger fellow students view "success"?

7. Why is the library what Elmore likes most about her work?

Structure

1. What is the purpose of paragraphs 1–5?

2. Explain how paragraphs 8–10, considered together, form an identifiable section of the article. Give this section a title.

Fact/Opinion

Classify each of the following statements as either a fact, an opinion, or a fact wrapped in an opinion. If the statement is a combination of fact and opinion, identify which part is fact and which opinion.

1. "On her 30th birthday, Lucille Elmore informed her husband that she was going through a crisis."

2. "She was not only the mother of two young children but also was working full time as an administrative assistant in a business-consulting firm."

3. "[Students who talk about 'the real world'] simply don't understand what the accumulation of knowledge and information means."

Inferences

In your responses to the following questions, incorporate some of the quotations you located in response to the Content questions. You may decide to use either all or only part of each quotation.

1. At one point Elmore says, "A line of Shakespeare challenges me more than half the jobs I'll be equipped for when I'm finished." And later she declares: "I think many people prefer the real world of everyday work because it's less frightening than the larger-than-life world of college." What do you think she means by these statements? Why is college "frightening"? Why is it "larger than life"?

2. How are the dual concerns discussed in paragraphs 9 and 10 related to the two worlds discussed in Barbara Damrosch's review of Bird's book? How are these concerns related to the subject matter of the Mount Holyoke "Principles" on the one hand and the concerns of Caroline Bird on the other?

3. Toward the end, Elmore says, "I certainly never understood what you had to know to even begin to think." What do you think she has in mind? To what extent do you agree with this sentiment?

Kate White

NINE SUCCESSFUL WOMEN TELL HOW COLLEGE CHANGED THEIR LIVES

Kate White, one of *Glamour* magazine's Top Ten College Women in 1972, graduated from Union College in Schenectady, N.Y. She is presently an executive editor for a national magazine and a freelance writer. White's subjects argue indirectly for the various benefits of a college education.

1   Twelve years have passed since I graduated from college, but, so far, those four years had the most important impact on my life. Some of it has to do with the hunger for experience that I felt — that we all feel — at eighteen; I held my plate out and was ready to taste anything that was put on it. Some of it has to do with the special kind of environment that college offers — a place where absolutely anything seems possible. College didn't open one door — but several. When Professor Gado read one of my short stories aloud in fiction class and remarked that it reminded him of Sherwood Anderson, my cheeks turned beet-red as I realized that maybe I *could* be a writer. Running for a seat on the college senate during such a turbulent time in history (the year was 1971) started an infatuation with politics that I've never lost. Finding out that I could remake myself in a new environment — from being high-school egghead to a popular girl on campus — was a lesson I used several times down the road. When I was chosen one of *Glamour's* Top Ten College Women in 1972,

it seemed to confirm what I already knew: College had given me my first real chance to be who I secretly wanted to be.

In this issue, we've followed up several other former winners to see how they view the college experience with the passage of time. Meet eight very successful women who have made their mark in a variety of fields.

Lillian Glass

Lillian Glass, a speech pathologist, coached Dustin Hoffman for Tootsie. *Winner 1974, graduated Bradley University, 1974.*

"College has had such an impact on my success. Of course, I've been through ten years altogether — undergraduate years, a master's degree, doctorate and post-doctoral work. Those years gave me determination: I felt that if I could get through with all the pressures, I could achieve anything in life.

"My undergraduate years were particularly special for me. Going off to college from Florida was my first introduction to the outside world. And my studies there convinced me that my dream of being a speech pathologist was the right dream for me. The professor I had in my first speech pathology class was so motivating that I left the room knowing that I had made the right decision. The clinical experience of working with patients made me even more enthusiastic, because in speech pathology you can see results very soon.

"I also saw what a difference I could make in people's lives because of the person I was. A computer can teach a person how to do certain things, but I learned that caring, warmth, a smile, were all extremely important.

"College also allowed me to pursue something else I'd been interested in: journalism. I was afraid I'd have to put it on a back burner, but I soon discovered that I could try my hand at journalism extracurricularly. I won first place in a women's television speaking contest in broadcast journalism.

"I was a very serious student and I studied hard but I didn't neglect my social life, my friends or my hobbies. I think that if a person can find that balance in college, she can take it with her into adulthood. In my own life I've found that I need that balance to be happy. When I saw some old friends from Bradley recently, they told me I was pretty much the person I was in college, only more so."

JoBeth Williams

JoBeth Williams, actress, whose films include The Big Chill *and* Poltergeist. *Winner 1969, graduated Brown University, 1970.*

3   "I absolutely loved college. The first semester I was very nervous because I was a little Texas girl and people laughed at my accent and said things like, 'Do they have any culture in Texas?' I was dealing with all these kids from the East Coast, most of whom were from families much better off than mine. But I began to realize that my own feelings of insecurity were hampering me more than anything other people were doing. I saw that everybody was scared no matter where they came from.

"I hadn't planned on getting involved in theater. I'd done musicals in high school, but my counselors said, it's all well and good that you like to act, but it's nothing that one does seriously in life. So I made a vow that I wasn't going to do any theater while I was at Brown.

"For the first six weeks I was very good. Then one day I went along with someone who was trying out for a play. I wound up auditioning, and I got the part and that was it. I spent all my time in the theater.

"I still vividly remember an early course in theater that I took, which was essentially the first time I'd had any kind of acting training. We each had to do a monologue in class and I chose one from a J. D. Salinger short story. While I was performing it, I began to cry. The professor was very gentle—he led me through and helped me. It was terribly frightening to have my emotions opened up that way, but it was also exciting—because I realized for the first time that there was a craft to acting.

"College in the sixties was the place to be. The peace movement was happening and we students were beginning to feel that we had power, that we were affecting things. We felt bound together, full of hope and enthusiasm. It gave me a sense of responsibility for what goes on in the world. Being an actress is by its nature selfish, but my experiences in school have affected the way I choose roles today. I want to do things that have impact, that affect people."

Zina Schiff

Zina Schiff is an award-winning concert violinist. Winner 1975, graduated University of California, Berkeley, 1975.

"As a musician I found college to be the   4 icing on the cake. I had gone to a music conservatory, Curtis Institute, instead of high school, and the typical thing for me to do would have been to go on to continue at Curtis where only music courses are offered. But instead I went to Berkeley, where I could try courses that I never would have considered at a specialized school.

"Berkeley was an extremely vibrant place. So much of the college experience there was walking between classes, seeing all the people. The whole atmosphere was stimulating.

"I still feel the impact of school today. All the developmental psychology courses I took have helped me as the mother of two daughters—and in my work. I travel a lot for concerts and I'm with many strangers in situations where unexpected things happen. I think I'm better prepared to deal with some of those experiences because of Berkeley. A lot of musicians live and breathe music; nothing else but music exists for them. College made me see that life is more interesting, that there are other things to talk about. It also gave me confidence. Though I'm still shy in certain situations, I'm very confident in my work. It's as though when I'm performing I'm back in college with the same kind of excitement."

Sheryl Lee Ralph

Sheryl Lee Ralph, actress, whose work includes the Broadway play Dreamgirls. *Winner 1975, graduated Rutgers University, 1975.*

5   "College made me realize what I wanted to do with my life. I was involved in drama in high school, but I went to college planning to be a doctor. I remember driving down to school with my father, and he told me that an actress spends most of her time looking for work, but a doctor has a certain amount of security. I had been raised in a very stable environment so I went for the security.

"But when I started taking pre-med and lab courses—and the thought of cadavers crossed my mind—I realized that it wasn't the path I wanted to take. I tried a semester of pre-law but that wasn't right for me either. All during this time I was involved with the theater department as an extracurricular activity and I got the role of Laura in *Tambourines to Glory*. It completely turned me around. I changed my major to theater and said goodbye to chemistry and cadavers. I knew for certain that my heart lay with the theater and that I had to take the chance. So, since I was young—I graduated from college at nineteen—I took the chance, and it was the right one.

"Several of my drama teachers had an important effect on me. There was one lovely old gruffy bear of a man who thought I was extremely talented. There was another who represented perfection to me and that made me want to strive for perfection. And working as a drama critic for the Rutgers *Daily Targum* gave me the chance to be on the other side and develop a different perspective.

"My theater courses had an important effect on me, but so did some of the courses I took in the humanities. I remember my first test in philosophy. The question on the page was simply 'Why?' I knew I wasn't going to sit there and write 15 million pages about why when I didn't know why *what.*" So I wrote 'Because' and handed in my paper as everyone else sat there writing. I got an A. I thought, 'Hey, this is the way it is.' I still use that lesson in life today: Sometimes you can go too deep looking for the answer; it may be right under your nose."

Carrie Francke

Carrie Francke is a Republican candidate in Missouri's 9th Congressional District. Winner 1976, graduated University of Missouri, 1976.

6   "Somewhere in high school I got the notion that I wanted to be in politics. I was senior class president and very active in the Albuquerque Youth Council. But when I got to college in 1972, I discovered that I was a little fish in a big pond. I just didn't know if I would be able to pull it off.

"One day, though, I went to a student-senate meeting. I can still remember watching the student-body president and thinking, 'That person isn't the kind of person who should be president. *I'm* going to be president in three years.' Soon after, I ran for senate from my dorm floor—and won. I got very involved in a number of student-government committees and did an internship my second semester in the General Assembly in Jefferson City. In my junior year I was elected student-body president, the first woman ever to hold the office at Missouri. It was hands-on training in politics and I decided I really loved it.

"As soon as I became active in student government I realized that politics gives you the power to change things. When I first started school there were city streets that ran right through campus and when you had only ten minutes to get from one building to another, you had to dodge traffic. So in my sophomore year a few of us decided that we wanted to have the streets closed during the school period. We first got students to say that's what they wanted, then we worked to get the university to agree. Then we went to the city council. There was such an uproar in the community that it had to go to a vote. It was a thrill when we won. And I knew I had a talent for that kind of work, for bringing forces together and being reasonable and finding a solution that everybody could live with. I knew for sure then that it was what I wanted to do with my life.

"There was a tendency for me to think that because I was meeting with people such as the university president and the board of curators, I was pretty important. But I learned to keep a healthy perspective by staying involved in clubs and with people who didn't live or die for student government. People who are going to make politics their life have to keep their feet in everyday activities so they don't lose perspective. That's what I try to do."

Kiron Skinner

Kiron Skinner is enrolled in the political science doctoral program at Harvard University. Winner 1981, graduated Spelman College, 1981.

7   "I think I am where I am today because of the nurturing environment of Spelman. I had a small department to work in and I got to know professors really well. I picked Spelman because I wanted to go to a small black college, and I wanted to go south, where I'd never been before.

"Spelman gave me more of a sense of identity as a black woman. It helped me

to understand the position that the black woman is put in in this country, as well as the fact that just because you are a black woman doesn't mean you *have* to have two strikes against you. Spelman gave me a good self-image, largely because of the role models there. The chairman of my department was a black woman with a doctorate in my field from The American University. Another professor I worked closely with, whose field was international politics, was a black woman. There were women in their thirties and forties who had overcome major obstacles to do the kinds of things I wanted to do. It encouraged me tremendously.

"I started out wanting to go to law school. Then I met the professor of international politics, and because of the things she was interested in—the reading lists she gave in class, her lectures—she changed my whole course of thinking about my future. She had the biggest impact on my decision to go into a graduate program and start my career in academics. I'm interested in bridging the gap between the academic community and the decision-making community. They need to work closely together on global issues.

"My extracurricular activities also helped to direct me. I was associate editor of the newspaper. I interned for former Senator Hayakawa in his district office, which expanded my interest in politics. And I had an internship in the district attorney's office, which confirmed the fact that I *didn't* want to be a lawyer.

"And my friends were really important, too, because once you get into a Ph.D. program you're working alone or with professors. My college friendships have helped me out personally more than anything else."

Nancy Glass

Nancy Glass is co-host and field producer of Evening *magazine in Philadelphia. Winner 1977, graduated Tufts University, 1977.*

8   "It was in college that I first discovered I wanted to be involved in television. Tufts didn't have any communications courses so I went to the dean and asked if I could become an intern at one of the local TV stations. She encouraged me. I worked first as an intern on a show called *Woman '75,* then the next summer I got involved in a management-trainee program, and after that I became a producer.

"If I hadn't been allowed to work while I was going to school, I wouldn't be doing what I'm doing now. In a way, it was good that Tufts didn't have a communications program because I might not have studied some of the things I did. I took a lot of courses that forced me to learn about the world. I also took a lot of fiction writing in college, which not only encouraged my writing but made me learn how to *think.* I still remember this one incident that happened in a writing course. One week a guy read aloud a story he'd written about a boy who went blind from an accident and later regained his sight. It wasn't written very well, and when the student was done, the professor said, "So what?" The guy replied, "It happened to me." And the professor said, "So what? If you don't tell it well, it has no impact." I learned then and there that the content will be lost if you don't tell it well.

"In high school your goal is to go to McDonald's or to the prom. I never even got invited to the prom. But in college your goal is to learn and to grow and, when that happens, it's terrific. While I was in college I just became aware there was so much to learn and to never give up on what you want."

Jean Harshbarger Arnold

Jean Harshbarger Arnold is an attorney with her own practice, specializing in school law. Particularly involved with rights of the handicapped. Winner 1973, graduated Virginia Polytechnic Institute, 1974.

9   "College students in the early seventies were very concerned about helping other people and caring about more than themselves. The particular focus down here then was the coal-mining population, as Blacksburg borders on Appalachia. On one project I helped raise money for the widows of coal miners who were deprived of benefits when their husbands died of black-lung disease. Such activities helped lead me to a law practice that deals with issues concerning *individuals.*

"Over the four years of college I did go through a transition in how I thought society's problems should be confronted. At first I wanted to fight the system, but by my senior year I believed in working for change *within* the system. I came to that conclusion in part from my student-leadership activities. In my sophomore year I was elected president of the class of '74, and held the position for three years. I sat in on every primary university committee, which gave me an excellent opportunity to observe the management of an educational institution. Observing the college president conduct the business of the university so effectively, so capably, really inspired me.

"Something else helped alter my views. At the end of my freshman year I was in a serious car accident that almost killed me, and I spent six weeks in the hospital. That was just an incredible time to reflect on where my life was going. And it seemed that the more realistic way to effect positive change in our society would be from the inside. Life's too short to take the idealistic, purist approach.

"My interest in helping the handicapped stemmed from my family experience. When I was very young, my mother went blind. She was employed as a laboratory technician and in conducting some test, she contracted a very rare eye disease. This was pre-workman's compensation, and I saw how that handicap affected her life. My work as a student leader stimulated my interest in the education field, and by the time I finished law school, I discovered that there was a new area developing in which those two interests—law and education—overlapped. It's very satisfying for me."

EXERCISE

Content

Select five quotations—either phrases or complete sentences—that illustrate important ideas in the preceding accounts.

ASSIGNMENT

A number of common threads run through these nine accounts, among them the following:

- Taking important courses
- Participating in an extracurricular activity
- Studying/working with an influential professor
- Experiencing a turning point, an important moment
- Having other crucial experiences and meeting people
- Developing a new sense of values
- Developing a sense of perspective, a sense of priorities
- Developing a sense of identity
- Developing new goals

Use some of these categories—or other categories of your own choosing—to organize some of the elements in these nine short accounts. Based on this categorization, develop an outline for an essay on the value of the college experience. After getting approval from your instructor, write this essay. Refer as necessary to Chapter 4 for help in dealing with multiple sources.

In your essay, try to explain how the points made by these women support or refute the contentions made by the authors of other articles in this unit (e.g., the Mount Holyoke "Principles," "College Is a Waste of Time and Money," "An Education System That Failed"). Consider also how the experiences of these women coincide with either the "utopian" aspect or the "practical" aspect of college (as discussed by Barbara Damrosch) or fall somewhere in between. Or aren't such categories relevant in light of the experiences of these nine women?

SUMMARY ASSIGNMENT

Write a summary of Caroline Bird's "College Is a Waste of Time and Money." (You may need to review the procedures discussed in Chapter 2.)

Begin by writing one-sentence section summaries. Then write a thesis for the article as a whole. Next combine your thesis and the section summaries into a coherent summary of the entire article.

We will help get you started by suggesting one way that the article can be divided into sections and by writing the first two one-sentence section summaries.

Section 1 (paragraphs 1–2)
Most college students are in college not because they want to be, but because they think they should be.

Section 2 (paragraphs 3–7)
The great college expansion of the 1950s and 1960s has come to an end, and now college administrators are desperate to attract new students and to satisfy the ones they have.

Section 3 (paragraphs 8–19)

Section 4 (paragraphs 20–23)

Section 5 (paragraphs 24–32)

Section 6 (paragraphs 33–39)

Section 7 (paragraphs 40–49)

Section 8 (paragraphs 50–52)

Section 9 (paragraphs 53–56)

Section 10 (paragraphs 57–61)

PAPER ASSIGNMENTS

1. Write a paper in which you argue a thesis of your choice. After you have formulated a thesis, read or reread the selections in this chapter with an eye to finding evidence that will support your thesis.
2. Why are you in college? Write an essay focusing on your own decision to go to college and on what you expect to get from a college education. Consider also whether your goals and expectations have changed over the past year or so. Wherever appropriate, draw on the opinions of the authors included in this chapter.
3. Susan Leslie is a high school senior. She has a G.P.A. of 2.6; her best subject is history; she is on the varsity swimming team; and she is vice-president of the drama club. Write an essay indicating the kinds of things she needs to keep in mind as she decides whether or not to apply to college. You may invent whatever other qualities and achievements for Susan that you like (including career inclinations, parental expectations, etc.); and you may also change those that are suggested here. You may even want to create other characters to compare or contrast to Susan. Draw on the selections in this chapter to provide support for your views.
4. Barbara Damrosch, in her review of Caroline Bird's book, suggests that there are two main opposing views of the purpose of college: the "utopian" view and the "practical" view. Other writers in this chapter

often support this idea. Write an essay, drawing on at least four of the selections in this chapter, in which you compare and contrast these two views of college.

5. Write an essay based on the responses to Caroline Bird's ideas. (See the assignment following the selection of letters to the editor on Bird's article.) You may also want to include material from Barbara Damrosch's review.

6. Write an imaginary letter from the author of one article in this chapter to the author of another article. In this letter argue against the positions expressed by the other author. For example, what might Lucille Elmore want to say to Harvey Rubenstein? Or vice versa? What might Rubenstein have to say to the faculty committee that drafted the Mount Holyoke "Principles"?

7. Write a letter to the editor responding to one of the selections in this chapter. In your letter, express your reaction to the ideas in the selection, *drawing support from material in other selections in the chapter.* (The difference between this assignment and the previous one is that in this assignment you are expressing *your own* views rather than what you believe to be the views of one of the authors in this chapter.)

8. Write a paper explaining the differences between Rubenstein's concerns and those expressed by the authors of the Mount Holyoke "Principles." Your paper might be neutral, it might be weighted toward Rubenstein's position, or it might be weighted toward the liberal arts view. Whatever your own position is, however, try to deal fairly with other positions.

9. Suppose the authors of the selections in this chapter (or the people written about, such as Lucille Elmore) took the quiz that appears in "Should You Go to College?" How do you think they would answer the questions? (Consider also the likely responses of the "nine successful women" in Kate White's article.) Write an essay summarizing what you think the results would be. Then draw conclusions about the meaning of these results.

10. Write your own paper assignment for this chapter. Find a common theme running through two or more articles, devise a topic based on this theme, and then write a question asking writers to draw on material in the selections that would support a thesis based on this topic. You might want to help your writers by suggesting some specific articles or even by getting them started with an outline for the paper.

CHAPTER 10

Anatomy of a TV Success: "Hill Street Blues"

Introduction

"Hill Street Blues," one of the most successful shows on television during the mid-1980s, was a flop during its first season (1981) and came perilously close to cancellation by its network, NBC. Although most of the critics raved and the show attracted a fanatically loyal band of devotees, it was simply not drawing enough of a mass audience to guarantee its survival. It was perhaps fortunate for "Hill Street Blues" fans that most of the other new shows on NBC that season were also flops. As NBC president Grant Tinker explained, "There's a limit to how much a network can cancel."

Fortunately, the network brass continued to back the show during its lean months, and loyal audiences begged NBC to keep it on the air. Some did more than beg. According to one article, "The president of an oil company in Texas warned that if 'Hill Street Blues' were canceled, he'd urge the show's growling Detective Belker, who bites people, to go after the NBC executives who pulled the plug." Happily, Belker's services were unnecessary. "Hill Street Blues" won eight Emmies in September 1981; and new audiences, curious about this acclaimed show they hadn't ever watched, tuned in and loved what they saw. And so "Hill Street Blues" became that TV rarity—a critical *and* a popular success.

Not all critics loved it. According to Tom Buckley, of the *New York Times:* "'Ten-thirteen' is the police-radio code for 'assist patrolman.' Too bad there isn't a signal for 'assist writers,' because 'Hill Street Blues' needs help badly." Buckley went on to charge that the first episode veered "back and forth between comic situations that aren't funny—serious matters such as the taking of hostages during a robbery and the shooting of two patrolmen—and a romance that is merely silly." Such confusion, he claimed, was the result of a "choppy script."[1] Ben Roberts, a successful TV producer, argued, "The show has no real spine.... There is no plot. It's a collection of brilliant middles; it puts character above plot. But dramatic structure requires a beginning, a middle and an end, and this you don't find on *Hill Street Blues.*" Although "brilliantly made," admitted Roberts, the show's structure is "something the audience can't accept":

> I'm hot for dramatic certainties. On *Hill Street,* you have an uneasy mixture of farce and reality. Truth is too hard to believe sometimes. That's why you have to turn it into art. I don't think it's fair to blame the audience if they don't like the show. Why should they? Characters aren't explained. It's emotionally mixed up. The stories don't end. There is no cleansing catharsis. I'm sure I'm like a lot of people. I love the characters, but I don't always know what's happening. You can't ask the audience to stay home every week just so they won't be confused.[2]

We've focused on the negative reactions to "Hill Street Blues" because we'd like to give you a chance to exercise your own critical abilities on a dramatic production with which you are probably quite familiar and about which you may even have strong feelings. Perhaps you'd like to challenge critics like Buckley and Roberts. Perhaps you'd like to challenge Mark Crispin Miller, who also dislikes "Hill Street Blues," for reasons he explains in his article reprinted later in this chapter. On the other hand, many critics, including Richard Jameson and Joyce Carol Oates (whose articles are also included), love the show; and you may want to use their arguments to help refute those of the negative reviewers. Two other articles in this chapter deal primarily with the creative problems of producing "Hill Street Blues," and these articles should give you further insight into how this show gets put together every week.

Whatever your reaction, it will probably not be indifferent. We invite you to let your enthusiasm—positive or negative—flow. Consider the unusual phenomenon of "Hill Street Blues," consider your own reactions to what you see, and with the assistance of some of the following articles, apply your critical abilities to what the show's editor has called "real filmmaking."

---

[1]Tom Buckley, "TV: 'Hill Street Blues,' New TV Series," *New York Times,* 17 January 1981, 48.
[2]Quoted in John Gabree, "Can 'Hill Street Blues' Keep Dodging the Nielsen Bullet?" *TV Guide,* 31 October 1981, 31–32.

Paper Assignment

Instead of presenting new organizing techniques in this chapter, we simply ask you to review the techniques you have learned in the previous two chapters for papers using example and argument. As you read the following passages, select evidence that will help you demonstrate *examples* of the distinctive qualities of "Hill Street Blues," and/or select evidence that will help you *argue* against the positions of the show's critics.

Richard T. Jameson

QUALITY UP THE WAZOO

Richard T. Jameson writes for *Film Comment*, where this article first appeared. Like the one that follows, it was written during the first season of "Hill Street Blues," before the show became a hit.

1   If my editor hadn't called my attention to it, the premiere episode of *Hill Street Blues* would very probably have come and gone without my notice. Hundreds of television series have. But he knew I liked *Lou Grant,* and this show "from the producers of *Lou Grant*" (the hypesters' phrase) was, on the basis of preview, similarly successful in "being funny when it wants to be funny, and dramatic when it wants to be dramatic" (his phrase), and maybe I should take a look. It was getting a modified mini-series send-off as part of NBC President Fred Silverman's last desperate bid to turn around his network's ever-worsening ratings drift and save his job. Who could say whether, if the numbers failed to materialize, Silverman wouldn't replace it with a jiggle epic, or his successors ashcan it in a combined spirit of slate-cleaning and revenge?

2   So I took the look. *Hill Street Blues:* Cop show. Thirteen series regulars identified up front, most of them unfamiliar and most of them frozen in slantwise TV grin. Handheld camera, Action News editing, and overlapping mutters on the soundtrack during the morning briefing that opens the show—

manneristic bad signs for the jaundiced viewer, though they did seem to make for an appropriate grab-shot naturalism here. What the hell, give it a chance.

3   The characters are introduced. No one is new to the precinct, Hill Street, except the viewer. Everyone lands running at full *shtick:* Furillo, the beleaguered precinct commander, compassionate, but with credible limits to his patience (Daniel J. Travanti, a warmer version of Roy Scheider); Esterhaus, the commandant's eternal sergeant, abrasive, avuncular, and tenderly in thrall to a high-school cheerleader (Michael Conrad, remembered as proudly Polish uncle to *All in the Family*'s Mike Stivic); shirt-sleeved cops, uniformed cops, plain-clothes cops; sweet-smiling black cop, hip black cop, simpatico Chicano cop, weary long-faced lady cop; plus a tanned, leggy beauty from the Public Defender's office, Joyce Davenport (Veronica Hamel), who opens and closes her mouth a lot; and Furillo's ex-wife Fay (Barbara Bosson), with no other departmental affiliation, who opens and closes *her* mouth a lot to shout her protest of inadequate alimony payments.

4   All right, so they have to get identified; even Lou Grant needed half an hour of his first show to get settled in at the *Trib.* And by the time that much of *Hill Street Blues*' first episode has gone by, all suspicion of ethnic and cuteness quotas have dissolved, a community has been defined, and these people

are simply who they are, neither more nor less "on" than they need to be to lead their professional and personal lives.

5   That's something many TV series — indeed, many feature films — never manage to do. Hand in hand with this achievement goes the series' amazing success at finding a narrative rhythm to accommodate its need to develop shaped dramatic events and at the same time honor the institutional imperative that the precinct's story, and the stories of the individuals in occupational orbit there, must be ongoing, beyond resolution. Over the five episodes televised as of this writing, interest has never flagged; yet I have never encountered another TV program that betrayed less sign of anticipating commercial breaks or straining to tie off tonight's episode.

6   "From the producers of *Lou Grant*" is true in a corporate sense merely: Both programs issue from the sterling MTM organization, but none of the key personnel responsible for the newspaper show are involved in *Hill Street Blues*. The series is the creation of its Executive Producers, Michael Kozoll and Steven Bochco, who have also written all episodes to date. Director is the veteran Robert Butler. Together they generate a density that not only puts standard over-lighted, emptied-out, programmatically written television drama to shame, but can hold its own against most recent movies.

7   As the denizens of Hill Street might put it in their verbally unfettered fashion, *Hill Street Blues* has texture up the wazoo. Any given space in the precinct house contains more bodies than should humanely be expected to occupy the same vicinity, and the flow of action and movement refuses to respect the conventional television inviolability of the fourth wall. Even the comparative sanctum of the Commander's office is open to invasion and congestion, and the panes of glass separating it from the general work area reflect additional off-screen hustle more often than they turn obligingly transparent for unhindered observation.

8   Butler's camera covers this and the endlessly various urban-ghetto milieux with an

intricacy and agility that never tips over into visual complication for its own self-displaying sake. We see clearly what we need to see, and at the same time see it in the context of the living flux — social, political, professional, interpersonal — which surrounds and defines it. The backs of shots are often as intriguing as the foregrounds, and there's no predicting when a background element is going to insinuate itself into the foreground. Likewise, the principals in one episode may serve as little more than occupational color, glorified extras, in the next, while an apparent walk-on may unexpectedly become a major focus of dramatic intensification.

9   There's no telling, either, where the action may lead, or when the comic and the dramatic are going to bleed into each other. In the premiere episode, Officers Hill (Michael Warren) and Renko (Charles Haid) answer a call to settle a violent family squabble. A black couple are feuding over the husband's attention to the wife's barely-adolescent daughter by a previous liaison. Hill talks soul-brother sense to the couple and warns them that "cohabitation" of this sort often leads to trouble. ("It ain't a habit," the husband protests, in a typically loopy scriptoral throwaway, "it only happened the one time.") The family unit settles down to the business of getting on with their lives, and the patrolmen depart, chewing over this latest manifestation of urban lunacy. The viewer is still marveling over the matter-of-factness with which incest has wafted into range and out again, when Hill and Renko arrive back at curbside to find their brand new squad car missing. It isn't the first time the cops have been in this absurd position and, the nearby call box having been ripped off as well, they mosey toward a semi-derelict building across the street in search of a public phone. They step through the door, the angle shifts to a dope pusher in the act of making a sale at the rear of the lobby, and before we or the cops can adjust to the surprise, the dealer has pulled a gun and shot both men down.

10   As it happens, the gunning-down of Hill and Renko (who survive to become the emo-

tional center of a drama of readjustment, mutual estrangement, and rapprochement in subsequent episodes) and the Emergency Action Team shootup of a street-gang siege elsewhere in the same program account for the only shots fired thus far in the series. Neither, mercifully, has there been a single car chase. Instead, *Hill Street Blues* has mostly concerned itself with the continuing, volatile complexities of urban peace-keeping, the bureaucratic infighting of various law-enforcement and other governmental agencies, and, above all, the lives and evolving characterizations of the regulars.

11   A few of these regulars are still waiting rounding-out at this point in the series. Belker (Bruce Weitz), the scurvy undercover officer who can out-growl vicious dogs and surly felons, has yet to transcend his role as house geek. (He can't live down the memory of having bitten the nose off a suspect— "One lousy nose!"—in the over-enthusiastic performance of his duty.) But even he has a mother, and may be humanized further by contact with the tender sex if he can just stop saying things like "I know ya must get dates up the wazoo." If EAT (disapproved acronym of Emergency Action Team) Commander Howard Hunter seems unlikely to advance even that far, James B. Sikking's hilarious stone-jawed performance nevertheless makes him welcome as the satiric joy of the season. Karate-chopping his way out of a jammed washroom cubicle to offer a chumly "*Comment ça -va?*" (pipe-stem raised in salute) and the advice that the streets are full of "environmentally handicapped types," Hunter represents a devastating fusion of sociopolitical Neanderthalism and polysyllabic fluency.

The show has a superb ensemble going 12 for it, but it's still possible to isolate stellar presences. Charles Haid (the rampaging skeptic in *Altered States*) can turn the buying of a candy bar into a fierce transaction; his barrel-chested Renko might readily have rigidified at the level of caricature, but he articulates this macho strutter in ways that suggest an ironical and vulnerable character who could become the heart of the show. That would mean eclipsing Travanti's Francis Furillo, of course; but Travanti not only wears quiet authority like one of Furillo's three-piece suits, he also has the delicious advantage of getting to conduct a clandestine, frankly observed affair with the lawyer lady who tilts with him during the daylight hours. Not all the warmth *Hill Street Blues* gives off is communal: any episode that fails to wend its way to Veronica Hamel's bed or bath is going to leave habitual viewers feeling erotically deprived.

Whether we're to be deprived in another 13 way is uncertain as this article goes to press. Have I written a rave or an obit? The numbers didn't materialize in the opening weeks and, although NBC did agree to pick up all of MTM's first twelve installments, *Hill Street Blues* is slotted into the infamous 10 P.M. Saturday graveyard. To be sure, Lou Grant took time to build an audience; also *All in the Family, Mary Tyler Moore,* and (to plunge to another level of reference) the present national craze, *Dallas.* They were fortunate enough to be berthed at CBS, which has a tradition of nurturing quality and idiosyncrasy. Can Silverman and NBC afford to do as much for a program that is already one of the best series ever developed for television?

EXERCISES

Content

    Recall the main ideas in this article by answering the following questions. Respond to some of the questions in your own words. Respond to others by finding quotations from the article that provide the answers.

1. What were some of the characteristic production qualities that Jameson first noted as he watched "Hill Street Blues"?

2. What is the main topic of paragraph 7?

3. For what qualities does Jameson give "Hill Street Blues" high praise?

4. Which characters, according to Jameson, still need "rounding-out"?

5. What is the main question posed in the final paragraph?

Structure

1. Explain how paragraphs 1–4, considered together, form an identifiable section of the article. Give this section a title.

2. How is paragraph 12 related to paragraph 11?

Fact/Opinion

Classify each of the following statements as either a fact, an opinion, or a fact wrapped in an opinion. If the statement is a combination of fact and opinion, identify which part is fact and which opinion.

1. "Butler's camera covers this and the endlessly various urban-ghetto milieux with an intricacy and agility that never tips over into visual complication for its own self-displaying sake."

2. "They step through the door, the angle shifts to a dope pusher in the act of making a sale at the rear of the lobby, and before we or the cops can adjust to the surprise, the dealer has pulled a gun and shot both men down."

3. "Hunter represents a devastating fusion of sociopolitical Neanderthalism and polysyllabic fluency."

Inferences

In your responses to the following questions, incorporate some of the quotations you located in response to the Content questions. You may decide to use either all or only part of each quotation.

1. In the first paragraph, Jameson uses two parenthetical phrases: "(the hypesters' phrase)" and "(his phrase)." Why?

2. What do you think is the purpose of the series of sentence fragments in paragraph 2?

3. In paragraph 3, Jameson mentions the show's "narrative rhythm." What does he mean by this?

4. Do you also see Howard Hunter as a "fusion of sociopolitical Neanderthalism and polysyllabic fluency"? Explain.

5. What is the meaning of the parenthetical phrase in paragraph 13 — "(to plunge to another level of reference)"?

Mark Crispin Miller

THE LIBERAL PIETIES OF "HILL STREET BLUES"

Mark Crispin Miller, a contributing editor of *The New Republic*, teaches English at the University of Pennsylvania. He has published articles on film directors Sam Peckinpah, Stanley Kubrick, and Alfred Hitchcock. This article was written in 1981, after the first season of "Hill Street Blues."

1   "Hill Street Blues" is not a hit. Out of 97 regular series in the 1980–81 season, the new police drama ranked only 83rd in popularity. Nevertheless, Fred Silverman, former head of NBC, claimed to like the show, and expected it to pick up next season. In this case, he probably was not relying on his instincts. Fred Silverman's instincts are a national disgrace, having brought us a number of emetic divertissements whose reruns will foul the airways for the next 30 years: "Charlie's Angels," "Fantasy Island," "The Love Boat," and too many more. "Hill Street Blues" is in a different class, and ordinarily would have a very short half-life, if subjected to Silverman's usual standards. For once, however, Silverman seemed to have heeded America's television critics, who have cheered the show with an outcry of defensive praise unprecedented in the history of television.

2   By and large, they like it for two reasons. First of all, it strikes them as very realistic, and so they tend, in their plaudits, to use certain adjectives that suggest the cast of characters in a porno remake of *Snow White:* "gutsy," "gritty," "racy," "raunchy," "punchy," "tough," and "steamy." And yet they also applaud the show's correctness as a liberal statement: the show is good because it contains little violence and no offensive ethnic stereotypes. While its characters are ethnically diverse, enthused one columnist in a recent issue of *TV Guide,* they are simply "a gathering of *human beings* who just happen to have widely different last names. (You know, like real life.)... All [these] characters are so genuine and worthy, it's impossible not to like them."

3   Now that's heart-warming, if not very steamy. In "real life," it seems, there are no ethnic traits, nor any such things as national character, regional identity, or class consciousness. And everyone is equally "genuine and worthy." This is gritty realism? In fact, "Hill Street Blues" is not both true to life and idealized, because such a combination is impossible. A work might either reflect "real life" or transcend it. As it happens, "Hill Street Blues" does neither. Although promising at first, the show soon settled down to do little more than promulgate a tired ideology.

4   Its "realism" is largely the quick result of a few well-worn cinematic devices. A hand-held camera, for example, lends many scenes the jerky immediacy of a documentary. There is also plenty of inner-city texture. The precinct-house is credibly seedy, the producers having worked hard to see that things break down: the furnishings are dim and battered, the heat goes out, the vending machines (a running gag) have to be beaten regularly. The streets are a mess, like many of the characters, who overrun this perfect squalor in endless sleazy multitudes. Actors jam the foreground, background, middle distance, and stream across the frame from points unknown. Surely no cop show has ever seemed this crowded; this is *French Connection III,* directed by Thomas Malthus. Even the soundtrack is cluttered. The background hubbub nearly drowns out the dialogue, which is no mean feat, since the characters generally bellow as if going deaf. (You know, like real life.) Their dialogue also overlaps, charging the action with the sort of rich confusion that we notice every day, in films by Robert Altman.

5   Although this kind of naturalistic din has suffused many American films since the 1960s, on television it seems like a novelty. The show is also structurally unlike the usual

prime-time item. Each episode is more fluid and various than the typical plot-and-subplot arrangement, sustaining at least three unrelated stories at a time. Moreover, things don't wind to a tidy close just before the final credits, but stray into subsequent episodes, as in a soap opera. Such open-endedness, and the anarchic milieu, create an impression of hectic vitality. The impression is not lasting. Once we spot the gimmicks, the air of "realism" disappears, leaving a tissue of clichés, artfully modernized.

6   The old-fashioned cop show, best represented by Jack Webb's early productions ("Dragnet," "Adam-12"), usually would go like this: two stern half-wits drive around Los Angeles, looking for "suspicious behavior." Although technically policemen, these dank prigs seemed more like social workers from beyond the grave, always butting in and moralizing with dead faces. No one could be whiter than these guardians of the norm, who protected their necropolis from the threat of a faint diversity (creeps, crooks, punks).

7   Such were the TV lawmen of another day, when boys liked girls, skies were blue, and blacks were Negroes. Now, of course, most (some?) of us laugh at those grim squares, preferring a groovier sort of policeman, hip, streetwise, and yet "caring," likably rebellious without losing his authoritative air, 100 percent American and still engagingly ethnic — Kojak, Baretta, Toma, Columbo. Collectively, these cops are not a force of clones, but as diverse an army as any band of bad guys, even as diverse as the very USA.

8   The Hill Street cops reflect this myth from the top down. The leadership is nicely varied. We have a Spanish-American lieutenant (Rene Enriquez) who runs the plainclothes division; the Polish-American sergeant Phil Esterhaus (Michael Conrad); and an Italian-American in Captain Frank Furillo (Daniel J. Travanti), the man in charge. Because this trio is acceptably motley, like the crowd in a United Way commercial, we are supposed to applaud it automatically. And just in case we miss the point, the show

includes a built-in satire of the thick-witted WASP in the character of Howard Hunter (James B. Sikking), commander of a SWAT-type outfit. A large, eager buffoon with an angular jaw and blinding teeth, Hunter is accoutered like Douglas MacArthur and sounds like one of Nixon's henchmen (E. Howard Hunter?), always singing the praises of excessive force in bizarre bureaucratese.

9   This devaluation of the straight white Hunter would seem to place "Hill Street Blues" opposite the likes of "Dragnet," but the shows have much in common. Under the surface of his slight ethnicity, for instance, Captain Furillo is as much a pill as Jack Webb's Sergeant Joe Friday. His heritage is a great device, allowing him the authenticity of being Italian, while letting him overcome the stereotype of being Italian. At first, his looks suggest a perfect synthesis of various streetwise types. (He looks like James Caan wearing Roy Scheider's nose.) But Furillo is no warm and explosive Mediterranean, like Travolta, De Niro, et al. On the contrary, he plays so intently against that type that he seems to be turning to cement right on camera. He never moves his neck, and rarely speaks above a soft, slurred monotone, as if afraid that, if he ever lets go, he might break out into an oily tan and start touching everybody.

10   Furillo's stiff joints are a sign of integrity. He is, of course, much purer than everyone above him. His superiors are always inviting him out to lunch or breakfast so they can harass him with corrupt advice: he should "play ball," etc. He'll never capitulate, or have a bite, but sits and eyes their loaded plates with monkish disapproval. On the other hand, he unbends slightly among his underlings, sometimes even permitting himself a tight little smirk over their wacky ways.

11   Furillo's function is to seem superior to everyone around him, so that we can feel superior by identifying with him. This strategy is obvious when it refers to those in power: Frank's various bosses and counterparts in the police establishment are all smooth toadies and pompous fools, easy targets like the

overdrawn Hunter. We are meant to look down on them because they are unenlightened. When it comes to the common man, however, the strategy becomes more insidious: through Furillo, we find all the little people—civilians as well as policemen—terribly colorful and cute. Each cop is just an amalgam of certain social and psychological tics, all of them stereotypic. We can look down on these characters because their "foibles" are at once laughable and easy to define.

12   Belker (Bruce Weitz) is a funky maniac who likes to bite off parts of suspects, yet always phones his mother (hostile/Jewish). There is patrolman Andy Renko (Charles Haid), a loud-mouthed northerner who puts on a Texas accent and always feels slighted (inferiority complex/"good ole boy"). Through this device, the show can include the obligatory cowboy without having to import a real one. J. D. LaRue has a drinking problem and is always scheming (alcoholic/white trash). They are lovably flawed, unglamorous, and weak, presented with the same affectionate contempt that imbues those TV commercials showing "real people" in all their droll impotence.

13   Not all the show's characters are so condescendingly drawn. The derision, in fact, is highly selective, expressing the liberal bias that has made the show a critical success. For instance, there is nothing funny about those cops who represent, however obliquely, the third world. There are two black officers, Hill (Michael Warren) and Washington (Taurean Blacque). One is handsome, diligent, brave, and upright, and so is the other one. (Washington is more flamboyant than Hill, and that's the only difference.) Ray, the Hispanic lieutenant, is another paragon, soft-spoken and attractive in a fatherly way.

14   The women are also the figments of some earnest liberal (male) imagination. Lucy (Betty Thomas) is a policewoman, not good-looking, but with a great personality: able and dedicated, yet vulnerable. On the other hand, high ratings demand a measure of tease, and so we have the well-groomed Veronica Hamel as Joyce Davenport, who spends her days in the Office of the Public Defender and her nights in the sack with the divorced Furillo. We are supposed to see Davenport as a liberated woman because she acts like an unfriendly man. In moments of post-coital repose, as Furillo lies back resting his neck, she bends grimly over some piece of homework, wearing her lover's shirt and man's glasses. She also calls him, not "Frank," but "Furillo." She is supposed to be much preferable to Furillo's ex-wife Fay, a shrill flake whose main function is to assault her ex-husband with labored quips: "Harvey is boiled beef, Frank," she complains of an erstwhile boyfriend. "I want escargot."

15   All the dialogue is painfully arch and overwritten, no matter who's speaking. Esterhaus's lines are all tortured circumlocution, a bad parody of Damon Runyon, and Conrad struggles mightily to make it funny. But his verbal mannerisms, like Fay's or Hunter's, get lost in the general flood of inept repartee. Aside from rank clichés ("I need you!" "I'd hate to see you get hurt." "It's OK to cry," etc.), there are stunningly clumsy attempts at clever banter: "Lots of workaholics, of which I consider you one, break out in hives at the mere thought of a vacation." "If you want to see battle scars, I've got a whole closetful." A promotion, says Davenport, will give Frank "more time for the better things in life, namely *moi.*" It's all meant to sound snappy and intriguing, like *interesting* people saying *interesting* things, but it only sounds like what you'd overhear in a singles bar for retarded television writers.

16   The show tries to cover its shallowness with these inanities, and with the various naturalistic techniques. So far, the viewers haven't bought it. Silverman and the critics have blamed the bad time-slot (Saturday at 10:00, 9:00 CST), assuming that a better one will make a big difference. It may not. And why? Because American viewers have such high standards, and consider "Hill Street Blues" overwritten and badly acted? That may seem unlikely. The millions who watch "Real People" or "The John Davidson Show"

are probably not too finicky about dramaturgy. On the other hand, they might reject the show's unmistakable smugness, its air of liberal righteousness, its propagandistic pitch disguised as something "gutsy." That is, they may disagree with all those critics who have been campaigning to save "Hill Street Blues" from cancellation: John Freeman (*San Diego Union*), Tom Shales (*Washington Post*), John Voorhees (*Seattle Times*), Tom Dorsey (*Louisville Courier-Journal*), Bill Carter (*Baltimore Evening Sun*), and many more. It could indicate a new awareness, because there are still too many shows like this, piously telling us how to think and "feel" while suggesting a subtle elitism. Such a rejection of "Hill Street Blues" would not be further evidence of any so-called "turn to the right," but simply the repudiation of something dated and offensive. As network television continues its slow decline, the failure of this show would be one more healthy sign of approaching death.

EXERCISES

Content

Recall the main ideas in this article by answering the following questions. Respond to some of the questions in your own words. Respond to others by finding quotations from the article that provide the answers.

1. According to Miller, what are the two main reasons most critics loved "Hill Street Blues"?

2. What are the "well-worn cinematic devices" that account for the show's "realism," according to Miller?

3. Why, according to Miller, is the impression of realism not long-lasting?

4. How are the "lawmen" of "Hill Street Blues" different from their counterparts in "the old-fashioned cop show"?

5. Why does Miller feel that a modern show like "Hill Street Blues" has much in common with an old-fashioned show like "Dragnet"?

6. According to Miller, the "selective derision" with which we are invited to view the characters on "Hill Street Blues" has a "liberal bias." What does he mean?

7. Why does Miller feel that the viewing public may have rejected "Hill Street Blues" during its first season?

Structure

1. What is the purpose of paragraph 2?

2. How are paragraphs 13 and 14 related to paragraphs 9–12?

3. How is paragraph 15 related to the thesis of the article?

Fact/Opinion

Classify each of the following statements as either a fact, an opinion, or a fact wrapped in an opinion. If the statement is a combination of fact and opinion, identify which part is fact and which opinion.

1. " 'Hill Street Blues' is not a hit."

2. "Fred Silverman's instincts are a national disgrace, having brought us a number of emetic divertissements whose reruns will foul the airways for the next 30 years."

3. "It's all meant to sound snappy and intriguing, like *interesting* people saying *interesting* things, but it only sounds like what you'd overhear in a singles bar for retarded television writers."

Inferences

In your responses to the following questions, incorporate some of the quotations you located in response to the Content questions. You may decide to use either all or only part of each quotation.

1. Miller asserts in paragraph 3 that " 'Hill Street Blues' is not both true to life and idealized, because such a combination is impossible." Why is it impossible? Do you agree with this statement? If not, why not?

2. What does Miller mean when he says in paragraph 4 that "this is *French Connection III,* directed by Thomas Malthus"?

3. Miller says, "The Hill Street cops reflect this myth [the ethnically diverse mix of modern police] from the top down." Why does Miller use the term "myth"? Do you agree with him? Explain.

4. Miller claims that "Furillo's function is to seem superior to everyone around him, so that we can feel superior by identifying with him." Do you think this is a fair assessment? Why or why not?

5. Explain the irony in the sentence in paragraph 13: "One [black cop] is handsome, diligent, brave, and upright, and so is the other one."

6. Miller says, "We are supposed to see Davenport as a liberated woman because she acts like an unfriendly man." Do you agree with that statement? Do you agree with the assumption that underlies it (i.e., that women who act like unfriendly men are liberated)?

7. Miller concludes by claiming that shows like "Hill Street Blues" are "piously telling us how to think and 'feel' while suggesting a subtle elitism." Is this a fair statement? Why or why not?

Beverly Gray

SINGIN' THE HILL STREET BLUES

Beverly Gray is a freelance writer whose articles, including the following, have appeared in *Theatre Crafts* magazine. In this piece, the author is concerned primarily with the technical aspects of "Hill Street Blues."

1   *Hill Street Blues,* the hour-long NBC dramatic series set in an inner-city police precinct, attracted few viewers when it made its debut in January 1981. But a record number of Emmy awards and nominations—several of them in technical categories—caused the public to take notice. Now in its second season, *Hill Street Blues* enjoys a large and loyal following, without having compromised on quality.

2   Conceived by Steven Bochco and Michael Kozoll, of the MTM organization, *Hill Street Blues* is unusual in the size of its running cast, which features 14 principals. Scripts are remarkably complex: several stories

are played out at once, often extending through four shows. Critics admire *Hill Street* for its gritty realism, to which the show's camerawork, sound, and art direction greatly contribute.

3   Supervising producer Gregory Hoblit remembers the evolution of *Hill Street*'s basic design concepts. He recalls being handed a pilot script "that in its very essence seemed to call for things being down and dirty and messy. It had a jumble of people — a boiling of cops and street people inside that precinct. It had colloquial dialogue, incomplete sentences, random thoughts, non sequiturs. And out of that came an inclination to make the film look grimy, to make it look like a *Serpico* or *Dog Day Afternoon*. That means downgrading the film. We shoot it in much lower candle power, almost half what your normal television show is shot at. They shoot at 125 to 150. We're down around 50 to 60. We put LCs on the lenses, a kind of orange filter that takes all that cleanness out of the film. We also push the film a stop, or half a stop, which tends to make it look a little more grainy." Hoblit says he told veteran cameraman William Cronjager that he wanted the film "to look like the negative had been rolled out on the deck in the morning and a truck had run over it, then stuck back in the camera and shot." What Hoblit terms Cronjager's "gutty shooting" won for the show one of its eight Emmies.

4   *Hill Street* cinematography is characterized, first of all, by the handheld camera, which imparts a sense of energy and documentary realism. Perhaps 25% of any one episode is filmed this way. Much use of cross-lighting (gaffer Dave Lee calls it "hard back cross light" or "model lighting") adds shadows for visual interest. And long lenses help to compress a scene. Explains Hoblit, "If you and I are sitting here talking and a 35mm lens is looking at us, it's going to show the distance between us. If the camera is back there on a 170 or 180 or a 125mm lens, it's going to look like we're right on each other." This technique of "stacking up the lens," combined with the use of cutting

pieces (parts of bodies, edges of furnitures) to deliberately clutter shots, makes for a jumble of images that Hoblit finds cinematically exciting.

5   The *Hill Street* pilot, directed by Robert Butler, set the pattern for subsequent episodes. From the first there were no time-consuming "shoe leather" shots of actors crossing to a ringing telephone or walking from car to doorstep. And conventional masters were replaced by what Hoblit calls "floating masters" and "split masters." A floating master eliminates the typical static sequence of establishing shot/two-shot/close-ups by having the camera follow one character into a scene. If the camera walks someone into a room, then settles in over his shoulder to pick up the person with whom he is dealing, says Hoblit, "what we've done is sold our geography. We've sold the room. We've shown the audience where the character is, gotten movement into the frame, and never been out at 35mm or 50mm — which is wide-angle and boring as hell — but kept it in tight." The split master is used when a number of characters occupy a small space. Again, a wide-angle establishing shot is avoided: the camera follows the actors to gradually build a picture of the entire situation. (*Hill Street*'s camera is Panaflex, and its lights chiefly Mole-Richardson).

6   Sound, too, has been handled innovatively from the start. To get a spontaneous quality, *Hill Street* puts heavy emphasis on overlapping dialogue. This requires placing a microphone squarely between two actors, or when using two separate mikes to boom them both. In complicated scenes, like the roll call that opens each show, ten or 12 separate voice tracks may be needed to record a roomful of characters all talking independently. Sound mixer William Marky, an Oscar winner for *Hello, Dolly!*, describes his job on *Hill Street* as "a nightmare." Beyond the problem of overlapped dialogue, Marky says, "we have two people in particular — Michael Conrad and Dan Travanti — both of whose voices are tremendously chesty. Every time they are in a scene, when they talk I

have to equalize for them as we shoot it." Marky is helped by Hank Garfield ("probably the best boom man in the business") and by a Sela 2880-BT mixing console. "I wouldn't use anything else but," he says. "They're bringing out a new panel and I'm going to be the one who premieres it in the western hemisphere."

7   Another aspect of the show's sound track is its multiple overlapping of background tracks. *Hill Street* is a constant hubbub of telephone calls both close and far away, police sirens, typewriters, and human voices. In addition, at *Hill Street* dubbing sessions members of the Off the Wall comedy group improvise wild lines to fit each episode. Summing up the ambitiousness of the show's stylistics, Marky insists that "this is not television. This is feature after feature after feature."

8   Although each *Hill Street* episode takes three or four weeks to write, technical departments receive scripts barely seven working days before shooting begins. Since the show shoots for seven days, when one episode is starting the next one is beginning to prep. This hectic schedule is one source of anxiety for the *Hill Street* crew. The high percentage of location filming (two to three days per episode) poses still other problems: Los Angeles must be made to resemble a large midwestern city, presumably, though not specifically, Chicago.

9   In his role as art director, Jeff Goldstein not only helps to choose locations, but is also in charge of the permanent set, built on Stage 15 (104′ × 140′, 35′ high) at CBS Studio Center in the San Fernando Valley.

10   Among Goldstein's initial design concepts was the use of glass partitions throughout the precinct house. These bring a feeling of openness. Says Goldstein, "One thing I try to do in sets is create interesting architecture, where things are happening in spaces beyond, so that the camera doesn't have to shoot into a flat wall." Shooting around and through glass is anathema to many cinematographers. But William Cronjager has handled the challenge with flair, and the partitions are now a *Hill Street* trademark— nearly every other episode features the shattering of a glass panel.

11   Goldstein's love for glass extends to his inclusion of windows wherever possible, since they give the cameraman an implicit light source. "In fact," notes Goldstein, "we even took license on the interrogation room, which normally would never have a window. We put one in, with bars on it and heavy security wire, to add a little bit of interest to what normally would be a very dead, drab room. Visual interest was important because they're in there a helluva lot."

12   Goldstein's other responsibilities include creating insignias for gang jackets, building convertible tenement houses on a swing stage (to cut down on location work), and adding new wild walls to the permanent set. This set was erected long before the stock exterior (a Chicago police station) was chosen. The building's entryway includes a stoop, a set of double doors, and, immediately inside, a steep flight of stairs; Goldstein designed a forced perspective to approximate this look on the soundstage.

13   Longtime set decorator Jim Cane, who for five years headed the decorating department at Lorimar, insists that *Hill Street* "is one of the toughest companies I've ever worked for in terms of sticking to authenticity." On location this often means shooting in filthy ghetto alleyways. But actors and crew cannot work amid stench and filth. So the alleys are washed down and "clean dirt" is added. "We shred up newspaper, and we find boxes and crush them, and we get some mattresses," Cane says. "Whenever necessary we put in breakaway broken glass."

14   Men's costumer Bob Harris, Jr., describes his job as "many hours of boredom punctuated by a few minutes of sheer terror." He and women's costumer Karen Hudson (who has an MA in costume design from the University of Texas) dress 50 to 100 actors every episode. About uniforms they can be somewhat sloppy and idiosyncratic. Explains Harris, "That's the way, generally, in any military-type organization—the harder the

duty the less regimented they are in uniforms, haircuts, shoeshines. If you work in
Beverly Hills, everybody looks supersharp. If
you work in the worst parts of LA, looks go
progressively downhill."

15 Because of the many violent sequences,
torn clothing is the norm; everything from
chemicals to an electric sander is used to, as
Harris says, "wear it down, put holes in it,
tear it, rip it, and rip it and patch it and re-rip
it." Garments have to be made with fabrics
that can take such abuse without falling
apart. For that reason Harris avoids polyester.

16 Hookers are stock characters on *Hill
Street,* and Karen Hudson has to outfit them.
"Ours are exaggerated," Hudson admits. "But
we have only a few seconds to sell a character. One difference between television and
theatre is that in TV you have only seconds to
give everybody an incredible amount of information. There's not the time for development you get in a play."

17 In the makeup department *Hill Street
Blues* requires proficiency in two areas: tattoos and wounds. As head makeup artist,
Bob Westmoreland draws a lot of gang tattoos. "What I use is a laundry marking pen
with a fine point on it. When you draw with
it, shade with it, and then powder it, it comes
up looking like a real tattoo."

18 Wounds are at least as important.
Makeup assistant Jerry Soucie praises the
producers for understanding the need for
graphic realism here: "If you're going to
write violence into a script, then I think you
have an obligation to show the results of

that violence," Soucie claims. *The Hill Street*
makeup kits contain products by Bob Tuttle,
Max Factor (touted by Soucie for its long
shelf life), Bob Kelly, Ben Nye ("The best
liner"), and John Chambers' plastics and
prosthetic pieces.

19 After shooting ends film editor David
Rosenbloom spends between 10 days and
2½ weeks preparing a final cut. Given the
many strands that make up a *Hill Street*
episode, Rosenbloom's primary responsibility is to direct the viewer's attention to each
week's central story line. In editing, he aims
"to key in on that story line and play it where
it needs to be played." At the same time, he
says "I don't have to hit the audience over
the head with story points."

20 "Meaningful" inserts (closeup of hand
holding gun, for instance) are avoided. Says
Rosenbloom, "You don't have to be as specific with this audience. If they're watching
the show they're a sophisticated audience."

21 Rosenbloom is, at 25, perhaps the
youngest film editor in the industry. He sees
the relative youth of *Hill Street*'s writers and
producers (many are in their 30s) as a major
factor in the show's success. In his opinion,
"It's all of us younger people who tend to
give the audience more credit than people
have given them in the past. We give them
credit for smarts. We trust them to pick up
complex themes." *Hill Street Blues,* he thinks
caters to a young, film-smart crowd who can
turn on the tube and realize, "There's real
film-making going on here."

| **EXERCISES** | |

Content

Recall the main ideas in this article by answering the following questions. Respond to
some of the questions in your own words. Respond to others by finding quotations from the
article that provide the answers.

1. What are some of the main factors that make "Hill Street Blues" different from other
TV series?

2. How is the grimy look of "Hill Street Blues" achieved photographically?

3. How does "stacking up the lens" help give "Hill Street Blues" a distinctive visual character?

4. How do the "floating master" and the "split master" (as opposed to conventional establishing shots) work to give "Hill Street Blues" a distinctive sense of space?

5. What accounts for the distinctive use of sound in "Hill Street Blues"?

6. What is "clean dirt"?

7. Why does a show like "Hill Street Blues" have special costuming requirements?

8. Why are "meaningful inserts" avoided by film editor David Rosenbloom? Why does the avoidance of such devices help account for the success of "Hill Street Blues" with a new generation of TV audiences?

Structure

1. Explain how paragraphs 6 and 7, considered together, form an identifiable section of the article. Give this section a title.

2. How do paragraphs 6 and 7 relate to the thesis?

3. Explain how paragraphs 9–12, considered together, form an identifiable section of the article. Give this section a title.

4. How is paragraph 18 related to paragraph 17?

Fact/Opinion

Classify each of the following statements as either a fact, an opinion, or a fact wrapped in an opinion. If the statement is a combination of fact and opinion, identify which part is fact and which opinion.

1. "Now in its second season, *Hill Street Blues* enjoys a large and loyal following, without having compromised on quality."

2. "We shoot [*Hill Street Blues*] in much lower candle power, almost half what your normal television show is shot at."

3. "The *Hill Street* pilot, directed by Robert Butler, set the pattern for subsequent episodes."

4. "Sound mixer William Marky, an Oscar winner for *Hello, Dolly!*, describes his job on *Hill Street* as 'a nightmare.'"

Inferences

In your responses to the following questions, incorporate some of the quotations you located in response to the Content questions. You may decide to use either all or only part of each quotation.

1. Gray's article focuses on the production values of "Hill Street Blues" — cinematography, sound, set design, costume, makeup, and editing. In what other TV shows (or in what feature films) is a special look and sound created? What accounts for these distinctive qualities? What effects do they have in terms of the dramatic purposes of these films?

2. If the production values are emphasized in this article, which values (that are often the focus of articles about TV shows or films) are *de-emphasized*? Do you think that Gray is downplaying the importance of such values?

3. To what extent do you think aspiring TV producers or writers could infer, from the qualities that appear to have made "Hill Street Blues" a success, the way to make other shows a success?

David Freeman

TELEVISION'S REAL A-TEAM

David Freeman is the author of the plays ***Jesse and the Bandit Queen*** **and** ***Creeps;*** **his books include** ***U.S. Grant in the City and Other True Stories of Pluggers, Swatters, and Whores; Battering Ram;*** **and** ***The Last Days of Alfred Hitchcock.*** **This article, which first appeared in** ***Esquire*** **in 1985, is concerned with the creation of the "Hill Street Blues" script.**

1   *"Seems like they hit you everywhere you turn these days, don't it? Accept this... accept that...cope with this...deal with that...understand where he's coming from... identify with his situation...I swear. I don't know anymore. It's just words, man...smoke and words. —Renko*

2   Nice, isn't it? From an existentialist French novel? Maybe a tony, academically acceptable off-Broadway play? Sorry, but it's from the heart of commercial television. I sometimes think that in our country we only honor movies with writing on the bottom of the screen or novels that *The New York Times* tells us are good or television shows in which all the characters drink a lot of tea. The last thing Americans seem ready to accept is art from the wrong places.

3   *Hill Street Blues* is primarily about the lives of the cops in a precinct in and around the Hill—a mostly black ghetto in a big, unnamed American city. There are more than sixteen fully drawn, breathing, sweating, fornicating, and fearing regular characters, as well as scores of miscreants, lunatics, bureaucrats, and politicians who move in and out of the life on the Hill. The show has a documentary look, open-ended scripts, and an obsession with showing real lives in credible situations. Everything seems crowded, starting with the lives of the characters. The squad room, jammed with cops, thugs, civic leaders, and angry citizens, is an apt correlative for the ghetto it serves. David Milch, the *Hill Street* writer who has ruminated the most on the show's meaning and its techniques, says "*Hill Street Blues* came along when there were rising expectations in the lower middle class; then the country couldn't make good on that implicit promise. That left a lot of people hungry for some sense of...insight. We try to provide that. That's what was new—those people, their frustrations, as the rightful focus of drama. The idea of cop shows—that, of course, was old."

4   Now in its fifth season, *Hill Street Blues* has had some celebrated ups and downs. It's a hit for NBC and MTM Enterprises, but it's been plagued by weak lead-ins (the show immediately preceding it on the air), and in its first season it aired on five different nights. Last season the network insisted on at least one story line that might have been more at home on the latest steamy mini-series. It was about prominent citizens, an expensive call girl (are there ever any discount ones?), and a secret videotape. It was not *Hill Street*'s finest hour. But in five seasons, the show has been nominated for seventy-six Emmys and has won twenty-five. *Hill Street* is a rarity on TV and certainly unusual at NBC—a program so popular with the critics that one swore it had replaced Proust as the favorite topic of New York literary cocktail chat.

5   The show is written by a collective: five scriptwriters under the leadership of the executive producer. They turn out one show a week, twenty-two a season. And though some

of the shows are written more by one person than another, the scripts are usually the result of a team effort by all the writers. There have been other writers on this show, and the current keepers of the flame are not the originators, but they have maintained *Hill Street*'s demanding pace and quality. They are: Roger Director, thirty-five; Mark Frost, thirty-one; Karen Hall, twenty-eight; Jeff Lewis, forty; and David Milch, thirty-nine. The executive producer is Steven Bochco, forty-one, who with Michael Kozoll conceived and created the show. Their foundation, reinforced by Bochco's ability to maneuver through the network thickets, provides the *Hill Street* writers with an extraordinary amount of freedom. Kozoll left after the second season to pursue a feature-film career. Writer-producer Anthony Yerkovich departed after the third season and has since gone on to create a new cop series, *Miami Vice*. Michael Wagner, for two and a half years a key *Hill Street* writer, made his exit only last season. Bochco, the boss of bosses, remains and runs the operation, and the writers see him as a heroic figure. Says David Milch, who on the brink of middle age found a second career as an Emmy Award–winning TV writer: "Bochco has allowed me to gain access to my imagination."

6   Bochco is a combination of poet and salesman that only Hollywood could produce. He survived the cutthroat, freeway-paced studio system at Universal for twelve years, writing a series of cop shows, including *The Name of the Game, Columbo,* and *McMillan and Wife. Hill Street* is clearly his escape, his triumph, and a formidable ongoing challenge.

7   Bochco coordinates the writing staff in his office, a sparely furnished suite of rooms at Studio Center in Studio City, the old Republic Pictures lot where John Wayne shot *The Sands of Iwo Jima*. Bochco stresses the ensemble nature of the work, saying, "I'm the boss, but really I'm the referee. You can't impose a story or a sensibility. It has to be understood or agreed to by the ensemble or it just won't work. If all the writers don't

really deep down live it and breathe it, then you have no ensemble and I think, inevitably, no scripts worth making." Bochco keeps a chest in his office with the vital tools of the writer's trade: two basketballs, a football, a Whiffle ball, and five bats. The group has been known to shoot baskets out the window until the muse intrudes. Or, as Jeff Lewis says, "We usually talk about girls if Karen's not there." Karen, on the other hand, says, "My presence just encourages them. I feel like I've just spent about six years in a locker room."

    Once a *Hill Street* writers' session is on 8 track, Jeff Lewis is the voice of the law. Lewis is in fact a lawyer, a graduate of Harvard Law School and a former assistant district attorney for New York County (Manhattan). Lewis came to Hollywood at thirty-six with some serious bridges burned and no new ones in sight. After floundering for a year, he wrote an over-the-transom letter to Bochco showing him some samples of his script work and suggesting he could bring a certain legal expertise to the show. Bochco, who seems to have twenty-twenty vision when he's looking at talent, hired him. Lewis ushered in an era of legally sophisticated scripts and an assortment of very real lawyers and judges. He was soon coproducing many of the shows.

    It was Lewis who persuaded David Milch 9 to come west and pitch a story to Bochco. Lewis and Milch, who have been friends for twenty years, were roommates at Trumbull College at Yale in the mid-Sixties. They make an unlikely combination: the tightly wrapped, coolly rational Lewis and the flamboyant, Rabelaisian Milch. Milch has become the heaviest hitter on the staff, earning his black belt in what fellow writer Roger Director calls "the judo of TV scene writing."

    Each *Hill Street* script is a little different, 10 but the writing process follows a well-established M.O.: Milch, Lewis, and Bochco work out a rough story line. In the script-writing game this is the heavy lifting. Then the trio will tell the story to the entire group. Each of the five writers will take a scene or two from each of the four acts (in TV-speak an act is the stuff between commercials), following a character or a plot strand. If there's more time, which is not often, a writer might be assigned an entire act and do a first draft. Each act must have its own internal rhythm and its own climax, and to make it live the writer must be ready to assume the identity of the characters—not acting, not doing what the performers will do, but reaching inside to feel the feelings, to know the characters' personal pain.

11   A few days after the initial conference, everyone reads their assigned scenes, and usually no one likes anything. After a group discussion, led by Bochco, the script is rewritten. The goal, of course, is for the collective whole to be greater than the sum of its individual parts. Given the size and complexity of the task, a writers' meeting can sound like a wisecracking group therapy session, with each person facing his or her vulgarity, vulnerability, childishness, racism, or whatever emotional qualities are required in the script. There is nothing polite about the process of writing this way. "It often goes beyond rudeness," says Jeff Lewis. "It can get nasty." Based on these encounter sessions, the script is rewritten, and after that, if it's still not working, which is usual, one person will do an initial polish. Though it could be anyone, it's frequently Milch or Lewis. This rewrite must also reflect production and budgetary notes.

12   All this is particularly dicey on *Hill Street* because the scripts, unlike those for most TV shows, are sprawling and almost aggressively messy. The stories don't have the usual neat beginnings, middles, and ends. A typical script will have several story lines that might go on for four weeks, while others start and end within one episode. The glue that binds it all together is a combination of character and mise-en-scène. "This show is like Rubik's Cube," says Roger Director, the most recently hired of the show's writers. "Each word and line has at least twelve different ways of fitting together. And each of those has a ripple effect throughout the rest of the hour and the season. You can spend the rest of your life trying to parse that."

For six people to formulate and agree   13 on these configurations is very unorthodox. In commercial TV it's more often just one or two persons who cook up the story line and perhaps a third to finish the job.

Time is one of the few constants in every   14 show. Each *Hill Street* episode runs for one day, from early-morning roll call (when the day's duties are assigned) to late at night. That doesn't mean every problem gets solved in one day—just that time runs out and the characters finally try for some sleep—the unsolved problems to be dealt with another time. Acting and writing on *Hill Street* have merged in an extraordinary way. Other cop shows have naturalistic acting, but it's usually on the order of "Hey, is that a new shirt?" "Yeah, you like it?" Then somebody robs a bank. We are talking about a higher order of things here. Credible and theatrical.

The show is never over when you think   15 it is. Repeatedly, a story line seems to have run its course, when something else happens that makes what precedes it feel like a prologue. Here's an example: A cop's mother pesters her unmarried son to call the daughter of a friend. Eventually he does. The cop is Belker, everybody's favorite mess, the one who bites suspects and is often brutal. Belker obeys his mom. The date is fine at first and maybe Mom was right. God knows Belker could benefit from a steady woman in his life, and Debbie looks like a likely candidate, except then it develops that she's sexually voracious, with a wide masochistic streak. Belker gets enough of hurting people in the streets, so he moves on. First you think it's through when he calls for the date to pacify his mom. Then you think, "Oh, that's nice, he's met a girl." Then she turns out to be weird. Neatly, ironically, that weirdness relates to the aspect of Belker's work he's most famous for—kicking ass—and it makes him unhappy.

"What we're supposed to be up here is the   16 one thing people can trust."—Furillo

If the show has a main artery, it's Captain   17 Furillo, the ultimate adult, played by Daniel J. Travanti. Furillo's a good man in a flawed world and a flawed man in an indifferent world. He does his best in a universe that's filled with venality and love, where people have names that end in vowels or -witz or -stein; his command is a neighborhood where people have accents and are mostly black or Hispanic. Some are good, but many are not. They're all looking for an edge they'll never find. Furillo remains stoic as all day long people try to get a word with him, each person in crisis, each one desperate for a moment of his time. Furillo stays as calm as he can, given the pressure and the chaos; all day he stifles his humor, or at least tries to. At night, in bed, he looks for a little human relief. His feelings are a pretty good model for the way we all feel about ourselves — torn, tired, keeping the world together with the glue of our own put-upon, overworked personalities. And that's why he's a hero even if he doesn't act like Achilles or John Wayne. We can identify with him even if we're not precinct captains. His humanity is ours, or so we would like to think as we flatter ourselves in our secret hearts that we too are trying to avoid the abyss.

18   *"Guys, cognizant as I am of the natural reluctance to part with one's vital organs, even in extremity, nevertheless, I might point out that you're not donating a part of your body to keep a stranger alive, he or she is donating everything else to keep a part of you alive...."* — Esterhaus

19   Michael Conrad, who played Sergeant Phil Esterhaus, the avuncular roll-call officer with the strangely baroque sense of language, died of cancer in 1983. Esterhaus was a character who could say something like "Come on, let's interface" to a group of angry citizens, and do it with a smile that seemed to admit: "I know it's silly, but it's fun to say." Jeff Lewis says of the character, "Nothing could blow that guy away. He gave everyone something to play off. He was the ballast, the center."

20   The roll-call device — the opening of each show, in which duties are assigned, news given, advice offered — gave Esterhaus his chance to glow, to philosophize, and of course to warn everyone "to be very careful out there." The roll call also sets up the plot possibilities for the hour to come. "It's like a menu," says David Milch. "There's a list of possibilities and you pick a few. It helps to know that what you're seeing is only part of what you might."

21   Conrad's death was written into the show. It was reported that Sergeant Esterhaus died in bed with his lover, a wonderful, sexy, fortyish decorator named Grace Gardner. "We were making love when he died," Grace told Furillo. "His great brave heart...exploded....He was a beautiful, simple, honorable man and I wanted to grow old with him."

22   Watching Conrad from week to week as he lost weight and his skin began to hang around his neck, you knew that it wasn't a diet that was wasting him. You couldn't help but feel that he wasn't just an actor up there, but a man, a cop, a lover, and a friend as well. The show in which his death was absorbed and reflected upon was surely about the writers' feeling for Conrad.

23   *Belker: Esterhaus was the law up here. And now that he's dead...I don't know. I'm scared. I feel like everything's going to unravel.*

Furillo: It's your job and mine to see that it doesn't.

24   This season the actor Robert Prosky plays a new roll-call officer, Sergeant Stanislaus Jablonski. Unlike Esterhaus, Jabbo takes a direct view of life and police work. Trying to stop a rumor, during his first roll call Jabbo insisted, "Stash Jablonski never cold-cocked no woman." Instead of Esterhaus's famous "Let's be careful out there," Jabbo signs off with "Let's get out there and do it to them before they do it to us."

25   Most action or cop shows on American television seem to have some pat formula for minority representation. If a bad guy is black, you can bet the next black guy will be a nuclear physicist. If a blond bimbo wanders through, we'll soon be subjected to several supermoms. *Hill Street* is one of the few places where blacks are portrayed with

genuine diversity and with no apparent scorecard. In its treatment of women, the show is possibly unique. There are three women who are real people. Joyce Davenport (Veronica Hamel), the public defender and once Furillo's clandestine lover, now his wife, is the paradigmatic Eighties woman: a fine, dedicated lawyer who is tough, smart, sexy, and straight. Fay Furillo (Barbara Bosson), Frank's ex-wife, is usually on the edge of hysteria when she's near her ex-husband. You just know she's a better person when Frank's not around, but she keeps coming back for more. Fay is the definition of a well-written, well-acted character: you're certain you know what she's like when she's not on screen. Lucy Bates (Betty Thomas), the only woman patrol sergeant, has to get along with a lot of rowdy men. She's smart, but not brilliant and certainly not able to articulate the complex problems she faces. The easy way out for Lucy is to be one of the boys. As a result, she's ready to pull her gun and use it if she has to. She's looking for a private life, but mostly she's fixated on her job.

26   The underlying assumptions that these writers bring to characters like Joyce, Fay, and Lucy are postfeminist. These women have lives outside their romances and marriages, but that doesn't mean they don't want men. Of course they do, the same way men want them. The characters rarely talk about feminism. I don't think the *Hill Street* staff thinks about it, it just comes out.

27
> *Furillo: This is the kind of crime that tears the city apart. It brings out what's savage in thousands of people. It has to be dealt with quickly.*
>
> *Davenport: So the book goes out the window?*
>
> *Furillo: I went by the book. I pushed a little hard at the bindings.*

28   There have been many memorable *Hill Street* episodes, but the best one, arguably, is "Trial by Fury," written by Milch. The script is packed with incident and character. There's a big melodrama—a nun raped and mur-

dered—that leads to a quieter personal drama: Furillo and Davenport's romance coming apart because of differing legal principles. It has jokes and it has dreams, and for a while it makes one murder feel less important than another—and then of course you realize that's wrong; all murders are important. There are few flashy passages, only a deep look into the guts of the characters.

29   The script pits Furillo against Davenport. Furillo has the nun's murderer and enough evidence for an indictment, but not a conviction. Outside there's a mob of concerned citizens ready to lynch. Furillo instructs the assistant D.A. to drop the charges, which means the killer can go free—right into the arms of the mob. The gentleman reconsiders and finally confesses. Davenport, as the legal defender, is infuriated. She feels Furillo has manipulated the law, something Furillo points out she does all the time. The coda has Furillo walking in the dark to some unnamed place that looks like a prison. There are bars and a face behind them. And Furillo says, "Forgive me, Father, for I have sinned." We might have thought he was right, but he knew in his heart he was wrong enough to feel guilty. So he goes to his own confession. You realize what a good cop he is. And what a fine script this is.

30   Some *Hill Street* scripts are more self-contained than others. The story line of "Trial by Fury" unfolds almost entirely within the hour, cathartic within itself. But even with that structure it embodies the paradox of *Hill Street*'s overall attitude: terrible things happen, and we spend our days trying to cope. Life can be wonderful or grim, but it's never fair. "We are making a collective hero of the lower middle class," Milch says. "By compressing the focus, we render our stories in more realistic dimensions. By telling multiple stories, we keep each on a credible scale. If we were to do only one story a show, it would be blown up to outsized proportions just to fill up the hour." These scripts don't spin inner-city fairy tales—the characters can't walk away easily, not out of their lives or their work, not into the next episode.

31   There are seventy-eight hours of *Hill Street Blues* now, and it all adds up to some vast nineteenth-century novel, teeming with life, full of characters, cliff-hangers, and themes that resonate, one with another — all creating a picture of urban life in the Eighties. If you bear in mind that it's written in week-to-week installments full of big, juicy, sloppy, emotional scenes, the shadow of Dickens is inescapable. *Hill Street* exists in a real city with snow and rain and lunatics in the street. This isn't Hollywood backlot, not *CHiPs* southern California, but a world we can live in, at least vicariously, more readily and with greater clarity than the one we actually inhabit. The precinct house here is as totemic of modern urban life as the cathedral was to another century. And when we watch the Hill from our TV privacy, our imagination is led to see the actual world with a deeper perception than before we tuned in, each Thursday night.

The Creators of "Hill Street Blues"

Steven Bochco, "The Boss," Age 41

Credits: Story editor for Name of the Game, Columbo, *and* McMillan and Wife; *producer of* Delvecchio; *executive producer and writer of* Richie Brockelman; *executive producer and co-creator of* Hill Street Blues; *executive producer and co-creator of* Bay City Blues.

The day he graduated from Carnegie Tech, Steven Bochco went west. Three days later he was on the Universal lot working as a writer. "I was one lucky cowboy," he says of his painless beginnings.

Bochco's ability to nudge, goad, order, and inspire the *Hill Street* writers to try again, to dig a little deeper, is famous in Hollywood. "You're always in the father business, I suppose," says Bochco, who is himself the father of a son and a daughter. (He has been married for fifteen years to Barbara Bosson, who plays Fay on the show.) Daddy or not, Bochco always reserves for himself the last polish of every scene. He doesn't always use it, but everyone writing a *Hill Street* script knows that Bochco's is likely to be the last typewriter involved.

Despite all appearances, Bochco balks at the idea of himself as the Captain Furillo of the writ-

ing staff. "I'm not the Captain Furillo of anything," he says. "He's genuinely middle management — lots of responsibility but little authority. I've got authority to go along with my responsibility. Except in the writing there is no boss. Nobody can arbitrarily say what goes. I'm glad to give my power to the writers. We all gain that way. Believe me, they're a very gifted and high-strung group. If you order them to do this or that, nothing good will come of it." Bochco's ability to maneuver *Hill Street's* frank and sometimes sexy or brutal scripts past NBC's censors led one observer to remark, "Bochco should get the Nobel Prize for dealing with Standards and Practices."

Jeff Lewis, "The District Attorney," Age 40

Credits: Class poet at Yale University; law degree from Harvard University; taught expository writing at Harvard; assistant district attorney for New York County.

A decade and a half ago Jeff Lewis could be found plea-bargaining in the courts of New York City. Today he's in Hollywood doing his bargaining with a somewhat more desirable group — the writing staff of *Hill Street Blues*. "We try to accommodate each other's needs," says Lewis of the *Hill Street* think tank, "but this isn't about being nice. If you start compromising to keep the peace, you'll wind up with lousy scripts and no peace anyway."

One of the things that the staff has consistently come up with since Lewis's 1980 arrival has been an increasing number of plots that turn on legal principle. How accurate is *Hill Street*? "We get it pretty close, it's never perfect, but there's a reasonable resemblance."

Lewis says he was never absolutely comfortable as a lawyer — "It was a product of my indecision about what to do with my life more than any driving need to practice law. What I'm doing now is terrific, and I feel at home." Asked which character is his favorite, he first declines to take sides, in a lawyerly way, but then the writer in him bubbles to the surface as he says, "I guess we all like writing LaRue. He appeals to the sleazebag in us all."

David Milch, "The Professor," Age 39

Credits: Yale University, Class of 1966 (Phi Beta Kappa); M.F.A. from Iowa Writers' Workshop (1970); worked with R. W. B. Lewis on The James Project.

In 1968 David Milch was in law school at Yale, fresh from a brilliant undergraduate career that won him the Chauncey Brewster Tinker Prize for highest achievement in English over four years. Then, one night. Milch went out with a shotgun and started blasting away at the revolving lights of a police car. "I was loaded, tripping, and just a jerk," he remembers, "but at least it got me out of law school." Milch became a heroin user in his early twenties and spent time in a Mexican jail. More recently, he has developed a taste for "mooning" friends, colleagues, and the occasional window washer. When clothed, Milch favors the racetrack and casinos from Las Vegas to Reno. This is the same man who taught creative writing at Yale between 1969 and 1982, published poetry in literary journals, was a protégé of Robert Penn Warren. In his first season as a *Hill Street* writer, Milch won an Emmy Award for his first script, "Trial by Fury." Says Steven Bochco: "It's his lunacy that does it, that makes it work, his willingness to be an outlaw."

While he may be an outlaw, he is also now a father and husband, and more likely to write about cop cars than shoot at them.

Roger Director, "The Journalist," Age 35

Credits: Award-winning writer for the New York Daily News; *sexual fantasy columnist for* Penthouse Publications; *contributor to* The New Yorker *and* National Lampoon; *scriptwriter for MTM's* Bay City Blues.

With the perfect name for a Hollywood scriptwriter, Roger Director languished in New York for his first thirty-three years. There he toiled in journalistic and theatrical sweatboxes of high and low repute—everyplace from *The Complete Handbook of Baseball* to the New York Shakespeare Festival. MTM brought Director cross-country for *Bay City Blues,* their ambitious spin-off about life in the minor leagues. He headed to California expecting "to wrench my back and come home." Instead, when the show was canceled after four episodes, he found himself being called up to TV's major leagues as a writer for *Hill Street.* Around the conference tables and water coolers at MTM, they call him Rocky.

None of this explains how a self-effacing Haverford graduate with an M.A. in English literature from Columbia is able to commune with the street wackos on the Hill. "I guess I have a journalist's cynicism, or maybe it's just a New Yorker's, and I've had some experience with city bureaucracies too, and street life, and street madness," explains Director, a slightly demented glint coming into his eyes. "I try to get that experience into

the show. You know, *Hill Street* isn't a dramatized op-ed page. We try to weld issues to characters." Apparently, Director is a character himself. His wife, Jan Cherubin, a writer for the *Los Angeles Herald Examiner,* reports: "Sometimes I turn around to talk to Roger and he's muttering to himself and I know he's not with me but with Frank and Joyce in the squad room."

Mark Frost, "The Playwright," Age 31

Credits: Wrote first, as yet unpublished, novel, The International Council for Peace and Justice, *at age eleven; scriptwriter,* The Six Million Dollar Man; *Literary Associate at the Guthrie Theater of Minneapolis.*

At the age of twenty, shortly after he dropped out of Carnegie Tech, Mark Frost was writing scripts for *The Six Million Dollar Man.* Then, in the middle of a gig many Hollywood writers would have clamored for, he bailed out. "I felt I was too young to be making so much money," he says, incredibly. So he headed back to the more impoverished stages of his youth at the Guthrie Theater, where as a Literary Associate he wrote two plays and copious program notes and "generally did grunt-level labor."

Meanwhile, back in L.A., Frost's friend, actor Charles Haid, was cast as Andy Renko, a redneck *Hill Street* cop with a hair-trigger temper and a big heart. When Frost was ready to return to L.A., he contacted producer Steven Bochco, who remembered Frost's precocious debut and hired him. In the show, Frost particularly enjoys conjuring up Howard Hunter, the Hill's SWAT team commander, a serious professional who loves guns and women and succeeds with only the former. "You know, the Roman comedy stock figure—*miles gloriosus?* The loudmouthed, self-absorbed soldier? That's Hunter," says Frost, "The danger is he can become a cartoon. My job is to keep him human."

Karen Hall, "The Criminologist," Age 28

Credits: B.A. in English from William and Mary (1978); temporary office worker in Los Angeles; story editor, Eight is Enough; *executive story consultant,* M*A*S*H.

In 1979 Karen Hall came from Chatham, Virginia (pop. 1,400), to Los Angeles, California (pop. 3,000,000), "twenty-one years old, broke, and naive." Eleven months later she was writing *M*A*S*H* and *Eight is Enough.* She was then twenty-two, not broke, and presumably still naive. "Wherever I went, I was the only woman," she now recalls. "At *M*A*S*H*, the guys would throw pencils on the floor so they could get down and look up my dress. At *Eight Is Enough,* they were more civilized." At twenty-eight, she relishes being the only woman in the *Hill Street* writing fraternity. "I like working with men, I really do," she says, "but there are times when it makes me crazy and I just want to go somewhere where there are no men. But the show is mostly men, so I write mostly men. No one thinks of me as 'the woman specialist.' At least, I don't think they do." In fact, they think of her as the blue-collar special-

ist. "I like to write inarticulate characters," she says, "where the emotions are stronger than the words they can think to say.... The thing that makes these characters sympathetic is their frustration...the frustration of trying to hold on to ideals in a career that does nothing to nurture them and everything to tear them down."

To work on the Hill, a writer's got to be passionate about issues and what they do to people. "My favorite subject on earth is capital punishment," she says. "I am obsessed with criminology and Bruce Springsteen's music."

EXERCISES

Content

Recall the main ideas in this article by answering the following questions. Respond to some of the questions in your own words. Respond to others by finding quotations from the article that provide the answers.

1. What is the "A-Team" of the title?

2. What makes "Hill Street Blues" a "rarity on TV"?

3. What is Jeff Lewis's role in the creation of "Hill Street Blues"?

4. How are the scripts of "Hill Street Blues" created? How is this process different from that of most other commercial-TV series?

5. In what way is time "one of the few constants in every show"?

6. In what way, according to Freeman, does Captain Furillo provide a role model for the way that we would like to think of ourselves?

7. What does "postfeminist" mean as defined by Freeman (paragraph 26)?

8. What are the dramatic advantages, according to David Milch, of telling multiple stories on each show?

9. Why does Freeman feel justified in comparing the seventy-eight hours of "Hill Street Blues" to a nineteenth-century novel?

Structure

1. What is the purpose of the italicized quotations interspersed throughout the article?

2. What is the purpose of paragraph 5?

3. How is paragraph 24 related to paragraphs 19–22?

4. How are paragraphs 28 and 29 related to the thesis of the article?

Fact/Opinion

Classify each of the following statements as either a fact, an opinion, or a fact wrapped in an opinion. If the statement is a combination of fact and opinion, identify which part is fact and which opinion.

1. "There are more than sixteen fully drawn, breathing, sweating, fornicating, and fearing regular characters, as well as scores of miscreants, lunatics, bureaucrats, and politicians who move in and out of the life on the Hill."

2. "The show is written by a collective; five scriptwriters under the leadership of the executive producer."

3. "Bochco is a combination of poet and salesman that only Hollywood could produce."

4. "A few days after the initial conference, everyone reads their assigned scenes, and usually no one likes anything."

Inferences

In your responses to the following questions, incorporate some of the quotations you located in response to the Content questions. You may decide to use either all or only part of each quotation.

1. What is Freeman's purpose in beginning with the quotation by Renko and in leading off the first paragraph as he does?

2. Freeman writes in paragraph 2: "I sometimes think that in our country we only honor movies with writing on the bottom of the screen or novels that *The New York Times* tells us are good or television shows in which all the characters drink a lot of tea." What does he mean? Do you think this is a fair statement? Explain.

3. David Milch, one of the "Hill Street Blues" writers, believes that "*Hill Street Blues* came along when there were rising expectations in the lower middle class; then the country couldn't make good on that implicit promise. That left a lot of people hungry for some sense of . . . insight. We try to provide that" (paragraph 3). Do you see "Hill Street Blues" in those terms? To what extent does this assessment throw light on particular episodes?

4. What does Freeman mean when he says, "*Hill Street* is one of the few places where blacks are portrayed with genuine diversity and with no apparent scorecard" (paragraph 25)? What does he mean by "no apparent scorecard"? Do you agree?

5. Why does Freeman feel that the script for "Trial by Fury" was a particularly fine one?

6. Freeman concludes by asserting that "when we watch the Hill from our TV privacy, our imagination is led to see the actual world with a deeper perception than before we tuned in." What kind of "deeper perception" do you think he means? Do you agree?

Joyce Carol Oates

FOR ITS AUDACITY, ITS DEFIANTLY BAD TASTE AND ITS SUPERB CHARACTER STUDIES

Joyce Carol Oates has authored short stories, novels, poetry, plays, and essays. Among her best-known works are *Marriages and Infidelities* (a collection of stories) and the novels *A Garden of Earthly Delights, Them, Childwold, A Bloodsmore Romance,* and, most recently, *Marya: A Life.* Oates has taught creative writing at the University of Detroit and the University of Windsor, Ontario, Canada, and is presently a visiting lecturer at Princeton University.

Perhaps because I came of age as television conquered America—in 1946, when I   1 was 8 years old, there were 15,000 sets in the country; in 1960 there were 50,000,000; and now?—I tend to associate television-watching with childhood and early adolescence. It was entertaining, often highly diverting, but not intellectually or emotionally stimulating, like serious literature. Quality television, too—by which I mean Sid Caesar, Ernie Kovacs, *See it Now,* live drama—rapidly declined after 1955, as mass-market tastes determined programming. Television simply passed out of my life; what I heard and read of it was not encouraging. Until a few years ago, my husband and I did not even own a set.

2   *Hill Street Blues* is the only television program I watch with any degree of regularity now, so perhaps it is presumptuous to call it my "favorite" program. In contrast to the lavishly produced BBC productions widely admired here, *Hill Street Blues* is unpretentious and unglamorous; simply a consistently rewarding series, intelligently conceived and executed, and performed with remarkable skill.

3   Immediately after its inauguration on NBC, in January 1981, the program won near-unanimous acclaim from television critics and any number of distinguished professional awards. It seems to be one of the few television programs watched by a fair percentage of my Princeton colleagues—arguably because it is one of the few current television programs that is as intellectually and emotionally provocative as a good book. In fact, from the very first, *Hill Street Blues* struck me as Dickensian in its superb character studies, its energy, its variety; above all, its audacity. And if, upon occasion, its humor is rather slapdash and broad, even outrageous (how many times have viewers been unwilling witnesses to the forcible extrication of pathologically obese men from tight quarters?), this, too, is in the solid Dickensian tradition. Melodrama, sentiment, defiantly bad taste, high seriousness—all are mixed together here and nearly always the mixture is just right. (In fact, this past season, the program seemed to rely less upon situation-

comedy routines and more upon comedy of character and theme. Officer Andy Renko [Charles Haid] was as brilliantly comic as ever, but others whose performances had begun to seem rather one-dimensional—Fay Furillo, Lee Schnitz, Mick Belker [Barbara Bosson, Robert Hirschfeld, Bruce Weitz], most obviously—were shifted to more serious material.

4   *Hill Street Blues* tells a profoundly disturbing story by way of numerous small stories that are braided deftly together. So typically rapid-fire is the dialogue, so cleverly interwoven the various tales, so swiftly does one scene cut to another, it is often remarked that new viewers find it difficult to follow any storyline at all. (It is helpful to give oneself two weeks' viewings before making any judgment.) At times one would like to know more about characters' motives and one would certainly like to know more about characters' fates—but the show has a relentless forward motion that mimics, one assumes, the unforgiving nature of "real life" in a city precinct station. This *is* a fair microcosm of the police world, set in a beleaguered urban environment the more convincing for being mysteriously anonymous. (The program is filmed in Los Angeles, though its opening shots and some transitional scenes are filmed in Chicago.)

5   At its most compelling, *Hill Street Blues* has the frantic, controlled air of ingenious improvisation. Except in the most extreme comic episodes, one is never conscious of actors "acting"; the performances are consistent but rarely predictable. The newer members of the cast—Mimi Kuzyk and Ken Olin as Detectives Mayo and Garibaldi, for instance—are developing well; Robert Prosky as the new sergeant is extraordinary; and it is impossible to find adequate praise for the more seasoned members of the cast—Capt. Frank Furillo (Daniel J. Travanti), his glamorous wife, public defender Joyce Davenport (Veronica Hamel), Lts. Henry Goldblume (Joe Spano) and Ray Calletano (René Enriquez). Dets. J. D. LaRue (Kiel Martin) and Neal Washington (Taurean Blacque),

Sgt. Lucy Bates (Betty Thomas), Officers Bobby Hill (Michael Warren), Andy Renko and Joe Coffey (Ed Marinaro), and all the rest.

6   *Hill Street Blues* is most moving when it deals directly with conflicts rising out of personal rather than social (or even criminal) issues. Recent episodes have dealt graphically with material that is surely controversial — police violence, for instance (perpetrated by a trigger-happy young officer under the authority of Lt. Howard Hunter [James B. Sikking] in one case, and by the otherwise gentlemanly Lt. Goldblume himself in another); the inability of police to protect their own witnesses; an on-camera electrocution of a black murderer-rapist (a powerful argument against capital punishment); the suicide by hanging of a young rookie following a crude hazing session; and the insensitivity of the police chief to that suicide. (If there is a dramatic flaw to Chief Daniels [Jon Cypher], it is simply that he is too one-note and predictable a character: always shallow, self-promoting, venal.)

7   One of the prevailing themes of the series is the depiction of the violent masculine world in which most of the policemen participate — "masculine" in the stereotypical sense of the word — and their efforts to transcend it, or to define themselves against it. So Renko and Hill are shown going through the considerable stress of breaking up their partnership of many years; Belker is often portrayed as sentimental, even rather sweet, despite the frequent coarseness of his persona; even the somewhat adolescent J. D. LaRue is capable of falling in love — however unwisely. In a recent episode, Joe Coffey is deeply agitated by being forced to arrest (on charges of solicitation) his former high-school football coach — a story that might have deteriorated into crude situation comedy had it not been so sensitively done.

8   While most of the interlocking stories are satisfactorily resolved, some are merely — minimally — resolved: the Hill Street police are figures of Sisyphus rolling their rocks up the hill and the next day rolling them up again, and again. Human effort and intelligence, action, risk, sudden eruptions of violence, sudden death — yet very little changes. It is always the next morning, it is always roll call.

9   In tone, *Hill Street Blues* is realistic melodrama, but it charts an unmistakably tragic course. Its message seems to be that the institutions of democracy have largely failed. Civilization depends upon a rigorous hierarchy of command — and upon distinctive personalities: men like Capt. Frank Furillo. (Yet Furillo is so clearly a special case: is there anyone else like him?) The precinct does not appear to be supported by the city, but is responsible for, and superior to, the city; the Hill is a region ruled by police, not governed by its own people — who scarcely exist except as victims and criminals.

10   It is probable that *Hill Street Blues* will continue to develop along its iconoclastic, disturbing lines. Are convicted murderers never convicted mistakenly? What of the volatile issues involving abortion, pro and con, in impoverished communities like the Hill? The questionable morality of undercover police work has been explored with commendable subtlety, but the ethics of entrapment need to be further explored: how do Detective Mayo and Sergeant Bates feel about disguising themselves as prostitutes, for instance? (Both these interesting women characters need to be developed in terms of contemporary feminism.)

11   Because of the high degree of respect it has earned, and its ongoing popularity, *Hill Street Blues* is not merely an hour's time slot in the television week, but a forum for provocative, timely issues. And it never fails to be entertaining — in the best, Dickensian sense of the word.

EXERCISES	

Content

Recall the main ideas in this article by answering the following questions. Respond to some of the questions in your own words. Respond to others by finding quotations from the article that provide the answers.

1. Why does Oates "tend to associate television-watching with childhood and early adolescence"? Why did television pass out of her life for many years?

2. Why do her Princeton colleagues like to watch "Hill Street Blues"?

3. Oates claims that "Hill Street Blues" is "Dickensian." What other writer in this chapter has compared "Hill Street Blues" to a Dickens novel? What qualities does Oates cite that are characteristically Dickensian?

4. At what times does Oates find "Hill Street Blues" most moving?

5. What is the dramatic flaw, according to Oates, in police chief Daniels?

6. In what ways do the "Hill Street" writers attempt to transcend the typically "masculine" world of the police?

7. According to Oates, what is the "tragic message" of "Hill Street Blues"?

8. What areas does Oates feel need further exploration by "Hill Street Blues"?

Structure

1. What is the purpose of paragraph 1?

2. Explain how paragraphs 2 and 3, considered together, form an identifiable section of the article. Give this section a title.

3. How is paragraph 10 related to paragraphs 4–9?

Fact/Opinion

Classify each of the following statements as either a fact, an opinion, or a fact wrapped in an opinion. If the statement is a combination of fact and opinion, identify which part is fact and which opinion.

1. "...in 1946, when I was 8 years old, there were 15,000 sets in the country; in 1960 there were 50,000,000...."

2. "Immediately after its inauguration on NBC,...the program won near-unanimous acclaim from television critics and any number of distinguished professional awards."

3. "Melodrama, sentiment, defiantly bad taste, high seriousness—all are mixed together here, and nearly always the mixture is just right."

4. "And [*Hill Street Blues*] never fails to be entertaining—in the best, Dickensian sense of the word."

Inferences

In your responses to the following questions, incorporate some of the quotations you located in response to the Content questions. You may decide to use either all or only part of each quotation.

1. Oates compares the Hill Street police to "figures of Sisyphus rolling their rocks up the hill and the next day rolling them up again, and again" (paragraph 8). What does she mean in terms of the dramatic structure of "Hill Street Blues"?

2. Do you think that Oates satisfactorily responds to the kind of objections to "Hill Street Blues" posed by Mark Crispin Miller in his article? If so, how? If not, why not?

3. After reading articles both favorable and unfavorable to "Hill Street Blues," after learning something about the way the show is made, have your impressions about the show been changed at all? If so, how?

 SUMMARY ASSIGNMENT

Write a summary of Beverly Gray's "Singin' the Hill Street Blues." (You may need to review the procedures discussed in Chapter 2.)

Begin by writing one-sentence section summaries. Then write a thesis for the article as a whole. Next combine your thesis and the section summaries into a coherent summary of the entire article.

We will help get you started by suggesting one way that the first part of the article can be divided into sections and by writing the first two one-sentence section summaries.

Section 1 (paragraphs 1–2)
The quality and complexity of "Hill Street Blues" make it an unusual television show.

Section 2 (paragraphs 3–4)
The distinctive cinematography of "Hill Street Blues" provides a feeling of gritty, "documentary realism."

Section 3 (paragraph 5)

Section 4 (paragraphs 6–7)

Section 5 (paragraph 8)

Section 6 (paragraphs 9–12)

 PAPER ASSIGNMENTS

1. Write an essay focusing on your own reactions to "Hill Street Blues." What kinds of things do you like most about the show? What do you like least or find annoying? Wherever appropriate, draw support from the articles included in this chapter.

2. Describe those aspects of "Hill Street Blues" that make it distinctive and unlike any other show on television. Draw heavily on the articles by Gray and Freeman (those concerned with the production of "Hill Street Blues"); but you may also want to bring in information from critical articles. It will be especially important for this assignment to develop a clear thesis and to present your evidence in a logical, well-organized manner.

3. Respond to two or more critics of "Hill Street Blues" with whose ideas you disagree. If you like the show, deal with the arguments of Mark Crispin Miller and also the comments of Tom Buckley and Ben Roberts, which appear in the introduction to this chapter. If you dislike the show, challenge the arguments made by critics like Jameson and Oates. In either case, explain *why* you think the critics you challenge are wrong. (For additional support, you may wish to summarize or quote the arguments of critics who believe as you do.)

4. Summarize the critical positions of those who like "Hill Street Blues" and those who dislike it. Arrange their arguments into categories (for example, what do they think of the fact that story lines continue from one episode to the next instead of being resolved in each episode?), but do not feel obligated to take a position yourself.

5. Write your own paper assignment for this chapter. Find a common theme running through two or more articles, devise a topic based on this theme, and then write a question asking writers to draw on material in the selections that would support a thesis based on this topic. You might want to help out your writers by suggesting some specific articles or even by getting them started with an outline for the paper.

CHAPTER 11

⌐⌐⌐ Children of Divorce

▬▬▬ Introduction

I remember it was near my birthday when I was going to be six that Dad said at lunch he was leaving. I tried to say, "No Dad, don't do it," but I couldn't get my voice out. My life sort of changed at that moment. I used to be always happy and suddenly I was sad. —*An eight-year-old girl*

In a way, I thought I'd made it happen. I thought maybe I was being punished by God. So I tried to be really good by not waking Mom before schooltime and getting my own breakfast and maybe God would change his mind. But it's been three years now. Sometimes, when I make a wish, though, I still wish for Dad to come home. —*A nine-year-old girl*

You never feel permanent anymore. You go from place to place. And I don't feel at home at Dad's. I feel very strange when his girlfriend is around. —*A 15-year-old girl*[1]

[1]Linda Bird Franke, "Children of Divorce," *Newsweek,* February 11, 1980, 58–66.

This is divorce from a subjective viewpoint. From an objective viewpoint, the facts are less moving, but more chilling. Over a million children under the age of 18 are involved in divorce every year in the United States. In the year 1900 the ratio of divorces to marriages was 8%. By 1950, it was 23%; and in 1976, for the first time, the ratio rose above 50%, meaning that one out of every two marriages was ending in divorce. If present trends continue, by 1990, fully half of all children will be living at some point with either a single parent or a stepparent.[2]

In this chapter we focus on the effects of divorce on children, a subject on which an increasing number of students have first-hand knowledge. You yourself may be a child of divorce; almost certainly you have friends and acquaintances who are such children. Thus you may be able to bring your own experiences and insights to bear on the subject.

The readings in this chapter fall roughly into two categories. One category consists of personal accounts of the effects of divorce by or about divorced parents or children of divorce. Included in this category is a moving short story, "Separating," by writer John Updike. The other category consists of analytical articles that offer insights into the ways that parents and children deal—or should deal—with divorce. Some articles fall into both categories, combining personal accounts of divorce with more objective commentaries.

To introduce you to this subject, let's consider one of the latter types of readings. In this question-and-answer column, Dr. Lee Salk, a professor of psychology in pediatrics and psychiatry at Cornell University Medical College, offers advice to parents who are either contemplating or experiencing the effects of divorce.

Dr. Lee Salk

HELPING CHILDREN DEAL WITH DIVORCE

1   *Question:* My husband and I have been having problems for some time now and have been talking about splitting up. We have two children, ages five and seven, who are both in school. My husband feels we should stay together until the boys are older, but I'm not sure this is the best thing for them. Can you help us?

2   *Answer:* Over the years I have found that, when couples stay together "for the sake of the children," it can make life miserable for everyone. Parents who continue to live together in a loveless marriage often experience a buildup of frustration that may lead to an increase in hostilities. Children who live in such an atmosphere receive little emotional satisfaction and frequently try to spend time in other people's homes where there is warmth and communication. Many of my adult patients whose parents stayed together under these circumstances tell me they couldn't wait to grow up and get away from home. These people developed a very negative view of marriage, and many of them said to me that they wish their parents had gotten divorced instead of remaining in a tense and

[2]Marilyn Webb, "The Joys and Sorrows of Joint Custody," *New York,* November 5, 1984.

empty marriage. On the other hand, many children and young adults I've seen whose parents did get divorced—and resolved their differences in a non-hostile way—were shown a far better model for dealing effectively with problems.

3   *Question:* I am in the middle of divorce proceedings with my husband. My nine-year-old son has been having nightmares almost every night. Is there anything I can do to help him?

4   *Answer:* Divorce is very traumatic for everyone involved. It is disruptive and brings forth basic anxieties about loss of love and separation from loved ones. Children often feel the brunt of divorce because they are generally powerless to do anything about it, yet may feel that in some way they were responsible. It's common for a child to feel that past arguments between his parents may have been the result of such things as his reluctance to do his homework, or even his forgetting to offer help with the dishes.

5   Children also worry about what will happen to them after their parents divorce. In the middle of divorce proceedings it is understandable for a child to wonder how his life will change: Where will he live? Will he still be able to see his friends? Will he have to change schools? If his parents have stopped loving each other, what assurance does he have that they will not stop loving him? Such concerns could easily bring about the nightmares your son has been having.

6   The best way to help is to give him an opportunity to talk about his feelings. But don't pressure him if he is reluctant to do so. And, at all costs, avoid burdening him with your problems or treating him like a counselor. Frequently, children find it easier to speak with someone who is outside the family and not involved in the situation itself. It might be wise to find a counselor or psychologist who is experienced in dealing with children of divorce.

7   *Question:* I was divorced several years ago and have recently remarried. My eight-year-old son has accepted my second hus-

band easily, but my ten-year-old daughter has not. She constantly talks about her father and tells us how wonderful he is. My husband is trying to be understanding, but she is becoming difficult to handle. What can we do?

8   *Answer:* It is important to remember that your ex-husband is still your daughter's father and she has an understandably strong attachment to him. Her feelings of admiration for her father should not be discouraged, nor should they be viewed as a rejection of your present husband. Any attempt on the part of either you or your husband to have him take the place of her father could easily cause her to resent you both.

9   I think the first step is to make it clear to your daughter that your new husband has no desire to take her father's place. Perhaps, if you suggest that she think of him not as a stepfather but simply as your new husband, it will be easier for her to accept him without feeling that it implies disloyalty to or rejection of her father.

10   You need to remember that it often takes time for some children to adjust to a new family situation. You can help your husband deal with the situation by getting him to understand that your daughter's relationship with her father is very important to her and that she may simply be afraid of having that relationship threatened. Encourage him to be patient with her and to acknowledge and accept her admiration for her father. In time, she will probably come to understand that it is possible to accept both her father and your husband, and your difficulties with her will in all likelihood subside.

11   *Question:* I have been divorced for two years now and have just begun to date other men. But my son and daughter, ages 12 and 15, have made me feel awkward about it. At times they giggle together and tease me about acting like a teenager; at other times they say things like "I hope you're not thinking of getting married again." How should I handle this?

12   *Answer:* First, you need to recognize that dating new men places you in a somewhat

different role than the one your children are used to. This is an awkward transition experienced by many divorced people, and your children's teasing, I'm sure, doesn't make matters any easier. However, their actions result from their own feelings of awkwardness and will gradually diminish as they come to recognize and accept this new and important step in your life. In the meantime, don't let their teasing deter you from dating—going along with it may even make it easier for everyone. Also, feel free to let them know that if you do find the right relationship, you certainly will think about marrying again. Assure them, however, that if you should decide to marry, you'll let them know in plenty of time.

Your children are at a stage in life when meeting members of the opposite sex is becoming increasingly important. Now, with you thinking along the same lines, they may have many conflicting feelings about it, from joy and happiness to a good deal of uncertainty. Let them know that it is important for you as a grown woman to have men friends and that by developing enjoyable relationships you will be a happier person, which in turn will enrich their lives as well.

Content

Each of the questions posed to Dr. Salk represents a particular, but typical, problem faced by a divorced or divorcing parent. (In fact, the writer of each question is a mother. Salk's column originally appeared in *McCall's,* which is geared to a female audience.) The first parent worries whether divorce would be in the best interests of the children. In the past, it was considered better, for the sake of the children, to hold a bad marriage together than to divorce. In the past, too, when divorces were far less common than they are today, the social stigma of being divorced or of being a divorced child was bad enough to deter many parents from divorce. Today, of course, the situation is very different; and, accordingly, Salk advises the writer that the effects on a child of growing up in a home atmosphere poisoned with hostility are far worse than the effects of divorce—provided the divorce is handled in a civilized manner.

The second writer, a mother in the midst of divorce, worries about her young son's frequent nightmares. Salk discusses the kind of anxieties—the child's sense of powerlessness, his sense of guilt that he may be to blame for the divorce, his uncertainty about the way his life will change—that could cause these nightmares, and explains that the best way to handle this problem is to have the child talk about his feelings, preferably with a counselor or psychologist.

The third parent, who has been divorced and is now remarried, is concerned because her ten-year-old daughter does not accept her new husband but remains emotionally attached to her natural father. Salk assures the parent that such an attitude is entirely normal and says that the child's feelings for her natural father should not be discouraged. He advises the woman to handle the situation with patience and understanding so as to assure both that her new husband does not feel rejected and that her child does not feel she must stop caring for her natural father.

The fourth parent faces another common problem: divorced for some time, she finds that her adolescent children tease her about dating new men. Salk advises the parent that her children's teasing—based on their ambivalent feelings toward their mother's dating—is a common phenomenon, that it will diminish in time (especially if she discusses the situation with them), and that she should certainly not be discouraged either from dating or from eventually contemplating remarriage.

Using Cause and Effect Analysis in Papers

Writers are concerned a great deal of the time with explaining *why* something has happened. Salk explains why the child of a divorcing mother may be having nightmares. A scientist explains why cancer is so deadly. A historian explains why the death of an obscure nobleman led to World War I. A professor of literature explains why George Orwell was so obsessed with the abuse of power.

When we answer the question "Why?" we attempt to link a cause or a set of causes to an effect. Many pieces of expository writing employ cause and effect analysis at some point; some deal with cause and effect exclusively. In the business world, an executive writes a report explaining why profits were down 10 percent last quarter. A group of military officers write an accident report explaining why an F-16 in apparently good condition stalled and crashed.

This chapter lends itself particularly well to cause and effect analysis since it has as its subject the *effects* of divorce on children. A comprehensive analysis describes the cause as precisely as possible, describes the effect(s) equally precisely, and, most important, establishes to the satisfaction of a reasonable person a convincing link between cause and effect.

Not all cause and effect analyses need be so comprehensive, however. Consider the following paragraph:

> Cutting through all age and sex distinctions is an obsessive desire to reunite the parents. One 2½-year-old in Chicago spent fretful hours trying to place his father's hand in his mother's hand. A nine-year-old New York girl spent all winter without a jacket on, trying to get sick enough so her parents would have to care for her—together. "All I did was get a lot of colds," she says ruefully.[3]

In this paragraph the writer establishes a link between particular effects (the boy trying to join his parents' hands, the girl trying to get sick) and their causes (both children wanted their parents back together again).

In these particular cases, the link between cause and effect is obvious to any reasonable person. In other cases, links between causes and effects are not so clear, and the writer must avoid certain pitfalls. One pitfall is to overgeneral-

---

[3]Franke, "Children of Divorce," *Newsweek*, February 11, 1980.

ize a cause to the point where it explains nothing. For example, suppose Salk had responded to the question from the woman who was concerned with her son's nightmares by saying, "Your child's behavior is a result of your divorce." Of course it is, but the mother already knows this. What she wants to know is not the ultimate cause (the divorce itself), but the *immediate* cause. (In this case the immediate cause is a complex of particular anxieties commonly experienced by children at the outset of a divorce.)

Often, explanations need to be lengthy and complex because proving that one thing caused another is difficult. Most situations contain enough variables to complicate any cause and effect analysis. If your car's engine failed thirty minutes after you filled the gas tank at a certain station, would you be justified in claiming that the gasoline was fouled and caused your engine to fail? To do so, you'd have to take into account such variables as the condition of the engine before you filled the tank; the level or condition of the oil; the frequency of service on your car; and an analysis of the gasoline in the tank (to see, for instance, whether or not it might have been contaminated with water). Only after you have considered many possible explanations and accounted for a wide range of variables can you claim with confidence that a cause and effect analysis is accurate.

In the case of divorce, numerous variables can account for the behavior and attitudes of a child of divorced parents. These include the home situation *before* the divorce, the way the breakup is explained to the child, how bitter the divorce is, the age of the child at the time of the divorce, the sex of the child (research seems to indicate that girls handle divorce better than boys), the custody arrangements, the frequency of visits with the absent parent, how well these visits go, and the mental health and the inner resources of the child before and during the divorce.

In the following passage, the writer attempts to establish a cause and effect relationship between two children's depression and the infrequent visits of their fathers:

> Lea...was an abnormally quiet girl whose teacher said she did not believe she could succeed at anything. We interviewed her at home. When asked about her father, she brought out a box containing all of the letters her father had written to her during the past three years. These letters, possibly 15 in number, were dog-eared, folded and refolded, and the interviewer wouldn't help but be reminded of a previous collection of love letters that had been read and reread with tears. The father had actually visited only once in the past two years.
>
> Peter, age nine, had not seen his father, who lives nearby, more than once every two or three months. We expected that he would be troubled, but we were entirely unprepared for the extent of this child's misery. The interviewer observed: "I asked Peter when he had last seen his dad. The child looked at me blankly and his thinking became confused, his speech halting. Just then, a police car went by with its siren screaming. The child stared into space and seemed lost in reverie. As this continued for a few minutes, I gently suggested

that the police car had reminded him of his father, a police officer. Peter began to cry and sobbed without stopping for 35 minutes.[4]

Here are two children who have withdrawn into themselves. Why? In the case of Lea, the account begins with a false cause (her teacher's assumption that Lea was not capable), the effects of her unhappiness are described through her actions, and at the conclusion of the paragraph, the presumed cause is provided: "The father had actually visited only once in the past two years." In the case of Peter, the cause of his unhappiness is provided at the outset (his father had visited him only once every two or three months), and then the effects are described in Peter's disturbed behavior. In both cases, the cause of the children's troubled behavior was their feeling that they were unloved and had been rejected by fathers who chose to visit them only at rare intervals.

We've seen one pitfall of cause and effect analysis—overgeneralizing the cause. Be on guard against other pitfalls. When claiming that an effect is the result of a particular cause, make sure that this "cause" is not simply an incidental (or coincidental) factor and that you have not overlooked more likely or more important causes. Children of divorce often make this mistake themselves: they assume that *they* are the cause of the divorce. They assume that they must be guilty of something, or their parents would not have decided to divorce. They may indeed be "guilty"—for instance, of not going to bed on time—but such behavior is certainly not the cause of the divorce.

A father who has lost custody of a teenage son whose grades begin to plummet may attribute the cause to his wife's sole custody of the child. This may be at least partially true—if links between the mother's custody and the son's low grades can be convincingly established. But there are likely to be other causes that may have nothing at all to do with the divorce—for example, a new love interest for the son or a demanding athletic schedule. People often jump to conclusions that are emotionally satisfying to them, conclusions that make them look good and others look bad. This is perhaps understandable, but it is not justifiable. Make sure that before you attribute a particular cause to a particular effect, you don't yourself have some emotional investment in establishing a connection, or some particular ax to grind—for example, that joint custody is almost *never* a good idea.

Assignment Preview

After you have finished reading the selections in this chapter, you will be asked to write a paper in which you draw one or more cause and effect relationships. (In this paper you may also decide to use techniques of description, example, and argument.) Select a thesis in advance or devise one as you read through the articles. Here are some topics to consider from which theses might be generated:

[4]Judith S. Wallerstein and Joan B. Kelly, "California's Children of Divorce," *Psychology Today,* January 1980, 72.

- The emotional effects of divorce on children
- The ways in which children can cope with the trauma of divorce
- The effect of divorce on parental relationships with children
- The ways in which divorced mothers or fathers attempt to forge new and better relationships with their children
- How some parents' ways of going about divorce are better than others'

Having formulated a thesis, read or reread the selections with an eye to finding evidence that will support your thesis. Questions following each selection will direct you to some of the important information and ideas.

Linda Bird Francke

GROWING UP DIVORCED

Linda Bird Francke, former general editor of *Newsweek,* a columnist for the *New York Times* since 1977, and an essayist whose work has appeared in numerous anthologies, is the author of *The Ambivalence of Abortion* and *Growing Up Divorced,* from which this passage is taken. It offers an insight into the effects of her own divorce on her children. Francke has said, "The thought on my life that consumes me these days is the glorious excitement of being a woman in contemporary America. For two-thirds of my life, I felt lesser and angrily frustrated because I was not born a male, the gender that seemed biologically destined to spawn the leaders, the movers, the producers. Now all is in the process of change and for the past twelve years, I have reveled in the joy and the privilege of being a woman."

1   It started off like any slightly chaotic family lunch. Caitlin, age seven, was lost in reading *Misty of Chincoteague* in her bedroom and had ignored three summonses to lunch. Tapp, five, was trying to coax her all-too-knowing cat out from under the porch so she could give her a bath and also pretended not to hear us call. And for once I was grateful for their contrariness. For this was to be no ordinary lunch. We—my husband and I, our two daughters, and twelve-year-old Andrew, then away at summer camp—were about to become a national statistic. It was time, my husband insisted, to tell the children that we were separating, that he was moving out, that we were never going to live again as an intact family.

2   And then we were finally at the table. What had prepared the children for this, I wondered numbly, listening to the girls squabble over who got the biggest piece of ham. To my knowledge they had never heard us have an argument, let alone a knock-down drag-out fight. Their father wasn't a drunk. Nor was I. He didn't beat me. Or them. Indeed, we really had a very happy family life, complete with a weekend house by the seashore, beach picnics, and a recent trip to Disney World. What differences my husband and I had were between us, not involving them. How could we do this to them, I anguished, longing to have it over with, longing for it never to happen.

3   And then, of course, it was time. Leaning over the bowl of cottage cheese, my husband reached for his daughters' hands on either side of him. "Give me your hands, girls," he said. "I have something very, very important to tell you." I listened in a daze to his words, which seemed to go on and on. He and I, he explained to the girls, had decided to live apart because we made ourselves unhappy living together. But it was very important, he went on, for the girls to realize he was not leaving them, that they were not in the least

responsible for the breakup. "I'll still be your father and I'll see you every weekend," he said, explaining that he was going to fix up his family's beach shack just two miles down the road. "The only difference in your lives is that sometimes you'll live with me, and sometimes you'll live with your mother."

4   I watched the tableau at the table with the damnable detachment that is bred into every journalist. Tapp seemed not to be listening to his words at all, but just kept asking "why, why, why" in a tone that was more of a squeak than a voice. Caitlin, being twenty months older, appeared to be listening very hard to every word and seemed frozen in the moment. Her fork hovered halfway between her plate and her mouth, and the bite of cottage cheese in her mouth remained unchewed. When he was finished, saying that he would pack and be out of the house before we returned from the Sunday matinee at the local movie theater, silence stretched over the table. Finally Caitlin swallowed and slowly put her fork back down. "I knew this happened to other kids," she said absently into the void. "I just never thought it would happen to me."

5   Variations on this scene are being played out in living rooms, dining rooms, backyards and kitchens across this country with stunning frequency. In 1963, according to the National Center for Health Statistics, 562,000 children under the age of 18 were involved in marital breakups. By 1980, the numbers had doubled to an annual rate of 1.18 million children. The suddenness of the divorce epidemic has taken everyone by surprise. Though the divorce rate has been rising steadily since World War II, with a brief respite in the fifties, the seventies saw the rate more than double, from a ratio of 47 per 1,000 married persons to 100 per 1,000 in 1980. And over half these couples have children under eighteen. Now, if you add up the total number of children whose parents are divorced, the sum rockets to over 12 million. Presently, nearly one out of every five children under the age of eighteen goes home to only one parent—the great majority be-

cause of divorce. And though divorce no longer carries the social stigma it used to, no longer makes outcasts of children, the shock and the personal significance to each family member have not been blunted. The words "I never thought it would happen to me" have become new echoes of childhood.

We settled down fairly quickly after that   6 separation announcement at lunch and the departure of my husband, as planned, before our return from *Star Wars*. For the next few months I worried about the children's reactions to his absence but was continually reassured by their silence about the subject and apparent reluctance to discuss it when I asked them how they felt. I realize now that their silence was a danger signal, but at the time, I was actually grateful that their seeming lack of distress eased what pain and guilt I felt toward them. My son seemed content at boarding school; my daughters continued to do well at their school, and no one started wetting her bed or having more nightmares than seemed appropriate for her age. And as promised, they saw their father every weekend.

Initially, when research came trickling   7 into the public sphere out of psychiatric literature, revealing that perhaps there was more to divorce and its effect on children than most people realized, it piqued only my professional interest. The evidence *was* startling. On the scale of childhood trauma, for example, divorce was second only to parental death. And though each child's circumstances were obviously different, certain reactions from children were almost universal: shock, followed by depression, denial, anger, low self-esteem, shame, and often, among younger children, a feeling that they were somehow responsible for their parents' splitup. Regardless of age, there also appeared to be an obsessive desire to reunite the parents.

I suggested a cover story on the children   8 of divorce to *Newsweek* magazine, where I was then a writer. There had been much to-do in the media about the plight of the single mother followed by the travails of the single father, all of which we had covered in the magazine. Wasn't it time we heard from the children, I suggested, to see how they felt about being part of the divorce epidemic? There were, after all, over one million children a year now going through the dissolution of their families. And though we all know the old saw that children are "resilient" and "flexible," "able to cope" with the most extraordinary adversities and "bounce back" better than ever, perhaps these children of divorce had a different story to tell.

9   I decided to begin my research with my own children, taking them out to dinner to interview them. At my fingertips were the snippets of information I'd gleaned about the effects of divorce, without ever thinking they would apply to my bright-eyed, seemingly well-adjusted children. It was, after all, three years since that fateful luncheon, and barring normal family crises like a couple of broken arms, a ruptured appendix and a few disagreements that had escalated into such epithets as "I hate you," we seemed as normal as any apple pie that is missing the "Daddy" slice.

10   The girls were delighted I was going to interview them, and we went to a local restaurant so the setting would be less homelike and more professional. Over our rounds of Shirley Temples, and bowls of chili, I took out my notebook and asked them how they had actually felt during that cataclysmic lunch three years before.

11   "I was very sad," Tapp said matter-of-factly. "I was going to say, 'No, Dad, don't do it,' but I couldn't get my voice out. I was too much shocked. I couldn't know why. I remembered once he came home late and you got mad at him, but I really thought you got along just fine.

12   "All the fun things we had done flashed right out of my mind like when he gave me piggy-back rides and when we picked apples and when we drove fast down the roller-coaster road and when we surprised you in the morning and jumped on you. All I could think of was the bad times and all the bad times stayed in my mind, like when he got mad at me and when he had to go to the hospital with his back. The bad thoughts just wouldn't go away.

13   "My life sort of changed at that moment. Like I used to be always happy and suddenly I was sad."

14   My pen skittered to a halt on the page. My youngest daughter had been going through all this suffering and I didn't even know? My mind went back to the divorce checklist. Shock. Depression. I looked at this child across the table, the chili spreading down her chin, and wondered if I really knew her after all. I pressed on. "What was it like when you went to school the next day?" I asked her, trying desperately to remember if I had called her teacher to tell her about the separation.

15   "I pretended it was a regular week and that I'd see Dad just like usual," she continued cheerfully. "I just put it out of my mind. I tried not to think about it. But I wouldn't tell anybody that you and Dad had got a separation. Not for ages and ages. I felt embarrassed."

16   Chalk up the next two. Denial. Shame.

17   In a very small voice now, I asked, "You didn't think you were the cause of our break-up, did you?"

18   "Oh, yes," she said merrily. "In a way I thought I'd made it happen. I thought maybe I'd acted mean to you and Caitlin and that you couldn't put up with me anymore. I felt I was being punished by God for being really bad, so I tried being really good so God would change His mind. I helped a lot in the house, I asked you if I could get your breakfast, I got up by myself for school without waking you up. I hoped that if I was really good God would change His mind and let Dad come home. I'm used to it now and it's okay. But sometimes when I have an eyelash to wish on, I still wish for Dad to come home."

19   I stared at this beautiful child, who was fidgeting now to get to the jukebox. She had opened wounds in me that she had closed in herself. In a detached way, I finished ticking

off the checklist. Low self-esteem. Responsibility for the breakup, a desire to reunite the parents. I was struck dumb by my maternal ignorance. How could I have failed to pick up the distress signals that she must have been sending out? I could have comforted her, reassured her, at least *listened* to her. And why hadn't she told me all this before? "Because you never asked," she said with a grin. "Can I have a quarter for the jukebox?"

20   It was Caitlin's turn now, my bright, puppy-hearted, super-sensitive nine-year-old who was two years ahead of herself in school. Like her sister, she had been totally unprepared for the announcement. "I never heard you have any fights. Never," she said firmly, this child who never loses an opportunity to uncover family secrets in bureau drawers, pocketbooks and file cabinets. "It came as a complete surprise. I always thought 'my parents will never get a divorce.'" Had she been reassured by her father's comforting and really very specific speech at the lunch table that though he was leaving me, he was not leaving them? "No," she continued just as firmly. "When I heard Dad say he wasn't going to live here anymore, I thought I was never going to see him again. I was in a daze. I didn't understand what was happening. Finally I heard him say he was coming out every weekend to see us. But I couldn't hear any of the other words."

21   Shock again, And again, a sense of responsibility for the breakup: "I was mad at myself. I thought you had been fighting about us, over who would get us if you ever got a divorce. I'd seen a show on TV where the parents were screaming at each other over who the kids would live with. I thought just by being alive I had made you and Dad split up."

All of this she, too, had kept to herself. 22 But being older than her sister, Caitlin had worked out at least a reasonable conclusion as to the "whys" of it all that satisfied her. "I just tried to live with it, really," she remembered, attacking her cheesecake. "I figured out that you weren't getting along because you spent a lot of time on your work and not on Dad, but I knew you didn't hate each other. So it was all right with me." Being an eternal optimist, Caitlin had even turned the separation into a plus. "After I got over being sad, I realized that we'd be better off separated because then I'd look forward to seeing Dad instead of just having him around all the time."

There it was. Not only were we part of a 23 national statistic, we were participants in a totally predictable series of emotional consequences. Sobered by how little I knew about my children, I got the check (Tapp proudly got the receipt for my expense account) and took the children home. Long after the children were asleep, I lay awake, wondering whether other divorced or separated parents knew what their children were thinking, feeling, fantasizing, scheming, suffering. For even though my children and I led very close and interdependent lives, I never had a clue any of this was going on.

EXERCISES

Content

Recall the main ideas in this article by answering the following questions. Respond to some of the questions in your own words. Respond to others by finding quotations from the article that provide the answers.

1. Imagining herself in her children's place, Francke acknowledges that the news of the breakup would probably come as a total surprise to them. Why?

2. In the months following the separation, what reassured Francke that her children were taking the situation well? Why was she thus reassured?

3. What is the typical sequence of children's reactions to their parents' divorce?

4. Why was Francke shocked when she interviewed her children?

5. In what way did Caitlin turn the separation "into a plus"?

6. After the interview, what was it that had made the biggest impression on Francke?

Structure

1. What is the purpose of paragraph 5?

2. Explain how paragraphs 9–22, considered together, form an identifiable section of the article. Give this section a title.

3. How is paragraph 23 related to the thesis of the article?

4. Write two more Structure questions and answer them.

Fact/Opinion

Classify each of the following statements as either a fact, an opinion, or a fact wrapped in an opinion. If the statement is a combination of fact and opinion, identify which part is fact and which opinion.

1. "Leaning over the bowl of cottage cheese, my husband reached for his daughters' hands on either side of him."

2. "In 1963, according to the National Center for Health Statistics, 562,000 children under the age of 18 were involved in marital breakups."

3. "It was, after all, three years since that fateful luncheon, and barring normal family crises like a couple of broken arms, a ruptured appendix and a few disagreements that had escalated into such epithets as "I hate you," we seemed as normal as any apple pie that is missing the 'Daddy' slice."

Inferences

In your responses to the following questions, incorporate some of the quotations you located in response to the Content questions. You may decide to use either all or only part of each quotation.

1. Why does Francke choose to interpose the statistics on divorce (paragraph 5) at the particular point she does? What information precedes this paragraph? What information follows?

2. Why do you think Francke had failed to realize what her children were going through?

3. Francke is a journalist, a writer for *Newsweek* magazine. How does this fact influence the way she reacts, the kinds of things she describes herself as thinking and doing in this piece?

4. What kind of inferences does Francke make after her interview with her children?

Rita Rooney

HELPING CHILDREN THROUGH DIVORCE

Rita Rooney is a freelance writer. Dr. Judith Wallerstein now heads the Center for the Family in Transition in Corte Madera, California, where she and others are converting the information gained from the Children of Divorce Project into concrete, short-term counseling help for couples about to divorce or remarry. The center's techniques are already being adapted in other parts of the country.

1   For some time now researchers have agreed that a couple's decision to divorce or remain together should not be governed by the impact on their children. Though divorce obviously changes the course of a child's life, it need not alter the child's whole outlook or capacity for happiness.

2   Until recently, however, professionals could only speculate about the long-range effects of divorce on children. There was no real evidence to substantiate how children respond, or to trace the changing relationships that typify a post-divorce family.

3   Then, in 1971, Doctors Judith Wallerstein and Joan Berlin Kelly began work on the California Children of Divorce Project, an exhaustive ten-year study funded by a private foundation and geared to develop guidelines for divorcing families. As Dr. Wallerstein, a psychologist at the University of California at Berkeley, explains, "A society that makes divorce so easy has a responsibility to help families through the inevitably difficult transitions."

4   The study began with interviews of 60 families, with a total of 131 children. Youngsters and their parents were first seen within a year of the initial separation; there were follow-up interviews a year later, again after five years, and then ten years later. To date, it is the largest, most intensive continuous study of the effects of divorce on children that has been done.

5   The researchers' basic conclusion is not surprising: Divorce does indeed leave scars on children that may never heal. Even after ten years, young people in the study continued to see themselves as "children of divorce," as if such a label identified them for all time.

6   Even so, Dr. Wallerstein says, this does not mean that couples should stay bound to a marriage that has become a source of anguish to one or both partners. "What it does mean," she points out, "is that parents who fail at married life owe it to their children not to fail at divorce." In other words, couples must learn to recognize the ways in which their divorce will affect their children — and handle the situation with sensitivity and love.

7   The first hurdle divorcing parents face with their children is breaking the news. Based on her research, Dr. Wallerstein advises that youngsters be told as soon as the decision is final, but not before. It is unfair, she contends, to drag a child through the painful deliberations that precede separation; but it is equally wrong for parents to announce a divorce and then continue living together, since most children will cling to a hope that the divorce won't happen.

8   If at all possible, parents should make the announcement together. Whether they tell the children individually or all at the same time is best determined by the age span involved. "If the children are close enough in age so that you can address them in the same way," Dr. Wallerstein says, "it's best to bring the whole family together. Youngsters support each other. But couples with a five-year-old and a teenager will probably want to tailor the explanation for each child."

9   The announcement itself is critical. Children have to be told what the divorce will mean to them. They should be told where

each family member will be living. If the house is to be sold, or if they will have to change schools, say so. A child's fear of disruption is often much worse than the disruption itself. All in all, it's best to be candid in admitting to children that divorce will bring a temporary upheaval to the family but that in time everything will settle down.

10   The only way a child can deal with the idea of divorce is to find a reason for it. If parents do not explain, youngsters must rely on their own fantasies—which, in the end, can hurt more than the truth. Most professionals agree that it's best to be honest with children within the boundaries of their understanding. Even a parent's infidelity should not be entirely skirted. While parents have to exercise some sensitivity to the issue, it's better to say up front that Daddy will be living in a new house with another woman than to have a child make his own shattering discovery.

11   Dr. Wallerstein also emphasizes the importance of parents telling their children, "We're sorry." "Don't be afraid of those words," she says, "Young people need to know that your separation is not an impulsive decision, that you have tried to make the marriage work and that you wish things had turned out differently. Give a child permission to be sad."

12   "Above all, make it clear that mothers and fathers may divorce but children never do. An alarming number of children are tragically torn between parents. They need reassurance that it's okay to love them both."

13   No matter how rationally parents explain the situation, however, most children will still refuse to accept the divorce. A seven-year-old, when told his parents are separating because they are not happy together, is likely to argue, "Stop being unhappy." And a teenager, confronted by a father's alcoholism, may reason, "All you have to do is stop drinking, get a job, and everything will be all right again."

14   According to Dr. Wallerstein, parents must override such objections with loving firmness, however difficult it may be for them. "Recognize the children's right to argue, but don't be drawn into the argument," she advises. "Tell them, 'I understand how you feel. If I were you, I'd feel that way, too. I wish I could take your advice, but that isn't possible.'"

15   On the basis of her research, Dr. Wallerstein believes the most important step divorced parents can take is to "finish the divorce." All too often, the issues that caused them to separate are reopened year after year. And though a man and woman who were married long enough to have children will probably always share an emotional tie, once they divorce they have to learn to keep their involvement to a minimum and to accept the fact that they are now separate and independent adults.

16   "We see couples who, whether they realize it or not, are holding on to their old relationship," she says. "This can be very hurtful to children." After five years of divorce, one woman in the study continued to call her ex-husband whenever their youngster visited him. "Be sure your son takes a shower," she would charge.

17   Parents who remain separated without divorcing, or who attempt periodic but unsuccessful reconciliations, cloud the issue for their children, increasing the uncertainty they already feel.

18   Though it is unlikely that any two youngsters will react in the same way to their parents' divorce, the study offers some guidelines to predictable behavior based on a child's age.

19   ■ Not surprisingly, preschoolers are especially vulnerable to the breakup of their family. And since most divorces occur in the sixth or seventh year of marriage, it is preschoolers who most frequently have to face this crisis.

20   The common denominator among these children appears to be anxiety, a fear of being abandoned by either or both parents. To a three-year-old, going across town can be as awesome as crossing the Sahara. Young chil-

dren worry that, when they go to visit Daddy, they may never get home again. Dr. Wallerstein calls this the Hansel and Gretel fantasy and suggests that mothers point out familiar landmarks along the way. "Look, there's the pretty church we saw last week" is the kind of offhand remark that may help a young child who is afraid of being "lost in the woods."

21   Even a new arrangement for being picked up at a baby-sitter's can be agonizing for a preschool child. Dr. Wallerstein talks of the value of giving the child subtle reassurance with a concrete timetable: "I'll come for you at five. We'll go home and have supper. Then we'll read a story."

22   One mother in the study noticed that her little girl was distressed each morning because she couldn't remember whether it was Mommy or Daddy who was scheduled to bring her home from kindergarten. The woman solved the problem by giving the child alternate lunch boxes — a blue one for Daddy's day, a pink one for Mommy's.

23   "Parents need to look for their own creative solutions," Dr. Wallerstein says.

24   ■ Slightly older children — around five and a half to eight years old — tend to demonstrate more open yearning for the absent parent. At this age, children feel abandoned by the parent who left — not by both parents, as younger children are apt to do. Boys, particularly, feel the loss of contact with their fathers and may be fearful of being left in the care of their mothers. Their logic is that the more powerful parent threw the weaker one out of the house, and they worry, Will I be next?

25   This is also the age during which little girls form a strong attachment to their fathers — and what many mothers fail to realize is that this attachment extends to *all* fathers, not just the good ones. Children of this age protect themselves with a fantasy that Daddy will return.

26   Dr. Wallerstein urges mothers not to crush this fantasy outright, but not to reinforce it, either. Instead, respond with under-

standing, saying, "I know you miss your dad." And emphasize again that the child still has her father: He left Mommy, not his children. She warns fathers, that their relationships with their children after divorce will not simply go along as they did before; a new bond must be formed and carefully nurtured. To both mothers and fathers she stresses that nothing can be gained by destroying a child's relationship with the other parent: "The only thing that's gained is destruction of the child."

27   ■ As a rule, children between nine and 12 years of age express open anger at their parents' divorce, usually out of a sense of desperation. They feel powerless and want to know why they were not consulted before the decision was made. Their anger is usually directed at the parent they think wants the divorce. Children of this age tend to divide the world into black and white: One parent is right, the other wrong. They identify with the parent they think of as victim, and often turn on the parent they were closest to during the marriage because, with their limited ability to understand the complexities of adult behavior, they feel abandoned by their protector. Unfortunately, many parents feed this moral indignation by establishing an unholy alliance with the child that pits him or her against the other parent.

28   "A youngster's anger won't go away by itself. It needs to be addressed," says Dr. Wallerstein. "But you don't have to give the child a hunting license in order to deal with his harsh judgment of the other parent."

29   ■ Adolescents and young people of college age may be the most neglected of all children of divorce. Historically, many couples wait "until the kids are grown" to separate. Yet it is these near-adults who are usually most depressed by parental separation. They question, "What about me?" They wonder who will send them to college. Often, they are thwarted in their need to establish autonomy outside the family by a parent's overreliance on them. Sometimes they are overwhelmed by what is going on in the

family and find it difficult to concentrate in school and maintain the friendships that are crucial to normal development.

30   If the divorce is grounded in a parent's infidelity, other problems arise, "Teenagers are preoccupied with their own burgeoning sexuality," Dr. Wallerstein points out. "They find it comforting to think of their parents as too old for sex. To be confronted with the suddenly visible sexual need of a parent can be traumatic."

31   Two important lessons for parents of adolescents seem clear. The first is that while one or both divorced parents may rely on an older child's emotional support, they must be careful not to intrude on the youngster's life outside the home. And, second, both parents must be alert to a breakdown of generational boundaries, aware that young people may be pushed across the threshold into adult behavior before they are able to handle the consequences.

32   Specifically, Dr. Wallerstein says, "Don't consult a teenager about the details of your social life or who you are dating. Parents often make the mistake of forcing young people into advisory roles they can't handle."

33   For children of any age, divorce does not end with a decree. Youngsters need continuing support from both parents to balance the impact of loss in their lives. Dr. Wallerstein recommends that parents work out a visitation policy, fine-tune it and stick with it. Don't let a child fret about weekend or holiday arrangements; let him know about them well in advance.

34   The biggest challenge of all for a child of divorce may be a parent's remarriage. Suddenly, there is not only a stepfather or stepmother but possible stepbrothers and -sisters as well. Dr. Wallerstein urges couples to give the new relationships time to set in. Two mistakes are common, she says: A remarried mothers expects her new husband to take over immediately as parent; and the new husband responds that they are *her* children, *her* problem. The same holds true for remarried fathers. What couples really need is time to get to know each other, time to define the new relationships.

35   Children are not comforted by the reassurance that, for an increasing number of people, divorce is a natural progression of family life. Knowing that several of her classmates have divorced parents is of no help to a little girl mourning the loss of her father. In fact, there is growing evidence that the high incidence of divorce intensifies children's anxiety about the hazards of loving someone. Teachers report that youngsters from intact families sometimes come to school after a parental argument and want to know, "Are my folks going to get a divorce?"

36   Children need help—from the time of separation throughout adolescence. They need the understanding and wisdom of parents who recognize that, while divorce may be the only solution for *them,* it is never a decision a child accepts easily. On the whole, children in the study who fared best were those who had continuing relationships with both parents and whose lives after the divorce were on a more even keel than before.

37   "In other words," Dr. Wallerstein says, "children do well when the divorce solves the problems it was meant to solve."

EXERCISES

Content

    Recall the main ideas in this article by answering the following questions. Respond to some of the questions in your own words. Respond to others by finding quotations from the article that provide the answers.

1. In what way was the Wallerstein-Kelly study unique?

2. Summarize the basic conclusion of the Wallerstein-Kelly study.

3. Why do Wallerstein and Kelly conclude that the timing of the divorce announcement is crucial?

4. Under what circumstances should children be told separately about the coming divorce?

5. What do Wallerstein and Kelly mean when they assert that divorced parents must "finish the divorce"? Why is this important?

6. Among which age group do divorces create the greatest anxieties? Why? What is the "Hansel and Gretel" fantasy?

7. According to Wallerstein, how should divorced mothers handle their daughter's fantasy that their father will eventually return?

8. Under what circumstances are parents advised not to depend too much on the support of their children?

9. In your own words, contrast the essential differences that children of various ages display in their reactions to divorce. Devote one sentence to each age group.

10. What kinds of problems arise for children when their custodial parent remarries?

Structure

1. Explain how paragraphs 7–14, considered together, form an identifiable section of the article. Give this section a title.

2. How is paragraph 28 related to paragraph 27?

3. How is paragraph 34 related to the thesis of the article?

Fact/Opinion

Classify each of the following statements as either a fact, an opinion, or a fact wrapped in an opinion. If the statement is a combination of fact and opinion, identify which part is fact and which opinion.

1. "Until recently...professionals could only speculate about the long-range effects of divorce on children."

2. "To date, [the Wallerstein-Kelly study] is the largest, most intensive continuous study of the effects of divorce on children that has been done."

3. "Parents who remain separated without divorcing, or who attempt periodic but unsuccessful reconciliations, cloud the issue for their children, increasing the uncertainty they already feel."

4. "In other words, Dr. Wallerstein says, 'children do well when the divorce solves the problems it was meant to solve.'"

Inferences

In your responses to the following questions, incorporate some of the quotations you located in response to the Content questions. You may decide to use either all or only part of each quotation.

1. How does Rooney's article expand on the information provided in Francke's article? What areas do both cover? What areas are new in this article?

2. This article is primarily a summary of parts of the Wallerstein-Kelly study. Why use such a summary instead of the study itself?

3. To what extent do you agree with the insights and advice presented in this article? To what extent do you disagree?

4. In paragraph 14, why does Wallerstein advise parents not to be "drawn into the argument" when children urge that they solve whatever problems have lead to the breakup?

5. How do you account for the characteristic differences in reaction to divorce by children of different ages?

6. What does Wallerstein mean when she says that "children do well when the divorce solves the problems it was meant to solve"?

Thomas J. Cottle

"GOODBYE, KIDS, MOTHER'S LEAVING HOME"

For information on Thomas J. Cottle, see the headnote on page 322. The following article is adapted from Cottle's book *Children's Secrets*. It offers another example of how the mishandling of divorce by parents can have traumatic effects on the child.

Divorce is the price our culture pays for the freedom we say we crave, including the freedom to recover from what we perceive as bad mistakes. When children are involved, their pain seems to come less from divorce itself than from a sense of abandonment. Such was the case with Willie Fryer, whose story follows.

1   Most families, for obvious reasons, would like to give the impression to the outside world, if not to their own members, that their home lives are ideal. Children, in the main, "appreciate" this myth, since the rumblings of parental wars and the threat of separation are hardly stabilizing influences on a child's personality. Parents and children alike "appreciate" the knowledge that arguments need not automatically end in separation or, for that matter, death, as children often imagine. The real and fantasized stability of the family helps all its members to believe in its ultimate strength and to have faith in the idea that families can wage war yet end up as allies.

2   Much of this is self-evident. It is also evident that families, adults and children alike, have begun to quake under the strain of ubiquitous divorces, although divorce rates lead to a series of myths of their own. That a growing percentage of marriages end in divorce has caused many couples to look upon their own marriages as far more frail, precarious, and strained than they ever recognized. Like microbes carrying vicious illness, the threat of divorce is in the air, and a not insignificant number of families now huddle together waiting for the disease to reach them. Equally important, as the nature of family life generally becomes more publicly discussed, the sacredness of marriage, and more particularly the marriage bond, is eroded, and marriage, in many people's eyes, becomes just another one of life's everyday institutions.

3   I am not suggesting that divorce is an innocuous event for the people involved. Quite the contrary. For these people, family stability may well remain a sacred concept and a hope. Despite the prevalence of divorce, it can cause great pain in the people

who institute it, not to mention in the people innocently victimized by it. As a notion, a practice, a reality, divorce is no longer something that people must keep secret. Yet, ironically, the very "speakableness" of divorce may be one of the matters that causes many people a special hurt: namely, one finds a tendency in our culture to substitute "speakability" for the successful resolution of human problems. All one has to do is speak about divorce, death, abortion, and one's tensions or misgivings, fears or doubts, are automatically dissipated. Letting a ghost out of a closet hardly guarantees the demise of the ghost. Secret closets may house other ghosts. In fact, secrecy itself generates ghosts.

4　My work with young people from divorced families is not easily summarized. Some children come out of a divorce psychologically wounded, and as the metaphor would suggest, the wound seems to heal over time. Other children do not emerge so fortunate; their scars are visible. In some instances I have found children flourishing after their parents' divorce, suggesting that life for them prior to the divorce had been unbearably stressful. Whether or not these children will someday reveal scars cannot yet be known, but for the moment, divorce, they claim, brought life-saving relief.

5　While divorce may be perceived by some children as abandonment, my own impression is that automatically equating divorce with abandonment is not necessarily helpful. Many divorced parents work hard not to show signs of abandonment, even though some of the children of these parents may speak about abandonment before they speak about family dissolution. In other words, a sense of abandonment may be heard in a child's early accounts of his or her parents' divorce, but eventually the new environment established for the child may help to dispel this sense. However, in the case of Willie Fryer, nothing about the "new" environment in which he found himself by dint of his parents' impending separation could possibly have counteracted the hurt *not* of divorce but of outright human abandonment.

And the fact that he was meant to keep these experiences and his feelings about them secret only exacerbated his despair.

6　Willie Fryer, seventeen years old, came from a well-to-do family, had long blond curls, a shaggy appearance, soft blue eyes, and broad hands. Willie Fryer's father was a professor of law, his mother a journalist. Both were talented, hardworking people. They loved their three children, but they wanted successful careers too. Their children (Willie was the second born) grew up with the knowledge that adults lead two lives, their work life and their family life, and there was no sense in children screaming for their parents between the hours of eight and six, Monday through Friday. They just wouldn't be there. Nor did the children think of the summer as a time when families vacationed together. The family typically stayed home; the children were sent to day camp. Everybody left the house at eight in the morning and returned at six in the evening. Still, it was a close family, even if its five members grew up leading separate lives.

7　Indeed, that was another thing the Fryers taught their children: Dependence is a dangerous stance. After the child reaches a certain age, there is no reason for him or her to be dependent on anyone, especially parents. People must learn to be self-sufficient, self-possessed. That way, the shock of life's vicissitudes, as Martin Fryer repeatedly reminded his son, will be reduced. Love people, he would tell his children, but never need them to the point of dependency. Shirley Fryer preached the same lesson, particularly to her daughters. Needing and loving are two foods, she would say. Too many people, and especially girls, confuse them. Don't let one substitute for the other. To Willie, she would add, "There is no man who can be happy, ultimately happy, when he's married to a woman who *needs* him rather than *loves* him. If she loves him she'll enrich his life. If she only needs him and pretends to love him to satisfy her need, she'll bring him down. She may be loyal, but if you want loyalty, marry a German shepherd!"

8   Willie Fryer was told many things by his parents, but his mother's remark about distinguishing between love and need remained the most prominent. The message made sense to him, although it carried a bit of fright as well, not that he could define this feeling. The idea that people who needed him would drag him down could not have been more dramatic. He could see it with his school friends. As a young teenager, he had close friends. But there was also a group who pretended to be his friends. In their way they expressed a need to be his friend, but his mother was correct. They were driven by a fascination for him, not by a concern for him. They were the people to look out for.

9   If further proof of his mother's statement was necessary, Sylvie Jenner provided it. Willie began dating her when they were in the eighth grade, and at seventeen Sylvie needed Willie, but it was love that held them together. Never did he feel brought down by her needs. He once asked her, "Do you love me 'cause you need me, or need me 'cause you love me?" Sylvie looked confused, "If I know what you're talking about," she answered, "I think I don't love you *or* need you. Or is that a song?" Willie remembers thinking the idea was right, but that it was just too soon to tell. When he told his mother of the exchange with Sylvie, Shirley Fryer laughed. Willie could see she approved of what he had tried to do. She agreed that it was too soon to tell. He would use the same words when he told me of his mother's decision to leave the family.

10   Willie Fryer did indeed have broad hands. When we went for beer at the Silver Parrot one afternoon, his hand was practically wrapped around the entire tall glass. I often remarked to myself on the contrast of that broad hand ready to crush the glass and the delicate manner with which Willie sipped his beer. He seemed somewhat self-conscious about sitting in a college hangout when he was a high school senior. Or perhaps the self-consciousness grew out of our conversation. The hand of a man, I would think, the drinking style of a boy.

11   In Willie's case, it was not important how we met, or what he felt the nature of our friendship to be. As he himself told Sylvie, the point was that if he didn't speak to someone soon, he was going to explode. He needed what he called an outsider. So we met on and off for several months, talking mostly about books, politics, and, as it was the autumn of his senior year, college applications and the things he might want to study in university. The subject of his mother's leaving, something I knew nothing about, arose with Willie saying: "I've got a little problem I thought you might be able to help me out with. I don't know exactly what you can do about it, but maybe you know somebody." This last phrase, so common among young people holding tightly to precious secrets, always sounds so poignant. "Maybe you know somebody." Somebody to do what? I always want to say. Listen? Fix it? Kiss the hurt? Or, in Willie Fryer's case, Love you but not need you? The noise in the Silver Parrot was so great I could barely hear Willie's words.

12   "About a year and a half ago my mom came to me with this little problem. Well, problem isn't the right word...listen, you got to stop me if you've heard this one before. I mean, I'm sure a lot of kids have stories like this one, so don't let me cry into your beer, okay? What I was saying, it wasn't really a problem, it was just a message. She had grown a little tired—that's the way she said it—of being a mother and a wife and a journalist. She couldn't do everything at once and be happy. So she had to give something up. It wasn't going to be journalism since that meant a lot to her, and we were all pretty much grown up so we didn't need a mother, like children need a mother, and besides, you know my mother and needing. So she had decided she was going to leave my father, and us. I tell you, when she said it, I felt like I was living in the middle of that expression, pulling the plug out. I mean, it was like somebody pulling the floor out, not the rug. I mean the floor, so you fall down, down, down, like into endless space.

13   "But here's the interesting thing: I must not have had any expression on my face. Just a look, like, go on, Mother, keep talking, I'm still listening. I couldn't even get the feeling I was feeling. It was just boom, except for one thing. She said it in a way that sort of made it impossible for me to say anything, or feel anything. Like, I had to keep anything I was thinking from her. So she said a little bit more, like how her leaving everybody didn't mean she didn't love us and that it was her work that was making her do it. She talked about how in the old days, when people weren't meant to live as long as they do now, it was all right for a man and woman to get married for life, but in modern times it's probably too long to stay together forever. It's nice to say it in a marriage vow and all that, but death, if you're lucky, doesn't come for a long, long time, so you could probably have a couple of families and still not be that old. She's talking on and on and I'm feeling like someone's choking the air out of my lungs but I'm not to let on I'm being choked. I didn't want to bother her. She'd obviously prepared her little speech, and I wasn't about to let it all come to nothing because this nice big fifteen-year-old kid—this was two years ago—was breaking down on the floor sobbing. And this was no big male thing on my part. I would have gladly cried if I thought I could have with her standing there. But if *she* could be calm, *I* could be calm. So I kept giving her the look, 'Keep going, Ma, I'm still listening.'

14   "Now comes the end of the speech: Don't tell Dad. The girls have known for a couple of weeks. They were told not to tell anybody, not even me, and now the three of us know but the old man doesn't. I mean the four of us know. Great game! And when does he find out? She's not sure. In time. She knows she has to make a break, but she's just not sure when, and she doesn't want to worry him because he's in the middle of a big project at work. So we get to keep a little secret. I'll tell you how I felt then, especially when she said, 'You want to tell me anything?' and all I could say was, 'Not really.

Maybe I'll think of something.' I felt like all the clocks in the world stopped and time went back to the beginning. All of us had to start all over again. It was like I was a new me. After all, no more mother; that makes me different from what I was when she came into my room. She went out the door and all the clocks stopped. I remember that night my younger sister looked at me and she didn't have anything written on her face. I couldn't tell what she was thinking. Then all of a sudden she has this big grin and she says, 'Merry Christmas, Lone Ranger.' I said, 'Merry Christmas, Tonto.' It was April then."

15   "So now the Fryers are leading a wonderful life. There's a little time bomb in the house, ticking away under my father's nose, maybe I should say in his bed, but he doesn't know it. At least he lets us *think* he doesn't know it. But he couldn't have known it and pretended like that. But none of us, not even my mother, knew when the time bomb was going off. Every night in bed, I'd say to myself, well, it wasn't today, maybe it won't happen. Then, as the time goes on, you begin to forget about it. Like, all secrets are fantastic, upsetting, whatever, in the beginning, but then the excitement wears off. Still, that feeling of, well, starting life all over again, and this time without a mother, I mean being born all over again without a mother, that didn't leave me. I was starting a second time, really a third time, and it was going to be a fourth time before it was over.

16   "When my mother gave me that speech, years before, about loving and needing, I think that's when I started to live life all over again. She was warning me, even if she wasn't aware of it. But knowing her, she probably was. I didn't know what was coming off, but I was being told, Stop the old clocks and start the new ones, pal, your old lady's going away one of these days. In a sense, that was like the first secret she was telling me. Be prepared: there's a time bomb being manufactured. Then the time bomb becomes real, which was when she told me she was leaving. The next time the clock stops and starts all over again is six months

after she made her little speech. Now both my parents come to me one night. My sister Patty is with me this time. They're both so straight-faced they look like they're going to ask me for the toothpaste. My father by now knows everything. The bomb went off and nothing. No one heard a noise. If it hit him, no one could have guessed by the way he was looking at us. So what can I think? They made their plans and they're neither delighted nor upset, and we're waiting around for the next step. Do they sell the house? Do we go with *her?* Do we go with *him?* Do they quit their jobs? No, that much I knew. Jobs come first after children reach six years old. So the clocks are going off again and I'm sitting on my bed feeling like a goddamn refugee. Just tell me when to pack and which country I'm supposed to walk to. And can I take my security blanket? This is all happening on Thanksgiving vacation. They waited until Thanksgiving vacation in case we got a little upset so we could take it easy a couple of days and not miss school. Thoughtful. Thoughtful people.

17   "Here's a funny thing. For a minute there, while the two of them like a couple of football coaches were giving us their half-time speech, how we're going to have to play a little better the second half—the second half of our life is more like it—I was actually feeling relieved. She waited so damn long she had me believing she wouldn't go through with it. It might have been better had she just said she was going and gone. But now I didn't have to keep the secret anymore. At least it was out in the open and we could talk about it. And don't think they didn't try to get us to talk about it. Probably because all the books said when you knife your kids in the back be sure they get a chance to talk about it with you; it makes them feel better. Except that Patty and I looked at each other and didn't have a thing to say. I don't think we talked about it for weeks. Fact, I don't *ever* remember talking about it. Patty said, 'Where do we go?' My mother said, 'You'll stay here with your father. I'll see you regularly.' But get this, she

tacked on the trailer, 'Willie, you must have some questions. You're never this quiet.' Oh yeah, man, I got a question. Do you think you could take your foot off my chest long enough so I could take a breath of air?

"It was really terrific. If anybody had   18 made a movie of us they could have sold it to television for one of these afternoon specials which are supposed to help children learn about *real* family problems, except we didn't have any problems because our family was breaking up amicably. That's my father's word. My mother called it *peaceably,* in case Patty or me didn't know the word amicably. Anyway, I felt relieved because no more secrets. I couldn't have said anything if they tortured me. But the more she kept saying, 'Willie, you must have something to say,' the more I could have killed her. She has a great way of not letting anybody express any emotion and she thinks they're purposely holding back. But she strangles us. That, maybe, is the biggest secret I was asked to keep in my entire life: my emotions. I *had* to keep them secret because she didn't have a way to deal with them, or the time. In fact, that may be why I keep saying that thing about time stopping and starting all over again. There never was time for our feelings. Our feelings were the big secret, *our* big time bombs, which weren't allowed to go off because Mommy and Daddy's work schedules would have been messed up. Can you imagine the three of us, the most wordy children in America, not saying a thing about what was going on? I mean, that has to go beyond a pledge of secrecy. She never said we couldn't talk to one another about it. Although she did, in her way. She kept us from raising anything with her, or with each other, or with anybody, that would keep her from getting where she wanted to go. This time she wanted to get out of the house. Can you see Patty and me exchanging Christmas greetings in the middle of the *spring?* 'Merry Christmas, Lone Ranger?' What the hell were we doing?"

"You want to hear the kicker? They take   19 one secret off the agenda for us, now they got another one. This time it's my father who's breaking the big news. He's just been told by my mother a couple of days before how she had decided to walk out. So what's on my father's mind? We shouldn't breathe a word of this to anyone. It was the right word for him to use too, because I couldn't breathe anymore at all. For his business and reputation, and her business and reputation, divorce wouldn't look good. My mother pointed out that when men leave women it doesn't look so bad as when women leave men. Either way, though, it ends up looking like there's something wrong with the woman. Either she's not good enough to keep her husband, or she's unstable and leaves him. So, there we were, pledged to secrecy all over again. And there was the clock stopping and starting again. I was beginning to feel like a car bumping along a dirt road without any gas.

20   "As you can see, I'm not doing all that well with my parents, but I've got to be among the world's top secret-keepers. I didn't tell Sylvie for a long, long time. When she'd come over she wouldn't ask where my mother was because she knew my parents worked. She didn't see anything different because the three little Fryers were such good secret-keepers, or is the word good liars! I didn't tell a soul; I led my life like a good little boy, and let myself choke on the whole scene. The secrets were still going strong in the Fryer home. If the split bothered anybody at 18 Willow Road, nobody could have told. But that's not really amazing. The amazing thing is that my parents kept up the secret, thanks to the sealed lips of their beloved children, one of whom's birthday was forgotten this year, and last year, too. They arranged to go to certain important social events together, the whole works, just to let people think they were together. People still wrote to her at home, thinking she lived at home. Great, huh? No one at their jobs knew, and the people they work with are the biggest gossips I've ever met. The fact is, the greatest family project the Fryers ever undertook was the keeping of that secret. My father must have known better than anyone how good we were at it, because we kept the one before it from him pretty darn well.

21   "That's my story. I still feel strangled to death, like I can't get air, and like every time I turn around I hear clocks stopping and starting and stopping and starting. I guess I feel too that I can't be young anymore, which isn't all that bad, not that I have any idea anymore who I am. Who I really am, I mean. No, that's a lie. I do know who I am, up to a point. I just can't put it into words; but I can sort of feel who I am. It's my parents I don't know. Talk about people you live with, or used to live with, or are *supposed* to live with, being strangers. Jesus, I don't know who they are, who they were, *what* they are. The big secret is the charade. The all-night, all-day drama playing over at Willow Road. The people are real, the events are real, only the emotions are fictitious to protect the innocent, as if anybody could be innocent after what's been going on.

22   "I think my parents are asking us to keep a far more important and dangerous secret than they think. Sometimes I think my mother's worse than my father, then I think he's worse. Both of them, in my eyes, are really sick people. They both need a team of psychiatrists working on them. But they don't see it, and nobody who is friends with them thinks there's anything wrong. Not telling anybody they're separated is a little matter next to the fact that their whole life is a lie. A lie when they were together, and when they're apart. That's what I can't tell anybody. Not even Sylvie. I have to be loyal to them. They think I'm loyal by not talking about their separation. They probably think I'm afraid to jeopardize their jobs because I may not have enough money for college, but that's a lot of crap! I couldn't care less about that. It's *them* I think about; not money for clothes and cars and college. And both my sisters are the same.

23   "I'm being loyal, acting the way I am, but the act is taking it out of me. It's changing me, which is all right, but it's making me think there are things I once thought I could

do that I don't think I can do anymore. It's cutting into my confidence. You can't grow up worrying about your parents or putting them out of your mind. It's normal for kids to grow up and find out that, well, your dad and mom aren't as great as you thought when you were small. Sure. But I have another problem. I have to grow up and put them behind me, or try to convince them that one of us is crazy, and I know it isn't me because *I'm* not going around asking people to keep secrets about *my* life. Believe me, I have a much healthier relationship with Sylvie than they ever had, and certainly better than that crazy business they have going between them now. Nobody goes through life with the strength they *could* have when their parents run around like that. This secret business is absolutely foolish, crazy. I say it's both. I also say I'm going to crack.

24   "You want the last straw? The secret-makers have just come up with their latest dandy. For the last six months they *have* been telling some people they're separated, although we're still not supposed to talk about it. But here's the latest: My mother is going to write a book about it. It, that means about us, the little counterspies of Willow Road. So now she really doesn't want me to talk about any of these things until I tell her how I've lived through the last few years. You want to see a grown man or almost grown man cry? I'd love to. But they've taken the tears out of me. I'd love to have a good old-fashioned cry, or laugh, or anything over this. But all that secret-keeping business, all that holding things in, I don't have a damn thing to let out. Maybe that's what I've been trying to say. The secrets took it all out of me. I told nothing in exchange for giving up every feeling I've had. Wow. I feel I've been talking a whole day. Tell me, after hearing this, you think I'm crazy? Or maybe I should ask, you think I *need* my parents, or *love* my parents?"

EXERCISES

Content

Recall the main ideas in this article by answering the following questions. Respond to some of the questions in your own words. Respond to others by finding quotations from the article that provide the answers.

1. In what ways has the growing rate of divorce been difficult even for intact families?

2. Cite two examples of metaphor used in the introductory section of this article (paragraphs 1–5) and explain their function.

3. Cite other examples of metaphor later in the article and explain their function.

4. In what way is the idea of abandonment associated with divorce? Does Cottle claim that divorce *is* abandonment?

5. How did Martin and Shirley Fryer distinguish between relationships based on love and those based on need?

6. How does Willie react to his mother's request that her decision be temporarily kept secret from her husband?

7. Why did Willie feel unable to say anything, either at the time of the announcement or afterward, to his sister?

8. Why are the children asked to keep the news of the divorce a secret?

Structure

1. Explain how paragraphs 1–3, considered together, form an identifiable section of the article. Give this section a title.

2. Explain how paragraphs 6–9, considered together, form an identifiable section of the article. Give this section a title.

Fact/Opinion

Classify each of the following statements as either a fact, an opinion, or a fact wrapped in an opinion. If the statement is a combination of fact and opinion, identify which part is fact and which opinion.

1. "Most families, for obvious reasons, would like to give the impression to the outside world, if not to their own members, that their home lives are ideal."

2. "Some children come out of a divorce psychologically wounded, and as the metaphor would suggest, the wound seems to heal over time."

3. "People must learn to be self-sufficient, self-possessed."

Inferences

In your responses to the following questions, incorporate some of the quotations you located in response to the Content questions. You may decide to use either all or only part of each quotation.

1. In the introduction to this article, Cottle asserts, "Divorce is the price our culture pays for the freedom to say we crave, including the freedom to recover from what we perceive as bad mistakes." Discuss the meaning of this statement.

2. To what extent does Willie Fryer's outward and inward reactions to the news of the coming divorce parallel Linda Bird Francke's daughters' reactions to similar news? To what extent does the behavior of those breaking the news (Martin Fryer and Francke's husband) contrast?

3. In paragraph 15, Fryer says, "'I was starting a second time, really a third time, and it was going to be a fourth time before it was over.'" What does he mean?

4. Fryer says (in paragraph 16) on the timing of the divorce announcement: "'Thoughtful. Thoughtful people.'" To what extent is he being ironic?

5. In what ways has keeping up with the charade, keeping the family secret, taken its toll on Willie?

6. At one point, (paragraph 22), Willie claims that his parents' whole life has been a lie. What does he mean?

7. Outwardly, Martin and Shirley Fryer seem to be decent parents who care about their children. They do want to keep the news of their divorce a secret, but as Cottle points out in the first sentence of this article, most families want to preserve at least a facade of well-being to the rest of the world. In view of this, do you think Willie is justified in regarding his parents as "really sick people"?

8. In some ways, Shirley Fryer bears comparison with Linda Bird Francke: both are journalists who were unaware for a long time of how their children felt about their divorce and both plan to write books about divorce and its effect on kids. What are the differences?

John Updike

SEPARATING

John Updike is one of America's foremost writers of short stories, novels, essays, and criticism. Among his many novels are *Rabbit Run*, *Couples*, *Rabbit Redux*, *Marry Me*, and *Rabbit Is Rich*. His short story collections include *Pigeon Feathers*, *The Music School*, *Bech: A Book*, and *Museums and Women*. The following story first appeared in *The New Yorker* in June 1975. Among other things, it shows the immediate effects of the news of marital breakup on children.

1   The day was fair. Brilliant. All that June the weather had mocked the Maples' internal misery with solid sunlight — golden shafts and cascades of green in which their conversations had wormed unseeing, their sad murmuring selves the only stain in Nature. Usually by this time of the year they had acquired tans; but when they met their elder daughter's plane on her return from a year in England they were almost as pale as she, though Judith was too dazzled by the sunny opulent jumble of her native land to notice. They did not spoil her homecoming by telling her immediately. Wait a few days, let her recover from jet lag, had been one of their formulations, in that string of gray dialogues — over coffee, over cocktails, over Cointreau — that had shaped the strategy of their dissolution, while the earth performed its annual stunt of renewal unnoticed beyond their closed windows. Richard had thought to leave at Easter; Joan had insisted they wait until the four children were at last assembled, with all exams passed and ceremonies attended, and the bauble of summer to console them. So he had drudged away, in love, in dread, repairing screens, getting the mowers sharpened, rolling and patching their new tennis court.

2   The court, clay, had come through its first winter pitted and windswept bare of redcoat. Years ago the Maples had observed how often, among their friends, divorce followed a dramatic home improvement, as if

the marriage were making one last effort to live; their own worst crisis had come amid the plaster dust and exposed plumbing of a kitchen renovation. Yet, a summer ago, as canary-yellow bulldozers gaily churned a grassy, daisy-dotted knoll into a muddy plateau, and a crew of pigtailed young men raked and tamped clay into a plane, this transformation did not strike them as ominous, but festive in its impudence; their marriage could rend the earth for fun. The next spring, waking each day at dawn to a sliding sensation as if the bed were being tipped, Richard found the barren tennis court — its net and tapes still rolled in the barn — an environment congruous with his mood of purposeful desolation, and the crumbling of handfuls of clay into cracks and holes (dogs had frolicked on the court in a thaw; rivulets had eroded trenches) an activity suitably elemental and interminable. In his sealed heart he hoped the day would never come.

3   Now it was here. A Friday. Judith was reacclimated; all four children were assembled, before jobs and camps and visits again scattered them. Joan thought they should be told one by one. Richard was for making an announcement at the table. She said, "I think just making an announcement is a cop-out. They'll start quarrelling and playing to each other instead of focusing. They're each individuals, you know, not just some corporate obstacle to your freedom."

4   "O.K., O.K. I agree." Joan's plan was exact. That evening, they were giving Judith a belated welcome-home dinner, of lobster and champagne. Then, the party over, they, the two of them, who nineteen years before would push her in a baby carriage along Fifth Avenue to Washington Square, were to walk her out of the house, to the bridge across the salt creek, and tell her, swearing her to secrecy. Then Richard Jr., who was going directly from work to a rock concert in Boston, would be told, either late when he returned on the train or early Saturday

morning before he went off to his job; he was seventeen and employed as one of a golf-course maintenance crew. Then the two younger children, John and Margaret, could, as the morning wore on, be informed.

5   "Mopped up, as it were," Richard said.

6   "Do you have any better plan? That leaves you the rest of Saturday to answer any questions, pack, and make your wonderful departure."

7   "No," he said, meaning he had no better plan, and agreed to hers, though to him it showed an edge of false order, a hidden plea for control, like Joan's long chore lists and financial accountings and, in the days when he first knew her, her too-copious lecture notes. Her plan turned one hurdle for him into four—four knife-sharp walls, each with a sheer blind drop on the other side.

8   All spring he had moved through a world of insides and outsides, of barriers and partitions. He and Joan stood as a thin barrier between the children and the truth. Each moment was a partition, with the past on one side and the future on the other, a future containing this unthinkable *now*. Beyond four knifelike walls a new life for him waited vaguely. His skull cupped a secret, a white face, a face both frightened and soothing, both strange and known, that he wanted to shield from tears, which he felt all about him, solid as the sunlight. So haunted, he had become obsessed with battening down the house against his absence, replacing screens and sash cords, hinges and latches—a Houdini making things snug before his escape.

9   The lock. He had still to replace a lock on one of the doors of the screened porch. The task, like most such, proved more difficult than he had imagined. The old lock, aluminum frozen by corrosion, had been deliberately rendered obsolete by manufacturers. Three hardware stores had nothing that even approximately matched the mortised hole its removal (surprisingly easy) left. Another hole had to be gouged, with bits too small and saws too big, and the old hole fitted with a block of wood—the chisels dull, the saw rusty, his fingers thick with lack of sleep. The sun poured down, beyond the porch, on a world of neglect. The bushes already needed pruning, the windward side of the house was shedding flakes of paint, rain would get in when he was gone, insects, rot, death. His family, all those he would lose, filtered through the edges of his awareness as he struggled with screw holes, splinters, opaque instructions, minutiae of metal.

10   Judith sat on the porch, a princess returned from exile. She regaled them with stories of fuel shortages, of bomb scares in the Underground, of Pakistani workmen loudly lusting after her as she walked past on her way to dance school. Joan came and went, in and out of the house, calmer than she should have been, praising his struggles with the lock as if this were one more and not the last of their long succession of shared chores. The younger of his sons for a few minutes held the rickety screen door while his father clumsily hammered and chiseled, each blow a kind of sob in Richard's ears. His younger daughter, having been at a slumber party, slept on the porch hammock through all the noise—heavy and pink, trusting and forsaken. Time, like the sunlight, continued relentlessly; the sunlight slowly slanted. Today was one of the longest days. The lock clicked, worked. He was through. He had a drink; he drank it on the porch, listening to his daughter. "It was so sweet," she was saying, "during the worst of it, how all the butchers and bakery shops kept open by candlelight. They're all so plucky and cute. From the papers, things sounded so much worse here—people shooting people in gas lines, and everybody freezing."

11   Richard asked her, "Do you still want to live in England forever?" *Forever*: the concept, now a reality upon him, pressed and scratched at the back of his throat.

12   "No," Judith confessed, turning her oval face to him, its eyes still childishly far apart, but the lips set as over something succulent and satisfactory. "I was anxious to come home. I'm an American." She was a woman.

They had raised her; he and Joan had endured together to raise her, alone of the four. The others had still some raising left in them. Yet it was the thought of telling Judith—the image of her, their first baby, walking between them arm in arm to the bridge—that broke him. The partition between his face and the tears broke. Richard sat down to the celebratory meal with the back of his throat aching; the champagne, the lobster seemed phases of sunshine; he saw them and tasted them through tears. He blinked, swallowed, croakily joked about hay fever. The tears would not stop leaking through; they came not through a hole that could be plugged but through a permeable spot in a membrane, steadily, purely, endlessly, fruitfully. They became, his tears, a shield for himself against these others—their faces, the fact of their assembly, a last time as innocents, at a table where he sat the last time as head. Tears dropped from his nose as he broke the lobster's back; salt flavored his champagne as he sipped it; the raw clench at the back of his throat was delicious. He could not help himself.

13   His children tried to ignore his tears. Judith, on his right, lit a cigarette, gazed upward in the direction of her too energetic, too sophisticated exhalation; on her other side, John earnestly bent his fact to the extraction of the last morsels—legs, tail segments—from the scarlet corpse. Joan, at the opposite end of the table, glanced at him surprised, her reproach displaced by a quick grimace, of forgiveness, or of salute to his superior gift of strategy. Between them, Margaret, no longer called Bean, thirteen and large for her age, gazed from the other side of his pane of tears as if into a shop-window at something she coveted—at her father, a crystalline heap of splinters and memories. It was not she, however, but John who, in the kitchen, as they cleared the plates and carapaces away, asked Joan the question: "*Why is Daddy crying?*"

14   Richard heard the question but not the murmured answer. Then he heard Bean cry, "Oh, no-oh!"—the faintly dramatized exclamation of one who had long expected it.

15   John returned to the table carrying a bowl of salad. He nodded tersely at his father and his lips shaped the conspiratorial words "She told."

16   "Told what?" Richard asked aloud, insanely.

17   The boy sat down as if to rebuke his father's distraction with the example of his own good manners. He said quietly, "The separation."

18   Joan and Margaret returned; the child, in Richard's twisted vision, seemed diminished in size, and relieved, relieved to have had the bogieman at last proved real. He called out to her—the distances at the table had grown immense—"You knew, you always knew," but the clenching at the back of his throat prevented him from making sense of it. From afar he heard Joan talking, levelly, sensibly, reciting what they had prepared: it was a separation for the summer, an experiment. She and Daddy both agreed it would be good for them; they needed space and time to think; they liked each other but did not make each other happy enough, somehow.

19   Judith, imitating her mother's factual tone, but in her youth off-key, too cool, said, "I think it's silly. You should either live together or get divorced."

20   Richard's crying, like a wave that has crested and crashed, had become tumultuous; but it was overtopped by another tumult, for John, who had been so reserved, now grew larger and larger at the table. Perhaps his younger sister's being credited with knowing set him off. "Why didn't you *tell* us?" he asked, in a large round voice quite unlike his own. "You should have *told* us you weren't getting along."

21   Richard was startled into attempting to force words through his tears. "We *do* get along, that's the trouble, so it doesn't show even to us—" *That we do not love each other* was the rest of the sentence; he couldn't finish it.

22   Joan finished for him, in her style. "And we've always, *especially*, loved our children."

23   John was not mollified. "What do you care about *us?*" he boomed. "We're just little

things you *had.*" His sisters' laughing forced a laugh from him, which he turned hard and parodistic: "Ha ha *ha.*" Richard and Joan realized simultaneously that the child was drunk, on Judith's homecoming champagne. Feeling bound to keep the center of the stage, John took a cigarette from Judith's pack, poked it into his mouth, let it hang from his lower lip, and squinted like a gangster.

24 "You're not little things we had," Richard called to him. "You're the whole point. But you're grown. Or almost."

25 The boy was lighting matches. Instead of holding them to his cigarette (for they had never seen him smoke; being "good" had been his way of setting himself apart), he held them to his mother's face, closer and closer, for her to blow out. Then he lit the whole folder—a hiss and then a torch, held against his mother's face. Prismed by tears, the flame filled Richard's vision; he didn't know how it was extinguished. He heard Margaret say, "Oh stop showing off," and saw John, in response, break the cigarette in two and put the halves entirely into his mouth and chew, sticking out his tongue to display the shreds to his sister.

26 Joan talked to him, reasoning—a fountain of reason, unintelligible. "Talked about it for years...our children must help us... Daddy and I both want..." As the boy listened, he carefully wadded a paper napkin into the leaves of his salad, fashioned a ball of paper and lettuce, and popped it into his mouth, looking around the table for the expected laughter. None came. Judith said, "Be mature," and dismissed a plume of smoke.

27 Richard got up from this stifling table and led the boy outside. Though the house was in twilight, the outdoors still brimmed with light, the lovely waste light of high summer. Both laughing, he supervised John's spitting out the lettuce and paper and tobacco into the pachysandra. He took him by the hand—a square gritty hand, but for its softness a man's. Yet, it held on. They ran together up into the field, past the tennis court. The raw banking left by the bulldozers was dotted with daisies. Past the court and a flat stretch where they used to play family base-ball stood a soft green rise glorious in the sun, each weed and species of grass distinct as illumination on parchment. "I'm sorry, so sorry," Richard cried. "You were the only one who ever tried to help me with all the goddam jobs around this place."

28 Sobbing, safe within his tears and the champagne, John explained, "It's not just the separation, it's the whole crummy year, I *hate* that school, you can't make any friends, the history teacher's a scud."

29 They sat on the crest of the rise, shaking and warm from their tears but easier in their voices, and Richard tried to focus on the child's sad year—the weekdays long with homework, the weekends spent in his room with model airplanes, while his parents murmured down below, nursing their separation. How selfish, how blind, Richard thought; his eyes felt scoured. He told his son, "We'll think about getting you transferred. Life's too short to be miserable."

30 They had said what they could, but did not want the moment to heal, and talked on, about the school, about the tennis court, whether it would ever again be as good as it had been that first summer. They walked to inspect it and pressed a few more tapes more firmly down. A little stiltedly, perhaps trying now to make too much of the moment, Richard led the boy to the spot in the field where the view was best, of the metallic blue river, the emerald marsh, the scattered islands velvety with shadow in the low light, the white bits of beach far away. "See," he said. "It goes on being beautiful. It'll be here tomorrow."

31 "I know," John answered, impatiently. The moment had closed.

32 Back in the house, the others had opened some white wine, the champagne being drunk, and still sat at the table, the three females, gossiping. Where Joan sat had become the head. She turned, showing him a tearless face, and asked, "All right?"

33 "We're fine," he said, resenting it, though relieved, that the party went on without him.

34 In bed she explained, "I couldn't cry I guess because I cried so much all spring. It

really wasn't fair. It's your idea, and you made it look as though I was kicking you out."

35   "I'm sorry," he said. "I couldn't stop. I wanted to but couldn't."

36   "You *didn't* want to. You loved it. You were having your way, making a general announcement."

37   "I love having it over," he admitted. "God, those kids were great. So brave and funny." John, returned to the house, had settled to a model airplane in his room, and kept shouting down to them, "I'm O.K. No sweat." "And the way," Richard went on, cozy in his relief, "they never questioned the reasons we gave. No thought of a third person. Not even Judith."

38   "That *was* touching," Joan said.

39   He gave her a hug. "You were great too. Very reassuring to everybody. Thank you." Guiltily, he realized he did not feel separated.

40   "You still have Dickie to do," she told him. These words set before him a black mountain in the darkness; its cold breath, its near weight affected his chest. Of the four children, his elder son was most nearly his conscience. Joan did not need to add, "That's one piece of your dirty work I won't do for you."

41   "I know. I'll do it. You go to sleep."

42   Within minutes, her breathing slowed, became oblivious and deep. It was quarter to midnight. Dickie's train from the concert would come in at one-fourteen. Richard set the alarm for one. He had slept atrociously for weeks. But whenever he closed his lids some glimpse of the last hours scorched them—Judith exhaling toward the ceiling in a kind of aversion, Bean's mute staring, the sunstruck growth in the field where he and John had rested. The mountain before him moved closer, moved within him; he was huge, momentous. The ache at the back of his throat felt stale. His wife slept as if slain beside him. When, exasperated by his hot lids, his crowded heart, he rose from bed and dressed, she awoke enough to turn over. He told her then, "Joan, if I could undo it all, I would."

43   "Where would you begin?" she asked. There was no place. Giving him courage, she was always giving him courage. He put on shoes without socks in the dark. The children were breathing in their rooms, the downstairs was hollow. In their confusion they had left lights burning. He turned off all but one, the kitchen overhead. The car started. He had hoped it wouldn't. He met only moonlight on the road; it seemed a diaphanous companion, flickering in the leaves along the roadside, haunting his rearview mirror like a pursuer, melting under his headlights. The center of town, not quite deserted, was eerie at this hour. A young cop in uniform kept company with a gang of T-shirted kids on the steps of the bank. Across from the railroad station, several bars kept open. Customers, mostly young, passed in and out of the warm night, savoring summer's novelty. Voices shouted from cars as they passed; an immense conversation seemed in progress. Richard parked and in his weariness put his head on the passenger seat, out of the commotion and wheeling lights. It was as when, in the movies, an assassin grimly carries his mission through the jostle of a carnival—except the movies cannot show the precipitous, palpable slope you cling to within. You cannot climb back down; you can only fall. The synthetic fabric of the car seat, warmed by his cheek, confided to him an ancient, distant scent of vanilla.

44   A train whistle caused him to lift his head. It was on time; he had hoped it would be late. The slender drawgates descended. The bell of approach tingled happily. The great metal body, horizontally fluted, rocked to a stop, and sleepy teen-agers disembarked, his son among them. Dickie did not show surprise that his father was meeting him at this terrible hour. He sauntered to the car with two friends, both taller than he. He said "Hi" to his father and took the passenger's seat with an exhausted promptness that expressed gratitude. The friends got in the back, and Richard was grateful; a few more minutes' postponement would be won by driving them home.

45   He asked, "How was the concert?"

46   "Groovy," one boy said from the back seat.

47   "It bit," the other said.

48   "It was O.K.," Dickie said, moderate by nature, so reasonable that in his childhood the unreason of the world had given him headaches, stomach aches, nausea. When the second friend had been dropped off at his dark house, the boy blurted, "Dad, my eyes are killing me with hay fever! I'm out there cutting that mothering grass all day!"

49   "Do we still have those drops?"

50   "They didn't do any good last summer."

    "They might this."

51   Richard swung a U-turn on the empty street. The drive home took a few minutes. The mountain was here, in his throat. "Richard," he said, and felt the boy, slumped and rubbing his eyes, go tense at his tone, "I didn't come to meet you just to make your life easier. I came because your mother and I have some news for you, and you're a hard man to get ahold of these days. It's sad news."

52   "That's O.K." The reassurance came out soft, but quick, as if released from the tip of a spring.

53   Richard had feared that his tears would return and choke him, but the boy's manliness set an example, and his voice issued forth steady and dry. "It's sad news, but it needn't be tragic news, at least for you. It should have no practical effect on your life, though it's bound to have an emotional effect. You'll work at your job, and go back to school in September. Your mother and I are really proud of what you're making of your life; we don't want that to change at all."

54   "Yeah," the boy said lightly, on the intake of his breath, holding himself up. They turned the corner; the church they went to loomed like a gutted fort. The home of the woman Richard hoped to marry stood across the green. Her bedroom light burned.

55   "Your mother and I," he said, "have decided to separate. For the summer. Nothing legal, no divorce yet. We want to see how it feels. For some years now, we haven't been doing enough for each other, making each other as happy as we should be. Have you sensed that?"

56   "No," the boy said. It was an honest, unemotional answer: true or false in a quiz.

57   Glad for the factual basis, Richard pursued, even garrulously, the details. His apartment across town, his utter accessibility, the split vacation arrangements, the advantages to the children, the added mobility and variety of the summer. Dickie listened, absorbing. "Do the others know?"

58   "Yes."

59   "How did they take it?"

60   "The girls pretty calmly. John flipped out; he shouted and ate a cigarette and made a salad out of his napkin and told us how much he hated school."

61   His brother chuckled. "He did?"

62   "Yeah. The school issue was more upsetting for him than Mom and me. He seemed to feel better for having exploded."

63   "He did?" The repetition was the first sign that he was stunned.

64   "Yes. Dickie, I want to tell you something. This last hour, waiting for your train to get in, has been about the worst of my life. I hate this. *Hate* it. My father would have died before doing it to me." He felt immensely lighter, saying this. He had dumped the mountain on the boy. They were home. Moving swiftly as a shadow, Dickie was out of the car, through the bright kitchen. Richard called after him, "Want a glass of milk or anything?"

65   "No thanks."

66   "Want us to call the course tomorrow and say you're too sick to work?"

67   "No, that's all right." The answer was faint, delivered at the door to his room; Richard listened for the slam that went with a tantrum. The door closed normally, gently. The sound was sickening.

68   Joan had sunk into that first deep trough of sleep and was slow to awake. Richard had to repeat, "I told him."

69   "What did he say?"

70   "Nothing much. Could you go say goodnight to him? Please."

71   She left their room, without putting on a bathrobe. He sluggishly changed back into his pajamas and walked down the hall. Dickie was already in bed, Joan was sitting beside him, and the boy's bedside clock radio was murmuring music. When she stood, an inexplicable light—the moon?—outlined her body through the nightie. Richard sat on the warm place she had indented on the child's narrow mattress. He asked him, "Do you want the radio on like that?"

72   "It always is."

73   "Doesn't it keep you awake? It would me."

74   "No."

75   "Are you sleepy?"

76   "Yeah."

77   "Good. Sure you want to get up and go to work? You've had a big night."

78   "I want to."

79   Away at school this winter he had learned for the first time that you can go short of sleep and live. As an infant he had slept with an immobile, sweating intensity that had alarmed his babysitters. In adolescence he had often been the first of the four children to go to bed. Even now, he would go slack in the middle of a television show, his sprawled legs hairy and brown. "O.K. Good boy. Dickie, listen. I love you so much, I never knew how much until now. No matter how this works out, I'll always be with you. Really."

80   Richard bent to kiss an averted face but his son, sinewy, turned and with wet cheeks embraced him and gave him a kiss, on the lips, passionate as a woman's. In his father's ear he moaned one word, the crucial, intelligent word: "*Why?*"

81   *Why*. It was a whistle of wind in a crack, a knife thrust, a window thrown open on emptiness. The white face was gone, the darkness was featureless. Richard had forgotten why.

EXERCISES

Content

Recall the main ideas in this story by answering the following questions. Respond to some of the questions in your own words. Respond to others by finding quotations from the article that provide the answers.

1. How does the weather "mock" the mood of Richard's misery?

2. Why have Richard and Joan decided to put off the separation?

3. What does Richard do to take his mind off the upcoming announcement?

4. What agreement have the couple made as to how the news of the separation should be broken? What is Joan's reasoning? Why does Richard only reluctantly agree?

5. Characterize, in your own words, Judith, the oldest child.

6. Characterize, in your own words, Margaret (Bean), the younger daughter, and John, the younger son.

7. Why do things not go according to plan at the dinner table?

8. How does each of the children react to the news of the separation?

9. About what else (besides the separation) is John upset?

10. At what point do we get the first hint that Richard is in love with another woman? At what point is this hint confirmed?

11. How does Dickie react to his father's news? How does Richard react to Dickie's response?

Structure

Indicate by paragraph numbers the sections into which this story seems divided. (*Hint:* New sections probably begin whenever there is a change of scene.) Then explain the function of each section in developing the story.

Inferences

In your responses to the following questions, incorporate some of the quotations you located in response to the Content questions. You may decide to use either all or only part of each quotation.

1. Based on the characterizations of the four children *before* the news is broken, did the different reactions of each one surprise you? Try to account for why each child reacted the way she or he did.

2. From what point of view is this story told? How does this particular point of view highlight the significance of the story? (Compare with the points of view in Francke's account and in Willie Fryer's account of how the news was broken to the children and the outward and inward reactions of the children.)

3. After the news has been broken and before Joan goes to sleep, she rebukes Richard for not sticking to the plan. Accusing her husband of making it seem as if she were kicking *him* out, she says, "You *didn't* want to [stop crying]. You loved it. You were having your way, making a general announcement." What does she mean by this?

4. Before he leaves to tell Dickie, Richard tells Joan, "If I could undo it all, I would." She replies, "Where would you begin?" What does she mean?

5. What is the significance of the ending?

6. How does the behavior of the parents in this story stack up against Wallerstein and Kelly's recommendations for parental behavior in such situations, as expressed in Rita Rooney's article "Helping Children Through Divorce"?

Dianna Booher

GAMES PARENTS AND CHILDREN PLAY

Dianna Booher has published numerous magazine articles and short stories and several books for young people. She reviews books for the *Houston Chronicle*, teaches creative writing at North Harris County College, and has worked extensively with young people, both as a teacher in public schools and together with her husband, who is a church youth director. This article, which originally appeared in her book *Coping...When Your Family Falls Apart,* shows how divorce can affect both parents and children in unexpected and insidious ways.

Games Parents Play

"People can hurt us in proportion to their meaningfulness to us, and the worst wounds are ever inflicted by those we love," says Willard Waller in *The Old Love and the New.*

That's unfortunate, but true. Families can hurt and scar each other for life by their careless words, actions, and attitudes. And the worst part of all is that most families don't realize the pain they're causing each other until it's too late.

Divorce is a situation in which painful games seem to be common. You can be on the lookout for the starting signals of some of these games and stop the action before it gets going.

4 Let's talk about games parents may try to play with you:

Poison

5 The object of this game is for one parent to try to poison your ideas and feelings about the other parent. Parents try to play this game because they've been hurt by the other parent and want to get even. Some play this game to make you think less of the other parent, so that you'll think more of them. Some parents play this game because they honestly think the other parent will harm you, and they want to protect you.

6 The rules to this game are simple. The poisoning parent simply tries to make every downgrading comment possible about the other. That parent comes out with statements like "Your daddy never did want you to have nice clothes. That's why he's late with the support payment." Or, "Your mother's a lousy housekeeper; it's a wonder you ever have any clean clothes to wear."

7 Another way to play Poison is for one parent to tell you all the details of the divorce, blaming the other parent, listing all the other's faults, and omitting all his or her own weaknesses.

8 Another variation of the game is for one parent to treat you "better" than the other parent so you will "realize" what a drab existence you have with the other or how "cruel" the other parent is to you.

9 If the parent wins this game, you will learn to despise or look down on your other parent. Or you may lose respect for both parents. It's easy to turn against the parent who is trying to poison you because you don't like what he or she is saying.

10 In the healthy family, comments from both parents about the other are counter-balanced. You can see the good and the bad, the strengths and weaknesses of each. When you only hear one side, things get lopsided for all concerned.

11 The best way to handle the game and blow the whistle before you all get hurt is just to simply tell your parent that you don't want to hear ugly, snide remarks about the other parent. Assure that parent of your love, but let him or her know that you love both of them and it upsets you to hear such comments. If telling a parent how you feel about the poisoning tactics doesn't help, then just leave the room when the remarks start flying.

12 You have lived with both parents and can pretty much decide for yourself what's true or untrue, regardless of what one parent might say. Use your judgment here and don't rely on the hurt parent's prejudiced statements.

13 Poison is a game with no real winners.

Scapegoat

14 The object of this game is to pour out all the anger and frustration of the marriage on the kids rather than own up to the responsibility as a husband or wife. This game is not played often because parents are very wary about hurting their children and risking their rejection. But still, a few parents play this game because they have a compulsion to punish or blame somebody.

15 The rules to this game are a little more difficult than poisoning. The parent may nag you for doing things which your other parent did. The parent may punish you for qualities you have that he or she dislikes in the other parent. The parent may punish you for no particular reason other than that the partner is not there to be punished. Fortunately, very, very few parents play this game because they do not want to lose a child's love.

16 If your parent plays this game, try to point out that you have been punished unjustly or that you are *not* your father or mother, and you want to be treated as the individual you are. A parent may be playing this game unconsciously, and pointing this out may be all that's necessary to stop it.

17 A parent may feel the winner at first when he gets rid of his resentment and frus-

trations. But in the end, he will have turned his children against him. Again, there are no winners.

Messenger

18   The object of this game is for parents to use you as a homing pigeon. The reason parents play this game is so they can say ugly things to each other through you without having to face each other. And at the same time, they have a chance to poison your thinking about the other parent.

19   This game is simple. They ask you to deliver messages such as: "Tell your dad that if he's late again to pick you up, I won't let you go with him." Or "Tell your mother you need new socks and to try to spend more of that support money on you rather than on herself."

20   The way to blow the whistle on this game is simply to refuse to give messages. Tell your parent that you want to stay out of it because their messages hurt you, and you don't want to be burdened with it. Parents won't have a choice about accepting your neutrality.

21   No winners again. Parents may think they're winning because they're taking a cut at the absent parent and feeding you poison at the same time. But in the end, they lose when you lose respect for them as mature adults. Or you may think you win by hurting a parent with the "message," but actually you only get caught in the battle and pick up a few stray bullets for the messages you deliver.

Spy

22   The object of this game is to gather data about the other parent to use as ammunition in court or to satisfy curiosity or feelings of jealousy.

23   Parents most often want to play Spy when they want to know who the other parent is dating, how the other parent is spending money, or how the other is managing the new household or job.

24   Some questions are direct, such as: "Is your mother dating the man from work?"

Other information is pried out of you more subtly, like: "I guess Dad is really having a hard time getting home-cooked meals, isn't he?" Such statements are supposed to bring some sort of comment from you about how the father is faring in the hopes that you may spill some other information in the details.

25   The best way to stop the spy game is just to refuse to talk about the other parent's personal matters. Tell your folks that such spying makes you uncomfortable, and to talk to one another directly.

26   On the surface, you feel like a winner in this game. You feel needed because one parent appreciates the "news" you've given. You feel important to have more knowledge about one parent than your other parent has.

27   But like the other games, this is unhealthy. First of all, it prolongs the hostility and fighting between parents. Knowledge about who the other is dating, how they're managing, whether or not they seem happy only adds fuel to the flames of jealousy and self-pity. Another hazard of the game is that both parents will come to distrust you. A parent in wiser moments will realize sooner or later that if you're telling personal things about one parent, surely you tell the other parent the same type of things. In the end, both parents may turn against you.

28   Another consequence of this game is that you lose respect for yourself because of playing such underhanded tricks.

29   If there's something you feel one parent needs to know about the other, discuss it in the presence of both. Or simply wait until the truth comes out.

30   Again, no winners.

Weapon

31   The object of this game is for one parent to use you as a weapon to punish the other parent. Parents play this game because they're angry, hurt, jealous, or helpless.

32   The way this game is played is to use visitation rights, housing arrangements, or money to punish the other parent. Your mother may refuse your father the right to visit with you if he is five minutes late pick-

ing you up. Or if he keeps you over the weekend longer than he was supposed to, she may refuse to let you visit for the following two weeks. The father may refuse to send your support checks so as to create a financial hardship for your mother. One or the other may mess up plans for vacations or holidays so as to purposely inconvenience the other.

33 It's very hard for you to stop this game between parents even though you're the weapon. Recognizing the game and being vocal about it helps. Try to point out to your parents that it's unfair for you to have to miss visits or get less money because of their battles. Be as tactful as possible, and try to avoid hurting their feelings.

34 No winners, only losers.

Substitute

35 The object of this game is for parents to use you as a substitute partner or friend. Parents play this game when they are feeling lonely or helpless.

36 The way this game is played is that the parent treats you like an equal in the family, leaning on you to help make important decisions, for protection, even to help figure out the finances.

37 A variation of this game is to treat you as a substitute friend. The parent may want you to call him or her by first name as a friend would. Also, the parent may talk about personal matters such as dates, inner feelings, and problems. The parent may even want to use you as a date for special occasions which call for couples only.

38 On the surface this seems like a harmless game. The parent is definitely the winner because he or she has someone to lean on and to share feelings with. In one respect, you seem like a winner, too, because you feel closer to the parent in such an open relationship.

39 But there are dangerous side effects for you. One is that your responsibilities will make you seem more mature and may turn your own friends off. They, or you, may get the feeling that you are beyond them, and a wall comes up between you. Also, being a parent/friend substitute can take time and effort away from developing friendships at your own age level. Either way, you fail to develop normally.

40 Another side effect of the game is the guilt you may feel when you need to break away from this relationship. When you find you are ready to leave home for college, a job, or marriage, you may feel guilty about leaving your parent without your emotional support. These feelings of guilt can color the rest of your future.

41 Another side effect is resentment. Often you come to resent having to sacrifice so much of your time and emotional energy to your parent. You may grow so tired from handling your parent's problems, you don't get around to handling your own.

42 To stop this game before it gets out of hand, explain to your parent that you can't handle knowing all those feelings and frustrations. Telling a parent that it depresses you and worries you to hear these personal things will usually work. When a parent asks you to be a date for a certain occasion, say no. Encourage your parent to get out and find other friends.

43 At first this game is flattering, and you feel like a winner. But eventually the "victory" of feeling needed, important, and mature turns into a burden.

Sky's the Limit

44 The object of this game is for parents to give you everything your heart desires in order to win your love and support and to rid themselves of any guilt about the divorce.

45 Parents play the game by giving you an abundance of material things like all the clothes you could possibly use, trips to wherever you want to go, lessons to learn whatever you want.

46 A variation of the game is to constantly and elaborately entertain you. Fathers often do this on visitation days. Another variation is to let you get away with murder; your parents' tolerance level is stretched to the sky.

47   Parents play this game for a number of reasons. They may be trying to prove to you how much they love you. They may be doing it because they feel guilty about hurting you in the divorce. They may be too weak to stand up against your demands. They may be trying to prove to outsiders or to the other parent what a super-parent they are. They may want to prove that any sympathy you may get from outsiders about the divorce is unwarranted because you're such a lucky kid and not at all deprived.

48   Whatever their reasons, parents come out the losers in this game as well as you. Parents find out that the more they give, the more is expected of them. And they obviously have less money, time, and energy to spend on themselves. They often feel like they're taken advantage of and martyred.

49   At first glance, you may look like a real winner in this game because of the extra money, attention, time, and freedom. But these, too, have their side effects. Too much of anything makes you appreciate it less. And when you constantly have more money to spend and less restrictions on your behavior than your friends do, a barrier develops between you. Laxity in discipline and too much freedom, too, soon can hamper your moral, physical, and psychological growth. And over a period of time, parents who feel they are sacrificing too much become resentful and look to you as the cause of their hardships.

50   When you realize that your parent has this anything-goes philosophy, you may have to be the one to put on the brakes. You can use good common sense about what you need in the way of clothes and spending money and can spend accordingly. If a parent is overindulging you out of guilt, he or she will be grateful that you don't expect such an effort. And exercising self-control in matters where your parent may be too trusting is really working to your own benefit.

51   Even though you may look like a winner in this game, in the end, it's only a draw.

52   Recognizing the game parents play with you is the first step in improving family rela-tionships. Refusing to play along is the next step and a much more difficult one.

53   As strange as it may seem, refusing to get in the game is the only way to win.

Games Kids Play

54   Parents are the bad guys in the last section, initiating all the harmful games with their kids. Some kids try games of their own, thinking they'll surely come out winners.

55   But just as with the parents' games, it doesn't often work that way. Let's talk about some of those games that sound most promising.

Bribery

56   The object of this game is to extort from parents as much money, time, attention, and privileges as possible.

57   This is an easy game to play with divorced parents because they feel guilty for any pain the divorce caused you. And because they're afraid of losing your love, or afraid of your loving the other parent more, they usually are unwilling participants in the game. Naturally, the game is attractive for kids with such grand prizes for the winners.

58   The game is played by withholding love from the parent (or at least not expressing it openly) unless the parent comes through with a reward. Kids say things like "I think maybe I'll just skip our visit and stay home this weekend if you're not planning anything special. I really would like to see the ball game, and Mother and her boyfriend will probably be watching it on TV." The idea is to get your dad to bribe you to visit him by offering to take you to the ball park or do something more fantastic than he originally planned.

59   Another such tactic might be: "Mother, if you're not going to let me go on that ski trip during Christmas vacation, I think I just might spend the holidays with Dad." Does Mom come through on the ski trip? Sometimes.

60   A variation of the game is to play one parent against the other. Such games usually start with "But Daddy always lets me stay out until…" Or, "But Mother thinks it's a neat idea to…" This is an easy game to play because parents are not together and can't easily verify facts with each other. If they always take your word on everything, the bribery works. When they do check out your facts, it backfires on you.

61   Another variation of the game is acting as spy for a bribe. Pretending to "tell all" about Dad's date or Mother's weekend makes you look like the good guy and like you're taking sides against the other parent. You can get extra rewards for this, depending on how bad the parent wants the information and how much you seem to know.

62   Still another variation of Bribery is to play on a parent's guilt. This is the old "You've caused me so much pain because of the divorce that you ought to bribe me so I don't mope." If your parents feel guilty enough, this works beautifully.

63   Another version of the same game is to pretend to or actually take sides. Of course, you have to switch sides often to keep the game going. One week you talk a lot about how awful your dad was to leave your mother with so little money, about how hard she's having to work to pay the bills while your dad is having such an easy time. The next week you do a lot of talking about how poor old Dad is suffering having to live in a dinky apartment while Mother gets the house, and about how Mother is such a nag all the time that you wish you could live with him. The week you sympathize with Mother, she gives the bribes. The week you sympathize with Dad, he gives the bribes.

64   You can see the almost limitless possibilities for variations of this game of Bribery. It has its rewards, no doubt about it. But most kids agree that the rewards are not worth the tactics it takes to get them.

65   Kids who bribe parents usually have a terrible feeling of guilt about using their parents this way. They realize that the money, at-tention, or love is given out of a parent's sickness or weakness and not out of genuine love. And besides the guilt, there's a point when parents will no longer be willing to sacrifice to buy a child's love and favor. Their bribes will turn to resentment and anger.

66   You may play along in style for a while, but the game gets rougher as you go.

Destroy

67   The object of this game is for kids to behave in a way destructive to parents, to themselves, or to both. Parents usually do not participate in this game as they do in the others. They are on the sidelines watching you play and trying to get you to stop. Kids play this game for various reasons—to punish their parents for the divorce, to get their parents' attention, to test parents' love, or to try to get parents back together again.

68   The rules of this game are wide open—almost anything goes. Kids can steal, set fires, run away from home, flunk out of school, try to get pregnant, overeat, or take drugs. The ways to destroy themselves or their parents are limited only by the limits of the imagination.

69   If kids want to punish parents, doing something to embarrass, humiliate, or worry them causes a lot of pain and suffering. If kids want to get a parent's attention, they may do these things to show the parent just how much they are hurting inside. Some kids do something destructive just to test the parents' love and see how much they will put up with. They think that the more parents tolerate, the more they are loved. Other kids destroy themselves to try to get their parents back together again. They think if they cause enough trouble, one parent alone can't cope and they'll have to get back together to handle the problem.

70   All this reasoning is faulty. Parents who have made up their minds to divorce will not get back together just because their teen is acting up. A child's poor behavior will only further complicate the parents' relationship. Nor is it reasonable to think a parent will

love you more if you cause more trouble. The only thing you can win is the punishment of your parents—your behavior can certainly cause them much heartache and guilt.

71   Of course, most kids don't consciously reason this all out. Usually these reasons are buried deep in the mind. But if warned about the potential danger, kids can figure out the real motives for their behavior and accomplish their purposes in a healthier, safer way.

72   Playing this game is like being a kamikaze pilot in World War II. You may accomplish your mission, but you kill yourself in the effort.

Poor Me

73   The object of this game is to use the divorce as an excuse for as many things as possible. Kids play this game because it relieves them of responsibility for their behavior, and they get sympathy.

74   Kids can play this game at home, school, or almost anywhere. They can decide not to do homework, to cut classes, or to cause a discipline problem in class. If they let it be known that there are "problems" at home, they can often avoid responsibility for their actions. Teachers, sponsors, and parents overlook things out of pity which they would otherwise punish.

75   Kids can use this game at home on parents by refusing to do chores, obey the house rules, or be cooperative. If the father was the one who generally enforced the rules, it's easy to play this game when only the mother is in command.

76   Although some kids really get carried away singing "poor, poor, pitiful me," as the country/western song goes, they finally lose the game. At first, they get by with a few things. But "getting-by" causes resentment in other kids who don't get away with the same behavior. And the "poor me" attitude causes a loss of self-respect. It also leads to adopting unhealthy attitudes like "The world owes me something."

77   Before too long others will lose patience with the "poor me" posture, parents included. Sympathy has its limits.

78   Bribery, Destroy, or Poor Me are all tempting games for kids of divorce to play because they promise shiny trophies. But the trophies tarnish quickly and are not worth the effort. When tempted to play one of these games with your parents, count the cost before you take the field.

| **EXERCISES** | |

Content

Recall the main ideas in this article by answering the following questions. Respond to some of the questions in your own words. Respond to others by finding quotations from the article that provide the answers.

1. Why is Poison played more frequently by parents than Scapegoat?

2. What is Booher's advice to children on how to handle most of the games played by parents?

3. Which parental game makes both sides feel, at first, like winners? Express in your own words the disadvantages of this game.

4. In what parental game do children *appear* to be the winners? Why is this appearance illusory?

5. In which kids' game do parents not participate?

Structure

1. How are paragraphs 11 and 12 related to paragraphs 5–10?
2. How is paragraph 19 related to paragraph 18?
3. How is paragraph 34 related to the thesis of the article?
4. What is the purpose of paragraph 78?
5. Write two more Structure questions and answer them.

Fact/Opinion

Classify each of the following statements as either a fact, an opinion, or a fact wrapped in an opinion. If the statement is a combination of fact and opinion, identify which part is fact and which opinion.

1. "Divorce is a situation in which painful games seem to be common."
2. "Poison is a game with no real winners."
3. "Parents play this game [Weapon] because they're angry, hurt, jealous, or helpless."

Inferences

In your responses to the following questions, incorporate some of the quotations you located in response to the Content questions. You may decide to use either all or only part of each quotation.

1. Booher begins her article by quoting Willard Waller: "People can hurt us in proportion to their meaningfulness to us, and the worst wounds are ever inflicted by those we love." Discuss this quotation, using specific examples.

2. Compare Booher's comments on the game Substitute with Rooney's comments in paragraphs 31 and 32 of "Helping Children Through Divorce."

3. Where do you find other parallels between particular games played by parents or children and Wallerstein and Kelly's conclusions, as expressed in Rooney's article?

4. Where do you find parallels in other articles in this chapter with some of the games described in Booher's article?

5. Write a brief essay, based on your own observations and experience, on how one or more of these games is played.

6. Can these games be played in the absence of divorce or separation?

7. Booher advises children to stop these games as early as possible. In which cases do you think it would be relatively easy for children to take this advice? In which cases would it be difficult? Why?

8. Rewrite Willie Fryer's experience (in Thomas J. Cottle's "Goodbye, Kids, Mother's Leaving Home") as if it were a game played by Fryer's parents. Use the same style as Booher uses in her article.

C. W. Smith

UNCLE DAD

C.W. Smith is a novelist whose works include *Country Music, Thin Men of Haddam,* and *The Vestal Virgin Room.* Here Smith describes the effects of his own divorce upon his children and himself.

1   Years ago I called a college buddy I hadn't heard from in a while. He had divorced his first wife but had remarried. I asked him how many kids he had now.

2   "Just the one."

3   "One? I thought you had two."

4   "*Aw* hell!" he snorted. "You're thinking of the ones I had with Judy. They don't count."

5   A silence several seconds wide dropped between us while I pictured those two fatherless children drifting into space without a tether. How could a man discount his children's existence with the indifference of a claims adjuster?

6   But now that I've lived for the last five years outside the home where my daughter and son are growing up, I don't judge my friend so harshly. Maybe "they don't count" meant that since he had botched that job, he could hope for a better grade on a new project, offer "the one" as evidence of his reformation. If he had stormy struggles over visitation arrangements, or if he wasn't allowed to help decide who would be his children's doctors, barbers, teachers, or playmates, or if his former wife moved them to another city without consulting him, then I can see why he says "they don't count." When we feel our efforts produce only the frustration of impotence, then we cease trying.

7   That's a comforting thought. But then, as I seem to remember C. S. Lewis once saying, "An explanation of cause is not a justification by reason." I keep thinking about that.

8   My father is a pipe-smoking Presbyterian who speaks in witty one-liners; he taught me to stand when ladies enter a room and how to handle hammers, and once, when I was twelve, I saw him rescue a drowning man, a father, from a river and walk away without giving anyone his name. A hero.

9   That he would have chosen to divorce my mother and walk out of our house to live elsewhere was inconceivable.

10   Walking out of my own house twenty-seven years later, I knew I had forfeited the right to be so admired by my own twin son and daughter. But because my parents had not divorced, I wasn't aware of how devastating it might be. And didn't want to know — I could dream the damage to my children would be minimal by watching other fatherless kids go about their daily lives: in the age of divorce, this seemed to have become oddly normal; there were thousands of such children, and they wore no bruises I could see.

11   I saw nothing to stop me from being the good father I had always been. Aside from the months I commuted to another state for work, I had been around the house constantly. With two "first" children, both my wife and I had to keep diapers changed, bottles washed and filled. For the two years that my wife was a television reporter, I stayed home to write, changed vacuum-cleaner bags, separated darks from whites in the wash, shuttled the kids to school, and greeted them all at the door at the end of the day in an apron, a wooden spoon in hand.

12   I read the kids Curious George and Dr. Seuss books. Once, when a heavy snowfall closed the schools, we made an igloo in the yard using a cardboard box as a mold. (The defense offers this, Exhibit A, to show that this worm was a good, liberated father before he bailed out of his marriage; he regrets that the flaming hulk landed in a school yard.)

13   Giving them a hug or an off-to-school scuff on the head, crooning the bedtime mantra ("Good night/Sleep tight/Wake up

bright in the morning light/To do what's right/With all your might"), making cheese toast, cheering while running beside my cycling-novice son with one hand clutching the waistband of his jeans — these humble pleasures vanished the moment I decided to leave. To provide, to protect, and to guide — like a service club motto, these had constituted the dogma of fathering I had learned as a son, and I didn't know that performing these ritual duties was such good spiritual nutrition until after I had prematurely nodded to the waiter and the plate was whisked from under my nose.

14 My lessons began immediately. Gay and I agreed, I thought, to pad the shock to the kids with a spirit of mutual cooperation. The day we decided to announce that we would separate, I presumed that we would sit them down and break the news, over their heads, together. The words would come hard, I knew. Every speech I rehearsed sounded lame and false; I couldn't frame any phrase that would make my leaving a necessity that could outweigh their claim to the pain of it. But as the parent who had chosen to go, the duty was rightfully mine, and the difficulty would be part payment for my guilt. Facing them would be both manly and fatherly.

15 But when I pulled into the driveway late that afternoon, they were huddled together on the sidewalk at the curb, looking stricken, two nine-year-olds waiting for the Dachau bus.

16 At the front door I knocked on the screen (that seemed strange — hours before, the house had belonged to me) and went inside to say that I was taking the kids to eat before we had our talk.

17 Then Gay reported that she had already told them we were going to separate. "I hope you don't mind," she offered politely. "After all, it's our problem now." *So you go on about your merry way and don't bother about us!*

18 Yes, I *did* mind — it's one thing to confess you're a scumbag and another to have the news precede your appearance. Obvi-

ously, part of my punishment would be to be denied any strategy I might devise for my absolution, however meager. My guilt also said I had no right to be angry.

19 "How'd they take it?"

20 "Okay," she said, "considering."

21 I slunk back to my car. My kids were already in it. My daughter sat in the front seat. Gray coils of mud were clinging to the rims of her tennis shoes. I almost told her to get out and wipe her shoes off but didn't, not because it would have seemed petty in juxtaposition with the news but because I had, in one stroke, lost my moral authority.

22 We went to Burger King. White tile, hard plastic benches, everything colored in the hues of chewable vitamins. I can't remember what was ordered, but it all came in paper cartons and was cold by the time the first of us had decided to bolt from the silence by stuffing his mouth with something handy.

23 "So what do you think?" I finally asked.

24 Keith shrugged, which I interpreted to mean indifference or stoic acceptance. Now I know he felt helpless, numb, and utterly confused.

25 "Just a separation," said Nicole.

26 "Yes," I said, "just a separation." A legalistic truth: I was 99-percent certain we would be divorced, but that remaining one percent permitted me the luxury of cowardice. "I'll see you all the time," I added. "I won't go away." Another lie, strictly speaking.

27 Nobody had an appetite. I couldn't make myself talk about anything important, and that also discouraged talking about anything inconsequential — it would have seemed vulgar. *The* subject sat on the table between us like a Venus's-flytrap the size of a basketball we were each pretending was only a private hallucination. Not knowing what to say, I was unpleasantly surprised by my own relief that Gay had already "explained" it to them. I asked "How was school?" and "Did you do your homework?" knowing that no child in his right mind could perform any productive work after having heard such crushing news.

28 "How about some ice cream?"

29   They shook their heads.

30   "*Aw,* come on, surely you want some ice cream?"

31   Surely you won't hate me for the rest of your lives?

32   My friend Elroy sent me an essay he had written. "I want to be a father again, with children growing up in my house..." he wrote. "I want to hear their voices among the voices of their friends on the front porch... I want schoolbooks on the living-room couch...I want half-eaten crackers-and-cheese on a plate in the kitchen and a package of oboe reeds on the buffet."

33   Elroy left his job, his friends, and the city where he had lived for twenty years to follow his children to the town they had moved to five hundred miles away. "I refused to become a stranger to these people, my children," he added in a letter, "who mean as much to me as I meant to myself."

34   Most of the divorced fathers I know still hang on in some way despite the trouble and pain. We form a legion of what novelist Bryan Woolley has termed the Uncle Dads. Unlike traveling dads, we never will come "home" to any welcome or to settle a quarrel or to hear an appeal, and our children gnaw on the suspicion that we've rejected *them;* unlike stepdads, we live in another house, or even in another city, perhaps with other children whom our "real" children suspect are getting the best of our attention.

35   Some of us pop irregularly into our children's lives, bearing an irrelevant or even inappropriate gift, disrupting routine, asking that our children's plans be changed to suit our brief visitation or hoping to be included in their activities.

36   We console ourselves with the notion of "quality time," the divorced parent's fondest way of coping with guilt. "I'm a remote kind of person," said one divorced father who takes his sons to a cabin every summer for two weeks, "so if I was living at home with my kids, I'd probably be removed; this way, I tend to pay more attention to them. I think of using this time for them to talk about any-thing serious that they want to, but so far," he joked, "nothing's come up."

37   The truth is, though, that children tend to talk seriously only when it's their choice, and that usually comes when the surface of daily routine is glassy, unruffled. They're helping us to bake cookies or to paint a cabinet, and out comes, "Dad, were you ever in love in the eighth grade?" Or, "Have you ever had a friend who was homosexual?"

38   When we're being honest, we admit that quality time is that rare moment when a stretch of ordinary time is interrupted by an unexpected burst of genuine rapport. To say "We will now have quality time" whether anybody feels like it or not is like saying, "We will now have fun, or else." We fear this truth: that the necessary preparation for quality time is quantity time, and that we can't give. Awakened by a nightmare that some disaster has befallen them miles away, or that they may be troubled by something that happened during the day, we're forced to recognize that there's no substitute for being there constantly; or rather, there are only substitutes for it.

39   So we live with a sadness that is pervasive and continual, like low-level radiation. Larry, a composer, told me: "There's always a slight little pain that's like that continuing E-string at the back of a score. I live across the street from an elementary school, and sometimes I might be writing a salute to mayonnaise or something and I'll hear some of the kids playing on a swing, and it really hits me. Or when I think of how I'm watching my kids grow up on Polaroids. When they're here, I measure them against the doorframe, and when they're gone I look at it and think I've got a yardstick of my kids growing up and I'm not there. Sometimes you just have to lie down until you feel better; then you get up."

40   But then there's hope. Dressed in clean jeans and sport shirts, we platoon up at Jetways on Friday evenings, waiting for the stewardesses to lead our mob of children — some wearing name tags like D.P.s — out of the tunnels to where we stand hoping they

haven't seen *Gremlins* yet. Upchuck Cheese Pizza is the last place we would ordinarily choose to dine, but the martyrdom of an awful meal is oddly comforting.

41   We yearn for things to go well. We're anxious. We fear our children's anger because it hurts us; we fear their love because we know it means they hurt. But we're also elated to have forty-eight hours to wedge slivers of ourselves into the chinks of their armor.

42   During the divorce negotiations I tried for joint custody but met stiff resistance. My greatest fear was that Gay might whisk them off to another city; the saddest men I knew were those whose children were literally out of reach, and I have one friend who arrived at his children's home one day to find the house empty and no forwarding address left. So I asked my lawyer if I could legally prevent this. He chuckled.

43   They stayed put, though, and I took furnished digs ten minutes away in an old, Mediterranean-style building said to have been the residence of the man who penned "Home on the Range" in the 1930s, the decade from which the dusty wooden blinds, the furniture, and the smelly mattresses doubtless dated. I was not supposed to have children here, my downstairs neighbors constantly reminded me. On overnights, Keith and Nicole slept in a sagging Murphy bed and fought over the covers. Looking out my bedroom window, they had a view onto an alley where the wan, androgynous denizens of a unisex hair boutique met during breaktime to compare rainbow-colored hair and to pass a joint, and sometimes each other's tongues, among them; I was cursed with the terror that my folly had led my own pink-cheeked babies out of innocence much too soon. My best hope was that years later they could tell their more sheltered peers about their lives with voices dripping with blasé sophistication; maybe they could wear all this like a badge.

44   In cold weather we stayed inside to play Monopoly on a rug so old, cross-hatched twine showed through the burgundy fuzz. If the weather was nice, I would walk them down to a nearby park to play Horse with a spongy basketball, or take them to the zoo, where I would see other Uncle Dads doing weekend duty. We could distinguish each other from the regular, full-time dads because they were allowed to look bored.

45   Once a week I drove Nicole to a town twenty miles away for gymnastic lessons; two afternoons a week I took my son to soccer practice or games. I took them to the movies and their pediatrician, showed up for PTA meetings, and talked to their teachers. I wanted to believe I was a good father, even from across town.

46   One evening when Gay was working late, Keith climbed onto the roof to rescue a mewling kitten and fell off, striking the air-conditioning unit. While he lay screaming on the driveway, Nicole ran up and down the block trying to find an adult who could help before she phoned for an ambulance. I discovered this twenty-four hours later. "I'm sure glad you weren't seriously hurt," I told Keith over the phone, as if I were a cousin across the continent. "You should be more careful." My words were altogether empty, coming so late and from one so remote that his name did not automatically spring to mind in an emergency.

47   I didn't worry about Nicole. She was gliding through her days on autopilot, so stunned I read her shock as acceptance. To make up for her broken home I got her an intact Barbie Townhouse where Ken and Barbie could all live happily with Francie; they had a working toilet and a pink-and-yellow van to take lots of fun family trips in. Barbie had a wedding dress and they could stay married as long as Nicole wanted them to.

48   Meanwhile, Keith was erupting in purple rages. Where before the divorce he had been a model child, he now roamed his neighborhood saying ugly things to adults and pelting people's houses with eggs. In family therapy I'd watch him braid his arms across his chest, clamp his jaws, and pretend he had nothing to say. His grades tumbled; he told his teach-

ers that when he tried to concentrate, all he could think about was the divorce.

49   Occasionally my ex would call to ask me "to do something with Keith"; he'd be ordered to the phone, and if I reproached him, he'd simply hang up on me. Sometimes she would tell him that if he didn't behave she would call me to come over to spank him. She never did, for which in retrospect I'm thankful: to have barged into my children's home for that reason would have been a terrible compounding of insult with injury.

50   He said he wanted to live with me. I was having the time of my mid-life living with my lover in an apartment over an elderly landlady, and I balked at dealing daily with my belligerent son, and that's the sorry truth. So I bought him a model airplane with a gasoline engine, something I had always wanted as a kid, and I thought it was good to give him what I had wanted (since I couldn't give him what *he* wanted), and I wanted to grab a little chunk of my own childhood back this way. Gee, Dad! the Beaver (Keith) would gush to Ward (me). Golly. It flies and it's got a real engine! He and I and Nicole went to the park, assembled the plane, got it started. I turned over the control lines to him, and he got dizzy turning on the plane's pivot after a few revolutions. Nicole took a turn, and the plane took a vertical swoop that arced into a loop that took it nose-down into the turf, where it exploded into pieces.

51   I bought Keith a BB gun to replace the airplane. He and a new friend, who had spiked hair and whose parents were also breaking up, chipped a garage window with a shot from the Daisy. The owner called the police and Keith's name probably went into a computer somewhere. I gave him a feeble lecture, but I knew that I shouldn't have bought the gun for him. "Keith says you're just trying to buy his love," Gay reported, obviously agreeing.

52   They were wrong. I knew I already had his love. I was trying to buy his forgiveness.

53   Three years after the separation, Gay announced that she was taking a job in Galve-

ston, three hundred miles away. I panicked. I didn't have room to keep both of them, but I invited Keith to live with me. He turned me down, whether from resentment or loyalty to his sister and his mother, I don't know.

54   For the three weeks that preceded their moving they both stayed in my apartment while their mother looked for a house in Galveston. I remember wanting to give them such a booster shot of myself that they'd never be able to get me out of their systems. I doled out allowances and lunch money just like a real dad, and labored over Sunday dinner so that when we all—my two children and my new wife—would sit down to eat, there'd be some faint reminder that family life was still possible. The Sunday before they left, when they balked at eating at the table (it seemed it was no longer required at home), I complained, hearing my mother's voice coming out of my mouth, that I had slaved in the kitchen for hours so that we could enjoy a Sunday family dinner. Keith retorted, "This isn't our family."

55   I signed up for Sprint and wrote to people I knew in Houston, fifty miles from Galveston, about jobs. On Tuesday, November 16, 1982, I helped them pack; then their mother came and took them.

56   When they were settled, I called them nightly. I kept saying to myself, *It won't be so bad,* but it was. I was tormented by not knowing what the house just off the beach there looked like, how the kids' rooms were decorated. I didn't know anything about their school, and none of their teachers had faces. Their teachers did not know me, either, and so my children were, to them, fatherless. They rode a school bus; on the phone I coaxed from my daughter a yard-by-yard description of the route, picturing how the bus passed over a bridge, with the water below "kind of glittery, you know, when it's early and sun is shining on it," she said.

57   I thought of Chappaquiddick. Frolicking in the surf, they were swept out to sea by riptides, undertow. Sharks cleaved their limbs from their bodies, leaving bloody joints and

stumps. Alone after school, they singed their palms on the stove burners and electrocuted themselves by turning on their hair dryers while standing in the tub.

58 But when I called, Keith was always "fine." Nicole was always "fine," too, even though, unknown to me, a great dark pterodactyl of depression was making a slow bank before gliding in to land on her rib cage. These telephone interrogations were, I suppose, typically fruitless. What did they do in school today? ("Nothing.") Who were their friends? ("Just some kids.") Where did these kids live? ("*Aw,* you know, everywhere.") What did they all do together? ("Just stuff.")

59 The phone was a crucial link. Sometimes I worked to hear in their voices all the minute aspects of their lives, the way I replay small night sounds in my inner ear to judge them malign or benign; while we talked I would ask them where they were sitting, what they had eaten that day, what they were wearing. (They had clothes I had never seen.)

60 To them these interrogations were a rip-roaring bore. I called some five times a week, and invariably they were about to watch *CHiPs,* to eat, to get a call from a friend, or had just gotten out of the shower, and answering my survey was as appealing as having a chat with a magazine-subscription peddler.

61 If there had been trouble at school, then I would not know about it, unless, say, Nicole happened to mention that Keith had been beaten up by some members of a gang *last week* or that he had called his band director an asshole, which Keith would instantly deny, then call Nicole a troublemaker and a liar, leaving me helpless to sort out the facts, let alone impose discipline.

62 Many times when I talked to them I felt I was hearing the kind of bland, remote, and superficial phrases about their lives I was accustomed to giving to my grandparents over the telephone on holidays at my house when I was a child, and this perspective on how little I counted would leave me sad and angry, especially when it was obvious they did not want to talk. "You're not letting them have any choice about when to talk to you," counseled my new wife. "Ease up and give them a chance to call you."

63 Once I waited for days, and finally broke down, convinced then that if I walked altogether out of their lives they would never miss me. "Why didn't you call me?" I whined. "Golly, Dad," they said, "I was going to."

64 Gradually I learned telephone technique. I'd check the TV schedule to avoid pulling them away from their "favorite" shows, though these appeared to be almost anything on prime time. Instead of grilling them I would talk about my day or my work or my car or my wife or my friends. Sometimes I would ask about movies they had seen. This worked especially well with Keith because all twelve-year-old boys have a gene that compels them to describe every frame of a movie orally. I would let the content of his speech wash over me; I would listen instead to his inflection, the structure of his sentences, and to his mood. My ear was a stethoscope pressed to his voice, listening for his heartbeat.

65 These telephone tricks didn't improve the quality of the information I got, but they did keep my frustration at a minimum and let me think that at least my calls were serving their main purpose—to let my children know I still loved them, still missed them, still thought about them. But my anxiety disappeared only when they were present during their monthly weekend visits to Dallas. High anticipation would make me step lightly, whistling, as I made my way down the halls of Love Field to where I would eagerly await their flight from Houston. How wonderful this will be! I would have made a few plans for "family" fun, but, invariably, no sooner would we hug and start to discuss them than things would begin to unravel. Keith would want to see one movie, Nicole another; Nicole would go roller-skating, but Keith wanted to go to a party. Now they were twelve, going on thirteen; they did not mind

using my house as a base of operations (although Keith was usually quick to let me know what offers he had turned down in Galveston), but they weren't enthusiastic about doing anything with Dad.

66 These are the normal aggravations of parenting made more difficult by abnormal circumstances. Playing chauffeur for forty-eight hours, opening my billfold, keeping as effaced as the most well-trained butler, I felt used. By Saturday night I would be soaking in self-pity; by Sunday morning I would be complaining about being mistreated (to which they might once again remind me of what they had given up to be there); by Sunday afternoon I would feel a wave of relief that they would be leaving, but by the time I would see them off, I could imagine how much they really needed me even if they didn't know it, and even some pale, innocuous heat lightning flickering through my windshield in the southern sky would be all I'd need to feel convinced I'd never see them alive again.

67 We Uncle Dads expect so much from these visits. And it's true of the kids too. My friend Jim said about his daughter's visits in the summer that "she's always anxious to get here as soon as possible after her school year is out. She'll start calling us long distance and writing us notes several weeks before she comes. She always sounds so excited about coming, but soon after she arrives a depression sets in."

68 We want these visits to be more "meaningful," like, say, an episode of *The Waltons,* where maybe a couple of orphans with bruised psyches show up and act pissy for two segments before Grandpa gives 'em what-for, Elizabeth charms them, Mary Ellen hugs them, Maw finds them a fine foster home, and John Boy says, "And so Huey and Louie discovered on Walton's Mountain what a family truly means."

69 Most of their visits that spring left me feeling depressed—I had frequent colds and viruses, my blood pressure rose. On Mondays I would struggle to start anew, over

the phone, the way you might hope to convince the hostess of Saturday night's party that some insult had been meant to be taken as a joke.

70 In the late spring disturbing hints seeped in like a slow water leak: What was that? Somebody found a partly smoked joint on the living-room carpet? When? And whose? "Not mine!" all the kids said. The neighborhood was a little wild. Then Nicole was said to have drunk a large glass of vodka once when she was alone in the house. *I just wanted to know what it was like.*

71 When Gay had to go out of town on business, I offered to stay in their house to take care of the kids. The house stood on stilts in a subdivision about a mile back from the beach; it had a high sun deck overlooking a canal laced with palms, and the location looked like every kid's dream—a short walk to the ocean, quiet streets for bike riding. Keith, I was happy to see, appeared to be doing well here. His friends had been teaching him to fish and to surf, and you could see him speeding off to a sandlot baseball game with his glove hooked over the handlebars of his bike. His friends wore run-down sneakers and T-shirts, and when you saw Keith and them with fishing poles over their shoulders they were a living Norman Rockwell *Post* cover. He seemed happy to see me and to introduce me to his friends. I was proud to be introduced, glad that we could claim kinship before people who mattered to him.

72 I found Nicole's new Schwinn ten-speed—this year's Christmas present—in the garage with two flat tires, the cables and spokes and gears corroded by salt spray and gummed with sand. Her room was papered with posters of heavy-metal rock groups on which sets of angry young men clad in black leather and spikes leered and postured. Clothes and papers and used tissue littered the floor; notes from friends were wadded or left lying about where even the most casual eye (and mine was not the most casual) could spot the horrific phrasing of minds just

discovering how to relish the vulgar. Drawings she had done of hollow-eyed, screaming Medusas filled a sketch pad. Behind the shut and locked door she played Pink Floyd at top volume (*"We don't need no ed-you-kay-shun...."*), and I had to pound on the door and scream to get her attention.

73   "Why don't you take better care of your bicycle?"

74   Shrug. Close door. She would shuffle out to fix herself a plate of food, then, moments later, disappear into the yard, and the odor of cigarette smoke would drift into the windows. On Friday night I took her to a dance program given by some of her classmates, where I met her friends; they all seemed older than her thirteen and were dressed in tight jeans and tight T-shirts, dangling earrings, and heavy blue eye shadow — the sort of girls a twenty-one-year-old red-neck cruising in his pickup would imagine to be an easy lay.

75   Saturday, Nicole went out to the sun deck and lay in a bikini on a beach towel. "Would you like to walk down to the beach with me?" I asked. "No," she said. "I just want to get some sun."

76   She looked very pale; her blonde's fair skin has never tanned easily, but in the strong yellow light she looked a cloistered white. Because I thought this might be an opportunity for us to talk, I took her bicycle up onto the sun deck to dismantle it, clean and oil the parts, and restore it to use. Lying prone, she feigned sleep as I scrubbed rust, salt, and sand from gears and cables. I took my time. I remembered how she slept belly down in her playpen, one cheek mashed against the quilt, the other plump and rosy, her Cupid's-bow mouth open and little bubbles of drool on her lip, her fat fingers fisted under her chin. And how I could lift her body with my palm across her chest and hold her over my head, and she would giggle and windmill her arms to imitate a bird. Even now she was still well under five feet tall and under one hundred pounds (and most of that in leg), but the invisible bell jar

she had placed around herself kept me from even trying to hug her. In only a matter of months she had become an utter stranger to me.

77   The next morning, Sunday, I worked in a stranger's kitchen preparing a send-off dinner for myself and them. Gay arrived two hours earlier than expected and I invited her to eat with us. This was the first time in almost two years that we had all sat at a table together. You could hear chewing, forks clinking on plates. Now and then she or I would say something polite, the way you small-talk with a stranger seated beside you on a plane.

78   Nicole picked at her food, then abruptly got up and left the table; just a few seconds later Keith asked to be excused, as though the discomfort of the occasion had caused him to recall his formal manners. I had the feeling they both hated me for the adult's pretense that nothing was different, nothing was wrong. *What right do you have to remind us that you aren't really here?* I ate far beyond hunger, and when I was finished with my own plate, I ate what was left on theirs.

79   I'm luckier than most divorced men, I thought. Four months after this upsetting trip, my children moved back to Dallas and began their eighth grade. Whatever happened now, I would be nearby; I could chauffeur them to malls for shopping, skating, or a movie. They could spend parts of weekends at my apartment without feeling I had stolen all of their leisure time, or I could have them over nights during the week.

80   But they were not the same children. They had contracted adolescence. They ran with a pack at shopping malls on Friday nights. They attended a tough urban school where a custom van with an ear-shattering stereo system showed up promptly at lunchtime to dispense the drug du jour to kids, and where small white boys like Keith were regularly threatened with an ass-kicking from gangs of low-riders. Half the time

he was afraid to go to school, but he learned the art of diplomacy by befriending very large black people.

81   Nicole's friend Alicia lived with her mother except when her mother was on a bender, when she'd go live with her father, a bricklayer, in a trailer park. She was dumb but friendly (rumor had it that she let college boys abuse her sexually). Nicole's friend Angie and her friend Denise dropped acid, stole some credit cards, and took off in a "borrowed" car with some eighteen-year-old boys and were caught two states away, for which Angie spent a month in juvenile detention. Nicole's friend Melissa was always so stoned that her friends had to prop her up in class and walk her down the halls, and she eventually spent several weeks in a drug rehabilitation program. They stole from their mothers' purses; they sniffed paint; they watched X-rated movies on cable. They all had a variety of parents but very little parenting.

82   They had no innocence of any kind, but they were ignorant. They could recite all the lyrics to any Van Halen album, but they didn't know if El Paso was a city or a state. Three of her teachers were very concerned about Nicole, but she was failing all of her classes.

83   And where was I? Largely in the dark. I saw her alarming report cards; I talked to her teachers, but mostly I was bewildered by her sullenness and her distance.

84   I was depressed, too. Having them back in town was not turning out as I had hoped. After a particularly grueling evening with them, I made notes for a new novel I suddenly wanted to write about a father with kids who do not live with him; it would be framed around a single weekend visitation.

85   *All-You-Can-Eat-Night at Pizza Inn. Or "Fat Night" because the buffet attracts all the local white fatties who come to chow down like hogs swathed in polyester stretch pants. The girl and boy have fought in the car on the way here, calling each other "asshole" and "bitch" between front and backseat while he murmurs, "Don't use words like*
that." They're all worn out from a long day, ragged with hunger. In truth, nobody seems to want to be here. They're doing him a favor; he hasn't bought the right to hear them talk about their lives.

86   *When their pizza finally comes, he has to call his son away from a video machine three times, then he tries to make conversation. "What'd you learn in English today?" he asks them. His son chortles. "Okay, here it comes," he says. "It's the family talk." The daughter smirks—you want English? "Dad?" she asks, "have the words bastard and shit been around long?" He could explain the etymologies but decides she's only mocking him.*

87   *He tells his daughter that he wants her to see a psychologist, and an argument breaks out. The son says this is stupid because counselors are stupid. "You want to know something," he says, "just ask me. I know everything there is to know about her." He looks at her. He's got something on her. What is it? He's hostile, belligerent, angry at her, and not too pleased to think that her bad behavior is going to earn her some extra attention. "There's nothing wrong with me," says the daughter to the father. "This is your idea, and I'll bet you'll even make Mom pay for the damn counselor."*

88   *He feels sorry for himself. They disappoint him; he disappoints them. He wants to be a fun dad but also wants to be respected and obeyed and loved; he wants his children to want to please him. The absence of these things in his children distresses him. Their indifference makes him feel ripped off, full of self-pity.*

89   What a baby! When I wasn't bathing in self-pity I could see we had to get Nicole into counseling. She agreed to it, partly out of curiosity and partly because she was a little worried about herself.

90   It was called "adolescent reactive adjustment syndrome," which means skipping school, flunking out, mouthing off, screwing up, getting drunk, taking drugs. Her psychologist was a pleasant and intelligent middle-aged woman who approached life

with a perpetual Happy Face. She gave Nicole a battery of tests about preferences, aptitudes, and attitudes toward parents, self, and peers. Part of the testing involved making up stories to pictures that looked like stills from old movies.

91 (1) *A man is looking out of the frame while a woman clutches at his bicep.* This story, according to Nicole, is about a man who is leaving the woman, his wife, for another woman. The other woman may be involved with the mob and needs to be rescued, but the man cannot tell his wife that. He leaves anyway, and years later when he comes back to apologize, the wife has remarried. There is a child, who is now traveling about playing with a rock band (but he doesn't know anything about that—he listens to jazz). He gets so discouraged that he goes off and buys a winery, becomes an alcoholic, and dies when his car runs into a parked car.

92 (2) *A girl is in a tree looking down onto a sidewalk where another girl is running by.* "Only the girl in the tree is real," says Nicole. The girl below is only an image the girl has of herself. She's wondering what she will be like in the future. The girl "is also running away from something and she doesn't know what it is."

93 (3) *A girl seated on a sofa is looking over her shoulder at a man who is smoking a pipe and leaning over the sofa toward her.* This is her father, and they are having an argument. But the father then goes away to avoid any more argument. "It only goes to show that you can't get anywhere with someone who thinks older means wiser."

94 After several sessions, the counselor reported that Nicole suffered from low self-esteem, and we were advised to accentuate the positive. But when you gave Nicole a compliment, she would counter with, "You're just saying that because *she* told you to make me feel good."

95 She continued to sneak out at night to join her friends; trapped at home, she'd closet herself in her room amid the hurricane winds of the stereo and draw that black-

and-white Fury I first saw in Galveston. The figure had wild, electrified hair, a square jaw, a Frankensteinian forehead, large hollow eyes without pupils, and a howling mouth.

96 What the counselor didn't know was that Nicole was stoned all the time. Her mother and I didn't know it, either. (Keith kept trying to tell us, but he had been caught at so many lies his credibility was low.) Arriving at school each day, she would load up with whatever drugs were available—speed, grass, Valium—and go blotto through her classes; she'd even attend her sessions with her psychologist three quarters under the influence of some chemical moon.

97 Then in April she took a horse tranquilizer (PCP) with the street name of "angel dust." It scrambled her brains. Voices in her head told her to hurt herself; she insisted the voices belonged to real people, characters to whom she gave fablelike names such as Bendikak. They looked like trolls when they popped into the frame of her vision. Some told her to do "good things," and some "bad things."

98 Her counselor advised hospitalization. While we looked for the right place, she was "sentenced" to stay at my house, out of reach of her friends and where my wife and I could keep close watch over her. She was furious and deadly silent. She kept drawing that face and broke off only to construct an odd tableau. Acting obsessed, she found an old Frisbee in the alley, washed it, and turned it rim up; she cut out a page from a magazine depicting a winter woods scene and attached it along one side of the Frisbee's rim like a backdrop; she glued silver glitter to the floor of the disk. I asked what it was. "Snow," she grunted. She next fashioned a small skirted figure out of tinfoil, a girl whose arms were spread in a cruciform position, and mounted it on the glitter-covered "stage." She then dug a clear plastic glass out of the trash and glued it in place mouth-down over the figure. She scissored an arm about the size of her little finger out of white paper and glued the shoulder joint to the top of the glass so that the arm waved

slightly with air currents. It was as if the girl inside the glass had an extra, detached limb which had somehow managed to penetrate to the outside of this otherwise unyielding surface.

99   It was an eerie little sculpture; it would easily have served to illustrate an edition of Sylvia Plath.

100   Going into the hospital was scary for her. A part of her welcomed it because she needed help and knew it might be an interesting experience, but when she realized that she would be kept behind locked doors, she balked. She could not eat or drink when or what she wanted to! She would not be allowed to take so much as a measly aspirin on her own! We were putting her in jail!

101   That night I slept soundly for the first time in two months. I was not only relieved that she was safe. The anxiety I had experienced over the last several weeks had finally equalized my guilt for having been responsible somehow for her condition, and having put her in the hospital gave me a sense of accomplishment. I had earned the right to sleep; I could tell my conscience that I had, for the moment, made payment in full.

102   Her mother, her teachers, her brother, her case workers, and I visited constantly, and we had to learn to deal with the personality that had been buried under that avalanche of chemistry. She was being treated for depression by nonchemical therapies; she had been numb for so long that when her feelings were finally allowed to flow, the wildly oscillating emotional upheaval alarmed her. She deeply resented our "help." Nobody knew her mind except her! Only she could solve her own problems! She didn't *have* any problems!

103   With each visit there were new, recent renderings of the Medusa taped to her wall.

104   But as the weeks went by, she grew more sunny, witty; she had a kooky sense of humor that endeared her to the staff. She made close friends with other girls who had similar problems. Some days she was more like the person I had known — and had all but forgotten — before she moved away to Galveston. She grew hospital-wise and ex-

pressed a desire to someday be a psychologist. ("I acted out in group today, didn't handle things well.")

105   I went to the parents' group, where I discovered the obvious, that such groups are composed of people who share the same problems and that you feel better the instant you realize that. We were a motley crew; we had nothing in common but our troubled children. There was an aging biker with tattoos who wore jeans and a Harley-Davidson T-shirt whose six-year-old son was in the ward; he sat in silence for three sessions, then one day he slumped forward and moaned, "I've been such a lousy father!"

106   Then there were Connie's parents. He wore plaid vested suits and wing tips and had the bland, rabbit-pink face of a midwestern preacher at an upscale Baptist church. His wife might have been a beauty queen at Baylor in the early Fifties. I thought they felt they really shouldn't be there, and I detested them for that. Connie had apparently fallen into bad company.

107   None of their friends had had problems with *their* children, nor, presumably, had any of their friends' friends. They were clearly concerned that Connie would be associating with problem children here at the hospital, and they were also very worried about what their friends would think should they learn about this. They had no idea where Connie was learning to say things such as "Piss off!" They had done everything right. "She's got everything a kid could want," he said. "We have good values."

108   I laughed. I relished their discomfort. I hated them for being so innocent; I hated them because they represented what I yearned to be: a guiltless parent. I acted up; I insulted them by telling them that obviously something had gone wrong somewhere. I should have been sympathetic to their complete bewilderment — they could not find a cause to blame. I could, in my daughter's case. And yet, seeing them agonize, it dawned on me that not everyone in the room was divorced, that such things happened to "nice" folks, too.

109   *Perhaps I was not altogether to blame!*

110 We who have left our children live with the burden of guilt that makes judgment more difficult. When something goes wrong, we immediately go for our own jugular. What I learned in group was that nobody knows for sure why kids go haywire; the causes could be emotional, chemical, spiritual, psychological, genetic, or social. (Or, as it was in Nicole's case, because of depression.) And yet it is obvious that wholesale rejection by a father of his children will most likely leave a lifelong emotional scar, something my old college buddy whose ex-children "don't count" may someday have to face. "Leaving" my children was not a necessary or even sufficient cause for it, but it certainly was a contributory one. My job was to minimize the damage. Whether I was in their home or not, I had better pay as close attention as I possibly could to how they were doing.

111 Nicole got out of stir with walking papers that pronounced her sound again, for which I am immensely grateful to the staff of that hospital. We kept her and her brother in constant motion over the summer — to camp, to Yosemite, to San Francisco, to Los Angeles, to Disneyland (she loved it!) — and she started ninth grade at a high school for the arts. Her first report card showed a string of B's interrupted only by a C in science.

112 Keith recently announced he was tired of living with women, so I invited him to live with me and my wife. He said that he would as soon as I moved into a house where he could have friends over and keep his dog. For a while Nicole kept drawing renditions of that Medusa, though each successive version seemed to represent something like stages of evolution out of the slime. One of the last she did she colored with pastel pencils: the woman has blond hair, high cheekbones with a slight peach flush. Her mouth is closed, and she has feminine lips; she isn't smiling, but the curve of her lips suggests repose. Her jaw has softened, and she has large, pale blue eyes with curving lashes. One brow goes up, the other down, in some faint intimation of melancholy. The old gal seems human now.

113 She gave that one to me. The inscription reads, "To Dad, a very special person who helped me through a lot of hard times. I love you."

114 As proud as I am for having earned those words, and as much as I'd like to end on that upbeat note, the truth is that no trauma is altogether erasable. The other night Nicole and I were talking about her future as an adult; she couldn't decide between being an artist or a psychologist. Well, there's your love life to consider, too, I said. "Oh, I think I'll just live with somebody," she said. "I don't think I'll get married." Why not? "Because then I might have kids and just get divorced."

Some of the names and certain details in this piece have been changed to protect privacy.

EXERCISES

Content

Recall the main ideas in this article by answering the following questions. Respond to some of the questions in your own words. Respond to others by finding quotations from the article that provide the answers.

1. What was the basic household arrangement at the Smith home before the breakup?

2. Who decided to leave, Smith or his wife? What was the plan for the announcement of the breakup? How did this plan turn out in reality? What was Smith's reaction?

3. Provide examples of language that Smith has carefully selected to indicate his feelings shortly after his children learned of the breakup.

4. After the news of the breakup, what "lies" were discussed by Smith and his children at the restaurant?

5. What is the meaning of the term "Uncle Dad"?

6. Who are Elroy and Larry? Why does Smith bring them into his article?

7. What is "quality time"? Why does Smith believe that "quality time," as applied to divorced fathers visiting their kids, is a myth?

8. Why did Smith feel so guilty when his son Keith was injured, even though he was not caring for Keith at the time?

9. What was Smith's domestic situation after the divorce?

10. Why did Smith buy Keith a model airplane? How does he mock himself for doing so?

11. At what point do we first get a hint that Nicole is about to have serious emotional problems?

12. Why were Smith's calls to his children, after they moved to Galveston, so frustrating? How did Smith attempt to lessen the frustration? Why were his kids' monthly visits to him equally depressing?

13. When Smith stays with his children in Galveston, what does he find most disturbing?

14. Why was the "family dinner" in Galveston so uncomfortable for Keith and Nicole?

15. What changes in his kids did Smith observe after they returned to Dallas?

16. What do the italicized paragraphs (85–88) represent?

17. Why is Nicole finally hospitalized? Why did Smith feel better once Nicole was in the hospital? How did she respond to treatment?

18. Why did Smith "detest" Connie's parents? Why did he take pleasure in their discomfort?

19. Why does Smith conclude at one point (paragraph 109), "*Perhaps I was not altogether to blame!*"?

20. What does Smith conclude about his ultimate responsibility for Nicole's condition? What does he decide to do about it?

21. Summarize, in your own words, Smith's feelings at the end of his article.

Structure

1. How are paragraphs 1–5 related to the thesis of the article?

2. Explain how paragraphs 36–38, considered together, form an identifiable section of the article. Give this section a title.

3. Explain how paragraphs 59–64, considered together, form an identifiable section of the article. Give this section a title.

4. Write two more Structure questions and answer them.

Fact/Opinion

Classify each of the following statements as either a fact, an opinion, or a fact wrapped in an opinion. If the statement is a combination of fact and opinion, identify which part is fact and which opinion.

1. "My friend Elroy sent me an essay he had written."

2. "The truth is, though, that children tend to talk seriously only when it's their choice, and that usually comes when the surface of daily routine is glossy, unruffled."

3. "Nicole picked at her food, then abruptly got up and left the table; just a few seconds later Keith asked to be excused, as though the discomfort of the occasion had caused him to recall his formal manners."

Inferences

In your responses to the following questions, incorporate some of the quotations you located in response to the Content questions. You may decide to use either all or only part of each quotation.

1. Why do you think Smith devotes a couple of paragraphs to his father (paragraphs 7 and 8)?

2. What do you think is the meaning of the parenthetical sentence in paragraph 12?

3. What does Smith mean when he says (in paragraph 13) that he "had prematurely nodded to the waiter and the plate was whisked from under my nose"?

4. Compare the announcement scene in Smith's article with the corresponding scenes in the selections by Francke, Cottle, and Updike.

5. Compare the reactions of Smith's children to the news of the divorce with the reactions of the children in the selections by Francke, Cottle, and Updike.

6. In paragraph 44, describing a visit with his kids to the zoo, Smith says, "We [the Uncle Dads] could distinguish each other from the regular, full-time dads because they were allowed to look bored." What does he mean?

7. In what way is the description of Nicole's present, the Barbie Townhouse (paragraph 47), shot through with irony?

8. What kind of games (in Booher's terms) do you detect between Smith, his ex-wife Gay, and their children?

9. What is the function of paragraph 57? ("I thought of Chappaquiddick...") in Smith's article? How is this paragraph related to the final sentence of paragraph 66?

10. In paragraph 82, Smith observes of his kids, "They had no innocence of any kind, but they were ignorant." What does he mean?

11. Discuss the significance of Nicole's Frisbee (paragraph 98). How does her drawing change over time?

Marvin Scott

WHAT MY CHILDREN TAUGHT ME ABOUT DIVORCE

Marvin Scott is a freelance writer. In this article a different perspective on divorce is presented.

1   I used to be a weekend father. Then I got divorced and discovered my two chil- dren and the joys of being a parent. I spend more time with them in divorce than I ever did in marriage.

2   Steven, now going on 13, and Jill, 9, re- acted much like the estimated one million other children who each year are told their

parents are splitting up. First there's shock, then denial and tears. For Jill, it was like a replay of an episode from the TV series *Dallas*. She angrily declared, "Oh, the two of you aren't going to get divorced. You're going to make up like Sue Ellen and J. R."

3　　It's not uncommon for children to engage in magical thinking when the world around them suddenly is collapsing. They were reassured of our love — told that we were divorcing each other, not them. "Mommy and Daddy have been unhappy for a long time, and we feel it is best to separate," their mother reasoned. The children cried themselves to sleep.

4　　I was filled with self-pity and guilt. After all, I was half to blame for this divorce. There were also fears of loneliness, of going broke from legal fees and alimony, and of losing the kids. Would our future be a limited, superficial one?

5　　The indignities of divorce left my estranged wife and me angry and embittered. We let out our frustrations on the children and unwittingly exploited them for emotional support. The lawyers got rich, and the children paid the price. Their schoolwork suffered, and their greatest fear was that Daddy would move far away and rarely see them.

6　　I was determined not to let that happen. And one day I stopped feeling sorry for myself and realized there was no reason to lose them. Even without custody, I could share the responsibility of their upbringing and remain a vital part of their lives.

7　　I began by making them an important part of *my* life. I let them pick out my new apartment — in the building next to theirs. My friends insisted I was crazy to be so close to my ex-wife, but it was one of the best decisions I ever made. It allayed the children's worst fears ... and mine. Being nearby gave them easy access to their father and provided stability during the most unstable period of their young lives. I had made a commitment to my children.

8　　Thus, out of the despair of the divorce, we began laying the foundation for a new

life. In the process, we also gained new insights into each other.

9　　I took advantage of my liberal visitation rights by no longer staying late at the office, or meeting friends for cocktails or dinner — as I had done previously to avoid returning to a home filled with marital tension and conflict. Now there was a reason to go home. And while it would have been easier to take the children out for dinner, I decided at the outset that when they were with me they would be served dinner in my home — their second home. But what did I know about cooking? Absolutely nothing! At most, I could heat a frozen dinner, open a can of tuna or, if I felt adventurous, scramble a couple of eggs.

10　　Could I satisfy my children's insatiable appetites? They became human guinea pigs as I groped through seemingly simple cookbooks with recipes that, to me, resembled formulas concocted by a chemist. I tossed the cookbooks aside and found that the best recipe was common sense — a dab of this and a dash of that. What was most important was that the children and I were sharing time at the dinner table, devoid of tension and without a TV in sight.

11　　The children enjoy helping Daddy prepare meals. They've attached names to some of my more "exotic" dishes, like Steak Marvin, Veal Jill and Shrimp Steven. And they regularly grade me on each new meal. My very first dinner — salad, meat patties and rice — garnered an A+ from Jill. My son gave me only a B+, and that, he explained, was because I gave him too much to eat. My lowest grade was a D for mashed potatoes, which I loused up after adding a gravy concentrate that transformed silky white potatoes into a brownish glob of mush. The greatest compliment came when my ex-wife asked for some of my recipes.

12　　The children teach me too. Like the night Jill admonished me for setting the table incorrectly. "Dad, the fork and napkin are placed to the *left* of the plate," she noted, rearranging the settings.

13　　What we have learned most since the divorce is how to communicate. The dinner table has become a place for nourishment of the mind and soul. In the beginning, it was an arena for letting out the anger over the divorce...mostly my anger. Sure, we talked about other things, but invariably I brought the conversation back to the divorce and bad-mouthed their mother. One evening Steven declared that he couldn't take it anymore: "Mom says bad things about you, and you say bad things about her. It's your divorce, not mine. You're angry with each other, and I love you both." He said he was glad when his mother and I argued on the telephone because "you get everything out, and I don't have to be a messenger." He added, "I don't like being a messenger. I'm a kid."

14 The bad-mouthing has stopped. The children are also discouraged from speaking badly of their mother when they are upset over her disciplinary actions. Dinner conversations these days focus more on what the children are up to — and, of course, on what I am doing. I listen a lot. I try to be reassuring, build their self-esteem and criticize constructively.

15 Children are naturally curious, and mine asked many questions about the breakup. It is not fair to taint a child's image of a parent — his role model. I resist the temptation to respond to questions and promise to tell my children whatever they want to know when they're older — perhaps 18 or so. "Maybe we won't want to know then," Jill exclaimed. Hopefully they won't.

16 They frequently ask sex-related questions. Since honesty is the foundation of a good relationship, I answer truthfully but discreetly. I'm often amazed about how much they already know. They also enjoy hearing about my girlfriends: Are they pretty, who do you like the best, and are you going to get married?

17 Some divorced fathers tend to act like social directors on a cruise ship, planning special activities to keep their children entertained during visits. Going to the movies, the theater or sporting activities are occasional treats, but I have found that doing simple

things at home is appreciated just as much and sometimes is more enjoyable. Steven and Jill love going through the picture albums with me. We do homework together, play trivia games and watch television. And they spend much time in their own room, playing with the computer I bought them for Christmas or with friends, whom they're encouraged to invite.

18 Vacations are also very special times. The first time we went away without their mother, I was petrified. But we made it a joint adventure, deciding together on our activities. That gave them a sense of responsibility. There were moments, however, when I thought I would lose my mind—when they would fight over the most inane things. Suddenly, I empathized with mothers everywhere, who put up with this every day. I exploded. Then I found the solution. I left the room. When I returned five minutes later, tranquility had been restored. I guess all kids instinctively have to put their parents to the tolerance test.

19 It rained a good deal on our vacation. But Steven put it in the right perspective when he said, "It doesn't matter if it rains. It'll be a good vacation because we're together." It was. I hated to bring them back.

20 Although I have no problem being a buddy to my children, I am first and foremost their father. And while there is a temptation to overindulge these children of divorce, there are times I have to get my hands dirty fathering. Children have to be disciplined for the right reasons. One of the ironies of child-rearing is that children who are allowed to do whatever they like end up feeling resentful. Disciplining may cause some tears and temporary tension, but most children subconsciously understand and get the message that the parent really cares. All of my judgment calls haven't been right, and I admit when I'm wrong. One night, I was particularly jumpy and ordered the children to bed. I immediately felt guilty for overreacting and apologized. My daughter comforted me. "It's OK, Daddy," she said. "Nobody's perfect."

21   Perhaps the most difficult adjustment for me was reaching a level of maturity that enabled me to invite my ex-wife to dinner. We discussed ways to heal the psychological scars we both had inflicted on our children. We began by calling a truce to our hostilities. We are now able to share special moments in the children's lives together.

22   I marvel over how Steven and Jill have matured in the two years since the separation. They are more resilient, independent and confident. And I am wiser and a much better parent than I ever thought I'd be.

EXERCISES

Content

Recall the main ideas in this article by answering the following questions. Respond to some of the questions in your own words. Respond to others by finding quotations from the article that provide the answers.

1. How did the divorce affect Scott's relationship with his children?

2. In what ways did the early dinner table scenes between Scott and his children resemble some of the games described by Booher in her article?

3. How have the dinners become a way for Scott and his children to forge a better relationship?

4. How has Scott handled the problem of discipline? How has this aspect of fathering also become a learning experience for him?

Structure

1. What is the purpose of paragraphs 4 and 5?

2. How are paragraphs 13–16 related to the thesis of the article?

3. Explain how paragraphs 18 and 19, considered together, form an identifiable section of the article. Give this section a title.

Fact/Opinion

Classify each of the following statements as either a fact, an opinion, or a fact wrapped in an opinion. If the statement is a combination of fact and opinion, identify which part is fact and which opinion.

1. "It's not uncommon for children to engage in magical thinking when the world around them suddenly is collapsing."

2. "Some divorced fathers tend to act like social directors on a cruise ship, planning special activities to keep their children entertained during visits."

Inferences

In your responses to the following questions, incorporate some of the quotations you located in response to the Content questions. You may decide to use either all or only part of each quotation.

1. What *did* Scott's children teach him about divorce?

2. What can you infer about the Scotts' family life before the divorce?

3. What connections do you see between Scott's account and other accounts in this unit of (a) the immediate effects on the children of the divorce and (b) the behavior of the parents during and after the divorce?

4. There are striking differences between this article's tone and some of the others (including Updike's) in this chapter. Scott's attitude toward the divorce and toward himself is also different. Explain some of these differences. How do they affect your own attitudes?

5. How do you account for the fact that Scott appears to have had an easier time forging good relationships with his children than did C. W. Smith ("Uncle Dad")?

6. What parallels do you find between the Wallerstein-Kelly recommendations (in Rooney's article) and Scott's handling of his children?

7. How do Scott's comments on discipline (paragraph 20) parallel what Booher says about games?

Michael Clayton

AFTER 30 YEARS OF MARRIAGE, MY PARENTS DIVORCED

Michael Clayton is a freelance writer. This article is concerned less with the effects of divorce on children than on the parents— after the children have left home.

1 My mother meets me at the airport wearing a smart new coat. She looks radiant and healthy. She hooks an arm in mine and juggles the car keys with her free hand as we cross the parking lot to a new car. My mother never drove until a year ago, and I ask her if she wants me to drive now.

2 "No, no," she insists jauntily.

3 We drive through town along the main street, lit by colored lights, flashing reindeer and bulbous Santas. It's Christmas Eve, and I'm home for the holidays. My mother is talking a mile a minute, and it pleases me that she's talking about herself.

4 The next morning I am gazing from the kitchen window at the snow-covered fields behind the house where I grew up. My mother is making breakfast. She has her back to me.

5 Eventually she breaks the silence and says, "Last summer your father seemed to lose interest in golf. From what I hear, he doesn't go to the club much anymore."

6 I wait, but nothing more is forthcoming. Having said what she wants to say, she changes the subject. When my mother talks about my father these days, she does so tactfully, economically and without an edge in her voice. This makes things a lot easier for both of us. After all, it's been three years now since they were divorced.

7 My parents split up after thirty years of marriage. My father moved to the other side of town and took up with a woman ten years younger than he. I called him before my arrival and told him I would spend Christmas Day with my mother. After breakfast I call him again, and we arrange to get together the next day.

8 It is snowing when he arrives to pick me up. He honks the car horn from the end of the driveway; I know he prefers not to come in. My parents have agreed that it's better this way. When they need to talk, they talk by phone.

9 It's a Saturday, and we drive across town to see my sister and her family. The kids make a big fuss over my father, and hardly recognize me, the stranger from the distant city. My father has a new camera, and he takes lots of pictures of the kids. Photogra-

phy is his new hobby, he says. He and my sister's husband talk about the play-offs, and I notice that my father never mentions golf, a passion of many years. In a way I can guess why: His life is taken up with new interests.

10   Around noon we drive into town. My father tells me he's thinking of retiring, packing in the business. I ask him why. To travel, he says. We drop by a car showroom to look at new cars and he inspects a few interiors. (He still believes he is being less than true to the American spirit if he doesn't trade in his car every two years.) I ask him when his friend, Jane, will have lunch ready. I make a point of always calling her by name now. Last time I was home, he criticized my reluctance to do so.

11   "We'll eat around one-thirty," he answers. As we leave the car showroom, he proceeds to tell me how good he's been feeling lately. I can see he means it. Something within him has caught fire, and there's new light in his eyes.

12   We're on our way again before he asks about my mother. He wants to know about her driving. I tell him she drives well. He chuckles, and I sense he is proud of her. My father wants to hear everything she's up to, so I tell him. He needs to know, and since there's nothing to gain or lose, I don't mind bringing him up to date.

13   Things have come a long way since the breakup; it wasn't always so easy. First there was the shock, the dislocation. Going home no longer meant the familiar reunion, old family jokes at the kids' expense, legacies of childhood. Going home meant running headlong into tension. In a way, my brother, sister and I were catapulted to a new phase of adulthood. Our parents could no longer pull rank. We became *their* parents almost, the arbiters of what constituted good judgment. They needed our endorsement and support, and we gave as we could.

14   It was a strange feeling when the breakup happened. It's a strange feeling to this day. Their split, as we all realized, could have come at any time in the previous five years. But despite the many omens, it was a

shock. My brother said, "Maybe we had stopped thinking of them as individuals." I understood what he meant. When we left home to pursue lives of our own, we wanted to believe that our parents occupied a quiet, contented cocoon. We were wrong. Without us to provide a strong focus in their lives, they examined each other and found their marriage lacking.

15   I live two thousand miles away from my parents, and they announced their breakup to me over the phone. Separate calls. The news hit me hard and I was unutterably depressed. I remember thinking: "Why can't they grow old gracefully?" I mumbled platitudes, asked if they weren't making a rash decision. After thirty years! At the time I felt that all that distinguished them, all that set them apart from the confusions of my generation, was being sacrificed in a way that belied their age and experience. To me, it seemed like they were undermining their own success.

16   When I got home that first Christmas, the new arrangements were already in place. My father had moved out. Two homes now existed, and neither one felt real. Over the next several days I listened to all their reasons. My father could hardly utter a sentence without some attempt at justification, for he carried a burden of guilt. Even though the decision had been mutual, I saw him as the primary instigator, and I couldn't help but feel angry at him. Still healthy and vigorous in his sixties, it had not taken him long to find a girlfriend.

17   My mother vented herself of many old grievances. She seemed bitter, and she needed to talk. Yet at times her criticisms were directed at herself, as much as at my father, for having allowed a situation to go on too long. On the one hand she felt "dumped" and got furious when my father wanted me to spend a day with him and his new friend. On the other hand, she concurred completely with the decision to break up. She would talk about her "right" to keep the house (which she did), then in the next breath she would acknowledge that my

father had been more than fair about the division of funds.

18   I listened to both of them in turn. I told them flat out that I wasn't taking sides, and my brother and sister each did the same. Occasionally, we siblings would have secret meetings to discuss our strategy. Throughout it all, I kept thinking of a boy in my fifth-grade class whose parents had gotten divorced and everyone knew about it. I remembered he was prone to sullen silences, then to sudden, periodic fits of anger. Thinking of that boy, I was glad I came to know the experience only of late, as a mature adult.

19   As I say, this was three years ago. Divorce is endemic to America, and in a way this helps. For years I had listened to friends' stories of the adjustments they had to make after their parents split up; the strange, often tumultuous circumstances of their growing up; the painful conflicts of loyalty. Now I understood some of their yearnings that their parents stay together. Yet I also understood, as they had told me, that reality eventually takes hold.

20   For me, reality means writing two letters home instead of one, or making two phone calls. When I tell one parent something, I make a mental note also to inform the other. It means being scrupulously fair. It also means keeping some distance while the fray is going on, yet dutifully listening at the same time.

21   It is never easy, but time passes and the new set of rules becomes routine. Then, strangely enough, one discovers that there are even benefits. My mother has taken up a wide range of new interests. My father is more candid than he ever was.

22   "What I have learned," my father told me last Christmas, "is that you can go a certain way for a long time, thinking you are enjoying life, without questioning it. Then you discover that maybe you are not. I thought growing a little vague was the price of growing older. Now I realize it doesn't have to be this way." And I realize that I have rediscovered my parents — perhaps as they rediscov-

ered themselves. My conversations with each of them have certainly improved. Occasionally, I am even asked for my opinion, a comparative rarity in a strong-willed family such as ours. And secrets have been disclosed. My father now tells me stories that he claims he could never tell in deference to my mother. Strangely enough, my mother says the same thing about the items *she* now shares with me.

23   My father, she claims, respected her intelligence, but never cared to see it fully applied if her views conflicted with his. Politics was one example. My father, self-made, would sooner have crossed a busy road blindfolded as vote for a Democrat. My mother was always a liberal at heart. Last year, she joined the local Democratic club. She's a very active member, and she doesn't care what my father thinks.

24   My mother was always better read than my father, and she is animated now as she talks about the current crop of books she's just finished. As I listen to her finely honed criticism, I see all that is alive in her, too. I interrupt to ask her if she has thought of dating other men. She insists that she has no inclination as yet. I believe her, but now I no longer see her aloneness as something to be pitied. . . . I am beginning to see her new life as she sees it: a possession that she values highly.

25   That night, after my mother has gone to bed, I stand at the window gazing at the snow. Already I am thinking of my return home, and I decide I want some photos to take back with me.

26   My mother keeps a box of pictures in an old chest. Digging through them I come across a photo of my parents at a small resort somewhere in northern Michigan. We kids are in the picture too, grinning inanely. The photo was taken in the fifties. We are a family struggling to get ahead. My father's suit is rumpled, my mother's dress is plain. The car in which we are seated is not a smart family sedan, but a broken-down Ford. We look as if we've just edged our way out of the Depression.

27   Yet my parents' faces reflect a sense of determination; a kind of fierce innocence. They are daring for something, and they will prevail. I see my parents now as they are in that picture. They have not undermined themselves—on the contrary. They are each pursuing something in their separate ways, but they are certainly not resigned. Perhaps they are experienced enough to know that there is value in defying the conventional at any age, and that if a person cheats the soul of its satisfactions, the soul has a way of winding down on its own.

EXERCISES

Content

Recall the main ideas in this article by answering the following questions. Respond to some of the questions in your own words. Respond to others by finding quotations from the article that provide the answers.

1. How has Clayton's mother weathered the divorce, three years after it has occurred?

2. In what way was the elder Claytons' divorce different from that faced by many of the other families described in this chapter?

3. Why did Clayton's mother and father split up? What was Clayton's reaction?

4. What does "reality" now mean for Clayton?

5. In what ways has divorce been beneficial for the elder Claytons? In what ways has it been beneficial for Michael Clayton?

Structure

1. What is the purpose of paragraph 7?

2. In which paragraph is the thesis of the article most clearly stated?

3. Explain how paragraphs 13–18, considered together, form an identifiable section of the article. Give this section a title.

4. Write two more Structure questions and answer them.

Inferences

In your responses to the following questions, incorporate some of the quotations you located in response to the Content questions. You may decide to use either all or only part of each quotation.

1. At what point do we learn that Clayton's mother has been divorced? Why do you think he waits for so long to tell us this crucial fact?

2. In paragraph 6, what can you infer about Clayton's mother's attitude toward her ex-husband soon after the breakup occurred? At what point do we learn more about this subject?

3. What can you infer about Clayton's early attitude toward his father's girlfriend?

4. In paragraph 12, Clayton recounts how his father asks for news of his mother. Does the father seem to be playing one of Booher's games—for example, Spy? Why or why not?

5. In paragraph 15, Clayton says that soon after the breakup his "parents could no longer pull rank." What does he mean? What parallels do you see between this situation and the one described by Smith in "Uncle Dad," paragraph 21?

6. What is the significance of the old family picture that Clayton describes at the end of the article? What is the meaning of the final sentence?

 SUMMARY ASSIGNMENT

Write a summary of Rita Rooney's "Helping Children Through Divorce." (You may need to review the procedures discussed in Chapter 2.)

Begin by writing one-sentence section summaries. Then write a thesis for the article as a whole. Next combine your thesis and the section summaries into a coherent summary of the entire article.

We will help get you started by suggesting one way that the first part of the article can be divided into sections and by writing the first one-sentence section summary.

Section 1 (paragraphs 1–6) The Wallerstein-Kelly study throws new light on the long-term effects of divorce on kids.

Section 2 (paragraphs 7–14)

Section 3 (paragraphs 15–17) transition (paragraph 18)

Section 4 (paragraphs 19–23)

Divide the rest of the article into sections, identifying each section with a one-sentence section summary.

PAPER ASSIGNMENTS

1. Write a paper in which you draw one or more *cause and effect* relationships about the children of divorce. (You may also decide to use techniques of description, example, and argument.) Here are some topics to consider from which theses might be generated:

   ■ The emotional effects of divorce on children
   ■ The ways in which children can cope with the trauma of divorce
   ■ The effect of divorce on parental relationships with children
   ■ The ways in which divorced mothers or fathers attempt to forge new and better relationships with their children
   ■ How some parents' ways of going about divorce are better than others'

Having formulated a thesis, read or reread the selections with an eye to finding evidence that will support your thesis.

2. If you are a child of divorce (or if you are a divorced parent), write an essay drawing on your own experiences. Wherever appropriate, refer also to the experiences of the people who are the subjects of this chapter.

3. Interview a friend who has experienced the effects of divorce. Then write an essay describing the relationships between his or her experiences and the experiences of some of the people discussed in this chapter. Show also how your friend's experiences fit (or do not fit) one or more of the patterns of behavior described in this chapter. You may wish to present your essay in the style of one of the articles you have read here.

4. *Describe* and give several *examples* of parents or children who experience comparable aspects of divorce. One such aspect might be the changed attitudes of the child or children toward one or both parents.

5. *Compare and contrast* the experiences of two of the parents in this chapter. Or compare and contrast the experiences of two of the children in this chapter. Consider such criteria as the announcement of the breakup, relations of parents and children during the weeks following the divorce, relations of parents and children during the months or years afterward, adjustment to living a new life, change for the better or worse.

6. In "Uncle Dad," paragraph 110, C. W. Smith discusses the *cause and effect* relationship between divorce and the emotional health of the affected children:

> We who have left our children live with the burden of guilt that makes judgment more difficult. When something goes wrong, we immediately go for our own jugular. What I learned in group [therapy] was that nobody knows for sure why kids go haywire; the causes could be emotional, chemical, spiritual, psychological, genetic, or social. (Or, as it was in Nicole's case, because of depression.) And yet it is obvious that wholesale rejection by a father of his children will most likely leave a lifelong emotional scar, something my old college buddy whose ex-children "don't count" may someday have to face. "Leaving" my children was not a necessary or even sufficient cause for it, but it was certainly a contributory one.

Review three or four of the other articles in this chapter and discuss the extent to which it is reasonable to draw cause and effect relationships between the actions of the parents and the effects on the children. In what cases does cause and effect seem clear? In what cases does it seem uncertain? In cases where it seems uncertain, what other causes could have contributed toward the observed effects?

7. *Argue* that divorce can be a beneficial thing for both parents and children if (as Wallerstein says) it "solves the problems it was meant to solve." Indicate also the conditions under which divorce would not be beneficial.

8. *Argue* that the experience of divorce can bring out both the best and the worst in people.

9. Reread Dr. Lee Salk's column, "Helping Children Deal with Divorce," in the introductory section of this chapter. Then, taking the point of view of one of the authors of the selections in the unit (for example, C. W. Smith) or one of the people written about (for example, one of the implied parents in Booher's article or one of the characters in Updike's story), write a letter to Dr. Salk outlining your problem. Compose also the reply that Salk might write. Note that in the original column, only women wrote to Salk, but you might try composing a letter from a man.

10. Write your own paper assignment for this chapter. Find a common theme running through two or more articles, devise a topic based on this theme, and then write a question asking writers to draw on material in the selections that would support a thesis based on the topic. You might want to help out your writers by suggesting some specific articles or even by getting them started with an outline for the paper.

CHAPTER 12

Ethnic Identity/ Cultural Assimilation

Introduction

Some years ago, Dr. James M. Washington, a professor of church history at New York's Union Theological Seminary, visited Africa on a faculty/student exchange project. Washington, a black man, left the United States at a time when he felt particularly alienated from the country of his birth, at a time when he felt that the West was "a vampire culture which sucks ideas from other cultures and pretends it owes them nothing."

In Africa he felt as if he were returning to his roots:

> As I traveled in, near, beyond the large cities, I told myself over and over again that these were indeed my people. Even though they often stared at me with an unfathomable curiosity, there was a conversation between us that resonated with the painful echoes of our kindred, exiled centuries ago. I was struck by the familiarity of the laughter, the faces, the gestures, the gentleness and the pride, too often mistaken for insolence. . . . Everywhere I turned I felt at home.

But this warm feeling was not to last long. In Ghana, a fourteen-year-old asked him, "'Mister, you an American?'"

> I said to myself, "Can't you see the color of my skin? Can't you see that I too am an African? I don't want to be different from you. I'm your distant cousin. Can't you read my mind? I'm one of you."
>
> I was too slow to answer. Thinking that I hadn't deciphered his broken English, this shrewd youngster put his question the way one finds it in a textbook: "Are you not an American?"
>
> The spiritual "There's No Hiding Place Down Here" came to my mind. He had discovered my secret. I forced a confession from myself and then tossed it toward him.
>
> "Yes," I said begrudgingly, "Yes, I'm one."
>
> With a sharp eye for a bargain, he asked, "You have any sneakers?" He had the undaunted confidence that all Americans are rich. When I told him that I was sorry, but I didn't, he smiled and walked away with his head raised with pride, despite his country's poverty. When he turned away, I realized for the first time that I was seen as a foreigner in my own ancestral land. I realized that I wasn't really at home after all. I was a welcomed guest, not a family member. I had never before experienced such estrangement and loneliness as I felt when I asked myself, "If this isn't home, then where is my home?"

And he came to the realization that "although I identified with Africa, I really did not belong to that great continent."[1]

Dr. Washington's surprise and dismay at being identified by African blacks not as one of them but rather as an American illustrate the personal plight that is central to this chapter—the identity crisis faced by those who are torn by the conflicting demands of ethnic identification and cultural assimilation. The United States is the most multiethnic society in the world. Its population derives from a vast diversity of cultural backgrounds. But America itself is a culture, with its own distinctive traditions and its own distinctive way of life; and for many immigrants and descendants of immigrants, this creates a dilemma. On the one hand, they take pride in their ethnic heritage and want to retain their ethnic identity. On the other hand, if they are to prosper in American society, they must become American, and this necessarily involves suppressing or de-emphasizing aspects of themselves that may be important. It is one thing for people to make a nostalgic visit to the old country. But, as Dr. Washington found, the old country is likely to treat them not as returning sons and daughters but rather as American visitors.

In this chapter we will focus on two of the largest ethnic groups in our culture: blacks and Hispanics. (Space limitations prevent us from devoting several readings apiece to other sizable ethnic groups in America—for example, Asians, Italians, Irish, and Jews.) We will also pay special attention to the requirements of the comparison-contrast essay.

---

[1] James Melvin Washington, "The Difficulty of Going Home: Reflections on Race and Modernity," *Christian Century*, August 15–22, 1984, 774–77.

To get started, read the following two articles focusing on the problem of ethnic identity and cultural assimilation faced by blacks.

Richard G. Carter

I HAVE A FLAG

1   One of the most difficult things most of us men can do in the interest of standing up for ourselves is to speak out on issues in which we really believe. But most of us never get the opportunity, as we go along doing our everyday things in our everyday way. This was especially true in the late 1950's, before Malcolm X, Muhammad Ali and Dr. Martin Luther King were so well known to us. Those of us who could manage it were employed, others of us treaded water, and still others went down and drowned in despair.

2   But life went on, and like many Black men, I thought *powerful* thoughts, made *powerful* plans but was *powerless* to put them into practice. I sat there, on my journalism degree, in the U.S. Post Office — then a den of hopelessness for college-educated Negroes (as we were called then) unable to find work in their fields.

3   Oh, I tried to get a job, but establishment, i.e., white, newspapers weren't hiring many Blacks 25 years ago, and Black papers, with few exceptions, couldn't provide the kind of security I needed with a wife and two children. So I played it safe.

4   And then, after four years of frustration, I heeded the advice of a good friend, bit the bullet and took a part-time job with a Black weekly, continuing to work nights at the post office. This led, two years later, to my first big-league journalism job, with the town's morning daily.

5   *At last,* I thought, as do so many of us when we finally "make it." I was so elated to have gotten over, I forgot what, besides ability, got me there. I forgot the kind of in-depth reporting on important issues I had

done for that Black weekly, the visibility I had had in that Black community — and proceeded, for the next two years, to throw no stones and make no waves. I reported what was requested and wrote what was expected.

6   You could have colored me *bland.*

7   But all that changed on a night in June 1965 when, as the only Black reporter on staff, I was dispatched to cover an impromptu visit to a new Muslim mosque by the newly crowned world heavyweight champion, Muhammad Ali. Almost as soon as I took my front-row seat, something began happening. It occurred to me, a northern-bred, college-educated "Negro," that this was the first time in my life I'd been part of such a large group of people of my own race. In Muhammad's Mosque No. 1 that night in Milwaukee, a largely white city with stringently segregated housing, it made me feel good. It made me feel like I truly belonged. It made me feel that, somehow, I'd been missing something. But there was more.

8   When Ali spoke, he said many of the things I'd been hearing Malcolm X say. But now they made more sense to me. Ali recalled how, after winning a gold medal at the 1960 Olympic Games in Rome, he was unable to get a cup of coffee at a restaurant in his hometown of Louisville, Kentucky, while an African man was served without incident. "I asked him how *he* could be served when Louisville was *my* home," Ali went on. "And the man told me he was served because he has a flag." Ali paused for a few seconds and then shouted, of his new Islamic religion: "Now *I* have a flag!" The audience of some 300 answered: "That's right!"

9   As the responses escalated, things began

to become clearer in my mind. Although I certainly was no Muslim and always had accepted the benevolence of most whites toward Blacks — despite the evidence of my own eyes — I was agreeing with more and more of what I was hearing on that hot, steamy night. I now was a Black man conscious of the fact I was not alone in a white world but surrounded by and united with other Black people who, like me, were proud.

10   Ali's words "I have a flag!" settled in my mind, along with the pride in being Black that for so long lay dormant beneath the surface of my consciousness — seeking an outlet but unsure when or how to get out. But then I knew I'd never again pass up an opportunity to tell others what I now knew: the truth as I saw it. I too now had a flag — not one of race or religion and not one of red, white and blue, but one of truth — of telling it like it is.

11   In the years since, I've found myself — despite leaving the day-to-day newspaper business for a corporate public-relations career three years after that night in 1965 — speaking out in other ways about my new pride in being a Black man. Over time, some of my flag waving has cost me promotions I deserved. I decline to simply be part of the woodwork, and I demonstrate my ability to

think through problems and come up with recommendations. So, I've gained respect — of the arm's-length variety.

12   And then, about six years ago, in that mystical way of fate, I once again found myself possessed of the means to wave my flag — I now write a weekly column for a newspaper chain in New York's Westchester County. Whether it's chiding white folks for seeking suntans "so they can look like us," or "repudiating" Walter Mondale for failing to consider a Black female running mate, or castigating Britain for granting citizenship to the white South African runner Zola Budd so she could compete in the recent Olympics or pointing out the professionalism of Black journalists — I'm in there, telling the truth as I see it.

13   But as anyone who writes for publication knows, *saying* it doesn't mean people are going to care about or believe it. The many hate letters I receive keep reminding me of this. Yet, every time I read one of them, I recall the night in Milwaukee nearly 20 years ago when I went from being a token Black man to an outspoken Black man — one who treads heavily and steps on a few toes along the way, who refuses to remain in the niche carved out for him by whites. A flag waver of truth.

Patrice Gaines-Carter

THE PRICE OF INTEGRATION

1   It was a subtle but powerful moment that got me thinking about integration and what Blacks have lost since it became a way of life.

2   I was visiting a friend in North Carolina. Her daughter had made the cheerleading squad at her junior high school, and my friend, a former cheerleader herself, was ecstatic. My girlfriend, our husbands and I

grinned as the 13-year-old took position in the living room to show us her cheerleading routine.

3   Our faces fell. The routine was something we couldn't sing, dance or relate to at all. And it wasn't because we're old; it was because my friend's daughter is a minority who has little input into the squad's cheerleading routine and is expected to assimilate.

4   We quickly regained our composure, though, because we know our children need encouragement—always. We clapped and yelled. Then when she left the room we talked about those days when big-legged Black cheerleaders chanted tunes such as "Be calm, be cool, and be collected" while doing a hip strut. Not only was a mother's cheer lost forever but also the common spirit that had surrounded it for generations. How could we face the possibility that our children might never know that those rhythms are good and correct for auditoriums, ball fields and boardrooms and not just for the dance floor?

5   I have always been a little leery of integration, having been the "victim" of the first school-busing effort in Prince Georges County, Maryland. I was forced to leave a tiny Black school to attend an all-white school three times that size.

6   I went from being wanted and known to being unwanted and unknown. I went from being an honor roll student to being a student barely passing each year. I was just as book-smart as ever, but education is more than books. My school-mates—those mirrors of myself who gave me strength to grow by saying that all I did was hip and correct—had been taken away. Being me was no longer acceptable.

7   I was well aware of the significance of what I was doing in integrating that school. To survive those days, I imagined myself a martyr who had sacrificed herself so that others might not have it so difficult. It's true: My child has not gone through most of the humiliation I had to bear when I attended a segregated school in the South. I'm thankful that she didn't have to experience what I endured in Beaufort, South Carolina, where my school rarely had heat. She has never had to watch the white students pass by on brand-new buses while she sat in a broken-down bus for the umpteenth time, waiting for a tow truck. Yet I really question whether she's any better for it. And if so, in what way?

8   It was in Beaufort that I learned to love myself and my folks with a passion, because we had only one another to depend upon. My mother knew all of my teachers because they lived within a rock's throw and they partied together too. We were family, and that togetherness and warmth cannot be duplicated in an integrated environment.

9   Today I try to supplement my daughter's public education by passing on that feeling I gained from a Black school and by instilling within her a love for her Black self. I make sure to expose her to TV shows, books, exhibits of Black talent and history. (I also make sure she observes Dr. King's Birthday.) Later I'll encourage her to attend a Black college so that she can immerse herself in the encouragement, love and support that can come from being in a Black institution. This would give her a chance to educate herself without adjusting to all those social changes she'd have to go through at a white school.

10   And I want her to know some pulsating Black cheers, the kind that used to make my spine tingle and my feet pat and make me jump up and shout, "*Oooweee,* baby!"

Content

Richard G. Carter's "I Have a Flag" and Patrice Gaines-Carter's "The Price of Integration" serve as a good introduction to the theme of this chapter. Both selections deal with the psychic costs of rejecting an ethnic heritage in the process of assimilating to a majority culture.

Richard Carter explains how, after getting a "big league–journalism job" on a white newspaper, he was careful to protect his status by not making any waves, by not doing or writing anything that would mark him as a black man, particularly as an outspoken black man. He was so happy to gain a professional foothold in a white-controlled world that he turned his back on the kind of reporting that had made him effective as a journalist on a black weekly and stopped speaking out on issues in which he believed. As he writes with some bitterness, "You could have colored me *bland.*"

A turning point in his life came when he heard world heavyweight boxing champion Muhammad Ali explain how he had become a convert to the Islamic religion. To Ali, his new religion served as a flag, as a source of pride in his blackness. Inspired, Carter realized that "I now was a Black man conscious of the fact that I was not alone in a white world but surrounded by and united with other Black people who, like me, were proud." Carter's new "flag" became the truth, as he saw it; and armed with his flag he proceeded to speak out on matters that were important to him as a black man. In his new public relations career and in a weekly newspaper column, he "went from being a token Black man to an outspoken Black man." Such outspokenness cost Carter some white support. But it regained for him the sense of pride he lost during the time he failed to speak the truth so that he could "fit into the niche carved out for him by whites."

Patrice Gaines-Carter also had an experience that made her realize how much had been lost by blacks who, anxious to fit into a white-dominated world, had rejected a part of their heritage. When visiting a friend in North Carolina, Gaines-Carter watched her friend's daughter go through her cheerleading routine. "Our faces fell," she recalled. "The routine was something we couldn't sing, dance or relate to at all. And it wasn't because we're old; it was because my friend's daughter is a minority who has little input into the squad's cheerleading routine and is expected to assimilate."

Though this particular incident was somewhat mundane, it caused Gaines-Carter to reflect on what had been gained and what had been lost in the process of assimilating to a white world. She recalled her own childhood in a segregated school in Beaufort, South Carolina, where black children had been humiliated and given second-rate services. While she is glad that her own daughter will not have to endure such indignities, there *were* advantages to growing up in Beaufort, for it was there "that I learned to love myself and my folks with a passion, because we had only one another to depend upon."

When Gaines-Carter moved to Maryland and was bused to an all-white school, "I went from being wanted and known to being unwanted and unknown.... Being me was no longer acceptable." Assimilation had been gained at the cost of identity and self-worth.

Gaines-Carter determined not to allow this to happen to her own daughter. She exposes her daughter as much as possible to black talent and black achievements and will encourage her to attend a black college. She knows that her daughter must assimilate to a white-controlled world, a world that she recognizes is less brutal than the one she knew as a child. At the same time, it will be a more spiritually impoverished world, unless Gaines-Carter is successful in "passing on that feeling I gained from a Black school and... instilling within her a love for her Black self."

Both of these narratives deal with the benefits and the costs of assimilation. Both are by blacks who in their early years endured rejection by whites, and who have since, by accommodating to the white-controlled world, become successful professionals. Both had to give up a part of themselves to achieve this success. For both individuals, particular events made them realize the costs of this "new set of values." For Carter, it was a speech by Muhammad Ali. For Gaines-Carter, it was a cheerleading routine by the daughter of a black friend. Each event became a turning point in the attitudes of the writer, a turning point that led to a new sense of awareness of black heritage, a new pride in black identity, and a rejection of total accommodation to the white world.

There are, of course, differences in the two experiences. First, what caused Carter to rethink his own life was an instance of black pride—the effect of ethnic identity. What caused Gaines-Carter to rethink hers was a soulless cheerleading routine—the effect of cultural assimilation. Second, Carter's new sense of black pride primarily affected his own work. Gaines-Carter's new attitude will primarily affect her daughter's life. What is most significant, however, is that both writers came to recognize the psychic cost of turning their backs on their own ethnic identity.

Using Comparison-Contrast in Papers

Comparing and contrasting is a common feature of daily life as well as of writing. How does your current romantic interest compare with your previous one? How does college English compare to high school English?

A comparison is a discussion of similarities, and a contrast is a discussion of differences between two or more people, places, or things. Comparison-contrast discussions encourage you to focus on details that illuminate the people, items, readings, or whatever else is being compared. If you were debating which of two brands of gloves to buy, you might compare the prices, the stitching, and the insulation. Based on these separate comparisons, you'd gain specific information about the gloves and then make your choice.

A comparative analysis makes sense only when you compare elements of the same substance or type. A comparison of the insulation of one glove with the stitching of the other glove would lead to no useful conclusion. Categories of comparison should also be significant. Why spend your time comparing the printing on the labels of the gloves? Choose categories for comparison that will allow you to make meaningful observations.

There are two principal ways of structuring a comparison and contrast essay. Here is the first, in outline form:

Method 1: Summary Approach

Topic sentence (if single paragraph) or thesis (if multiparagraph essay)

Summary of A's (the first person's, place's, or thing's) significant features

Summary of B's significant features

Comparisons of A and B

Contrasts of A and B

Optional: Repetition at the end of the paragraph of the claim made in the topic sentence or thesis

If you turn back to our discussion of the readings in the previous section, "Content," you will see that it has been organized in exactly this manner.

The first paragraph introduces the subject and includes the topic sentence: "Both selections deal with the psychic costs of rejecting an ethnic heritage in the process of assimilating to a majority culture." The next two paragraphs deal with the significant features of "A" — Richard Carter's "I Have a Flag." The next three paragraphs deal with the significance of "B" — Patrice Gaines-Carter's "The Price of Integration."

In the next paragraph (beginning "Both of these narratives...") we compare A and B — that is, we point out the similarities between them. In the last paragraph, we point out two contrasts — differences between the two main articles. Finally, we reiterate the main idea — "both writers came to recognize the psychic cost of turning their backs on their own ethnic identity."

As you can see, this method of comparing and contrasting involves summarizing each item and then discussing the similarities and differences. Generally, the summary approach works best with brief discussions.

The second method of structuring a comparison-contrast essay is to use an element-by-element approach. This method works best with lengthier, more complex discussions. Here it is in outline form:

Method 2 (Element-by-Element Approach)

Topic sentence or thesis

Significant element 1: Compare and contrast A and B with respect to element 1

Significant element 2: Compare and contrast A and B with respect to element 2

Significant element 3 and so on

Optional: Repetition at the end of the essay of the claim made in the topic sentence or thesis

We will get you started on a comparison-contrast paper of these readings and then give you the opportunity to write the rest of the paper.

What are some of the significant elements that are common to the two main readings? There are several. Both readings deal with blacks who in their early years were treated as second-class citizens in a white world. Later, both writers successfully assimilated to white culture. Both writers recount particular incidents that made them realize that their assimilated life, for all of its gains, had involved significant losses as well. Both writers came to see the costs of the conflicting demands of ethnic identity and cultural assimilation. Both writers came to a new recognition of their ethnic heritage and their pride in being black. And both writers had resolved their dilemmas to their own satisfaction (implying that their readers can do the same).

Here's a sample paragraph that deals with the early lives of both writers:

> Both writers recall their earlier years with bitterness and pain. Although he had a journalism degree, Carter was unable to get a job on a white newspaper and had to support himself and his family by working in the U.S. Post Office — "then a den of hopelessness for college-educated Negroes." He did find a job on a black newspaper, but the pay was low, and he had to continue working nights at his Post Office job. Gaines-Carter endured insults and deprivations at a segregated school in Beaufort, South Carolina. Later, when she attended a barely integrated school in Maryland, she found herself deprived of the kind of encouragement and support from her black classmates that had sustained her in Beaufort. As a result, she "went from being an honor roll student to being a student barely passing each year."

Now complete the essay, using as significant elements the suggestions made above (or use significant elements of your own choosing). Include an introductory paragraph. Be sure to point out both similarities (comparisons) and differences (contrasts). And use transitional expressions to help link the comparisons and contrasts.

Four transitional expressions are used to establish a *comparison:*

and   also

as well   similarly

A number of transitional expressions are commonly used to establish *contrasts:*

although	however	while
but	others	yet
by contrast	some	on the one hand
even though	whereas	on the other hand

The transitional words "while," "even though," "although," and "whereas" are subordinate constructions that establish a contrast *within* a sentence:

> *Whereas* Ms. Jones believes that all new employees should enroll in special orientation classes, Mr. Thompson believes that they can learn whatever they need to know on the job.

The other transitional expressions establish a contrast *between* sentences:

> Ms. Jones believes that all new employees should enroll in special orientation classes. *However,* Mr. Thompson believes that they can learn whatever they need to on the job.

Assignment Preview

After you have finished reading the selections in this chapter, write a paper that uses techniques of comparison-contrast. (You may also use other techniques such as description, argument, and cause and effect.) Select a thesis in advance or devise one as you read through the articles. Here are some topics to consider from which theses might be generated:

- The nature of ethnic identity and ethnic pride
- The costs of ethnic identity
- The nature of assimilation
- The costs of assimilation
- A delicate balance between two worlds
- Making adjustments and compromises
- Generational conflicts
- Personal crises
- Redefining one's self
- Resolutions of crises
- The limits of ethnicity
- The limits of assimilation
- Social implications
- Feelings of self-worth and self-hatred

Having formulated a thesis, read or reread the selections with an eye to finding evidence that will support your thesis. Questions following each selection will direct you to some of the important information and ideas.

Nathan Glazer ■ Daniel Patrick Moynihan

BEYOND THE MELTING POT

Sociologist Nathan Glazer has taught at the University of California at Berkeley, Bennington College, Smith College, and, since 1968, Harvard. He is the author (with David Riesman and R. Denny) of the landmark study *The Lonely Crowd* and has also written *American Judaism, Affirmative Discrimination,* and *Ethnic Dilemmas.* Since 1973 he has been coeditor of *The Public Interest* magazine. Daniel Patrick Moynihan, since 1977 a U.S. senator from New York, is equally at home in academia and government. He was a director for the Joint Center for Urban Studies at M.I.T. and Harvard, has taught at the Kennedy School of Government at Harvard, and served as American ambassador to India from 1973 to 1975 and as American ambassador to the United Nations from 1975 to 1976. Among his books are *Maximum Feasible Misunderstanding, A Dangerous Place, Counting Our Blessings,* and *Loyalties.* He is the editor of *Ethnicity: Theory and Experience.* The following selection is from Glazer and Moynihan's co-authored book, *Beyond the Melting Pot: The Negroes, Puerto Ricans, Jews, Italians, and Irish of New York City* (1963).

1   The idea of the melting pot is as old as the Republic. "I could point out to you a family," wrote the naturalized New Yorker, M-G. Jean de Crèvecoeur, in 1782, "whose grandfather was an Englishman, whose wife was Dutch, whose son married a French woman, and whose present four sons have now four wives of different nations. *He* is an American, who leaving behind him all his ancient prejudices and manners, receives new ones from the new mode of life he has embraced. . . . Here individuals of all nations are melted into a new race of men. . . ." It was an idea close to the heart of the American self-image. But as a century passed, and the number of individuals and nations involved grew, the confidence that they could be fused together waned, and so also the conviction that it would be a good thing if they were to be. In 1882 the Chinese were excluded, and the first general immigration law was enacted. In a steady succession thereafter, new and more selective barriers were raised until, by the National Origins Act of 1924, the nation formally adopted the policy of using immigration to reinforce, rather than further to dilute, the racial stock of the early America.

2   This latter process was well underway, had become in ways inexorable, when Israel Zangwill's play *The Melting Pot* was first performed in 1908. The play (quite a bad one) was an instant success. It ran for months on Broadway; its title was seized upon as a concise evocation of a profoundly significant American fact.

3   Behold David Quixano, the Russian Jewish immigrant—a "pogrom orphan"—escaped to New York City, exulting in the glory of his new country:

> . . . America is God's Crucible, the great Melting Pot where all the races of Europe are melting and reforming! Here you stand, good

folk, think I, when I see them at Ellis Island, here you stand in your fifty groups with your fifty languages and histories, and your fifty blood hatreds and rivalries, but you won't be long like that brothers, for these are the fires of God you've come to—these are the fires of God. A fig for your feuds and vendettas! German and Frenchman, Irishman and Englishman, Jews and Russians—into the Crucible with you all! God is making the American.

. . .

...The real American has not yet arrived. He is only in the Crucible, I tell you—he will be the fusion of all the races, the coming superman.

4   Yet looking back, it is possible to speculate that the response to *The Melting Pot* was as much one of relief as of affirmation: more a matter of reassurance that what had already taken place would turn out all right, rather than encouragement to carry on in the same direction.

5   Zangwill's hero throws himself into the amalgam process with the utmost energy; by curtainfall he has written his American symphony and won his Muscovite aristocrat: almost all concerned have been reconciled to the homogeneous future. Yet the play seems but little involved with American reality. It is a drama about Jewish separatism and Russian anti-Semitism, with a German concertmaster and an Irish maid thrown in for comic relief. Both protagonists are New Model Europeans of the time. Free thinkers and revolutionaries, it was doubtless in the power of such to merge. But neither of these doctrines was dominant among the ethnic groups of New York City in the 1900's, and in significant ways this became less so as time passed. Individuals, in very considerable numbers to

be sure, broke out of their mold, but the groups remained. The experience of Zangwill's hero and heroine was *not* general. The point about the melting pot is that it did not happen.

6   Significantly, Zangwill was himself much involved in one of the more significant deterrents to the melting pot process. He was a Zionist. He gave more and more of his energy to this cause as time passed, and retreated from his earlier position on racial and religious mixture. Only eight years after the opening of *The Melting Pot* he was writing "It was vain for Paul to declare that there should be neither Jew nor Greek. Nature will return even if driven out with a pitchfork, still more if driven out with a dogma."

7   We may argue whether it was "nature" that returned to frustrate continually the imminent creation of a single American nationality. The fact is that in every generation, throughout the history of the American republic, the merging of the varying streams of population differentiated from one another by origin, religion, outlook has seemed to lie just ahead—a generation, perhaps, in the future. This continual deferral of the final smelting of the different ingredients (or at least the different white ingredients) into a seamless national web as is to be found in the major national states of Europe suggests that we must search for some systematic and general causes for this American pattern of subnationalities; that it is not the temporary upsetting inflow of new and unassimilated immigrants that creates a pattern of ethnic groups within the nation, but rather some central tendency in the national ethos which structures people, whether those coming in afresh or the descendants of those who have been here for generations, into groups of different status and character.

EXERCISES	

Content

Recall the main ideas in this article by answering the following questions. Respond to some of the questions in your own words. Respond to others by finding quotations from the article that provide the answers.

1. In what way has immigration been restricted, starting in the late nineteenth century?

2. Express in your own words the main idea(s) behind Quixano's speech in Zangwill's *The Melting Pot*.

3. What evidence do Glazer and Moynihan provide that Zangwill himself later became disillusioned with the idea of the melting pot?

4. What has been suggested as a reason that it has taken so long for the various ethnic, religious, and national groups in America to merge into one? To what extent do Glazer and Moynihan accept this reason as valid?

Structure

1. Explain how paragraphs 2–6, considered together, form an identifiable section of the article. Give this section a title.

2. How is paragraph 6 related to paragraph 5?

Fact/Opinion

Classify each of the following statements as either a fact, an opinion, or a fact wrapped in an opinion. If the statement is a combination of fact and opinion, identify which part is fact and which opinion.

1. "The idea of the melting pot is as old as the Republic."

2. "'America is God's Crucible, the great Melting Pot where all the races of Europe are melting and reforming!'"

3. "The point about the melting pot is that it did not happen."

Inferences

In your responses to the following questions, incorporate some of the quotations you located in response to the Content questions. You may decide to use either all or only part of each quotation.

1. Why do you think that Zangwill's vision of the melting pot did not work out as he and so many others imagined it would?

2. Why was it important for people like Zangwill to believe in the idea of the melting pot?

3. Explain what Zangwill meant when he declared (paragraph 6), "'It was vain for [Saint] Paul to declare that there should be neither Jew nor Greek. Nature will return even if driven out with a pitchfork, still more if driven out with a dogma.'"

Gary Soto

LOOKING FOR WORK[1]

Gary Soto is a poet and a professor of Chicano Studies and English at the University of California at Berkeley. Among his collected editions of poetry are *The Tale of Sunlight*, *Father Is a Pillow Tied to a Broom*, and *Black Hair*. He has also written a collection of essays, *Living Up the Street*, from which the following selection is taken. While reading this article, compare Soto's present attitudes (you will have to infer them) with his attitudes as a child toward his ethnic heritage.

1   One July, while killing ants on the kitchen sink with a rolled newspaper, I had a nine-year-old's vision of wealth that would save us from ourselves. For weeks I had drunk Kool-Aid and watched morning reruns of *Father Knows Best,* whose family was so uncomplicated in its routine that I very much wanted to imitate it. The first step was to get my brother and sister to wear shoes at dinner.

2   "Come on, Rick—come on, Deb," I whined. But Rick mimicked me and the same day that I asked him to wear shoes he came to the dinner table in only his swim trunks. My mother didn't notice, nor did my sister, as we sat to eat our beans and tortillas in the stifling heat of our kitchen. We all gleamed like cellophane, wiping the sweat from our brows with the backs of our hands as we talked about the day: Frankie our neighbor was beat up by Faustino; the swimming pool at the playground would be closed for a day because the pump was broken.

3   Such was our life. So that morning, while doing-in the train of ants which arrived each day, I decided to become wealthy, and right away! After downing a bowl of cereal, I took a rake from the garage and started up the block to look for work.

4   We lived on an ordinary block of mostly working class people: warehousemen, egg candlers, welders, mechanics, and a union plumber. And there were many retired people who kept their lawns green and the gutters uncluttered of the chewing gum wrappers we dropped as we rode by on our bikes. They bent down to gather our litter, muttering at our evilness.

5   At the corner house I rapped the screen door and a very large woman in a muu-muu answered. She sized me up and then asked what I could do.

6   "Rake leaves," I answered, smiling.

7   "It's summer, and there ain't no leaves," she countered. Her face was pinched with lines; fat jiggled under her chin. She pointed to the lawn, then the flower bed, and said: "You see any leaves there—or there?" I followed her pointing arm, stupidly. But she had a job for me and that was to get her a Coke at the liquor store. She gave me twenty cents, and after ditching my rake in a bush, off I ran. I returned with an unbagged Pepsi, for which she thanked me and gave me a nickel from her apron.

8   I skipped off her porch, fetched my rake, and crossed the street to the next block where Mrs. Moore, mother of Earl the retarded man, let me weed a flower bed. She handed me a trowel and for a good part of the morning my fingers dipped into the moist dirt, ripping up runners of Bermuda grass. Worms surfaced in my search for deep roots, and I cut them in halves, tossing them to Mrs. Moore's cat who pawed them playfully as they dried in the sun. I made out Earl whose face was pressed to the back window of the house, and although he was calling to me I couldn't understand what he was trying to say. Embarrassed, I worked without looking up, but I imagined his contorted mouth and the ring of keys attached to his belt— keys that jingled with each palsied step. He scared me and I worked quickly to finish the flower bed. When I did finish Mrs. Moore gave me a quarter and two peaches from her tree, which I washed there but ate in the alley behind my house.

9   I was sucking on the second one, a bit of juice staining the front of my T-shirt, when

Little John, my best friend, came walking down the alley with a baseball bat over his shoulder, knocking over trash cans as he made his way toward me.

10   Little John and I went to St. John's Catholic School, where we sat among the "stupids." Miss Marino, our teacher, alternated the rows of good students with the bad, hoping that by sitting side-by-side with the bright students the stupids might become more intelligent, as though intelligence were contagious. But we didn't progress as she had hoped. She grew frustrated when one day, while dismissing class for recess, Little John couldn't get up because his arms were stuck in the slats of the chair's backrest. She scolded us with a shaking finger when we knocked over the globe, denting the already troubled Africa. She muttered curses when Leroy White, a real stupid but a great softball player with the gift to hit to all fields, openly chewed his host when he made his First Communion; his hands swung at his sides as he returned to the pew looking around with a big smile.

11   Little John asked what I was doing, and I told him that I was taking a break from work, as I sat comfortably among high weeds. He wanted to join me, but I reminded him that the last time he'd gone door-to-door asking for work his mother had whipped him. I was with him when his mother, a New Jersey Italian who could rise up in anger one moment and love the next, told me in a polite but matter-of-fact voice that I had to leave because she was going to beat her son. She gave me a homemade popsicle, ushered me to the door, and said that I could see Little John the next day. But it was sooner than that. I went around to his bedroom window to suck my popsicle and watch Little John dodge his mother's blows, a few hitting their mark but many whirring air.

12   It was midday when Little John and I converged in the alley, the sun blazing in the high nineties, and he suggested that we go to Roosevelt High School to swim. He needed five cents to make fifteen, the cost of admission, and I lent him a nickel. We ran home for my bike and when my sister found out

that we were going swimming, she started to cry because she didn't have the fifteen cents but only an empty Coke bottle. I waved for her to come and three of us mounted the bike — Debra on the cross bar, Little John on the handle bars and holding the Coke bottle which we would cash for a nickel and make up the difference that would allow all of us to get in, and me pumping up the crooked streets, dodging cars and pot holes. We spent the day swimming under the afternoon sun, so that when we got home our mom asked us what was darker, the floor or us? She feigned a stern posture, her hands on her hips and her mouth puckered. We played along. Looking down, Debbie and I said in unison, "Us."

13   That evening at dinner we all sat down in our bathing suits to eat our beans, laughing and chewing loudly. Our mom was in a good mood, so I took a risk and asked her if sometime we could have turtle soup. A few days before I had watched a television program in which a Polynesian tribe killed a large turtle, gutted it, and then stewed it over an open fire. The turtle, basted in a sugary sauce, looked delicious as I ate an afternoon bowl of cereal, but my sister, who was watching the program with a glass of Kool-Aid between her knees, said, "Caca."

14   My mother looked at me in bewilderment. "Boy, are you a crazy Mexican. Where did you get the idea that people eat turtles?"

15   "On television," I said, explaining the program. Then I took it a step further. "Mom, do you think we could get dressed up for dinner one of these days? David King does."

16   "Ay, Dios," my mother laughed. She started collecting the dinner plates, but my brother wouldn't let go of his. He was still drawing a picture in the bean sauce. Giggling, he said it was me, but I didn't want to listen because I wanted an answer from Mom. This was the summer when I spent the mornings in front of the television that showed the comfortable lives of white kids. There were no beatings, no rifts in the family. They wore bright clothes; toys tumbled from their closets. They hopped into bed with kisses and woke to glasses of fresh or-

ange juice, and to a father sitting before his morning coffee while the mother buttered his toast. They hurried through the day making friends and gobs of money, returning home to a warmly lit living room, and then dinner. *Leave It To Beaver* was the program I replayed in my mind:

17   "May I have the mashed potatoes?" asks Beaver with a smile.

18   "Sure, Beav," replies Wally as he taps the corners of his mouth with a starched napkin.

19   The father looks on in his suit. The mother, decked out in earrings and a pearl necklace, cuts into her steak and blushes. Their conversation is politely clipped.

20   "Swell," says Beaver, his cheeks puffed with food.

21   Our own talk at dinner was loud with belly laughs and marked by our pointing forks at one another. The subjects were commonplace.

22   "Gary, let's go to the ditch tomorrow," my brother suggests. He explains that he has made a life preserver out of four empty detergent bottles strung together with twine and that he will make me one if I can find more bottles. "No way are we going to drown."

23   "Yeah, then we could have a dirt clod fight," I reply, so happy to be alive.

24   Whereas the Beaver's family enjoyed dessert in dishes at the table, our mom sent us outside, and more often than not I went into the alley to peek over the neighbor's fences and spy out fruit, apricot or peaches.

25   I had asked my mom and again she laughed that I was a crazy *chavalo* as she stood in front of the sink, her arms rising and falling with suds, face glistening from the heat. She sent me outside where my brother and sister were sitting in the shade that the fence threw out like a blanket. They were talking about me when I plopped down next to them. They looked at one another and then Debbie, my eight-year-old sister, started in.

26   "What's this crap about getting dressed up?"

27   She had entered her profanity stage. A year later she would give up such words and

slip into her Catholic uniform, and into squealing on my brother and me when we "cussed this" and "cussed that."

28   I tried to convince them that if we improved the way we looked we might get along better in life. White people would like us more. They might invite us to places, like their homes or front yards. They might not hate us so much.

29   My sister called me a "craphead," and got up to leave with a stalk of grass dangling from her mouth. "They'll never like us."

30   My brother's mood lightened as he talked about the ditch—the white water, the broken pieces of glass, and the rusted car fenders that awaited our knees. There would be toads, and rocks to smash them.

31   David King, the only person we knew who resembled the middle class, called from over the fence. David was Catholic, of Armenian and French descent, and his closet was filled with toys. A bear-shaped cookie jar, like the ones on television, sat on the kitchen counter. His mother was remarkably kind while she put up with the racket we made on the street. Evenings, she often watered the front yard and it must have upset her to see us—my brother and I and others—jump from trees laughing, the unkillable kids of the very poor, who got up unshaken, brushed off, and climbed into another one to try again.

32   David called again. Rick got up and slapped grass from his pants. When I asked if I could come along he said no. David said no. They were two years older so their affairs were different from mine. They greeted one another with foul names and took off down the alley to look for trouble.

33   I went inside the house, turned on the television, and was about to sit down with a glass of Kool-Aid when Mom shooed me outside.

34   "It's still light," she said. "Later you'll bug me to let you stay out longer. So go on."

35   I downed my Kool-Aid and went outside to the front yard. No one was around. The day had cooled and a breeze rustled the trees. Mr. Jackson, the plumber, was watering his lawn and when he saw me he turned

away to wash off his front steps. There was more than an hour of light left, so I took advantage of it and decided to look for work. I felt suddenly alive as I skipped down the block in search of an overgrown flower bed and the dime that would end the day right.

EXERCISES

Content

Recall the main ideas in this article by answering the following questions. Respond to some of the questions in your own words. Respond to others by finding quotations from the article that provide the answers.

1. Why did Soto like to watch such shows as *Father Knows Best* and *Leave It to Beaver?*

2. Why did Soto ask his brother and sister to wear shoes to dinner? What was Rick's response? What other dress suggestion does he later make to his mother?

3. What was Miss Marino's seating arrangement at the Catholic school Soto attended? Where did Soto sit?

4. How does Soto contrast the life of his own family with the life of the typical American TV family?

Inferences

In your responses to the following questions, incorporate some of the quotations you located in response to the Content questions. You may decide to use either all or only part of each quotation.

1. Why do you think "looking for work" was so important to the young Soto?

2. Would you say that Soto had a happy childhood? Why or why not?

3. To what extent were Soto's values and his self-image formed by what he saw on TV?

4. How did Soto view David King?

5. What differences in attitude do you detect between the elder Soto who is narrating this account and the younger Soto who is one of its subjects? How, for instance, do you think the elder Soto now views his ambitions for himself and his family? How does he view the difference in lifestyles between his own family and Beaver's family? How does he use juxtaposition to highlight those differences?

6. To what extent do you think the families in *Father Knows Best* and *Leave It to Beaver* represented actual family life in the United States?

Richard Rodriguez

THE EDUCATION OF RICHARD RODRIGUEZ

Born in San Francisco to Mexican immigrant parents and raised in Sacramento, Richard Rodriguez eventually earned a Ph.D. in English at the University of California at Berkeley. Subsequently, he refused several attractive offers of teaching positions at

prestigious universities and is now a writer living in San Francisco. Rodriguez has published articles in his area of academic expertise, Renaissance studies, but he became well known as a result of his first—and highly controversial—book, *Hunger of Memory: The Education of Richard Rodriguez* (1982). Although the book won high praise for its power as autobiography and for its sentiments on bilingual education (a subject on which Rodriguez has lectured widely), it was also bitterly attacked, particularly by Mexican Americans, for those same ideas. One of these negative reviews is reprinted following the Rodriguez selection. Together, these two passages epitomize the conflict between ethnic identity and assimilation.

1

1   I remember to start with that day in Sacramento—a California now nearly thirty years past—when I first entered a classroom, able to understand some fifty stray English words.

2   The third of four children, I had been preceded to a neighborhood Roman Catholic school by an older brother and sister. But neither of them had revealed very much about their classroom experiences. Each afternoon they returned, as they left in the morning, always together, speaking in Spanish as they climbed the five steps of the porch. And their mysterious books, wrapped in shopping-bag paper, remained on the table next to the door, closed firmly behind them.

3   An accident of geography sent me to a school where all my classmates were white, many the children of doctors and lawyers and business executives. All my classmates certainly must have been uneasy on that first day of school—as most children are uneasy—to find themselves apart from their families in the first institution of their lives. But I was astonished.

4   The nun said, in a friendly but oddly impersonal voice, "Boys and girls, this is Richard Rodriguez." (I heard her sound out: *Rich-heard Road-ree-guess.*) It was the first time I had heard anyone name me in English. "Richard," the nun repeated more slowly, writing my name down in her black leather book. Quickly I turned to see my mother's face dissolve in a watery blur behind the pebbled glass door.

5   Many years later there is something called bilingual education—a scheme proposed in the late 1960s by Hispanic-American social activists, later endorsed by a congressional vote. It is a program that seeks to permit non-English-speaking children, many from lower-class homes, to use their family language as the language of school. (Such is the goal its supporters announce.) I hear them and am forced to say no: It is not possible for a child—any child—ever to use his family's language in school. Not to understand this is to misunderstand the public uses of schooling and to trivialize the nature of intimate life—a family's "language."

6   Memory teaches me what I know of these matters; the boy reminds the adult. I was a bilingual child, a certain kind—socially disadvantaged—the son of working-class parents, both Mexican immigrants.

7   In the early years of my boyhood, my parents coped very well in America. My father had steady work. My mother managed at home. They were nobody's victims. Optimism and ambition led them to a house (our home) many blocks from the Mexican south side of town. We lived among *gringos* and only a block from the biggest, whitest houses. It never occurred to my parents that they couldn't live wherever they chose. Nor was the Sacramento of the fifties bent on teaching them a contrary lesson. My mother and father were more annoyed than intimidated by those two or three neighbors who tried initially to make us unwelcome. ("Keep your brats away from my sidewalk!") But despite all they achieved, perhaps because they had so much to achieve, any deep feeling of ease, the confidence of "belonging" in public was withheld from them both. They regarded the people at work, the faces in crowds, as very distant from us. They were

the others, *los gringos.* That term was interchangeable in their speech with another, even more telling, *los americanos.*

8   I grew up in a house where the only regular guests were my relations. For one day, enormous families of relatives would visit and there would be so many people that the noise and the bodies would spill out to the backyard and front porch. Then, for weeks, no one came by. (It was usually a salesman who rang the doorbell.) Our house stood apart. A gaudy yellow in a row of white bungalows. We were the people with the noisy dog. The people who raised pigeons and chickens. We were the foreigners on the block. A few neighbors smiled and waved. We waved back. But no one in the family knew the names of the old couple who lived next door; until I was seven years old, I did not know the names of the kids who lived across the street.

9   In public, my father and mother spoke a hesitant, accented, not always grammatical English. And they would have to strain — their bodies tense — to catch the sense of what was rapidly said by *los gringos.* At home they spoke Spanish. The language of their Mexican past sounded in counterpoint to the English of public society. The words would come quickly, with ease. Conveyed through those sounds was the pleasing, soothing, consoling reminder of being at home.

10   During those years when I was first conscious of hearing, my mother and father addressed me only in Spanish; in Spanish I learned to reply. By contrast, English (*inglés*), rarely heard in the house, was the language I came to associate with *gringos.* I learned my first words of English overhearing my parents speak to strangers. At five years of age, I knew just enough English for my mother to trust me on errands to stores one block away. No more.

11   I was a listening child, careful to hear the very different sounds of Spanish and English. Wide-eyed with hearing, I'd listen to sounds more than words. First, there were English (*gringo*) sounds. So many words

were still unknown that when the butcher or the lady at the drugstore said something to me, exotic polysyllabic sounds would bloom in the midst of their sentences. Often, the speech of people in public seemed to me very loud, booming with confidence. The man behind the counter would literally ask, "What can I do for you?" But by being so firm and so clear, the sound of his voice said that he was a *gringo;* he belonged in public society.

12   I would also hear then the high nasal notes of middle-class American speech. The air stirred with sound. Sometimes, even now, when I have been traveling abroad for several weeks, I will hear what I heard as a boy. In hotel lobbies or airports, in Turkey or Brazil, some Americans will pass, and suddenly I will hear it again — the high sound of American voices. For a few seconds I will hear it with pleasure, for it is now the sound of *my* society — a reminder of home. But inevitably — already on the flight headed for home — the sound fades with repetition. I will be unable to hear it anymore.

13   When I was a boy, things were different. The accent of *los gringos* was never pleasing nor was it hard to hear. Crowds at Safeway or at bus stops would be noisy with sound. And I would be forced to edge away from the chirping chatter above me.

14   I was unable to hear my own sounds, but I knew very well that I spoke English poorly. My words could not stretch far enough to form complete thoughts. And the words I did speak I didn't know well enough to make into distinct sounds. (Listeners would usually lower their heads, better to hear what I was trying to say.) But it was one thing for *me* to speak English with difficulty. It was more troubling for me to hear my parents speak in public: their high-whining vowels and guttural consonants; their sentences that got stuck with "eh" and "ah" sounds; the confused syntax; the hesitant rhythm of sounds so different from the way *gringos* spoke. I'd notice, moreover, that my parents' voices were softer than those of *gringos* we'd meet.

15   I am tempted now to say that none of this mattered. In adulthood I am embarrassed by childhood fears. And, in a way, it didn't matter very much that my parents could not speak English with ease. Their linguistic difficulties had no serious consequences. My mother and father made themselves understood at the county hospital clinic and at government offices. And yet, in another way, it mattered very much—it was unsettling to hear my parents struggle with English. Hearing them, I'd grow nervous, my clutching trust in their protection and power weakened.

16   There were many times like the night at a brightly lit gasoline station (a blaring white memory) when I stood uneasily, hearing my father. He was talking to a teenaged attendant. I do not recall what they were saying, but I cannot forget the sounds my father made as he spoke. At one point his words slid together to form one word—sounds as confused as the threads of blue and green oil in the puddle next to my shoes. His voice rushed through what he had left to say. And, toward the end, reached falsetto notes, appealing to his listener's understanding. I looked away to the lights of passing automobiles. I tried not to hear anymore. But I heard only too well the calm, easy tones in the attendant's reply. Shortly afterward, walking toward home with my father, I shivered when he put his hand on my shoulder. The very first chance that I got, I evaded his grasp and ran on ahead into the dark, skipping with feigned boyish exuberance.

17   But then there was Spanish. *Español:* my family's language. *Español:* the language that seemed to me a private language. I'd hear strangers on the radio and in the Mexican Catholic church across town speaking in Spanish, but I couldn't really believe that Spanish was a public language, like English. Spanish speakers, rather, seemed related to me, for I sensed that we shared—through our language—the experience of feeling apart from *los gringos.* It was thus a ghetto Spanish that I heard and I spoke. Like those whose lives are bound by a barrio, I was reminded by Spanish of my separateness from *los otros, los gringos* in power. But more intensely than for most barrio children—because I did not live in a barrio—Spanish seemed to me the language of home. (Most days it was only at home that I'd hear it.) It became the language of joyful return.

18   A family member would say something to me and I would feel myself specially recognized. My parents would say something to me and I would feel embraced by the sounds of their words. Those sounds said: *I am speaking with ease in Spanish. I am addressing you in words I never use with* los gringos. *I recognize you as someone special, close, like no one outside. You belong with us. In the family.*

19   (*Ricardo.*)

20   At the age of five, six, well past the time when most other children no longer easily notice the difference between sounds uttered at home and words spoken in public, I had a different experience. I lived in a world magically compounded of sounds. I remained a child longer than most; I lingered too long, poised at the edge of language—often frightened by the sounds of *los gringos,* delighted by the sounds of Spanish at home. I shared with my family a language that was startlingly different from that used in the great city around us.

21   For me there were none of the gradations between public and private society so normal to a maturing child. Outside the house was public society; inside the house was private. Just opening or closing the screen door behind me was an important experience. I'd rarely leave home all alone or without reluctance. Walking down the sidewalk, under the canopy of tall trees, I'd warily notice the—suddenly—silent neighborhood kids who stood warily watching me. Nervously, I'd arrive at the grocery store to hear there the sounds of the *gringo*—foreign to me—reminding me that in this world so big, I was a foreigner. But then I'd return. Walking back toward our house, climbing the steps from the sidewalk, when

the front door was open in summer, I'd hear voices beyond the screen door talking in Spanish. For a second or two, I'd stay, linger there, listening. Smiling, I'd hear my mother call out, saying in Spanish (words): "Is that you, Richard?" All the while her sounds would assure me: *You are home now; come closer, inside. With us.*

22   "*Sí,*" I'd reply.

23   Once more inside the house I would re-sume (assume) my place in the family. The sounds would dim, grow harder to hear. Once more at home, I would grow less aware of that fact. It required, however, no more than the blurt of the doorbell to alert me to listen to sounds all over again. The house would turn instantly still while my mother went to the door. I'd hear her hard English sounds. I'd wait to hear her voice re-turn to soft-sounding Spanish, which assured me, as surely as did the clicking tongue of the lock on the door, that the stranger was gone.

24   Plainly, it is not healthy to hear such sounds so often. It is not healthy to distin-guish public words from private sounds so easily. I remained cloistered by sounds, timid and shy in public, too dependent on voices at home. And yet it needs to be emphasized: I was an extremely happy child at home. I re-member many nights when my father would come back from work, and I'd hear him call out to my mother in Spanish, sounding re-lieved. In Spanish, he'd sound light and free notes he never could manage in English. Some nights I'd jump up just at hearing his voice. With *mis hermanos* I would come run-ning into the room where he was with my mother. Our laughing (so deep was the pleasure!) became screaming. Like others who know the pain of public alienation, we transformed the knowledge of our public separateness and made it consoling—the reminder of intimacy. Excited, we joined our voices in a celebration of sounds. *We are speaking now the way we never speak out in public. We are alone—together,* voices sounded, surrounded to tell me. Some nights, no one seemed willing to loosen the

hold sounds had on us. At dinner, we in-vented new words. (Ours sounded Spanish, but made sense only to us.) We pieced to-gether new words by taking, say, an English verb and giving it Spanish endings. My mother's instructions at bedtime would be lacquered with mock-urgent tones. Or a word like *sí* would become, in several notes, able to convey added measures of feeling. Tongues explored the edges of words, espe-cially the fat vowels. And we happily sounded that military drum roll, the twirling roar of the Spanish *r*. Family language: my family's sounds. The voices of my parents and sisters and brother. Their voices insist-ing: *You belong here. We are family mem-bers. Related. Special to one another. Listen!* Voices singing and sighing, rising, straining, then surging, teeming with pleasure that burst syllables into fragments of laughter. At times it seemed there was steady quiet only when, from another room, the rustling whis-pers of my parents faded and I moved closer to sleep.

2

Supporters of bilingual education today   25 imply that students like me miss a great deal by not being taught in their family's lan-guage. What they seem not to recognize is that, as a socially disadvantaged child, I con-sidered Spanish to be a private language. What I needed to learn in school was that I had the right—and the obligation—to speak the public language of *los gringos*. The odd truth is that my first-grade classmates could have become bilingual, in the conven-tional sense of that word, more easily than I. Had they been taught (as upper-middle-class children are often taught early) a second lan-guage like Spanish or French, they could have regarded it simply as that: another pub-lic language. In my case such bilingualism could not have been so quickly achieved. What I did not believe was that I could speak a single public language.

Without question, it would have pleased   26 me to hear my teachers address me in

Spanish when I entered the classroom. I would have felt much less afraid. I would have trusted them and responded with ease. But I would have delayed—for how long postponed?—having to learn the language of public society. I would have evaded—and for how long could I have afforded to delay?—learning the great lesson of school, that I had a public identity.

27   Fortunately, my teachers were unsentimental about their responsibility. What they understood was that I needed to speak a public language. So their voices would search me out, asking me questions. Each time I'd hear them, I'd look up in surprise to see a nun's face frowning at me. I'd mumble, not really meaning to answer. The nun would persist, "Richard, stand up. Don't look at the floor. Speak up. Speak to the entire class, not just to me!" But I couldn't believe that the English language was mine to use. (In part, I did not want to believe it.) I continued to mumble. I resisted the teacher's demands. (Did I somehow suspect that once I learned public language my pleasing family life would be changed?) Silent, waiting for the bell to sound, I remained dazed, diffident, afraid.

28   Because I wrongly imagined that English was intrinsically a public language and Spanish an intrinsically private one, I easily noted the difference between classroom language and the language of home. At school, words were directed to a general audience of listeners. ("Boys and girls.") Words were meaningfully ordered. And the point was not self-expression alone but to make oneself understood by many others. The teacher quizzed: "Boys and girls, why do we use that word in this sentence? Could we think of a better word to use there? Would the sentence change its meaning if the words were differently arranged? And wasn't there a better way of saying much the same thing?" (I couldn't say. I wouldn't try to say.)

29   Three months. Five. Half a year passed. Unsmiling, ever watchful, my teachers noted my silence. They began to connect my behavior with the difficult progress my older sister and brother were making. Until one Saturday morning three nuns arrived at the house to talk to our parents. Stiffly, they sat on the blue living room sofa. From the doorway of another room, spying the visitors, I noted the incongruity—the clash of two worlds, the faces and voices of school intruding upon the familiar setting of home. I overheard one voice gently wondering, "Do your children speak only Spanish at home, Mrs. Rodriguez?" While another voice added, "That Richard especially seems so timid and shy."

That Rich-heard!   30

31   With great tact the visitors continued, "Is it possible for you and your husband to encourage your children to practice their English when they are home?" Of course, my parents complied. What would they not do for their children's well-being? And how could they have questioned the Church's authority which those women represented? In an instant, they agreed to give up the language (the sounds) that had revealed and accentuated our family's closeness. The moment after the visitors left, the change was observed. "*Ahora,* speak to us *en inglés,*" my father and mother united to tell us.

32   At first, it seemed a kind of game. After dinner each night, the family gathered to practice "our" English. (It was still then *inglés,* a language foreign to us, so we felt drawn as strangers to it.) Laughing, we would try to define words we could not pronounce. We played with strange English sounds, often over-anglicizing our pronunciations. And we filled the smiling gaps of our sentences with familiar Spanish sounds. But that was cheating, somebody shouted. Everyone laughed. In school, meanwhile, like my brother and sister, I was required to attend a daily tutoring session. I needed a full year of special attention. I also needed my teachers to keep my attention from straying in class by calling out, *Rich-heard*—their English voices slowly prying loose my ties to my other name, its three notes, *Ri-car-do.* Most of all I needed to hear my mother and father speak to me in a moment of seriousness in broken—suddenly heartbreaking—English.

The scene was inevitable: One Saturday morning I entered the kitchen where my parents were talking in Spanish. I did not realize that they were talking in Spanish however until, at the moment they saw me, I heard their voices change to speak English. Those *gringo* sounds they uttered startled me. Pushed me away. In that moment of trivial misunderstanding and profound insight, I felt my throat twisted by unsounded grief. I turned quickly and left the room. But I had no place to escape to with Spanish. (The spell was broken.) My brother and sisters were speaking English in another part of the house.

33   Again and again in the days following, increasingly angry, I was obliged to hear my mother and father: "Speak to us *en inglés*." (*Speak.*) Only then did I determine to learn classroom English. Weeks after, it happened: One day in school I raised my hand to volunteer an answer. I spoke out in a loud voice. And I did not think it remarkable when the entire class understood. That day, I moved very far from the disadvantaged child I had been only days earlier. The belief, the calming assurance that I belonged in public, had at last taken hold.

34   Shortly after, I stopped hearing the high and loud sounds of *los gringos*. A more and more confident speaker of English, I didn't trouble to listen to *how* strangers sounded, speaking to me. And there simply were too many English-speaking people in my day for me to hear American accents anymore. Conversations quickened. Listening to persons who sounded eccentrically pitched voices, I usually noted their sounds for an initial few seconds before I concentrated on *what* they were saying. Conversations became content-full. Transparent. Hearing someone's *tone* of voice—angry or questioning or sarcastic or happy or sad—I didn't distinguish it from the words it expressed. Sound and word were thus tightly wedded. At the end of a day, I was often bemused, always relieved, to realize how "silent," though crowded with words, my day in public had been. (This public silence measured and quickened the change in my life.)

At last, seven years old, I came to believe   35 what had been technically true since my birth: I was an American citizen.

But the special feeling of closeness at   36 home was diminished by then. Gone was the desperate, urgent, intense feeling of being at home; rare was the experience of feeling myself individualized by family intimates. We remained a loving family, but one greatly changed. No longer so close; no longer bound tight by the pleasing and troubling knowledge of our public separateness. Neither my older brother nor sister rushed home after school anymore. Nor did I. When I arrived home there would often be neighborhood kids in the house. Or the house would be empty of sounds.

Following the dramatic Americanization   37 of their children, even my parents grew more publicly confident. Especially my mother. She learned the names of all the people on our block. And she decided we needed to have a telephone installed in the house. My father continued to use the word *gringo*. But it was no longer charged with the old bitterness or distrust. (Stripped of any emotional content, the word simply became a name for those Americans not of Hispanic descent.) Hearing him, sometimes, I wasn't sure if he was pronouncing the Spanish word *gringo* or saying gringo in English.

Matching the silence I started hearing in   38 public was a new quiet at home. The family's quiet was partly due to the fact that, as we children learned more and more English, we shared fewer and fewer words with our parents. Sentences needed to be spoken slowly when a child addressed his mother or father. (Often the parent wouldn't understand.) The child would need to repeat himself. (Still the parent misunderstood.) The young voice, frustrated, would end up saying, "Never mind"—the subject was closed. Dinners would be noisy with the clinking of knives and forks against dishes. My mother would smile softly between her remarks; my father at the other end of the table would chew and chew at his food, while he stared over the heads of his children.

39   My *mother!* My *father!* After English became my primary language, I no longer knew what words to use in addressing my parents. The old Spanish words (those tender accents of sound) I had used earlier — *mamá* and *papá* — I couldn't use anymore. They would have been too painful reminders of how much had changed in my life. On the other hand, the words I heard neighborhood kids call *their* parents seemed equally unsatisfactory. *Mother* and *Father*; *Ma, Papa, Pa, Dad, Pop* (how I hated the all-American sound of that last word especially) — all these terms I felt were unsuitable, not really terms of address for *my* parents. As a result, I never used them at home. Whenever I'd speak to my parents, I would try to get their attention with eye contact alone. In public conversations, I'd refer to "my parents" or "my mother and father."

40   My mother and father, for their part, responded differently, as their children spoke to them less. She grew restless, seemed troubled and anxious at the scarcity of words exchanged in the house. It was she who would question me about my day when I came home from school. She smiled at small talk. She pried at the edges of my sentences to get me to say something more. (What?) She'd join conversations she overheard, but her intrusions often stopped her children's talking. By contrast, my father seemed reconciled to the new quiet. Though his English improved somewhat, he retired into silence. At dinner he spoke very little. One night his children and even his wife helplessly giggled at his garbled English pronunciation of the Catholic Grace before Meals. Thereafter he made his wife recite the prayer at the start of each meal, even on formal occasions, when there were guests in the house. Hers became the public voice of the family. On official business, it was she, not my father, one would usually hear on the phone or in stores, talking to strangers. His children grew so accustomed to his silence that, years later, they would speak routinely of his shyness. (My mother would often try to explain: Both his parents died when he was eight. He was raised by an uncle who treated him like little more than a menial servant. He was never encouraged to speak. He grew up alone. A man of few words.) But my father was not shy, I realized, when I'd watch him speaking Spanish with relatives. Using Spanish, he was quickly effusive. Especially when talking with other men, his voice would spark, flicker, flare alive with sounds. In Spanish, he expressed ideas and feelings he rarely revealed in English. With firm Spanish sounds, he conveyed confidence and authority English would never allow him.

41   The silence at home, however, was finally more than a literal silence. Fewer words passed between parent and child, but more profound was the silence that resulted from my inattention to sounds. At about the time I no longer bothered to listen with care to the sounds of English in public, I grew careless about listening to the sounds family members made when they spoke. Most of the time I heard someone speaking at home and didn't distinguish his sounds from the words people uttered in public. I didn't even pay much attention to my parents' accented and ungrammatical speech. At least not at home. Only when I was with them in public would I grow alert to their accents. Though, even then, their sounds caused me less and less concern. For I was increasingly confident of my own public identity.

42   I would have been happier about my public success had I not sometimes recalled what it had been like earlier, when my family had conveyed its intimacy through a set of conveniently private sounds. Sometimes in public, hearing a stranger, I'd hark back to my past. A Mexican farmworker approached me downtown to ask directions to somewhere. "*¿Hijito . . . ?*" he said. And his voice summoned deep longing. Another time, standing beside my mother in the visiting room of a Carmelite convent, before the dense screen which rendered the nuns shadowy figures, I heard several Spanish-speaking nuns — their busy, singsong overlapping voices — assure us that yes, yes, we were remembered, all our family was remembered in their prayers. (Their voices echoed faraway family sounds.) Another day, a dark-

faced old woman—her hand light on my shoulder—steadied herself against me as she boarded a bus. She murmured something I couldn't quite comprehend. Her Spanish voice came near, like the face of a never-before-seen relative in the instant before I was kissed. Her voice, like so many of the Spanish voices I'd hear in public, recalled the golden age of my youth. Hearing Spanish then, I continued to be a careful, if sad, listener to sounds. Hearing a Spanish-speaking family walking behind me, I turned to look. I smiled for an instant, before my glance found the Hispanic-looking faces of strangers in the crowd going by.

43   Today I hear bilingual educators say that children lose a degree of "individuality" by becoming assimilated into public society. (Bilingual schooling was popularized in the seventies, that decade when middle-class ethnics began to resist the process of assimilation—the American melting pot.) But the bilingualists simplistically scorn the value and necessity of assimilation. They do not seem to realize that there are *two* ways a person is individualized. So they do not realize that while one suffers a diminished sense of *private* individuality by becoming assimilated into public society, such assimilation makes possible the achievement of *public* individuality.

44   The bilingualists insist that a student should be reminded of his difference from others in mass society, his heritage. But they equate mere separateness with individuality. The fact is that only in private—with intimates—is separateness from the crowd a prerequisite for individuality. (An intimate draws me apart, tells me that I am unique, unlike all others.) In public, by contrast, full individuality is achieved, paradoxically, by those who are able to consider themselves

members of the crowd. Thus it happened for me: Only when I was able to think of myself as an American, no longer an alien in *gringo* society, could I seek the rights and opportunities necessary for full public individuality. The social and political advantages I enjoy as a man result from the day that I came to believe that my name, indeed, is *Rich-heard Road-ree-guess*. It is true that my public society today is often impersonal. (My public society is usually mass society.) Yet despite the anonymity of the crowd and despite the fact that the individuality I achieve in public is often tenuous—because it depends on my being one in a crowd—I celebrate the day I acquired my new name. Those middle-class ethnics who scorn assimilation seem to me filled with decadent self-pity, obsessed by the burden of public life. Dangerously, they romanticize public separateness and they trivialize the dilemma of the socially disadvantaged.

My awkward childhood does not prove   45 the necessity of bilingual education. My story discloses instead an essential myth of childhood—inevitable pain. If I rehearse here the changes in my private life after my Americanization, it is finally to emphasize the public gain. The loss implies the gain: The house I returned to each afternoon was quiet. Intimate sounds no longer rushed to the door to greet me. There were other noises inside. The telephone rang. Neighborhood kids ran past the door of the bedroom where I was reading my schoolbooks—covered with shopping-bag paper. Once I learned public language, it would never again be easy for me to hear intimate family voices. More and more of my day was spent hearing words. But that may only be a way of saying that the day I raised my hand in class and spoke loudly to an entire roomful of faces, my childhood started to end.

```
┌─────────────────┬──────────────────────────────────────────────┐
│   EXERCISES     │                                              │
└─────────────────┴──────────────────────────────────────────────┘
```

Content

Recall the main ideas in this article by answering the following questions. Respond to some of the questions in your own words. Respond to others by finding quotations from the article that provide the answers.

1. What kind of relationships did the Rodriguez family in Sacramento have with its neighbors?

2. Who were *gringos*? What kind of connotation does the word carry?

3. What were Rodriguez's first experiences with the English language? How did the sound of English affect him? How was he affected by the way his parents spoke English?

4. What does Rodriguez mean when he says that for him Spanish was a private language and English a public language?

5. Why was leaving and reentering his home such a significant, emotionally fraught experience for Rodriguez?

6. In what way did language serve to bind the Rodriguez family closer together?

7. Why is Rodriguez opposed to bilingual education?

8. Why did the three nuns come to the Rodriguez home one day? What significant change in the household developed from that meeting? In what way did this change represent a benefit? In what way did it represent a loss?

9. What was the effect on Rodriguez's mother of the "Americanization" of her children?

10. How did Rodriguez's growing skill with English affect his relationship with his parents?

11. What does Rodriguez mean when he says that "Hearing Spanish...I continued to be a careful, if sad, listener to sounds"?

Structure

1. How is paragraph 4 related to paragraph 3?

2. How is paragraph 16 related to paragraph 15?

3. Explain how paragraphs 29–35, considered together, form an identifiable section of the article. Give this section a title.

4. What is the purpose of paragraph 45?

5. What indications do we have that this passage by Rodriguez is part of a longer structure (a book)?

6. Write two more Structure questions and answer them.

Fact/Opinion

Classify each of the following statements as either a fact, an opinion, or a fact wrapped in an opinion. If the statement is a combination of fact and opinion, identify which part is fact and which opinion.

1. "[Bilingual education] is a program that seeks to permit non-English-speaking children, many from lower-class homes, to use their family language as the language of school."

2. "In public...full individuality is achieved, paradoxically, by those who are able to consider themselves members of the crowd."

Inferences

In your responses to the following questions, incorporate some of the quotations you located in response to the Content questions. You may decide to use either all or only part of each quotation.

1. In what way does the boy teach the adult, as Rodriguez implies in paragraph 6?

2. Why do you think Rodriguez says of his parents (in paragraph 7), "They were nobody's victims"?

3. After his father talked with the gas station attendant, why did Rodriguez, "the very first chance that I got,...[evade] his grasp and [run] on ahead into the dark, skipping with feigned boyish exuberance"?

4. Why is it "not healthy," as Rodriguez asserts, "to distinguish public words from private sounds so easily"?

5. Why do you think it is necessary for Rodriguez to insist that he "was an extremely happy child at home"?

6. Maurice Ferre, the mayor of Miami, has said that Hispanics will demand "maintenance teaching of Spanish at all taxpayers' expense." He explains:

> ...we recognize that culture is vitally important if we are going to be able to solve our problems. The thing that rescues people is pride — pride in their religion, their family, their tradition, their language. As I see it, what is great about America is the system of the Constitution and citizenship. It works because citizenship is what makes us all Americans. Language is not necessary to the system. Nowhere does the Constitution say that English is our language. (Quoted in Thomas P. Morgan, "The Latinization of America," *Esquire,* May 1983, 55–56)

With whom are you in greater agreement on the subject of bilingual education — Ferre or Rodriguez? Explain.

7. What did Rodriguez mean when he says (in paragraph 27) that "I couldn't believe that the English language was mine to use. (In part, I did not want to believe it.)"?

8. Rodriguez notes that once his family started speaking English, he began, increasingly, to stop hearing English and that he was "often bemused, always relieved, to realize how 'silent,' though crowded with words, my day in public had been." What does he mean, and how does this fact reinforce Rodriguez's arguments against bilingual education?

9. In what way is bilingual education a product of the concerns Glazer and Moynihan address in "Beyond the Melting Pot"?

10. Rodriguez says that in public, "full individuality is achieved, paradoxically, by those who are able to consider themselves members of the crowd." What does he mean?

11. Of those who would encourage immigrants and children of immigrants to celebrate their ethnic heritage, Rodriguez says, "Those middle-class ethnics who scorn assimilation seem to me filled with decadent self-pity, obsessed by the burden of public life. Dangerously, they romanticize public separateness and they trivialize the dilemma of the socially disadvantaged." Evaluate this statement. In particular: (a) Why *middle class* ethnics? (b) Why "dangerously"? (c) What does "romanticize" mean in this context? (d) How are these middle-class ethnics "trivializing" a dilemma?

Arturo Islas

REVIEW OF "THE EDUCATION OF RICHARD RODRIGUEZ"
NOBODY'S VICTIM: THE "SCHOLARSHIP BOY" AS WRITER

Arturo Islas earned his Ph.D. at Stanford University and is now a professor in the Stanford English Department. He teaches courses in American literature, autobiography, the novel, and creative writing for bilingual students.

1   Richard Rodriguez is from Sacramento, California. His parents are working class, Mexican immigrants. "They were nobody's victims," Mr. Rodriguez tells us in the first chapter of his autobiography *Hunger of Memory,* recently published by· David Godine of Boston. They reared him and his brother and sisters among the *gringos* and far from the Mexican south side of town. Despite his parents' achievements, "the confidence of 'belonging' in public was withheld from them both." And though their children were educated by nuns whose students were mostly the white sons and daughters of doctors, lawyers and business executives, Mr. and Mrs. Rodriguez retained their distance from *los gringos* who were also *los Americanos.*

2   Their son Richard (or *"Rich-heard"* as the nuns called him) has spent most of his thirty-odd years aware of that distance. His story (told in six chapters and a short prologue) is a description of how his education has made him a "public" person who now feels very uncomfortable in his parents' company. They do not understand why after all those years of education in some of the most prestigious universities in the country—Stanford, Columbia, Berkeley—their son has chosen to leave academic life altogether to write articles about himself and them, as well as about the evils of bilingual education and affirmative action programs.

3   Although he dedicates his book to his parents ("to honor them"), he explicitly states that he is writing "to the *gringos.* " And he writes for those *gringos* who believe that the admission of minority students (especially Blacks and Chicanos) into the privileged educational institutions of the country is a kind of reverse racism. Still, Mr. Rodriguez readily admits that at every opportunity, even after publicly voicing his objections to affirmative action, he willingly reaped the benefits of such programs. As he describes it, his condition is a curious one: he is a "scholarship boy" (a central idea he borrows from Richard Hoggart's *The Uses of Literacy*), who has been "Americanized." Falsely, he accepted minority status in order to be admitted into and rewarded by the very universities who, up until affirmative action programs were established, had systematically excluded students from his background. His education has "changed" him and removed him from the private domain of his parents' home and propelled him into the public realm. He now writes, is a featured speaker at conferences, travels to London, Paris and New York and, no longer self-conscious, jogs without worrying that the sun will darken his skin even more. (An entire chapter is devoted to "Complexion.")

4   In Richard Rodriguez's world, English is "public" and Spanish is "private." Having to learn one language *necessarily* excludes the other, which explains why he is so against bilingual education and feels so alienated from his parents. "Bilingual education is worthless," he said several years ago at a meeting of the English Speaking Union in San Francisco and received the most enthusiastic ovation of the entire conference. It does not occur to him or to those who applaud him that if a nonminority person made such a statement, its impact would be less; they are listening to a "minority student" who has been a good boy and not spoken Spanish on the school grounds. That fact makes Richard Rodriguez, dark and with the face of a Mayan (his description), appealing. They also do not realize that bilingual education as it has been implemented is not a program that

teaches students fluency in two languages; it is a kind of stepping stone program whose basic aim is to teach Spanish-speaking students the *English* language. That it did not work for Mr. Rodriguez does not mean it has not worked for others. And politics aside, any intellectual worthy of the name—and he calls his book an "intellectual autobiography"—can hardly argue against the notion that a truly well-educated person is one who is fluent in more than one language. (Given the extent of the Indo-Hispanic influence in North America, and particularly the western and southwestern regions of this country where Mr. Rodriguez has enjoyed most of his educational opportunities, and given that it is the language of most of the nations of the Western hemisphere, does it not make sense that all members of the university community learn the Spanish spoken on this side of the Atlantic and its *American* dialects and permutations? What is so threatening or fearful about that?)

5   In the almost ten years since his essays against bilingual education and affirmative action programs began appearing with regularity in prestigious North American journals, some of us who have a profound interest in the plight of Hispanics in higher education and who teach courses in "minority" or "ethnic" literature, have been wondering how Richard Rodriguez would work out his continuing and personally constructed dichotomy between public and private language. His autobiography offers no resolution: instead, he is still paralyzed by the dichotomy, unable to reconcile his interest in Milton with the reality of his position as one of the few from his background who has achieved so much, and surely not simply because he was a "minority student."

6   Rodriguez' stance to reject any teaching position until affirmative action programs no longer influence university policy strikes me as sophomoric, as it did his graduate advisor. In his decision to give up academic life, Mr. Rodriguez describes a conversation with a fellow graduate student, Jewish, who has not been offered similar teaching positions. In response to his colleague's charge of injus-

tice, Mr. Rodriguez dismisses as "frantic self defense" the very good reasons that occur to him for such a state of affairs. "The importance of cultural diversity; new blood; the goal of racial integration" become lies to him in the face of the anger focused on him by another minority student whose history of exclusion from Western culture has been part of the curriculum and media for as long as most of us can remember. (When I was one of a few, if not the only, "Spanish surnames" in the 1960 graduating class at Stanford, the Jewish students were the "minority" group fighting against admissions quotas and for more representation on the faculty.) Even if some agree that affirmative action can work unfairly and that it can present philosophical problems for the beneficiaries of it, have we forgotten the years of excluding Blacks and Chicanos from places like Yale and Stanford that gave rise to such policies?

7   His father's response to Mr. Rodriguez' decision is poignant and right on target. "Silent for a moment, he seemed uncertain of what I expected to hear. Finally, troubled, he said hesitantly, 'I don't know why you feel this way. We have never had any of the chances before.'" Exactly. Unassimilated, not fully "Americanized," Rodriguez' father is not afflicted with historical amnesia. Mr. Rodriguez' assessment of his father's puzzlement is characteristic of how the son educated by nuns consistently uses *language* to alienate himself from others. "*We,* he said. But he was wrong. It was *he* who never had any chance before." And his parents, remember, were "nobody's victims." According to their son, it was their fault that they remained unassimilated in the private world of Spanish. Never mind that, like thousands of Hispanic parents of that generation, they were spending most of their time working to support their children's education as much as they could before as well as during the time of affirmative action funding. It is to their son's credit that he brings them to life and pays tribute to them in ways neither he nor they seem to be aware of. What dignity his parents possess, what modesty, how compassionate they are, and always without a

trace of self-pity. All in contrast to the tone of "irony sharpened by self-pity" with which Mr. Rodriguez describes his condition as a "minority student."

8   "Why do you need to tell the *gringos*?" his mother writes in a letter quoted in the last chapter of his book, "Mr. Secrets." And she continues, "Why do you think we're so separated as a family? Do you really think this, Richard?...Do not punish yourself for having to give up our culture in order to 'make it' as you say. Think of all the wonderful achievements you have obtained. You should be proud. Learn Spanish better. Practice it with your dad and me. Don't worry so much." Why, indeed? Exactly for his portrayal of his parents, I am glad he has written about his family. And, yes, he ought to learn (relearn?) his Spanish, even if only to broaden his knowledge of English literature of the renaissance (Spanish influences and connections abound). And to both mother and son, one wants to say that "culture" is not a static condition.

9   The greatest irony at work about this book is that it will be read not so much by the *gringos* into whose society *Rich-heard* wants so desperately to be admitted (in some ways, this book is more about *social* equality than political or economic equality); it will be read and examined closely by those very beneficiaries of affirmative action and bilingual programs who are now beginning to populate universities in increasing numbers. Where would they be, what would have become of them without such programs, including those students Rodriguez dismisses as "middle-class ethnics"?

10   For all its contradictions, *Hunger of Memory* is a well-written description of how an intelligent person can paralyze himself with an intellectual dichotomy. Now and then, Rodriguez wants too much to impress the reader with his sensitivity and erudition (he lists with delight how many books he read as a very young student) and for this reason, his language is occasionally precious and self-conscious in its attempt to beatify the act of writing. (Without realizing how patronizing they sound, critics from outside Mexican-American culture seem surprised that someone with a name like Rodriguez can write English so well.) Mostly, his language touches on surfaces, hovers above the personal but does not allow itself to sink into it. Using English as a weapon, Rodriguez examines the institutions that have shaped his public persona. He has an unquestioned respect for authority and order: his views on policemen, his love for the Catholic Church before it abandoned Latin in favor of the language of "the people," his coy description of the smiling friends who wonder why he is more than an hour late for Sunday brunch, are presented to the reader as pronouncements from on high. Rodriguez makes no attempt to face his fears or to understand deeply his father's silence or to consider seriously why it is that right-wing politicians pay him such tribute. His tone throughout is that of authority, spoken from behind that public mask which he has accepted as real and which allows him to assume the kind of power and confidence he sees the masters possess.

11   How Rodriguez writes his premature autobiography (where will he take it from here now that he has virtually done away with anything private?) offers an interesting twist to what is usually regarded as the most personally revealing of literary genres. His words want passionately to remain removed from the "private" and to consider "public" issues in a "public" way. In the end, we know next to nothing about Richard Rodriguez, the private self, except that it has been wilfully sacrificed in favor of a public persona richly rewarded for giving up its past. He does not understand that the masters are not interested in the private lives of their servants, or that the servant remains a servant because he believes their indifference is divinely ordained.

12   I will ask the students in my classes in minority literature as well as my seminar on "American" autobiography to read this book. Mr. Rodriguez' failure to come to terms with his dichotomies as well as his feelings of alienation from his family are pitiable and ought to be studied carefully.

EXERCISES	

Content

Recall the main ideas in this article by answering the following questions. Respond to some of the questions in your own words. Respond to others by finding quotations from the article that provide the answers.

1. To what contradiction does Islas call attention in paragraph 3?

2. According to Islas, what is the purpose of bilingual education? What is *not* its purpose?

3. How does Islas defend bilingual education programs?

4. Why does Islas want the students in his minority literature class to read Rodriguez's book when he disagrees so much with it? What does he expect them to get out of Rodriguez's ideas?

Structure

1. How is paragraph 9 related to paragraph 3?

2. In which paragraph is Islas's overall assessment of Rodriguez's book stated most clearly?

Fact/Opinion

Classify each of the following statements as either a fact, an opinion, or a fact wrapped in an opinion. If the statement is a combination of fact and opinion, identify which part is fact and which opinion.

1. "Richard Rodriguez is from Sacramento, California."

2. "In Richard Rodriguez' world, English is 'public' and Spanish is 'private.'"

3. "That it did not work for Mr. Rodriguez does not mean it has not worked for others."

4. "His father's response to Mr. Rodriguez' decision is poignant and right on target."

Inferences

In your responses to the following questions, incorporate some of the quotations you located in response to the Content questions. You may decide to use either all or only part of each quotation.

1. What are Islas's main objections to Rodriguez's ideas?

2. Has Islas's review changed your reactions to the Rodriguez passage? Explain.

3. Do you agree with Islas's charge that Rodriguez (and his supporters) have misunderstood the aims of bilingual education?

4. What is the "dichotomy" that Islas claims has paralyzed Rodriguez? Do you agree with Islas? Do you think Rodriguez would agree?

5. Islas implies that Rodriguez has been afflicted with "historical amnesia." What does he mean?

6. Toward the end of his review Islas writes that Rodriguez "does not understand that the masters are not interested in the private lives of their servants, or that the servant remains a servant because he believes their indifference is divinely ordained." What do you think he means by this, in terms of Rodriguez's experiences?

7. Another reviewer of Rodriguez has written: "...the acceptance [Rodriguez] has gained, the public identity he has achieved: was it worth his alienation from his family, from the language of his childhood...need such a high price have been paid?" To this reviewer (Carlos Hortas, writing in the *Harvard Educational Review*), the answers to these questions are clearly "no." What is your opinion? (Do you think Hortas's questions have been fairly phrased?)

Armando Rendón

KISS OF DEATH

Armando Rendón has been affiliated with the U.S. Civil Rights Commission and is the author of *Chicano Manifesto* (from which the following excerpt is taken) and *The Chicano Press: A Status Report on the Needs and Trends in Chicano Journalism*. Like Soto and Rodriguez, Rendón uses his personal history to express his attitudes toward his ethnicity.

1   I nearly fell victim to the Anglo. My childhood was spent in the West Side barrio of San Antonio. I lived in my grandmother's house on Ruiz Street just below Zarzamora Creek. I did well in the elementary grades and learned English quickly.

2   Spanish was off-limits in school anyway, and teachers and relatives taught me early that my mother tongue would be of no help in making good grades and becoming a success. Yet Spanish was the language I used in playing and arguing with friends. Spanish was the language I spoke with my *abuelita,* my dear grandmother, as I ate *atole* on those cold mornings when I used to wake at dawn to her clattering dishes in the tiny kitchen; or when I would cringe in mock horror at old folk tales she would tell me late at night.

3   But the lesson took effect anyway. When, at the age of ten, I went with my mother to California, to the San Francisco Bay Area where she found work during the war years, I had my first real opportunity to strip myself completely of my heritage. In California the schools I attended were all Anglo except for this little mexicanito. At least, I never knew anyone who admitted he was Mexican and I certainly never thought to ask. When my name was accented incorrectly, Réndon instead of Rendón, that was all right; finally I must have gotten tired of correcting people or just didn't bother.

4   I remember a summertime visit home a few years after living on the West Coast. At an evening gathering of almost the whole family—uncles, aunts, nephews, nieces, my *abuelita*—we sat outdoors through the dusk until the dark had fully settled. Then the lights were turned on; someone brought out a Mexican card game, the Lotería El Diablito, similar to bingo. But instead of rows of numbers on a pasteboard, there were figures of persons, animals, and objects on cards corresponding to figures set in rows on a pasteboard. We used frijoles (pinto beans) to mark each figure on our card as the leader went through the deck one by one. The word for tree was called: *Arbol!* It completed a row; I had won. Then to check my card I had to name each figure again. When I said the word for tree, it didn't come at all as I wanted it to; AR-BOWL with the accent on the last syllable and sounding like an Anglo tourist. There was some all-around kidding of me and good-natured laughter over the incident, and it passed.

5   But if I had not been speaking much Spanish up until then, I spoke even less afterward. Even when my mother, who speaks both Spanish and English fluently, spoke to me in Spanish, I would respond in English. By the time I graduated from high school and prepared to enter college, the break was nearly complete. Seldom during college did I admit to being a Mexican-American. Only when Latin American students pressed me

about my surname did I admit my Spanish descent, or when it proved an asset in meeting coeds from Latin American countries.

6   My ancestry had become a shadow, fainter and fainter about me. I felt no particular allegiance to it, drew no inspiration from it, and elected generally to let it fade away. I clicked with the Anglo mind-set in college, mastered it, you might say. I even became editor of the campus biweekly newspaper as a junior, and editor of the literary magazine as a senior—not bad, now that I look back, for a tortillas-and-beans Chicano upbringing to beat the Anglo at his own game.

7   The point of my "success," of course, was that I had been assimilated; I had bought the white man's world. After getting my diploma I was set to launch out into a career in newspaper reporting and writing. There was no thought in my mind of serving my people, telling their story, or making anything right for anybody but myself. Instead I had dreams of Pulitzer Prizes, syndicated columns, foreign correspondent assignments, front-page stories—that was for me. Then something happened.

8   A Catholic weekly newspaper in Sacramento offered me a position as a reporter and feature writer. I had a job on a Bay Area daily as a copyboy at the time, with the opportunity to become a reporter. But I'd just been married, and there were a number of other reasons to consider: there'd be a variety of assignments, Sacramento was the state capital, it was a good town in which to raise a family, and the other job lacked promise for upward mobility. I decided to take the offer.

9   My wife and I moved to Sacramento in the fall of 1961, and in a few weeks the radicalization of this Chicano began. It wasn't a book I read or a great leader awakening me, for we had no Chávezes or Tijerinas or Gonzálezes at the time; and it was no revelation from above. It was my own people who rescued me. There is a large Chicano population in Sacramento, today one of the most activist in northern California, but at the time factionalized and still dependent on the social and church organizations for identity. But together we found each other.

10   My job soon brought me into contact with many Chicanos as well as with the recently immigrated Mexicans, located in the barrios that Sacramento had allocated to the "Mexicans." I found my people striving to survive in an alien environment among foreign people. One of the stories I covered concerned a phenomenon called Cursillos de Cristiandad (Little Courses in Christianity), intense, three-day group-sensitivity sessions whose chief objective is the re-Christianization of Catholics. To cover the story properly I talked my editor into letting me make a Cursillo.

11   Not only was much revealed to me about the phony gilt lining of religion which I had grown up believing was the Church, but there was an added and highly significant side effect—cultural shock! I rediscovered my own people, or perhaps they redeemed me. Within the social dimension of the Cursillo, for the first time in many years I became reimmersed in a tough, *macho ambiente* (an entirely Mexican male environment). Only Spanish was spoken. The effect was shattering. It was as if my tongue, after being struck dumb as a child, had been loosened.

12   Because we were located in cramped quarters, with limited facilities, and the cooks, lecturers, priests, and participants were men only, the old sense of *machismo* and *camarada* was revived and given new perspective. I was cast in a spiritual setting which was a perfect background for reviving my Chicano soul. Reborn but imperfectly, I still had a lot to learn about myself and my people. But my understanding deepened and renewed itself as the years went by. I visited bracero camps with teams of Chicanos; sometimes with priests taking the sacraments; sometimes only Chicanos, offering advice or assistance with badly needed food and clothing, distributed through a bingo-game technique; and on occasion, music for group singing provided by a phonograph or a guitar. Then there were barrio organization

work; migrant worker programs; a rural self-help community development project; and confrontation with antipoverty agencies, with the churches, with government officials, and with cautious Chicanos, too.

13   In a little San Francisco magazine called *Way,* I wrote in a March, 1966, article discussing "The Other Mexican-American":

> The Mexican-American must answer at the same time: Who am I? and Who are we? This is to pose then, not merely a dilemma of self-identity, but of self-in-group-identity.... Perhaps the answer to developing a total Mexican-American concept must be left in the hands of the artist, the painter, the writer, and the poet, who can abstract the essence of what it is to be Mexican in America....When that understanding comes...the Mexican-American will not only have acculturized himself, but he will have acculturized America to him.

If anyone knew what he was talking   14
about when he spoke of the dilemma of who he was and where he belonged, it was this Chicano. I very nearly dropped out, as so many other Mexican-Americans have, under the dragging pressure to be someone else, what most of society wants you to be before it hands out its chrome-plated trophies.

And that mystique—I didn't quite have   15
it at the time, or the right word for it. But no one did until just the last few years when so many of us stopped trying to be someone else and decided that what we want to be and to be called is Chicano.

I owe my life to my Chicano people.   16
They rescued me from the Anglo kiss of death, the monolingual, monocultural, and colorless Gringo society. I no longer face a dilemma of identity or direction. That identity and direction have been charted for me by the Chicano—but to think I came that close to being sucked into the vacuum of the dominant society.

EXERCISES

Content

Recall the main ideas in this article by answering the following questions. Respond to some of the questions in your own words. Respond to others by finding quotations from the article that provide the answers.

1. At what point in Rendón's life did he begin to leave his Mexican heritage behind?

2. Why does Rendón recount the incident of the card game (paragraph 4)?

3. What event served as a turning point in Rendón's life, away from assimilation and back toward his ethnic heritage?

4. What are the "Cursillos de Cristiandad"? Why were they important to Rendón?

Structure

1. Explain how paragraphs 3–7, considered together, form an identifiable section of the article. Give this section a title.

2. What is the purpose of paragraphs 8 and 9?

3. Which paragraph contains the thesis of the article?

4. Write two more Structure questions and answer them.

Fact/Opinion

Classify each of the following statements as either a fact, an opinion, or a fact wrapped in an opinion. If the statement is a combination of fact and opinion, identify which part is fact and which opinion.

1. "My childhood was spent in the West Side barrio of San Antonio."

2. "There was some all-around kidding of me and good-natured laughter over the incident, and it passed."

3. "A Catholic weekly newspaper in Sacramento offered me a position as a reporter and feature writer."

4. "I found my people striving to survive in an alien environment among foreign people."

Inferences

In your responses to the following questions, incorporate some of the quotations you located in response to the Content questions. You may decide to use either all or only part of each quotation.

1. In what ways were Rendón's childhood experiences similar to Rodriguez's? In what ways different? How is Rendón's rediscovery of his ethnicity similar to Richard G. Carter's ("I Have a Flag")?

2. What kind of distinction does Rendón make (in paragraph 13) between "self-identity" and "self-in-group identity"?

3. What do you think Rendón means when he says that when the proper understanding comes, "the Mexican-American will not only have acculturized himself, but he will have acculturized America to him"?

4. What kind of things do you think Rendón is thinking about when he refers to the "chrome-plated trophies" that society hands out (paragraph 14)? Do you think that Richard Rodriguez is after "chrome-plated trophies"?

5. What do you think accounts for the difference between earlier groups of ethnics, who wanted nothing else quite so much as to be assimilated into the American way of life, and people like Rendón, who, finally, turned with revulsion from "being sucked into the vacuum of the dominant society"?

Irving Howe

THE LIMITS OF ETHNICITY

Irving Howe, author, historian, and critic, has taught at Brandeis University, Stanford University, City University of New York, and Hunter College. Among his books are *Politics and the Novel*, *Steady Work*, *Thomas Hardy*, and *World of Our Fathers*, for which he received a National Book Award. The following article first appeared in *The New Republic*.

Americans have often defined themselves   1
through an unwillingness to define themselves. In the work of our greatest writers, notably Melville and Whitman, the refusal to succumb to fixity of definition comes to seem a cultural signature.

In opposition there has arisen a native   2
industry of American-definers who offer a maddening plenitude of answers. But people

in a hurry with answers have usually not even heard the questions. And finally it all comes to the same thing: many answers equal no answer.

3   All through the nineteenth century there was a lot of talk in America about our national character, our unique emerging culture, our new kind of man. Most of it was no more than talk. But the real cultures of America were meanwhile being built up as *regional* cultures, defining themselves apart from and sometimes in opposition to the idea of a single national culture. Our best writers, enraptured with particularities of speech and place, felt that in local custom they might find an essence of the new nation.

4   With time, the regions came to be replaced by immigrant communities. The heterogeneity of nineteenth century America, consisting of regions often at considerable physical and spiritual distance from one another, was followed by the heterogeneity of industrial America, consisting of immigrant subcultures, plebeian and urban, which clung to some indeterminate condition between the remembered Old Country and the not-so-friendly New World.

5   The most recent sign of American heterogeneity has been a turn toward ethnicity. In part, this is mere fashion concocted by TV, publicity and other agencies of deceit. In part, it releases deep impulses of yearning. No one quite knows what ethnicity means: that is why it's so useful a term. For if we will not define ourselves as Americans, we can at least define ourself as fractional or hyphenated Americans, making of that hardy hyphen a kind of seesaw of cultural ambivalence. Or we will define ourselves as pre-Americans, claiming recognition for what can barely still be recognized in us — the heritage of European nationhood and culture.

6   There are plenty of symptoms. There is my own recent book about immigrant Jews [*World of Our Fathers,* 1976], written, I must plead, in innocence of the uses to which it may be put. There is another recent book about the ordeal of black slaves and the journey that one of their descendants made back home. No doubt there will be many more books on such themes, some of them serious and others devoted to making a quick buck.

7   It is all astonishing. In a country long devoted to dulling the sense of the historical past and denying the continuity of experience from Europe to America; in a country where the young can hardly remember the name of Franklin Delano Roosevelt and are by no means sure in which century World War I was fought, or who fought in it — in this very country groups of people now seek to define themselves through a deliberate exclusion from the dominant native stock which, only yesterday, had been taking pains to exclude them. These ethnic groups now turn back — and as they nervously insist, "with pride" — to look for fragments of a racial or national or religious identity that moves them to the extent that it is no longer available. Perhaps, also, *because* it is no longer available.

8   Some of this turning-back strikes me as a last hurrah of nostalgia. Each day, necessarily, it keeps getting weaker and sillier. Traveling around the country recently, I encountered middle-class Jewish ladies intent on discovering their family genealogies. I suggested to them, not very graciously, that if they were serious they would first try to learn their people's history and then they might see that it hardly mattered whether they came from the Goldbergs of eastern Poland or the Goldbergs of the western Ukraine. Other segments of the Jewish community are turning back to the immigrant experience. Some time ago I attended a pageant in an eastern city recreating the Lower East Side: pushcarts, onion rolls, flexibly-priced suits, etc. Someone asked me whether anything was missing and I answered, again not very graciously, that a touch of reality might have been added by a tubercular garment worker spitting blood from his years of exhaustion in a sweat shop.

9   Sentimentalism is the besetting sin of the Jewish turn to ethnicity, a sentimentalism that would erase memories of ugliness and pathology, disputation and radicalism. Among

the blacks things are different. Having been deprived of their history in more brutal ways than anyone else in our society, they have to engage in more extreme measures to retrieve it. Still, one wonders whether some recent assertions of roots are a conquest of history or an improvisation of myth. Tens of thousands of black Americans are expected to be visiting Gambia this summer, and while that is likely to be a boon for the tourist industry of a country that needs every break it can get, one is less certain about what it will do for the tourists. Will it lead to a growing moral strength with which to confront American realities or will it constitute a pleasant style of evasion?

10   Still, I would be the last to deny that there are serious meanings behind ethnic nostalgia. We are all aware that our ties with the European past grow increasingly feeble. Yet we feel uneasy before the prospect of becoming "just Americans." We feel uneasy before the prospect of becoming as indistinguishable from one another as our motel rooms are, or as flavorless and mass-produced as the bread many of us eat.

11   We are losing the passions, the words, the customs of the old countries. Having savored the richness of bilingualism, we find it distressing to be reduced to one language — at most. And so we reach back, clumsily, to a past we know cannot be regained.

12   To the grandeur of the American idea we want to connect the historical substance of the Jewish or black or Slavic experience. All of these subcultures add a little flavor to modern American life, which certainly can use it. Walk into Little Italy and you feel an enclosingness of human bonds that you're not likely to feel in many other parts of New York City. Watch the Greek-Americans parade on Fifth Avenue, with their garish floats evoking symbols not many of the paraders could identify, and you feel, well, let them cling to as much of their past as they can. And as for black culture as an avenue for difference in America — one that brings us into greater sadness and suffering than Americans can

usually confront — that has by now become a virtual cliche of our culture and thereby properly subject to skepticism by blacks themselves.

The famous melting-pot of American 13 society could grow very hot, indeed, too hot for those being melted. Usually it was the immigrants and their children who were the meltees, while the temperature was being regulated by the WASP melters. So by now many of us are rightly suspicious about easy notions concerning cultural assimilation, what might be called the bleaching of America. Some of us remember with discomfort our days in high school when well-intentioned but willful teachers tried to smooth the Jewish creases out of our speech and our psyches. We don't want to be smoothed out — at least entirely, at least not yet. We don't want to yield ourselves completely to that "destruction of memories" which the great sociologist, W. I. Thomas, once said was the essence of the Americanizing process.

Neither should we succumb to the cur- 14 rent uncritical glorification of ethnicity. The ethnic impulse necessarily carries with it dangers of parochialism: the smugness of snug streets as against the perilous visions of large cities, the indulgent celebration of habitual ways simply because they are habitual. The ethnic community always runs the danger that it is not really preserving the riches of an old-world culture; it is merely clinging to some scraps and debris of that culture which were brought across the ocean. At a time when the fate of mankind is increasingly, for better or worse, an *international* fate, the ethnic community too often shuts its eyes or buries its head while clinging anxiously to received customs — as if there were no more important things in the world than customs!

When one thinks a little about the culture 15 of our time, the force of these cautions regarding ethnicity is magnified. At its best and most troubling modernist expression, the culture of the twentieth century has broken past borders of nationhood, race and speech. There is a characteristic pattern here: province runs smack against metropolis, decaying tradition jostles metropolitan experiment—and the result is that brilliant nervousness, that fierce and restless probing we identify with modernist culture. Cavafy from the streets of Alexandria, Faulkner from the hills and villages of Mississippi, Sholom Aleichem from the east European *shtetl* [small town or village], Eliot from a provincial midwestern city, Joyce from the rigid precincts of Dublin—our greatest twentieth century writers leave behind them, though finally they remain deeply stamped by, the limitations of the provincial. The province, the ethnic nest, remains the point from which everything begins and without which, probably, it could not begin; but the province, the ethnic nest, is not enough, it must be transcended.

16   Finally, however, the great weakness of the turn to ethnicity is that it misreads or ignores the realities of power in America. The central problems of our society have to do, not with ethnic groupings, but with economic policy, social rule, class relations. They have to do with vast inequities of wealth, with the shameful neglect of a growing class of subproletarians, with the readiness of policy makers to tolerate high levels of unemployment. They have to do with "the crisis of the cities," a polite phrase masking a terrible reality—the willingness of this country to dump millions of black (and white) poor into the decaying shells of once thriving cities.

17   Toward problems of this kind and magnitude, what answers can ethnicity offer? Very weak ones, I fear. Common action by the poor, major movements for social change require alignments that move past ethnic divisions. They require a tougher perception of the nature of American society than the ethnic impulse usually enables. The dominant powers of American society would be perfectly delighted if, for example, American

blacks were to divert themselves over the next ten or twenty years in seeking their roots in distant Africa, especially if this meant that blacks would thereby lessen their pressure for the jobs, the housing, the opportunities they need here. (Who can say with any assurance that the vivid, if coarse, evocation of the black ordeal in the recent TV version of *Roots* did very much, or anything at all, to persuade white Americans that this society owes a debt to its black minority? Who can say that it raised the consciousness of TV viewers regarding current social policy rather than giving them a momentary *frisson*, an inexpensive thrill of horror?) Social militancy may not always be undermined, social solidarity may not always be threatened, by ethnic or racial consciousness; but too often, in the past, they have been.

In principle, is there any reason why   18 discovering that "black is beautiful" shouldn't lead to the conclusion, "well, if we're beautiful, or even if we're not, we deserve a bigger share of the pie than America has thus far let us get"? No, of course not—in principle. Nor is there any preordained reason why the white ethnic groups could not move from a reconquest of identity to union with other plebeian communities in behalf of shared needs, thereby helping a little to right the wrongs of our society.

This is not just a problem in social   19 strategy; it has also to do with human awareness and self-definition. We want to remain, for the little time that we can, whatever it was that we were before they started pressurizing us in those melting pots. So let's try, even if the historical odds are against us. But there is also another moral possibility, one that we call in Yiddish being or becoming a *mensch*. The word suggests a vision of humanity or humaneness; it serves as a norm, a possibility beckoning us. You don't have to be Jewish (or non-Jewish), you don't have to be white (or black) in order to be a *mensch*. Keeping one eye upon the fading past and the other on the unclear future, enlarging ethnic into ethic, you can become a man or woman of the world, even as you remember, perhaps because you remember, the tongue your grandfather and grand- mother spoke in, though in fact the words themselves are fading from memory.

| **EXERCISES** | |

Content

Recall the main ideas in this article by answering the following questions. Respond to some of the questions in your own words. Respond to others by finding quotations from the article that provide the answers.

1. Howe sees several stages of what he calls "American heterogeneity." What are they?

2. From what sources, according to Howe, does the "turn toward ethnicity" derive? (See paragraphs 10–12 as well as paragraph 5.)

3. Why does Howe feel that he is at least partially to blame for what he sees as an undesirable trend?

4. What does Howe find especially surprising — even paradoxical — about this current trend?

5. What does Howe mean by sentimentalism? Why does he find that people tracing their ethnic origins or participating in ethnic festivals are often being sentimental? Why are blacks less susceptible to such sentimentality than Jews?

6. In what way does the trend toward ethnicity constitute "a pleasant style of evasion"?

7. What does Howe see as the dangers of "the current uncritical glorification of ethnicity"?

8. Why does Howe cite writers like Faulkner, Aleichem, Eliot, and Joyce? What do these writers have in common that ties in with the theme of this article?

9. What does Howe see as the real domestic problems of our time? Why does he find ethnicity as offering few solutions to such problems? Why does he believe that the impulse toward ethnicity can, in fact, prolong such problems?

Structure

1. Explain how paragraphs 3–5, considered together, form an identifiable section of the article. Give this section a title.

2. What is the purpose of paragraph 8?

3. How is paragraph 10 related to the thesis of the article?

4. How is paragraph 14 related to paragraph 13?

5. How is paragraph 17 related to the thesis of the article?

6. Write two more Structure questions and answer them.

Fact/Opinion

Classify each of the following statements as either a fact, an opinion, or a fact wrapped in an opinion. If the statement is a combination of fact and opinion, identify which part is fact and which opinion.

1. "Americans have often defined themselves through an unwillingness to define themselves."

2. "All through the nineteenth century there was a lot of talk in America about our national character, our unique emerging culture, our new kind of man."

3. "The most recent sign of American heterogeneity has been a turn toward ethnicity."

4. "Sentimentalism is the besetting sin of the Jewish turn to ethnicity, a sentimentalism that would erase memories of ugliness and pathology, disputation and radicalism."

Inferences

In your responses to the following questions, incorporate some of the quotations you located in response to the Content questions. You may decide to use either all or only part of each quotation.

1. What does Howe mean when he says, in the opening sentence, "Americans have often defined themselves through an unwillingness to define themselves"? Do you agree with him? Explain.

2. What does Howe imply when he says (at the end of paragraph 7), "Perhaps...*because* it [a racial, national, or religious identity] is no longer available"?

3. Often Howe appears to be looking at particular situations with a cynical eye—that is, he either states or implies that people's motives for behaving or thinking in certain ways are less honorable or idealistic than they would have others believe. What specific evidence do you find of this cynicism? Do you share this cynicism? Why or why not?

4. With what other writers in this unit would Howe seem to be most in sympathy? Least? Explain.

5. In what way do you think that the "Americanizing process" requires what sociologist W. I. Thomas has called the "destruction of memories"?

6. Why are the "historical odds" against our remaining "unmelted"?

7. Discuss the meaning of the final sentence. What does it mean to enlarge "ethnic into ethic"? What does it mean to remember the language our grandparents spoke, "though...the words themselves are fading from memory"?

8. Have you been convinced by Howe's argument that we must transcend ethnicity? Why or why not?

Dennis A. Williams with Tenley-Ann Jackson,
Diane Weathers, Nadine Smith, and Monroe Anderson

ROOTS III: SOULS ON ICE

Dennis A. Williams is a staff writer for *Newsweek*, where this article first appeared. One of the several subjects of comparison-contrast here is between young black attitudes toward their ethnicity now and their attitudes a generation ago.

One ever feels his twoness—an American, a Negro; two souls, two thoughts, two unreconciled strivings; two warring ideals in one dark body, whose dogged strength alone keeps it from being torn asunder. —W. E. B. Du Bois, "The Souls of Black Folk"

Chad Clark, a 15-year-old sophomore at Walter Johnson High School in Bethesda, Md., is popular, well adjusted, good-looking and smart. Nevertheless, his parents, both of whom are lawyers, are worried about his sense of identity. "I have no black friends," Chad says evenly. "Every day I am surrounded by white people." For him, that's no big deal; he is simply living the life his parents wanted for him. What they did not want, however, was for their children to become so integrated into the white community that they have no awareness of their blackness. "Look, I know we didn't come here on the Love Boat," says Chad, who dismisses his parents' concerns as "anachronistic." "I know there are differences beyond skin color. But racist thought is disappearing." His brother Kamani agrees. "I'm in the seventh grade," he says with all the wisdom of his 12 years, "but I haven't seen any racism."

2   Andrea Wilson, 19, knows that racism exists because her mother told her about it. But Andrea grew up admittedly pampered in a totally integrated neighborhood of San Francisco. The first time she visited Mills College across the bay in Oakland, which she now attends, she was "shocked" by the blackness of that city. Many of her Lacoste-and-Calvin Klein black friends remain intimidated by the streets and huddle in the shelter of the campus, largely ignoring racial issues. "I guess we don't even talk about Jesse Jackson or apartheid in South Africa," Wilson says apologetically. "Those issues are brought up by radical white kids."

3   They used to call it "passing": blacks pretending to be white to avoid racial discrimination. Now a lot of black parents, educators and social scientists are worried about what might be considered accidental passing. Too many black children and young adults, they fear, end up knowing little about black history and culture. "They have had a lot of exposure to white America and very little exposure to black America," frets DeLois Scott, a Chicago social worker and mother of three children raised in suburban Highland Park. The Scotts, like other families who have fought their way into mainstream America, are left to wonder if the price of integration is "deracination"—an isolation from one's native culture.

The Ultimate Fear

The deracination process often begins 4 when black parents move to white neighborhoods so their kids can attend the best schools. They send them off like Moses in the bulrushes and then begin worrying about whether they will be accepted academically and socially. For the last seven years Courtney Arrington has traveled across town from Boston's black Roxbury section to the Winsor prep school. Although she was elected class president twice and participates in school activities, Courtney's life has not been without sacrifices. "She has had no social life at all," says her mother, Jackie. "She didn't have to stand against the wall at too many socials before realizing there was no point in going." To some parents, full socialization may be even worse: they watch in horror as young Malik and Nzingha begin dressing like Boy George, talking like Valley girls or grooving to Van Halen.

And always there is the ultimate fear 5 that their child will be called a nigger—or treated like one—and won't understand why or know how to handle the hurt. "Parents worry that without the benefit of knowing who they are culturally, historically and politically, their kids will not understand how they are perceived by the world at large," says New York psychologist Charles Jamison. "And they will not have the resources with which to combat those perceptions."

The problem arises because so many 6 youngsters, like Kamani Clark, haven't felt racism's sting. Born after the *Brown v. Board of Education* school-desegregation case, after the Selma voting-rights march, the Newark riots and the assassination of Martin Luther King Jr., they may never have seen an American race riot on TV, may never have heard stories of lynchings and probably wonder who that guy Jim Crow was anyway. Not only are they lacking negative memories of struggle and repression, but they also missed out on the positive reinforcement of the black-pride movement that once inspired even the most middle-class blacks to abandon white fashion for Afros and dashikis. What they inherited instead was a sense of well-being and belonging unprecedented among their ancestors on these shores. John Lewis, former head of the Student Nonviolent Coordinating Committee (SNCC), is not so sure that assimilation is necessarily such a bad thing. "I think that was one of the goals of the civil-rights movement," he says, "to move us beyond the question of race in this society."

7   Though black assimilation may have muted the question of race for some, it has heightened questions of class. Not too long ago, as Lewis notes, it didn't matter whether you were black and wealthy or black and poor; you couldn't buy a hamburger in downtown Atlanta. But when restrictions were eased, black neighborhoods, like those of other ethnic groups, began to fracture along class lines. "The black middle class moved out in droves," says Jamison—to begin their quest for the American Dream. The results have been significant. In 1983, 27.2 percent of black families reported incomes of $25,000 or more; 11 percent of the total college population in 1981 was black, compared with 7 percent in 1970; black home ownership between 1970 and 1980 soared 45 percent. Still, for many of those who moved on up there is a lingering unease: adults who remember the way it was may suspect that a sudden economic reversal could topple them from prosperity. "The position of the black middle class is much more tenuous" than it was even a few years ago, argues University of Chicago sociologist William Julius Wilson.

Black Yuppies

8   The precarious position of some middle-class black families is one more reason why many believe it is important for children to understand how they got where they are. Berkeley sociologist and '60s activist Harry Edwards charges that Buppie (black Yuppie) parents have lied to their kids "out of love,"

seeking to protect them from the hardships they themselves endured. "It's natural that my kids are not as racially conscious as I was," Edwards allows. "I couldn't eat at the Woolworth lunch counter in East St. Louis." But he believes it is his duty to put things in perspective for them, from presidential politics to Bo Derek's cornrow. Having done that, he says, he doesn't mind if his 12-year-old daughter wants to tack Bruce Springsteen's poster up alongside one of Tina Turner.

9   But life for many young blacks isn't always put in neat perspective. Jacqueline Gray, 23, a project officer for the U.S. Information Agency, recalls her New Jersey childhood cynically as that of a Black American Princess in "integration land." Believing as a teen-ager that she had been deprived of the "real" black experience, Gray and a similarly curious boyfriend used to hop into his Corvette and drive over to the projects, just to get a sense of how other blacks lived.

10   Growing up in the pale of Cedar Rapids, Iowa, Ronnie Webb seemed to have his social life under control. "I didn't have any problems whatsoever in going out with white girls," says Webb. "Those were the only girls I knew." The problem was *keeping* a girlfriend; parental intervention caused them to lose interest quickly. "It took me a while," he says, "to figure out what was going on." That rejection persuaded Webb to attend a college where he could meet more black students. Now a junior at Harvard, he dates only black girls who, he has decided, "are even prettier than white girls."

11   As tricky as personal relationships can be, some black parents are even more concerned about what may happen to their children in the working world. "These kids are just not prepared," says Atlanta mother Shereka Osorio. "They are not going to think they're being rejected because they're black. They're going to take it personally." That is not to say that any black person who is turned down for a job should automatically scream racism. It would be silly, however, not to be aware of the possibility that race might have had something to do with it. San

Francisco psychiatrist Price Cobbs sees a resurgence of racial awareness among highly credentialed, upwardly mobile young blacks who had never considered race to be much of a factor in their lives. Cobbs tells of a black man in line for a corporate vice presidency who was told by the chairman that the company wasn't "ready" for that yet. "When my father told me it happened that way in 1957, I didn't believe him," the crushed executive told Cobbs.

12   In order to foster black awareness in their marooned offspring, parents are turning in greater numbers to family-oriented clubs. Founded in the days of rigid segregation, those clubs allowed middle-class blacks to enjoy activities, from theater parties to cotillions, from which they had been excluded by white society. The clubs lost favor in the power-to-the-people '60s because they were seen as "seditty" cliques of high-toned folks trying to mimic whites. Now, ironically, instead of reaffirming their middle-class status in the black community, members seek to reaffirm their blackness in the midst of white enclaves.

13   Beverly Blake, a public-school teacher, enrolled her daughter in a private, nearly all-white school — shortly *after* she signed her up in Jack and Jill, the oldest and largest of the social clubs. There are 110 families in the Chicago chapter, and this year the group received 44 applications for 14 openings. Yvonne Horton, who lives in the Chicago suburb of University Park, organized a chapter of Jack and Jill six years ago when her son James was two. That South Suburban chapter, now including 80 families with children 2 to 19, is only 1 of 4 suburban-Chicago Jack and Jill branches to spring up in the last decade. "I never thought I'd do that to one of my kids," says Horton, who grew up in Philadelphia and says she was "born into Jack and Jill"; her mother was national president of the organization. "Then, it was something that your mother made you

go to," she says. "Little did I know that I would be living in one of those neighborhoods where we're isolated and scattered."

The search for roots may revitalize   14 another neglected institution as well: the black college. Pam Scott of Highland Park, Ill., resolved her confusion about her suburban upbringing by attending Spelman College, where she is a senior. "I had never seen so many black people in one place before," she says, many of them, like herself, from predominantly white schools. "I found that my self-confidence went up and that I was able to relate to whites on a whole different level as well as to blacks," she says. Mary Oliver of New York's Westchester County was delighted when her 17-year-old son Ed decided to attend Morehouse College this fall. When he first visited, his mother says, "He found that the students were serious; they were not just finger-popping, break-dancing young bloods." Psychologist Jacqueline Fleming, author of *Blacks in College,* argues that the atmosphere at black colleges enhances students' academic performance as well as their self-image. "The kids in black schools were just more alive; they seemed to be more interested in things," says Fleming. "There was more warmth, but I also felt more intelligence. The kids at Ivy League schools were terrific kids and they tried real hard, but there was just something missing."

What seems to be missing from the lives   15 of many young middle-class blacks is a sense of balance — and a measure of truth. The truth is that racism continues to exist, and any preparation for success without that acknowledgment is incomplete. And, as pediatrician and psychiatrist Phyllis Harrison-Ross cautions, "If we allow people to artificially whitewash us, then we are allowing them to say they don't recognize a big part of us." That part, the black souls of folks, is something that enriches not only the individual but the society as well.

EXERCISES

Content

Recall the main ideas in this article by answering the following questions. Respond to some of the questions in your own words. Respond to others by finding quotations from the article that provide the answers.

1. What is "accidental passing," as defined by Williams?

2. What is "deracination"? When does it occur?

3. Why do black parents often have mixed feelings about their children's socialization by white schools and other institutions of white-dominated culture?

4. Why are the experiences and memories of black children today often different from those of their parents?

5. For many blacks the process of assimilation has caused the problems of race to be replaced with what other major factor in social success?

6. Why are black social clubs, like Jack and Jill, and black colleges like Morehouse, enjoying a resurgence among black parents in the 1980s?

Structure

1. What is the purpose of paragraphs 1 and 2?

2. How is paragraph 11 related to paragraph 10?

3. How is paragraph 14 related to the thesis of the article?

4. Write two more Structure questions and answer them.

Fact/Opinion

Classify each of the following statements as either a fact, an opinion, or a fact wrapped in an opinion. If the statement is a combination of fact and opinion, identify which part is fact and which opinion.

1. "Chad Clark, a 15-year-old sophomore at Walter Johnson High School in Bethesda, Md., is popular, well adjusted, good-looking and smart."

2. "The problem arises because so many youngsters, like Kamani Clark, haven't felt racism's sting."

3. "What seems to be missing from the lives of many young middle-class blacks is a sense of balance — and a measure of truth."

Inferences

In your responses to the following questions, incorporate some of the quotations you located in response to the Content questions. You may decide to use either all or only part of each quotation.

1. Why do you think the article begins with the quotation by Du Bois and then the brief accounts of Chad Clark and Andrea Wilson?

2. What do you imagine would be Richard Rodriguez's reaction to the kinds of problems discussed in "Roots III: Souls on Ice"?

3. To what extent do you believe the apprehensions of many black parents justified as to the precariousness of their children's positions in white-dominated society?

4. Compare and contrast the feelings of some of the parents described in this article with those of Patrice Gaines-Carter in "The Price of Integration."

5. Based on your own knowledge and experience, evaluate Williams's assertion that "what seems to be missing from the lives of many young middle-class blacks is a sense of balance—and a measure of truth."

Bebe Moore Campbell

BLACKS WHO LIVE IN A WHITE WORLD

Bebe Moore Campbell writes regularly for *Essence* and *Black Enterprise* and occasionally for *Savvy*, *Ms.*, and the *New York Times Magazine*. This article first appeared in *Ebony*.

1   When Rodney Butler joined the Pittsburgh office of the Gulf Corp. in 1971 at 24, he became one of the few professional Blacks in the company. He hadn't been there long when a friend from the old days paid him a visit, bringing a touch of jitterbug to the conservative bulwark of billion dollar deals. "My man, Rod. S'happening, Bro." Several days later, an older Black manager took Butler aside. He didn't give him "five." Instead, he provided the corporate novitiate with advice on how to succeed in big business: "Cut your Afro, stay married, go to lunch and socialize with White managers, and stop running around with funny-looking Black people."

2   Butler doesn't discard friends. But in the months that followed, he trimmed his hair, switched from round wire frames to a more conservative style of glasses, and purchased his first pair of wing tips. In his dark, three-piece suit, externally, he resembled the legions of other young corporate managers on the rise. Except, of course, for his color.

3   The story of the transformation of Rodney Butler is the story of ambitious Black men and women who have infiltrated the ranks of major corporations and who live today in a mostly White world.

4   Throughout American history, Blacks and Whites have lived in mostly separate worlds. Lively church services, "do-wopping" on the corner, partying heartily and living in relative poverty among other Blacks are part of the Black world's definition, though not necessarily exclusive to it. Most Black professionals have functioned, for the most part, within that world. Many professions have been the exclusive domain of Whites. Big business is an example.

5   But in the last 15 years, the number of professional Blacks in large corporations has been slowly increasing. In 1972, 1.4 percent of all managers and administrators in manufacturing were Black; in 1981, 2.4 percent were Black.

6   For Black managers, the impact of the corporation goes far beyond the office. To climb the corporate ladder includes social interaction with peers and supervisors, and entree into a life-style where people are introduced at obligatory cocktail parties by name and profession, and where managers are clustered in exclusive neighborhoods and attend very quiet churches. There are those who assert that for Blacks to make it in the corporate world, they must exchange a Black lifestyle for a totally White one. Most Black managers dispute the assertion, but

they candidly admit (although some require a cloak of anonymity) that Blacks in big business have a double task: to become professionally, as well as culturally, acclimated.

7 The corporation is a pressure cooker. The days can be long, weekends may mean just another work day at the office, and transfers are common and sometimes frequent, removing managers from communities where they've established ties. "If the company needs you in Jablip, you go to Jablip," complained the wife of an East Coast railroad executive. The company is a political arena where gamesmanship is the key to climbing the rungs of the corporate ladder. The rewards are tangible: fat paychecks, healthy insurance policies and power in an arena where clout matters.

8 The corporation's professionals must adhere to codes of dress and behavior that project them as irreproachable representatives of companies worthy of their investors' dollars. Blacks aren't singled out for conformity or special duties. Indeed, many Whites fail at juggling the pressures of big business. While there are parallels managers can draw from their Black experience—i.e., there is a dress code at most Black churches—the superficial and intrinsic values of the corporation are different from the world most of them grew up in. The parents of most Black managers lack the experiences needed to prepare their children for big business. Peers can't help because there are so few professional Blacks participating in private industry. While some credit military experience and attending a predominantly White college for somewhat preparing them for a corporate environment, most of the managers who've entered the ranks of big business over the last 15 years (when affirmative action programs opened some corporate doors) have come armed with college degrees and maybe a little street savvy. If their interview was a good one, they have that to draw from, but probably not much else. They quickly learn that big business isn't going to adjust to them. Black managers have gone through changes.

9 For some there was initial ambivalence toward being a part of "the system."

10 Marchand Alphran, 49, formerly a manager with a large food processing corporation, recalls his decision to join big business. "I went through an intense debate with myself. At the time, I was with a Black business and I had some guilt about leaving that company." Others find it intimidating to suddenly be surrounded by Whites. Says a 32-year-old female engineer who joined a communications corporation in Richmond, Va., in 1971, "I grew up in the rural South. Basically, I'd always perceived of White folks as people I was subservient to. Before I accepted the job, I'd lived a totally Black existence."

11 Some felt that there was racism at their offices. Says the female engineer, "I didn't know how to handle it when a co-worker announced that he wouldn't attend a business meeting if he had to be seen going into a hotel with me." A 30-year-old manager with a large energy corporation in Richmond, Va., says, "If I asked a question, my supervisor would give me a basic answer. If my White counterpart asked a question, they'd give him the whole picture." Most didn't go public with charges of racism; they were too immersed in learning corporate jargon, dress codes and politics to have time to go to the Equal Employment Opportunity Commission.

12 One of the few Blacks at NASA (National Aeronautics and Space Administration), Dudley McConnell, Ph.D., assistant administrator of the space application program, says, "The bureaucracy in private industry and government isn't significantly different. There is some pressure to conform at NASA. There is subtle pressure to socialize because you work in a team, but after five, the government couldn't care less what you do and where you live."

13 The corporation does care. Says one middle manager at Gulf in Houston, a man who earns close to $60,000 annually, "You're evaluated for the life you lead away from the job. My current boss told me, 'Once you reach a certain level, you're never off.' The bosses have made innuendoes: what clothes

to buy, that I need to belong to a country club. Whenever I'm transferred, the boss has always suggested areas where I should look for a house. There are required social outings that I have to attend. After my next promotion, I'll have to learn to play golf with the big boys. Been a long time since I sat on the steps and drank beer."

14 Managers on the lower echelon, where most Blacks are clustered, don't have as many dictates to follow as those on higher rungs of the ladder, but, the higher they climb, the more ambitious Blacks are forced to make choices. Do they hang out in the old neighborhood for after-work drinks or accompany their White co-workers to the bar down the street? Do they go to their boss' cocktail party or their main man's house party? As corporate demands mount, they begin to realize that they haven't been to a fraternity or sorority meeting, a real party, a concert or church in months. A few time management experts somehow squeeze in everything, but, sooner or later, even the priorities of the superorganized are challenged. Whites are confronted too, but while it may be a simple time squeeze for them, for Blacks it's far more isolating. As their daily interaction becomes more and more limited to White people, it begins to mean more than just trimmed Afros and wing tips. For many Black managers, the question of cultural conflict arises.

15 Black managers strive to excel, perhaps even harder than their White counterparts. Ronald Brown, Ph.D., a psychologist with Pacific Management Systems in San Francisco, a management development corporation that trains White managers to deal with minority employees and teaches career development to Blacks, women and Hispanics, says, "Initially, Black managers succumb to the 'work twice as hard ethic' feeling that if they give 200 percent, they'll climb the ladder." The manager from Richmond recalls his early days. "I wanted to overcome the racial stereotypes for myself and all Black people. I tried to be superlative in every capacity. I almost burned myself out." "After a year,"

says Dr. Brown, "when the time crunch comes down, people start to ask themselves, 'Am I losing my Blackness? I wonder what I'm giving up?'"

16 There is no one answer to that question. Certainly, all Black managers don't feel conflicted; the corporate experience is as varied as the people. Kim Clark, 25, a middle manager responsible for administrative support, including staffing, revenue planning, sales and technical support for 350 people at AT&T Long Lines in Parsippany, N.J., grew up in an integrated environment in Belmar, N.J. She's enthusiastic about her career and takes in stride being in a corporate environment and a town where there are few Blacks. "I've always been aware of the Black and White issue, but I didn't see it as a deterrent in trying to accomplish my goals," she says.

17 William Donan, 34, a vice-president at American Hospital Supply Corp. in San Francisco, where he supervises a staff of 90 and handles a multimillion/dollar budget for marketing and sales activities, says, "It became immediately obvious that the company was White. I had no expectations that there would be a problem. I just did my job."

18 Ludwick Hayden's former job as manager of community affairs at Gulf in Houston, Texas gave him extensive involvement in Black and Hispanic communities. He is currently area director of public affairs for Gulf in Philadelphia, Pa., and feels that his corporate experience hasn't caused a departure from his Black lifestyle.

19 But transitions aren't so smooth for all. When Reba and Melvin Poulson, both in their late 20s, decided to leave Richmond so that Melvin could take a job as a quality control chemist with the Upjohn Co. in Kalamazoo, Mich., a town with a small Black population, they found it jolting being the only Blacks on the street at times and having to wait until Saturday for the weekly four hours of Black radio music. For the railroad executive and his wife, company social events are dreaded. Says the wife, "A lot of them are being exposed to Blacks for the first time. We have a heavy burden. Whatever

we do, they'll feel it's what all Blacks do. You can't feel free, because you're being watched." The manager in Houston is still adjusting to "coldness." "I've never had a good social time on the job. They do, but then, it's their world."

20 That's debatable. But one thing isn't: to hold onto working definitions of Blackness that don't serve the company's interests is to end a corporate career. The Houston manager recalls, "There was a guy who used to come to work dressed like the Temptations at showtime: platform shoes, green suit. In my presence, his White supervisor told him, 'How can we put faith in what you're saying when you look like Bozo the clown?' He didn't last long." Says Donan: "There was a Black sales rep who couldn't or wouldn't relate to the White people he had to do business with. He wanted to be Joe Brother to everybody and that didn't make it."

21 "I can still think of instances when Black managers have had problems dealing with White supervisors' criticisms. Because of racism, Blacks can sometimes be hypersensitive," says Hayden. "Sometimes you cause yourself to see everything as racism; using racism can become a defense mechanism."

22 At some point, a choice must be made. Most Black managers, highly motivated, goal-oriented people, are willing to be flexible in order to gain the rewards that the corporation has to offer. "Somewhere along the line," says Donan, "I made a conscious or subconscious decision. I wanted other things. I found out what gets goals accomplished . . . it became obvious what was necessary. I had to do certain things to get them. Call it conforming or adapting."

23 But the choice for corporate life isn't a rejection of a Black lifestyle. Certainly, there are those who "lose their Black identity," but most feel strongly about keeping their Blackness intact and, after a while, they begin to understand how to do that for who they are, and where they are a lot better than they did at the beginning of their careers.

24 They don't cross over, they *criss* cross. If the corporate social interaction is obligatory, they learn to squeeze in Black social outlets, too. If their children attend predominantly White schools, they take them to where other Black children are. If a Cadillac is too flashy a symbol of corporate success, they buy big Fords. They read Fortune, but they read Black publications, too. They're aware of the politics of their work environment, so they change their style. Most don't sell their souls.

25 "I'm only going to change to a certain extent," says the female engineer. The Poulsons make a point of attending the AME church every Sunday and socialize regularly with other Black couples. Butler, now 34 and a recruiting manager for Sohio in Cleveland, remarks, "I feel more in control. I don't let the corporation overstep its bounds. Today you couldn't pay me to wear a pair of wing tips; my feet are too big." It isn't a coincidence that self-confidence grows as Blacks become highly rated, seasoned professionals with something to offer any company.

26 If Blacks go through changes initially, after a few years they find their stride. Those who stay make significant contributions to the corporation, and by their very presence go far beyond affirmative action in eroding the stereotypes of Blacks' inability to excel in business. Says the Houston manager, "When I first came, a lot of the White supervisors didn't want to deal with me. After a while, they were singing a different tune."

27 The Black managers' definition of Blackness isn't as monolithic as it once was. They are older, more experienced and richer; they've left their home-towns and expanded their horizons. Combined with their corporate experience, these factors have reshaped their views of themselves and the world.

28 Says Dr. Brown, "What I see in large seminars is that most Blacks in the corporation have very *Black* perspectives, though they may appear 'White' to other people." Dr. Brown instructs managers to move away from superficial definitions of Blackness and define the corporate reality of Blackness. In their environment, supporting each other through formal and informal networks, "men-

toring" newcomers, and having the clout to help other Blacks get jobs or promotions is very Black.

29   Says Donan: "During the maturation process, behavior takes on differing levels of importance. At 10, it was important for me to say, 'Hey, man' and sing on the corner. But not at 20. Today, my Blackness makes me feel prouder of my successes, and if I ever had any sense of inferiority to Whites, I don't have it now." He adds, "I don't consciously try to 'soak up' Blackness. I probably should. I choose not to forget where I came from."

30   "You take Blackness with you," says Hayden's wife, Barbara. "Consciousness is automatic. Blackness puts a perspective on any situation and makes sense of it."

31   In the last 15 years, the first generation of Blacks to play a role in the wheeling and dealing that make the world go round has emerged. They've made the trade-offs that have made sense for them and are becoming accustomed to a definition of Blackness that includes affluence and, to some extent, power. Their experience has changed most of them; it has bleached only a few. As Black America seeks survival definitions in the '80s, Black managers are abandoning self concepts that ghettoize, but are not abandoning their roots. Success in big business, they say, can come in *their* shade.

EXERCISES

Content

Recall the main ideas in this article by answering the following questions. Respond to some of the questions in your own words. Respond to others by finding quotations from the article that provide the answers.

1. Why has the growing participation of blacks in the executive echelons of corporate America also affected their lives outside of work?

2. In what ways do blacks require more of an adjustment to corporate life than do whites?

3. Why have the past fifteen years brought about the kinds of problems and conflicts discussed in this article?

4. What are some of the particular difficulties that some blacks encounter on first entering the corporate world?

5. Why did Reba Poulson, the wife of the quality control chemist, feel that she and her husband were no longer "free," that they were being "watched"?

6. In what kind of situations does charging racism become a defense mechanism?

7. How have some black managers been able to resolve the cultural dilemmas that corporate life generates?

Structure

1. What is the purpose of paragraph 1?

2. Explain how paragraphs 7 and 8, considered together, form an identifiable section of the article. Give this section a title.

3. How is paragraph 13 related to paragraph 12?

4. Write two more Structure questions and answer them.

Fact/Opinion

Classify each of the following statements as either a fact, an opinion, or a fact wrapped in an opinion. If the statement is a combination of fact and opinion, identify which part is fact and which opinion.

1. "Throughout American history, Blacks and Whites have lived in mostly separate worlds."

2. "But in the last 15 years, the number of professional Blacks in large corporations has been slowly increasing."

3. "The corporation is a pressure cooker."

4. "Managers on the lower echelon, where most Blacks are clustered, don't have as many dictates to follow as those on higher rungs of the ladder, but, the higher they climb, the more ambitious Blacks are forced to make choices."

Inferences

In your responses to the following questions, incorporate some of the quotations you located in response to the Content questions. You may decide to use either all or only part of each quotation.

1. To what extent does this article parallel the previous one by Dennis A. Williams, "Roots III: Souls on Ice"?

2. Why do you think Campbell began the article with the anecdote about Rodney Butler?

3. Parallel the experiences of blacks like the manager at Gulf Oil (paragraph 13) and Ronald Brown (paragraph 15) with those of Richard Rodriguez.

4. What do you think Richard Carter ("I Have a Flag") would advise many of the blacks discussed in this article? How would they be likely to respond?

5. Why does paragraph 20 begin with the sentence "That's debatable"? In what way is it debatable?

6. What solutions, if any, do you believe there are for problems such as those discussed in this article?

7. What does Campbell mean by saying (in paragraph 31): "Their experience has changed most of them; it has bleached only a few"?

8. Compare and contrast the concerns of this article with those of "Roots III: Souls on Ice." What are the major conflicts discussed in each article? On which groups of blacks does each article focus? What are the attitudes of each author toward his subject? How do you think the author of each article has been influenced by the readership of the magazine in which his article appeared ("Roots III" appeared in *Newsweek;* "Blacks Who Live in a White World" appeared in *Ebony*)?

Stanley Sanders

I'LL NEVER ESCAPE THE GHETTO

Born and educated in the Watts district of Los Angeles, Stanley Sanders became president of the student body at Whittier College, went to Oxford University as a Rhodes **scholar, and then to Yale Law School. He was a cofounder of the Watts Summer Festival in 1966 and, later, director of the Summer Work Project for Youth in Watts. He has pub-**

lished articles in *The Nation* and in numerous education journals. **This article, which first appeared in *Ebony*, may be compared and contrasted with Rendón's.**

1   I was born, raised and graduated from high school in Watts. My permanent Los Angeles home address is in Watts. My father, a brother and sister still live in Watts. By ordinary standards these are credentials enough to qualify one as coming from Watts.

2   But there is more to it than that. I left Watts. After I was graduated from the local high school I went away to college. A college venture in Watts terms is a fateful act. There are no retractions or future deliverances. Watts, like other black ghettos across the country, is, for ambitious youths, a transient status. Once they have left, there is no returning. In this sense, my credentials are unsatisfactory. To some people, I am not from Watts. I can never be.

3   The Watts-as-a-way-station mentality has a firm hold on both those who remain and those who leave. Such as it is, the ghetto is regarded as no place to make a career for those who have a future. Without exception, the prime American values underscore the notion. Negroes, inside it or out, and whites too, behave toward the ghetto like travelers.

4   Accordingly, I was considered one of the lucky ones. My scholarship to college was a ticket. People did not expect me to return. Understanding this, I can understand the puzzlement in the minds of those in Watts when I was home last summer, working in the local poverty program. Rumors spread quickly that I was an FBI agent. I was suspect because I was not supposed to return. Some people said I was either a federal agent or a fool, for no reasonable man, they said, returns to Watts by choice. Outside of Watts, reports stated that I had "given up" a summer vacation to work in Watts. For my part, I had come home to work in my community, but to some people I could not come home to Watts. To them I was no longer from Watts.

5   My own state of mind, when I left Watts eight years ago to take up the freshman year at Whittier College, was different. It was to me less of a departure; it was the stepping-off point of an Odyssey that was to take me through Whittier College and Oxford University, to Yale Law School, and back to Watts. I had intended then, as now, to make Watts my home.

6   A career in Watts had been a personal ambition for many years. In many ways the career I envisioned was antithetical to ghetto life. In the ghetto, a career was something on the outside. In Los Angeles, this meant a pursuit founded in a world beyond Alameda Street, at a minimum in the largely Negro middle-class Westside of Los Angeles. The talk among the ambitious and future-minded youth in Watts was on getting out so that careers could begin. And they did just that. The talented young people left Watts in droves. The one skill they had in common was the ability to escape the ghetto.

7   I was especially intrigued by a career in Watts because it was supposed to be impossible. I wanted to demonstrate that it could be done more than anything else. I recall a moment during a city-wide high school oratorical contest when one of the judges asked whether anything good could come out of Watts. Our high school won the contest. We showed that judge. I saw that achievement as a possible pattern for the entire ghetto. I was pleased.

8   I had not realized in leaving for Whittier College that, however worthy my intention of returning was, I was nevertheless participating in the customary exodus from Watts. It was not long after leaving that my early ambitions began to wear thin. The stigma of Watts was too heavy to bear. I could easily do without the questioning looks of my college classmates. I did not want my being from Watts to arouse curiosity.

9   I followed the instructions of those who fled Watts. I adopted the language of escape. I resorted to all the devices of those who wished to escape. I was from South Los Angeles, thereafter, not Watts. "South Los Angeles," geographically identical to Watts, carried none of the latter's stigma. South Los

Angeles was a cleaner — safer — designation. It meant having a home with possibilities.

10   It never occurred to me at the time what I was doing. I thought of it only as being practical. It was important to me to do well in college. Community identity was secondary, if a consideration at all. Somehow, the Watts things interfered with my new college life. Moreover, Negro college youth during those undergraduate years had none of its present mood. Its theme was campus involvement. Good grades, athletics, popularity — these were the things that mattered. The word "ghetto" had not even entered the lexicon of race relations. Students were not conscious of the ghetto as a separate phenomenon. Civil rights, in the Southern sense, was academically fashionable. But the ghetto of the North was not. The concern for the ghetto was still in the future.

11   It was to occur to me later, at the time of the Watts riots, two years after I graduated from college, if my classmates at Whittier realized that the epochal conflagration taking place was in the home of one of their very own student body presidents. They had no reason to think it was. I had never told them that I was from Watts.

12   A lot of things changed during the two years at Oxford. My attitude toward home was one of them. It was there, ironically enough, that the Odyssey turned homeward. Those years were bound to be meaningful as a Yankee foreign student or Rhodes Scholar. I knew that much. But I would never have imagined when receiving the award that Oxford would be significant as a Negro experience. After all, it was part of the faith gained during four years at Whittier that everything concerning me and Watts would remain conveniently buried.

13   It emerged in an odd context. England then, for the most part, was free of the fine distinctions between blacks and whites traditionally made in America. Except for some exclusive clubs in London, there were few occasions where racial lines were drawn. The color-blindness of England was especially true in the student life at Oxford. (This relatively mild racial climate in England during the last three years has, with the large influx of blacks from the West Indies and Southern Asia, adopted some very American-like features.) It was in such a relaxed racial atmosphere that all my defenses, about race and home, came down. At Oxford, I could reflect on the American black man.

14   My ghetto roots became crucially important in this examination. Englishmen were not concerned about the distinctions I was making in my own mind, between Watts and "South Los Angeles," between Watts and Whittier. They were not imagined distinctions. I was discovering that I could not escape the ghetto after all. A fundamental change was taking place in the ghettos, the Wattses, across the country. These changes were making the distinction. I realized I was a part of them, too.

15   By far the most traumatic of the new changes was ghetto rioting. I was studying at the University of Vienna, between semesters at Oxford, during the summer of 1964. News of Harlem rioting jolted the multinational student community there. The typical European response was unlike anything I had seen before. They had no homes or businesses to worry about protecting. They wanted to know why Negroes did not riot more often. As the only Negro in the summer session I felt awkward for a time. I was being asked questions about the black man in America that no one had ever asked me before. I was embarrassed because I did not have any answers.

16   My own lack of shame in the rioting then taking place in America surprised me. In one sense, I was the archetype of the ghetto child who through hard work and initiative, was pulling himself toward a better life. I was the example, the exception. It was my life that was held up to Watts youth to emulate.

17   In another sense, however, my feelings toward the rioting were predictable. I had always been bothered by the passivity of the ghetto. The majority of black men in the North had remained outside the struggle. Nothing was happening in the ghettos. No

one was making it happen. Ghetto rioting then was the first representation I perceived of movement and activity among the mass of Negroes in the North. It marked a break with the passive tradition of dependency and indifference. The ghetto was at least no longer content with its status as bastard child of urban America. The currents set in motion had a hopeful, irreversible quality about them. The ghetto wanted legitimation. That was a beginning.

18   The parallel between a single individual's success and the boot-strap effort of the mass of ghetto youth is and remains too tenuous to comport with reality. This was made clear to me during the discussions of the Harlem riots on those hot summer days in Vienna. It shattered the notion that my individual progress could be hailed as an advance for all Negroes. Regrettably, it was an advance only for me. Earlier I had thought the success I had won satisfied an obligation I had to all Negroes. It is part of the lip service every successful Negro is obliged to pay to the notion of race progress whenever he achieves. In the face of mass rioting, the old shibboleths were reduced to embarrassing emptiness. I was enjoying the privileges of studying at the world's finest universities; Negroes at home were revolting against their miserable condition. To them, my experience and example were as remote as if I had never lived or been there. At best, only the top students could identify with my example—but they were few. And besides, the top students were not the problem.

19   When I returned to Oxford in the fall, following a spate of summer rioting in Eastern cities, I was convinced that some momentous changes had been wrought for all Negroes, not just those in the ghetto. It certainly meant a new militancy and a militancy of action, not the passive fulminations of the demi-militants. This was for Watts.

20   I returned home in August, 1965, from two years at Oxford just in time for the beginning of the Watts riots. As I walked the streets I was struck by the sameness of the community. There were few changes. Every-

thing seemed to be in the same place where I had last seen it. It was unsettling for me to recall so easily the names of familiar faces I saw on the street. It was that feeling one gets when he feels he has done this one same thing before.

21   Streets remained unswept; sidewalks, in places, still unpaved. During this same time the growth rate in the rest of Southern California had been phenomenal, one of the highest in the country. L. A. suburbs had flourished. Watts, however, remained an unacknowledged child in an otherwise proud and respectable family of new towns.

22   The intellectual journey back to Watts after the Vienna summer and during the last year at Oxford had partly prepared me for what was soon to erupt into revolutionary scale violence. My first reaction after the riot began was to have it stopped. But I was not from Watts for the past six years. I, nor anyone outside of Watts, was in no moral position to condemn this vicious expression of the ghetto.

23   I enrolled in Yale Law School in the fall after the riots. This time I did not leave Watts. Nor did I wish to leave Watts. Watts followed me to Yale. In fact, Watts was at Yale before I was. The discussions about riots and ghettos were more lively and compelling than the classroom discussions on the law. There were no word games or contrived problems. The questions raised were urgent ones.

24   Not surprisingly, Watts, too, was in the throes of painful discussion about the riots. It was beginning to look as though the deepest impact of the riots was on the people of Watts themselves. Old attitudes about the community were in upheaval. There were no explanations that seemed complete. No one knew for sure how it all began. There was no agreement on how it was continued as long as it was—and why. We only knew it happened. What I had often mistaken for pointless spoutings was in reality a manifestation of this desperate search for a truth about the riots.

25   The new intellectual climate in Watts was hard-wrought. It was rich enough to support

even a communist bookstore. Writers, poets, artists flourished. I was handed full manuscripts of unpublished books by indigenous writers and asked to criticize them. I have not seen during eight years of college life as many personal journals kept and sketches written than in Watts since the 1965 riots. A new, rough wisdom of the street corner was emerging.

26   I suspected at the time and now realize that the riots were perhaps the most significant massive action taken by Northern Negroes. It was a watershed in the ghetto's history. Before the riots, the reach of the Negro movement in America seemed within the province of a small civil rights leadership. Now Watts, and places like Watts, were redefining the role of black men in their city's life.

27   I have affectionate ties to Watts. I bear the same mark as a son of Watts now that I did during that oratorical contest in high school. I may be personally less vulnerable to it today, but I am nevertheless influenced by it. While a group in Whittier, Calif. may regard it as unfortunate that its college's first Rhodes Scholar comes from Watts, I, for my part, could not feel more pride abut that

than I do now. I feel no embarrassment for those who think ill of Watts. I had once felt it. Now I only feel the regret for once having been embarrassed. "South Los Angeles" is a sour memory. Watts is my home.

Then I have my logical ties to Watts, too.   28 My interest in the law stems from a concern for the future of Watts. The problem of the poor and of the city in America, simplified, is the problem of the ghetto Negro. I regard it as *the* problem of the last third of this century. Plainly, Watts is where the action is. The talents and leadership which I saw leave Watts as a child are the very things it needs most today. Many of the ghetto's wandering children are choosing a city to work in. My choice was made for me — long ago.

There is a difference between my   29 schooling and the wisdom of the street corner. I know the life of a black man in Watts is larger than a federal poverty program. If there is no future for the black ghetto, the future of all Negroes is diminished. What affects it, affects me, for I am a child of the ghetto. When they do it to Watts, they do it to me, too. I'll never escape from the ghetto. I have staked all on its future. Watts is my home.

EXERCISES

Content

Recall the main ideas in this article by answering the following questions. Respond to some of the questions in your own words. Respond to others by finding quotations from the article that provide the answers.

1. Why would some people consider that Sanders is *not* from Watts? Why was there so much surprise and disbelief when Sanders returned to Watts?

2. In what way was a career considered "antithetical to ghetto life"?

3. Why was Sanders interested in returning to Watts after college?

4. Why was Sanders's experience at Oxford University crucial to his rediscovering his heritage?

5. In what way was the reaction of Europeans to the rioting in the black ghettos different from the reaction of the Americans? How did this reaction affect Sanders?

6. Why did Sanders feel a sense of shame in Vienna when he read about the Harlem riots?

7. Why did Sanders consider the riots a good development?

8. What does Sanders mean when he says, "Watts followed me to Yale"?

9. What "logical ties" does Sanders feel he has to Watts?

Structure

1. What is the purpose of paragraph 1?

2. How is paragraph 25 related to paragraph 24?

3. In what paragraph does the thesis of this article appear?

4. Write two more Structure questions and answer them.

Fact/Opinion

Classify each of the following statements as either a fact, an opinion, or a fact wrapped in an opinion. If the statement is a combination of fact and opinion, identify which part is fact and which opinion.

1. "The Watts-as-a-way-station mentality has a firm hold on both those who remain and those who leave."

2. "The talented young people left Watts in droves."

3. "The currents set in motion had a hopeful, irreversible quality about them."

4. "There is a difference between my schooling and the wisdom of the street corner."

Inferences

In your responses to the following questions, incorporate some of the quotations you located in response to the Content questions. You may decide to use either all or only part of each quotation.

1. Compare and contrast the experiences of Sanders and Rendón. Consider especially important turning points in their lives.

2. Compare and contrast the experiences of Sanders and Rodriguez.

3. What does Sanders mean when he writes (paragraph 10): "Civil rights, in the Southern sense, was academically fashionable. But the ghetto of the North was not." Why do you think this was the case?

4. What does Sanders mean when he says, "I, nor anyone outside of Watts, was in no moral position to condemn this vicious expression of the ghetto." Do you agree with this statement?

5. What is the significance of the statement "'South Los Angeles' is a sour memory?"

6. Compare the following two quotations:

> No man is an island, entire of itself; every man is a piece of the continent, a part of the main. If a clod be washed away by the sea, Europe is the less, as well as if a promontory were, as well as if a manor of thy friend's or of thine own were. Any man's death diminishes me, because I am involved in mankind. And therefore never send to know for whom the bell tolls; it tolls for thee.
> —John Donne, *Devotions upon Emergent Occasions*

If there is no future for the black ghetto, the future of all Negroes is diminished. What affects it, affects me, for I am a child of the ghetto. When they do it to Watts, they do it to me, too.

—Stanley Sanders, "I'll Never Escape the Ghetto"

Are Donne and Sanders writing about the same thing? If Sanders had not returned to Watts, would his sentences be less valid?

Alice Walker

EVERYDAY USE

for your grandmamma

Alice Walker, born in Georgia in 1944, has been a voter registration worker in Georgia, a worker in the Head Start Program in Mississippi, and a staff member of the New York City Welfare Department. She has lectured at Jackson State College, Tougaloo College, Wellesley College, University of California at Berkeley, and Brandeis University. She is most well known, however, for her stories and poems. Her fictional works include *The Third Life of Grange Copeland, In Love and Trouble: Stories of Black Women* (from which "Everyday Use" is taken), and *The Color Purple,* which was adapted into a film by Steven Spielberg. Her collections of poetry include *Once; Revolutionary Petunias and Other Poems;* and *Goodnight, Willie Lee, I'll See You in the Morning.* She has also written *Langston Hughes: American Poet,* a children's biography, and has edited *The Third Woman: Minority Women Writers of the United States.* While reading this story, be especially alert for the differences in attitude between Dee, on the one hand, and her mother and sister, on the other.

1   I will wait for her in the yard that Maggie and I made so clean and wavy yesterday afternoon. A yard like this is more comfortable than most people know. It is not just a yard. It is like an extended living room. When the hard clay is swept clean as a floor and the fine sand around the edges lined with tiny, irregular grooves, anyone can come and sit and look up into the elm tree and wait for the breezes that never come inside the house.

Maggie will be nervous until after her 2 sister goes: she will stand hopelessly in corners, homely and ashamed of the burn scars down her arms and legs, eying her sister with a mixture of envy and awe. She thinks her sister has held life always in the palm of one hand, that "no" is a word the world never learned to say to her.

You've no doubt seen those TV shows 3 where the child who has "made it" is confronted, as a surprise, by her own mother and father, tottering in weakly from backstage. (A pleasant surprise, of course: What would they do if parent and child came on the show only to curse out and insult each other?) On TV mother and child embrace and smile into each other's faces. Sometimes the mother and father weep, the child wraps them in her arms and leans across the table to tell how she would not have made it without their help. I have seen these programs.

Sometimes I dream a dream in which 4 Dee and I are suddenly brought together on a TV program of this sort. Out of a dark and soft-seated limousine I am ushered into a bright room filled with many people. There I meet a smiling, gray, sporty man like Johnny Carson who shakes my hand and tells me what a fine girl I have. Then we are on the stage and Dee is embracing me with tears in her eyes. She pins on my dress a large orchid, even though she has told me once that she thinks orchids are tacky flowers.

5   In real life I am a large, big-boned woman with rough, man-working hands. In the winter I wear flannel nightgowns to bed and overalls during the day. I can kill and clean a hog as mercilessly as a man. My fat keeps me hot in zero weather. I can work outside all day, breaking ice to get water for washing; I can eat pork liver cooked over the open fire minutes after it comes steaming from the hog. One winter I knocked a bull calf straight in the brain between the eyes with a sledge hammer and had the meat hung up to chill before nightfall. But of course all this does not show on television. I am the way my daughter would want me to be: a hundred pounds lighter, my skin like an uncooked barley pancake. My hair glistens in the hot bright lights. Johnny Carson has much to do to keep up with my quick and witty tongue.

6   But that is a mistake. I know even before I wake up. Who ever knew a Johnson with a quick tongue? Who can even imagine me looking a strange white man in the eye? It seems to me I have talked to them always with one foot raised in flight, with my head turned in whichever way is farthest from them. Dee, though. She would always look anyone in the eye. Hesitation was no part of her nature.

7   "How do I look, Mama?" Maggie says, showing just enough of her thin body enveloped in pink skirt and red blouse for me to know she's there, almost hidden by the door.

8   "Come out into the yard," I say.

9   Have you ever seen a lame animal, perhaps a dog run over by some careless person rich enough to own a car, sidle up to someone who is ignorant enough to be kind to him? That is the way my Maggie walks. She has been like this, chin on chest, eyes on ground, feet in shuffle, ever since the fire that burned the other house to the ground.

10   Dee is lighter than Maggie, with nicer hair and a fuller figure. She's a woman now, though sometimes I forget. How long ago was it that the other house burned? Ten, twelve years? Sometimes I can still hear the flames and feel Maggie's arms sticking to me, her hair smoking and her dress falling off her in little black papery flakes. Her eyes seemed stretched open, blazed open by the flames reflected in them. And Dee. I see her standing off under the sweet gum tree she used to dig gum out of; a look of concentration on her face as she watched the last dingy gray board of the house fall in toward the red-hot brick chimney. Why don't you do a dance around the ashes? I'd wanted to ask her. She had hated the house that much.

11   I used to think she hated Maggie, too. But that was before we raised the money, the church and me, to send her to Augusta to school. She used to read to us without pity; forcing words, lies, other folks' habits, whole lives upon us two, sitting trapped and ignorant underneath her voice. She washed us in a river of make-believe, burned us with a lot of knowledge we didn't necessarily need to know. Pressed us to her with the serious way she read, to shove us away at just the moment, like dimwits, we seemed about to understand.

12   Dee wanted nice things. A yellow organdy dress to wear to her graduation from high school; black pumps to match a green suit she'd made from an old suit somebody gave me. She was determined to stare down any disaster in her efforts. Her eyelids would not flicker for minutes at a time. Often I fought off the temptation to shake her. At sixteen she had a style of her own: and knew what style was.

13   I never had an education myself. After second grade the school was closed down. Don't ask me why: in 1927 colored asked fewer questions than they do now. Sometimes Maggie reads to me. She stumbles along good-naturedly but can't see well. She knows she is not bright. Like good looks and money, quickness passed her by. She will marry John Thomas (who has mossy teeth in an earnest face) and then I'll be free to sit

here and I guess just sing church songs to myself. Although I never was a good singer. Never could carry a tune. I was always better at a man's job. I used to love to milk till I was hooked in the side in '49. Cows are soothing and slow and don't bother you, unless you try to milk them the wrong way.

14   I have deliberately turned my back on the house. It is three rooms, just like the one that burned, except the roof is tin; they don't make shingle roofs any more. There are no real windows, just some holes cut in the sides, like the portholes in a ship, but not round and not square, with rawhide holding the shutters up on the outside. This house is in a pasture, too, like the other one. No doubt when Dee sees it she will want to tear it down. She wrote me once that no matter where we "choose" to live, she will manage to come see us. But she will never bring her friends. Maggie and I thought about this and Maggie asked me, "Mama, when did Dee ever *have* any friends?"

15   She had a few. Furtive boys in pink shirts hanging about on washday after school. Nervous girls who never laughed. Impressed with her they worshiped the well-turned phrase, the cute shape, the scalding humor that erupted like bubbles in lye. She read to them.

16   When she was courting Jimmy T she didn't have much time to pay to us, but turned all her faultfinding power on him. He *flew* to marry a cheap city girl from a family of ignorant flashy people. She hardly had time to recompose herself.

17   When she comes I will meet — but there they are!

18   Maggie attempts to make a dash for the house, in her shuffling way, but I stay her with my hand. "Come back here," I say. And she stops and tries to dig a well in the sand with her toe.

19   It is hard to see them clearly through the strong sun. But even the first glimpse of leg out of the car tells me it is Dee. Her feet were always neat-looking, as if God himself had shaped them with a certain style. From the other side of the car comes a short, stocky man. Hair is all over his head a foot long and hanging from his chin like a kinky mule tail. I hear Maggie suck in her breath. "Uhnnnh," is what it sounds like. Like when you see the wriggling end of a snake just in front of your foot on the road. "Uhnnnh."

20   Dee next. A dress down to the ground, in this hot weather. A dress so loud it hurts my eyes. There are yellows and oranges enough to throw back the light of the sun. I feel my whole face warming from the heat waves it throws out. Earrings gold, too, and hanging down to her shoulders. Bracelets dangling and making noises when she moves her arm up to shake the folds of the dress out of her armpits. The dress is loose and flows, and as she walks closer, I like it. I hear Maggie go "Uhnnnh" again. It is her sister's hair. It stands straight up like the wool on a sheep. It is black as night and around the edges are two long pigtails that rope about like small lizards disappearing behind her ears.

21   "Wa-su-zo-Tean-o!" she says, coming on in that gliding way the dress makes her move. The short stocky fellow with the hair to his navel is all grinning and he follows up with "Asalamalakim,* my mother and sister!" He moves to hug Maggie but she falls back, right up against the back of my chair. I feel her trembling there and when I look up I see the perspiration falling off her chin.

22   "Don't get up," says Dee. Since I am stout it takes something of a push. You can see me trying to move a second or two before I make it. She turns, showing white heels through her sandals, and goes back to the car. Out she peeks next with a Polaroid. She stoops down quickly and lines up picture after picture of me sitting there in front of the house with Maggie cowering behind me. She never takes a shot without making sure the house is included. When a cow

---

*A Muslim greeting.

comes nibbling around the edge of the yard she snaps it and me and Maggie *and* the house. Then she puts the Polaroid in the back seat of the car, and comes up and kisses me on the forehead.

23   Meanwhile Asalamalakim is going through motions with Maggie's hand. Maggie's hand is as limp as a fish, and probably as cold, despite the sweat, and she keeps trying to pull it back. It looks like Asalamalakim wants to shake hands but wants to do it fancy. Or maybe he don't know how people shake hands. Anyhow, he soon gives up on Maggie.

24   "Well," I say. "Dee."

25   "No, Mama," she says. "Not 'Dee,' Wangero Leewanika Kemanjo!"

26   "What happened to 'Dee'?" I wanted to know.

27   "She's dead," Wangero said. "I couldn't bear it any longer, being named after the people who oppress me."

28   "You know as well as me you was named after your aunt Dicie," I said. Dicie is my sister. She named Dee. We called her "Big Dee" after Dee was born.

29   "But who was *she* named after?" asked Wangero.

30   "I guess after Grandma Dee," I said.

31   "And who was she named after?" asked Wangero.

32   "Her mother," I said, and saw Wangero was getting tired. "That's about as far back as I can trace it," I said. Though, in fact, I probably could have carried it back beyond the Civil War through the branches.

33   "Well," said Asalamalakim, "there you are."

34   "Uhnnnh," I heard Maggie say.

35   "There I was not," I said, "before 'Dicie' cropped up in our family, so why should I try to trace it that far back?"

36   He just stood there grinning, looking down on me like somebody inspecting a Model A car. Every once in a while he and Wangero sent eye signals over my head.

37   "How do you pronounce this name?" I asked.

38   "You don't have to call me by it if you don't want to," said Wangero.

39   "Why shouldn't I?" I asked. "If that's what you want us to call you, we'll call you."

40   "I know it might sound awkward at first," said Wangero.

41   "I'll get used to it," I said. "Ream it out again."

42   Well, soon we got the name out of the way. Asalamalakim had a name twice as long and three times as hard. After I tripped over it two or three times he told me to just call him Hakim-a-barber. I wanted to ask him was he a barber, but I didn't really think he was, so I didn't ask.

43   "You must belong to those beef-cattle peoples down the road," I said. They said "Asalamalakim" when they met you, too, but they didn't shake hands. Always too busy: feeding the cattle, fixing the fences, putting up salt-lick shelters, throwing down hay. When the white folks poisoned some of the herd the men stayed up all night with rifles in their hands. I walked a mile and a half just to see the sight.

44   Hakim-a-barber said, "I accept some of their doctrines, but farming and raising cattle is not my style." (They didn't tell me, and I didn't ask, whether Wangero (Dee) had really gone and married him.)

45   We sat down to eat and right away he said he didn't eat collards and pork was unclean. Wangero, though, went on through the chitlins and corn bread, the greens and everything else. She talked a blue streak over the sweet potatoes. Everything delighted her. Even the fact that we still used the benches her daddy made for the table when we couldn't afford to buy chairs.

46   "Oh, Mama!" she cried. Then turned to Hakim-a-barber. "I never knew how lovely these benches are. You can feel the rump prints," she said, running her hands underneath her and along the bench. Then she gave a sigh and her hand closed over Grandma Dee's butter dish. "That's it!" she said. "I knew there was something I wanted to ask you if I could have." She jumped up

from the table and went over in the corner where the churn stood, the milk in it clabber by now. She looked at the churn and looked at it.

47   "This churn top is what I need," she said. "Didn't Uncle Buddy whittle it out of a tree you all used to have?"

48   "Yes," I said.

49   "Uh huh," she said happily. "And I want the dasher, too."

50   "Uncle Buddy whittle that, too?" asked the barber.

51   Dee (Wangero) looked up at me.

52   "Aunt Dee's first husband whittled the dash," said Maggie so low you almost couldn't hear her. "His name was Henry, but they called him Stash."

53   "Maggie's brain is like an elephant's," Wangero said, laughing. "I can use the churn top as a centerpiece for the alcove table," she said, sliding a plate over the churn, "and I'll think of something artistic to do with the dasher."

54   When she finished wrapping the dasher the handle stuck out. I took it for a moment in my hands. You didn't even have to look close to see where hands pushing the dasher up and down to make butter had left a kind of sink in the wood. In fact, there were a lot of small sinks; you could see where thumbs and fingers had sunk into the wood. It was beautiful light yellow wood, from a tree that grew in the yard where Big Dee and Stash had lived.

55   After dinner Dee (Wangero) went to the trunk at the foot of my bed and started rifling through it. Maggie hung back in the kitchen over the dishpan. Out came Wangero with two quilts. They had been pieced by Grandma Dee and then Big Dee and me had hung them on the quilt frames on the front porch and quilted them. One was in the Lone Star pattern. The other was Walk Around the Mountain. In both of them were scraps of dresses Grandma Dee had worn fifty and more years ago. Bits and pieces of Grandpa Jarrell's Paisley shirts. And one teeny faded blue piece, about the size of a penny matchbox, that was from Great Grandpa Ezra's uniform that he wore in the Civil War.

56   "Mama," Wangero said sweet as a bird. "Can I have these old quilts?"

57   I heard something fall in the kitchen, and a minute later the kitchen door slammed.

58   "Why don't you take one or two of the others?" I asked. "These old things was just done by me and Big Dee from some tops your grandma pieced before she died."

59   "No," said Wangero. "I don't want those. They are stitched around the borders by machine."

60   "That'll make them last better," I said.

61   "That's not the point," said Wangero. "These are all pieces of dresses Grandma used to wear. She did all this stitching by hand. Imagine!" She held the quilts securely in her arms, stroking them.

62   "Some of the pieces, like those lavender ones, come from old clothes her mother handed down to her," I said, moving up to touch the quilts. Dee (Wangero) moved back just enough so that I couldn't reach the quilts. They already belonged to her.

63   "Imagine!" she breathed again, clutching them closely to her bosom.

64   "The truth is," I said, "I promised to give them quilts to Maggie, for when she marries John Thomas."

65   She gasped like a bee had stung her.

66   "Maggie can't appreciate these quilts!" she said. "She'd probably be backward enough to put them to everyday use."

67   "I reckon she would," I said. "God knows I been saving 'em for long enough with nobody using 'em. I hope she will!" I didn't want to bring up how I had offered Dee (Wangero) a quilt when she went away to college. Then she had told me they were old-fashioned, out of style.

68   "But they're *priceless!*" she was saying now, furiously; for she has a temper. "Maggie would put them on the bed and in five years they'd be in rags. Less than that!" "She can always make some more," I said. "Maggie knows how to quilt."

69   Dee (Wangero) looked at me with hatred. "You just will not understand. The point is these quilts, *these* quilts!"

70   "Well," I said, stumped. "What would *you* do with them?"

71   "Hang them," she said. As if that was the only thing you *could* do with quilts.

72   Maggie by now was standing in the door. I could almost hear the sound her feet made as they scraped over each other.

73   "She can have them, Mama," she said, like somebody used to never winning anything, or having anything reserved for her. "I can 'member Grandma Dee without the quilts."

74   I looked at her hard. She had filled her bottom lip with checkerberry snuff and it gave her face a kind of dopey, hangdog look. It was Grandma Dee and Big Dee who taught her how to quilt herself. She stood there with her scarred hands hidden in the folds of her skirt. She looked at her sister with something like fear but she wasn't mad at her. This was Maggie's portion. This was the way she knew God to work.

75   When I looked at her like that something hit me in the top of my head and ran down to the soles of my feet. Just like when I'm in church and the spirit of God touches me and I get happy and shout. I did something I never had done before: hugged Maggie to me, then dragged her on into the room, snatched the quilts out of Miss Wangero's hands and dumped them into Maggie's lap. Maggie just sat there on my bed with her mouth open.

76   "Take one or two of the others," I said to Dee.

77   But she turned without a word and went out to Hakim-a-barber.

78   "You just don't understand," she said, as Maggie and I came out to the car.

79   "What don't I understand?" I wanted to know.

80   "Your heritage," she said. And then she turned to Maggie, kissed her, and said, "You ought to try to make something of yourself, too, Maggie. It's really a new day for us. But from the way you and Mama still live you'd never know it.

81   She put on some sunglasses that hid everything above the tip of her nose and her chin.

82   Maggie smiled; maybe at the sunglasses. But a real smile, not scared. After we watched the car dust settle I asked Maggie to bring me a dip of snuff. And then the two of us sat there just enjoying, until it was time to go in the house and go to bed.

EXERCISES

Content

Recall the main ideas in this story by answering the following questions. Respond to some of the questions in your own words. Respond to others by finding quotations from the article that provide the answers.

1. Why is Maggie envious of Dee and awestruck by her?

2. In what way is the final sentence of paragraph 4 characteristic of the theme of the story?

3. What are the physical differences between Maggie and Dee? Why is Maggie lame? Of what are her lameness and scars symbolic?

4. Why is Dee's first appearance so startling to the mother and to Maggie?

5. Why did Dee change her name?

6. What does Dee (Wangero) plan to do with the churn and the dasher?

7. What accounts for the change in Dee's attitude toward the quilts from before she went to college to the present time? What does Dee plan to do with the quilts? What does Maggie plan to do with them? How is the difference tied in to the central concern of this chapter?

Inferences

In your responses to the following questions, incorporate some of the quotations you located in response to the Content questions. You may decide to use either all or only part of each quotation.

1. What is the central conflict of this story?

2. Discuss the significance of the title — "Everyday Use" (the phrase occurs also in paragraph 66). Then attempt to summarize the meaning of the story.

3. Discuss the contrast that is set up in paragraph 5 and explain how it anticipates the theme of the story.

4. In paragraph 6, who is "them"?

5. Compare and contrast Dee's behavior toward her mother (in paragraph 11) with Rodriguez's toward his parents as he became more fluent in English.

6. Why does the mother emphasize Dee's word "choose" in paragraph 14?

7. Why does Dee (Wangero) make a point of taking pictures that include the house (and even a cow) as background?

8. What is the significance of Dee's protest (paragraph 66): "Maggie can't appreciate these quilts! . . . She'd probably be backward enough to put them to everyday use." In what way does Dee "appreciate" the quilts? What indicates that the author (Alice Walker) is handling Dee ironically? Discuss also the ironic treatment of Dee in paragraphs 80 and 81.

9. What "hits" the mother just before she gives Maggie the quilts?

10. To what extent can you sympathize with Dee? What kind of attitude or cultural trend does she represent?

11. Leaving aside for the moment Dee's treatment of her family, which other authors in this chapter would be most sympathetic to her? Which would be least sympathetic?

12. Consider what happens (or some of what happens) in "Everyday Use" in relation to the discussion in one of the other articles in this chapter. Then write a sentence or two summarizing "Everyday Use" that could be inserted at a particular point in the other article as an example of its author's thesis. Do the same with one or two other articles, trying to select pieces with different viewpoints. Discuss how your story summaries change with each attempt to fit them into the context of articles with differing viewpoints.

13. To what extent do you think Irving Howe ("The Limits of Ethnicity") would approve of the mother's behavior in "Everyday Use" while disapproving of Dee's? Explain, using particular sections of Howe's arguments to back up your explanation.

14. If you have read Alice Walker's novel *The Color Purple* (or if you have seen the film), identify some similar thematic concerns between that work and "Everyday Use." Which characters are similar? How so? What kinds of conflicts or tensions do we find in the two works? How are they resolved?

SUMMARY ASSIGNMENT

Write a summary of Bebe Moore Campbell's "Blacks Who Live in a White World." (You may need to review the procedures discussed in Chapter 2.)

Begin by writing one-sentence section summaries. Then write a thesis for the article as a whole. Next combine your thesis and the section summaries into a coherent summary of the entire article.

We will help get you started by suggesting one way that the first part of the article can be divided into sections and by writing the first one-sentence section summary.

Section 1 (paragraphs 1–3)
   Like many other blacks in corporate America, Rodney Butler discovered that he could climb the executive ladder only by denying part of his ethnic heritage.

Section 2 (paragraphs 4–8)

Section 3 (paragraphs 9–11)

PAPER ASSIGNMENTS

1. Write a paper that uses techniques of comparison-contrast to develop one of the following topics:

   - The nature of ethnic identity and ethnic pride
   - The costs of ethnic identity
   - The nature of assimilation
   - The costs of assimilation
   - A delicate balance between two worlds
   - Making adjustments and compromises
   - Generational conflicts
   - Personal crises
   - Redefining one's self
   - Resolutions of crises
   - The limits of ethnicity
   - The limits of assimilation
   - Social implications
   - Feelings of self-worth and self-hatred

   You may also use other techniques such as description, argument, and cause and effect. Having formulated a thesis, read or reread the selections with an eye to finding evidence that will support your thesis.

2. Depending on your own ethnic background, the theme of this chapter may be particularly relevant to your own experiences. If this is the case

(or if it is the case with your parents or grandparents), write an essay discussing how the conflict between ethnic identity and cultural assimilation has been a problem for you or for someone in your family. Discuss also the ways you have found for dealing with and possibly resolving this problem. Wherever possible, draw on the works in this chapter.

3. Select two articles in this chapter that appear to represent opposite viewpoints and *compare and contrast* them. (Review the material on pages 433–435 of this chapter for advice on comparison-contrast essays.)

4. Write an essay describing of some of the anxieties and difficulties experienced by people caught in the dilemma of ethnic identity and cultural assimilation. (Review the material on page 212 of Chapter 7 for advice on using descriptions to support a thesis.)

5. Write an essay giving examples of crucial moments experienced by people discussed in articles in this chapter that caused them to change their attitudes (including the way they thought about themselves) and/or the way they behaved in regard to their ethnic heritage or their relation to the majority culture. (Review the material on pages 238–239 of Chapter 8 for advice on using examples to support a thesis.)

6. *Argue* either that minorities need primarily to find ways of reaffirming their ethnic pride or that they need primarily to find ways of assimilating. Use at least three of the articles in this chapter in support of your position. (Review the material on pages 294–296 of Chapter 9 for advice on using argument to support a thesis.)

7. Using assignment number 6 as a basis, write an essay that emphasizes the dangers of taking the wrong course.

8. To a great extent people often behave in ways that other people expect them to behave, rather than in ways that they would like to behave. Write an essay showing how this is true, using examples from articles in this chapter. Include in your essay a discussion of the various consequences of behaving (and of not behaving) according to the expectations and standards of others.

9. Write an essay focusing on the crucial ways that formal education often changes the way one defines one's own self and one's relationship to the rest of the world. Use examples from articles in this chapter.

10. Discuss the ways that conflicts between parent and child highlight the ethnic identity-cultural assimilation dilemma. Use examples from articles in this chapter.

11. Based on the passages you have read in this chapter, compare and contrast the problems faced by Hispanics with those faced by blacks in assimilating to the majority culture. Pay particular attention to the problems faced in childhood (in terms of education, for example) and those faced in adulthood.

12. *Compare and contrast* the experiences of Armando Rendón and Stanley Sanders, using their articles.

13. Based on the material in this chapter, summarize the positions of those writers who favor *assimilation* (or who think that assimilation is inevitable) and the positions of those who favor retaining as much as possible of one's ethnic heritage (or who think that assimilation is *not* inevitable). Draw your own conclusions at the end of your paper. To begin, ask yourself which writer (or writers) best represents the assimilationist position? Which one (or ones) best represents the anti-assimilation position?

14. Write an *objective* account of Rodriguez's ideas together with Arturo Islas's criticisms of these ideas. Write this account as if it were to be a newspaper or newsmagazine story. (If you are interested in learning more about the reactions to Rodriguez's book, look up the list of reviews in the *Book Review Digest* for 1982 and 1983.)

15. Write your own paper assignment for this chapter. Find a common theme running through two or more articles, devise a topic based on this theme, and then write a question asking writers to draw upon material in the selections that would support a thesis based upon this topic. You might want to help out your writers by suggesting some specific articles or even by getting them started with an outline for the paper.

CHAPTER 13

The Assassination of Abraham Lincoln

Introduction

The assassination of Abraham Lincoln at Ford's Theater on April 14, 1865, by the actor John Wilkes Booth is one of the most dramatic and significant events in the history of the American republic. It is dramatic because Lincoln was the first president to be assassinated and because he was killed at the height of his triumph—five days after the end of the Civil War and the victory of the North that assured the preservation of the Union. It is significant not only because Lincoln has come to be almost universally regarded as the greatest American president but also because, had he lived, the terrible wounds of the Civil War might have been much quicker to heal and the nation might have been spared much of the bitterness and division that characterized the Reconstruction period and that persists in various forms even today.

In this chapter we are going to look very closely at the assassination of Lincoln. We will not be as concerned with the causes of the assassination or its effects as with the central event itself. In other words, we will be less concerned with the *why* than with the *what*. You may think that *what* happened

491

should be clear enough and that there is little point in looking very closely at the assassination itself. But we may get as many different impressions of what happened as there are different people to tell us about it — each of the tellers is likely to color his or her description with his or her own emotional response. Consider the mixture of fact and opinion in these brief descriptions of the assassination from history books:

> At the Cabinet on the 14th [Lincoln] spoke of Lee and other Confederate leaders with kindness, and pointed to the paths of forgiveness and goodwill. But that very night as he sat in his box at Ford's Theatre a fanatical actor, one of a murder gang, stole in from behind and shot him through the head. The miscreant leapt on the stage, exclaiming *"Sic semper tyrannis,"** and although his ankle was broken through his spur catching an American flag he managed to escape to Virginia, where he was hunted down and shot to death in a barn.[1]

> [Lincoln] was preparing for a reconciliation when, on April 15, 1865, he died at the hands of an assassin — John Wilkes Booth — a martyr to the cause he had served so singleheartedly.[2]

> [Lincoln's] theme was reconciliation and the reconstruction of loyal government in the defeated states. On the evening of April 14 he went to Ford's Theater in Washington and as he sat looking at the stage he was shot in the back of the head and cruelly murdered by an actor named Booth, who had some sort of grievance against him, and who had crept into the box unobserved.[3]

> But Providence seems to have looked aside. That same evening the Great Emancipator, at long last the hero of the victorious Union and, ironically, the last, lorn hope of the South, was assassinated at Ford's Theater in Washington by the mad John Wilkes Booth.[4]

Notice how, in each of these accounts, it's difficult to separate the *what* of the event from *how* the writer feels about it. (Note such emotionally laden language as "the miscreant leapt on the stage," "a martyr to the cause he had served so singleheartedly," "cruelly murdered," "the last, lorn hope of the South.") And this is a very common phenomenon.

Consider the following scene: A teacher is leading a discussion. Suddenly a student breaks into the room and begins questioning the teacher about a bad grade he has received on a paper. While the class looks on in amazement, the angry student starts to yell at the teacher, refusing to listen to any response. The teacher insists that the student leave, telling him that he will discuss the matter in private later that day. This only infuriates the student more and he begins shoving the teacher. When the teacher makes a move to defend himself, the student knocks him down. Then he runs out the door. For a few moments, the class is too stunned to move or speak. Then the teacher calmly picks him-

*Thus ever to tyrants.

[1] Winston S. Churchill, *A History of the English Speaking Peoples*, v. 4, *The Great Democracies* (New York: Dodd, Mead, 1958), 262.

[2] Charles A. Beard and Mary R. Beard, *A Basic History of the United States* (New York: Doubleday, 1944), 286.

[3] H. G. Wells, *The Outline of History* (New York: Garden City Books, 1949), 1012.

[4] William Miller, *A History of the United States* (New York: Dell, 1958), 244.

self up. The angry student comes back in the room, smiling. He and the teacher, also smiling now, shake hands. The teacher then turns to his class and tells them that they are to write a detailed account of the scene they have just witnessed—for it *was* a scene, staged for their benefit. The student actor leaves the room. Still shaken, the students begin to write. With various degrees of difficulty they try to remember exactly what they saw, exactly what was said. And their accounts of the scene differ significantly. Some have the teacher saying, "Leave the room, now!"; some have him saying, "Get out!" Some think the angry student wore a blue shirt; some don't remember the color at all. Some think the teacher was simply defending himself; some thought they saw a counterattack. In many cases, it is difficult for students to write an account of the "facts" that is separate from their strong emotional response to what they have seen.

One of the facts of the Lincoln assassination is that after Booth shot Lincoln, he jumped from the president's box to the stage of the theater, breaking his leg in the process. Almost every account of this event differs slightly in emphasis from every other account. Here, for example, is an account by Louis J. Weichmann, a contemporary, who was not at Ford's Theater that evening but who lived at the same boardinghouse as Mary Surratt, one of the conspirators later hanged for her part in the conspiracy:

> As he was descending, the spur in his left boot caught on to the flag which had been draped in front of the President's box, in honor of his presence, and clung to it, causing his left foot to partially turn under him as he struck the stage, and thereby one of the bones of his leg was broken. The height of the stage was twelve feet. Had it not been for this accident, Booth would doubtless have made his escape into Virginia, within the Confederate lines, and possibly out of the country; and thus it was that the national flag was a mute instrument in the vengeance which overtook the President's murderer. Booth, as he fled across the stage, turned partially, faced the audience, threw up his hands, holding aloft the gleaming knife, and exclaimed "Sic semper tyrannis."[5]

As we will see later, there is considerable disagreement over whether Booth did, in fact, exclaim "Sic semper tyrannis" on the stage of the theater; but what is interesting here is how Weichmann makes the flag a moral agent in the revenge of the nation against its president's murderer.

Here is another account by an actual eyewitness, a restaurant owner named James Ferguson:

> I heard some one halloo out of the box, "Revenge for the South!" I do not know that it was Booth, though I suppose it must have been; it was just as he was jumping over the railing. His spur caught in the blue part of the flag that was stretched around the box, and as he went over, it tore a piece of the flag, which dragged half way across the stage on the spur of his right heel.[6]

[5]Louis J. Weichmann, *A True History of the Assassination of Abraham Lincoln and of the Conspiracy of 1865,* ed. Floyd E. Risvold (New York: Knopf, 1975), 152.
[6]James Ferguson, *The Assassination of President Lincoln and the Trial of the Conspirators,* ed. Benn Pitman (New York: Moore, Wilstach and Baldwin, 1865), 76.

Ferguson's account is the only one we have encountered that mentions the detail of the flag being dragged across the stage on Booth's spur.

A more recent account is given here by Larry Starkey (Major Henry Rathbone, mentioned in this account, was Lincoln's guest that evening and, with his fiancée, Clara Harris, occupied the same box as the president and Mrs. Lincoln):

> Even given the height of the box, the jump would have been a simple one for the athletic Booth and, with only a single actor on the stage, would have been the first of an easy escape. But Rathbone's interference hadn't been counted into the plan, and the Union officer's grip on the young actor's coat threw him off balance, forcing him to kick away from the box rather than to leap. The spur of Booth's right boot caught in the Treasury Guard's flag and then scratched across the carefully framed portrait of George Washington, causing Booth to land even more off stride. He hit hard and off balance, and felt pain in his lower leg as he sank down hard against it until the bone split upward against his weight.[7]

Starkey focuses on the physical aspects of Booth's escape, emphasizing Rathbone's role in throwing the assassin off balance as he jumped.

Finally, here is an even more recent account, by Gore Vidal, from his novel *Lincoln:*

> Miss Harris shrieked, as Booth shoved past her and jumped onto the railing of the box. Then, with the sort of athletic gesture that had so delighted his admirers in this same theater, he leapt the twelve feet from box to stage. But, as on several other occasions when Booth's effects proved to be more athletic and improvised than dramatic and calculated, he had not taken into account the silken bunting that decorated the front of the box. The spur of one boot got entangled in the silk, causing him to fall, off-balance, to the stage, where a bone in his ankle snapped.[8]

Notice that while Starkey gives Rathbone's resistance as the main cause of the bad fall, Vidal attributes the accident to the "improvised" nature of Booth's jump—the kind of improvisation that he says was common for this particular actor. The sentence itself, in fact, seems to be a kind of sardonic criticism of Booth's acting style—an unusual approach for those who write about this topic.

In *Twenty Days* Dorothy Meserve Kunhardt and Philip B. Kunhardt give a variety of additional versions—some bizarre—of Booth's escape from the presidential box:

> Booth put one hand on the box rail, vaulted over it, and sailed through the air the twelve feet to the stage. In jumping, his right spur turned the framed engraving of Washington completely over, snagged the blue Treasury guard's flag festooned around the front of the box, and a shred of the blue

[7]Larry Starkey, *Wilkes Booth Came to Washington* (New York: Random House, 1976), 118–19.

[8]Gore Vidal, *Lincoln: A Novel* (New York: Ballantine, 1984), 648.

Two Versions of the Lincoln Assassination

material fluttered behind his heel all the way. Booth rose, flourished his dagger, shouted "Sic Semper Tyrannis," and strode out of sight.

Some said that the blue flag was not draped around the box, but up on a staff that stood straight up against the box's central pillar, but Booth managed to flip his spurred heel up there and make the tear, then he grasped the flagpole, slid his hands down its length and dropped the eight feet to the stage. Booth rode the rail first as though it were a saddle and his gait crossing the stage was a slow limp. He also coasted down the front of the box as though he were sledding, ran at top speed to the exit opposite and didn't say a word. He landed on his hands first; he was hurt dreadfully; he went by, moaning with pain. He soared fifteen feet from a crouched position, sauntered slowly to the footlights as though he were part of the troupe, flashed his knife blade in the gaslight, hissed "Sic Semper Tyrannis," with deathly pale face and eyes glittering, almost emitting fire, turned and with defiantly unhurried stage gait stalked off the stage.

In two curious variations, Booth hopped across the stage like a toad and the blue cloth hopped along just out of time behind him. And he was so completely paralyzed from the fall that his helpers had to throw a rope to him and he was pulled off behind scenes.

A young girl eyewitness contributed the fact that Booth had asked her just the day before whether "tyrannis" was spelled with two r's or two n's. She agreed with the versions of Booth's swift escape, but added an extra morsel — the maddened crowd had heaved her up on the stage and in a half-faint she realized the actor who played Lord Dundreary was fanning her with his wig. He volunteered that he had been standing alone in center stage when Booth fell heavily exactly beside him. But the actor Harry Hawk was also volunteering that he had been alone on the stage when Booth fell heavily.

In this chapter, then, you will read a variety of accounts of Lincoln's assassination. Although the time period covered will differ in each piece, we will focus on the period between the time Booth first entered Ford's Theater that evening (or the time that the Lincoln party arrived) and the time that the dying president was carried out of Ford's Theater and brought to a bed at the nearby roominghouse where he spent his last few hours.

As you read these selections, you may wish to consider some of the broader questions they raise. What is truth? Why does truth appear to vary according to the writer or speaker? How is history written? How can we trust what is written as "history"? How do we evaluate historical data? And, finally, why should any of this matter?

Mark E. Neely, Jr.

THE ASSASSINATION OF ABRAHAM LINCOLN

Mark E. Neely, Jr., is the director of the Louis A. Warren Lincoln Library and Museum in Fort Wayne, Indiana. The following passage, from his book, *The Abraham Lincoln Encyclopedia*, provides a historical overview of the assassination.

1   On April 14, 1865, Abraham Lincoln became the first American President to be assassinated. Indeed, there had been only one previous assassination attempt against a President. In 1835 Samuel Lawrence, a house painter born in England, tried to shoot Andrew Jackson because he believed that Jackson had denied him the crown of England. Even after the Baltimore Plot (and perhaps because the precautions taken then proved so embarrassing to Lincoln), the administration showed little outward fear of assassination. Secretary of State William H. Seward assured John Bigelow in a letter written July 15, 1862, that

> Assassination is not an American practice or habit, and one so vicious and so desperate cannot be engrafted into our political system. This conviction of mine has steadily gained strength since the Civil War began. . . . The President, during the heated season, occupies a country house near the Soldiers' Home, two or three miles from the city. He goes to and fro from that place on horseback, night and morning, unguarded.

Lincoln himself tended to be fatalistic; he felt that no security system could exclude assassins who would very likely be Southerners, one's own countrymen. Security precautions were minimal, therefore, and there was opportunity aplenty to assassinate President Lincoln.

2   John Wilkes Booth first revealed his plot to kidnap President Lincoln to his boyhood friends Samuel B. Arnold and Michael O'Laughlin in Barnum's Hotel in Baltimore in late August or early September 1864. In a sense, it was a second "Baltimore Plot," for Booth and his two original coconspirators were from the Baltimore area. Like the first plot, too, it was hatched at a time of great political excitement; the Democratic nominating convention was held in late August 1864. Maryland was fertile ground for opposition to Lincoln. A slave state in a country fighting slavery, it had been the scene of the first violence of the Civil War. On April 19, 1861, Massachusetts soldiers on their way to protect Washington were involved in a melee in Baltimore which saw 12 Marylanders and 4 Federal soldiers killed. Maryland Governor Thomas H. Hicks had written a letter to Congressman Edwin H. Webster, an officer in the Maryland militia, at about the time of Lincoln's election in 1860:

> [I have] no arms at hand to distribute, at earliest possible moment you shall have arms. . . . Will they [your militia company] be good men to send out to kill Lincoln and his men. If not, I suppose the arms would be better sent South.

The letter is controversial and must have been facetious, but it shows how easily such an idea came to mind in Maryland's fevered politics.

3   James Ryder Randall's famous poem "Maryland, My Maryland," written soon after the Baltimore riot, warned that "The despot's heel is on thy shore, Maryland." The Maryland House of Delegates debated the "gross usurpation, unjust, oppressive tyrannical acts of the President of the United States — and Booth's cry after he assassinated Lincoln would be *Sic semper tyrannis.*"

4   There was nothing unique about the political thought of John Wilkes Booth. In a long letter left with his sister in Philadelphia in 1864, Booth said that he had "ever held the South were right," and added: "People of the North, to hate tyranny, to love liberty and justice, to strike at wrong and oppression, was the teaching of our fathers. The study of our early history will not let me forget it, and may it never."

5   Like many others in the North, Booth denounced Lincoln's racial policies, claiming that "This country was formed for the *white,* not for the black man." He considered slavery "one of the greatest blessings (both for themselves and us) that God ever bestowed upon a favored nation." He claimed that Lincoln's policy toward blacks was "only preparing a way for their total annihilation." Maryland Congressman John W. Crisfield told the House of Representatives the same thing, that Negroes must be kept in slavery, for oth-

erwise "degradation, poverty…and ultimate extinction" would befall them.

6   Since April 1864 General Ulysses S. Grant had refused to exchange Confederate prisoners. Booth planned to kidnap Lincoln on his way to the Soldiers' Home, take him to Richmond, and exchange him for Confederate prisoners. Arnold and O'Laughlin agreed, and over the next few months Booth calculated his plot rationally. He tidied up his personal affairs by going to Montreal, Canada, where he consigned his $15,000 theatrical wardrobe to an agent who would try to run it through the blockade to the Confederacy. He obviously thought he would resume his career in the South after the successful kidnapping. On returning to Washington, Booth explored southern Maryland in November and December, claiming to be in the market for land, but actually looking for escape routes and recruits. He picked up a valuable accomplice on December 23 in John H. Surratt, who, as runner for the Confederate "mail" between Baltimore and Richmond, knew the likely escape routes in Maryland and shared Booth's Confederate sympathies. Surratt provided entree to the network of disloyalists in Washington and southern Maryland, among them David E. Herold and George A. Atzerodt. Herold hunted partridges in southern Maryland and claimed to know the area of escape; Atzerodt ferried Confederate spies across the Potomac and was knowledgeable about the route as well. Finally, on March 1, 1865, Booth added the dangerous, strong, and violent Lewis Thornton Powell (better known by the alias Lewis Payne, or Paine), an escaped Confederate prisoner from Florida.

7   The motivation of the conspirators was clear. Arnold, O'Laughlin, and Powell had been Confederate soldiers. Surratt and Atzerodt had served the Confederacy in surreptitious roles. All but Powell were Marylanders, and Powell had found a congenial board in Baltimore. Only Herold came from Washington, and he spent considerable time hunting in southern Maryland. Each had

more than reasons of political sympathy to join Booth. Arnold was unemployed, as was Herold; Powell was broke and desperate in a strange land. Surratt loved adventure and had learned not to fear Federal detectives. Atzerodt and all the others probably enjoyed the notoriety of associating with the famous Booth; Louis J. Weichmann, a key government witness at the trial of the assassins, claimed most of them were in it for the money. Booth was a wealthy man and supported members of the group in Washington and provided them with horses. The conspirators also expected to become Southern heroes.

8   By the time Booth had enough men to kidnap the President, his opportunity was gone, for the season of hot weather in Washington was gone, and the President no longer traveled regularly to the Soldiers' Home. Therefore, Booth changed his plans — still kidnapping, but now from Ford's Theatre while Lincoln watched a play. Booth's coconspirators did not like the idea; in the words of Samuel Arnold, they "wanted a shadow of a chance for" their lives. When Booth revealed the plan in March, serious disagreement followed, and Arnold swore to leave the plot in a week.

9   Under the pressure of Arnold's ultimatum, Booth tried to capture the President on March 17 when he was supposed to go out of Washington to a theatrical performance. Booth's information proved erroneous, and the conspirators rode out in vain. After the attempt, Arnold and O'Laughlin left Washington and the plot, and Surratt resumed his activities for the Confederacy. Booth now had too few men to kidnap even so loosely guarded a President as Lincoln.

10   By April 3 there was no Richmond government to which to take a kidnapped Lincoln. By noon of April 14, Booth decided to kill the President while he watched *Our American Cousin* at Ford's Theatre; the performance starred Laura Keene, famed comedienne who first produced the play in New York in 1858. Booth had free run of the

theater and even picked up his mail there. That afternoon, apparently, Booth bored a peephole in the door of the President's box and prepared a pole to jam the door so it could not be opened behind him once he entered the box.

11   Booth decided to kill Vice President Andrew Johnson and Secretary of State Seward too, probably because, as he later related to a woman who helped him escape, he thought it might lead to a political revolution in the North that would benefit the South. He did not assign his coconspirators their roles until 2 hours before the crime. In an 8:00 p.m. meeting at the Herndon House, he instructed Atzerodt to kill Johnson, Powell to kill Seward, and Herold to lead the Floridian Powell out of Washington. Atzerodt failed even to try to kill Johnson. Herold, too, failed: he fled without helping Powell, and Powell's inability to leave the city led to his capture.

12   Booth asked Edman Spangler, a scene changer, to hold his horse behind the theater. Spangler gave the job to "Peanut John" Burroughs. Booth encountered no obstacle from Lincoln's guard, John F. Parker, who apparently left the door to Lincoln's box unguarded to watch the play. In any case, such a famous actor as Booth would have had no trouble getting in to see a President notoriously fond of theater. Armed with a dagger and a single-shot Deringer [*sic*] pistol, Booth committed a crime that bore the idiosyncratic marks of his own personality. He guaranteed its theatricality by committing it in a theater. Lincoln was shot from behind while sitting in his private box overlooking the stage. The assassin, famous for his athletic acting, then leaped some 12 feet to the stage. Most accounts agree that he shouted "*Sic semper tyrannis!*" Thus the political motive was on his mind at the moment of the crime.

13   Powell came very near killing Seward as well. Pretending to deliver medicine, Powell forced his way into Seward's home. He injured the Secretary's son Frederick, stabbed Seward's cheek and neck, and might well have killed the Secretary but for the heavy brace the bedridden man wore on his neck as the result of a recent carriage accident. Seward's nurse, George Robinson, also helped save the Secretary, but not without serious injury to himself. On his way out, the dangerous Powell wounded another of Seward's sons, Augustus, and a State Department messenger who happened to be on the first floor.

14   Thus ended America's first successful presidential assassination. The shabbily run trial wreaked considerable hysterical vengeance on the perpetrators (and perhaps on some of their innocent acquaintances as well), but it failed to clear up all the circumstances of the assassination because it focused primarily on the idea that the crime was a Confederate plot.

15   Over the years, the motives of the conspirators were obscured in popular writings. The great effort to bring the nation back together was not aided by memories that Lincoln was killed by a group of Confederate sympathizers, disloyal spies, and ex-Confederate soldiers. To ease sectional tensions, the real political motive tended to be forgotten. Moreover, few were concerned enough about racism to remember or care that the crime had been motivated by racist hatred for Lincoln's policies toward the Negro. The real reasons for the crime receded so far from popular memory that Booth came to be seen as a madman, the perpetrator of an irrational crime.

16   Sensationalists and misguided zealots supplied reasons for the crime that made Booth's group the mere tools of persons with larger motives; Jefferson Davis, Catholics, and even a member of Lincoln's Cabinet have been accused of being the true perpetrators. But the conspirators' motive and opportunity are entirely explained by their Confederate sympathies and race hatred and by the loose security measures of the Lincoln administration.

EXERCISES	

Content

Recall the main ideas in this article by answering the following questions. Respond to some of the questions in your own words. Respond to others by finding quotations from the article that provide the answers.

1. What previous president was the target of an assassination attempt?

2. Why was the security provided to Lincoln so loose by today's standards?

3. What was the nature of Booth's first plot against Lincoln, hatched in Baltimore?

4. Why was Maryland, technically a Union state, considered hostile to Lincoln?

5. What was Booth's main objection to Lincoln?

6. Why were people like John Surratt and David Herold important to Booth as he devised his plot against Lincoln?

7. Why, according to Louis J. Weichmann, did the other conspirators agree to support Booth?

8. Why did the attempts to kidnap Lincoln fail? Why did Booth decide finally to kill Lincoln instead of to kidnap him?

9. What preparations did Booth make at Ford's Theater on the afternoon of the assassination day?

10. What other jobs were the conspirators to accomplish while Booth was killing Lincoln?

11. How did Booth get past Lincoln's guard in the theater?

12. Why did the plot against Secretary of State Seward fail?

13. Why did the assassination trial "[fail] to clear up all the circumstances of the assassination"?

14. What has tended to be the assumed motives behind the assassination? What was the real motive?

Structure

1. How is paragraph 3 related to paragraph 2?

2. Explain how paragraphs 6–9, considered together, form an identifiable section of the article. Give this section a title.

3. What is the purpose of paragraphs 15 and 16?

Fact/Opinion

Classify each of the following statements as either a fact, an opinion, or a fact wrapped in an opinion. If the statement is a combination of fact and opinion, identify which part is fact and which opinion.

1. "On April 14, 1865, Abraham Lincoln became the first American President to be assassinated."

2. "Lincoln himself tended to be fatalistic; he felt that no security system could exclude assassins who would very likely be Southerners, one's own countrymen."

3. "Booth decided to kill Vice President Andrew Johnson and Secretary of State Seward too, probably because, as he later related to a woman who helped him escape, he thought it might lead to a political revolution in the North that would benefit the South."

4. "But the conspirators' motive and opportunity are entirely explained by their Confederate sympathies and race hatred and by the loose security measures of the Lincoln administration."

Inferences

In your responses to the following questions, incorporate some of the quotations you located in response to the Content questions. You may decide to use either all or only part of each quotation.

1. John Wilkes Booth is often characterized in histories and in the popular mind as mad or deranged. Does Neely's account support this view? Why or why not?

2. In paragraph 5, Neely quotes Booth and Maryland Congressman John W. Crisfield. What is the purpose of these quotations?

3. Find a history book or a book about Lincoln that describes the Lincoln assassination, and compare this description with Neely's. What differences in fact or interpretation do you find? How do you account for these differences?

Dorothy Meserve Kunhardt ■ Philip B. Kunhardt, Jr.

GOOD FRIDAY IN WASHINGTON

Dorothy Meserve Kunhardt had a successful career as an author of children's books but became a historian after inheriting from her father, Frederick Hill Meserve, the greatest collection in existence of photos of Lincoln, his contemporaries, and his times. Together with her son Philip B. Kunhardt, Jr., a former managing editor of *Life* magazine and author of *My Father's House*, she wrote *Twenty Days: A Narrative in Text and Pictures of the Assassination of Abraham Lincoln and the Twenty Days and Nights That Followed*, from which the following excerpt is taken. She later collaborated with her son on *Matthew Brady and His World*. In 1983, four years after Dorothy Kunhardt died, Philip Kunhardt published *A New Birth of Freedom: Lincoln at Gettysburg*. This passage covers the last few hours before the assassination and ends the instant before Booth pulls the trigger.

1   At eleven-thirty that Good Friday morning of April 14, 1865, less than eight hours before curtain time, a White House messenger arrived at Ford's Theatre with the welcome news that the President accepted the management's invitation to attend that evening's performance of *Our American Cousin*. Ever since John Ford had bought the old First Baptist Church of Washington in 1859 and turned it into a theatre, it had been a focal point in the city. When the building burned to the ground on December 30, 1862, Ford built an even finer brick theatre, at which he presented the best actors and actresses of the time. Lincoln attended plays there often, finding rest and distraction in watching such noted actors as Edwin Forrest, James H. Hackett and Edwin Booth. He liked Shakespeare, but remarked dryly that Shakespeare's characters did talk a great deal while they were dying. Sometimes he was so weary, as he was on April 14, that just getting to the theatre seemed too great an effort. As he said after seeing Edwin Booth in *The Merchant of Venice*, "I had a thousand times rather read it at home if it were not for Booth's playing."

2   Now Ford was away on a trip to Richmond and the news of Lincoln's attendance that evening was received by his brother James, business manager of the theatre. A third brother, twenty-one-year-old

Harry, realizing that a presidential visit during the week of national victory was an occasion, personally set about furnishing and decorating the ample space provided by throwing boxes Numbers Seven and Eight together. He used a sofa, flags, a framed engraving of George Washington, two stuffed chairs on casters, and a rocking chair, which he thought the President would find comfortable, and six straight-legged chairs for possible guests. The rocking chair was part of a Victorian set, and it was such a comfortable chair that when it had been stored downstairs the ushers had lounged in it and their hair had made a greasy spot on the figured dark-red satin with which the chair was upholstered. So the spot would not get worse Harry had kept it upstairs in his own room. Now, feeling that the disfigurement would not be noticed in the few rays of gaslight which would penetrate the presidential box with its double curtaining of lace and satin, he got a theatre errand boy to carry it on his head to the dress circle. Harry then placed the chair where its long rockers exactly fitted, in the left-hand corner.

3   At eleven-thirty that morning John Wilkes Booth, the actor — he was Edwin's younger brother — had arrived at the theatre to pick up his mail, a privilege he had been given by his close friend, John Ford. There he learned of the President's visit. He seemed casual as he sat down on the theatre steps to read his letter but everyone who saw him from that moment on noticed he was deathly pale — thought he looked sick. He left soon to begin a day of frenzied preparation. No one has ever pinpointed the hour at which Booth stole back into the theatre, made a hole in the wall for a bar to jam the door of the box, and bored a peephole in the door, grinding through the wood with a large iron-handled gimlet, then carving it out to the size of a finger with a pen-knife. Through it he had a dead-eye view of the back of the rocking chair.

4   The President and Mrs. Lincoln had had a hard time assembling guests for their the-atre party. Besides their son Robert they had invited twelve people to go with them and at the end had had just two acceptances.

5   Even though it had been announced in the papers that General and Mrs. Grant would be in the theatre box that evening with the President and his lady, as the afternoon began Mrs. Grant did her best to release herself from the prospect of an unpleasant three hours. At City Point, a few days before, Mrs. Lincoln had refused to step on shore until the Grants' boat was swung out from the dock and the Lincoln vessel maneuvered into the place of honor — she would not set foot on the Grants' deck. And when the General's wife sat down on a coil of ropes on board a war vessel she had been asked, "How dare you sit in the presence of the wife of the President of the United States?"

6   General Grant finally told Mr. Lincoln with apologies that he and Mrs. Grant were so longing to see their daughter, at school in New Jersey, that they could not wait until the next day but would leave by train immediately.

7   Mrs. Stanton, wife of the Secretary of War, also took every opportunity to avoid the First Lady — as she put it, succinctly and coldly, "I do not call on Mrs. Lincoln." Mr. Stanton declined for himself and his wife, though he gave as his reason his strong disapproval of the President's risking his life by appearing in a public place at a time when passions ran high.*

*"It's incontestable that in the afternoon [of April 14, 1865] Lincoln went to the War Department and requested that Major Thomas Eckert accompany him as bodyguard to the theater that night. Eckert, Lincoln said, could break iron pokers over his arm.

"Stanton denied the request, saying he had pressing work for Eckert that evening. Lincoln then asked Eckert himself, who said he followed Stanton's orders. In fact, Eckert only went home that evening, while Stanton called on Seward and then went home himself. However many questions their excuses raised later, the President acquiesced that afternoon." (James McKinley, *Assassination in America* [New York: Harper and Row, 1977], 15)

8   The Lincolns had picked up their last-minute substitute guests, Major Henry Reed Rathbone and his stepsister and fiancée, Clara Harris, at the Harris home and driven them in their carriage to the theatre—with Edward Burke, their coachman, in livery up on the box and Charles Forbes, the President's personal attendant, beside him. It was just a month since the Lincolns had last invited Clara to go with them to the theatre, and Mrs. Lincoln seemed to have forgiven her father, Ira Harris, a prominent lawyer of Albany who had been elected to the Senate in 1861, for asking the blunt question one day in the White House—"Why isn't Robert in the army?"

9   Major Rathbone was twenty-eight years old and had only recently been appointed by the President as Assistant Adjutant General of Volunteers. Obviously he had not had it impressed upon him that he was to watch out for the President's safety that evening, for he sat on the sofa in the far front of the box slightly behind Clara but nowhere near the President. A seat behind Lincoln would have placed him in the path of the box door by which Booth was to enter.

10   The presidential party was so late that evening that the curtain had to go up without the Lincolns and their guests. In about half an hour they were seen in the dress circle approaching their box, and the play stopped, the audience rose and applauded and the orchestra struck up "Hail to the Chief." The First Lady was all smiles, but Mr. Lincoln seemed weary and his face was serious. The audience had settled down for an evening of laughter at a silly play, and now the President's melancholy mood would be a poor match for the high spirits of the crowd.

11   It was true that Lincoln had experienced one of his swift changes from confident hope to depression. Late that afternoon he had walked to the War Department with his guard, William Crook, as he had done so many times before, and had said something that he had never said before.

12   "Crook, do you know," he said, "I believe there are men who want to take my life." Then he lowered his voice, as though talking to himself. "And I have no doubt they will do it."

13   "Why do you think so, Mr. President?" asked Crook.

14   "Other men have been assassinated," Lincoln answered. "I know no one could do it and escape alive. But if it is to be done, it is impossible to prevent it."*

15   And a little later when he left for the theatre in his carriage, for the first time, the guard remembered later, Lincoln said, "Good-by, Crook," instead of the usual "Good night." The newly hired White House guard, John Parker, who was a patrolman on the Metropolitan Police Force, had been charged with Lincoln's protection for the evening. Parker had gone on ahead to the theatre—there was no official protection for the President throughout the short drive.

16   On the night of April 14 Laura Keene was playing the part of the young girl Florence Trenchard in *Our American Cousin* for more than the thousandth time. By her grace and natural style of acting in an age when many characters were played in a stylized manner, she managed to give a pleasing illusion of youth. Laura Keene had shiny auburn curls, a creamy complexion, and dark brown eyes which were a little on the beady side. When she first presented *Our American Cousin* in New York in 1858 at the Olympic Theatre she had the benefit of being supported by the famous actors E. A. Sothern, as Lord Dundreary, and Joseph Jefferson, as Asa Trenchard. But now, on tour, Harry Hawk was proving a very well-received Asa, the comically eccentric backwoodsman.

---

*"Lincoln not only spoke of his premonitions of death; he saw himself dead. Within a month of April 14 he'd had, and remarked on, a dream in which he saw a corpse lying in state in the East Room. The dreaming President asked a guard who was dead in the White House. He answered, "The President; he was killed by an assassin." Surely this was in the President's mind on the fourteenth, when he conducted his 11 A.M. Cabinet meeting." (McKinley, *Assassination in America,* 15)

17   Harry Hawk was a permanent member of Laura Keene's company and toured with her as her manager as well as principle comedian in the plays she presented. During this Good Friday performance both Laura Keene and Harry Hawk as well as the Ford's Theatre orchestra leader, William Withers, could see the Lincoln party up in the box enjoying the play. While Mrs. Lincoln laughed openly and heartily at every joke, her husband frequently leaned forward and rested his chin in one hand, seemed to be thinking of something not present. There were people in the audience who watched, guessing that he was pondering his greatest problem, how to welcome back the Southern states and make them feel at home in the Union, from which he held they had never been absent. His own instruction to his officers, given only a few days before, was still his consuming wish: "Let 'em down easy."

18   The First Lady was oblivious of the fact that the President's thoughts were straying from the performance. She was to be questioned closely as to what Mr. Lincoln's exact last words had been, and she would ultimately take refuge in remembering two completely opposite versions, which she told alternately.

19   First, she recalled that her hand had been on Mr. Lincoln's knee and she had been leaning across the arm of his chair, over very close to him, so close that she had asked rather apologetically, with a look at the engaged couple in the front of the box, "What will Miss Harris think of my hanging on to you so?" The last words were the pronouncement, "She won't think anything about it."

20   But then later Mrs. Lincoln was sure the President had turned to her just before Booth's shot and remarked earnestly, "How I should like to visit Jerusalem sometime!" This was an odd sequence of thought as the play had been following a less than spiritual course and convulsing the audience as a wildly caricatured American backwoodsman arrived to visit his English cousins. The

Lincolns had heard Binny the butler ask Asa Trenchard if he would like to have a "baath," heard Asa tell Binny to "absquatulate—vamose!"—that he was a "tarnal fat critter—swelling out his bosom like an old turkey cock in laying time," had heard the butler's answer, "I suppose I shall be a hox next, or perhaps an 'ogg." Down in the drawing room Our American Cousin offered to mix a drink for a young lady invalid and promised his concoction "would make a sick girl squirm like an eel in a mud bank." Two minutes before Booth's shot sounded in the box Asa warned the girl who was flirting with him, thinking him a rich catch, "Don't look at me that way...if you do I'll bust. I'm biling over with affections which I'm ready to pour all over you like apple sass over roast pork." The actual last speech before the assassination was by the American Cousin in answer to the scheming mother who had just found out he was not rich and called out angrily that Asa did not know the manners of good society. Asa was alone on the stage and for the final time Abraham Lincoln heard the sound of a human voice. "Don't know the manners of good society, eh? Well, I guess I know enough to turn you inside out, old gal—you sockdologizing old mantrap."

21   If Abraham Lincoln had been given time to turn around in his rocking chair that night in the theatre, he would have instantly recognized his assassin. Twenty-six-year-old John Wilkes Booth was one of the country's promising actors though no one expected him to come near the genius of his father, Junius Brutus Booth, or his incomparable brother, Edwin Booth. Lincoln had seen him perform, seen that handsome pale face, the thick, raven hair, the deep-set eyes, black as ink and filled with a strange, wild fire. Only a few months before, the President had been at Ford's Theatre in his usual box watching Booth play the part of a villain, and whenever the Maryland actor had anything ugly and threatening to say he had stepped up near the presidential box and shaken his

finger toward Lincoln and said the lines directly to him. "He looks as if he meant that for you," the President's companion said, and Lincoln replied, "Well, he does look pretty sharp at me, doesn't he?"

EXERCISES

Content

Recall the main ideas in this article by answering the following questions. Respond to some of the questions in your own words. Respond to others by finding quotations from the article that provide the answers.

1. Why did the management of Ford's Theater have good reason to believe that the president would be interested in attending a performance of *Our American Cousin?*

2. What special preparations were made by the theater management for Lincoln's visit?

3. Why did John Wilkes Booth have such easy access to Ford's Theater?

4. What did the General and Mrs. Grant give as an excuse for not accompanying the Lincolns to the theater that night? What, according to the authors, was the real reason?

5. Who were the chief players in *Our American Cousin* on that evening?

6. In what way were Mrs. Lincoln's memories of the president's last words inconsistent?

7. What kind of play is *Our American Cousin?*

Structure

1. Explain how paragraphs 4–8, considered together, form an identifiable section of the article. Give this section a title.

2. What is the purpose of paragraph 8?

3. What is the purpose of paragraphs 11–15?

4. Write two more Structure questions and answer them.

Fact/Opinion

Classify each of the following statements as either a fact, an opinion, or a fact wrapped in an opinion. If the statement is a combination of fact and opinion, identify which part is fact and which opinion.

1. "When [the first Ford's Theater] burned to the ground on December 30, 1862, Ford built an even finer brick theatre, at which he presented the best actors and actresses of the time."

2. "The President and Mrs. Lincoln had had a hard time assembling guests for their theatre party."

3. "There were people in the audience who watched [Lincoln], guessing that he was pondering his greatest problem, how to welcome back the Southern states and make them feel at home in the Union, from which he held they had never been absent."

Diagram of the Stage of Ford's Theater
at the Time of Lincoln's Assassination

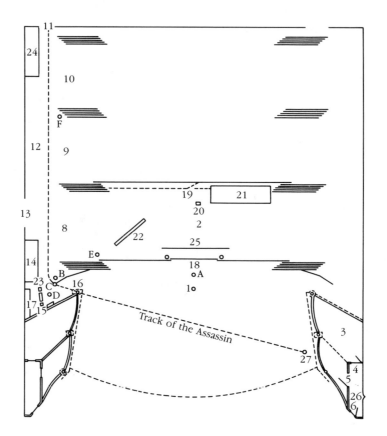

A. 'Asa Trenchard' (Mr. Harry Hawk)	right (figure missing from original diagram)	18. Center door in scene
B. Miss Laura Keene		19. Fence, with gate
C. Mr. Ferguson	8. Second entrance to right	20. Martin-house
D. Gas Man		21. Set dairy (12 ft. by 12 ft., 3 feet deep)
E. Stage Manager (Mr. Wright)	9. Third entrance to right	22. Bench
F. Mr. Wm. Withers, Jr., (Leader of Orchestra)	10. Fourth entrance to right	23. Small table and two chairs
	11. Back door to alley	24. Covered stairway to basement
1. First scene	12. Scenery in pile	25. Set piece, to mask center door
2. Second scene	13. Door to dressing-rooms	
3. Box of President	14. Scenery in pile	26. Hole in the wall, to fasten door (3 ft. 6 in. from corner)
4. Door to box	15. Governor to gas-lights	
5. Door to box	16. Prompter's desk	27. Torn place in carpet (two feet from lower box)
6. Entrance to passage	17. Scenery in pile	
7. First entrance to		

Inferences

In your responses to the following questions, incorporate some of the quotations you located in response to the Content questions. You may decide to use either all or only part of each quotation.

1. Based on the information in this selection, what can you gather about the differences in temperament between Abraham Lincoln and his wife?

2. How do the authors suggest that Major Rathbone was guilty of negligence?

3. What other factors (besides John Wilkes Booth) appear to be contributory factors in Lincoln's assassination?

AWFUL EVENT

This is the lead story in the April 15, 1865, edition of the *New York Times*.

AWFUL EVENT.
President Lincoln Shot
by an Assassin.
The Deed Done at Ford's Theatre Last Night.

The Act of a Desperate Rebel.

The President Still Alive at Last Accounts.

No Hopes Entertained of His Recovery.

Attempted Assassination of Secretary Seward.

Details of the Dreadful Tragedy.

[Official]

War Department

Washington, April 15, — 1:30 a.m.

1 This evening at about 9:30 p.m., at Ford's Theatre, the President, while sitting in his private box with Mrs. Lincoln, Miss Harris, and Major Rathborn, was shot by an assassin, who suddenly entered the box and approached behind the President.

2 The assassin then leaped upon the stage, brandishing a large dagger or knife, and made his escape in the rear of the theatre.

3 The pistol ball entered the back of the President's head and penetrated nearly through the head. The wound is mortal. The President has been insensible ever since it was inflicted, and is now dying.

4 About the same hour an assassin, whether the same or not, entered Mr. Seward's apartments, and under the pretense of having a prescription, was shown to the Secretary's sick chamber. The assassin immediately rushed to the bed, and inflicted two or three stabs on the throat and two on the face. It is hoped the wounds may not be mortal. My apprehension is that they will prove fatal.

5 The nurse alarmed Mr. Frederick Seward, who was in an adjoining room, and hastened to the door of his father's room, when he met the assassin, who inflicted upon him one or more dangerous wounds. The recovery of Frederick Seward is doubtful.

6 It is not probable that the President will live throughout the night.

7 Gen. Grant and his wife were advertised to be at the theatre this evening, but he started to Burlington at 6 o'clock this evening.

8 At a cabinet meeting at which Gen. Grant was present, the subject of the state of the country and the prospect of a speedy peace was discussed. The President was very cheerful and hopeful, and spoke very kindly of Gen. Lee and others of the Confederacy and of the establishment of government in Virginia.

9   All the members of the Cabinet except Mr. Seward, are now in attendance upon the President.

10   I have seen Mr. Seward, but he and Frederick were both unconscious. — **Edwin M. Stanton, Secretary of War.**

Detail of the Occurrence

Washington, Friday, April 14 — 12:30 a.m.

11   The president was shot in a theatre tonight, and is, perhaps, mortally wounded.

12   Secretary Seward was also assassinated.

Second Dispatch.

Washington, Friday, April 14

13   President Lincoln and his wife, with other friends, this evening visited Ford's Theatre for the purpose of witnessing the performance of the "American Cousin."

14   It was announced in the papers that Gen. Grant would also be present, but he took the late train of cars for New-Jersey.

15   The theatre was densely crowded, and everybody seemed delighted with the scene before them. During the third act, and while there was a temporary pause for one of the actors to enter, a sharp report of a pistol was heard, which merely attracted attention, but suggesting nothing serious, until a man rushed to the front of the President's box, waving a long dagger in his right hand, and exclaiming "*Sic semper tyrannis,*" and immediately leaped from the box, which was in the second tier, to the stage beneath and ran across to the opposite side, making his escape amid the bewilderment of the audience from the rear of the theatre, and mounting a horse, fled.

16   The screams of Mrs. Lincoln first disclosed the fact to the audience that the President had been shot, when all present rose to their feet, rushing toward the stage, many exclaiming "Hang him! hang him!"

17   The excitement was of the wildest possible description, and of course there was an abrupt termination of the theatrical performance.

18   There was a rush toward the President's box, when cries were heard: "Stand back and give him air," "Has any one stimulants." On a hasty examination, it was found that the President had been shot through the head, above and back of the temporal bone, and that some of the brain was oozing out. He was removed to a private house opposite to the theatre, and the Surgeon-General of the army, and other surgeons sent for to attend to his condition.

19   On an examination of the private box blood was discovered on the back of the cushioned rocking chair on which the President had been sitting, also on the partition and on the floor. A common single-barreled pocket pistol was found on the carpet.

20   A military guard was placed in front of the private residence to which the President had been conveyed. An immense crowd was in front of it, all deeply anxious to learn the condition of the President. It had been previously announced that the wound was mortal; but all hoped otherwise. The shock to the community was terrible.

21   The President was in a state of syncope,* totally insensible, and breathing slowly. The blood oozed from the wound at the back of his head. The surgeons exhausted every effort of medical skill, but all hope was gone. The parting of his family with the dying President is too sad for description....

22   The entire city tonight presents a scene of wild excitement, accompanied by violent expressions of indignation, and the profoundest sorrow — many shed tears. The military authorities have dispatched mounted patrols in every direction, in order, if possible to arrest the assassins. The whole metropolitan police are likewise vigilant for the same purpose.

23   The attacks both at the theatre and at Secretary Seward's house took place at about the same hour — 10 o'clock — thus showing a preconcerted plan to assassinate those gentlemen. Some evidence of the guilt of the party who attacked the President are in the possession of the police.

24   Vice-President Johnson is in the city, and his headquarters are guarded by troops.

*unconsciousness

Another Account

Special Dispatch to the New York-Times
Washington, Friday, April 14, 11:15 p.m.

25   A stroke from Heaven laying the whole of the city in instant ruins could not have startled us as did the word that broke from Ford's Theatre a half hour ago that the President had been shot. It flew everywhere in five minutes, and set five thousand people in swift and excited motion on the instant.

26   It is impossible to get at the full facts of the case, but it appears that a young man entered the President's box from the theatre during the last act of the play of "Our American Cousin," with pistol in hand. He shot the President in the head and instantly jumped from the box upon the stage, and immediately disappeared through the side scenes and rest of the theatre, brandishing a dirk knife and dropping a kid glove on the stage.

27   The audience heard the shot, but supposed it fired in the regular course of the play, did not heed it till Mrs. Lincoln's screams drew their attention. The whole affair occupied scarcely half a minute, and then the assassin was gone. As yet he has not been found.

28   The President's wound is reported mortal. He was at once taken into the house opposite the theatre.

29   As if this horror was not enough, almost the same moment the story ran through the city that Mr. Seward had been murdered in his bed.

30   Inquiry showed this to be so far true also. It appears that a man wearing a light coat, dark pants, slouch hat, called and asked to see Mr. Seward, and was shown to his room. He delivered to Major Seward, who sat near his father, what purported to be a physician's prescription, turned, and with one stroke cut Mr. Seward's throat as he lay on his bed, inflicting a horrible wound, but not severing the jugular vein, and not producing a mortal wound.

31   In the struggle that followed, Major Seward was also badly, but not seriously wounded in several places. The assassin rushed down the stairs, mounted the fleet horse on which he came, drove his spurs into him, and dashed away before any one could stop him.

32   Reports have prevailed that an attempt was also made on the life of Mr. Stanton.

Midnight

33   The President is reported dead. Cavalry and infantry are scouring the city in every direction for the murderous assassins, and the city is overwhelmed with excitement. Who the assassins were no one knows, though every body supposes them to have been rebels.

Saturday — 1 o'clock

34 The person who shot the President is reported as about 30 years of age, five feet nine inches in height, sparely built, of light complexion, dressed in dark clothing, and having a genteel appearance. He entered the box, which is known as the State box, being the upper box on the right hand side from the dress-circle in the regular manner, and shot the President from behind, the ball entering the skull about in the middle, behind, and going in the direction of the left eye; it did not pass through, but apparently broke the frontal bone and forced out the brain to some extent. The President is not yet dead, but is wholly insensible, and the Surgeon-General says he cannot live till day-break. The assassin was followed across the stage by a gentleman, who sprang out from an orchestra chair. He rushed through the side door into an alley, thence to the avenue and mounted a dark bay-horse, which he apparently received from the hand of an accomplice, dashed up F, toward the back part of the city. The escape was so sudden that he effectually eluded pursuit. The assassin cried "*sic sempre*" in a sharp, clear voice, as he jumped to the stage, and dropped his hat and a glove.

35   Two or three officers were in the box with the President and Mrs. Lincoln, who made efforts to stop the assassin, but were unsuccessful and received some bruises. The whole affair, from his entrance into the box

to his escape from the theatre, occupied scarcely a minute, and the strongest of the action found everybody wholly unprepared. The assault upon Mr. Seward appears to have been made almost at the same moment as that upon the President. Mr. Seward's wound is not dangerous in itself, but may prove so in connection with his recent injuries. The two assassins have both endeavored to leave the city to the north west, apparently not expecting to strike the river. Even so low down as Chain Bridge, cavalry have been sent in every direction to intercept them.

Saturday, 1:30 o'clock a.m.

36 The President still lies insensible. Messrs. Stanton, Wells, McCullough, Speed and Usher are with him, as also the Vice-President, the Surgeon-General, and other Surgeons.

37 There is a great throng about the house, even at this hour.

2 o'clock a.m.

38 The President still lives, but lies insensible, as he has since the first moment, and no hopes are entertained that he can survive.

39 The most extravagent stories prevail, among which one is to effect, that Gen. Grant was shot while on his way to Philadelphia, of course, this is not true.

40 Another is that every member of Mr. Seward's family was wounded in the struggle with the assassin there. This also is untrue. Mr. Fred. Seward, the Assistant Secretary, and Major Clarence Seward, of the army, were wounded, neither of them dangerously.

The Condition of the President
Saturday, April 15 — 2:12 a.m.

41 The President is still alive; but he is growing weaker. The ball is lodged in his brain, three inches from where it entered the skull. He remains insensible, and his condition is utterly hopeless.

42 The Vice-President has been to see him, but all company, except the members of the Cabinet and of the family, is rigidly excluded.

43 Large crowds still continue in the street, as near to the house as the line of guards allows.

EXERCISES

Content

Recall the main ideas in this article by answering the following questions. Respond to some of the questions in your own words. Respond to others by finding quotations from the article that provide the answers.

1. Does Stanton believe that the same man who shot the president also shot Seward?

2. How seriously did Stanton believe that Seward had been wounded when he wrote this report?

3. At what point in the play was Lincoln shot?

4. According to this report, when did the audience first become aware that something was wrong?

5. Was it clear, at this point, that Booth had hurt his leg?

6. Where was Lincoln taken after the shooting?

7. What item did the assassin leave at the murder scene? What did he drop on the stage?

8. How did the public react to the news of the president's shooting?

9. How did the police know that Lincoln's assassination and the shooting of Seward were connected?

10. At this point, how much was known of the assassin himself?

11. Why did the audience not respond to the sound of the pistol shot?

12. What misinformation about Lincoln's condition was reported at midnight?

13. What assumption was immediately made about the assassins?

14. How did the assassin make his escape?

15. What misinformation is provided in the "Midnight" story about the people in Lincoln's box just before the shooting?

16. In the 2 A.M. story, what other rumors are reported?

Inferences

In your responses to the following questions, incorporate some of the quotations you located in response to the Content questions. You may decide to use either all or only part of each quotation.

1. In what way is the first report of the president's assassination (paragraphs 1–10) different from the kind of report that would appear in a contemporary newspaper?

2. In what other ways do you find the reporting of this story different from what you would expect in a comparable modern story?

3. What indication does Stanton give at this early point that Lincoln's assassination would seriously affect the Reconstruction period?

4. Why do you think no mention is made of the name of Lincoln's assassin?

TESTIMONY FROM EYEWITNESSES

The following selections are statements from individuals who had direct knowledge of the people and events surrounding the assassination of Abraham Lincoln. These statements are derived from the testimony collected by the nine-member military commission that tried the conspirators. John Wilkes Booth himself was not tried, having been shot to death by Union cavalry on April 26, 1865 (eleven days after the assassination), while hiding in a barn with fellow conspirator David Herold. The other conspirators undergoing trial were Lewis Paine (formerly Powell), George Atzerodt, Mrs. Mary Surratt, Dr. Samuel Mudd (who treated Booth's broken leg), the stagehand Edward Spangler, Samuel Arnold, and Michael O'Laughlin. (See Mark Neely's article, "The Assassination of Abraham Lincoln," paragraphs 6–7, for descriptions of the conspirators.) Herold, Paine, Atzerodt, and Surratt went to the gallows on July 7, 1865. Arnold, O'Laughlin, Spangler, and Mudd were sentenced to imprisonment at Fort Jefferson in the island of Garden Key, Florida. John Surratt, Mary's son, who had fled the country immediately after the assassination, was brought back to the United States to stand trial in 1867, but the trial ended in a hung jury and Surratt was freed. O'Laughlin died at Fort Jefferson of yellow fever in 1867. The remaining conspirators, Arnold, Spangler, and Mudd, were pardoned by President Andrew Johnson in 1869.

Benn Pitman, recorder to the military commission, arranged and reordered the trial testimony, eliminating repetition and converting the question and answer transcript (represented by the Samuel Knapp Chester testimony below) to statement form. In an article he wrote in 1900 Pitman describes his work schedule during the trial:

My duties commenced at 9 o'clock in the morning and I rarely left the War Department until between 10 and 11 at night.... At the trial of the assassins over four hundred witnesses were examined. The proceedings on the busy days required the services of six reporters.... When fewer witnesses were examined, I reported the entire proceedings. Two press copies were taken of the transcribed notes.... The original formed the court record, one copy was kept at the War Department, and the other was afterward confided to the writer for the compilation and publication of the proceedings of the trial.

The extract from John Wilkes Booth's diary, following the trial testimony, is reprinted from Philip Van Doren Stern's edition of the trial testimony edited by Pitman.

Samuel Knapp Chester

A witness called for the prosecution, being duly sworn testified as follows:—

By the Judge Advocate.*—

Q. Your profession is that of an actor?

A. Yes, sir.

Q. Have you known J. Wilkes Booth a good many years?

A. I have known him about ten or eleven years, since I first met him.

Q. Quite intimately, I suppose?

A. For about six or seven years intimately.

Q. Can you recall a conversation which you are supposed to have had with him in November last in New York?

A. Yes, sir.

Q. What time in the month was it?

A. I think it was in November that I had a conversation with him.

Q. What time in November? State about the period of time.

A. I cannot think of the exact date, but was in the early portion of November: one day we were in conversation, and I asked him why he was not acting, and he told me that he did not intend to act in this portion of the country again: that he had taken his wardrobe to Canada, and intended to run the blockade.

Q. Did you meet him after that, and have some conversation with him in regard to oil speculations, or was it at the same time?

A. No, sir; the next time I met him was about the time we were in the play *Julius Caesar,* which we did play on the 25th of November; and it was either on the 24th or 25th that he asked me to take a walk with him, or asked if I knew some costumers, where he might get some dressers from his character in that play; and I asked him where his own wardrobe was.

Q. Was that in the city of New York?

A. Yes; I never had any conversation with him relative to this affair out of New York; he said it was still in Canada, in charge of a friend, and I think he said, named Martin; I will not be positive, but I think he said it was in Montreal; he did not say anything to me at all about the oil business then, that I remember.

Q. Did he not ask you how you would like to go into the oil business with him?

A. Not in the oil business; he never mentioned that.

*Brigadier General Joseph Holt, in charge of the prosecution.

Q. He told you he had a big speculation on hand?

A. Yes, sir.

Q. Did he ask you to go in with him?

A. Yes, sir; I met him, and he was talking with some friends, and they were joking with him about the affair; I met him on Broadway; after he left them he said he had a better speculation than that on hand, and one they would not laugh at; some time after that I met him again and he again talked of this speculation, and asked me how I would like to go in with him; I told him I was without means, that I could not; and he said it did not matter, he always liked me and would furnish the means; the next time I heard from him he was in Washington.

Q. State the whole of the conversation in which he urged you to go into this speculation in New York.

A. As well as I can remember, I will tell you from beginning to end. He left me then in New York, and I received several letters from him from Washington, telling me he was speculating in farms in lower Maryland and was sure to coin money; that I must go with him to Virginia, and still telling me that I must join him; that I paid very little attention to it. Then about the latter part of December or early in January, I will not be positive which it was, but late in December or early in January, he came to New York; I then lived at No. 45 Grove street; he asked me to take a walk with him; I did so; we went out and went into a saloon known as the House of Lords, in the Houston street; we remained there a considerable time; I suppose an hour, eating and drinking; he had often mentioned this affair; that is, his speculation; but would never say what it was; if I would ask him what it was he would say he would tell me by-and-by. We left there and went to another saloon under the Revere House, and ate some oysters. We then started up Broadway; I thought it was time to

go home, and my way was down Bleecker street, that is, up Broadway from the corner of Houston, and I had to turn down Bleecker street to get to Grove street; I bade him good night. He asked me to talk a piece further up the street with him, and I did so; I walked a square, that is, to Fourth street because Broadway was crowded; he said Fourth street was not so full of people as Broadway, and he wanted to tell me about that speculation; I walked up there with him, and when we got into an unfrequented portion of the street, he stopped and told me then that he was in a large conspiracy to capture the heads of the Government, including the President, and take them to Richmond; I asked him if that was what he wished me to go in; he said it was; I told him I could not do it, that it was an impossibility; only to think of my family; he said he had two or three thousand dollars that he could leave them; I still said I could not do it; he urged it, and talked with me for, I suppose, twenty minutes or half an hour, and I still refused; he then told me that at least I would not betray him, and said I dare not; he said he could implicate me in the affair, any how; he said that the party were sworn together, and that if I attempted to betray them I would be hunted down through life, and talked some more about the affair; I cannot remember it now; but still urging me, saying I had better go in; I told him no, and bade him goodnight, and I went home.

Q. Did he indicate to you what part he wished you to play in carrying out the conspiracy?

A. Yes, sir.

Q. What did he say?

A. That I was to open the back door of the Theatre at a signal.

Q. Did he indicate at what Theatre this was to occur?

A. Yes; he told me at Ford's Theatre; because it must be some one acquainted or connected with the Theatre who could take part in it.

Q. Ford's Theatre in Washington?

A. Yes, sir.

Q. Did he urge you upon the ground that it was an easy affair, and that you would have very little to do?

A. Yes, he said that; that was all I would have to do, he said. He said the thing was sure to succeed.

Q. What preparations did he say, if any, had been made toward the conspiracy?

A. He told me that everything was in readiness; that it was sure to succeed, for there were parties on the other side ready to co-operate with them.

Q. Did you understand from him that the Rebel Government was sanctioning what he was doing?

A. He never told me of that.

Q. What do you mean by parties on the other side?

A. I imagined that they were on the other side, but he did not say who they were; I mean they were those people; he said on the other side.

Q. Did he mention the probable number of persons engaged in the conspiracy?

A. He said there were from fifty to a hundred; he said that when he first mentioned the affair to me.

Q. Did he write to you?

A. He wrote about this speculation, and then he wrote to me again; that must have been in January.

Q. Have you those letters?

A. I never kept my letters; every Sunday I devote in answering my correspondents, and generally destroy their letters then.

Q. Did he or not make you any remittance with a view of enabling you to come to Washington?

A. Oh yes, sir; after I had declined going, had refused him, I got a letter from him stating that I must come; this was the letter in which he told me it was sure to succeed; I wrote back that it was

impossible; I would not come; then, by return mail, I think, I got another letter with $50 inclosed, saying I must come, and must be sure to be there by Saturday night; I did not go; I had not been out of New York since last summer.

Q. Can you remember the time you received the last letter with the $50 in it?

A. That was in January, I think.

Q. You say he said he had $1000 to leave to your family?

A. That was before, at the first interview.

Q. Did he, at the time he sent you the first $50, mention any more?

A. In the letter he did not.

Q. Did he speak of having plenty of funds for the purpose?

A. Not in his letter.

Q. Did he in his conversation?

A. In his conversation after he came to New York again.

Q. What did he say then?

A. When he came to New York he called on me again and asked me to take a walk with him, and I did so; he told me that he had been trying to get another party to join him named John Matthews, and when he told him what he wanted to do that the man was very much frightened, indeed, and would not join him, and he said he would not have cared if he had sacrificed him; I told him I did not think it was right to speak in that manner; he said no, he was a coward, and was not fit to live; he then asked me again to join him; he told me I must do so; he said that there was plenty of money in the affair; that if I would do it I would never want again as long as I lived; that I would never want for money; he said that the President and some of the heads of Government came to the theatre very frequently during Mr. Forrest's engagements; I still urged him not to mention the affair to me; to think of my poor family; he said he would provide for my going with him; I still refused; he said he would ruin me in the profession if I did not go; I told him I could not help that, and begged him not to mention the affair to me; when he found I would not go, he said he honored my mother and respected my wife, and he was sorry he had mentioned this affair to me, and told me to make my mind easy, he would trouble me about it no more; I then returned him the money he sent me; he said he would not allow me to do so, but that he was very short of funds—so very short that either himself or some of the party must go to Richmond to obtain means to carry out their designs.

Q. He said, however, that there was plenty of money in the enterprise?

A. Yes, sir.

Q. When did this last conversation occur?

A. That, I think, was in February.

Q. Did he have any conversation with you at a later period, after the inauguration, as to the opportunity which he had for the assassination of the President? Did he speak of that?

A. Yes, sir; on Friday, one week previous to the assassination, he was in New York.

Q. What did he say then?

A. We were in the House of Lords at the time, sitting at a table, and had not been there long before he exclaimed, striking the table, *"What an excellent chance I had to kill the President, if I had wished, on Inauguration Day"; that was all he said relative to that.

Q. Did he explain what the chance was?

A. No; he said he was as near the President on that day as he was to me; that is all he said.

Q. Can you tell at what time in February he said it would be necessary to send to Richmond for money?

A. No, sir; I cannot tell positively.

Cross-examined by Mr. Clampitt.*—

Q. Did he mention any names of those who were connected with him in this

plan as communicated to you in reference to the assassination of Mr. Lincoln?

A. No, sir, not that I am aware of.

Q. You never heard him mention any names?

A. I never did.

Cross-examined by Mr. Ewing.†—

Q. Do I understand you to say that he spoke to you of a plan to assassinate the President and to capture him?

A. To capture him.

Q. Did he say anything to you as to how he would get him off?

A. No.

Q. As to where he would take him?

A. To Richmond.

Q. By what route?

A. He did not say.

Q. He spoke of there being persons "on the other side"?

A. Yes, sir.

Q. Did he use just simply that expression, or did he explain what he meant by "the other side"? What did you understand him to mean?

A. He did not explain it at all, but I supposed it was in the South.

Q. Across the lines?

A. Yes, sir.

Q. Across the river?

A. Across the Potomac.

Q. Did he say nothing to you as to the means he had provided or purposed to provide for conducting the President after he should be seized?

A. No, sir; on one occasion he told me that he was selling off horses after he had told me that he had given up this project.

Q. When did he say to you that he had abandoned the idea of capturing the President?

A. In February, I think.

Q. Did he say why he had abandoned it?

A. He said the affair had fallen through owing to some of the parties backing out.

*John W. Clampitt, a defense counsel.

†Thomas Ewing, a defense counsel.

Q. On what day was it he said to you what an excellent chance he had for killing the President?

A. That was on a Friday, one week previous to the assassination.

Q. On what day of April was that?

A. The 7th.

Q. Did he say anything to you then as to why he did not assassinate the President?

A. No, sir; that was the only exclamation he made use of relative to it.

Q. State his exact words, if you can.

A. He said, "what an excellent chance I had, if I wished, to kill the President on inauguration day; I was on the stand as close to him nearly as I am to you." That is as near his language as I can give.

Q. State how far he explained to you his project for capturing the President in the theatre.

A. I believe I have stated as far as I know.

Q. Did he ever indicate how he expected to get him from the box to the stage without being caught?

A. No, sir.

Q. Did he say how many were to help him in seizing the President?

A. No, sir.

Q. Did he name any other officials who were to be seized besides the President?

A. No; the only time he told me, he said *"the heads of the Government, including the President."*

By the Judge Advocate. —

Q. I understood you to say that he stated that the particular enterprise of capturing the President and heads of Government had been given up, and that in consequence he was selling off the horses he had bought for the purpose?

A. Yes, sir.

Q. He did not state to you what mode of proceeding had been substituted for that, but simply that that one had been given up?

A. He told me that they had given up the affair.

Q. That it had fallen through?

A. Yes, sir.

E. A. Emerson.

The actor in *Our American Cousin,* E. A. Emerson, said that Booth had whacked him over the shoulder with a cane breaking it in four pieces and saying of Lincoln — "Did you hear what that old scoundrel did the other day — he went into Davis' home in Richmond and threw his long legs over the arm of a chair and squirted tobacco juice all over the place. Someone ought to kill him."[1]

Samuel P. Jones.*

For the Prosecution. — May 12

I resided in Richmond during a part of the war. I have often heard the officers and

men of the Confederate army conversing respecting the assassination of President Lincoln. I have heard it discussed by rebel officers as they were sitting around their tents. They said they would like to see him brought there, dead or alive, and they thought it could be done. I heard a citizen make the remark that he would give from his private purse ten thousand dollars, in addition to the Confederate amount offered, to have the President of the United States assassinated, and brought to Richmond, dead or alive. I have, besides that, heard sums offered to be paid, with the Confederate sum, for any person or persons to go north and assassinate the President. I judge, from what I heard, that there was an amount offered by the Government in their trashy paper, to assassinate any officials of the

*Jones was blind.

[1] Quoted in Dorothy Meserve Kunhardt and Philip B. Kunhardt, Jr., *Twenty Days* (New York: Harper & Row, Publishers, Inc., 1965), 199.

United States Government that were hindering their cause.

James W. Pumphry.

For the Prosecution.—May 15

I reside in Washington City, and keep a livery stable. I was acquainted with J. Wilkes Booth. He came to my stable about 12 o'clock of the 14th of April last, and engaged a saddle-horse, which he said he wanted about 4 or half-past 4 that day. He had been in the habit of riding a sorrel horse, and he came to get it, but that horse was engaged, and he had in its place a small bay mare, about fourteen or fourteen and a half hands high. She was a bay, with black legs, black mane and tail, and a white star in the forehead. I think the off front foot had white spots. I have never seen the mare since. He asked me to give him a tie-rein to hitch the horse. I told him not to hitch her, as she was in the habit of breaking the bridle. He told me he wanted to tie her while he stopped at a restaurant and got a drink. I said, "Get a boy at the restaurant to hold her." He replied that he could not get a boy. "O," said I, "you can find plenty of boot-blacks about the streets to hold your horse." He then said, "I am going to Grover's Theater to write a letter; there is no necessity of tying her there, for there is a stable in the back part of the alley; I will put her there." He then asked where was the best place to take a ride to; I told him, "You have been some time around here, and you ought to know." He asked, "How is Crystal Spring?" "A very good place," I said, "but it is rather early for it." "Well," said he, "I will go there after I get through writing a letter at Grover's Theater." He then rode off, and I have never seen Booth since.

About six weeks before the assassination, Booth called at my stable, in company with John H. Surratt. He said he wanted a good saddle-horse. I said, "Before you get him you will have to give me reference; you are a stranger to me." He replied, "If you don't know me you have heard of me; I am John Wilkes Booth." Mr. Surratt spoke up and said, "This is John Wilkes Booth, Mr. Pumphry; he and I are going to take a ride, and I will see that you are paid for the horse." I let him have the horse, and I was paid.

James J. Gifford.

For the Prosecution.—May 19

I was the builder of Ford's Theater, and am stage-carpenter there. I noticed Mr. Harry Clay Ford in the President's box, on the 14th of April last, putting flags out; I think I saw Mr. Raybold with him. When I was in the box on Saturday, the 15th, I saw the large rocking-chair. I do not know whether or not it has been previously used this season, but I saw it there last season. It was part of a set of furniture—two sofas and two high-backed chairs—one with rockers and one with castors. I have sometimes seen the one with castors in the box this season, but not the rocking-chair. The last time I saw the chair before it was placed in the President's box was in Mr. Ford's room, adjoining the theater.

On Monday morning, after the assassination, I was trying to find out how the door of the President's box had been fastened, when I first saw the mortise in the wall. The Secretary of War came down to the theater to examine the box, and he told me to bring a stick and fit it in the door. I found that a stick about three feet six inches long, if pressed against it, would prevent the door from being opened on the outside, but if the door was shaken, the stick would fall. The mortise in the plastering looked as though it had been recently made, and had the appearance of having been made with a knife. Had a chisel or hammer been used, it would have made a sound, but with a knife it could have been done quietly. It might have required some ten or fifteen minutes to make it. I had not been in the box, I think, for a week. Had the marks been there then, I think I should have observed it, as I am particular in looking around to see the place is clean. It was the duty of Mr. Raybold, the upholsterer, to decorate the box; but he had a stiff neck, and got Mr. Clay Ford to do it for him, so he told me afterward.

At the moment of the assassination I was in front of the theater; twenty minutes before, I was behind the scenes where I saw Spangler; he was then waiting for his business to change the scene.

Cross-examined by Mr. Ewing.

The passage on each side of the entrances is always kept free. The entrances are always more or less filled with tables, chairs, etc. The passage way through which Booth passed to the outer door is about two feet eight inches to three feet wide; some places a little wider, some a little narrower; but it is never obstructed, except by people when they have a large company on the stage; never by chairs, tables, etc. It is necessary to keep this passage way clear to allow the actors and actresses to pass readily from the green-room and dressing-rooms to the stage.

. . .

Everybody about the house, actors and all, were friendly with Booth; he had such a winning way that he made every person like him. He was a good-natured, jovial kind of man, and the people about the house, as far as I know, all liked him…He had access to the theater by all the entrances, just as the employees of the theater had. Spangler appeared to be a sort of drudge for Booth, doing such things as hitching up his horse, etc.

Sergeant Joseph M. Dye.

For the Prosecution.—May 15

On the evening of the 14th of April last, I was sitting in front of Ford's Theater, about half-past 9 o'clock. I observed several persons, whose appearance excited my suspicion, conferring together upon the pavement. The first who appeared was an elegantly-dressed gentleman, who came out of the passage, and commenced conversing with a ruffianly-looking fellow; then another appeared, and the three conversed together. It was then drawing near the second act. The one that appeared to be the leader, the well-dressed one, said, "I think he will come out now," referring to the President, I supposed. The President's carriage was standing in front of the theater. One of the three had been standing out, looking at the carriage, on the curbstone, while I was sitting there, and then went back. They watched awhile, and the rush came down; many gentlemen came out and went in and had a drink in the saloon below. After the people went up, the best-dressed gentleman stepped into the saloon himself; remained there long enough to get a drink, and came out in a style as if he was becoming intoxicated. He stepped up and whispered to this ruffian, (that is, the miserablest-looking one of the three), and went into the passage that leads to the stage from the street. Then the smallest one stepped up, looked at the clock in the vestibule, called the time, just as the best-dressed gentleman appeared again. Then he started up the street, remained there awhile, and came down again, and called the time again. I then began to think there was something going on, and looked toward this man as he called the time. Presently he went up again, and then came down and called the time louder. I think it was ten minutes after 10 that he called out the last time. He was announcing the time to the other two, and then started on a fast walk up the street, and the best dressed one went inside the theater.

I was invited by Sergeant Cooper to have some oysters; and we had barely time to get seated in the saloon and order the oysters, when a man came rushing in and said the President was shot.

[A photograph of J. Wilkes Booth was handed to the witness.]

That was the well-dressed man; but his moustache was heavier and his hair longer than in the photograph, but these are his features exactly.

The ruffianly man I saw was a stout man, with a rough face, and had a bloated appearance; his dress had been worn a considerable time. The prisoner, Edward Spangler, has the appearance of the rough-looking man, except that he had a moustache.

The one that called the time was a very neat gentleman, well dressed, and he had a moustache.* I do not see him among the prisoners. He was better dressed than any I see here. He had on one of the fashionable hats they wear here in Washington, with round top and stiff brim. He was not a very large man, about five feet, six inches high; his coat was a kind of drab color, and his hat was black.

Joseph Burroughs, *alias* "Peanuts."

For the Prosecution. — May 16

I carry bills for Ford's Theater during the daytime, and stand at the stage-door at night. I knew John Wilkes Booth, and used to attend to his horse, and see that it was fed and cleaned. His stable was immediately back of the theater. On the afternoon of the 14th of April, he brought his horse to the stable, between 5 and 6 o'clock. He hallooed out for Spangler; when he came, Booth asked him for a halter. He had none, and sent Jake up stairs after one. Jim Maddox was down there too. Between 9 and 10 o'clock that night, I heard Debonay calling to Ned [Edward Spangler] that Booth wanted him out in the alley. I did not see Booth come up the alley on his horse, but I saw the horse at the door when Spangler called me out there to hold it. When Spangler told me to hold the horse, I said I could not; I had to go in to attend to my door. He told me to hold it, and if there was any thing wrong to lay the blame on him; so I held the horse. I held him as I was sitting over against the house there, on a carpenter's bench.

I heard the report of the pistol. I was still out by the bench, but had got off when

*Dye later identified this "neat gentleman" as John Surratt. (See headnote to these selections.)

Booth came out. He told me to give him his horse. He struck me with the butt of a knife, and knocked me down. He did this as he was mounting his horse, with one foot in the stirrup; he also kicked me, and rode off immediately.

I was in the President's box that afternoon when Harry Ford was putting the flags around it. Harry Ford told me to go up with Spangler and take out the partition of the box; that the President and General Grant were coming there. While Spangler was at work removing it he said, "Damn the President and General Grant." I said to him, "What are you damning the man for — a man that has never done any harm to you?" He said he ought to be cursed when he got so many men killed.

J. L. Debonay.

For the Defense [of Edward Spangler]. — May 31

By Mr. Ewing.

I was playing what is called "responsible utility" at Ford's Theater at the time of the assassination. On the evening of the assassination, Booth came up to the alley door and said to me, "Tell Spangler to come to the door and hold my horse." I did not see his horse. I went over to where Mr. Spangler was, on the left-hand side, at his post, and said, "Mr. Booth wants you to hold his horse." He then went to the door and went outside, and was there about a minute, when Mr. Booth came in. Booth asked me if he could get across the stage. I told him no, the dairy scene was on, and he would have to go under the stage and come up on the other side. About the time that he got upon the other side, Spangler called to me, "Tell Peanut John to come here and hold this horse; I have not time. Mr. Gifford is out in the front of the theater, and all the responsibility of the scene lies upon me." I went on the other side and called John, and John went there and held the horse when Spangler came in and returned to his post.

I saw Spangler three or four times that evening on the stage in his proper position. I saw him about two minutes before the shot was fired. He was on the same side I was on—the same side as the President's box. About five minutes after the shot was fired I again saw Spangler standing on the stage, with a crowd of people who had collected there.

I saw Booth when he made his exit. I was standing in the first entrance on the left-hand side. When he came to the center of the stage, I saw that he had a long knife in his hand. It seemed to me to be a double-edged knife, and looked like a new one. He paused about a second, I should think, and then went off at the first entrance to the right-hand side. I think he had time to get out of the back door before any person was on the stage. It was, perhaps, two or three seconds after he made his exit before I saw any person on the stage in pursuit. The first person I noticed was a tall, stout gentleman, with gray clothes on, I think, and I believe a moustache. Booth did not seem to run very fast across the stage; he seemed to be stooping a little when he ran off. The distance he ran would be about thirty-five or forty feet; but he was off the stage two or three seconds before this gentleman was on, and of the two, I think Booth was running the fastest.

Mary Jane Anderson (colored).

For the Prosecution.—May 16

I live right back of Ford's Theater, adjoining Mrs. Turner's house. I knew John Wilkes Booth by sight. I saw him on the morning of the 14th of April down by the stable, and again between 2 and 3 o'clock in the afternoon, standing in the theater back-door, in the alley, talking to a lady. I stood in my gate and looked right wishful at him.

He and this lady were pointing up and down the alley, as if they were talking about it. They stood there a considerable time, and then Booth went into the theater.

After I had gone up stairs that night, a carriage drove up, and after that I heard a

horse step down the alley. I looked out of the window, and it seemed as if the gentleman was leading the horse down the alley. He did not go further than the end of it, and in a few minutes he came back up to the theater door, holding his horse by the bridle. He pushed the door open, and said something in a low voice, and then in a loud voice he called "Ned" four times. There was a colored man up at the window, who said, "Mr. Ned, Mr. Booth wants you." This is the way I came to know it was Mr. Booth, for it was dark and I could not see his face. When Ned came, Mr. Booth said, in a low voice, "Tell Maddox to come here."

Then Ned went back and Maddox came out, and they said something to each other. Maddox then took off the horse from before my door, round to where the work bench was, that stood at the right side of the house. They both then went into the theater. The horse stood out there a considerable time, and kept up a great stamping. After awhile, the person who held the horse kept walking backward and forward; I suppose the horse was there an hour and a half altogether. Then I saw Booth come out of the door with something in his hand, glittering. He came out of the theater so quick that it seemed as if he but touched the horse, and it was gone like a flash of lightning. I thought to myself that the horse must surely have run off with the gentleman. Presently there was a rush out of the door, and I heard the people saying, "Which way did he go?" I asked a gentleman what was the matter, and he said the President was shot. I asked who shot him. Said he, "The man who went out on the horse."

Major Henry R. Rathbone.

For the Prosecution.—May 15

On the evening of the 14th of April last, at about twenty minutes past 8 o'clock, I, in company with Miss Harris, left my residence at the corner of Fifteenth and H Streets, and joined the President and Mrs. Lincoln, and went with them, in their carriage, to Ford's

Theater, on Tenth Street. On reaching the theater, when the presence of the President became known, the actors stopped playing, the band struck up "Hail to the Chief," and the audience rose and received him with vociferous cheering. The party proceeded along in the rear of the dress-circle and entered the box that had been set apart for their reception. On entering the box, there was a large arm-chair that was placed nearest the audience, farthest from the stage, which the President took and occupied during the whole of the evening, with one exception, when he got up to put on his coat, and returned and sat down again. When the second scene of the third act was being performed, and while I was intently observing the proceedings upon the stage, with my back toward the door, I heard the discharge of a pistol behind me, and, looking round, saw through the smoke a man between the door and the President. The distance from the door to where the President sat was about four feet. At the same time I heard the man shout some word, which I thought was "Freedom!" I instantly sprang toward him and seized him. He wrested himself from my grasp, and made a violent thrust at my breast with a large knife. I parried the blow by striking it up, and received a wound several inches deep in my left arm, between the elbow and the shoulder. The orifice of the wound was about an inch and a half in length, and extended upward toward the shoulder several inches. The man rushed to the front of the box, and I endeavored to seize him again, but only caught his clothes as he was leaping over the railing of the box. The clothes, as I believe, were torn in the attempt to hold him. As he went over upon the stage, I cried out, "Stop that man." I then turned to the President; his position was not changed; his head was slightly bent forward, and his eyes were closed. I saw that he was unconscious, and, supposing him mortally wounded, rushed to the door for the purpose of calling medical aid.

On reaching the outer door of the passage way, I found it barred by a heavy piece of plank, one end of which was secured in the wall, and the other resting against the door. It had been so securely fastened that it required considerable force to remove it. This wedge or bar was about four feet from the floor. Persons upon the outside were beating against the door for the purpose of entering. I removed the bar, and the door was opened. Several persons, who represented themselves as surgeons, were allowed to enter. I saw there Colonel Crawford, and requested him to prevent other persons from entering the box.

I then returned to the box, and found the surgeons examining the President's person. They had not yet discovered the wound. As soon as it was discovered, it was determined to remove him from the theater. He was carried out, and I then proceeded to assist Mrs. Lincoln, who was intensely excited, to leave the theater. On reaching the head of the stairs, I requested Major Potter to aid me in assisting Mrs. Lincoln across the street to the house where the President was being conveyed. The wound which I had received had been bleeding very profusely, and on reaching the house, feeling very faint from the loss of blood, I seated myself in the hall, and soon after fainted away, and was laid upon the floor. Upon the return of consciousness I was taken to my residence.

In a review of the transactions, it is my confident belief that the time which elapsed between the discharge of the pistol and the time when the assassin leaped from the box did not exceed thirty seconds. Neither Mrs. Lincoln nor Miss Harris had left their seats.

[A bowie-knife, with a heavy seven-inch blade, was exhibited to the witness, stains of blood being still upon the blade.]

This knife might have made a wound similar to the one I received. The assassin held the blade in a horizontal position, I think, and the nature of the wound would indicate it; it came down with a sweeping blow from above.

[The knife was offered in evidence.]

James P. Ferguson.

For the Prosecution.—May 15

I keep a restaurant, adjoining Ford's Theater, on the upper side. I saw J. Wilkes Booth, on the afternoon of the 14th, between 2 and 4 o'clock, standing by the side of his horse—a small bay mare; Mr. Maddox was standing by him talking. Booth remarked, "See what a nice horse I have got; now watch, he can run just like a cat;" and, striking his spurs into his horse, he went off down the street.

About 1 o'clock Mr. Harry Ford came into my place and said, "Your favorite, General Grant, is to be at the theater to-night, and if you want to see him you had better go and get a seat." I went and secured a seat directly opposite the President's box, in the front dress-circle. I saw the President and his family when they came in, accompanied by Miss Harris and Major Rathbone.

Somewhere near 10 o'clock, during the second scene of the third act of "Our American Cousin," I saw Booth pass along near the President's box, and then stop and lean against the wall. After standing there a moment, I saw him step down one step, put his hands on the door and his knee against it, and push the door open—the first door that goes into the box. I saw no more of him until he made a rush for the front of the box and jumped over. He put his left hand on the railing, and with his right he seemed to strike back with a knife. I could see the knife gleam, and the next moment he was over the box. As he went over, his hand was raised, the handle of the knife up, the blade down. The President sat in the left-hand corner of the box, with Mrs. Lincoln at his right. Miss Harris was in the right-hand corner, Major Rathbone sitting back at her left, almost in the corner of the box. At the moment the President was shot, he was leaning his hand on the railing, looking down at a person in the orchestra; holding the flag that decorated the box aside to look between it and the post, I saw the flash of the pistol right back

in the box. As the person jumped over and lit on the stage, I saw it was Booth. As he struck the stage, he rose and exclaimed, *"Sic semper tyrannus!"* and ran directly across the stage to the opposite door, where the actors come in.

I heard some one halloo out of the box, "Revenge for the South!" I do not know that it was Booth, though I suppose it must have been; it was just as he was jumping over the railing. His spur caught in the blue part of the flag that was stretched around the box, and, as he went over, it tore a piece of the flag, which was dragged half way across the stage on the spur of his right heel.

Just as Booth went over the box, I saw the President raise his head, and then it hung back. I saw Mrs. Lincoln catch his arm, and I was then satisfied that the President was hurt. By that time Booth was across the stage. A young man named Harry Hawk was the only actor on the stage at the time.

I left the theater as quickly as I could, and went to the police station on D Street, to give notice to the Superintendent of Police, Mr. Webb. I then ran up D Street to the house of Mr. Peterson, where the President was taken. Colonel Wells was standing on the steps, and I told him that I had seen it all, and I knew the man who jumped out of the box.

Next morning I saw Mr. Gifford, who said, "You made a hell of a statement about what you saw last night; how could you see the flash of the pistol when the ball was shot through the door?" On Sunday morning Miss Harris, accompanied by her father, Judge Olin, and Judge Carter, came down to the theater, and I went in with them. We got a candle and examined the hole in the door of the box through which Mr. Gifford said the ball had been shot. It looked to me as if it had been bored by a gimlet, and then rimed round the edge with a knife. In several places it was scratched down, as if the knife had slipped. After this examination, I was satisfied that the pistol had been fired in the box.

Mr. Gifford is the chief carpenter of the theater, and I understood had full charge of it. I recollect when Richmond was surrendered I said to him, "Have you not got any flags in the theater?" He replied, "Yes, I have; I guess there is a flag about." I said, "Why do you not run it out on the roof?" He answered, "There's a rope, isn't that enough?" I said, "You are a hell of a man, you ought to be in the Old Capitol." He didn't like me any how.

Captain Theodore McGowan.

For the Prosecution. — May 15

I was present at Ford's Theater on the night of the assassination. I was sitting in the aisle leading by the wall toward the door of the President's box, when a man came and disturbed me in my seat, causing me to push my chair forward to permit him to pass; he stopped about three feet from where I was sitting, and leisurely took a survey of the house. I looked at him because he happened to be in my line of sight. He took a small pack of visiting-cards from his pocket, selecting one and replacing the others, stood a second, perhaps, with it in his hand, and then showed it to the President's messenger, who was sitting just below him. Whether the messenger took the card into the box, or, after looking at it, allowed him to go in, I do not know; but, in a moment or two more, I saw him go through the door of the lobby leading to the box, and close the door.

After I heard the pistol fired, I saw the body of a man descend from the front of the box toward the stage. He was hid from my sight for a moment by the heads of those who sat in the front row of the dress-circle, but in another moment he reappeared, strode across the stage toward the entrance on the other side, and, as he passed, I saw the gleaming blade of a dagger in his right hand. He disappeared behind the scenes in a moment, and I saw him no more.

I know J. Wilkes Booth, but, not seeing the face of the assassin fully, I did not at the time recognize him as Booth.

William Withers, Jr.

For the Prosecution. — May 15

I am the leader of the orchestra at Ford's Theater. I had some business on the stage with our stage-manager on the night of the 14th, in regard to a national song that I had composed, and I went to see what costume they were going to sing it in. After talking with the manager, I was returning to the orchestra, when I heard the report of a pistol. I stood with astonishment, thinking why they should fire off a pistol in "Our American Cousin." As I turned round I heard some confusion, and saw a man running toward me with his head down. I did not know what was the matter, and stood completely paralyzed. As he ran, I could not get out of his way, so he hit me on the leg, and turned me round, and made two cuts at me, one in the neck and one on the side, and knocked me from the third entrance down to the second. The scene saved me. As I turned, I got a side view of him, and I saw it was John Wilkes Booth. He then made a rush for the back door, and out he went. I returned to the stage and heard that the President was killed, and I saw him in the box apparently dead.

Where I stood on the stage was not more than a yard from the door. He made one plunge at the door, which I believe was shut, and instantly he was out. The door opens inward on the stage, but whether he opened it, or whether it was opened for him, I do not know. I noticed that there was nothing to obstruct his passage out, and this seemed strange to me, for it was unusual.

Jacob Ritterspaugh.

. . .

Recalled for the Prosecution. — May 30

I was a carpenter in Ford's Theater down to the 14th of April last, and was there on that night when the President was shot. He occupied the upper box on the left-hand side of the stage, the right as you come in from the front. My business was to shift wings on the stage and pull them off, and fetch things out of the cellar when needed.

I was standing on the stage behind the scenes on the night of the 14th, when some one called out that the President was shot, and directly I saw a man that had no hat on running toward the back door.

He had a knife in his hand, and I ran to stop him, and ran through the last entrance, and as I came up to him he tore the door open. I made for him, and he struck at me with the knife, and I jumped back then. He then ran out and slammed the door shut. I then went to get the door open quick, and I thought it was a kind of fast; I could not get it open. In a moment afterward I opened the door, and the man had just got on his horse and was running down the alley; and then I came in. I came back on the stage where I had left Edward Spangler, and he hit me on the face with the back of his hand, and he said, "Don't say which way he went." I asked him what he meant by slapping me in the mouth, and he said, "For God's sake, shut up;" and that was the last he said.

The man of whom I speak is Edward Spangler, the prisoner at the bar. I did not see any one else go out before the man with the knife. A tall, stout man went out after me.

Cross-examined by Mr. Ewing.

When I heard the pistol fired I was standing in the center of the stage, listening to the play, and Spangler was at the same place, just about ready to shove off the scenes; I stood nearest the door. I am certain we both stood there when the pistol was fired. I did not at first know what had happened. Some one called out "Stop that man;" and then I heard some one say that the President was shot, and not till then did I know what had occurred. When I came back, Spangler was at the same place where I had left him. There was a crowd in there by that time, both actors and strangers. When Spangler slapped me there were some of the actors near who had taken part in the play; one they called Jenny—I do not know what part she took—was standing perhaps three

or four feet from me; I do not know whether she heard what he said; he did not say it so very loud. He spoke in his usual tone, but he looked as if he was scared, and a kind of crying. I heard the people halloo, "Burn the theater!" "Hang him and shoot him!"

. . .

I saw Booth open the back door of the theater and shut it, but I did not know who he was then; I did not see his face right. I was the first person that got to the door after he left; I opened the door, but did not shut it. The big man that ran out after me might have been five or six yards from me when I heard him, or it might have been somebody else, call out, "Which way?" I cried out, "This way," and then ran out, leaving the door open. By that time the man had got on his horse and gone off down the alley. I saw the big man outside, and have not seen him since. I did not take particular notice of him; but he was a tolerably built tall man. It might have been two or three minutes after I went out till I came back to where Spangler was standing, and found him kind of scared, and as if he had been crying. I did not say any thing to him before he said that to me. It was Spangler's place, with another man, to shove the scenes on; he was where he ought to be to do the work he had to do. I did not hear any one call Booth's name. It was not till the people were all out, and I came outside, that I heard some say it was Booth, and some say it was not. Spangler and I boarded together; we went home to supper together on the evening of the assassination, at 6 o'clock, and returned at 7.

Joseph B. Stewart.

For the Prosecution.—May 20

I was at Ford's Theater on the night of the assassination of the President. I was sitting in the front seat of the orchestra, on the right-hand side. The sharp report of a pistol at about half-past 10—evidently a charged pistol—startled me. I heard an exclamation, and simultaneously a man leaped from the

President's box, lighting on the stage. He came down with his back slightly toward the audience, but rising and turning, his face came in full view. At the same instant I jumped on the stage, and the man disappeared at the left-hand stage entrance. I ran across the stage as quickly as possible, following the direction he took, calling out, "Stop that man!" three times. When about twenty or twenty-five feet from the door through which the man ran, the door slammed to and closed.

. . .

I saw several persons in the passage way; ladies and gentlemen, one or two men, perhaps five persons.

Near the door on my right hand, I saw a person standing, who seemed to be in the act of turning, and who did not seem to be moving about like the others. Every one else that I saw but this person, seemed intensely excited, literally bewildered; they were all in a terrible commotion and moving about except this man. As I approached the door, and only about fifteen feet from it, this person was facing the door; but, as I got nearer, he partially turned round, moving to the left, so that I had a view of him as he was turning from the door and toward me.

[The witness was directed to look at the prisoners, to see if he recognized among them the person he saw standing at the door.]

That man [pointing to Edward Spangler] looks more like the person I saw near the door than anybody else I see here. He recalls the impression of the man's visage as I passed him. When the assassin alighted on the stage, I believed I knew who it was that had committed the deed; that it was J. Wilkes Booth, and I so informed Richards, Superintendent of the Police, that night. I knew Booth by sight very well, and when I was running after him, I had no doubt in my mind that it was Booth, and should have been surprised to find that it was anybody else. I felt a good deal vexed at his getting away, and had no doubt when I started across the stage that I could catch him.

From the time I heard the door slam until I saw the man mounting his horse, was not over the time I could make two steps.

I am satisfied that the person I saw inside the door was in a position and had an opportunity, if he had been disposed to do so, to have interrupted the exit of Booth, and from his manner, he was cool enough to have done so. This man was nearest of all to the door, and could have opened and gone out before I did, as it would have been but a step to the right and a reach to open it.

Cross-examined by Mr. Ewing.

The man I have spoken of stood about three feet from the door out of which Booth passed; I noticed him just after the door slammed. From the position in which he stood, he might have slammed it without my noticing it. The lock of the door, as I approached it, was on the right-hand side, the hinges to the left. If the door had been open and I had not been stopped, I could have got the range of the horse outside.

. . . Coming up to the door, I touched it first on the side where it did not open; after which I caught hold at the proper place, opened the door, and passed out. The last time that I exclaimed "Stop that man," some one said, "He is getting on a horse at the door;" and almost as soon as the words reached my ears I heard the tramping of a horse. On opening the door, after the temporary balk, I perceived a man mounting a horse. The moon was just beginning to rise, and I could see any thing elevated better than near the ground. The horse was moving with a quick, agitated motion—as a horse will do when prematurely spurred in mounting—with the reins drawn a little to one side, and for a moment I noticed the horse describe a kind of circle from the right to the left. I ran in the direction where the horse was heading, and when within eight or ten feet from the head of the horse, and almost up within reach of the left flank, the rider brought him round somewhat in a circle from the left to the right, crossing over, the horse's feet rattling violently on what seemed to be rocks. I crossed in the same direction, aiming at the rein, and was now on the right flank of the horse. He was rather gaining on me then, though not yet in a forward movement. I could have reached his flank with my hand when, perhaps, two-thirds of the way over the alley. Again he backed to the right side of the alley, brought the horse forward and spurred him; at the same instant he crouched forward, down over the pummel of the saddle. The horse then went forward, and soon swept rapidly to the left, up toward F Street. I still ran after the horse some forty or fifty yards, and commanded the person to stop. All this occupied only the space of a few seconds.

From the Diary of John Wilkes Booth

[The two fugitives remained hidden in a thicket on Cox's farm from Sunday, April 16, until Friday, April 21, when they started out across the Potomac in a rowboat which Jones had obtained for them. During these six days, Jones brought them food and — more important than anything else — newspapers which told Booth what had happened after he fled from Washington.

Booth had with him a small pocket diary for 1864. After reading the newspapers, he made the following entries on some of the diary's unused pages:]

April 13, 14, Friday the Ides — Until today, nothing was ever thought of sacrificing to our country's wrongs. For six months we had worked to capture. But our cause being almost lost, something decisive and great must be done. But its failure was owing to others, who did not strike for their country with a heart. I struck boldly and not as the papers say. I walked with a firm step through a thousand of his friends, was stopped, but pushed on. A colonel was at his side. I shouted *Sic semper* before I fired. In jumping broke my leg. I passed all his pickets. Rode sixty miles that night, with the bone of my leg tearing the flesh at every jump.

I can never repent it, though we hated to kill. Our country owed all her troubles to him, and God simply made me the instrument of His punishment. The country is not what it was. This forced Union is not what I have loved. I care not what becomes of me.

I have no desire to outlive my country. This night (before the deed) I wrote a long article and left it for one of the editors of the *National Intelligencer* in which I fully set forth our reasons for our proceeding. He or the gov'n —

[Booth was doubtless interrupted here, for the entry ends abruptly. The next entry is several days later:]

Friday, 21. — After being hunted like a dog through swamps and woods, and last night being chased by gunboats till I was forced to return, wet, cold, and starving, with every man's hand against me, I am here in despair. And why? For doing what Brutus was honored for — what made William Tell a Hero; and yet I, for striking down an even greater tyrant than they ever knew, am looked upon as a common cutthroat. My act was purer than either of theirs. One hoped to be great himself; the other had not only his country's, but his own, wrongs to avenge. I hoped for no gain; I knew no private wrong. I struck for my country, and her alone. A people ground beneath this tyranny prayed for this end, and yet now see the cold hands they extend to me! God cannot pardon me if I have done wrong; yet I cannot see any wrong, except in serving a degenerate people. The little, the very little, I left behind to clear my name, the Government will not allow to be printed. So ends all! For my country I have given up all that makes life sweet and holy — to-night misfortune upon my family, and am sure there is no pardon for me in the heavens, since man condemns me so. I have only heard of what has been done (except what I did myself), and it fills me with horror. God, try and forgive me and bless my mother. To-night I will once more try the river, with the intention to cross; though I have a greater desire and almost a mind to return to Washington, and in a measure clear my name, which I feel I can do.

I do not repent the blow I struck. I may before my God, but not to man. I think I have done well, though I am abandoned, with the curse of Cain upon me, when, if the world knew my heart, that one blow would have made me great, though I did desire no greatness. To-night I try once more to escape these bloodhounds. Who, who, can read his fate? God's will be done. I have too great a soul to die like a criminal. Oh! may He spare me that, and let me die bravely. I bless the entire world. I have never hated nor wronged any one. This last was not a wrong, unless God deems it so, and it is with Him to damn or bless me. And for this brave boy, Herold, here with me, who often prays (yes, before and since) with a true and sincere heart, was it a crime in him? If so, why can he pray the same? I do not wish to shed a drop of blood, but I must fight the course. 'Tis all that's left me.

[This diary was taken from Booth's body when he died at Garrett's farm. It was brought back to Washington with his other personal effects and turned over to the War Department.]

EXERCISES

Content

Recall the main ideas in this testimony by answering the following questions. Respond to some of the questions in your own words. Respond to others by finding quotations from the testimony that provide the answers.

Chester

1. Where did Booth conduct all his conversations with Chester?

2. What was the plan Booth discussed with Chester on Fourth Street?

3. What was Chester's role in the plot to be?

4. How many people did Booth claim were involved in the conspiracy?

5. What written evidence existed of this conspiracy? What became of it?

6. How did Booth attempt to persuade Chester to join the conspiracy?

7. What had Booth planned to do with Lincoln after capturing him?

8. Why did Booth finally abandon the kidnapping plot?

9. On what other occasion did Booth have an opportunity to murder Lincoln?

10. According to Chester, did Booth bring up the subject of assassinating Lincoln before or after he dropped the plan to kidnap him?

11. Write a one-paragraph summary of the essential information presented in this testimony.

Jones

1. How does Jones throw light on the assassination of Lincoln?

2. Does Jones implicate Booth in any manner?

3. At what point does Jones give an indication of what he thinks about the Confederacy?

Pumphry

1. How long had Pumphry known Booth?

2. What business did Booth have with Pumphry on the day of the assassination?

3. Write a brief summary of Pumphry's testimony.

Gifford

1. The information provided by Gifford in paragraph 1 corroborates what other information provided elsewhere in this chapter?

2. What material evidence did Gifford discover on the Monday following the assassination? What made him sure that the marks he found were recently made?

3. What additional evidence does Gifford provide about John Wilkes Booth?

4. Write a brief summary of Gifford's testimony.

Dye

1. Who was the "elegantly-dressed gentleman" Dye reports seeing? Who was the "ruffian"?

2. Why was the behavior of the three men suspicious to him?

3. Why was the "neat gentleman" man calling out the time? After the time was called out the last time, what did the elegantly dressed man do?

4. About how long after the last occasion on which the time was called out did the assassination occur?

5. Write a brief summary of Dye's testimony.

Burroughs

1. In what capacity did Burroughs know Booth?

2. Did Burroughs see Booth on the evening of the assassination before Booth had shot the president?

3. What was Burroughs doing while the assassination was in progress?

4. Write a brief summary of Burroughs's testimony.

Debonay

1. Why did Debonay tell Booth he could not cross the stage?

2. Why could Spangler not hold Booth's horse, according to Debonay?

3. What indication of Booth's injury does Debonay note?

4. Write a brief summary of Debonay's testimony.

Anderson

1. Did Anderson see Booth on the night of April 14 before the assassination?

2. How did Anderson know that Booth's horse was outside the theater for about an hour and a half?

3. Write a brief summary of Anderson's testimony.

Rathbone

1. Did the Lincoln party arrive before or after the performance had started?

2. At what point did Rathbone first notice Booth in Lincoln's box?

3. How did Rathbone receive the wound on his arm?

4. What did Rathbone do after glancing back toward Lincoln?

5. Why did Rathbone have difficulty getting to the outer passageway?

6. How soon does Rathbone estimate that Booth jumped out of the box after shooting Lincoln?

7. Write a brief summary of Rathbone's testimony.

Ferguson

1. Does Ferguson's account of Booth's horse tally with Pumphry's account earlier in this section? If so, in what particulars?

2. Why was Ferguson well placed to witness the assassination?

3. Did Ferguson appear to find Booth's actions before the assassination suspicious?

4. Was Ferguson an actual eyewitness to the shooting of the president? Explain.

5. How does Ferguson's account of what Booth said after shooting Lincoln tally with Rathbone's account?

6. What made Ferguson realize that Lincoln had been wounded?

7. Why did Gifford express doubt about the truth of Ferguson's statement to the police?

8. How does Ferguson's account of Booth's preparation of the president's box tally with Gifford's?

9. Write a brief summary of Ferguson's testimony.

McGowan

1. Why did McGowan notice Booth that evening?

2. What did he notice Booth doing before he disappeared into the lobby leading to the box?

3. Did McGowan get a clear view of Booth after the assassination? Explain.

4. Write a brief summary of McGowan's testimony.

Withers

1. Did Withers see the assassination?

2. How did Withers get hurt that evening?

3. Write a brief summary of Withers's testimony.

Ritterspaugh

1. What was Ritterspaugh doing at Ford's Theater that evening?

2. What do all of the eyewitnesses agree that Booth was carrying in his hand as he made his escape?

3. Was Ritterspaugh injured by Booth that night?

4. How does Ritterspaugh appear to implicate Spangler in the conspiracy?

5. Who did Ritterspaugh hear crying "Stop that man"?

6. Did Ritterspaugh know that the man running out the door was Booth?

7. Ritterspaugh claims to have been the first person to do what?

8. Write a brief summary of Ritterspaugh's testimony.

Stewart

1. To what extent was Stewart a witness to the assassination?

2. What time does he say the shooting occurred?

3. How does Stewart's description of the condition of the door to the street tally with Ritterspaugh's?

4. In what way does Stewart appear to implicate Spangler in the crime?

5. Under what circumstances does Stewart think he might have stopped Booth from escaping?

6. How close did Stewart get to Booth's horse before the actor escaped into the night?

7. Write a brief summary of Stewart's testimony.

Booth's Diary

1. What reasons does Booth give for assassinating Lincoln?

2. How does Booth's account of the assassination square with those of other eyewitnesses?

3. In what way was Booth unprepared for the reaction to the assassination?

4. What were Booth's conflicting intentions at the time he made his last entry?

5. Write a brief summary of Booth's diary entries.

Combined Testimony

Combine your summaries of the separate testimonies and of Booth's diary entries into a smooth, coherent account of the Lincoln assassination.

Philip Van Doren Stern

THE MAN WHO KILLED LINCOLN

Philip Van Doren Stern has written many historical books, including several on the Civil War. His works include *The Life and Writings of Abraham Lincoln; Tin Lizzie: The Story of the Fabulous Model T Ford; An End to Valor: The Last Days of the Civil War; Beyond Paris: A Touring Guide to the French Provinces; The Annotated Walden;* and *Edgar Allan Poe: Visitor from the Night of Time. The Man Who Killed Lincoln* (from which the following passage is taken), a novel focusing on John Wilkes Booth, was written in 1939. It deals with the assassination from an unusual point of view — the assassin's.

1   Booth's horse clattered down the narrow alley that led to the open space in back of the theater. Negro women, sitting on the steps of their shanties, ceased talking as they heard the horse approach. It was completely dark except for the light of a single lamp over the stage entrance at the far end of the alley. No one was in sight near the theater. Booth dismounted and led his horse to the doorway. He stepped inside, holding the reins over his arm. A man was standing in the passageway near the door.

2   "Tell Ned Spangler to come out here for a minute, will you?" Booth asked quietly.

3   The man recognized him and sauntered off in search of Spangler. Booth examined the mare's saddle-girth. He made sure that the deringer was in his pocket and he loosened his bowie knife in its sheath. Then he looked up at the narrow slit of sky where the stars were shining between scattered clouds. Rain would be fatal. It would turn the clay roads of southern Maryland into a morass of sticky impassable mud. There were so many

things beyond his control, he thought, so many things that could defeat him. Courage, even reckless courage, was not enough. The little gods of chance that can cause a pistol to misfire, or a blundering guard to get in the way, must withhold their spitefulness now, or he would fail and be lost.

4   The Negro women began to talk again. He could hear the soft murmur of their voices coming from the darkness beyond the circle of light around the stage door. He patted the smooth flank of his horse, and she turned her head inquiringly to look at him.

5   Now the moment is fast approaching, he said to himself, forming the words on his lips as though he were speaking to another person. When I come out of this doorway I shall have finished forever with the role of the admired young actor, John Wilkes Booth, and I shall have thrust upon me a new part wherein I play the fugitive with a snarling, shouting crowd at my heels. The hatred of twenty million Northerners will follow me always, and wherever I go men will look at me and whisper: "He is the man who killed Lincoln."

6   The narrow alley, with its odor of stables and shanties, seemed to him to be a ludicrously inappropriate waiting place for an actor who was about to take the leading role in a drama of world-shaking importance. The occasion called for a more impressive background. He remembered Shakespeare's description of what had taken place in Rome on the eve of Caesar's death.

7   He closed his eyes, shutting out the commonplace scene before him. As the magic words coursed through his mind, the fiery warriors fighting in the clouds and the ghosts shrieking and squealing in the Roman streets, became as real to him as they had been to Calphurnia. There should be some portent, some omen in this placid Washington sky, he thought. What I am going to do is no less than what Brutus did.

8   He opened his eyes suddenly, half-expecting to see something unusual. But only the brick wall of the theater was in front of him, pierced by the dark rectangle of the stage doorway. He stared at the opening, and as he looked fixedly into its blackness, the thought occurred to him that he had lived through this moment before. Somewhere he had waited like this, waited to kill. The face and figure of a man rose up out of his memory, and he felt that he would now at last be able to find out who it was. Then Spangler came out of the doorway, cursing angrily, and the image he had been trying to recall was rudely shattered.

9   "Damn it! I can't be ordered out here like this, Mr. Booth," the man was saying. "I've got to be on the stage. They'll be changing sets in a few minutes. I can't stand here holding a horse."

10   "Then get somebody who can," Booth told him peremptorily. "I have business here that can't wait. But be sure the horse is held here for me."

11   He thrust the reins into Spangler's unwilling hands and asked him if the President had arrived. The man nodded sullenly. Booth swung around and entered the theater.

12   "May I cross the stage now?" he whispered to someone standing inside.

13   "No. The dairy scene has just gone on, and the stage is open all the way back. You can't get across. Go down underneath."

14   He stood for a few minutes in the wings, looking out at the brilliantly lighted stage. The actors moved about busily, eager to catch a laugh from the audience seated out in the black void beyond the footlights. Tall piles of scenery were stacked around him, and he could smell the familiar odor of paint, hot gaslight and freshly cut lumber.

15   The sight of the play being enacted before him gave him new courage. What he had to do seemed very simple now. He had only to walk on to play his part as he had done a thousand times before. He had killed dozens of men with sword and pistol — on the stage. He had made all sorts of desperate gestures — on the stage. What he was about to do now could not be so very different. He had only to wait for his cue: "Don't know the manners of good society, eh?" And there was plenty of time, plenty of time before he

would be called upon to act. He would have a chance to reinforce himself with brandy as he always did before undertaking the performance of a new and difficult part.

16   He went down the stairs to the understage passage and walked through, groping in the darkness. He could hear the shuffling of feet on the boards overhead, and the players' voices came to him as disembodied sounds, permeating the blackness with the strange senseless quality of words chattered in delirium. Words like these were too dangerously close to the echoes of sounds that sometimes rose up from the depths of his own mind, terrifying him with their insistent urging, their dark summoning.... He was glad when he got beyond their reach into the open street in front of the theater.

17   The sidewalk was brightly illuminated. Two soldiers were sitting on the wooden carriage platform under a flaring gas lantern. The downward rays of the lamp threw their features into strong relief, making their eyes seem like black holes, and drawing heavy lines of shadow across their mouths. They stopped talking and stared at Booth.

18   Immediately he sensed danger. Perhaps these men were special guards detailed to the theater. The War Department might have learned something.... The image of Weichmann, waiting furtively in the hallway of Mrs. Surratt's house, came back to him. Could these soldiers have been sent here to watch the theater? And then he realized why they were looking at him. Why, of course! He was John Wilkes Booth, the famous actor. What could be more natural than for these yokels to gape at a celebrity? He turned away, stroking his mustache impressively. He had forgotten his own fame.

19   He looked at the clock in the lobby. It was still early. He stood and watched the scene on the sidewalk. Some curiosity-seekers, attracted by the advertised presence of the President as the guest of honor, were gazing at the playbills posted in front of the house. "Benefit and last night of Miss Laura Keene, the distinguished Manageress, Authoress and Actress ... in Tom Taylor's celebrated eccentric comedy, as originally produced in America by Miss Keene, and performed by her upwards of one thousand nights, entitled *Our American Cousin.*" And there were announcements of a benefit for Miss Jennie Gourlay in *The Octoroon,* to be held on Saturday, April 15, and notices of a forthcoming engagement of Edwin Adams — for twelve nights only.

20   Poor devils! Booth thought. They would surely never play their scheduled performances. He smiled grimly. The thunderbolt imprisoned in his pocket would shatter not only the lives of the great; little people, too, would have their petty plans twisted and thwarted by its mighty detonation.

21   He was like a god now with the power of life and death in his hands. Like a great sword, the swift force of his will would descend upon the world, cleaving through the flesh of these lesser mortals. Down, down, down, the bright blade falling, all resistance swept away before it. What did these scurrying insects matter? They were spawned upon the earth only to die. What were a few days more of their trivial existences worth? Away with them! Only he triumphant, bending a nation to his will, driving on the defeated to a new victory by the force of his example.

22   He paced up and down on the sidewalk. By God, at this moment he should be on the stage! Never had he felt the vast surge of energy so tremendous within him. He could move an audience to tears, to shouts, to wild salvos of applause. It was a pity that he had to wait until after ten o'clock. He wished that he could leap upon the stage now, to stand defiant before the footlights, bringing the flaming spirit of war and vengeance to these Yankees who were sitting in the theater, smug with the thought that victory was already theirs. But they would never forget this coming moment, never forget this single figure who would fling the cry "Unconquered!" in their faces while they sat helpless in the very heart of their own Northern citadel.

23   And then beside him, someone walking, someone speaking to him. He stopped abruptly. It was Lewis Carland, the costumer

of the theater, a soft little man with the low whining voice of one who is destined to life's perpetual defeats. He was puffing on a cigar that seemed enormous in his small silly mouth. Booth felt that he would like to pick the fellow up and break him between his hands like a pulpy log of rotted wood.

24 Carland backed away, taking the cigar from his mouth. His face, in the white glare of the street light, looked like some monstrous-eyed fish with its mouth gaping open.

25 "What's the matter, Mr. Booth?" he said, still moving away. "Is something wrong?"

26 Booth smiled, and in the soft voice of conciliation said: "Wrong? Why, no, of course not, Mr. Carland. You simply surprised me while I was going over my new part."

27 Carland laughed nervously. "Oh, you actors—always trying to live your parts. I know how you are. I'd have gone in for acting seriously myself if I had only had the figure for it. It was a pleasure to play with you in *The Apostate*. You were magnificent." He had been pressed into service in one of the minor roles of this play when Booth had acted here for a single performance during the previous month. It was evident that he would never forget the experience.

28 Booth kept walking. Carland tagged along at his heels.

29 "What sort of part are you going to play, Mr. Booth? I'll bet it's a tragic part, isn't it? Tragedy suits you best, you know. Comedy parts are all right for men like Harry Hawk, but they never really get you anywhere—" He waved his short little arm in a circle. "You were really superb as Pescara." He stopped, drew back his foot and thrust out his hand as though he had a sword in it. "Ha! ha! a Moor—one of that race we have trodden down from empire's height and crushed—a damned Morisco!... Rise, Spaniards, rise! Rush on these slaves and revel in their blood!" People were staring at him, but he was oblivious of the attention he was attracting.

30 "I see that you have a just appreciation of the tragic role," Booth said gravely.

31 Carland laid his hand on Booth's arm. Booth gently pulled his own arm away and stepped back from the round perspiring face. Carland's eyes fell.

32 "Tell me what sort of role you're preparing for now, Mr. Booth," he said. "I'll design a costume for it that will do you justice."

33 "I'm awfully sorry, but I can't say anything about it yet. I've promised not to discuss it with anyone."

34 "I understand. You shouldn't either. There's a lot of nasty jealousy in our profession. It doesn't pay to tell everyone of your plans, but you know I can be discreet...."

35 "I'm sorry. I really can't tell you. You startled me into mentioning the fact that I was preparing a new part, or I wouldn't have said anything about it at all. Please don't tell anyone...."

36 "Of course, of course." Carland sighed heavily. "Well, anyway," he said finally, "we expect great things of you, Mr. Booth. You have a magnificent tradition to carry on. I remember your father, although I was only a boy when I saw him. A wonderful man. You are living in a more fortunate era. The theater is going to have a period of prosperity now that the war is over. People will want entertainment, art, fine things.... You'll see. Even the poor bleeding South will rebuild her temples to our art."

37 Booth had always suspected that Carland was a Southern sympathizer, but he had refrained from discussing political matters with him because he felt that the man was a fool, unworthy of trust. He began to walk again. Carland followed him.

38 Carland threw out another feeler. "You will surely return to the stage in Richmond and New Orleans, won't you? Those cities will be glad to welcome you again...."

39 Booth motioned vaguely. Damn the fellow! Would he never stop talking? Why did he have to listen to the endless babbling of this dapper little tailor?

40 Gifford, the stage carpenter, walked toward them, solid, substantial, puffing energetically at his pipe as he came. His stubby-bearded face broke into a momentary smile of greeting.

41 "Talking about the war, I'll wager."

42 Carland nodded curtly. Gifford took his

pipe from his mouth and spat into the gutter.

43   "Well, there isn't much else worth talking about these days, is there? I suppose Mr. Carland here has been describing the finer strategic points of the recent campaign in Virginia," he said to Booth as he knocked the ashes out of his pipe. "He's the one to do it, too. The man is a born general—he certainly should be in the field. I never could understand how a man like him could stay out of the army."

44   Carland shifted about uneasily. Gifford, evidently enjoying himself, went on speaking. "Of course, I never could quite figure out just which side General Carland would fight on, but that really doesn't matter much, does it? I'm sure either side would be glad to have him. It's a shame—such a waste of talent." He rubbed some tobacco briskly between his hands in order to fill his pipe which he seldom allowed to cool.

45   Carland looked up at Booth as if seeking his support. Booth's face was stonily unresponsive. Carland turned to Gifford. "The science of military tactics has nothing to do with fighting in the field," he began. Gifford guffawed. "Besides we weren't talking about the war," he went on feebly. "We were discussing the South—her chances for recovery, and—and things like that."

46   "Aye, it's time to stop talking of war now, I suppose," Gifford said, cramming the tobacco into his pipe. "Recovery, reconstruction, rebuilding, reconciliation—all 'R's' too, aren't they?—anyway, they're the order of the day now. Well, it's going to be a hard time ahead of us, a precious hard time. I shouldn't like to have the job of the man who's sitting in the state box of this theater right now. There's too much bitterness about, and a hard cruel bitterness it is that will go on for generations. This country can never be the same again. The old easy days are gone forever."

47   "But there's great prosperity ahead, too," Carland said hotly. "We'll have to build up the country again—"

48   "We'll build it up all right. Nothing will stop this country from growing; but mark my words, the days to come are going to be hard ones, with hard, selfish men in control. I've watched what's been happening. I've seen how some men have made fortunes from this war. They're going to keep right on making fortunes, and God help anyone who gets in their way!"

49   He lighted his pipe, drew on it and blew out a cloud of smoke that hung in the windless air. Booth shrugged his shoulders. This philosophical carpenter had amused him in the past, but he only irritated him now.

50   He looked at the lobby clock that was marking away the minutes to ten o'clock. They would be talking about him tomorrow, these philosophical carpenters and strategy-minded tailors. His name would be on the lips of every cracker-barrel commentator in the country. They would all have a new factor to contend with in their discussions of the problems of war and peace.

51   He turned away from the two men to look down the street toward Pennsylvania Avenue. Someone in uniform was approaching, beckoning to him as he came. Booth stepped quickly away from Gifford and Carland and put his hand in the pocket where he had placed his pistol. The man in uniform entered the circle of lamplight, calling out a hearty greeting to Booth. It was Captain Williams of the Washington police force, a man whom Booth knew very well.

52   "What's the matter, Wilkes?" he said, surprised by the startled expression on Booth's face. "You look as if you expected me to arrest you. And I must say that you seem to be prepared to make a desperate stand."

53   Booth laughed nervously and held out his hand to his friend.

54   "I thought you might want to step in somewhere for a drink with me," Williams said. "I have a wonderful little story to tell you about a certain lady who is playing right now in a theater not a million miles away from here."

55   Booth smiled at him, and clasped his shoulder with a show of good nature. "It breaks my heart to turn down an invitation like that, Captain, but Keene will be on the

stage in a minute and I promised to look in on her performance tonight."

56   Williams lingered a moment, trying to persuade Booth to come with him. Finally, he went on his way, and Booth's tensed muscles relaxed. What terrible coincidence had caused this man to cross his tracks at this crucial instant? And was it a coincidence? He looked again at the two soldiers sitting on the carriage platform. They were no longer paying any attention to him, he noticed with relief.

57   Gifford and Carland were still talking together, but Booth gave up even the pretense of listening to them. Damn all these people who kept getting in his way! It had been a close shave with that fellow Williams.... He looked up at the lobby clock. The minute hand had crept forward to five minutes to ten. Paine and Herold should be riding through the streets toward Lafayette Square now....

58   Carland and Gifford clung to him, arguing between themselves. When he moved, they moved with him as though he were a necessary audience to what they were saying. *Why do these two fools talk about the war as if it were all over?* Atzerodt's frightened face recurred to him. What was the fellow doing now? He should never have trusted him. Perhaps Paine was right. One must be ruthless in matters where great issues are concerned.

59   Carland suddenly announced that he had to go backstage to inspect Laura Keene's costume before she went on. Gifford still hovered about, talking now about the imminence of Johnston's surrender to Sherman. It surely must be ten o'clock, Booth thought. He tried to disengage himself from the carpenter's clutches.

60   "I'm going inside to see Keene's performance," he said. "Will you excuse me?"

61   Gifford protested that she would not be on the stage for another fifteen minutes. In desperation, Booth mumbled something about not wanting to miss her entrance and hurried toward the lobby. One minute to ten.

62   Buckingham, the theater's tall lanky doorkeeper, was standing with his back to the lobby. His arm barred the entrance way. Booth touched his hand lightly. Buckingham turned around, scowling.

63   "I guess you don't need a ticket from me, do you?" Booth asked pleasantly. The doorkeeper's long homely face cracked into a wide grin.

64   "No, sir, I should say not. Fact is you couldn't buy a ticket here if you wanted to. Courtesy of the house, sir." He bowed sweepingly. "Go right on in." He was proud of his acquaintance with this young star who was so democratic in his relationships with the theater's people.

65   He lowered his arm and stepped back, still grinning good-naturedly. Booth entered the theater. The house was well filled with an audience in which blue army uniforms predominated. The stage lights filtered back into the auditorium with a soft glow that emphasized the white shoulders of women and brought out the metallic gleam of epaulets and army insignia on the men.

66   The dairy set, which was used for the first scene of the third act, was on the stage, but the scene still had some time to run. Booth walked to the rear row of seats and stood behind it. The state box was brightly lighted by one of the two big chandeliers that hung over the stage, but it was difficult to see inside the box. Flags and lace curtains concealed the opening. He could just make out the forms of an army officer and a young girl in evening dress, and he could see a rather stout woman who was probably Mrs. Lincoln. Lincoln himself was hidden from the audience by the front wall of the box. Evidently the rocking chair had not been moved.

67   Booth walked over to look into the boxes on the other side of the stage. They were all empty. This was so unusual that it frightened him for a moment. Could there be some purpose in not selling any of the seats in the other boxes? Then he realized that this had probably been done for the protection of the President, and the idea gave him a certain grim pleasure. It was a fortunate thing, after all, since no one could look directly across the stage into

the rear part of the state box where Lincoln was seated.

68 Booth walked across the theater again and went up the dress-circle stairs. As he reached the top, his eyes immediately sought the little white door leading into Lincoln's box. He expected to find a guard seated at the entrance. A chair was standing there beside the door, half-hidden in the darkness, but it was empty and no one was near it. The guard had evidently wandered off in search of a better seat from which to watch the performance. All the little gods of chance were with him now, he felt, and they had even given him this unforeseen opportunity of entering the box without being challenged.

69 He went down the stairs, exulting. Surely destiny was on his side! Second by second the clocks of the world were eating away the life of the man he was going to kill. Paine and Herold were moving at this minute toward the Seward residence, and somewhere in the dimly lighted corridors of the Kirkwood House, Atzerodt was lying in wait for Johnson. Even Surratt, miles away from him now and speeding northward, was safely on the train with Grant.

70 As Booth re-entered the lobby, Buckingham was waiting eagerly to present a group of his friends to him. Booth glanced at the clock while the introductions were being made. Three minutes after ten. Not much longer to wait now. He bowed mechanically to the men as they were presented. Buckingham offered him a chew of tobacco, which he accepted. He bit into the sweet-smelling brown cake.

71 "When are you going to play a Shakespearean role again, Mr. Booth?" asked one of the men who were crowding around him in an admiring circle. He spoke with a pompous air through a great black beard that lent dignity to everything he said.

72 "Very soon, I hope," Booth replied, smiling politely at the huge beard. "Very soon indeed."

73 "That is very good news," the beard enunciated slowly. "I saw you play with your brothers in New York last November in *Julius Caesar.* A great performance, sir, a great performance, even though it was marred by the despicable attempts of the rebels to fire the city." The words came out importantly, discouraging the other men from trying to speak at all. Booth ignored his reference to the rebel plot and bowed in acknowledgment of the compliment. "You should bring a cast like that to our fair city," the man continued, speaking with solemnity. "You would be richly rewarded, I assure you."

74 Booth thanked him. It was four minutes after ten.

75 Buckingham was grinning happily at his friends. In less than ten minutes the fatal second scene of the third act would be on. Booth decided that he needed a drink.

76 One of the men offered him a cigar, a thin evil-looking stogie. He declined it gracefully, excused himself and sauntered out to the street, where he promptly got rid of the chewing tobacco. He could hear the boom of the black-beard's voice follow him as he went. Gifford was still waiting on the sidewalk, but, fortunately, he had turned away to look toward the Lincoln carriage, which was standing at the curb near F Street. Booth managed to slip past him unnoticed, to seek shelter in Peter Taltavul's barroom.

77 The far end of the long bar was still covered with glasses left by the theatergoers during the last intermission. Taltavul was leisurely putting the glassware on a tray. He walked forward and greeted Booth cordially.

78 "What'll it be this evening?" he asked, wiping the surface of the bar in front of Booth with a beerstained rag.

79 "Same as usual, Peter. The brandy bottle and a glass of water."

80 "Quite an honor having the President next door," Taltavul commented cheerfully. "I wish he'd come oftener. It's good for business. There's a fine crowd there tonight." He pushed a bottle of brandy toward Booth and filled a glass with water.

81 Booth indicated that he was glad the President's visit was good for business.

82 "Well, to tell the truth, I can't complain about business anyway," Taltavul said, wringing out the wet rag. He leaned on the bar

and thrust his grizzled face toward Booth. "Business has been very good. Yes, sir, very good. This celebration, you know...." He winked solemnly. "A lot of liquor went down the nation's gullet when Richmond fell."

83   Booth finished two glasses of brandy and then stepped back to see the clock at the front of the bar. Seven minutes after. They would be changing scenes in a few minutes now. Just time for another drink. He filled his glass again. This was the last drink he would ever be able to take in the city of Washington. He lifted the glass in a silent toast to the Confederacy. So many people were counting on him...so much human happiness depended on his success...the South...the old South—God bless her!

84   Taltavul was still talking about the celebration. Booth realized that he was asking him a question.

85   "Sorry, Peter," he said. "I didn't hear you. What did you say?"

86   "Thinking about the ladies again, eh, Mr. Booth?" Taltavul chuckled. "Well, I can't blame you. I do myself sometimes. I was just asking you, did you think they would hold a big parade—you know, bring all the soldiers here to march down the Avenue, maybe?"

87   "Undoubtedly...undoubtedly." Booth took up the water glass and drank from it, staring at the barkeeper over its rim. Victory, victory, victory—all these filthy little shopkeepers were thinking of nothing but victory and their own profits.

88   "God, wouldn't that be magnificent?" Taltavul said gleefully. "All them soldier boys brought here to Washington, and every one of 'em thirsty."

89   Booth put some money down on the wet bar. Taltavul started to make change, but his customer had already left the saloon, humming a tune as he went.

90   The air outside was cool and fresh. Most of the loiterers had gone, but Gifford was still waiting. He seemed surprised to see Booth come out of Taltavul's saloon, but he immediately collared him and tried to engage him in conversation again. Booth felt that it was impossible even to attempt to be polite to the man now—he had to get rid of him quickly. The play inside was moving on, line by line, to the moment when his cue, "Don't know the manners of good society, eh?" would be spoken. He had to be in the theater before then, and he could allow nothing to stop him.

91   Gifford was standing in the lobby entrance, blocking his way. Booth interrupted his flow of meaningless words and asked him abruptly: "Can you see the time on the lobby clock?"

92   Gifford turned to look, and Booth took advantage of his movement to slip past him.

93   "Ten minutes after ten," Gifford announced in a loud voice. "What's your hurry?" he asked in surprise. "Miss Keene won't be on for at least five minutes yet."

94   Booth felt Gifford's hand touch his arm. This restraining gesture drove him to such fury that the thought of knocking the man down occurred to him. Then he controlled himself, and in a normal voice said: "I want to find a comfortable seat somewhere—if there is one." He paused, using up some of his time which had now become precious. "You can understand that, can't you?" he said, smiling ingratiatingly. "I don't often have the privilege of seeing a play from the front of the house, you know."

95   Gifford grinned sympathetically and released his arm. Booth went through the lobby, bowing as he walked past Buckingham and his friends. Still some few minutes yet. The second scene of the third act was about to begin. The big flat with the large doorway had already been dropped. He stood watching the actors make their entrances upon the stage. The whole performance at that moment seemed so utterly nonsensical that he wondered, for the first time in his life, what it was that brought the public to see a play. What sort of pleasure could people possibly get from looking at other human beings go through the empty gestures of living, when life itself was so much richer, so much more exciting than any counterfeit a dramatist could conceive? The actors' lines sounded as if they had been learned by rote, and to him they seemed especially artificial

because he knew every word and he could foretell every gesture. A child could see through this pretense—these characters had not even the semblance of life.

96   He watched the actors wearily, waiting for his moment to come. The play moved on with deadly slowness. I am tired of the life of the theater, he thought. I have had enough of being Macbeth, Hamlet, Brutus, Pescara, and all the others who strut the stage for an hour, mouthing another man's words. I have become death's emissary in order to rid myself of the many ghosts I have caused to walk the earth again, speaking through my voice, living in my body. Away with them! They are as insubstantial as everything else in this world that I have dreamed. I lent them reality for a moment, as I lend it now to these people here around me. . . .

97   On the stage, Mrs. Montchessington began to advise her daughter, Augusta, to set her cap for the wealthy Yankee, Asa Trenchard. I have seen all this happen before, Booth thought. I know what these people said during the first act, what they are going to say now, what they would say in the next scene, if I were to let it go on. Have I lived through my own part too, and is all this that I am now doing only a repetitious and meaningless action that goes on forever, over and over again? He knew then he must go up the stairs to the dress circle. He turned to the left of the orchestra pit, and with slow deliberate steps began the ascent. He could see the image of the lobby clock before him as he went, and it seemed to him that his own feet were keeping time with the monotonous beat of its heavy pendulum. As he stepped on to the dress-circle floor he saw Harry Hawk appear on the stage to play Asa Trenchard's part.

98   "Ah, Mr. Trenchard, we were just talking of your archery powers," Mrs. Montchessington said in a voice that seemed to be even louder and more raucous than usual.

99   He could hear Asa Trenchard answer in the drawling Yankee tones that reminded him of Lincoln's homely accents. "Wal, I guess shooting with bows and arrows is just about like most things in life. All you've got to do is keep the sun out of your eyes, look straight—pull strong—calculate the distance, and you're sure to hit the mark in most things as well as shooting."

100   Well spoken, Harry! Good advice even if you don't realize what your words suggest at this moment, Booth thought. He leaned against the back wall of the theater and looked around the house. The guard's chair at the entrance to the President's box was still vacant.

101   The play dragged on, its unreal comedy lines drawing unreal laughter from the audience. Like puppets pulled with strings the actors moved and gesticulated before the absurdly painted flat with its two huge vases and its writhing, tangled mass of drapery. Booth waited motionless, patient—although consumed with a vast impatience—his eyes intent upon the President's box. He saw Lincoln's hand reach out and place itself on the box-rail. His own hands were hot with sweat, and he kept digging his fingers into his palms.

102   Now the moment was very near. Mrs. Montchessington was learning that Asa Trenchard was not the millionaire she had imagined him to be. "No heir to the fortune, Mr. Trenchard?"

103   "Oh, no."

104   Augusta cried out: "What, no fortune?"

105   "Nary red," Trenchard told her cheerfully, "it all comes to their barking up the wrong tree about the old man's property."

106   These were the lines that came just before his cue. In a few seconds Harry Hawk would be alone upon the stage. Booth unhurriedly began his progress across the back of the dress circle. His feet made no sound on the carpeted floor, and he glided along the wall, hands outstretched, feeling his way in the semidarkness. His black-clad, high-booted figure moved stealthily toward the door that led to the President's box. Asa Trenchard's sallies filled the house with laughter as he went. (A droll fellow, this Yankee, he'll put the English snobs in their places before he's through.) Down the steps

now, the white door beckoning. Booth's face was rigid as his jaw muscles clenched, and his eyes stared into the darkness ahead of him. Step by step, nearer and nearer — the door was close to him now. He seized the knob and pushed his knee against the panel.

107 A man seated near the box entrance suddenly rose and approached him. Booth's hand reached under his coat for his knife. Then he realized what he was doing, and he turned, ready to placate this inquisitive stranger. He drew out his cardcase and showed the man one of Senator Hale's calling cards. The man backed away, apologizing.

108 Now the way is clear. Trenchard's remarks sweep the house with laughter again. The door swings open and Booth is inside the passageway at last. He closes the door behind him and stands there with his hand on the knob, his heart pounding, and his breath coming in short spasmodic gasps. There is no light inside the narrow passage, and he is alone in utter darkness. He feels for the wooden bar he had left in the corner behind the door, and his fingers close around its smooth square sides — only a moment's work to slip it in place, closing the only entrance to the box against all intruders. Quickly, quickly now. There is no time to be lost. That fellow outside the door has made him lose precious seconds. The voices on the stage, muffled and far away, have been speaking, and he listens to them carefully for his first cue.

109 "Augusta, dear, to your room."

110 "Yes, Ma. The nasty beast!"

111 "I am aware, Mr. Trenchard, that you are not used to the manners of good society —"

112 The words send a sudden quiver through him. He knows that he will hear them again, and then he will have to act. Mechanically he moves toward the second door. The hole he had cut in the panel gleams in the darkness — a single malignant eye, unblinking and steady, drawing him toward it. He peers into the box — the high back of the armchair is in front of him, and he can see a dark head rising above it. Mrs. Lincoln is leaning toward her husband,

speaking to him. Beyond them the lights from the stage shine through the lace curtains that hang like a mist in the background.

113 It is time for the two women to leave the stage now, and Booth listens for Asa Trenchard's words that will tell him when they are gone.

114 Now the final summons is about to be spoken!

115 The Yankee voice gives him the words: *"Don't know the manners of good society, eh?"*

116 There can be no hesitation. This is the moment! His final cue has been spoken, and he must make his entrance. His pistol is ready in his hand. His breath rushes into his lungs — can they hear the terrible sound of it? His left hand turns the doorknob — the door opens, letting in the light — his feet move silently on the carpet. . . . The people in the box are all watching the stage. They do not notice him. He steps forward, raising his hand with the deringer in it. He holds it close to that hated head. There must be no chance of missing. Now! Now! Asa Trenchard's voice still drawls on: "Well, I guess I know enough to turn you inside out, you sockdologizing old mantrap —"

117 And then the report, sharp and loud — the pistol almost seemed to go off by itself, kicking his hand upward. *"Sic semper tyrannis!"* he cries. He has done it! He has done it! He has killed Lincoln! The man in the chair never moves. He sits there, his head sagging forward, white smoke billowing around him. Mrs. Lincoln's face, upturned and startled, looks into Booth's for an instant. The officer at the other end of the box is standing up, and Booth sees him coming toward him. He drops his empty pistol and draws his knife. The officer lunges at him. Booth slashes quickly with the dagger. He feels the blade tear through cloth and flesh. The man clutches for an instant at his own arm, but he makes another attempt to seize Booth, snatching at his coat-tails as he turns toward the edge of the box. The knife jabs back again and Booth is free. Over the box-rail now to the stage, the light burning in his

eyes, and a tearing sound as he jumps — one of his spurs has caught in the flag draping the box, and he is thrown off balance. He lands on the stage heavily, all his weight on his left foot. It crumples under him, and he sprawls on the floor, half unconscious from the terrible stab of pain.

118   He gets up and almost falls again. Harry Hawk has stopped speaking and is looking at him wonderingly. Booth is up now, and he begins to run across the stage, forcing himself to bear the pain that is crippling him. The lines he had intended to speak at this supreme moment are forgotten; he struggles desperately to reach the protection of the wings. The audience, puzzled by what has happened, and thinking that perhaps it is all part of the play, watches him in silence.

119   And then there comes a scream from the President's box. A man sitting in the front row of the orchestra scrambles up on the stage and runs after Booth. Laura Keene comes out from the wings. Booth rushes past her, nearly colliding with a young actor who is just behind her. The audience begins to shout. Mrs. Lincoln is still screaming.

120   Booth runs with uncertain steps into the long passage that leads to the stage door. Someone tries to bar his way. He strikes with his knife, and the man scuttles out of his path. He is at the stage door now, tugging frantically at its handle. He hears the heavy tread of a running man behind him. The door opens with a rush of cool night air, and the quiet darkness of the theater alley lies before him.

121   A boy is lying on a bench near the stage door idly holding the mare's reins. He tries to get up, but Booth pushes him violently away and strikes at him with the handle of his knife. The horse shies. Booth seizes the reins, and the frightened animal stands still long enough to permit him to get his foot into the stirrup. As he springs up to mount the horse, the weight of his body on his injured foot sends another paralyzing wave of pain through him. He manages to scramble into the saddle, clutching in agony at the pommel. The horse starts off with a clatter of hoofs, tossing its head at this sudden strange treatment. The man who has followed him out of the theater tries to grasp the reins, but the horse is too quick for him. Booth kicks her side with his right foot and heads her down the alley, out into the broad expanse of F Street, which lies muddy and deserted in the darkness.

EXERCISES

Content

Recall the main ideas in this article by answering the following questions. Respond to some of the questions in your own words. Respond to others by finding quotations from the article that provide the answers.

1. Why would rain have been bad news for Booth?

2. What impressions did Booth have of the setting for his crime?

3. What, according to Stern, gave Booth new courage to carry out the murder?

4. Why did Booth leave the theater again after he had first entered it that evening?

5. Why, did Booth finally conclude, were the soldiers staring at him after he came out of the theater?

6. In general, what was Booth's mood that evening, according to Stern?

7. How is Lewis Carland characterized, in Booth's mind?

8. What did Gifford emphasize in his comments to Carland and Booth?

9. What excuse did Booth give for not accepting Williams's offer of a drink?

10. What class of people formed much of the audience at Ford's Theater that evening?

11. What alarmed Booth as he surveyed the boxes in the theater?

12. Who did Booth encounter when he came out into the lobby once again?

13. Why did Gifford become a source of worry to Booth before he went back into the theater for the last time?

14. What were Booth's thoughts, according to Stern, as he watched the dramatic action before going to Lincoln's box?

15. What lines of the play did Booth think were appropriate to what he was about to do?

16. According to Stern, did Booth yell anything while he was on stage?

17. Based on your knowledge of the trial testimony, who was the "man sitting in the front row of the orchestra [who] scramble[d] up on the stage and [ran] after Booth"?

18. Who was the "boy...lying on a bench near the stage door idly holding the mare's reins"?

Inferences

In your responses to the following questions, incorporate some of the quotations you located in response to the Content questions. You may decide to use either all or only part of each quotation.

1. Based on the factual evidence you have read prior to this selection, do you think Stern is justified in making the inferences he does about what Booth was thinking on that evening? Cite examples of passages that you believe are justified. Cite examples that you believe may carry "poetic license" too far.

2. Based on your knowledge of what the other sources say actually *happened* on that evening (as opposed to what Booth was *thinking*), has Stern been faithful to the facts? If not, at what point(s) has he deviated?

3. Booth asks "someone" if he can cross the stage. Based on your reading of the trial testimony, who was that "someone"?

4. In paragraph 20, Stern has Booth thinking: "The thunderbolt imprisoned in his pocket would shatter not only the lives of the great; little people, too, would have their petty plans twisted and thwarted by its mighty detonation." What does he mean?

5. Why do you think Stern inserts the episode involving Carland?

6. What is our impression of Gifford when we first meet him, especially after we read what he has to say about Carland? Do you notice any inconsistencies in character between the Gifford portrayed by Stern and the Gifford who provided testimony at the trial?

7. Why do you think Stern places Gifford in his narrative?

8. Why do you think Stern places Captain Williams in the narrative?

9. Here is tavernkeeper Peter Taltavul's testimony about Booth's visit on the evening of April 14, 1865:

> I was acquainted with John Wilkes Booth. I kept the restaurant adjoining Ford's Theater, on the lower side. Booth came into my restaurant on the evening of the

14th of April, I judge a little after 10 o'clock, walked up to the bar, and called for some whiskey, which I gave him; he then called for some water, which I also gave him; he placed the money on the counter and went out. I saw him go out of the bar alone, as near as I can judge, from eight to ten minutes before I heard the cry that the President was assassinated. (*The Assassination of President Lincoln and the Trial of the Conspirators,* compiled and arranged by Benn Pitman [New York: Wilstach and Baldwin, 1865], 72)

Compare and contrast this account with Stern's (paragraphs 77–89).

10. At what point does the *tense* of Stern's narrative change? (What has happened immediately before? What happens immediately afterward?) How do you account for the change?

11. How does Stern use the on-stage drama to increase the suspense of the off-stage drama?

Jim Bishop

THE DAY LINCOLN WAS SHOT

Journalist Jim Bishop wrote best-selling journalistic-style accounts of significant historical events. Starting as a copy boy for the *New York Daily News*, Bishop worked for the *New York Daily Mirror*, *Collier's* magazine, *Liberty* magazine, and *Catholic Digest*. In addition to *The Day Lincoln Was Shot*, the source of the following passage, Bishop's books include *The Day Christ Died*, *The Day Christ Was Born*, *A Day in the Life of President Kennedy*, *A Day in the Life of President Johnson*, *The Day Kennedy Was Shot*, *The Days of Martin Luther King, Jr.*, *F.D.R.'s Last Year*, and two autobiographical works, *Jim Bishop, Reporter*, and *A Bishop's Confession*. This passage showcases Bishop's journalistic skills in detailing, moment by moment, the steps leading to the assassination and the immediate aftermath. Unlike a typical piece of journalism, however, it also offers some historical perspective (many of the details Bishop discusses were not uncovered for months or even years afterward) and a polished writing style.

1   The night air cleared. The mists rolled away with theatrical speed and, in the gaps between the scudding clouds, the signals of far-off stars could be seen tapping blue dots and dashes. The moon was due to rise at 10:02 P.M. but the men at the Naval Observatory up beyond Rock Creek saw nothing in the east except the silvered edges of clouds over the Maryland shore.

2   The roisterers were still in the streets, and public singing was plentiful and cheap. At Lichau House, Mike O'Laughlin sang a flat baritone which most customers thought was good, and sad, or perhaps good and sad. In the freshly washed night air, the Capitol dome looked like a picture postcard and lights were on in many homes at an hour when most good families were in bed.

3   At Surratt House, the widow kissed Anna good night and began the job of turning off the kerosene lamps in the downstairs dining room and the upstairs sitting room, taking the last lighted lamp with her along the hall to the bedroom she shared with Honora Fitzpatrick. If she gave a thought to her son John, she thought of him in Canada, but, in reality, he was in northern New York State, in a small town where thousands of Southern prisoners were kept. He was on a final mission for the Confederate States of America.

4   George Atzerodt trotted his horse up Tenth Street again and he looked at Ford's Theatre as though fascinated. He saw the President's carriage and he saw off-duty soldiers lounging and he saw a few civilians on

the sidewalk. He rode back to Kirkwood House to kill the Vice President but his feet carried him into the bar and he drank and looked at the clock and drank some more.

5   In the theater, the play was more than half over. The second scene of the third act had begun. President Lincoln, momentarily distracted from the action onstage, watched a portly officer come down the right-hand orchestra aisle. He knew the man. It was General Ambrose E. Burnside, an officer who did not believe that he was big enough to command the army of the Potomac and, when Lincoln gave it to him, proved it. The President watched him come down front, split the tails of his uniform coat, and sit. Lincoln may have wondered what kept him so late. The presidential attention reverted to the stage.

6   Booth came out of Taltavul's and stood talking to Lewis Carland, the theater costumer. Mr. Carland was a sponge; he absorbed the moods of his friends. James J. Gifford, the stage carpenter, came out puffing a freshly lighted pipe and joined the conversation. A singer named Hess came down from F Street and asked what time it was. Someone looked at the lobby clock and said "ten." Hess returned a few minutes later and asked the same question. He was scheduled to go on, just before the last scene, and sing in concert with a young lady and another man "All Honor to Our Soldiers," the new song composed by Professor Withers.

7   Another man walked up from E Street to join the conversation. He was Captain William Williams of the Washington Cavalry Police. The captain was an admirer of John Wilkes Booth. He invited his idol into Taltavul's for a drink, but Booth looked at his watch, and declined with thanks.

8   "Keene," he said, "will be onstage in a minute and I promised to take a look for her."

9   He bowed and left the group and walked in the main entrance to the theater. Absent-mindedly, John Buckingham, ticket taker, held out his hand, and Booth said, in mock shock: "You will not want a ticket from me?"

10   Buckingham laughed and bowed. "Courtesy of the house," he said. The actor looked at the lobby clock. It read 10:07. He saw Buckingham chewing, and borrowed a bite of tobacco. Buckingham said that, if Mr. Booth did not mind, he would like to introduce a few friends. The actor winked, and said: "Later, John." He turned and bounded up the stairs to the Dress Circle.

11   In Boston, his brother was, on this night, playing the part of Sir Edward Mortimer and, with a declaiming sweep of his hand, moaned: "Where is my honor now?"

12   Here in the dress circle, a man and a little girl were disappointed. James Ferguson, restaurateur, occupied the extreme left seat in the front row solely to see Abraham Lincoln and General Ulysses S. Grant. He did not want to see the play. He had brought the little neighbor's girl along because she too had an appreciation of historical figures which matched his. With her own eyes, she wanted to see the President of the United States and the man who had won the war.

13   All evening long, he had studied the State Box and the right-hand aisle. The President was in the box but, except for one brief moment when he had leaned forward to look down in the orchestra, they had not seen him. The general was not present and Mr. Ferguson kept telling the little girl that Grant was sure to be along at any moment. Now he saw a figure move down the right-hand aisle and he squeezed the little girl's hand. She followed his glance and saw a man step down the broad steps with easy grace. Ferguson shaded his eyes against the glare of the stage lights and, after a look, smiled sadly and said that it wasn't General Grant after all; it was a famous actor named Booth.

14   Almost as though to assuage the disappointment, James Ferguson noticed that, at the same time, President Lincoln was leaning forward in the box, with his left hand on the ledge, looking at the people below. It was the first time that Ferguson had seen Lincoln come into plain view, and he nudged the little girl and pointed. She looked steadily, and nodded. For the first time in her life she

had seen, with her own eyes, the President of the United States.

15   John Wilkes Booth, slightly ahead of schedule, came down the dress circle steps slowly. He heard the lines onstage and he knew that he had about two minutes.

16   Asa Trenchard walked onstage and Mrs. Mountchessington said: "Ah, Mr. Trenchard, We were just talking of your archery powers."

17   Asa, who was played by Harry Hawk, was a slender drawling Yankee.

18   "Wal," he said, "I guess shooting with bows and arrows is just about like most things in life. All you have got to do is to keep the sun out of your eyes, look straight, pull strong, calculate the distance, and you're sure to hit the mark in most things as well as shooting."

19   Booth looked down at the little white door and saw the empty chair. Confused, he looked at patrons sitting in dress circle seats as though wondering which one was the President's guard. He saw the two army officers and he moved by them. For the first time, he realized that he was going to get into that box with no trouble; no challenge; no palaver; no argument; no fight; no stabbing. He was going to be able to walk in as though Lincoln had been expecting him.

20   He walked down to the white door, and stood with his back to it. He studied the faces nearby, men and women, and he saw some of them glance briefly at him. A real wave of laughter swept the theater and attention reverted to the stage.

21   Mrs. Mountchessington had just learned that Asa Trenchard was not a millionaire.

22   "No heir to the fortune, Mr. Trenchard?"

23   "Oh, no," he said.

24   "What!" young Augusta shrieked. "No fortune!"

25   "Nary a red," said Asa brightly. "It all comes from their barking up the wrong tree about the old man's property."

26   Now was the time. Booth knew that, in a few seconds, Asa would be alone on the stage. He turned the knob, pushed the door, and walked into the darkness. The door closed behind him. He found the pine board, held it against the inside of the door, and tapped the other end down the wall opposite until it settled in the niche he had carved for it. Pursuit could not come from that direction. Nor interference.

27   He moved toward the door of Box 7* in the darkness. A tiny beam of yellow light squeezed through the gimlet hole in the door and made a dot on the opposite wall.

28   Wilkes Booth could still hear the actors faintly. Mrs. Mountchessington had just said: "Augusta, to your room!"

29   And Augusta said: "Yes, ma. The nasty beast!"

30   "I am aware, Mr. Trenchard," said Mrs. Mountchessington in her frostiest tone, "that you are not used to the manners of good society—"

31   The conspirator crouched and pressed his eye against the gimlet hole. What he saw

---

*An interesting commentary on the fates of people in the presidential box has been provided by John G. Nicolay and John Hay, private secretaries to Abraham Lincoln:

The glitter of fame, happiness, and ease was upon the entire group, but in an instant everything was to be changed with the blinding swiftness of enchantment. Quick death was to come on the central figure of that company—the central figure, we believe, of the great and good men of the century. Over all the rest the blackest fates hovered menacingly—fates from the which a mother might pray that kindly death would save her children in their infancy. One was to wander with the stain of murder on his soul, with the curses of a world upon his name, with a price set upon his head, in frightful physical pain, till he died a dog's death in a burning barn; the stricken wife was to pass the rest of her days in melancholy and madness; of those two young lovers, one was to slay the other, and then end his life a raving maniac. (*Abraham Lincoln: A History* [New York: The Century Co., 1914], 295)

In his *Abraham Lincoln Encyclopedia* Mark E. Neely explains,

In 1867 [Major Henry] Rathbone married his stepsister [Clara Harris]. Twenty years later President Grover Cleveland appointed him consul to Hanover, Germany. There Rathbone, Clara, and their three children lived until 1894, when Rathbone, who had become mentally ill, apparently grew jealous of his wife's attentions to the children and murdered her. German authorities convicted him of murder and committed him to an asylum for the criminally insane, where he died in 1911. (256)

was clear. The high back of the horsehair rocker was in plain view and the silhouette of a head above it. He waited. Three persons were on the stage. In a matter of seconds, Augusta would be offstage, followed by her irate mother. That would leave Harry Hawk (as Trenchard) alone and he would begin to drawl: "Don't know the manners of good society, eh?..."

32   Booth kept his eye to the gimlet hole. The head in front of him barely moved. The universe seemed to pause for breath. Then Trenchard said: "Don't know the manners of good society, eh?" Booth did not wait to hear the rest of the line. The derringer was now in his hand. He turned the knob. The door swung inward. Lincoln, facing diagonally away toward the left, was four feet from him. Booth moved along the wall closest to the dress circle. The President had dropped Mrs. Lincoln's hand and there was a little space between their chairs. The major and his Clara were listening to the humorous soliloquy of the actor onstage:

33   "Wal, I guess I know enough to turn you inside out, you sockdologizing old mantrap!"

34   The derringer was behind the President's head between the left ear and the spine. Booth squeezed the trigger and there was a sound as though someone had blown up and broken a heavy paper bag. It came in the midst of laughter, so that some people heard it, and some did not. The President did not move. His head inclined toward his chest and he stopped rocking.

35   Mrs. Lincoln turned at the noise, her round face creased with laughter. So did Major Rathbone and Miss Harris. A chrysanthemum of blue smoke hung in Box 7. Booth, with no maniacal gleam, no frenzy, looked at the people who looked at him and said, "Sic semper tyrannis!" It was said in such an ordinary tone that theatergoers only fourteen feet below did not hear the words.

36   The conspirator forced his way between the President and his wife. Mrs. Lincoln's laughter dissolved in confusion. She saw the young man towering above her, but she did not know who he was or what he wanted. The major saw the cloud of smoke and, with-

out understanding, jumped up and tried to grapple with the intruder. Booth dropped the derringer and pulled out his knife. The major laid a hand on his arm and the assassin's arm went high in the air and slashed down. Rathbone lifted his left arm to counter the blow, and the knife sliced through his suit and flesh down to the bone.

37   The assassin moved to the ledge of the box and the major reached for him with his right arm. Booth shoved him and said loudly: "Revenge for the South!" Mrs. Lincoln began to rub her cheek nervously. She glanced at her husband, but he seemed to be dozing.

38   Harry Hawk faltered in his lines. He looked up at the State Box indecisively. In the wings, W. J. Ferguson, an actor, heard the explosion and looked up at the box in time to see a dark man come out of the smoke toward the ledge. In the dress circle, James Ferguson and his little friend saw Booth climb over the ledge of the box, at a point near where Boxes 7 and 8 met at the picture of George Washington and watched him turn his back to the audience and, by holding on with his arms, let himself down over the side.

39   As he dropped, he pushed his body away from the box with his right hand. This turned him a little and the spur of his right foot caught in the Treasury regiment flag. As the banner ripped, and followed him to the stage in tatters, the actor, by reflex, held his left foot rigid to take the shock of the fall, plus two outstretched hands. He landed on the left leg, and it snapped just above the instep. He fell on his hands, got up, and started to run across the stage to the left. He passed Harry Hawk and headed for the wings.

40   The audience did not understand. They watched the running actor, and he fell again. He stood and, as he got offstage, he was limping on the outside of his left foot; in effect, walking on his ankle.

41   Hawk, stupefied, did not move. His arms were still raised in half gesture toward the wings through which the women had departed. Laura Keene, in the Green Room, noticed that the onstage action had stopped

and she came out in time almost to bump into Booth. She brushed by him, wondering what had happened to Harry Hawk. An actor stood in Booth's way and he saw a knife flash by his face.

42   A piercing scream came from the State Box. This was Mrs. Lincoln. Clara Harris stood and looked out at the people below and said "Water!" Major Joseph B. Stewart, sitting in the front row of the orchestra with his wife and his sister, got up from his seat and climbed over the rim of the stage. He was a big man, looking bigger in a pale fawn suit, and he got to his feet, rushed by Harry Hawk, and yelled "Stop that man!"

43   The conspirator hobbled to the back door, opened it, and shut it behind him. Johnny Peanut was lying on the stone step with the mare's bridle in his hand. Booth's face was snowy and grim as he pulled his foot back and kicked the boy in the chest.

44   He took the bridle and limped toward the animal. She began to swing in a swift circle as he tried to get his good foot up in the stirrup. When he made it, Booth pulled himself across the saddle, threw his left leg over, and was just settling in the saddle when Major Stewart came out the back door yelling "Stop! Stop!" He reached for the rein as Booth spurred the horse and turned out of the alley.

45   The course he chose was not up to F Street, where the gate would have to be unlatched. He swung toward the side of the T, out through Ninth Street, then right toward Pennsylvania Avenue. His job was to put that first mile between him and his pursuers; he must be ahead of the news he had created. So he spurred the little mare hard, and she laid her ears back and ran. The conspirator was in little pain. He knew that his leg had been hurt, but the pain was not great now. He leaned his weight on the right stirrup and sat with the left thigh half up on the saddle. The mare turned into Pennsylvania Avenue and headed toward the Capitol. To the right of the House wing, a moon two days shy of being full was showing.

46   At Capitol South, he passed another horseman, trotting in the opposite direction.

The speed of the mare attracted the lone rider's attention. As Booth turned into New Jersey Avenue, he slowed the mare. This was a shanty section, so dark that, unless the United States Government knew his escape route, no one would look for him here. At Virginia Avenue, he turned left, and was now close to the bridge.

47   When Booth swung away from the rear of Ford's Theater, Johnny Peanuts rolled in the alley, moaning: "He kicked me. He kicked me." Major Stewart turned to go back into the theater and was met by a rush of theater people coming out. Backstage, Jacob Ritterspaugh ran out of the wings and grabbed Ned Spangler by the shoulders.

48   "That was Booth!" he shouted. "I swear it was Booth!"

49   Spangler swung and smashed Ritterspaugh in the face.

50   "Be quiet!" he said. "What do you know about it?"

51   The audience began to buzz. Some of the men stood and began to ask others what did this mean. The people sensed now that this was not a part of the play and they felt vaguely alarmed. Major Rathbone pointed dramatically toward the dead wings and roared: "Stop that man!" Out of the State Box came a second scream, a shriek that chilled the audience and brought a large part of it to its feet. This again was Mrs. Lincoln. It had penetrated her mind that Mr. Lincoln could not be aroused. To the West, many farmers testified that, at this time, the moon emerged from behind clouds blood red.

52   In the orchestra, one man stood and brought to mouth the question everyone was asking: "For God's sake, what is it? What happened?" Miss Shepard, the letter writer, stood and saw that Miss Harris was leaning over the ledge of the box wringing her hands and pleading for water. Someone in the box, a man, yelled:

53   "He has shot the President!"

54   All over the theater, hoarse voices shouted, "No! No!" "It can't be true!" In a trice, Ford's resembled a hive immediately after the queen bee has died. The aisles were

jammed with people moving willy-nilly. The stairs were crowded, some trying to get up to the dress circle, others trying to get down. Some were up on the stage. Harry Hawk stood in stage center and wept. A group of men tried to force their way through the white door, but, the harder they pushed, the more firmly it held. James Ferguson, choking with horror, picked the little girl up and said that he would carry her out of the theater. Actors in make-up ran on the stage begging to know what had happened.

55 "Water!" Miss Harris begged from the box. "Water!"

56 Some of the patrons got out on the street and spread the word that Lincoln had been shot. The President, they said, is lying dead in the box inside. Tempers flared. A crowd collected. From E and F Streets, people came running. Many tried to get into the theater as others were trying to get out. Inside, a few women fainted and the cry for water could be heard from different parts of the theater.

57 Rathbone, soaked with blood, went back into the corridor and tried to open the door. He found the wooden bar and yelled for the men on the other side to stop leaning against the door. After several entreaties, he was able to lift the bar and it fell to the floor, stained with his blood. The major pleaded that only doctors be admitted. A short, handsome man in sideburns and mustache yelled from the rear of the mob that he was a doctor. Men pushed him forward until he got inside the corridor. He was Dr. Charles Leale, Assistant Surgeon of United States Volunteers, twenty-three years of age.

58 Someone, below the stage, turned the gas valve up and hundreds of faces were revealed to be in varying stages of fright and anger. On the street, a man shouted, "I'm glad it happened!" In a moment, he was scuffed underfoot, most of his clothes ripped from his body, and he was carried toward a lamp post. Three policemen drew revolvers to save his life.

59 In the State Box, President Lincoln's knees began to relax and his head began to come forward. Mrs. Lincoln saw it,

moaned, and pressed her head against his chest. Rathbone asked Dr. Leale for immediate attention. "I'm bleeding to death!" he said. The blood had soaked his sleeve and made a pool on the floor. The doctor lifted Rathbone's chin, looked into his eyes, and walked on into the box.

Miss Harris was hysterical. She was begging everyone to please help the President. The doctor looked at her, then lifted Mrs. Lincoln's head off her husband's chest. The First Lady grabbed the hand of medicine and moaned piteously. 60

"Oh, Doctor! Is he dead? Can he recover? Will you take charge of him? Oh, my dear husband! My dear husband!" 61

"I will do what I can," the doctor said, and motioned to the men who crowded into the box behind him to remove her. She was taken to the broad sofa in Box 8, and Miss Harris sat beside her, patting Mrs. Lincoln's hand. 62

At first, Leale thought that the President was dead. He pushed the shoulders back in the rocker so that the trunk no longer had a tendency to fall forward. Then he stood in front of the President and studied him from head to foot. With the attitude of one who knows that he will be obeyed, he said to the gawking men: "Get a lamp. Lock that door back there and admit no one except doctors. Someone hold matches until the lamp gets here." 63

These things were done, as Dr. Leale knew that they would be. He was the first person to bring order around the dying President. The eyes of the patient were closed. There was no sound of breathing. There was no sign of a wound. Men held matches and looked open-mouthed as Leale placed the palm of his hand under the whiskered chin of the President, lifted it, and then permitted it to drop. 64

In the crowd peering in from the corridor, he saw a few soldiers. "Come here," he said to them. "Get him out of the chair and put him on the floor." Half afraid, they did as he told them to. The body was relaxed. They placed it on the floor and stepped away. Leale was going to look for the wound. He 65 was sure that it was a stab wound because, as he was passing the theater on his way back to the army hospital, he heard a man yell something about the President and a man with a knife. Further, he had seen that Major Rathbone sustained a knife wound.

66   Dr. Leale crouched behind Lincoln's head and lifted it. His hands came away wet. He placed the head back on the floor and men in a circle held matches at waist level as the doctor unbuttoned the black coat, the vest, unfastened the gold watch chain, and, while trying to unbutton the collar, he became impatient and asked for a pocket knife. William F. Rent had a sharp one, and Doctor Leale took it and slit the shirt and collar down the front.

67   He tore the undershirt between his hands and the chest was laid bare. He saw no wound. The doctor bent low, and put his ear to the chest. Then he lifted the eyelid and saw evidence of a brain injury. He separated his fingers and ran them through the patient's hair. At the back, he found matted blood and his fingers loosened a clot and the patient responded with shallow breathing and a weak pulse.

68   Onstage, men lifted another doctor into the box. This one was Dr. Charles Taft. He was senior to Leale, but he placed himself at Leale's disposal at once as an assistant. Leale lifted the body into a slumped sitting position and asked Dr. Taft to hold him. In the saffron flicker of the matches, he found what he was looking for. His fingers probed the edges of the wound and he pulled the matted black hair away from it. It was not a knife wound. The President had been shot behind the left ear and, if the probe of a pinky meant anything, the lead ball moved diagonally forward and slightly upward through the brain toward the right eye. Dr. Leale felt around the eye to see if the ball had emerged. It had not. It was in the brain.

69   Gently, he lowered the great head to the floor. He knew that Lincoln had to die. Leale acquainted Dr. Taft with his findings, and his feeling. He straddled the hips and started

artificial respiration. His business was to prolong life — not to try to read the future — and so he raised the long arms up high and lowered them to the floor — up and back — forward and down — up and back — forward and down. For a moment, he paused. Rudely, he pushed the mouth open and got two fingers inside and pushed the tongue down to free the larynx of secretions.

70   Dr. Albert F. A. King was admitted the box. Leale asked each doctor to take an arm and manipulate it while he pressed upward on the belly to stimulate the heart action.

71   A few soldiers started to clear the box of people. From onstage, questions flew up to the box. Mostly, they were unanswered. "How is he?" "What happened?" "Was he stabbed?" "Who did it?" "Is he breathing?" "Did anyone see who did it?"

72   For the first time, someone uttered the name of John Wilkes Booth. The name moved from the stage down into the orchestra, was shouted across the dress circle and out of the half-empty theater into the lobby and cascaded into Tenth Street. "Booth!" "Booth did it!" "An actor named Booth!" "The management must have been in on the plot!" "Burn the damn theater!" "Burn it now!" "Yes, burn it!" "Burn!"

73   Grief spirals to insanity.

74   Dr. Leale sat astride the President's hips and leaned down and pressed until these strangers met, thorax to thorax. Leale turned his head and pressed his mouth against the President's lips, and breathed for him in a kiss of desperation. Then he listened to the heart again and, when he sat up, he noticed that the breathing was stronger. It sounded like a snore.

75   "His wound is mortal," he said to the other doctors. "It is impossible for him to recover."

76   One of the soldiers began to get sick. Two others removed their uniform caps. A lamp arrived. Dr. Leale saw a hand in front of him with brandy. He dripped a small amount between the bluish lips. Leale watched the Adam's apple. It bobbed. The liquid had been swallowed and was now retained.

77   He paused in his labors to wipe his face with a kerchief.

78   "Can he be removed to somewhere nearby?" Leale said.

79   "Wouldn't it be possible to carry him to the White House?" Dr. King said.

80   "No," Dr. Leale said. "His wound is mortal. It is impossible for him to recover."

81   On the couch, Mrs. Lincoln sat quietly, rocking slightly. Miss Laura Keene had come into the box and was now sitting with her and with Miss Harris. All three heard Dr. Leale's words, but only Mrs. Lincoln seemed not to comprehend. She sat between them, rocking a little and looking across the theater at the other boxes.

82   Miss Keene came over, and asked the doctor if she could hold the President's head for a moment. He looked at her coldly, and nodded. She sat on the floor and placed his head on her lap.

83   "If it is attempted," said Leale, still thinking about the White House, "he will be dead before we reach there."

84   Dr. Taft asked an officer to run out and find a place nearby — a suitable place — for President Lincoln. He called four soldiers to carry the body — at first it was decided to try seating the body in the rocker and carrying it that way — but Leale said that there were too many narrow turns and besides, it would not hurt him to be carried as long as the open wound was downward.

85   Four men from Thompson's Battery C, Pennsylvania Light Artillery, drew the assignment. Two formed a sling under the upper trunk; the other two held the thin thighs. Dr. King held the left shoulder. Dr. Leale followed behind and held the head in cupped hands. Miss Keene sat, oblivious to the dark stain on her dress, watching. At the last moment, Leale decided that headfirst would be better and he walked backward with Lincoln's head in his hands, his own head twisted to see ahead.

86   "Guards!" he yelled. "Guards! Clear the passage!"

87   From somewhere, a group of troopers came to life and preceded the dismal party, shoving the curious to one side. "Clear out!" they yelled at one and all. "Clear out!"

88   At the head of the stairs, Leale shouted orders as the party began the slow descent. Ahead, they could hear the cries of the crowd in Tenth Street. Downstairs in the lobby, a big man looked at the great placid face, and he blessed himself. Tenth Street was massed with humanity as far as the eye could see.

89   A short paunchy captain of infantry impressed more soldiers to duty and ordered them double-ranked to precede the body. He drew his sword and said: "Surgeon, give me your commands and I will see that they are obeyed." Leale looked at the houses across the street, private homes and boardinghouses, and asked the captain to get them across.

90   For the first time, the crowd saw the shaggy head and the big swinging feet. A roar of rage went up. Someone in the crowd yelled "God almighty! Get him to the White House!" Leale shook his head no. "He would die on the way," Leale said. Men in the crowd began to weep openly. The little party pressed through, inch by inch, the faces of the mob forming a canopy of frightened eyes over the body. The crowd pressed in ahead, and closed in behind.

91   The paunchy captain swung his sword and roared: "Out of the way, you sons of bitches!"

92   The night, now, was clear. The mist gone. The wind cool and gusty. The moon threw the shadow of Ford's Theatre across the street.

93   Every few steps, Leale stopped the party and pulled a clot loose. The procession seemed to be interminable. When they got across the street, the steady roar of the crowd made it impossible to hear or to be heard. Leale wanted to go into the nearest house, but a soldier on the stoop made motions that no one was home and made a helpless pantomime with a key. At the next house toward F Street, Leale saw a man with a lighted candle standing in the doorway, motioning. This was the William Petersen

house at 453 Tenth Street. Mr. Petersen was a tailor.

94 Lincoln was carried up the steps and into the house. Part of the crowd followed. The man with the candle motioned for the doctors to follow him. They moved down a narrow hall. To the right was a stairway going up to the second floor. To the left was a parlor, with coal grate and black horsehair furniture. Behind it, also on the left, was a sitting room. Under the stairway was a small bedroom.

95 Here, the President was placed on a bed. A soldier on leave, who had rented the room, picked up his gear and left. He was Private William T. Clark of the 13th Massachusetts Infantry. The room measured fifteen feet by nine feet. The wallpaper was oatmeal in character. A thin reddish rug covered part of the floor. There were a plain maple bureau near the foot of the bed, three straight-backed chairs, a washstand with white crock bowl, a wood stove. On the wall were framed prints of "The Village Blacksmith" and Rosa Bonheur's "The Horse Fair." The bed was set against the wall under the stairway.

96 It was too small for the President. Leale ordered it pulled away from the wall. He also asked that the footboard be taken off, but it was found that, if that was done, the bed would collapse. The body was placed diagonally on the bed, the head close to the wall, the legs hanging off the other end. Extra pillows were found and Lincoln's head was propped so that his chin was on his chest. Leale then ordered an officer to open a bedroom window—there were two, facing a little courtyard—and to clear everybody out and to post a guard on the front stoop.

97 At the back end of the room, Leale held his first formal conference with the other doctors. As they talked in whispers, the man who had held the candle went through the house lighting all the gas fixtures. The house was narrow and deep, and behind this bedroom was another and behind that a family sitting room which spread across the width of the house.

98 Leale, in the presence of the other doctors, began a thorough examination. As he began to remove the President's clothing, he looked up and saw Mrs. Lincoln standing in the doorway with Miss Keene and Miss Harris. He looked irritated and asked them to please wait in the front room. The patient was undressed and the doctors searched all of the areas of the body, but they found no other wound.

99 The feet were cold to the touch up to the ankles. The body was placed between sheets and a comforter was placed over the top. A soldier in the doorway was requisitioned as an orderly and the doctors sent him for hot water and for heated blankets. They sent another soldier for large mustard plasters. These were applied to the front of the body, covering the entire area from shoulders to ankles.

100 Occasionally, the President sighed. His pulse was forty-four and light; breathing was stertorous; the pupil of the left eye was contracted; the right was dilated—both were proved insensitive to light. Leale called a couple of more soldiers from the hallway, and sent them to summon Robert Lincoln, Surgeon General Barnes, Dr. Robert K. Stone, President Lincoln's physician, and Lincoln's pastor, Dr. Phineas D. Gurley.

101 The death watch began.

EXERCISES

Content

Recall the main ideas in this article by answering the following questions. Respond to some of the questions in your own words. Respond to others by finding quotations from the article that provide the answers.

1. Where was Booth immediately before he went into Ford's Theater to kill Lincoln?

2. Why had James Ferguson and his neighbor's daughter come to Ford's Theater that evening?

3. Whom did Ferguson first mistake John Wilkes Booth for, as the actor walked down the aisle?

4. What surprised Booth as he approached the outer door of the president's box?

5. For what moment was Booth waiting to enter Lincoln's box?

6. What did Booth do immediately after entering the outer door?

7. At what moment in the play's action did Booth pull the trigger?

8. According to Bishop, when did Booth say "Sic semper tyrannis!"? At what point did Booth next speak, and what did he say?

9. According to Bishop, did W. J. Ferguson, the actor, see the actual assassination?

10. Exactly how did Booth exit the box?

11. What were Leale's first assumptions about Lincoln's condition? What facts appeared to justify these assumptions?

12. As soon as Leale had ascertained Lincoln's condition, what did he do?

13. How was Lincoln removed from the theater?

14. Into whose house was the president conveyed?

Structure

1. What is the purpose of paragraphs 1–3?

2. Explain how paragraphs 12–14, considered together, form an identifiable section of the article. Give this section a title.

3. How is paragraph 73 related to paragraph 72?

4. Explain how paragraphs 84–95, considered together, form an identifiable section of the article. Give this section a title.

5. Write two more Structure questions and answer them.

Fact/Opinion

Classify each of the following statements as either a fact, an opinion, or a fact wrapped in an opinion. If the statement is a combination of fact and opinion, identify which part is fact and which opinion.

1. "The universe seemed to pause for breath."

2. "To the West, many farmers testified that, at this time, the moon emerged from behind clouds blood red."

3. "In a trice Ford's resembled a hive immediately after the queen bee has died."

4. "Grief spirals to insanity."

5. "His pulse was forty-four and light; breathing was stertorous; the pupil of the left eye was contracted; the right was dilated—both were proved insensitive to light."

Inferences

In your responses to the following questions, incorporate some of the quotations you located in response to the Content questions. You may decide to use either all or only part of each quotation.

1. How does the exchange between Booth and Buckingham, the ticket taker (paragraphs 9–10), tally with the corresponding exchange in Stern's account (paragraphs 63 and 64)?

2. Compare and contrast paragraph 19 in Bishop's account and paragraph 68 in Stern's account.

3. To what extent does Bishop's account of Booth's escape tally with those of Ritterspaugh and Stewart in their testimony?

4. Select examples of events that must have happened exactly as Bishop describes them (e.g., "Wilkes Booth could still hear the actors faintly"). Select examples of events that Bishop must have reconstructed and that may or may not have happened exactly as he describes them (e.g., "Booth's face was snowy and grim as he pulled his foot back and kicked the boy in the chest").

5. Why were Mrs. Lincoln and the others in the box so slow to realize what had happened to Lincoln?

6. Compare and contrast paragraph 26 in Bishop's account and paragraph 108 in Stern's account.

7. Compare and contrast paragraphs 32 and 33 in Bishop's account and paragraph 116 in Stern's account.

8. Here is novelist Gore Vidal's account of Booth's attack on Rathbone:

> Major Rathbone threw himself on Booth, who promptly drove his dagger straight at the young man's heart. But Rathbone's arm deflected the blade. (Vidal, *Lincoln,* 648)

Compare and contrast Vidal's account with biographer Carl Sandburg's account of the same moment:

> Major Rathbone leaps from his chair. Rushing at him with a knife is a strange human creature, terribly alive, a lithe wild animal, a tiger for speed, a wildcat of a man bare-headed, raven-haired—a smooth sinister face with glaring eyeballs. He wears a dark sack suit. He stabs straight at the heart of Rathbone, a fast and angry lunge. Rathbone parries it with his upper right arm, which gets a deep slash of the dagger. Rathbone is staggered, reels back. The tigerish stranger mounts the box railing. (*Abraham Lincoln: The War Years* [New York: Harcourt, 1939], 281)

What are the differences in *attitude* implied by these two accounts? (See also Bishop, paragraph 36, and Stern, paragraph 117.)

9. Compare Bishop's account of Booth's exit from Lincoln's box with those quoted in the introduction to this chapter. What similarities and differences do you detect?

10. What appears to indicate that Booth was thinking clearly as he rode off on his horse?

11. How does Bishop characterize Mrs. Lincoln and Dr. Leale?

12. How does Bishop characterize the public reaction to Lincoln's shooting? What events does he report that support this characterization?

SUMMARY ASSIGNMENT

Write a summary of Jim Bishop's "The Day Lincoln Was Shot." (You may need to review the procedures discussed in Chapter 2.)

Begin by writing one-sentence section summaries. Then write a thesis for the article as a whole. Next combine your thesis and the section summaries into a coherent summary of the entire article.

We will help get you started by suggesting one way that the first part of article can be divided into sections.

Section 1 (paragraphs 1–3)

Section 2 (paragraphs 4–5)

Section 3 (paragraphs 6–11)

 PAPER ASSIGNMENTS

1. Compare and contrast the treatment by two or more writers of a particular incident or aspect of Lincoln's assassination. Consider not only what is said to have happened (or not happened) but also *why* the particular writers present the version that they do. How is their version of the event(s) consistent with the rest of their presentation?

2. Reconstruct a portion of the action before, during, or after the assassination, drawing on at least three sources. If there are conflicts or differences among sources, try to account for them.

3. What kind of man was John Wilkes Booth? Using the accounts presented here, develop a character portrait of the assassin of President Lincoln. Base your conclusions on what Booth said, on what he did, and on how other people appear to have viewed him. You may use Stern's fictional account if you wish, but be sure to attribute this particular view of Booth to Stern. (For example, use explanatory phrases, such as "According to Stern..." or "As Stern has reconstructed this incident....")

4. Discuss the various approaches used by those who have written (or given testimony about) the Lincoln assassination to tell the story. Consider the style in which the pieces are written — emotional, poetic, straightforward, methodical. Consider also what the writers *don't* say; in other words, account for the different *emphases* of the various accounts. Finally, consider *who* is telling the story (what are their backgrounds, their points of view, their purposes?) as a way of accounting for the differences.

5. For film buffs only: Write a portion of a screenplay for a new film based on the life of Lincoln. You may choose to focus on the period from the time Booth first appeared at Ford's Theater on the evening of April 14, 1865, to the time he escaped, or you may choose to focus on a particular

portion of this period. If you are not familiar with basic film conventions (cuts, closeups, long shots, tracking shots, zooms, etc.), look them up in a film text.

Before you begin writing, decide on your basic approach. Is the part of the film dealing with the assassination to be highly dramatic? Matter of fact? Will you focus primarily on Booth? On the Lincoln party? Will you cross-cut between them (and the action on stage), building up suspense? You can get an idea of what is involved by reading three or four of the accounts of one particular moment (perhaps Booth's dropping from the box to the stage and breaking his leg) and translating each account into a film version. Or you may simply want to concentrate on one or two versions—perhaps Stern's and one other.

6. One of the pieces in this chapter was the *New York Times* reportage of the assassination. Of course, the *Times* coverage was limited to what was known at the time the stories were written—three to four hours after the shooting. Imagine now that a great deal more was known at that time; imagine that you had available much of the information in the sources you have read in this chapter. Write another newspaper account of the assassination as it might appear in a modern newspaper. Include interviews with eyewitnesses as well as with others (such as military and police officers and doctors who know about head injuries). Include a new headline. (Before you start this assignment, read some model newspaper stories and see how they are put together. Even better, read a newspaper account of the John F. Kennedy assassination.) You might have to reconstruct one or two things that your sources don't mention; you might even have to use your imagination a little. But for the most part, stick to the facts as reported in your sources.

7. At the beginning of this chapter, we suggested that the various accounts of the assassination of Abraham Lincoln raise some interesting questions. Among them: What is truth? Why does truth appear to vary, according to the writer or speaker? How is history written? How can we trust what is written as "history"? How do we evaluate historical data? And, finally, why should any of this matter?

    Write an essay on the topic of the "truth" of history. Use the material you have read on Lincoln's assassination to *exemplify* what you say. Your real topic, however, is not the assassination but the nature of historical truth, whether or not it is possible to know the truth, and if so, how?

8. Write your own paper assignment for this chapter. Find a common theme running through two or more articles, devise a topic based on this theme, and then write a question asking writers to draw on material in the selections that would support a thesis based on the topic. You might want to help your writers by suggesting some specific articles or even by getting them started with an outline for the paper.

pp. 272–274: Margaret Atwood. "Just Like a Woman," from *Harper's Magazine,* June 1985, pp. 27–28; *Ms.* Magazine, August 1986, p. 98., by Margaret Atwood. Reprinted by permission of the author and Phoebe Larmore, literary agent.

pp. 274–279: Margo Jefferson. "Books and Their Readers: Sweet Dreams for Teen Queens," from *The Nation,* May 22, 1986. Reprinted by permission of The Nation Magazine/Nation Associates Inc.

pp. 286–289: "Does College Really Matter Anymore?" Reprinted with permission from *Changing Times* Magazine, © 1979 Kiplinger Washington Editors, Inc., Nov. 1979. This reprint is not to be altered in any way, except with permission from *Changing Times.*

pp. 296–298: Anne Nelson. "Should You Go to College?" From *Senior Scholastic.* Copyright © 1979 by Scholastic Inc. Reprinted by permission of Scholastic Inc.

pp. 299–300: "Principles of the Liberal Arts College." From "Principles of the College" from *Mount Holyoke College Bulletin,* 1985–1986. Reprinted by permission of Mount Holyoke College.

pp. 302–309: Caroline Bird. "College Is a Waste of Time and Money." First appeared in *Psychology Today,* May 1975 and *Signature* Magazine, June 1975. Reprinted by permission of the author.

pp. 312–315: Letters to editor in response to Caroline Bird's article. Reprinted with permission from *Psychology Today* Magazine. Copyright © 1975. American Psychological Association.

pp. 316–317: Barbara Damrosch. Review of Caroline Bird's *The Case Against College.* The Nation, July 5, 1975. Reprinted by permission of The Nation Magazine/Nation Associates Inc.

pp. 318–321: Harvey Rubenstein. "An Education System That Failed." Originally published as "Unemployed Youth: A Ticking Bomb." Reprinted from *USA Today* Magazine. July 1978. Copyright 1978 by Society for the Advancement of Education. Used by permission of the Society for the Advancement of Education.

pp. 322–323: Thomas J. Cottle. "Overcoming an Invisible Handicap." Reprinted with permission from *Psychology Today* Magazine. Copyright © 1980. American Psychological Association.

pp. 325–329: Kate White. "9 Successful Women Tell How College Changed Their Lives." *Glamour,* August 1984. Reprinted by permission of the author.

pp. 335–337: Richard T. Jameson. "Quality Up the Wazoo." Originally appeared as "Television: Quality Up the Wazoo" in *Film Comment,* March–April, 1981. Reprinted by permission of the author.

pp. 339–342: Mark Crispin Miller. "The Liberal Pieties of 'Hill Street Blues' ", originally published as "Off the Prigs" in *The New Republic,* July 18, 1981. Reprinted by permission of *The New Republic.*

pp. 343–346: Beverly Gray. "Singin' the Hill Street Blues," from *Theatre Crafts,* May 1982. Reprinted by permission of *Theatre Crafts.*

pp. 348–355: David Freeman. "Television's Real A-Team." Copyright © 1985 by David Freeman. First appeared in *Esquire.* Reprinted with permission of the author.

pp. 356–358: Joyce Carol Oates. "For Its Audacity, Its Defiantly Bad Taste and Its Superb Character Studies." Reprinted by permission of the author and her agent Blanche C. Gregory, Inc. Copyright © 1985 by The Ontario Review, Inc. Reprinted with permission from *TV Guide*® Magazine. Copyright © 1985 by Triangle Publications, Inc., Radnor, Pennsylvania.

pp. 362, 366: Linda Bird Francke. Excerpted from "Children of Divorce" by Linda Bird Francke, *Reader's Digest,* May 1980. Condensed from *Newsweek.* Copyright 1980, by Newsweek, Inc. All Rights Reserved. Reprinted by Permission.

pp. 363–365: Lee Salk. "Helping Children Deal with Divorce." *McCalls,* October 1983. Reprinted with permission of *McCalls.*

pp. 367–368: Judith S. Wallerstein and Joan Berlin Kelly. Excerpted from "California's Children of Divorce" in *Psychology Today,* January 1980. Excerpted from *Surviving the Breakup: How Children and Parents Cope with Divorce* by Judith S. Wallerstein and Joan Berlin Kelly. Copyright © 1980 by Judith S. Wallerstein and Joan Berlin Kelly. Reprinted by permission of Basic Books, Inc., Publishers.

pp. 369–372: Linda Bird Francke. "Growing Up Divorced." Copyright © 1983 by Linda Bird Francke. Reprinted by permission of Linden Press, a division of Simon & Schuster, Inc.

pp. 374–377: Rita Rooney. "Helping Children Through Divorce," *McCalls,* April 1984. Reprinted by permission of Rita Rooney.

pp. 379–385: Thomas J. Cottle. "Goodbye Kids, Mother's Leaving Home," *The Atlantic,* March 1980. Reprinted by permission of the author.

pp. 387–393: John Updike. "Separating." Copyright © 1975 by John Updike. Reprinted from *Problems and Other Stories* by John Updike, by permission of Alfred A. Knopf, Inc. Originally appeared in *The New Yorker.*

pp. 394–400: Dianna Booher. "Games Parents and Children Play." Originally "Games Children Play" and "Games Parents Play." From *Coping... When Your Family Falls Apart.* Copyright 1979 by Dianna Daniels Booher. Reprinted by permission of Julian Messner, a division of Simon & Schuster, Inc.

pp. 402–413: C. W. Smith. "Uncle Dad." From *Esquire,* March 1985. Reprinted by permission of C. W. Smith © 1985–March and Elaine Markson Literary Agency, Inc.

pp. 415–418: Marvin Scott. "What My Children Taught Me About Divorce." From June 23, 1985 *Parade.* Reprinted with permission of the author.

Art Credits